UNDERSTANDING THE
EUROPEAN UNION

We work with leading authors to develop the
strongest educational materials in history and
politics, bringing cutting-edge thinking and
best learning practice to a global market.

Under a range of well-known imprints, including
Longman, we craft high quality
print and electronic publications which help
readers to understand and apply their content,
whether studying or at work.

To find out more about the complete range of our
publishing please visit us on the World Wide Web at:
www.pearsoneduc.com

UNDERSTANDING THE
EUROPEAN UNION

Sir William Nicoll
Trevor C. Salmon

An imprint of **Pearson Education**

Harlow, England · London · New York · Reading, Massachusetts · San Francisco
Toronto · Don Mills, Ontario · Sydney · Tokyo · Singapore · Hong Kong · Seoul
Taipei · Cape Town · Madrid · Mexico City · Amsterdam · Munich · Paris · Milan

Pearson Education Limited
Edinburgh Gate
Harlow
Essex CM20 2JE
England

and Associated Companies throughout the world

Visit us on the World Wide Web at:
http://www.pearsoneduc.com

First published 2001

© Pearson Education Limited 2001

ISBN 0 130 20838 8

British Library Cataloguing-in-Publication Data
A catalogue record for this book is available from the British Library

Library of Congress Cataloging-in-Publication Data
A catalog record for this book is available from the Library of Congress

10 9 8 7 6 5 4 3 2 1
04 03 02 01 00

Typeset by 42 in Janson
Printed in Great Britain by Henry Ling Ltd., at the Dorset Press, Dorchester, Dorset

CONTENTS

PREFACE

THIS TITLE is *not* a revised edition of our *Understanding the European Communities* or *Understanding the New European Community*. Listening to the feedback from our readers, we have changed the angle of approach to our subject, while preserving the features of which they approved. In brief, we have updated the account we give of the European Union to incorporate the changes introduced by the Inter-governmental Conference and the Treaty of Amsterdam and we have enlarged the analysis we make of the Community's and Union's policies. It remains our aim to encourage reliance on the texts of treaties, which establish the components of the European Union, and to counteract misinformation about them.

To forestall disappointment, or contrariwise to encourage the readership, we need to explain that we have not set out to write a treatise on integration theory. There are textual references to theoretical underpinnings and to writings on theory in the notes and bibliography.

The plan of this work is as follows:

Part 1 is a concise history of the building of European Union, pointing out some of the countervailing pressures that have existed from time to time. Part 2 describes the institutions, their functions and interactions that produce Community and European Union policy. Parts 3 and 4 analyse the policies of the first, second and third pillars of the European Union. Part 5 examines the attitudes of the existing fifteen Member States of the European Union and explores some of the issues relating to the enlargement of that Union. There is also an Extended Glossary that seeks to give rather more detail on specific points and to note features not in the text.

By virtue of Article 12 of the Treaty of Amsterdam, which came into force on 1 May 1999, the articles of the Treaty on European Union and of the Treaty establishing the European Community are renumbered. We have used the new numbering throughout, with a reminder of the better known numbering of the older versions.

Most money values are given in ECUs, as they were originally presented. The sterling value of the ECU fluctuated, as has the value of the euro. There is no fixed £/euro rate but in the first half of 1999 the euro was roughly equal to 65–70 pence.

The signing off point for the book was the end of autumn 1999 and the nomination of the Prodi Commission.

We are grateful to the European Commission for permission to reproduce source material. We are also grateful to Liz Mackie of Aberdeen University European Documentation Centre and Janet Michaelsen for all the help provided.

Sir William Nicoll
Trevor C. Salmon

LIST OF BOXES

LIST OF TABLES

LIST OF FIGURES

LIST OF ABBREVIATIONS

ACP	Africa-Caribbean-Pacific
AG	Advocate-General
BSE	Bovine Spongiform Encephalopathy
CAP	Common Agriculture Policy
CCP	Common Commercial Policy
CE	Compulsory expenditure
CEEC/CCEE	Countries of Eastern and Central Europe
CES	Economic and Social Committee
CET	Common External Tariff
CFI	Court of First Instance
CFSP	Common Foreign and Security Policy
CFP	Common Fisheries Policy
CJHA	Co-operation on Justice and Home Affairs
CoR	Committee of the Regions
Coreper	Committee of Permanent Representatives
Coreu	Correspondents européens (fax-line)
CU	Customs Union
DG	Director(ate) General
EAGGF	European Agricultural Guarantee and Guidance Fund
EC	European Community/ties
ECB	European Central Bank
ECJ	European Court of Justice
Ecofin	Economic and Finance Council
Ecosoc	Economic and Social Committee
ECSB	European System of Central Banks
ECSC	European Coal and Steel Community
ECU	European Currency Unit
EDC	European Defence Community
EEA	European Economic Area
EEC	European Economic Community
EFTA	European Free Trade Area
EIB	European Investment Bank
EMS	European Monetary System

EMU	Economic and Monetary Union
EP	European Parliament
EPC	European Political Co-operation
EPP	European People's Party
ERDF	European Regional Development Fund
ERM	Exchange Rate Mechanism
ESC	Economic and Social Committee
ESF	European Social Fund
EU	European Union
Euratom	European Atomic Energy Community
Eurostat	Commission Statistical Office
Euro-XI	Council of EMU participants
Feoga	French version of EAGGF
GAG	General Affairs Group
GATT	General Agreement on Tariffs and Trade
IGC	Inter-governmental Conference
JHA	Justice and Home Affairs
K4	Co-ordinating Committee of CJHA
MCA	Monetary Compensation Amounts
MEP	Member of the European Parliament
MFN	Most favoured nation
NATO	North Atlantic Treaty Organisation
NCE	Non-compulsory expenditure
NTB	Non-Tariff Barrier
OECD	Organisation for Economic Co-operation and Development
OJ	Official Journal
OOP	Office for Official Publications
OPEC	Organisation of Petroleum Exporting Countries
OSCE	Organisation for Security and Co-operation in Europe
PDB	Preliminary Draft Budget
Phare	Assistance to CEECs
QMV	Qualified Majority Vote/Voting
SEA	Single European Act
SEM	Single European Market
TAC	Total Allowable Catch
TACIS	Technical Assistance to Commonwealth of Independent States
TEN	Trans-European Network

TEU	Treaty on European Union
WEU	Western European Union
WTO	World Trade Organisation

1952 Eur 6

The European Community was originally founded by six states – Belgium, France, Germany, Italy, Luxembourg and the Netherlands – which were joined by Denmark, Ireland and the United Kingdom in 1973, Greece in 1981, and Spain and Portugal in 1986.

In 1990, the new east German *Länder* were incorporated.

In 1992, the Member States decided to form a European Union, which was enlarged in 1995 to include Austria, Finland and Sweden.

1973 Eur 9

1981 Eur 10

1986 Eur 12

1990 Eur 12

xxi

THE PATH TO THE TREATIES OF ROME

'EUROPA', daughter of the King of Tyre, was abducted by Zeus and taken to Crete to become queen and found a dynasty. The kingdom of Tyre was seen as the ancestor of European civilisation and the womb of different religions and cultures. The Greeks came to apply the name not only to their own territory, but also to the lands situated to the north and west. Europe was originally little more than a predominantly geographical construct, but the Roman legacy of language, culture and values gave the concept of Europe a wider foundation, as did Charlemagne's empire (founded AD 800), the Holy Roman Empire (962–1806) and Christianity. The divisions of Christianity, the Reformation and Counter Reformation weakened the concept of Europe, as did the concomitant theories of state, state sovereignty and, later, nationalism.

Nonetheless, the idea of Europe remained as a political and cultural entity, although it clearly possessed both diversity and unity: diversity in geography with rivers and mountains dividing territory, diversity in language despite the Grecian Roman inheritance, and diversity in political authority as states sought and pursued their own interests leading to wars, destruction and death. But there was unity too in certain values and a religious, cultural and philosophical inheritance. This tension between diversity and unity persisted. Questions still arise as to what is Europe; this uncertainty has taken on a new importance with the potential enlargement of the European Union from its current fifteen to twenty-one early in the new century.

This issue has also arisen in other European organisations like the Organisation for Security and Co-operation in Europe (OSCE), which has fifty-five members, including Canada and the United States, as well as Armenia, Azerbaijan, Georgia, Kazakhstan, Kirghizia, Moldova, Turkmenistan and Izbekistan.[1] This poses the question of where does the boundary of Europe lie; and is it a geographical or some other boundary? 'Europe' has often been referred to as if it were synonymous with the EC or EU, but this was and is not true. It is worth recalling that there were only six original founders of the EC/EU: Belgium, France, Federal Republic of Germany, Italy, the Netherlands and Luxembourg.

3

EARLY MUSINGS

The idea of some form of common ground among Europeans can be traced back to Dubois in the fourteenth century who argued that there could only be peace if there were institutions to preserve it with arbitration. Suarez, in 1612, wrote of the human race as part of a universal community requiring law to direct it; Grotius, in 1625, sought some sort of body to adjudicate between parties and to try to force them to come to some agreement; Cruce, in 1623, was the first to emphasise trade; the Duc de Sully, writing at the turn of sixteenth and seventeenth centuries was the first statesman to make proposals for: (a) the creation of a *Conseil très chrétien*, with full powers to arbitrate in disputes between members, and supported by an army of over 125,000 to enforce its decisions; (b) a Europe divided into more or less fifteen equal states; and (c) a Europe with preferably one religion and no more than three. Other schemes followed: William Penn, Montsequieu, the Abbé de Saint-Pierre, Rousseau, Bentham, Kant, the Comte de Saint-Simon, Mazzini, and Proudhon. But these ideas were of negligible influence. Napoleon was not so philosophical and suggested that he had 'not succeeded to the throne of Louis XIV, but to that of Charlemagne'. Mazzini in the nineteenth century was an interesting ardent advocate of both Italian and European unity.[2]

The roots of action

It was not philosophies that made the difference but the impacts of practicalities, and in particular the impacts of the industrial revolution, the French Revolution, and Napoleon. Prior to the first there was limited mass production and communications were poor and dangerous. The industrial revolution instigated a major increase in the flow of people, goods and services between states, and began the informal integration of the European and world economies. The French Revolution and the legacy of Napoleon created trends pushing in the opposite direction – pressure for national self-determination and, consequently, nationalism and the decreasing permeability of state boundaries. The first led to transnational ties and functional co-operation and the latter gave states a greater role as 'gate-keepers' with regard to the movement of people, goods and services.

To resolve these apparently contradictory tendencies, where both freedom of movement and control of it were desired, international organisations were invented, providing for freedom of movement under a set of rules which were negotiated, determined and enforced by the governments of states. Therefore, the first international organisations were developed to help the state to fulfil its functions, not to do away with them.

In addition to these pragmatic responses to national and international developments, the nineteenth century saw an increasing awareness that war was gore as well as glory. The inadequacies of the international system were also becoming more and more apparent, fuelling a growing perception that there was a need for new bodies to (a) serve state interests and (b) serve the interests of the system as a whole; although there was to be no attack on sovereignty.

The Concert of Europe and the Zollverein

The twin tracks of focus upon economic relationships and concern with peace are reflected in the examples of the Concert of Europe and the Zollverein in the nineteenth century. The Concert of Europe came about after twenty-two years of war. The origins of system lay in the alliance against France, and the 1814 Treaty of Chaumont that symbolised the alliance of Austria, Prussia, Russia and Britain. In the Treaty it was agreed that they should 'concert together . . . as to the means best adapted to guarantee to Europe, and to themselves reciprocally, the continuance of Peace . . .'.[3] The Congress of Vienna (1814–15) sought to find ways of implementing the Chaumont agreement. The participating states agreed to build upon the connections that existed between them for the purpose of pursuing their common interests and of finding ways of providing for the repose, peace and prosperity of Europe. In fact, after a short time there were no regular meetings and no real system, but nonetheless a certain pattern, level of expectation and habit of consultation were established. This was not always successful and could not, for example, prevent the Crimean War of 1854–56. By the end of the century, however, the hardships of war and the costs of war and preparations for war were being taken much more seriously, and in 1899 and 1907 the two Hague Conferences attempted to mitigate the costs and increase the possibilities of prevention. Their limited success can be seen in the fact that the third Hague Conference scheduled for 1915 did not take place because of the Great War of 1914–18.[4]

The Prussian-based Zollverein of 1834 was a customs union among 23.5 million 'Germanic' people. It played a part in the unification of Germany, although again its primary purpose served national interests and the pursuit of national economic advantage for most participants. Several states only joined because of economic depression and empty exchequers, and the perception that resistance to Prussia was difficult if not impossible.[5]

Practical steps

The other initial tentative moves to create international organisations were in very specific mundane areas which were not overtly political or controversial, what came to be called later 'low politics', in the areas of river navigation, posts and telegraphs. The International River Commissions on the Rhine, Danube, Elbe, Douro, Po and Pruth, the International Telegraphic Association and the Universal Postal Union, were all rooted in genuine need, and laid the foundations of experience, expertise, formats and institution-building that were crucial precursors to twentieth-century developments.

The nineteenth century laid the foundations of permanent international secretariats manning the network of technical, administrative functional agencies; the periodic, almost institutionalised meetings of the great powers; the introduction of the notion that the other powers should also meet together to discuss matters of common concern; the growth of arbitration; and an economic integration. These seeds laid the foundations for the League of Nations, albeit that there was no direct line of descent.[6]

War

A major impetus, of course, in that next century was the horror of the First World War. The carnage of that war saw 8.5 million dead [5 million Allies and 3.5 million of the Central Powers] and 21 million wounded. But it was not just the scale of the deaths, it was their manner: the trench warfare, the gas attacks, the mass slaughter of conscripts for the advance of metres that might be lost the next day. It became difficult to argue any longer that 'bloodshed is a cleansing and a sanctifying thing, and the nation that regards it as the final horror has lost its manhood'.[7]

The spirit of the times was better captured by Wilfred Owen in 'Dulce Et Decorum Est' that finishes:

> And watch the white eyes writhing in his face,
> His hanging face, like a devil's sick of sin;
> If you could hear, at every jolt, the blood
> Come gargling from the froth-corrupted lungs,
> Obscene as cancer, bitter as the cud
> Of vile, incurable sores on innocent tongues, –
> My friend, you would not tell with such high zest
> To children ardent for some desperate glory,
> The old Lie: Dulce et decorum est
> Pro patria mori.[8]

The League

This spirit led to the League of Nations coming into being in 1920; there being a widespread sense that something had to be done. The League was intended to meet two basic objectives: to build a durable peace through collective security and disarmament and to consolidate the Versailles settlement of 1919. It originally had little emphasis on functional socio-economic activity, although ironically some of its later successes were in this area rather than in its prime purpose of preventing war. In addition to the absence of the United States and other problems relating to universality, a critical weakness of the League was that it could not order its Member States to take action; it could only recommend. Ultimately, like the Concert before it, it fell foul of its lack of appropriate structures, especially in the area of decision-making capacity; of its lack of sustained political will after the initial enthusiasm had waned; of changes in the international environment in which it had to operate; and of changes in the domestic, political and social environments. The League proved to be incapable of fulfilling the hopes vested in it.[9]

More musing

Some of these weaknesses were recognised in the inter-war period. Richard Coudenhove-Kalergi in 1923 founded the 'Pan-Europa' movement. He believed in a united Europe, excluding Britain and the USSR, a two-chamber parliament, and an internationalist, cosmopolitan and multiracial approach. The new Europe should start with a security pact before moving to a customs union and single economic area, with the crowning act, the constitution of a United States of Europe on the model of the United States of America.[10] These ideas struck a chord with Aristide Briand, sometime Foreign and Prime Minister of France. In 1928 Briand had been instrumental in the Briand–Kellogg Pact which sought to entrench the principle of the renunciation of war as an instrument of policy. In September 1929 he spoke to the League of his plan for a permanent federal organisation in Europe to handle specifically European problems, although he also spoke of maintaining national sovereignty. In the socio-economic and political areas it was clear to him that there were advantages in the states of Europe working together. He was asked to put his ideas in a memorandum to be circulated to League members for comment. It was met with little enthusiasm, although a study group was established.[11] In 1932 Briand died but already by then circumstances were conspiring against the proposal with the fears generated by the Wall Street crash and important electoral victories for the Nazis in Germany. In the years that followed, European life was marked by increasing national economic protectionism and by the emergence of nationalist movements.

Another war

The totalitarian and dictatorial nature of fascism and National Socialism pushed the idea of European union into the background and, indeed, into another catastrophic war in which between 15 and 20 million combatants and between 9 and 10 million civilians, including 6 million Jews, were to die. This war was to finish with the explosion of nuclear devices over Hiroshima on 6 August 1945 and over Nagasaki on 9 August 1945, the first killing 68,000 and the second 38,000, although by the end of the year the total fatalities were at least double these figures. If anyone was prone to thinking that conventional warfare was a comfortable alternative, the bombing raid on Dresden in February 1944, killing 135,000 people, and the bombing of Tokyo in March 1944, which saw 80,000 killed, 40,000 wounded and 16 square acres destroyed, demonstrated that was an chimera. No wonder that, after the war, Winston Churchill would refer to Europe as a 'charnel-house', a pile of bones.

The failure of pre-war appeals had a cathartic effect, leading to the questioning of the basis of the international political system – that is, the emphasis upon independence and sovereignty. The system created after the Treaty of Westphalia system in 1648, which had ended the Thirty Years' War but which also laid the basis for the sovereign state system in Europe, had now demonstrably failed to maintain international order, peace and security, and the lives and prosperity of the citizens of its component states. Indeed, the French and Germans had now fought in 1870, 1914–1918 and 1939–1945. This had profound implications because the state's very *raison d'être* was precisely to bring about the objectives of peace and prosperity.

NEW THINKING

Given this failure, even before the war had ended radical thinking was taking place in the resistance movements of Europe, as those involved did not want a return to the past. One leading radical was Altiero Spinelli [1907–86], imprisoned by the Italian Fascist government in 1927 on the island of Ventotene. Later a member of the European Commission and European Parliament, Spinelli attacked passionately the ideology of national independence, totalitarianism and capitalist imperialism. He wanted to see the 'final abolition of the division of Europe into sovereign national States' and for that system to be replaced by a European federation, founded by a constituent assembly for the new Europe.[12] Others in the resistance were equally radical, although the movement was profoundly ideologically divided. Nonetheless, for many there was a deep hope that the camaraderie of the wartime resistance movements would last and be the basis for a new order in Europe. Some of those involved rejected previous solutions as having been too weak, the institutions created lacking the ability to implement decisions or to be independent of, or even superior to, the Member States. By 1944 some of the groups meeting in Geneva were arguing:

> It is a most urgent task to end this international anarchy by creating a European Federal Union . . . in view of the failure of the League of Nations, the States must irrevocably surrender to the Federation their sovereign rights in the sphere of defence, relations with powers outside the Union, international exchange and communications.

Only a Federal Union it was claimed would allow:

- the German people to play a full role without being a threat to others;
- the resolution of minorities issues;
- the protection of democracy; and
- the reconstruction of the economy.

It would require three essential features:

1. A government responsible not to the governments of the various member States but to the peoples, who must be under its direct jurisdiction in the spheres to which its powers extend.
2. An army at the disposal of this government, no national armies being permitted.
3. A Supreme Court acting as authority in interpreting the Constitution and deciding cases of conflict between the Member States or between the Member States and the Union . . . .[13]

Monnet

As early as 1917, one visionary had begun writing memoranda on what needed to be done to win a war, and began very quickly to identify some of the same principles as the most appropriate way for relations between states to be organised. Jean Monnet

(1888–1979) at this time was already beginning to argue passionately that there was a need for collective action to solve problems that no state could deal with on its own: initially, this was to be co-ordination of war efforts based on the principle that 'the unity of views and of actions which is indispensable', but subsequently this principle was to be applied to more positive situations, and Monnet himself declared that he set no *a priori* limits to the principle.[14]

By 1919, Monnet was writing:

> Co-operation between nations will grow from their getting to know each other better, and from interpenetration between their constituent elements and those of their neighbours ... so that they come to see the problems that face them, not from the viewpoint of their own interests, but in the light of the general interest ... if each interested party ... is presented with the problem as a whole, there can be no doubt that all parties' points of view will be modified. Together, they will reach a solution that is fair.[15]

This became the general rule: 'look at the problem as a whole and in the light of the general interest.'[16]

Going back to old solutions:

That was tried in 1919; we all know the result.[17]

But this thinking was not to have negligible effect as had so much of what had gone before. It had a direct impact on concrete plans that became the basis of the concrete proposals made in the Schuman declaration of 9 May 1950,[18] which was the basis of the first Community, the European Coal and Steel Community, which in turn led to the European Economic Community and, in 1993, the European Union. But before those ideas could fully take root, the intellectual and political environment had to change too.

POST-WAR MOTIVATIONS: A NEW MOOD?

It was not only the horror of war that allowed radical thinking in the mid- and late-1940s and early 1950s and reinforced the potency of the European ideal, but the concern to avoid the perceived mistakes of the period after the First World War, which many, as well as Monnet, saw as directly contributing to the origins of the Second World War. In addition, by the mid-1940s there was the clear perception, at least on the part of many on the continent of Europe, that the nation-state, that nineteenth epitome of political development, had failed to deliver peace and prosperity. It was also clear that the nature of war and of the socio-economic environment was being transformed by technological innovation; that the scale of the damage caused by war, and thus of the necessary reconstruction, was unparalleled; and that that there was already looming the prospect of another war as a result of the ideological political and military division between the victorious former Allies and the onset of the Cold War.

In the post-war period, at least five factors played an important role in the creation of a new mind set. The first was the 'mood' of the times. The ideas that had been mooted took on a new urgency and found a favourable environment. A major development was the coming together of a variety of transnational groups who felt that the post-war political system required to be radically different from its pre-war predecessor. In 1947 an effort was made to co-ordinate these groups, bearing fruit in 1948 in the Congress of Europe at The Hague, a meeting of over 800 prominent public figures. They attended in their private capacities, but brought with them considerable political authority – twelve former Prime Ministers were present (as well as François Mitterrand, a future President of France). The Congress issued a number of resolutions. The Political Resolution argued that it was:

> the urgent duty of the nations of Europe to create an economic and political union in order to assure security and social progress ... that the time has come when the European nations must transfer and merge some portion of their sovereign rights so as to secure common political and economic action for the integration and proper development of their common resources.

It also called for the urgent convening of a European Assembly, nominated by national Parliaments to

> examine the juridical and constitutional implications arising out of the creation of such a union or federation and their economic and social consequences; to prepare the necessary plans.

An Economic Resolution called for 'an economic union in Europe', which should include 'the unification of currencies' and the 'abolition of all barriers to the movement of goods between the countries of the union'.[19]

The mood meets pragmatism

In many ways The Hague Congress marked a false dawn, since the proposals which were taken up by the French and Belgian governments were watered down in the negotiations that led to the formation of the Council of Europe in May 1949. Those involved were still so keen to include the anti-federal British, that instead of the far-reaching Hague proposals, the Council of Europe was based upon inter-governmentalism. Although it could discuss almost everything (apart from defence), it was fundamentally a traditional international inter-governmental organisation, with every state having a veto over decisions. The nature of the compromise was reflected in the Statute of the Council, which noted the need for 'closer unity between all like-minded countries of Europe', and thus acknowledged that it was 'necessary forthwith to create an organisation which will bring European States into closer association'. The aim was to 'achieve a greater unity'.[20] This was not quite the language nor the organisation that those at The Hague had had in mind. Nonetheless, the mood was for change and it came by May 1950, with the Schuman declaration, which launched the European Coal and Steel Community (ECSC). What did not change was the tension between the federalist approach to European co-operation and those who argued for the tradition of national sovereignty. To some extent the battle lines drawn up in the debates about the functions and powers of the Council of Europe have continued through to the current day.

Physical reality and need

A powerful motivation to action was the really urgent need, in and after 1945, to address the issue of physical and economic reconstruction. It is difficult now to picture the state of much of continental Europe in 1945, but Richard Mayne gives one vivid description:

> In the cities, the skyline was jagged with destruction: amid the ruins and craters, rubble and wreckage, blocked the streets . . . machinery rusted in the bombed-out factories . . . Roads were pitted with shell-holes . . . Much of the countryside was charred and blackened . . . in some areas, unchecked by peasant bows and arrows, herds of wild pigs roamed the land for forage. Yet amid the destruction there were people . . . Sheds of weekend vegetable plots became houses; cellars and caves were turned into houses . . . The survivors . . . for them, this wasteland of rubble, rags and hunger was a prison without privacy or dignity; and like all prisons it smelled . . . of sweat and vomit, dirty socks and excrement; of decay and burning and the unburied dead.[21]

People starved, roads and rail tracks were destroyed and economies devastated. In reality, there was not just the question of reconstruction for its own sake, but the powerful added incentive of the perceived need to act, since these abysmal conditions were regarded as creating fertile conditions for the appeal of communist ideology, which appeared to offer a better future. A major response to this fear came on 5 June 1947 when the American Secretary of State, George Marshall, launched what became the European Recovery Programme, otherwise known as the Marshall Plan. Marshall explicitly spoke of:

> the dislocation of the entire fabric of European economy . . . Our policy is directed . . . against hunger, poverty, desperation, and chaos. Its purpose should be the revival of a working economy in the world so as to permit the emergence of political and social conditions in which free institutions can exist. Such assistance . . . must not be on a piecemeal basis as various crises develop . . . there must be some agreement among the countries of Europe as to the requirements of the situation and the part those countries themselves will take . . . The programme should be a joint one, agreed to by a number, if not all, European nations . . . .[22]

The offer was made to the whole of Europe. Although Marshall had stressed it was not directed against any state or ideology, Stalin of the Soviet Union turned the offer down and insisted that the Soviet's satellites in Eastern and Central Europe did the same, reinforcing the economic and political division represented by the Iron Curtain. Although sixteen states created the Organisation for European Economic Co-operation in May 1948,[23] to co-ordinate the European response, the more important feature of what happened is that the sixteen received between them some $13,150 million in grants and loans.

11

The importance of defence (and the USA)

These states were not just concerned with economic recovery. They also feared for their survival, given the perceived animosity and ideological missionary zeal of the Soviet Union under Stalin, with its apparent juggernaut of the Red Army.

While this perception may have been exaggerated, it was real. Another necessary step in creating new confidence in Europe was the attempt to move to collective defence, since leading policy-makers believed that their states were too weak to defend themselves individually. In 1947 the Americans again took a lead, on this occasion in a speech by President Truman, that came to be known as the Truman Doctrine, when he asserted that:

> it must be the policy of the United States to support free peoples who are resisting attempted subjugation by armed minorities or by outside pressure.[24]

The initial response was the granting of $400m to Greece and Turkey, who both faced problems. More generally, the Truman Doctrine became a basis of United States policy towards Western Europe for a generation. It was followed by five European states (Belgium, France, Luxembourg, the Netherlands and the United Kingdom) taking steps towards helping themselves with the 'Treaty of Economic, Social and Cultural Collaboration and Collective Self-Defence' on 17 March 1948, which was the basis of the Brussels Treaty Organisation, and which, in modified form, is still the basis of the Western European Union (WEU).[25] If the five were concerned with self-defence, they were also concerned with demonstrating to the United States that they were making every effort to help themselves, with the hope that this might attract American support. It did, in the form of the Vandenberg Resolution, passed by 64 to 4 in the American Senate in June 1948. This Resolution made clear that the Senate would welcome:

> the association of the United States, by constitutional process, with such regional and other collective arrangements as are based on continuous and effective self-help and mutual aid.[26]

In less than a year the USA had signed the North Atlantic Treaty, the basis of NATO, and with the famous Article V commitment:

> The Parties agree that an armed attack against one or more of them in Europe or North America shall be considered an attack against them all and consequently they agree that, if such an armed attack occurs, each of them ... will assist the Party or Parties so attacked by taking forthwith ... such action as it deems necessary, including the use of armed force ....[27]

By 1949 the basic security positions in Europe until 1989 had been established, although the formal response to the North Atlantic Treaty did not occur until 1955, when the Soviet Union and its allies signed the Warsaw Treaty. It is clear from today's perspective that with regard to both the immediate economic reconstruction objective and the preoccupation with survival against the perceived Soviet threat, the steps taken in the late 1940s were successful.

An international voice?

Another basic concern of leading West European states was how to recover their position as leading actors in the international political system. The European great powers had dictated the fortunes of the globe before 1939; it was they who decided issues of war and peace locally and globally. Now they had to adjust to loss of world standing and empire, to the transfer of decisive power to Washington and Moscow, and to Europe becoming an object of the great power game rather than a participant in it. Stutteringly, they had to adjust to this new reality, and gradually they came to believe that only a united Europe could recover the continent's old greatness, significance and influence. By the time the Six met at Messina in 1955 to discuss the way forward beyond the ECSC, they had become convinced that the path of unity was indispensable if Europe was to maintain her position in the world, regain her influence and prestige.[28]

Despite this clear recognition of the problem, they have continued to find it difficult to achieve as much in this sphere of activity as in their economic co-operation (see Chapter 12 for discussion of the CFSP). Nonetheless, the members of the European Union have made strides in this direction, pursuing two avenues: the first is through an integral part of the original Treaty of Rome, the Common Commercial Policy; and the second was through European Political Co-operation, now the CFSP. By the mid-1990s, excluding intra-EU trade, the EU had just under a 19% share of world imports and just over 19% share of world exports, compared to the American and Japanese figures of 15.5% and 12% for exports and 20% and 8% for imports. The European Community is a world economic power. The attempt to match that politically has not been so successful.

The EU clearly has an identifiable presence in the world, as is further exemplified by the relationship between the fifteen EU Member States and the African, Caribbean and Pacific States via the Lomé conventions. Whatever the criticisms of the relationship, the strength of the relationship has endured over the years. In addition, the EU has clearly proved to be a magnet to others, not just those who have joined with the original Six since 1951, but to those who are currently on the waiting list for admission, and those states throughout the world that recognise that the EC/EU cannot be ignored in either international economic or political relationships.

Independent interdependence on the USA?

A further motivation behind economic integration was that West Europeans should gradually be in a position where they were not so dependent on the USA not only for security, but also for economic prosperity. Indeed, despite the welcome for Marshall aid, there was some concern about the dangers of being swamped by American economic power, technology and investment. These fears were classically expressed in 1967 in *Le Défi Américain*, which expressed concern at the dangers of American technological and economic penetration.[29] While these fears have periodically reappeared, by the late 1980s and the approach of the Single Internal Market of 1992, it was the Americans who were becoming worried about Europe's economic weight.

THE FOUNDATION OF THE FIRST COMMUNITY

Despite the potency of these motivations, actual progress seemed almost to have stalled by early 1950, and the disappointment occasioned by the compromise over the Council of Europe was palpable. It was at this moment that a new radical idea was promoted, and this time it had both political clout behind it and a determination that there would be no more fatal compromises with the British. It was Jean Monnet who made the original move.

Since 1946 Monnet had been the First Commissioner of the French National Economic Plan. Previously he had played leading roles in wartime planning in both world wars, had been Deputy Secretary-General of the League of Nations and a key figure behind the 1940 abortive proposal for an Anglo-French Union. By 1949 Monnet was beginning to think again about planning on a European basis, especially thinking about how to embed France and Germany in a common interest so as to make another conflict impossible.

In April 1950, reflecting on an allied conference to be held in London on 10 May 1950, he contemplated ways to avoid France coming under pressure to ease restrictions on Germany. Using lateral thinking, he came up with a radical and novel solution, and submitted a memorandum to the Foreign Minister, Robert Schuman. The memorandum began by expressing the fear that war in Europe appeared to be accepted as inevitable; indeed, in some ways it appeared as if Europe was already at war. Given this, 'concrete and resolute action' was required, and this action had also to reassure those in France worried about the resurgence in German economic power. Monnet thus proposed:

> By the pooling of basic production [in coal and steel] and the establishment of a new High Authority whose decisions will be binding on France, Germany, and the countries that join them, this proposal will lay the first concrete foundations of the European Federation which is indispensable to the maintenance of peace.[30]

Schuman accepted Monnet's idea for a Franco-German Coal and Steel Pool and on 9 May 1950 launched the idea of a European Coal and Steel Community in his historic Declaration:

> Europe will not be made all at once, or according to a single plan. It will be built through concrete achievements that first create a *de facto* solidarity . . . [French Government] proposes that Franco-German production of coal and steel as a whole be placed under a common High Authority, within the framework of an organisation open to the participation of the other countries of Europe . . . a first step in the federation of Europe . . . The solidarity in production thus established will make it plain that any war between France and Germany becomes not merely unthinkable, but materially impossible . . . .[31]

In the aftermath of the Schuman Declaration an exchange of notes and views took place between the British and French governments, which revealed their different approaches to European co-operation. The key stumbling block was French insistence that all those negotiating on the proposals accepted in advance a commitment to the principles of 'pooling' of production and the institution of a new high authority with real and effective decision-making powers.

The simple 'authority' model of Monnet and Schuman was quickly modified during the negotiations. Monnet himself proposed that there be a parliamentary assembly to meet annually to review the work of the High Authority and, if necessary, sack its members. It also became clearer that this enterprise was fundamentally political and therefore needed more than technical machinery. In July 1950 the Belgian and Dutch governments proposed that the High Authority's actions be subject to review by some forum comprising government representatives. After some discussion this became the Special Council of Ministers, whose official task was to harmonise the actions of the national governments with those of the High Authority.

The basic structure is laid

The resultant pattern:

> High Authority
>   + Special Council of Ministers
>   + Common Assembly
>   + European Court of Justice

became *the* institutional pattern for the European Economic Community and the European Atomic Energy Community created by the two Treaties of Rome of March 1957. Both of these Communities initially shared the Court and Assembly with the ECSC, although there were separate Councils and two new Commissions. The 1965 Merger Treaty merged the three Councils formally into one, and the High Authority and the two Commissions of the EEC and Euratom into one Commission. The Treaty only merged the institutions, not the Communities *per se*. The merger of the institutions came into effect in July 1967.

Even before the Merger Treaty, a significant change had taken place in the description and definition of the character of the common higher authority. A unique feature of the Treaty of Paris of April 1951, which created the European Coal and Steel Community, was that:

> The members of the High Authority . . . shall refrain from any action incompatible with the supranational character of their duties.

By the two Treaties of Rome in 1957 this had been diluted to:

> The members of the Commission . . . shall refrain from any action incompatible with their duties.[32]

not that it had ever been clear what supranational actually meant or implied, and indeed, despite the initial plan, the Council increasingly acted as a check upon the High Authority, particularly after the emergence of a major crisis in the coal market – that is, a coal glut.

A BLOW TO THE APPARENT INEVITABILITY OF PROGRESS ───────

The apparent and early success of the ECSC kindled hopes that movement towards a united Europe might accelerate and proposals began to be made for an Agricultural Community and a European Transport Authority, although they came to nothing. More significant, at least initially, was the proposal for a European Defence Community. Indeed, on 27 May 1952 a European Defence Community Treaty was actually signed by the Six states that had signed the Paris Treaty in 1951. The idea for such a Community was a response to the success of the ECSC negotiations, the desire to give a political dimension to the enterprise the Six had embarked upon, and, more immediately, the alarm bells rung by the invasion of South Korea by North Korea on 25 June 1950. Given the excited atmosphere of the times, many regarded this attack as part of the giant communist conspiracy to draw limited Western forces to the east as a prelude to a Soviet attack on Berlin or as the first move in a global Soviet offensive. Western Europe felt vulnerable to the perceived might of the Soviet Union, and it was argued in the search for solutions that in order to find matching manpower Germans must be re-armed. This was political dynamite given that victory in Europe had only been declared in May 1945 and that occupation had only ended in the winter of 1944–45. The solution that began to appeal was that of the ECSC model: there should be a European army tied to the creation of the new political institutions of a united Europe. It should be possible to arm Germans but not Germany, since the authority over the forces created would reside with the new European Defence Community (EDC), and not with Germany. The EDC Treaty referred to:

> a European Defence Community, supranational in character, comprising common
> institutions, common armed forces, and a common budget.[33]

Four of the Six ratified the Treaty, although it was very controversial in West Germany, but in August 1954 the French National Assembly, on a procedural motion, decided to move to next business and thus defeated it. The Italians were proceeding to ratification, but with the Paris result, they did not pursue the matter. There were numerous reasons for the French verdict, including fears concerning arming Germans and Germany, a change in the landscape of domestic French politics and a preoccupation with difficulties being experienced in the French possessions overseas, especially in Indo-China.[34] To accompany this new Community, and its nature, there was to have been an associated Political Community, which was to have among its objectives the co-ordination of the members' foreign policies and 'the progressive development of a common market'.[35]

Another compromise

With this defeat, the high hopes of advancing to a federal Europe received what appeared to be a knockout blow. While the European idea was to be relaunched, the EDC defeat was a blow from which those aspirations have never fully recovered. In the

immediate situation, the problem of German rearmament was patched up through modifications to the Brussels Treaty of 1948, which transformed it into the Western
European Union in 1954 allowing for a re-armed West Germany to become a member of
NATO in 1955, but with restrictions, which were to be monitored by the WEU of its
weapons programme, it not being allowed to develop or obtain atomic, biological or
chemical weapons.[36] The WEU was a very traditional, inter-governmental (not supranational) organisation, and as such the British felt able to support it.

RELAUNCH

With the failure of the EDC, and by implication the radical proposals for a European
Political Community, Europeans moved away from 'high politics'.[37] When in 1955 the
attempt was made to 'relaunch Europe', three factors had changed the view as to the right
approach to be adopted:

- the chastening experience of the EDC débâcle;
- the nature of the tasks to be undertaken, in particular the idea of focusing on a
  common market; and
- the practical experience of the ECSC institutions, which demonstrated that although
  there had been some difficulties, the general approach adopted could work.

In the background also relevant was the growing awareness of the weakness of the old
colonial powers, and that a state's influence was intimately related to its economic
strength, its rate of technological progress and its economic dynamism.

It was now clear, however, that an overtly federalist or supranational approach was
unacceptable, ironically particularly to the French, but to a lesser extent to other states
also. As economies recovered, as life became a little less awful for the citizens, and as
physical reconstruction began to be completed, more traditional concerns with empire,
nationalism and status began to reassert themselves, and there was less perceived need for
supranational intervention into national areas of activity. The relaunch, therefore, was
concerned with a less ambitious agenda than in the immediate past. The Dutch, picking
up the idea of a European customs union from the abortive Political Community, and
working with Paul-Henri Spaak of Belgium, called for joint studies of transport problems, energy questions and of the steps necessary to create a common market, but made
no initial attempt to define any institutional structures.

When the Foreign Ministers met at Messina on 1–2 June 1995 they too were cautious,
but they agreed to an inter-governmental conference to draft treaties on the 'development of common institutions, the gradual merging of national economies, the creation
of a common market, and the gradual harmonisation of their social policies'. The study
of the common market was to address such issues as the degree of co-ordination of
monetary policies necessary for the operation of a common market, the implications of
freedom of movement of workers, and the nature of competition policy. They thought
it necessary to develop large-scale communications facilities (what might now be termed

Box 1.1 Key dates in the history of European integration, 1945–57

1945	May	End of the Second World War in Europe: Britain victorious.
1947	March	Treaty of Dunkirk: Britain and France against possible German aggression.
		Truman Doctrine: USA ready to provide support to those threatened by communist aggression or subversion.
	June	Marshall speech offering economic aid to Europe if Europeans co-operate with each other.
1948	March	Brussels Treaty: Britain, France plus Benelux states. A treaty of collective defence against Soviets (and initially Germany).
	April	Organisation for European Economic Co-operation (1960 OECD) formed by sixteen European states plus USA/Canada (1960).
	May	Congress of Europe by federalists of The Hague.
1949	April	North Atlantic Treaty signed in Washington by twelve states.
	May	Statute of Council of Europe signed in Strasbourg by ten states.
1950	May	In a speech inspired by Jean Monnet, Robert Schuman, the French Foreign Minister, proposes that France, the Federal Republic of Germany and any other European country wishing to join them should pool their coal and steel resources.
	June	Attack by North Korea on South Korea, leads to proposals for a European army or a European Defence Community.
1951	April	The Six sign the Paris Treaty establishing the European Coal and Steel Community (ECSC).
	May	**The Treaty establishing the European Defence Community (EDC) is signed in Paris by ECSC Six.**
1952	July	ECSC starts work.
1954	August	The French parliament rejects the EDC Treaty.
	October	Following the London Conference, agreements on a modified Brussels Treaty are signed in Paris, and the Western European Union (WEU) comes into being.
1955	June	The foreign ministers of the Six, meeting in Messina, decide to extend European integration to all branches of the economy.
1957	March	The Treaties establishing the European Economic Community and the European Atomic Energy Community are signed in Rome.
		Mauding OEEC talks between the Six and other OEEC members.

trans-European networks), and cheaper energy (especially looking to the nuclear field).[38] The ground was to be prepared by a committee of government delegates assisted by experts, under the chairmanship of a leading political figure (who it emerged was Paul-Henri Spaak, previously twice Prime Minister of Belgium and at Messina as Belgian

Foreign Minister). It thus became known as the Spaak Committee. The subsequent Spaak Report was the basis of the negotiations among the Six leading to the two Treaties of Rome of 25 March 1957. The British, as members of the WEU and associates of the ECSC, were invited to attend the Spaak Committee. They sent an official, whilst the others were represented by Ministers. There still remains some difference of recollection as to whether the British official, Mr Bretherton, was pushed out or withdrew in November 1955. The Spaak Report was presented to the Six Foreign Ministers in Venice in May 1956. Expected French objections did not materialise. It was accepted that the report should be the basis for drafting of the Common Market and Euratom treaties.

A major issue in the ensuing difficult treaty negotiations was that of the nature and power of the institutions to be created, particularly given that much of the debate in 1954 over the EDC had been about the powers of central institutions, and a rejection of supranationalism. On the other hand, there was also the belief that any new arrangements had to move beyond the unanimity rule which prevailed in the Council of Europe. The small states feared domination by the more powerful and were strong advocates of institutions with some independence from governments. The ECSC model set something of a precedent, but by 1956–57 there was a determination that a Council of Ministers, made up of representatives of the Member States, should be the prime decision-making body, with the High Authority, or as it was now to be known, the Commission, acting as the initiator of policy in an independent manner. It was also to ensure the carrying out of treaty obligations and the administration of certain escape clauses. There was to be a gradual movement towards majority voting, but this was to be weighted in such a way as to ensure that the three larger states would not automatically gain their way.

Although the inclusion of agriculture was never in doubt since it was so crucial to the economies of key states – in France over 20% and in Italy over 30% of the working population worked on the land – its inclusion did cause difficulties. These could only be resolved by agreeing on general objectives to be attained by the end of a transitional period. Euratom raised problems, because of the links between the peaceful and defence-related uses of nuclear energy. In fact, this was to remain a difficulty for many years after 1957 and partly explains why Euratom never lived up to its original promise. A thorny issue during the negotiations proved to be the relationship between the Six and their overseas territories, that is, their former colonies. This was only resolved at the last minute at a Heads of Government meeting, and only then because the French were able to argue that without an outcome satisfactory to them, there would be little prospect of successful ratification in France. There were other troublesome issues, such as the pace of harmonisation, especially of social policy. The two new treaties were signed on 25 March 1957 in Rome. Ratification proceeded without setbacks and the two new Communities came into being in January 1958.

The history of the integration of Europe from 1945 to 1957 is summarised in Box 1.1.

THREE COMMUNITIES, ONE PURPOSE

EACH OF the three separate communities – ECSC, EEC and Euratom – had its own distinct legal base. Although the Communities that were created covered coal and steel, atomic energy and a customs union and common market, their work programme was purely economic and there was always a political motive behind their creation. While partly influenced by the perceived Soviet threat, these political motives more importantly remained in the tradition of the Resistance manifesto, Spinelli, The Hague and the Schuman Plan.

That preoccupation was reflected, for example, in the grandiloquent Preamble to the Treaty of Paris of 1951 creating the ECSC:

> Considering that world peace can be safeguarded only by creative efforts commensurate with the dangers that threaten it, . . .
> Convinced that the contribution which an organised and vital Europe can make to civilization is indispensable to the maintenance of peaceful relations, . . . Resolved to substitute for age-old rivalries the merging of their essential interests; to create, by establishing an economic community, the basis for a broader and deeper community among peoples long divided by bloody conflicts; and to lay the foundations for institutions which will give direction to a destiny henceforward shared. . . .[39]

By 1957 the aspiration was more muted, but the Preamble to the EEC Treaty recorded that the Member States were

> Determined to lay the foundations of an ever closer union among the peoples of Europe . . . Resolved by thus pooling their resources to preserve and strengthen peace and liberty, and calling upon the other peoples of Europe who share their ideal to join in their efforts. . . .[40]

Nonetheless, what began to become clear was the tension between the realisation that there were important gains to be made from working together and the will to do so, and increasingly growing concerns about fundamental and traditional issues of politics and international politics: where was power to lie, who was to exercise it, and who were to

21

gain or lose in terms of resources and values. In the period since 1951 and 1957 these issues have been at the forefront of developments in the European Communities, or have lain not far from the surface of arguments that superficially appeared to be about other things. That continues to be the case today, as the central issues of the two Inter-governmental Conferences of the 1990s, Agenda 2000 and the fifth enlargement are about the issues of power, resources and the very vision of the future shape of the European enterprise.

EARLY SUCCESS

The new European Economic Community was fortunate initially in that its launch occurred in a period with a benign economic environment. Industrial producers felt able to invest and expand production and the more than expected rate of reduction of tariffs further instilled confidence. By the summer of 1961 the British government moved to apply for membership of what it had formerly regarded as unworkable and undesirable. It had noted that within three years of its origins the EEC had cut its internal tariffs by 30% (a year ahead of schedule), with further accelerated cuts in the pipeline, and that rate of economic growth in EEC states had outstripped that of Britain. A British White Paper recorded that between 1954 and 1960 total output grew faster in the EEC states, except in Belgium, than in Britain, and that industrial output grew by over 50% in the EEC states in that period compared to 20% in Britain.[41] It was also clear that this economic success was beginning to result in a changing pattern of inward investment from the USA, with the EEC states now beginning to take the 50% plus share that had previously been enjoyed by Britain. This economic progress continued throughout the 1960s, and in July 1968 the Member States managed to achieve the formal completion of the creation of the customs union – that is, the final abolition of customs duties on goods traded within the Six and the introduction of the Common Customs Tariff towards the rest of the world – some 18 months ahead of schedule.

Another primary task of the EEC was to put flesh and bones on the Common Agricultural Policy (CAP), Articles 38 to 46 of the EEC Treaty only having set out the general outlines of such a policy: defining the products to which it should apply and laying down its objectives in the most general terms. In July 1958 at a conference in Stresa the Foreign Ministers began the task of teasing out the CAP's guiding principles and laying the basis of subsequent legislation on CAP. It took a further two years to reach full agreement on the basic principles of:

- the single market (free movement of agricultural goods);
- joint financial responsibility (that is, an agricultural budget);
- Community preference (over imports).

The CAP was established in July 1962. It came into force progressively between 1962 and 1968. The question of how it was to be funded was a factor behind one of the biggest crises the EC has ever known, the so-called Empty Chair crisis of 1965–66. Prior to that crisis, the new EEC was widely regarded as a great success:

- trade and investment grew;
- rapid progress was made to dismantling tariffs;
- the CAP was established;
- agreement on a Value Added Tax (VAT) system was reached;
- free movement of people began;
- there was the beginnings of a competition policy; and
- the EEC began to make its mark on the world economy. In the Kennedy Round (1964–1967) of the General Agreement on Tariffs and Trade [GATT], for example, the European Commission under Article 113 represented the EEC with a negotiating mandate given to it by the Council.

There was also the beginnings of a different relationship with the African territories linked to the Member States, this being reflected in the Yaoundé Convention association agreement between the Community and 18 African states in July 1963, followed by another agreement in 1969.

All of this seemed to demonstrate that powerful centripetal forces were at work and that, perhaps, some determinism was occurring leading inexorably to ever-closer union among the Member States or the people of the European Community.

The initial phases of the Community were also aided by the dynamic political leadership exhibited by Walter Hallstein, the Commission President from 1958 to 1967. Hallstein was no shrinking violet, on one occasion commenting to journalists that he could be regarded as a kind of Prime Minister of Europe. He demonstrated what a Commission President with a clear treaty mandate, political leadership skills and the support of Member States could achieve, although by 1965 he was also to demonstrate what could happen when these were challenged. The 1965–66 crisis also suggested that there was nothing inevitable about the progress of the EEC and that powerful centrifugal forces could challenge the apparently effortless spill-over and progress that some had foreseen.

Blows to apparently inexorable progress

It was the French President, de Gaulle, who challenged the emerging conventional wisdom. De Gaulle (President of France 1958–69) had a very definite view of the place of France in the world and what it meant to be French. He understood both to mean that France could not be beholden or subordinate to any other entity, be it another state or a European organisation. For example, in March 1966 he announced that France was leaving the integrated military structure of NATO. Even before then he had asserted his authority in the EEC on three significant occasions: vetoing British membership in 1963 (and subsequently in 1967); proposing an inter-governmental alternative to the Community method and system in the French-inspired Fouchet negotiations; and challenging the whole ethos of the Community and the role of the Commission in the Empty Chair crisis of 1965–66.

Britain applied for membership of the EEC on 31 July 1961, and the negotiations to identify the terms on offer had commenced on 10 October 1961. On 14 January 1963, the day before two scheduled meetings were due to take place, de Gaulle announced to a press conference that in the French view the British were not ready to accept the conditions of EEC membership. The Commission, however, later issued an analysis that suggested that substantial progress had been made in the negotiations and that, contrary to de Gaulle's assertions, Britain had demonstrated a willingness to accept the Treaty of Rome. The Commission Report implied that the negotiations might have eventually succeeded, and that it was possible to envisage solutions to the major unresolved issues. De Gaulle felt, however, that the British had not severed their dependence upon and allegiance to the United States and perhaps also felt, as it was put by one of his ministers:

> Now, with six members, there are five hens and a rooster. If you join (with the other countries), there will perhaps be seven or eight hens. But there will be *two* roosters. That isn't as agreeable.[42]

That is, French leadership of the Community would be challenged. De Gaulle did not consult his five partners over this veto.

In the second crisis de Gaulle began to lay out an alternative vision of how the Member States should co-operate. In February 1961 at a European summit, or more formally Heads of State or Government meeting, it was agreed to establish an Inter-governmental Committee on Political Union under the chairmanship of M. Christian Fouchet, a French career diplomat, to examine the issue of political co-operation. In Bonn that summer the Member States agreed to seek to meet regularly and to try to concert their foreign policies. When the Fouchet committee began its work it quickly became apparent that those involved had very different ideas about the nature of the political union, and that the French wished to take the opportunity to re-model the Community in de Gaulle's preferred inter-governmental model. The French talked of a Union of *States* not of *People*, a significant difference, and even in a second draft maintained the essentials of their position, despite the hostility of the other members. They even sought to include economic matters in the remit of the new Union, a blatant challenge to the Commission and the other Member States. In fact, the talks eventually faltered over the perennially disputed issues of whether to move away from supranationalism and how far, whether to circumvent the EEC Commission, and whether to deal with defence outside NATO and the American umbrella, something that all but France bitterly opposed. Despite the failure of the Fouchet initiative it proved to be indicative of de Gaulle's thinking. His major challenge provoked the crisis of 1965–66.

Although the Empty Chair crisis grew out of the need to find appropriate financial arrangements for the CAP, it actually went much deeper. It represented an attempt by de Gaulle to uphold the authority of the Member States at the expense of the Community, but more especially at the expense of the Commission, and to seek to postpone or halt the movement – provided by the treaty – to more majority voting with the end of the transition phase in December 1965. The Commission had been asked to submit proposals for financing the CAP, something dear to French hearts. In its proposals it argued not only that the CAP should be fully financed but that to do this the Community should have its 'own resources', and that given that there would be no national parliamentary control over these resources, the European Parliament (known at the time as the

Assembly) should acquire budgetary control powers. It was hoped that French interest in the first part of the proposal would sweeten the pill of the other two aspects. It did not, and especially in the context of the approach of more majority voting the French decided to take a stand. Discussions were pursued until France, coincidentally holding the Presidency of the Council and thus chairing the meeting, decided that progress was nil and closed the proceedings on 15 June 1965. France then boycotted Community meetings (apart from CAP Management meetings), and listed ten complaints it had against the Commission, the Decalogue. It was only in January 1966 – after de Gaulle had failed to obtain a sufficient majority in the first round of the French presidential elections in December 1965 – that France agreed to attend a meeting to discuss these issues. As a sign that it was not a normal Community meeting, it was held in Luxembourg, not Brussels. Fundamentally, the outcome was an agreement to disagree. The French continued to maintain that individual states must have a veto on matters that they considered important. The Five argued that while every effort should be made to reach agreements acceptable to all, talks could not go on indefinitely. In fact, political reality meant that it was always unlikely that a major state would have something to which it objected imposed upon it. The difference of view was apparent in the communiqué:

> When if the case of decisions which may be taken by a majority vote on a proposal from the Commission very important interests of one or more partners are at stake, the members of the Council will endeavour, within a reasonable time, to reach solutions which can be adopted by all the members of the Council, while respecting their mutual interests and those of the Communities ... With regard to the previous paragraph, the French delegation considers that where very important interests are at stake the discussion must be continued until unanimous agreement is reached. The six delegations note that there is a divergence of views on what should be done in the event of a failure to reach complete agreement. The six delegations nevertheless consider that this divergence does not prevent the Community's work being resumed in accordance with the normal procedure.[43]

Subsequently the Council behaved as if all had accepted the French demand.

ANOTHER RELAUNCH

Some ten years after it came into operation, the blossom appeared to be fading from the cheeks of the EEC's achievements as it appeared that centrifugal forces were stronger than the previously supposed invincible centripetal forces. But just as the 1949 crisis over the Council of Europe had been followed by the Schuman initiative of 1950 and the apparent catastrophe of the EDC failure of 1954 had been followed by the relaunch of 1955–57, so the trauma of de Gaulle was ended with his resignation in April 1969 and was followed by the revitalisation of the Community process at The Hague summit of December 1969, another meeting of the Six Heads of State or Government. French standing had been severely diminished by the domestic crisis of 1968 when the French government came close to collapse, and the new German government, of a different political persuasion from all previous German governments, was in any case no longer willing to play a subordinate role to French leadership. The message from The Hague summit rang out for many years in the three words, drafted by M. Jean-Pierre Brunet, a French official at the meeting: completing, deepening, widening.

Completing meant initially essentially securing a proper financial basis for the CAP, something still not achieved by 1969. It became much later the single market programme. *Deepening* involved the production of two reports in 1970: the Davignon Report of July on the problems of political unification, which picked up on the previous abortive efforts towards foreign policy co-operation, as had been attempted in the Fouchet Plan, and which led to European Political Co-operation, the forerunner of the CFSP,[44] and the Werner Report of October, the 'Report to the Council and Commission on the Realization by Stages of Economic and Monetary Union in the Community'. The Werner Committee said that they considered 'that economic and monetary union is an objective realizable in the course of the present decade', that is, by 1980, but added with prescience, 'provided the political will ... is present'.[45] In fact, this was to be yet another case of centrifugal and centripetal forces contending with one another, or rather, the economic imperatives coming into conflict with the political and national interests of key Member States, namely France and Germany.

Widening meant enlargement, in particular that serious negotiations would now be entered into in a positive spirit with the four applicant states: Britain, Denmark, Ireland and Norway. The negotiations commenced on 30 June 1970. The applicants had to 'accept the Treaties and *their political aims*, [and] the decisions taken since the entry into force of the Treaties and the options adopted in the sphere of development'.[46] By early 1971 the negotiations were running into difficulties, but a crucial meeting in May 1971, between President Pompidou of France and Prime Minister Heath of Britain made clear that this time the political will existed to find solutions, and in June the remaining four big issues in the British negotiations were resolved: the UK budgetary contribution; the length of the transitional phase; the problem of British Commonwealth sugar's access to the British market; and the issue of the access of and prices for New Zealand lamb and dairy produce. The Irish, given their inordinate dependence on the British for imports and exports, felt they had to join if the British did, although they also hoped for gains from the CAP and increased foreign investment. There was also the prize of the negotiated Protocol No. 30 in the Treaty of Accession, which noted that regional imbalances between parts of the Community would need to be addressed, which the Irish interpreted as a commitment to a far-reaching regional policy. The Danes too joined because they felt they had little economic alternative, fearing that key economic decisions that affected them were taken without their participation. The Irish and Danes joined after referendums: the Irish voted by 83% to 17% and the Danes 63.3% to 36.7% in favour. The British joined by parliamentary vote, although in a referendum in June 1975, two-and-a-half years after membership, 67.2% voted for continued membership. All four states signed the Treaties of Accession in Brussels on 22 January 1972, but in a referendum in Norway in September 1972 the people rejected membership on the terms on offer by

53.49% to 44.51%. The Norwegians stopped attending meetings to which they had been invited prior to their assumed membership, and returned all the documents they had received since January 1972. This again serves as a salutary warning that the progress of integration was not uniformly smooth or progressive.

A summary of the developments between 1958 and 1972 is given in Box 2.1.

Box 2.1   Key dates in the history of European integration, 1958–72

1958	January	The Treaties of Rome come into force and the EEC and Euratom Commissions are set up in Brussels.
1959	January	First EEC tariff cuts.
1960	January	The Stockholm Convention establishing the European Free Trade Association is signed on the initiative of the United Kingdom.
	December	OEEC becomes OECD and includes USA and Canada.
1961	July-August	Ireland, Denmark and the United Kingdom apply for membership of EEC.
1962	July	The Common Agricultural Policy is introduced.
1963	January	General de Gaulle announces at a press conference that France will veto the United Kingdom's accession to the Community.
	July	An association agreement is signed between the Community and eighteen African countries in Yaoundé.
1965	April	A treaty merging the executives of the three Communities is signed in Brussels. It comes into force on 1 July 1967.
	July	France begins boycott of Community institutions.
1966	January	The 'Luxembourg compromise' is agreed, France resuming its seat in the Council in return for retention of the unanimity requirement where very important interests are at stake.
1967	May	Denmark, Ireland and the United Kingdom re-apply for Community membership.
	July	Fusion Treaty takes effect.
	December	Six fail to agree on enlargement.
1968	May	Crisis in France.
	July	Remaining customs duties in intra-Community trade in manufactured goods are abolished eighteen months ahead of schedule and the Common External Tariff (CET) is introduced.
1969	December	At The Hague Summit the Community's Heads of State or Government decide to bring the transitional period to an end by adopting definitive arrangements for the Common Agricultural Policy and agreeing in principle to give the Community its own resources. They also paved the way for enlargement, EPC and discussion of EMU.

Box 2.1 (*cont.*)

1970	April	A treaty providing for the gradual introduction of an own resources system is signed in Luxembourg. It also extends the budgetary powers of the European Parliament.
	June	Negotiations with four prospective Member States (Denmark, Ireland, Norway and the United Kingdom) open in Luxembourg.
1972	January	The Treaty on the Accession of Denmark, Ireland, Norway and the United Kingdom is signed in Brussels.
	April	The currency 'snake' is set up, the Six agreeing to limit the margin of fluctuation between their currencies to 1.25%.
	September	Norway withdraws its proposed membership following a referendum.

A HOPEFUL PARIS AGENDA

Centrifugal pressures in a new environment

The new Community of Nine came into being on 1 January 1973, amid great optimism about the future. Not only had the Six enlarged, but in Paris in October 1972 the Six and the three new members had agreed an ambitious agenda of work for the next few years:

- A renewal of commitment to economic and monetary union by 1980.
- A commitment to address regional imbalances by the creation of a Regional Development Fund.
- A new emphasis upon improving the quality of life of its citizens, which was partly reflected in a new emphasis upon Social Policy and the Social Fund.
- A new emphasis upon providing a uniform foundation for industry throughout the Community, by focusing on the removal of technical barriers, etc.
- A decision to establish Community environment and energy policies.
- An intensification of political co-operation, as expressed in the attempt to co-operate in the area of foreign policy.
- Some attempts to make the institutions more effective, and especially to strengthen the supervisory powers of the European Parliament.[47]

It appeared as if the Community was moving to a new phase of its development.

But, again, there was to be no plain sailing or inexorable progress. The Norwegian referendum had dented confidence a little, and the general economic circumstances had begun to be somewhat less benign. Even more importantly, before the first year of the life of the new Community was complete, a major shock occurred to the Community and international system, namely the consequences of the October 1973 Yom Kippur war between Israel and its Arab neighbours, which completely changed both the political and economic environment within which the Community operated.

These consequences included an embargo on the supply of oil to those who had supported Israel, most notably in the EC, the Netherlands, and this was coupled with the partially related Organisation of Petroleum Exporting Countries (OPEC) decision to quadruple the price of oil. The result was crisis in Western Europe. Crucially there was insufficient Community solidarity to defend a fellow Member State. The UK and France were quick to make oil deals with the Arab states. The Community was shown to have little backbone when Arab ministers turned up in Copenhagen in December 1973, making a series of demands, just as the Nine were issuing a 'Declaration on European Identity', which spoke of them speaking 'increasingly with a single voice' in international affairs.[48]

Not only was there shown to be little political solidarity, but the economic climate now changed significantly for the worse: economic growth, which had averaged 4.8% in the previous decade now dropped to 3.4% in the mid-1970s; unemployment rose by 400% in the decade after 1973 and inflation doubled in 1973 compared to the 1960s average, and doubled again in 1974, inflation in Britain reaching 25% in 1975. Not helping the situation, as narrow national interests held sway, the limited agreement reached in Luxembourg in 1966 was being invoked on a whole range of issues, usually far broader than any normal understanding of 'very important interests'. The Commission appeared to have become intimidated by the legacy of the 1965–66 crisis, and after Hallstein's departure in 1967 lacked skilful political leadership. Perhaps not surprisingly, in 1983 some academics expressed concern that:

> Western Europe is drifting . . . the existence of the European Community is under serious threat. In sharp contrast to only a decade ago, the position of Western Europe seems to be challenged from all sides. If nothing is done, we are faced with the disintegration of the most important European achievement since World War II.[49]

To confound matters, after the British election of 1979, the leaders of the Community had to contend with Mrs Thatcher as the Prime Minister of the United Kingdom. Mrs Thatcher not only held firm, almost Gaullist ideas, about the nation-state and the appropriate roles of national governments and European officials, but also expressed a determination to win Britain's 'money back'. Britain's financial contribution had been an issue in the pre-accession negotiations and in the re-negotiation of 1974–75 which paved the way for the 1975 referendum. This time five years of acrimonious debate and negotiation followed Mrs Thatcher's November 1979 declaration to the Fontainebleau European Council in June 1984. Part of the difficulty was the sense of *déjà vu* among the other Member States, given the previous British concern on the issue, and partly it was a question of the tone adopted by Mrs Thatcher.

The arguments were sometimes very bitter and often crowded other matters off the agenda of European Council meetings. These meetings, which were supposed to chart a strategy for the future of the European Community, became bogged-down in haggling. This was, in addition, a traditional political battle about 'who pays and who loses'. The atmosphere was further exacerbated by British disputes with their partners over the failure to reform the CAP and the fixing of prices for agricultural produce. Indeed, in May

1982 Britain attempted to veto price increases of, on average, 11%, partly because it objected to them and partly as part of the battle over the budgetary contributions. The partners rebuffed this linkage, and in a unique event at the time, decided to vote on a matter that the British considered to be covered by the Luxembourg compromise of 1966. Not only were they agitated by the British approach, but some also felt that having supported Britain a matter of weeks previously over the Falklands war, Britain should have been rather more open to compromise on other issues. Perhaps typical of the sclerosis that appeared to be settling into the arteries of European integration at this time, in February 1982, following home rule for Greenland from Denmark and a referendum in Greenland, Greenland withdrew from the Communities.

The centrifugal forces appeared to be in the ascendant, and this was partly reflected in the reaction to and the outcome of a bold attempt to move the European Community forward, the Genscher–Colombo Plan, or the 'Draft European Act submitted by the government of the Federal Republic of Germany and the Italian Republic'.[50] Towards the end of 1981 the German Foreign Minister, Genscher, anticipating the German Presidency in the first half of 1983, launched a new initiative for European Union, with immediate support from his Italian counterpart. Discussions lasted eighteen months before the Solemn Declaration of European Union was adopted at Stuttgart, at the end of the Germany Presidency in June 1983.[51] But what should have been a bold leap forward proved to be a hesitant step, since the Solemn Declaration, unlike the originally proposed Draft Act, had no treaty or legal status, and had no immediate effect, although traces of it were to reappear in both the Single European Act of 1986 and the Treaty on European Union of 1992. The Genscher–Colombo Plan spoke of:

- creating a 'European Union';
- a common foreign policy
- the co-ordination of security policy to safeguard Europe's independence;
- closer cultural co-operation;
- a more effective decision-making structure, including attempts to restrict the invocation of 'very important interests'; and
- a comprehensive political and legal framework capable of development, including the merging of the structures of the EC and the EPC under the umbrella of the European Council.

As noted, at least in the immediate time frame, the outcome was disappointing. While elements of the Genscher–Colombo Plan remained, by 1983 it had become mostly rhetoric, significantly the 'merging' of the EC and the EPC was dropped; 'security' was defined as the 'political and economic aspects' but not the military or defence aspects; no restrictions on the Luxembourg compromise came into being; and no formally binding legal framework was adopted.

Some therefore remained disturbed by the power of the forces of stagnation, or even worse, of pressures for renationalisation. In 1983 the prospects for further integration appeared to have receded significantly. It was not all bad news, but even some signs of progress, which appeared to support the continuation of progress towards integration, were in fact mixed. Indeed, with Mrs Thatcher's hostility to the Commission and the Labour Party's move in opposition to a position of calling in their 1983 General Election manifesto for 'British withdrawal from the Community' within the next five years, the atmosphere was not encouraging.

Even the holding of the first direct elections in June 1979 to the European Parliament was not as positive an event as had been anticipated when the idea was first mooted. The election was held on different days (Thursday 9 June and Sunday 12 June), there were a variety of electoral systems, despite the Treaty of Rome requirement [Article 138.3] that there be 'elections by direct universal suffrage in accordance with a uniform procedure in all Member States', and the campaigns were overwhelmingly national in character, fought on a national not a European agenda. Also disappointing for European enthusiasts was the turnout at 63%, which hardly suggested a public passion for the Community or the Parliament. Since 1979 the turnout has continued to drop. On the other hand, it could be argued that this still represents a larger percentage of voters than USA Presidential elections.

COUNTERVAILING SIGNS OF SUCCESS

The turnout in the European Parliament elections of 1979 ought perhaps not to divert attention from the fact that such elections to a common parliamentary body were actually taking place, and the coming together of the MEPs (now 626), has enormous symbolic importance, especially given their ability to question the actions (and inaction) of Member State governments and the Commission, to thwart the will of governments over some aspects of the budget and with increasing powers to be awkward about the passage of Community legislation. Similarly, despite the continuing British recalcitrance, the 1975 referendum meant that Britain was clearly going to remain a member. That had important consequences for the Irish too, since a British 'No' in 1975 would have made continuing Irish membership problematic.

There were other developments in the 1980s that had positive and negative effects. One such was the enlargements of 1981 to take in Greece and of 1986 to include Portugal and Spain. In some ways, the three had many experiences in common, especially recent experience of dictatorship and levels of economic development well below the Community average. However, the Community of Nine felt a strong political and moral obligation to endeavour to consolidate the move to democracy in these states.

Greece had undergone a turbulent domestic political scene since 1945, with civil war, arguments about monarchy or republic and fiercer than usual domestic arguments between left and right. This had culminated in April 1967 when units of the Greek army staged a coup and began the 'Rule of the Colonels'. This regime lasted until July 1974, when an attempt by the regime to influence events in Cyprus backfired and led to a Turkish invasion of the island and the downfall of the Colonels. Greece returned to democracy.

Prior to the Junta taking power, Greece had had an Association Agreement with the Community that included the prospect of later membership. This Agreement was

31

suspended until after the Junta fell. The new government applied for full membership in June 1975 and in 1976 the Commission issued its Opinion. This made it quite clear that:

> the Commission has been deeply conscious of the obligation that lies on the Community to find a fitting and appropriate response to the Greek request for membership . . . It is clear that the consolidation of Greece's democracy that is a fundamental concern not only of the Greek people but also to the Community and its Member States, is intimately related to the evolution of Greece's relationship with the Community. It is in the light of these considerations that the Commission recommends that a clear affirmative reply be given to the Greek request and that negotiations for Greek accession be opened.[52]

In other words, the political imperative, not the level of economic development of the Greek economy, was the crucial factor: politics not logic or other criteria ruled the day. Greece finally became a member in 1981.

Much the same occurred in the context of the Iberian enlargement to include Portugal and Spain. Portugal had not been a democracy for decades, democracy only being restored in the spring of 1974. The new Portugal applied for membership in March 1977. Spain had undergone the dictatorship of Franco for forty years, and it was only after his death in the autumn of 1975 that membership of the Community became a possibility, with Spain applying in June 1977. The negotiations with Spain and Portugal were long drawn out, partly because they involved some vested economic interests on the part of some members such as wine and olive oil, but more importantly because the Nine were preoccupied with their own internal problems, especially but not only finance. Portugal and Spain became members in 1986. It is interesting to note that in the latter cases there was a considerable time-lag between application and adhesion, and that in all three cases the principal arguments for were political and notions of reinforcing democracy in these states, not what their contribution to the cause of integration might be. Indeed, the admission of Greece was to cause some problems, with a change of government there within the first year of membership. The new government, formed by the Panhellenic Socialist Party (PASOK), set a radical nationalist agenda. Relations reached a nadir in 1983 when the PASOK regime vetoed the proposal in the EPC to condemn the Soviet Union for shooting down a South Korean civilian airliner.

This is illustrative of the problems that enlargement can cause in increasing the heterogeneity of the Community, and that even the increase in size itself causes problems in reaching decisions. The 1973 enlargement brought in Britain and Denmark, the former almost immediately seeking to renegotiate, causing five years of difficulty over its budgetary contribution, and the latter, in its attempts to renegotiate the Single European Act, demonstrating by the mid-1980s that it wished to exercise a brake on certain aspects of the integration endeavour. The Community also discovered in the 1980s that a Community of Ten or Twelve was very different from one of Six. Seeking the consent of Six to almost anything and everything was difficult as the 1965–66 crisis showed, but Nine, Ten and Twelve, let alone Fifteen plus, was always going to be inherently difficult. It is also true that all of the enlargements caused hiccups in the

Commission administration and staffing. It is not clear that these problems were success-fully addressed in the 1970s or 1980s or later.

CENTRIPETAL FACTORS RE-EMERGE

Nonetheless, the expansion from Six to Twelve was a sign of success, that the Community idea, experience and progress could act as a magnet to others, even previous doubters; the British referendum had secured the place of a significant political, security and economic actor in the Community, and that of Ireland; the budgetary issue was resolved; there had been an expansion of the scope of the EPC to include the 'political and economic aspects of security'; and the EPC process had seen a strengthening of its framework.

There were other positive developments too, most particularly, as after the crises of the early and mid-1970s, the Member States began to move forward on the monetary union front, albeit initially more cautiously than previously. This was the train of events that was to lead to the European Monetary System (EMS), with its Exchange Rate Mechanism (ERM), and in 1985–86 the launching of the initiative to seek to achieve a Single European Market by the end of 1992. This stream of development was born out of the realisation in 1977 that something needed to be done to rescue the Community from the drift that it appeared to have fallen into.

In January 1977 Roy Jenkins of Britain had become the President of the Commission. Jenkins had long supported the cause of European integration, even defying a Labour Party whip in the 1971 parliamentary vote on whether to accept the Conservative gov-ernment's negotiated terms of entry. In 1977, as the President of the Commission, Jenkins was looking for a new initiative to move the Community and the debate on. He decided to proclaim afresh the goal of monetary union, and to do so not by advocating the tradi-tional path of incrementalism, but by proposing a quantum leap.[53] In November 1977 the Commission sent a communication to the Council on the prospects for economic and monetary union. Although it contained no specific proposals, it argued that the project was stagnating and that this in itself was a reason for a new effort. The European Council in December welcomed the initiative and in the spring of 1978 France and Germany work-ing together sought to develop the idea. They sought British participation, but when the British government declined to enter into commitments, their involvement ceased. By the Bremen European Council, held during the German Presidency in July 1978, the French and Germans had a scheme ready for discussion. At the end of the year in Brussels the European Council (still under the German Presidency) adopted the European Monetary System. Three states contended that they were special cases – Britain, Ireland and Italy – which caused delay, but after special financial arrangements to help Ireland and Italy were agreed, they joined the full EMS. Britain joined the EMS but not its ERM component, from which it remained aloof for another decade.

While, therefore, EMS was generally a positive development, it also saw the first step and acceptance of a two-tier, or to use a phrase that was developed later, a *flexible* Europe.

Again the centripetal factors were not alone, and in this case the seeds of later centrifugal devices and pressures were also laid. This saga also, however, again demonstrated what could be achieved if the political will was there, if ideas had significant actors supporting them – in this case the Commission President (although the result was not entirely the one that Jenkins had sought, nor was the final system the one proposed by the Commission) – and when the German Chancellor and the French President worked hand in glove.

The EMS started to operate in March 1979. In essence, it was an attempt to regulate the exchange rates of the participating states and to build a zone of monetary stability in Western Europe. It contained two elements: an Exchange Rate Mechanism (ERM) and a European Currency Unit (ECU). The ERM linked national currencies together in a structure that imposed limits on how far each currency could fluctuate against its counterparts. For some this was 6%, but for most there was a narrower 2.25% band. Two states belonged to the EMS without belonging to the ERM – Britain and Greece. The former joined eleven years later in October 1990, but Greece remained outside until 1998. Initially the ERM worked as flexibly as intended, and gradually moved to a situation in the late 1980s where there were no significant parity changes. It was deemed a success, contributing to greater stability in the exchange rates and to the lowering of inflation, although in the early 1990s it ran into trouble. The other element of the EMS was the European Currency Unit (ECU), a basket of the currencies of all the Member States, weighted for their economic importance, which was also used as a measure to trip action if a currency deviated more than 75% from the currency's possible fluctuation under the bilateral parity grid of the ERM (see pp. 249–50). The experience of the EMS was to provide a powerful factor in the later development of plans for Economic and Monetary Union (EMU). An even more powerful stimulant was the evolution of the Single Market. That in turn was part of the wider developments associated with the Single European Act of 1986, which was also a direct attempt to cure the apparent malaise of the European Community. Thus the strands behind the Single European Act (SEA) were both political and economic.

THE SINGLE EUROPEAN ACT

Apart from resolving the British budgetary problem, the Fontainebleau European Council meeting of June 1984 decided to set up two new committees to prepare reports on the future of the Communities. One was the Committee on 'Citizen's Europe' chaired by a former Italian MEP, Adonnino. This was a reflection of a continuing concern that developments at the European level did not seem to be capturing the popular imagination and, indeed, many people in Europe could not see any direct connection between what occurred in the European Community and their own lives. This Committee did not resolve the issue,[54] which was to become a recurrent theme for the next decade or more.

More significant in its impact on integration was the second committee, the ad hoc Committee on Institutional Affairs, chaired by the former Irish Foreign Minister, Jim

Dooge. The Dooge Committee did not set out to be consensual, and its final report was littered with dissenting footnotes. There were thirty-seven reservations and two closing unilateral declarations. The mainstream report looked towards a single market by the end of the decade; the improvement of competitiveness; the promotion of common values (including cultural); the search for external identity (including security and defence); more regular recourse to voting in decision-making (while safeguarding the veto for very important interests); strengthening the role of the Commission; the participation of the European Parliament in legislating (including co-decision in certain defined matters); and operationally the convocation of an Inter-governmental Conference (IGC) to draft a treaty of European Union.[55] The Dooge Committee reported to the European Council meeting in Brussels in March 1985. Three months later at Milan the European Council did not act on Dooge directly but rather adopted Franco-German drafts and a British draft prepared for other purposes as the working basis for an IGC. The Italian Presidency took a snap vote to call the Inter-governmental Conference suggested by Dooge, but to which the British, Danes and Greeks objected. The Italians contended that the procedural decision to consult the European Parliament on convening a conference could be taken by a simple majority. The conference was subsequently convened. Crucially, of course, those who objected had the knowledge that any outcome of an IGC suggesting changes to the treaties required their consent; nothing could be changed without unanimity.

Parallel to this development, the Commission was busy preparing proposals for the Single Market, in effect seeking to make a reality of the Treaty of Rome objective of a frontier-free market for goods, services and people, that is, having by and large eliminated tariffs and quantitative restrictions, there was a need to eliminate non-tariff restrictions. The Common Market created by the Customs Union was still fragmented by a vast range of restrictions on intra-Community trade in goods and services. By the mid 1980s many different groups and individuals, including the European Parliament, which in February 1984 adopted the 'Draft Treaty establishing the European Union'[56] (in practice having the effect of exhortation rather than any constitutional significance), were pressing for action, but the decisive players turned out to be the President and Vice-President of the European Commission, Jacques Delors and Lord Cockfield. The intellectual justification was provided later by the Cechinni Report, an econometric study of the benefits to be won from the completion of a proper Single Market.[57] Rather like his predecessor Roy Jenkins, Jacques Delors (Commission President 1985–94) was looking for something to provide impetus and a new agenda, and Cockfield came from a de-regulatory Conservative government in Britain. Together Cockfield and Delors combined to produce a Commission White Paper 'Completing the Internal Market'[58] in June 1985 which set out an annotated, precise and timed programme for the completion of the Single Market by the end of 1992. Against opposition and faint-heartedness they pushed through the bulk of the 300 measures or so needed to eliminate frontier controls on the circulation of goods, services, capital and people.

In the second half of 1985 an IGC agreed the Single Market programme and wrote the Single Market into the treaties. The Single European Act was signed on 17 February 1986 by nine Member States, followed on 28 February by Denmark, Italy and Greece. It is the

'Single' Act because it contains both the necessary revisions of the three founding treaties of the three Communities and separate treaty provision, for the first time, on European Political Co-operation. The SEA extended qualified majority voting, formalised Community concern with research and development, introduced the 'co-operation procedure' between the Council and the European Parliament, and gave the Parliament the right to grant or withhold assent on the entry of new members and on association agreements. Its major features, however, were the articles providing the basis for the Single Market, especially the new Article 100A, which provided for qualified majority voting, perceived by all, including Mrs Thatcher, to be necessary to bring it into being. It also formalised EPC, largely by codifying existing practice, expanding the scope of topics to be discussed and introducing a limited secretariat for this activity.

The SEA was the result of a series of compromises and of the political environment. There was a convergence of national interests among leading states. Britain was keen on the apparent deregulatory aspects of the SEA, while others appreciated the decision-making improvements prior to the accession of Portugal and Spain. Britain also had begun to fear exclusion from the first division of developments. Originally, Mrs Thatcher described the SEA as a 'modest decision' but in fact it operated as a dynamic for Community development, and the goals of the internal market were largely completed by the end of 1992. The British tended to view the Single Market as the culmination of a process of economic integration. Others, however, saw it as a beginning, since they came to argue that it would be incomplete without an economic and monetary union (EMU). The Danish government was required by its parliament, the Folketing, to seek a renegotiation of the Act before signing, but it was told by its partners that no revision would be acceptable. The Danes accepted it, and this was subsequently confirmed by a referendum when the Danish people voted 56.2% in support of the SEA. The SEA itself only came into operation on 1 July 1987 after a delay caused by a constitutional challenge to certain of its provisions on European Political Co-operation in Ireland.

The main developments in the integration of Europe between 1973 and 1986 can be see in Box 2.2.

Box 2.2   Key dates in the history of European integration 1973–86

1973	January	Accession of Denmark, Ireland and United Kingdom.
	October	Yom Kippur war in Middle East leading to oil and economic crises in Europe and elsewhere.
1974	April	First Gymnich informal meeting of foreign ministers.
	December	At the Paris Summit the Community's Heads of State or Government decide to meet three times a year as the European Council, give the go-ahead for direct elections to the European Parliament and agree to set up the European Regional Development Fund (ERDF).

Box 2.2 (*cont.*)

1975	February	A first Convention between the Community and 46 states in Africa, the Caribbean and the Pacific is signed in Lome.
	March	Dublin – First European Council meeting.
	June	'Yes' to continued membership in United Kingdom referendum; Greece applies for membership.
	July	A treaty giving the European Parliament wider budgetary powers and establishing a Court of Auditors is signed. It enters into force on 1 June 1977.
1977	March	Portugal applies for Community membership.
	July	Spain applies for Community membership.
1978	July	At the Bremen European Council, France and the Federal Republic of Germany present a scheme for closer monetary co-operation (the European Monetary System) to replace the currency 'state'.
1979	March	The EMS starts to operate.
	May	The Treaty on the Accession of Greece is signed.
	June	The first direct elections to the European Parliament are held.
	October	A second Convention between the Community and 58 states in Africa, the Caribbean and the Pacific is signed in Lome.
	December	European Parliament for first time does not approve proposed Community budget.
1981	January	Greek accession to Community.
	October	'London Report' on EPC.
1983	June	Stuttgart 'Solemn Declaration on European Union'.
1984	February	European Parliament Draft Treaty establishing the European Union.
	June	Direct elections to the European Parliament are held for the second time. At the Fontainebleau European Council, the Ten reach an agreement on the compensation to be granted to the United Kingdom to reduce its contribution to the Community budget.
	December	A third Lome Convention between the Ten and the ACP states, now numbering 66, is signed in Togo.
1985	June	Commission publishes its White Paper *Completing the Internal Market*. Milan European Council accepts Commission White Paper and calls an Inter-governmental Conference.
	December	At the Luxembourg Council the Ten agree to amend the Treaty of Rome and to revitalise the process of European integration by drawing up a 'Single European Act'.
1986	January	Spain and Portugal join the Community.
	February	The Single European Act is signed in Luxembourg.

ANOTHER LEAP FORWARD

In the negotiations leading to the conclusion of the Single European Act, the Commission and a majority of delegations wanted to lay the Treaty foundations for an economic and monetary union. Although there are oblique references to EMU in the Single European Act, there was no substance or commitment to further development. But in January 1988 the French Finance Ministry circulated a paper on EMU and the German Presidency took up the idea, suggesting a committee to study a monetary area, a central bank and a programme of complementary measures. At the European Council meeting in Hanover in June 1988 it was agreed to establish a committee to examine and propose concrete stages on how economic and monetary union might be realised. It was to be chaired by Delors. The British hoped to use the study to limit the enthusiasm, but they were to be disappointed. In theory the report was not a discussion of 'whether EMU' but of how to bring it into being if a political decision were taken. The report was unanimous in setting out a scheme for EMU; its substantive sections stated the implications of EMU: complete freedom of movement for people, goods, services and capital; and irrevocably fixed exchange rates among national currencies. The report did not specifically recommend a single currency, but this was the logical extension of monetary union. A transfer of decision-making power from the Member States to a European system of central banks would also be necessary, as responsibility for the single monetary policy would need to be assigned to a new body, described as being of a federal nature, because it would work through national central banks but its decisions would be centralised and collective.

Meeting in Madrid in June 1989, the European Council commissioned work, to be based on the Delors' Report, on the preparation of an IGC to lay down the second and third stages of EMU: the first being the completion of the single internal market; the second seeing the setting up of the European Central Bank, to be preceded by a European Monetary Institute; and the third and final stage seeing the introduction of the single currency and the full transfer of competence for monetary policy to the European System of Central Banks. The British did not dissent but made a unilateral declaration to the effect that there was nothing automatic about the timing and content of the third stage. In addition, Britain laid down the conditions on which it might enter the ERM, although this became a matter of dispute between Mrs Thatcher and some of the key members of her cabinet. In October 1990, with John Major as Chancellor, Britain did decide that the 'time was right' and entered the ERM.

The preparatory work for the IGC was undertaken by a group of national experts, headed by a special adviser to President Mitterrand of France, Mme Guigou. The European Council meeting in Strasbourg in December 1989 saw Mitterrand as President declare that a simple majority existed in favour of convening an IGC on EMU, and after further discussions in Rome in October 1990, a detailed agenda for the IGC on EMU was agreed. That was to begin in Rome on 14 December 1990. Mrs Thatcher, having described her European colleagues as living in 'cloud cuckoo land' and having poured cold water on ideas about currency union, found her power base at home had been undermined, and her leadership challenged, bringing her resignation.[59] She was replaced at the Rome December meeting by John Major, who on essentials carried on her policy.

REVOLUTION IN THE EAST: THE COMMUNITY SEEKS TO RESPOND

While this process towards an IGC on economic and monetary union was taking place, the most extraordinary developments were taking place in Eastern and Central Europe, and in the divided Germany. In 1989 the whole European system, which had endured for about forty years, was shaken by the revolution which swept through Eastern and Central Europe and which, by the end of 1991, had even claimed the very existence of the Soviet Union and of communism as a political and socio-economic system. In Germany events developed very rapidly:

- On 7 October 1989 the East German regime celebrated its fortieth anniversary, but by the end of the month their long-time leader, Honecker, had been ousted.
- On 9 November 1989 the Berlin Wall, the physical and symbolic monument to the division of Germany and Europe, was breached by the people.
- On 31 August 1990 there was the signature of the Treaty of Union between the two Germanies.
- On 12 September 1990 the treaty of the Final Settlement with Respect to Germany was signed between the four occupying powers and the two Germanies.
- On 3 October 1990 German unification took place with the accession of the five Eastern Länder (the former East Germany) to the Federal Republic of Germany.

Elsewhere in Eastern and Central Europe the events were just as surprising, as rapid and as revolutionary. In addition, the extra-European environment was altered in August 1990 by the Iraqi invasion and annexation of Kuwait.

On 18 April 1990, on the eve of a European Council meeting in Dublin, President Mitterrand and Chancellor Kohl issued a statement in which they underlined that the upheavals in Europe and the fulfilment of the internal market, along with the plans for EMU, made it necessary to accelerate the political construction of Europe, and transform relations among the Member States into a European Union. Kohl, in particular, was aware of the hostility and apprehension regarding German unification and the speed of events in 1989–90, and wanted to demonstrate that the new Germany would be a 'European Germany'. The letter was discussed at Dublin on 28 April 1990, where it was agreed that there should be a

> detailed examination . . . on the need for possible Treaty changes with the aim of strengthening the democratic legitimacy of the union, enabling the Community and its institutions to respond effectively to the demands of the new situation, and assuring unity and coherence in the Community's international action.

It was agreed that the Foreign Ministers would do this and report to the next European Council in June 'with a view to a decision on the holding of a second inter-governmental conference to work in parallel with the conference on economic and monetary union'. The European Council in June duly agreed to a second IGC 'on political union', which was to open in Rome on 14 December 1990.[60]

THE 1990s: CENTRIFUGAL AND CENTRIPETAL FORCES COMPETE

THE TWO 1990–91 INTER-GOVERNMENTAL CONFERENCES

THE TWO IGCs were rather different. The EMU IGC had been extensively pre-prepared, and although some disagreements persisted, there was a certain understanding about what the IGC was going to achieve and what the end result would be, EMU. The political union IGC was, by way of contrast, unprepared, apart from the much earlier work on Political Union and a recent Belgium memorandum on the subject. Over 300 proposals of different sorts were made to the IGC on political union. The two IGCs were officially launched in Rome in December 1990 but the work was really begun under the Luxembourg Presidency in the first half of 1991. The Dutch took over the Presidency in the second half of 1991 and with it the responsibility for the IGC, which came to a conclusion at Maastricht in the Netherlands on 9–10 December 1991. The two IGCs were officially distinct but they were closely co-ordinated and there was a linkage between them. The new Treaty, the Treaty on European Union, was officially signed in Maastricht on 7 February 1992. After delays in the ratification process, it finally came into operation on 1 November 1993.

In the IGCs of 1990–91, and indeed the IGC of 1996–97, the negotiations started from very heterogeneous positions on the part of Member States. In addition, key figures in the Presidency, the Commission and leading Member States were to become distracted by a number of other issues, not least of which was the dissolution of the Federal Republic of Yugoslavia, and the Gulf crisis and war of 1990–91.

The main issues in the negotiations were:

- The vocation of the European enterprise: (a) was the Union working towards a federal or inter-governmental objective? (b) what was to be the distribution of power between the Member States and the Union? and (c) what was to be the distribution of power between the institutions of the Union themselves? – issues which were to return in 1996–97.

41

- Progress towards the single currency.
- The precise changes to be made to European Political Co-operation (EPC) as it was transformed into the Common Foreign and Security Policy (CFSP): what should the CFSP cover and what should be the system of decision-making, that is, should it include 'defence' and should any decisions be made by qualified majority voting, or some other system of special majority?
- Which other areas of activity should the new European Union move into, and should those areas be organised around the Community method employed since 1952, or was some inter-governmental model (based on the EPC system) to be applied?
- Was the new Union to take seriously the question of economic and social cohesion, and if it was, how was this to be done?
- Could it be agreed that, to make the enterprise more relevant to the people of Europe, they might be granted 'citizenship' of the new Union, with concomitant rights?
- Although enlargement was not specifically on the agenda, there was a clear understanding that one of the key issues facing the IGC was: what steps should the existing members and institutions take in order to be prepared for future enlargements?

THE OUTCOME: THE TREATY ON EUROPEAN UNION

Much of the outcome was opaque and involved deliberate and studied ambiguity. It is important to note that it is the Treaty *on* not *of* European Union. It was also clear that many key issues were unresolved; indeed, the Treaty on European Union itself contained provision for review in 1996 (Article N.2). The treaty takes the form of a treaty within a treaty, since most of its 250+ pages concern the European Community (the new official name of the European Economic Community), but there is also the creation of the CFSP and Justice and Home Affairs pillars as part of the new European Union. The key features of the Treaty on European Union were:

- The creation of the European Union.
- The timetable and criteria for Economic and Monetary Union.
- The creation of a 'pillar' structure; that is, parallel to the European Community system, two new structures were created, both with separate policy and decision-making systems and both with substantially reduced or even no role for Community institutions. This new structure was allegedly to be held together by a 'single institutional framework' [Article C TEU] but all that involved was the European Council sitting at the apex of the three structures; and the two new pillars, which were deliberately inter-governmental, adopting the titles of the institutions of The Community but not the same functions or decision-taking procedure.
- The innovation of these pillars: the Common Foreign and Security Policy pillar and the Justice and Home Affairs pillar.
- The introduction of 'union citizenship' (a Spanish invention).

- New statements of competence for the European Community, especially in consumer protection, public health, visa policy, the establishment of trans-European networks, development co-operation, industrial policy, social cohesion, education, culture, environmental protection, and social policy.
- Increased power for the European Parliament, especially co-decision in some areas, the right to prior approval of a new Commission and the power of assent for all major international agreements.
- The formal introduction of the principle of subsidiarity, which by one definition meant that 'decisions are taken as closely as possible to the citizen' [TEU Common Provisions Article A].

MORE PROBLEMS

The conclusion of the Maastricht agreement was greeted with a good deal of 'Europhoria' across Europe and it was expected that ratification would be completed by 1 January 1993, coinciding with the completion of the Single Internal Market at the end of 1992. The first jarring note was on 2 June 1992, when in a referendum in Denmark, by a majority of 42,000 votes (less than 1% of the electorate) the Danish people voted against ratification. This should have killed the Treaty, just as the French 'No' in 1954 killed the European Defence Community Treaty. Nevertheless, on this occasion the other Member States decided to proceed with their own ratification procedures on the basis that the Danes might not have spoken their final word. In June 1992 the Irish gave a 68.7% 'Yes' endorsement of the Treaty and attention turned to France.

Also in June 1992 the French had completed the required constitutional procedures for ratification, having successfully put the Treaty to a joint gathering of the *Assemblée Nationale* and the Senate. President Mitterrand, however, decided that following the Danish rebuff, the French people should offer a popular endorsement of the Treaty (and incidentally of their government which had played a leading role in the IGC), and relaunch the drive for European integration. In fact, it turned out differently, with strong nationalist opposition to the Treaty growing over the summer and some taking the referendum as an opportunity to demonstrate their disillusionment with Mitterrand. In the event the French only approved Maastricht by a majority of less than 2% in September 1992.

Difficulties also began to appear in Britain and Germany. In Britain the Danish 'No' had given new hope to opponents of the Prime Minister John Major in his own Conservative Party. Given his slim overall majority in the House of Commons, this made ratification difficult. Mr Major's problems were exacerbated by the undignified forced withdrawal from the ERM on 16 September 1992, which represented a reversal of government policy and proved to Maastricht's opponents that the Maastricht plans in general and on EMU in particular were too ambitious and unworkable, as well as being an unwarranted attack on sovereignty. It finally required John Major to make the ratification of the Treaty a matter of confidence in his government in the summer of 1993 before he could secure the necessary majority. In Germany, there were also difficulties because of the attachment to the Deutschmark, the federal system (with the Länder fearing loss of power over areas reserved to them in the Constitution), and a legal challenge on the question of whether Maastricht was compatible with the German constitution. Ironically, Germany was the last state to ratify.

In June 1992 the Danes and their partners ruled out the re-negotiation of the Treaty on European Union, since to have reopened issues affecting Denmark would have led potentially to a reopening of all the issues that had consumed the 1990–91 IGC, and released chaos. However, sophisticated attempts began to be made to devise some from of 'addition' or 'clarification', which did not compromise the text of the Treaty but could be regarded as interpreting it. Late in October 1992 the Danish government, having negotiated with the numerically superior opposition at home, published its proposals for the reassurances which it thought the population required. They appeared to want legally binding provisions for Denmark to opt out of the single currency, of Union citizenship and of an eventual common defence policy. The TEU already went some way to meet these problems but the demand for legally binding statements raised precisely the problem of whether Denmark could not be satisfied except by renegotiation. Eventually, at the European Council meeting in Edinburgh in December 1992, the Heads of State and Government steered by the British Presidency, agreed a 'decision' concerning the Danish demands:

- It was declared that European Union citizenship did not take the place of national citizenship, an individual's nationality being a matter for national law.
- The TEU gave Denmark the right to decide for itself on its participation in the third stage of EMU, and at Edinburgh Denmark gave notice that it would not participate (a decision confirmed in the summer of 1998).
- It was also agreed that Denmark would not participate in decisions and actions of the Union which have defence implications.[61]

A question arose as to the interpretation of the status of the European Council 'decision', a measure not known to Community law. One view was and is that the decision was simply a clarification of things already decided, there being no renegotiations and no treaty amendment. An alternative view, upheld by the British, is that while the Treaty was not amended, the decision has the status of an international agreement and is therefore binding international law on how the parties will behave with respect to the Treaty. This appeared to satisfy the Danes and in May 1993 the Danish people in a second referendum approved ratification of the Treaty on European Union by 56.8% to 43.2%.

As if this crisis was not enough, a major crisis of confidence affected the British pound sterling in September 1992, and led after a sustained run on the pound to the British leaving the ERM after two years' membership. The British government was forced to announce that it did not expect to re-enter the ERM soon, and that there were 'fault lines' in the ERM system that needed to be corrected. Given the general state of unhappiness in the governing party, the Conservatives and the narrow parliamentary majority, the government also announced that it would not proceed to ratification of the TEU until the Danish position became clear and until there was greater clarification about the principle of subsidiarity, which had been introduced in the Treaty. These latter two questions were in effect resolved at the Edinburgh European Council meeting, but that meeting also had to resolve the disagreement among the Member States over the future financing of the Community (Delors II), problems in the Community position in the Uruguay round of the General Agreement of Tariffs and Trade talks, and some unfulfilled aspects of the move to the Single Internal Market which was supposed to have been completed by December 1992.

The British Presidency managed to secure a substantial new statement on subsidiarity, running to 16 pages, and which focused on the three legal concepts of:

- 'the Community should only act where given the power to do so . . .';
- 'the Community should only take action where an objective can be better attained at the level of the Community than at the level of the individual Member State . . .';
- 'the means to be employed by the Community should be proportional to the objective pursued . . .'.[62]

Other matters settled at Edinburgh included:

- Future financing of the Community for seven years ahead and new Financial Perspectives for 1993–99, including a Cohesion Fund worth 16,150 billion ECUs at 1992 prices over seven years. (Spain nearly brought the entire Edinburgh Council and all entire package of agreements to collapse on this issue, and negotiations on it took the meeting past its scheduled ending.)
- An increase in the number of MEPs for the new Germany.
- The negotiations for the accession of Austria, Finland and Sweden should open at the beginning of 1993.
- There should be no change in the locations of the various seats of Community institutions.[63]

ANOTHER ENLARGEMENT

Edinburgh authorised the opening of negotiations for the fourth enlargement. Traditionally, Austria, Finland, Sweden and Switzerland had shied away from membership of the Community on the grounds of a perceived incompatibility with their policies of neutrality, and in the Finnish case because of the inhibitions generated by their location next to the Soviet Union, a superpower which had made clear its antipathy to Finland having too close ties to the Community. But they, and Norway, which had voted against membership in 1972, had to reassess their position given the approach of the Community's Single Market by the end of 1992, from which they feared exclusion and the potential of new barriers to trade, and given the revolutionary upheavals which had and were taking place in Eastern and Central Europe, with the collapse of a whole system and of the basis of European affairs since 1945.

Initially, the Community had been preoccupied with its own problems and development. At the end of the 1980s the idea of these states negotiating in effect to join the Single Market but not the Community began to take hold and negotiations opened in June 1990, being concluded in February 1992. Some in the Community hoped that this might end the matter. The Community, Austria, Finland, Iceland, Norway, Liechtenstein and Sweden constructed the European Economic Area (EEA), which extended the four freedoms of the Single Market (freedom of movement of goods, services, capital and people), and its heart, to the Area. The states participating had all had previous relationships with the Community via their membership of the European Free Trade Association (EFTA), created in 1960. The Swiss put the Agreement to a referendum in December 1992, and it was rejected by their voters, with the result that Switzerland withdrew and also suspended its interest in pursuing negotiations for membership of the European Community. The expectation that the EEA would define the relationship between the Community and these states for a period of time was not fulfilled. Four of them applied for membership of the Community: Austria in 1989, Sweden in 1991, and Finland and Norway in 1992.

The Member States of the Community decided at Maastricht that they would address enlargement when they had concluded their own negotiations over such sensitive issues as future financing and related issues. By the spring of 1992 at Lisbon this had been narrowed to the resolution of the two issues of TEU ratification and conclusion of discussions of the Delors II package (the proposed spending of the Community for the next five years). Given the Edinburgh outcome and in the expectation of successful ratification, negotiations for accession opened formally on 1 February 1993. In each case it was assumed that the applicants accepted everything in the Treaty on European Union and all the accumulated legislation and decisions the Community had taken over the years, the *acquis*. A potential problem, that of the compatibility of neutrality with membership, failed to materialise, as the three neutrals, as Austria, Finland and Sweden accepted the new Common Foreign and Security Policy (CFSP), without looking for any concessions or opt-outs. A significant factor about this enlargement was that the four states seeking to join were relatively wealthy and on joining what in November 1993 had become the European Union were expected to contribute some 6,000 million ECUs between them to the Union budget but only to receive 4,500 million ECUs in return, a favourable balance for the Union of 1,500 million ECUs. Only Finland would receive more than it gave. The negotiations proceeded quickly and were concluded by April 1994, a record for such negotiations. There was in reality not much to negotiate about.

Accommodations were found on such questions as Arctic and Alpine agriculture (partly by allowing derogations from the common price regimes) and on the Austrian insistence on retaining restrictions on the transit of lorries across the Alps in order to reduce the pollution levels. Where the applicants had higher environmental standards than those agreed by the Union, they were to be allowed to maintain them for four years, during which time the Union was to review its own standards. None of the applicants sought opt-outs on the single currency/EMU, or any other aspect of EU policy. The only permanent opt-out from the *acquis communautaire* granted in any enlargement negotiations was in favour of a distinctive type of Swedish snuff.

The real issue became whether the people would support their membership in the referendums that they were committed to holding. In fact, the results were as given in Table 3.1.

Table 3.1 1994 referendums

State	% Yes	% No	% Turnout
Austria	66	34	81
Finland	57	43	74
Norway	48	52	89
Sweden	52	48	82

Norway had rejected membership in 1972 and now, given its levels of economic prosperity, its oil and fisheries resources, and its attachment to the history of independence from foreign rule, the people again said 'No', involvement in the EEA being seen as enough to meet their needs. Not only had the applicant states to vote for their accession, but following the TEU it was also necessary to gain the support of the European Parliament. Although the Parliament voted positively (380 for Sweden, 377 for Finland and 374 for Austria, and incidentally 373 for Norway) and well in excess of the required 259 votes, the vote was more contentious than anticipated since about 150 MEPs supported an earlier motion to postpone consideration of the application to allow time for negotiations with the Council on Parliament's demands for more democracy and majority voting in decision-making. But this was defeated by 305 MEPs voting against. It was also necessary to secure the approval of existing Member States, which occurred without incident (although the Spanish successfully linked approval to gaining access to British and Irish fishing waters from which they had been excluded, but which were to be opened up to Sweden).

Austria, Finland and Sweden became members of the European Union on 1 January 1995, taking the membership of the Union to fifteen, although already by the summer of 1995, there was a reduction in public support for membership in Austria and Sweden.

Economic problems change the environment

By early 1994 unemployment in the existing twelve Member States of the Union had reached 17 million, and this became more and more of an issue for the rest of the 1990s. In 1994 this level of unemployment was one factor behind the fall in turnout for European Parliament elections, as voters began to ask what direct benefit to them did the Union bring and what could the Parliament actually do to make a difference in their lives. Already by the end of 1993 the Commission had responded to a request from the European Council meeting in Copenhagen in June 1993 to produce a White Paper on 'Growth, Competitiveness, Employment'. The White Paper opened with the question: 'Why this White Paper? The one and only reason is unemployment.'[64] The White Paper set out a list of possible actions, but dismissed traditional remedies such as protectionism, increased government spending and cuts in wages. Despite much discussion, little real progress was made and in most of the Member States, despite some signs that the recession was ending, unemployment continued to rise, making this an issue that had to be returned to in the 1996–97 IGC.

THE 1996–97 IGC: DIVIDED VIEWS ABOUT THE FUTURE

The Inter-governmental Conference of 1996–97, by its nature as an IGC, was about treaty reform and therefore a number of matters of controversy were not covered in that set of negotiations, although they were very much part of the environment in which the negotiations took place. These included: EMU, the *Growth, Competitiveness, Employment* White Paper, completion of the Single Internal Market (SIM), reform of the Common Agricultural Policy (CAP) and a number of policies with an impact on yet another enlargement, such as the reform of the Structural funds.

As the negotiations progressed, senior figures were distracted to some extent by the time and effort that needed to be paid to the problems of the approaching EMU. The IGC negotiations saw the re-emergence of the differences over the scope, pace, objectives and methods of integration. The 1996 IGC dragged on to become the 1996–97 IGC, concluding in Amsterdam in June 1997. The treaty was signed at the beginning of October 1997. Even after the negotiations and signing the treaty still faced the test of ratification, which could not be assumed after the rough ride the TEU received in 1992, although most commentators would agree that there was little of substance in the Treaty of Amsterdam and certainly no new initiatives on the scale of EMU, CFSP or JHA. In fact, the Treaty was ratified and it came into operation on 1 May 1999. One of the reasons for the modest results of the IGC was that as with any international treaty it was the result of numerous compromises and could be vetoed by any Member State which considered that its requirements had not been met. In some states the changes required to be approved by referendums.

In the negotiations the broad general issues were:

- Questions remaining about the general direction of the EU and whether it was still about the The Hague or Schuman dream or whether Mrs Thatcher's practical and limited agendas had acquired more legitimacy, despite her own departure from the political scene. This debate, as with many others, had taken on a slightly different form by 1996–97, but still remained at the heart of many disputes.
- A series of questions about how to organise the EU, especially in terms of the institutional balance between:
  - the EU institutions themselves; and
  - the EU and the Member States, in effect the recurring argument about how much power an independent European body, the Commission, should have over policy decisions and the way forward for the Union as a whole, and how much power, and over what matters, should reside with the Member States.
- The function and power of individual institutions, especially whether the European Parliament should become co-equal with governments in the legislative decision-making and whether the European Court of Justice had become too powerful and too prone to make law rather than administer it.
- Arguments about striking the right balance between efficiency and democracy and transparency in decision-making, especially given that a gap in democratic

accountability had arisen because national parliaments were deemed to have lost power to Brussels but there had not been sufficient parliamentary compensation at the European level.

- A fundamental dispute over whether more decisions should be made by 'qualified majority voting' (QMV), where some Member States on some issues could suffer decisions being taken which became law in their own states although they opposed the measure.

- Continuing arguments about whether the 'pillar' structure agreed in the TEU was appropriate, and whether some functions in the highly inter-governmental Co-operation on Justice and Home Affairs pillar – that is, where decisions still required the consent of all Member States – might be transferred to the European Community pillar.

- Within the CFSP and JHA pillars themselves there were also important differences that needed to be resolved, such as the continuing issues of whether the European Union should become directly involved in defence tasks, and, if it did, what they should be in the first instance, and what its relationship to NATO and the WEU should be – indeed some argued very strongly that the WEU should be incorporated into the European Union itself; and in the Justice and Home Affairs field, the powers of the European Court of Justice.

- A further issue, again not new but emerging in a slightly different form, was whether the EC/EU was fundamentally a Europe for business focusing on such issues as the Single Market and the EMU, or whether there should not be a more direct connection with the everyday lives and concerns of the people of Europe, in other words a 'Citizens' or 'Social' Europe. This had become an issue because of the high levels of unemployment the EU was suffering in the mid/late 1990s and an increasing sense that there appeared to be little connection between what went on in the Union and what mattered to individuals. The issue had taken on a new emphasis with the apparent apathy or even antagonism manifested towards Europe in the TEU ratification saga and in declining turnouts for the direct elections to the European Parliament. In the TEU the issue had been partly addressed by the inclusion of a 'Social Chapter' at the end of the Treaty and in an arrangement which applied to all the Member States save Britain. The Social Chapter, which touched on working conditions, workers' health and safety (including hours of work), the consultation of workers, and the right of association, but not wages and social security, was regarded as a threat to competitiveness in the world economy by the British. But in May 1997 a new Labour government policy changed British policy and it was agreed at Amsterdam that the Chapter was to be included within the EU's remit. In the 1996–97 IGC the general concerns about a social 'caring' Europe were manifested through the introduction into the treaties of an 'Employment' Title.

49

AMSTERDAM: MODERATE PROGRESS OR STANDING STILL? ———

What advances were incorporated in the Amsterdam Treaty?

- There is the new Title on Employment, which says that the Member States will seek to co-ordinate their strategies for employment, particularly the areas of promoting a skilled, trained and adaptable workforce; and that they will seek to achieve a high level of employment throughout the Union. This is to be a matter of joint examination of national policies and dissemination of best practices, but it does not involve Community legislation. It likewise does not speak of 'full employment', as some Member States would have wished.
- It incorporates the Social Chapter into the main body of the EC Treaty, following the abandonment of the British opt-out. Provisions in this area still, however, give primacy to consensus.
- Reflective of the need to bring Europe closer to the citizens, it lays the foundation for an area of 'freedom, security and justice' by:
  - providing for common rules on immigration, asylum and visa policy;
  - transforming Justice and Home Affairs into 'Provisions on Police and Judicial Co-operation in criminal matters', that is, focusing on enhancing co-operation between the law and order authorities in the Member States to combat international crime, fraud, corruption and drug-trafficking as well as terrorism, and this co-operation will remain inter-governmental, that is, all decisions have to be unanimously agreed by all Member States; and
  - with the exceptions of Britain, Ireland and Denmark, removing frontier checks on the circulation of people at the Union's internal borders between Member States.

The granting of exceptions is a recognition that not all Member States need or wish to be involved in all activities – an acceptance of flexibility. Indeed, instead of all states being committed to the same objectives and final outcomes, some may now permanently exclude themselves.

- Reflective of the concerns that the EU was not making its voice heard sufficiently on the world stage, particularly in the context of its failure to deal adequately with the Yugoslav crises and wars, Amsterdam introduced procedures to improve the ability of the Member States to arrive at common assessments of their own and common interests, in particular, the new policy planning and early warning unit (for more on this and the CFSP see Chapter 12).
- It changed the decision-making procedure by:
  - extending the power of co-decision of the European Parliament into more areas (that is, allowing the Parliament the power to veto decisions made by the Member States acting together in certain areas) and allowing the Parliament a co-equal role in the appointment of the Commission President; and confining the co-operation procedure to EMU; and

- extending qualified majority voting to new areas in the Council.
- It introduced formally into the treaties the concept of flexibility, or 'Provisions on Closer Co-operation' as it is formally put. These provisions allow certain groups of states (but the membership of those groups will be varied) to deepen their integration and co-operation and at a faster rate than some others in certain policy areas, as long as this does not pose a threat to the integrity of the Union or infringe on the rights of other Member States. To safeguard this latter concern, a Member State not willing or able to take part in the proposed closer co-operation in certain areas, will be able to veto such a development from taking place.[65]

For all this, Amsterdam produced a modest result and failed to address a number of issues:

- Its decision-making changes were so limited that the Union remained unprepared for a planned enlargement to twenty-one Member States; the existing Members having been unable to agree to radical changes:
  - to the composition of the Commission's membership;
  - to the weighting of votes in the Council of Ministers when it is a matter subject to qualified majority voting; and
  - to the vexed question of a significant reduction in the areas where Member States have a legally and treaty enshrined right to veto proposed measures and actions of which they disapprove.
- The progress on social and employment issues was limited, making legislative action still dependent on the consensus of all Member States and other national action subject only to peer review. In other words, much of the progress in the social and citizen Europe areas is largely rhetoric.
- Flexibility, while it may allow a repeat of the Six experience, where a group of European states decided no longer to allow themselves to be held hostage by Britain and decided that they would be a role model and pathfinders to others, may also be an implicit confirmation that the EU is no longer on a path whereby it is seeking to create a unified, collective coherent political and socio-economic identity, even a kind of United States of Europe, but will become increasingly fragmented as states begin to pick and choose those activities in which they will or will not become involved – an *à la carte* Europe, not a federal or unified Europe. This does not appear to be the current intention, but the opt-outs granted already on the third stage of EMU, Denmark and defence, Britain and the Social Chapter, and the new opt-outs on complete and genuine freedom of movement for citizens have already put down markers; it would be strange if, at a later date and on other issues, other Member States did not make use of these precedents, especially in the context of the next enlargement significantly increasing the heterogeneity of the Member States.

Reform is difficult because it requires the unanimous consent of all the existing Member States. In 1997 this was fifteen, and, as discussed above, they are not in agreement on a number of fundamentals. The IGC was a negotiation in which not all states achieved all that they wished, individual states had to decide on what they were or were not willing to compromise and where the point of acceptable compromise was. The final text is inelegant and esoteric precisely because it was not written by one hand but as the evolving outcome of many hands over an eighteen-month period. In addition, all participants were mindful of the 1992 difficulties and had to be aware of what their parliaments, people and, in the German case, their Constitutional court would accept.

AN AREA OF GOVERNANCE

The Treaty on European Union 1992 and the Treaty of Amsterdam 1997 have crystallised the general areas of governance of the Union for the next few years as:

- Amsterdam made clear that the Union is founded 'on the principles of liberty, democracy, respect for human rights and fundamental freedoms and the rule of law'.[66] To reinforce the concern with these issues, the Treaty of Amsterdam modified Article O (TEU) to make it clear that applicant states must respect these principles. It also introduced a new Article (Article 7) which allows the Council, meeting in the composition of Heads of State or Government, to suspend a Member State if it is in 'serious and persistent breach' of these principles. Although the European Union as such has still not acceded to the European Convention for the Protection of Human Rights and Fundamental Freedoms, the 1992 Treaty on European Union did include the provision that the Union would respect the fundamental rights enshrined in that Convention and those resulting from the 'constitutional traditions common to the Member States'.[67]

Amsterdam also inserted a new paragraph confirming the 'attachment' of the Member States to 'fundamental social rights' as defined in the Council of Europe's 1961 European Social Charter and the 1989 Community Charter of the Fundamental Social Rights of Workers, although these are of a declaratory rather than legally binding nature.[68] The Amsterdam Treaty also inserted as a task of the European Community 'equality between men and women'[69] and allowed the European Community to 'take appropriate action to combat discrimination based on sex, racial or ethnic origin, religion or belief, disability, age or sexual orientation'[70] if all the Member States agree.

The Treaty on European Union of 1992 created 'Citizenship of the Union', although the rights of the citizens were rather restricted to include:

- 'the right to move and reside freely within the territory of the Member States' within limits;
- the 'right to vote and stand' as candidates in municipal and European Parliament elections on the same terms as nationals of the state where the citizen resides, although again, there were some qualifications;

- provisions allowing citizens to register complaints against instance of mal-administration to an Ombudsman (again with limitations); and
- provisions for the wider diplomatic protection of Member State nationals by entitling individuals to consular facilities of other Member States if their own had no representation.[71]

Amsterdam added little of substance, although it did make clear that 'Citizenship of the Union shall complement and not replace national citizenship'.[72] Thus the integration process has seen a movement towards an extension of competence by the granting of economic rights, and moved through to selected, and limited, political rights.

- 'An area of freedom, security and justice', under provisions for free movement of persons, asylum and immigration (which were moved from the Justice and Home Affairs pillar to the EC pillar by Amsterdam), and allowing the people of the Union to benefit fully from the freedom which the development of the Union was supposed to make possible, while at the same time, allowing the people to live without fear or threat to their personal safety and security.[73]
- A move beyond simply a customs union or Single Market or a narrow range of 'common policies' such as the Common Agricultural Policy (CAP), to inclusion of concern but not common polices for the preoccupations of its citizens in their daily lives including: employment, social policy, environment, public health, education, culture, the rights of citizenship, and consumer protection.
- The move to a coherent external policy, covering both external economic relations and the more high politics area of the Common Foreign and Security Policy (CFSP), which is now to include 'all questions relating to the security of the Union, including the progressive framing of a common defence policy ... which might lead to a common defence' if all Member States agree. In the first instance the issues to be covered under this rubric are: 'humanitarian and rescue tasks, peacekeeping tasks and tasks of combat forces in crisis management, including peacemaking'.[74]

It remains true that the European Union and its constituent elements – the EC (and the ECSC and Euratom), the CFSP and the Provisions on Police and Judicial Co-operation in Criminal Matters (the new version of Justice and Home Affairs emanating from Amsterdam) – cover only those matters which are accorded to them under the founding treaties of Paris and Rome, the Single European Act, the Treaty on European Union and the Treaty of Amsterdam. Since the Union is founded on law, and since Commission proposals require a treaty base, and since the Council and Member States can only act where legitimised by the treaties and, in many cases, by their own national laws and constitutional requirements, the Union cannot act in every nook and cranny of the lives of the citizens of the Union; to do so would be *ultra vires*, as well as politically dangerous.

A NEW AGENDA OR UNRESOLVED BUSINESS AFTER AMSTERDAM?

The IGC did not address several issues that will have more profound effects on the future of the European Union and European integration than some of the specifics in the Amsterdam Treaty. Three in particular can be identified: EMU, enlargement, and the consequent reforms of policies and funds in connection with enlargement.

Economic and Monetary Union had been the cornerstone of the Treaty on European Union of 1992. Without going into the economic and monetary detail here (see Chapter 10), two key points about the TEU arrangements have been particularly important: firstly, the TEU laid down a timetable by which the three stages were to be completed and by which certain key decisions were to be made; and, secondly, it laid down a number of convergence criteria that the states had to meet to be eligible for participation in the third and final stage of the process.

The 1997 timetable for the third and final stage of EMU slipped, but an enormous political investment was put into complying with the convergence criteria in order to ensure compliance with the fallback programme under which the founder members of EMU would adopt the single currency by January 1999. It was a matter of some controversy as to which states would and did meet the convergence criteria.

Several states experienced great difficulty in fulfilling the criteria. Some appear to have resorted to creative accounting to make their figures match the appropriate targets, and some had to change their public expenditure plans significantly to achieve the targets, despite political pressure for measures to be taken to alleviate unemployment, a consequence of which has been increased unemployment and unpopularity for both governments and the EU. Nonetheless, in May 1998, ironically during the British Presidency, it was agreed at a special European Council in Brussels, that eleven states met the criteria and would join the monetary union. Greece did not meet the criteria and three states (Britain, Denmark and Sweden) had already declared that they did not wish to participate whether or not they satisfied the criteria at the appropriate time.[75]

Another big issue surrounding the IGC, Amsterdam and the whole future of the EU in the period 1997 to 2005–7 was that of enlargement. Enlargement is not a new phenomenon for the EC/EU, but the next enlargements are generally regarded as qualitatively different because of the number of states and the challenge that their entry will pose to both them and the Union.

As the 1995 enlargement was being negotiated, Poland and Hungary both applied for membership, and they were followed by applications from the other Eastern and Central European states (Romania, Bulgaria, the Czech Republic, Slovenia and Slovakia) and the Baltic states (Estonia, Latvia and Lithuania), applications already having been received from Malta, Cyprus and much later Turkey. As early as June 1993 in Copenhagen the EC had declared that it was ready to consider applications if the applicants were able to 'assume the obligations of membership by satisfying the economic and political conditions required'.[76] It went further and said that the following conditions had to be met by applicants:

stability of institutions guaranteeing democracy, the rule of law, human rights and respect for and protection of minorities, the existence of a functioning market economy as well as the capacity to cope with competitive pressure and market forces within the Union ... [the] ability to take on the obligations of membership, including adherence to the aims of political, economic and monetary union (the 'Copenhagen criteria').

In addition, it has been made clear that the applicants need to be able to meet and fulfil the so-called *acquis*, namely, to accept all the decisions of the EC/EU since their inception – subject to periods of transition. The applicants have to accept conditions that not all current members accept, given the 1990s vogue for flexibility.

Meeting these requirements will not be at all easy for the applicants and indeed in mid-July 1997 the Commission gave its view (*avis*) on the ability of the various applicants to meet the criteria set out earlier and it issued independent opinions on each (Turkey, Cyprus and Malta having already been advised upon). The Commission concluded as a result of detailed analysis that accession negotiations should begin with the Czech Republic, Estonia, Hungary, Poland and Slovenia,[77] the Member States having already agreed to open talks with Cyprus six months after the signing of the Amsterdam Treaty in October 1997. These negotiations symbolically opened in April 1998 with no target date being set for their conclusion. The first round-the-table negotiations did not take place until November 1998.

At the same time as it issued its detailed *avis* on each applicant, the Commission also issued 'Agenda 2000: For a stronger and wider Union'[78] which sought to identify the challenges facing the Union both in terms of its policies and enlargement 'Agenda 2000' gave some indication of the size of the adjustments that will be necessary (see Table 3.2).

There is no need to be a technical expert to be able to understand the message: all the states in Table 3.2 are a long way below the European Union average in terms of economic development and wealth. For Poland, the fastest growing, to catch up with the poorest current EU member, Greece, would require it to have an annual growth of over 6% for more than ten years.

Table 3.2 Central and Eastern European states recommended for the opening of negotiations: Gross Domestic Product (GDP) and EU Member States Basic Data (Year 1995)

State	GDP at purchasing power standards (in ECUs per head as %age of EU average)
Hungary	37
Poland	31
Estonia	23
Czech Republic	55
Slovenia	59

Source: 'Agenda 2000: For a stronger and wider Union', *Bulletin of the European Union*, Supplement 5/97 (OOP, 1997) p.138.

The Commission in Agenda 2000 made generous assumptions about economic growth in the EU (economic growth was forecast to be running at 2.5% a year for the period 2000–2006 for the existing EU states and at 4% a year between 1997 and 2006 for the applicant states) and managed to argue that by the end of the period the EU would have potential additional resources of over £16 billion available to help in the new members' adjustment. Most commentators regarded these forecasts with great suspicion, if not incredulity.

The applicants have already started preparing by beginning to adjust to the requirements of the Single Market, and by seeking to converge their laws in a whole swathe of areas to make them compatible with the requirements of the EU *acquis*, subject only to transitional derogations.[79] But the task is large and there are questions as to the ability of socio-economic, administrative and political systems that had to cope with the traumatic seismic changes in and since 1989 to cope with another set of upheavals.

Partly, but not exclusively, because of the prospect of enlargement, the EU needs to examine a number of its policies and to begin a process of reform. The major areas for reform are: Cohesion and Structural Funds, and the Common Agriculture Policy, partly because together they account for over 80% of the EU budget, the CAP taking nearly 45%; Cohesion (agreed in 1992 exclusively for the benefit of the four less developed Member States) about 3%; and the Structural Funds (the European Regional Development Fund, European Social Fund and the Guidance aspects of the European Agricultural Guidance and Guarantee Fund) about 33%.[80]

The agenda is large and difficult since many existing policies reflect the particular vested interests of certain states, indeed even the parochial and domestic electoral interests of governments and political parties. In addition, reform of these policies is intimately related to arguments about winners and losers – that is, who pays money into the EU budget and who receives money. By early 1999 progress was slow and problems were multiplying.

A brief history of European integration from 1987 to 1999 is given in Box 3.1.

Box 3.1   Key dates in the history of European integration, 1987–99 (June)

1987	April	Turkey applies for EC membership.
	July	Single European Act comes into force.
1988	June	Hanover European Council creates Delors' Committee to study EMU.
1989	April	Delors' Committee presents its report.
	June	Third direct elections to European Parliament.
		Madrid European Council agrees that Stage I of EMU will begin on 1.7.90.
	July	Austria applies to join EC.

Box 3.1 (*cont.*)

	September–December	Collapse of Soviet-control of Eastern and Central Europe.
	November	Opening of Berlin Wall.
	December	Negotiations begin between EC and EFTA states on forming European Economic Area (EEA).
		Strasbourg European Council agrees to establish IGC on EMU.
1990	April	Special Dublin European Council confirms its commitment to political union and instructs Foreign Ministers to prepare proposals.
	June	Dublin European Council agrees to convene two IGCs on EMU and political union in December 1990.
	July	Stage I of EMU begins.
		Cyprus and Malta apply to join EC.
	September	Signing of 'Two Plus Four Treaty' laying basis for unification of Germany.
	October	Five Eastern Länder join Federal Republic of Germany.
		UK joins ERM.
	December	IGCs formally opened in Rome.
1991	July	Sweden applies to join EC.
	December	Maastricht negotiation and agreement of draft Treaty on European Union.
		'Europe Agreements' signed by EC and Poland, Hungary and Czechoslovakia.
		Demise of Soviet Union (USSR).
1992	February	TEU formally signed.
	March	Finland applies to join EC.
	May	European Economic Area agreement signed.
		Switzerland applies to join EC.
	June	Danes vote by 50.7 % to reject TEU.
		Irish vote by 68.7% to accept TEU.
	September	'Black Wednesday' – Britain and Italy leave the ERM.
		French vote by 51.04 % to accept TEU.
	November	Norway applies to join EC.
	December	Swiss vote against participation in the EEA and suspend EC application.
		Edinburgh European Council.
		Completion of Single Market (nearly).
1993	February	Accession negotiations open with Austria, Finland and Sweden.
	April	Accession negotiations open with Norway.
	May	Danes vote 56.8% for TEU.
	June	Copenhagen European Council lays down criteria for enlargement.

Box 3.1 (*cont.*)

	November	TEU enters into force: European Union begins its existence.
	December	Uruguay Round of GATT successfully negotiated.
	January	Stage II of EMU begins.
		EEA enters into force.
	April	Hungary and Poland apply to join EC.
	June	Fourth direct elections to European Parliament.
		Austrians vote 66% in favour of accession to EU.
	October	Finns vote 57% in favour of accession to EU.
	November	TEU enters into force: European Union begins its existence.
		Swedes vote 52% in favour of accession to EU.
		Norwegians vote 'No' with 52% against.
1995	January	Austria, Finland and Sweden become members of EU.
	March	Schengen enters into force between Benelux, France, Germany, Portugal and Spain.
	June	Romania and Slovakia apply to join EU.
		Group of Reflection created.
	October	Latvia applies to join EU.
	November	Estonia applies to join EU.
	December	Lithuania and Bulgaria apply to join EU.
		Madrid European Council adopts name 'euro' for new currency.
1996	January	Czech Republic applies to join EU.
	March	BSE ban.
		IGC opens in Turin.
	June	Slovenia applies to join EU.
1997	May	New government in Britain.
	June	Amsterdam conclusion to IGC.
	July	Commission publish 'Agenda 2000'.
		Commission publish ten *avis* on applicant states.
	October	Treaty of Amsterdam signed.
1998	January–June	UK Presidency.
	March	'European Conference' between EU states and eleven applicants. (Turkey declined to attend.)
	April	EU launches negotiations with six applicant states and opens accession process for five others.
	May	Brussels European Council agrees that eleven Member States meet convergence criteria for EMU, and appoints Wim Duisenberg to be President of the ECB.
		Danes vote 55.1% in favour of Amsterdam.
		Irish vote 61.7% in favour of Amsterdam and 94% in favour of 'Good Friday agreement' on Northern Ireland.

Box 3.1 (*cont.*)

	June	Cardiff European Council.
	September	Elections in Malta lead to re-activation of application to join EU.
	November	'Informal' meeting of EU Defence Minister during Austrian Presidency.
1999	January	1.1.99 Stage III of EMU into force; eleven states enter EMU and adopt the 'euro'.
		European Parliament censure motion on Commission rejected by 293 to 232 with 27 abstentions.
	March–June	NATO/Yugoslav conflict over Kosovo.
	March	Commission resigns following publication of 'First report on allegations regarding fraud, mismanagement and nepotism in the European Commission'.
		Berlin European Council agrees Agenda 2000 reform package.
	June	Fifth direct elections with lowest turnout in twenty years.
		Cologne European Council agreed to an IGC on institutional reform in 2000.

CENTRIPETAL AND CENTRIFUGAL TENDENCIES AND PRESSURES

What the 1990s debates have been about, like many of the debates before them apart from the specific details of policy areas, is the heart and soul of the European enterprise. If the goal was once clear in the minds of the founding fathers, the implementation and achievement of it has not been straightforward. There has been a tendency, with hindsight, to see the progression from ECSC to EEC to customs union to single internal market to European Union to economic and monetary union as somehow inexorable and progressing in a steady path towards a predetermined goal. It has not been like that:

- The Council of Europe in 1949 had already demonstrated a fatal compromise between Britain and supporters of a strong central decision-making authority.
- The European Defence Community Treaty signed in 1952 was not ratified.
- The negotiations for the Treaty of Rome in 1957 had to reconcile strongly divergent viewpoints with no guarantee of success, and certain problems were only resolved at the very last minute in March 1957.
- President de Gaulle of France twice vetoed enlargement (in 1963 and 1967 with particular reference to Britain but with a direct impact also upon the other applicants: Denmark, Ireland and Norway) and caused the biggest constitutional crisis in the European Community/Union's history in 1965 when France began its

'empty chair' strategy of absenting itself from key meetings of the premier decision-making bodies and challenged the whole institutional set-up.

- In June 1992 Denmark put the whole movement towards European Union in jeopardy when it initially rejected the Treaty on European Union by referendum (a decision they reversed a year later).
- The British have consistently sought to block both the easement of decision-taking and the monetary union; have crowded out the agendas by insisting on budgetary rebates; and under a Conservative government dissented from much of the will of the other Member States in the 1996–97 IGC. The view expressed in 1998 at Bruges by Mrs Thatcher that:

willing and active co-operation between independent sovereign states is the best way to build a successful European Community[81]

is not too far from a bipartisan British position, although new Labour would never borrow Mrs Thatcher's words.

Thus while there are and have been pressures for more integration there have also been pressures in the other direction. In the 1990s there have been and are differences of opinion about the internal arrangements of the European Union; fundamentally about the point of decision and where power should lie – disputes about the institutional power of the EU's central institutions and about the relationship between those institutions and the Member States.

These arguments took on new force in the aftermath of the débâcle of the resignation of the whole Commission in the wake of the Committee of Independent Experts 'First Report on Allegations Regarding Fraud, Mismanagement and Nepotism in the European Commission' of 15 March 1999. Leaving aside individual cases, the most damning elements in the Report were in its 'Concluding Remarks':

the Committee has observed that Commissioners sometimes argued that they were not aware of what was happening in their services . . . such affirmations . . . represent a serious admission of failure . . . tantamount to an admission of a lack of control by the political authorities over the Administration they are supposedly running. This loss of control implies at the outset a heavy responsibility for both the Commissioners individually and the Commision as a whole. [para. 9.2.1–9.2.2]

and in the final paragraph:

The studies carried out by the Committee have too often revealed a growing reluctance among the members of the hierarchy to acknowledge their responsibility. It is becoming difficult to find anyone who has even the slightest sense of responsibility. [para. 94.25][82]

Further pressures have been evident on a variety of issues.

- While 'partners' in the EU, the Member States are also economic rivals both on the world stage and in terms of competition within the European market; and this causes them semi-permanently to seek to construct, define and implement policies to their own advantage – a good example is the rivalry and bitter antagonism that has been generated between British and Spanish fishery fleets.

- From the beginning there have been disputes about 'who pays?' Initially the Federal Republic of Germany was more or less willing to pay more than might have been expected but there have always been arguments about 'winners and losers' and with British entry this became a problem made famous by Mrs Thatcher's handbag as she fought for five years to reclaim 'my money'. The issue has come to the fore again with the prospect of enlargement to include six new states who will all be a drain on the Union's budget, the German disinclination to continuing to pay disproportionately, and the release for the first time of figures by the Commission in the autumn of 1998, which identify those states in 1996 and 1997 which made net contributions (gross payments minus receipts) to the Union budget – Germany, France, Italy, the Netherlands, Austria, Sweden and the United Kingdom (see the discussion of the budget on pp. 316–17 below for more on this). Given that the essence of politics is choices about the distribution of values and resources, the question of the nature of and the distribution of the EU budgetary funding lies close to the hearts of states, especially the net contributors, and of interest groups and individuals within them.

- Divergences also arise because of geography and not just because Britain and Ireland are islands. As the Community/Union enlarges, the divergence of interests and concerns between, say, Austria, Greece and Sweden, given their different geopolitical positions, also becomes an issue as tension increases between, say, a Mediterranean orientation and an orientation towards Central Europe; not to mention particular local concerns such as Greece's concerns with Turkey.

- These concerns are exacerbated by differences of historical experience: imperial Britain, Belgium, the Netherlands, Portugal and France compared to the experience of Ireland; the different experiences between 1939 and 1945 – France, Belgium and the Netherlands routed in days, Germany and Italy defeated, Britain triumphant and Sweden and Ireland as non-participants. In addition, there are the divergent experiences and socio-cultural traditions on such issues as religion and Church/State relations.

- These issues have affected profoundly attitudes to national identity and perceptions of the nature of sovereignty; not least, for example, in German attitudes to the importance of the stability of their currency, given the ravages inflicted by inflation in the late 1920s and early 1930s and the connections between that and the rise of the Nazi Party. It is a cliché to see a link between British attitudes and the British wartime experience.

- These divergences partly came home to roost in the problematic ratification of the Maastricht Treaty (Treaty on European Union 1992) in 1992–93 with particular, and to some extent divergent, difficulties in Denmark, France, Britain and Germany. This trend carried over into the second Inter-governmental Conference of the 1990s in 1996–97 and into the debate about the composition of and nature of economic and monetary union, which occupied so much political time and energy in the late 1990s.

61

But clearly this assessment is too bleak since, as noted above, the pressures have not all been one way. There have been, and are, pressures towards further integration.

- There remains a strong, though perhaps declining, sense of mission or commitment to the 'ideal' of European integration as a vehicle for resolving issues of peace and war; a sense perhaps reinforced by the too close to home experiences of the Yugoslav horrors of war in the 1990s.
- There is continuing, even growing, awareness of the potential economies of scale if European enterprises can work together – a sentiment reinforced by the concerns about European competitiveness in the world economy: concerns which prompted the movement towards the Single Market between 1985 and 1992 (and beyond as it still needs to be completed in some areas) and the European Commission to publish a White Paper in 1994 on *Growth, Competitiveness, Employment: The Challenges and Ways Forward into the 21st Century*.[83]
- Whatever caveats there may be about the notion that European integration is an inexorable process, leading to 'a kind of United States of Europe',[84] it is clear that there has been spill-over in both the economic and political areas since the foundation of the ECSC by the Treaty of Paris in 1951: there has been movement from the original coal and steel foundation to a wide range of Community/Union competencies: economic concerns with employment, the single market and economic and monetary union and a range of specific policy areas such as agriculture and transport, as well as funding for a series of measures to bring about economic and social cohesion to educational exchange schemes, to co-operating in foreign and security policy (the Common Foreign and Security Policy) and to co-operation in the fields of Justice and Home Affairs. This spill-over has occurred partly because it has been discovered that to perform adequately in one area of activity requires involvement in adjacent areas – that is, rationalisation of the coal and steel industries led to concerns with retraining, as do concerns about EU's competitive position *vis-à-vis* the rest of the world. There has also been the feature that some policies that might have been deemed 'domestic' have actually had significant external implications; most notably this has proved to be true of the Common Agricultural Policy (CAP) since the USA has perceived it to be very protectionist and harmful to American interests and this has split over into other aspects of American relations with some of its European partners.
- It must also be remembered that one of the founding motivations for the EEC was a concern that a politically fragmented and insecure Western Europe would be unable to exercise real power in an international environment apparently dominated by the United States and the Soviet Union. Although that environment has been radically transformed, the concern to have a voice on the international stage has remained significant and has been an important motivation behind the initial development of European Political Co-operation (the attempt to co-ordinate the Member States' foreign policies between 1970 and 1993) and the post-1993 development of the Common Foreign and Security Policy (CFSP).

- Similarly the pressures for common action have been reinforced by not only economic tensions between the United States and the members of the EU, but the growing political distance that has developed in the last twenty-five years (although this is very much a relative development and the relations through NATO are still close). Following the Vietnam War débâcle, the forced resignation of President Nixon in 1974, the perceived vacillation and weak presidency of Jimmy Carter and doubts about the capability of successive American Presidents, many Europeans increasingly lost confidence in American leadership and wisdom. In addition, as they have regained their strength since 1945 and more recently as the threat posed by the Soviet empire and its perceived ambitions has abated, there has been increasing questioning of American hegemony. Fundamentally, the question being increasingly asked is what do the Europeans and Americans have in common?

- A further pressure for unity is the so-called 'German question'. Part of the genius of Jean Monnet, to a large extent the 'brains' behind the European Community approach and the originator of the Schuman proposals of 1950, was to recognise that the traditional methods of trying to deal with the relationship between France and Germany had failed – in 1870, 1914 and 1939 – and in the aftermath of these events in trying to secure the peace. He, therefore, proposed that instead of Germany being treated unilaterally or being required to face singular restrictions on its activities, it should only be required to forgo what France and other states were willing to forgo – that is, Germany would give up as much sovereignty in the same areas as other West European states, most noticeably France. With the unification of Germany in 1990 and the emergence of a Germany that had a population of 79 million, compared to those of France, Britain and Italy of 56, 57, and 58 million respectively, in addition to its unique geopolitical position at the centre of Europe, the problem arose in many minds of how to ensure the emergence of a 'European Germany' and not a 'German Europe'[85] – concerns that the former Chancellor of Germany, Helmut Kohl, appeared to have shared himself. The answer adopted, not least by a majority of mainstream German politicians, was the Monnet solution – Germany would be tied into the European integration movement via both moves towards political and economic and monetary union. This was a significant motive behind the inter-governmental conferences (IGCs) on these two topics in 1991, the second IGC in 1996–97 and the political determination to press ahead with economic and monetary union in 1997–98, despite a number of economic doubts.

- It is also the case that a powerful factor working for integration in the 1990s was the record of achievement of the Six (1951–73), the Nine (1973–81), the Ten (1981–86), the Twelve (1986–95) and the Fifteen (1995–). Despite the internal criticisms, the European integration experiment has shown that such a system can work institutionally and it can be argued that it has played a major role in the economic reconstruction of the Member States.

- Moreover, as the continual stream of third parties that expressed an interest in joining or having some other relationship with the EC/EU continued to expand, it was clear that in the world at large the EC/EU was and is a pole of attraction and is often recognised as an economic giant if not always so powerful in all other areas of activity.

• Finally, there are the residual aspects of the shared inheritance intellectually, culturally and philosophically – that is, the idea of a common heritage, a feature particularly of liberal, pluralist, democratic and industrial Western Europe, all the more so since 'the West' appeared to have won the Cold War and many believed the ideological arguments associated with it. The 'end of ideology' was actually the victory of one side.

• Despite some noises off-stage, it is inconceivable that any Member State will secede.

THE 1990s DEBATES

These conflicting pressures, the individual significance of which waxed and waned over the years, continued to have resonance in the debates about the nature and future of European integration in the 1990s. There continued to be a continuum of views and a range of possible decisions from the choices available.

At the most stark the divergence of views ranges from profound differences as to the very nature of the enterprise that Europeans have embarked upon. As just noted, Mrs Thatcher in 1988 gave, as her first guiding principle for the future of Europe, 'willing and active co-operation between independent sovereign states is the best way to build a successful European Community' instead of concentrating 'power at the centre of a European conglomerate ... working together does not require power to be centralised in Brussels or decisions to be taken by an appointed bureaucracy'.[86]

This contrasts rather starkly with the declarations issued by supporters of federalism in The Hague in 1948 which argued it was:

> the urgent duty of the nations of Europe to create an economic and political union in order to secure security and social progress ... European nations must transfer and merge some portion of their sovereign rights so as to secure common political and economic action for the integration and proper development of their common resources ... [must] bring about the necessary economic and political union of Europe ....[87]

It is also clearly at variance with the aspirations of Schuman in May 1950, the hopes of the Treaty of Paris in 1951, the determination in the Treaty of Rome to 'lay the foundations of an ever closer union among the peoples of Europe', the Stuttgart and Single European Act commitment to continue the work to 'transform the relations as a whole among their States into a European Union', the draft Dutch Treaty of September 1991 reference to the European Union having a 'federal vocation' (albeit that that was expunged at the insistence of Prime Minister John Major) and indeed, the renewed commitment to 'creating an ever closer union among the peoples of Europe, in which the decisions are taken as closely as possible to the citizen' in both the TEU and the Amsterdam Treaty.

More subtly, the 1990s saw a debate about whether the Member States still saw themselves as striving for a common goal at all, this being expressed most starkly by a British Foreign Secretary, Malcolm Rifkind, in September 1995 when he argued that:

> What we must not do is suppress important national interests in order to construct an artificial consensus, a bogus unity, that lacks credibility or conviction . . . Variable geometry is already well established . . . Sometimes one hears this described as a potential two-speed Europe. But that is unwise. It implies a common destination arrived at in different time-scales. That is certainly relevant to enlargement but may not be relevant to social policy or to a Single Currency. There may be some areas of integration that even in the long term will not be attractive or acceptable to a number of Member States. As the European Union increases from fifteen to twenty and then, perhaps, to twenty-five States that is bound to become more and more likely. If this reflects the reality of different interests, then the European Union will need to respond in a sensitive and flexible manner . . . .[88]

That theme of flexibility had been brought to the fore somewhat earlier in a paper published by the German CDU/CSU parties (the majority parties in the German coalition government at the time) in September 1994, when in context of the German Presidency and of federal German elections approaching, they worried about the current state of integration and the prospect of the Union becoming 'in essence . . . a loosely knit grouping of States restricted to certain economic aspects and composed of various sub-groupings', being no more than a 'sophisticated' free trade area. To avoid this, they suggested five things needed to be done:

- further development of the EU's institutions;
- a strengthening of the EU's 'hard core';
- the renewal of Franco-German leadership;
- improved capacity in the CFSP; and
- enlargement.

Most intriguing was the reference to a hard core of those 'oriented to greater integration and closer co-operation'. It consisted at present of five or six states, although it was to be open to 'every Member State willing and able to meet its requirements'. This core was to provide a strong centre to 'counteract centrifugal forces', and to that end the states participating 'must not only participate as a matter of course in all policy fields, but should also be recognisably more Community-spirited in their joint action than others, and launch common initiatives aimed at promoting the development of the Union', in the expectation that this would act as a motor for integration and a magnet for others, just as the Six had done originally.[89]

The British firmly opposed the German ideas as suggesting that some were more equal than others, and as opening up the possibility of Britain's permanent exclusion from an inner directorate, albeit that that exclusion would be of its own volition. Britain strongly preferred a Europe where there would be several circles of overlapping and different memberships, to some extent as was already happening and evolving; not a system of a fixed inner circle, which might force it to choose between whole-hearted participation or exclusion.[90]

More subtly still were the arcane, esoteric and often internecine debates over the precise meaning of concepts such as federalism, subsidiarity, inter-governmentalism, and variable geometry which in itself could be subdivided into ever more precise, but often nearly synonymous, words and phrases. In addition, the new Amsterdam Treaty saw legitimisation of 'flexibility' as a working principle, although not in the manner intended in the 1994 German paper.

Proposals for a federal Europe have been made over the centuries, and have ranged widely in scope, precision, and distribution of competencies. One of many difficulties with the concept is that it encompasses both a strategy for achieving the desired outcome of a united Europe and a definition of the desired end-situation itself. This is further complicated by the fact that the founders of the integration process included outright federalists like Spinelli, who wished to see a decisive, almost once in a lifetime, movement towards a federal system and those like Monnet who were much more pragmatic and who took the view expressed by Schuman in his May 1950 speech that:

> Europe will not be made all at once, or according to a single plan.[91]

It appears that this strategy has borne fruit, but the more federalist critic would argue that the current problems or malaise is precisely because those individual steps have proved so successful in fulfilling limited objectives that there is little or no inclination to proceed to the radical step of creating a federal Europe.

There is also the difficulty that there is widespread confusion and disagreement about what a federal Europe would or should look like. Classic definitions of a federal system suggest:

> Federal government exists when the powers of government for a community are divided substantially according to the principle that there is a single independent authority for the whole area in respect of some matters, and that there are independent regional authorities for other matters, each set of authorities being co-ordinate with, and not sub-ordinate to the others within its prescribed sphere.[92]

The difficulty is that the distribution of power between these independent centres of authority can vary over time and place, so that no two federal systems are exactly alike, and even a well-established federal system such as the United States of America has seen the relative power of centre and constituent elements change as a result of changing political and economic circumstance. Even the more recent example of the Federal Republic of Germany illustrates that federal systems are not static, as the German Länder in the 1990s sought to assert their rights *vis-à-vis* the central government in Bonn and in some cases successfully argued that Bonn was attempting to encroach upon their independent sphere of authority. Indeed, this argument was put forward in the debate about the ratification of the Maastricht Treaty in Germany and required concessions from the Bonn government.

One difficulty, then, is that there is no clear unambiguous view of what a federal Europe would actually look like and consist of; that is a matter of choice and of negotiation. It can, however, perhaps be suggested that any such new entity would reflect certain boundary conditions that might distinguish a European Union from the current state of affairs:

- All the component states or regions are full participants in all of the Union's activities.
- Federal systems have basic constitutional documents which attempt to delineate the respective powers of the centre and constituent elements, what matters are to be entrenched, and gives some indication of how any disputes between the two are to be resolved.
- In most federal systems, and perhaps a minimal distinguishing attribute of European Union, the centre practises economic management in regard to the level of employment, prices and growth. However, although this might be central management, it need not be over-centralised – there could be a lot of devolution. In addition, there is usually some redistribution of wealth between the constituent parts, although this does not mean that they all have the same standards of living or levels of prosperity. As long ago as 1977 the MacDougall Report on the 'Role of Public Finance in European Integration'[93] suggested that, in a small public sector federation, central expenditure would need to be about 5–7% of GNP, plus a further 2.5–3% if defence were included. In the late 1990s the European Union is still spending less than one-third of that 5–7%. In addition to general economic management, federal systems also include an economic and monetary union, including at a minimum, decisions on public spending and on the levels of credit to be available.
- Federal systems also possess a single foreign policy, as only the central state authority is recognised as the *sovereign* state in international relations and is eligible for membership of international organisations such as the United Nations, or even the Organisation for Security and Co-operation in Europe (OSCE) or the European Union. To accompany this foreign policy, states have a single defence policy – that is, there would be no separate foreign or defence policies – and, moreover, an attack on one part of the Union would automatically be regarded as an attack on all elements of the Union.

It is possible for disagreement to exist about some of these elements. It is even more possible to disagree when one begins to go beyond what might be a minimalist interpretation. Thus, even in the 1990s some could regard a federal Europe as the epitome of centralisation and others could use the same word to envisage a decentralised Europe, where a great deal of power resided not only with the Member States of the Union but even to devolved areas within the Member States, perhaps even one day a 'Europe of the Regions'. No wonder that the attempt to say that the Europe had a 'federal vocation' ran into some difficulty in the autumn of 1991 – did it imply centralisation (the British Conservative interpretation) or the opposite?

It is clear from the foregoing that a true federal system need not imply a 'supranational' system of decision-making. The concept of 'supranational' appeared in the Paris Treaty of 1951 and the EDC Treaty of 1952, although after the EDC débâcle it disappeared from the treaty lexicon. Literally *above* national, supranationality, like other concepts, has been defined in a variety of ways but in essence it suggests that central authorities have real authority to deal directly with the citizens and economic agents of the society and make decisions affecting them on some matters traditionally handled solely by the state. This was already too controversial and powerful an image by 1957 and the writing of the two Rome treaties, and even with respect to the ECSC it was removed by the Fusion or Merger Treaty of 1965.

By 1991 just as the word 'supranational' had previously been replaced in 1957 and 1965, so the notion of the European Union having a 'federal vocation' was replaced by the incorporation of the concept of subsidiarity – a concept that became fashionable again after President Delors used it ten times in a speech in 1989 that sought to reply to Mrs Thatcher's onslaught on the perceived centralisation tendencies of the Community.[94] The European Parliament's Draft Treaty on European Union in 1984 had also invoked it without using the word.[95] In Article A, second paragraph of the TEU, it is described as a system 'in which decisions are taken as closely as possible to the citizen', which is further elaborated and qualified in Article 3b, second paragraph:

> In areas which do not fall within its exclusive competence, the Community shall take action, in accordance with the principle of subsidiarity, only if and in so far as the objective of the proposed action cannot be sufficiently achieved by the member states and can, therefore, by reason of the scale or effects of the proposed action, be better achieved by the Community.

Subsidiarity is part of the social teaching of the Roman Catholic Church. According to this doctrine, the people should be closely involved in decisions that affect them, and the bodies that take decisions should be close to them. It might be basically expressed as the principle that decisions should be taken as low in the political hierarchy as possible. It could be regarded as another way of expressing one version of the federal principle of decentralisation. However, it differs in at least one important respect from that principle: there is no constitutionally entrenched principle and no clear division of labour in the system. Indeed, there can be endless arguments about what level of decision-making obtains the best results, viz. the arguments in the United Kingdom about the merits of devolution. The Union has gone through endless contortions since 1992 as it has tried to put flesh on what subsidiarity actually means. Interestingly, and in the light of the politico-social arguments of German Catholic theologians after the popular revolution of 1648, subsidiarity can also be interpreted to mean respect for higher authority rather than power to the people. The people decide what they can, but some decisions are properly beyond their reach. They are 'subsidiary' to higher levels.

The conclusions of the special Birmingham European Council and the 16-page document agreed at the Edinburgh European Council in 1992 were not the end of the matter, nor was the 'Interinstitutional Agreement of 28 October 1993 between the European

Parliament, the Council and the Commission on procedures for implementing the principle of subsidiarity'.[96] There is further elaboration and qualification of subsidiarity in
the 'Protocol on the application of the principle of subsidiarity and proportionality' of
the Treaty of Amsterdam 1997. In sum,

- all European Community institutions must apply the principles of subsidiarity and
  proportionality;
- in any proposed Community legislation, the 'reasons for concluding that a
  Community objective can be better achieved by the Community must be
  substantiated by qualitative or, wherever possible, quantitative indicators';
- it must be clear that 'the objectives of the proposed action cannot be sufficiently
  achieved by Member States' and 'can therefore be better achieved by action on the
  part of the Community';
- this means, the 'issue under consideration has transnational aspects . . . [which] cannot
  be satisfactorily regulated' by Member States, or where Member State action 'alone or
  lack of Community action would conflict with the requirements of the Treaty', or
  where 'action at Community level would produce clear benefits by reason of its scale
  or effects compared with action at the level of the Member States';
- the 'Community shall legislate only to the extent necessary', with directives being
  preferred to regulations or detailed measures;
- 'Community measures should leave as much scope for national decision as possible';
  and
- where the application of subsidiarity leads to no action by the Community, the
  Member States must still ensure that they fulfil their obligations under the European
  Community Treaty.

This analysis is scarcely illuminating or even coherent.

Another way of way of limiting the power of the centre is to consciously limit the
authority that the centre has and the fields of activity in which it can legitimately
become involved. One way of achieving this is to stress inter-governmentalism, which
has been a feature of the European experience since the introduction of European
Political Co-operation in 1970, and which was reinforced substantially in the Treaty of
European Union's introduction of and provisions on the second and third pillars. The
CFSP and Justice and Home Affairs[97] pillars are inter-governmentalism writ large; no
key decisions can be made unless all the Member States agree. Inter-governmentalism is
a mode of action that preserves the authority of member states, because it rests upon
unanimity and seeks in the CFSP and the JHA to escape the jurisdiction of the European
Court of Justice and to minimise the involvement of Commission and Parliament in the
process. A further way of achieving an equivalent outcome is by opting out of areas of
activity, then nothing that is agreed can formally be imposed upon the state that opted
out, although such a state might find that what the participants plan to do or decide has
consequences for them anyway.

These tendencies have also been developed in more subtle ways to include conceptions of variable geometry – a generic term. Near synonyms are 'multi-speed Europe',

'two-speed Europe' and 'Europe à la carte'.[98] An important distinction between the latter and the former two is that the latter does not imply that all the Member States are striving to achieve the same objective, a point emphasised by Rifkind's remarks noted earlier. This has assumed significance in that it is by no means clear that all the Member States are committed to the single currency or to the implementation of the Schengen agreement, despite the Treaty of Amsterdam incorporating the Schengen *acquis* into the framework of the European Union.

Most significantly, of course, the Treaty of Amsterdam incorporates the principle of 'flexibility' into the constitutional framework of both the European Community and the European Union. Amsterdam inserts into the Treaty on European Union a new Title, Title 'VII Provisions on Closer Co-operation', and a new Article 11 in the Treaty establishing the European Community setting out additional prerequisites that 'Member States which intend to establish closer co-operation between themselves' must fulfil. Interestingly, these provisions do not follow the German 1994 proposals, since the Title VII provisions (Article 4.3.1(h)) requires that any movement in this direction must also meet the criteria laid down in the EC Treaty Article 11, which stipulates that if a Member State:

> declares that, for important and stated reasons of national policy, it intends to oppose the granting of an authorisation by qualified majority [to allow some members to establish closer co-operation between themselves utilising Union institutions, procedures and mechanisms], a vote shall not be taken. The Council may, acting by a qualified majority, request that the matter be referred to the Council, meeting in the composition of the Heads of State or Government, *for decision by unanimity.*[99]

The original proposal was directed against the British, but the Amsterdam wording means that any state can stop the others proceeding to closer co-operation among themselves if that co-operation involves Community or Union competencies, institutions or procedures. More importantly, the language perhaps further entrenches the principle and legitimacy that not all states are going in the same direction or at the same speed, since some may choose to remain permanently outside the arrangement. While this privilege applies to existing member states, it is not to apply to those applicant states that have begun to negotiate entry – they are required to participate fully in all existing Community and Union activities. Once in, they could join or not join closer co-operation arrangements.

Title VII spells out a number of hurdles that have to be overcome before states that wish to establish closer co-operation can do so. That co-operation must:

- 'be aimed at furthering the objectives of the Union . . .';
- '[respect] the principles of the Treaties and the single institutional framework of the Union';
- be 'only used as a last resort';
- involve 'a majority of Member States';
- 'not affect the *acquis communautaire*';

- 'not affect the competencies, rights and interests' of those that choose not to participate;
- be 'open to all'; and
- meet the 'specific additional criteria laid down on Article 11' of the European Community Treaty.

This stipulates that such closer co-operation:

- cannot be in areas 'which fall within the exclusive competence of the Community';
- must 'not affect Community policies, actions or programmes';
- must 'not concern the citizenship of the Union or discriminate between the nationals of Member States'
- must remain 'within the limits of the powers conferred upon the Community'; and
- must 'not constitute a discrimination or a restriction of trade . . . [or] competition . . .'.

The German proposals were thus effectively neutered by the need to secure sufficient support to reach agreement in Amsterdam and it will be interesting to observe whether any significant use is made of this mechanism, although the incorporation of the Schengen *acquis* may be a portent of the future. The 'Provisions on Closer Co-operation' are yet another example of measures that could either be indicative of a commitment to further integration, or be used to halt progress not only in general but also with respect to those who wish to go further and deeper.

CONCLUSION

There is no blueprint or grand plan for the future of the European Union or of European integration. While some have tended to see inexorable progress and can point to the growth in numbers from Six to Fifteen and beyond and the apparently relentless, if not effortless, movement into new areas of policy and activity, there is another perspective:

- Twice in the 1990s the Member States have failed to make the necessary changes to the decision-making capacity of the Community and Union to cope with current difficulties and future enlargements.
- As later generations are not influenced by direct experience of war on their native land, the commitment to 'ever closer union' and radical, even federal, solutions appears to be waning.
- This is exacerbated by the danger that the EC/EU has become a victim of its own success, in that since it has largely achieved many of its original objectives, especially in the economic sphere, a feeling has developed which basically questions why the state needs to be brought into question when it works, if not perfectly, then at least well enough for most purposes.
- With this development, a return to political stability, the triumph in the Cold War, has come the renewed arrogance of national political systems and some desire to

71

restore as much autarky as is possible in an interdependent world: a confusion has arisen between the illusion of sovereignty, or the formal constitutional status of sovereignty and the capacity of states to exercise freedom of action and decision in a meaningful way.

• Whatever the merits and political need to enlarge (partly because of a sense of obligation following the applicant states' experience during the Cold War and partly because of a belief that their membership will increase the zone of economic and political stability in Europe), it must be recognised that enlargement involves the European Union becoming more and more heterogeneous compared to the relative homogeneity of the Six, who shared geographical propinquity, and in some cases coal seams running beneath their shared border. If a Community of Six could come close to being torn apart in the 1965–66 crisis and fail to meet numerous deadlines for decision, and, as noted, the EC/EU of Twelve and Fifteen failed in the 1990s, what chance for a European Union of twenty-one or more in the years to come?

• In answer to the above queries it sometimes seems to be assumed that the project of European integration will survive because there is an implicit assumption that there is something inexorable or even economically deterministic about the past and future of integration, at least in the economic sphere. Is there some hidden hand moving integration from coal and steel to customs union to single market to economic and monetary union? Is the progress towards integration so entrenched that there will be no significant repatriation of powers and policy areas? Will the *acquis* survive?

• Have 'flexibility', subsidiarity, à la carte choices and variable geometry destroyed the heart of the enterprise?

• Is the EU anachronistic since it has already been left behind by the pressures of globalisation on the one hand and the emergence of subnational political systems on the other?

It could be argued that far from inexorability, what has actually been occurring is the increased obduracy of Member States, for the reasons given above and that there is now a lack of sufficient political will to take the necessary hard decisions. This leads to the question of whether the European Union is the model for the future development of Europe? Since a fratricidal war between the Member States of the European Union is now unthinkable, and since there is no credible external military threat, has integration gone as far as it can or needs?

D DISCUSSION QUESTIONS

1. What elements of the pre-twentieth-century precursors in the development of international organisations have any relevance to the structure and nature of the European Union?
2. Is the European Union on an inexorable path to a federal Europe?
3. How important was the 1965–66 crisis in shaping the future development of the European Community and European Union?

4. Does the failure of the European Defence Community suggest that there are some areas of policy that are not suited to integration?
5. Did the IGCs in the 1990s make substantial changes to how the Community/Union work and did they prepare the Union for the next enlargements?

BIBLIOGRAPHY

Corbett, R. (ed.): *The Treaty of Maastricht: from Conception to Ratification*, Harlow: Longman, 1993.

Dinan, D.: *Ever Closer Union: an Introduction to the European Community*, London: Macmillan, 1994.

Duchêne, F.: *Jean Monnet: the First Statesman of Interdependence*, New York: W.W. Norton, 1994.

Duff, A., (ed.): *The Treaty of Amsterdam: Text and Commentary*, London: Federal Trust 1997.

Haas, E.: *The Uniting of Europe*, Stanford: Stanford University Press, 1958.

Hinsley, F.H.: *Power and the Pursuit of Peace*, Cambridge: Cambridge University Press, 1963.

Laursen, F. and Vanhoonacker, S. (eds): *The Ratification of the Maastricht Treaty: Issues, Debates and Future Implications*, Dordrecht: Nijhoff 1994.

Milward, A.: *The European Rescue of the Nation-State*, London: Routledge, 1992.

de Rougemont, D.: *The Meaning of Europe*, London: Sidgwick & Jackson, 1965.

Salmon, Trevor C. and Nicoll, Sir William: *Building European Union: a Documentary History and Analysis*, Manchester: Manchester University Press, 1997.

Urwin, D.: *The Community of Europe: a History of European Integration since 1945*, London: Longman, 1991.

Urwin, D.: *A Political History of Western Europe since 1945*, London: Longman, 1997.

Westlake, M. (ed.): *The EU beyond Amsterdam*, London: Routledge, 1998.

NOTES

1. The Federal Republic of Yugoslavia is a member, but its membership is suspended

2. Lord Gladwyn, *The European Idea*, Weidenfeld & Nicolson, 1966, p. 32, see passim 1–40, and also F.H. Hinsley, *Power and the Pursuit of Peace*, Cambridge University Press, 1967, passim.

3. John Lowe, *The Concert of Europe: International Relations 1814–70*, Hodder & Stoughton, 1990, p. 39.

4. See J.S. Brown, *The Hague Peace Conference of 1899 and 1907*, Johns Hopkins UP, 1909 and J.H. Choate, *The Two Hague Conferences*, Princeton UP, 1913.

5. W.O. Henderson, *The Zollverein*.

6. Gerard J. Mangone, *A Short History of International Organization*, McGraw-Hill, 1954 passim, and Hinsley, op. cit.

7. Padraig Pearse, a hero of the Easter uprising in Dublin in 1916, quoted in F.S. Lyons, *Ireland Since the Famine*, Fontana/Collins, 1973 (revised edition), p. 336.

8. Wilfred Owen, 'Dulce Et Decorum Est', in C.D. Lewis (ed.), *The Collected Poems of Wilfred Owen*, Chatto & Windus, 1964, p. 55.

9. F.P. Walters, *A History of the League of Nations*, Oxford University Press, 1969.

10. Richard Coudenhove-Kalergi, *Pan-Europe: Publications de l'institut universitaire d'études européennes*, Presse Universitaire de France, 1988.

11. *International Conciliation: Documents for the Year 1930*, Special Bulletin, Carnegie, 1930, pp. 325–46 and *International Conciliation: 'European Federal Union: Replies of Twenty-Six Governments of Europe to M. Briand's Memorandum of May 17*, 1930, No. 265; see also Trevor C. Salmon and Sir William Nicoll, *Building European Union: a documentary history and analysis*, Manchester University Press, 1996, pp. 9–16.

12. Altiero Spinelli, *The Manifesto of Ventotene*, Associazione Italiana per il consiglio dei Communi d'Europa, the Centro Italiano Formazione Europea, and Movimento Federalista Europea, 1981; Altiero Spinelli and Ernesto Rossi, 'Gli Stati Uniti d'Europa e le vaire tendenze politiche', in Eugenio Corloni (ed.); Altiero Spinelli and Ernesto Rossi, *Problemi della federazione europea*, Rome, 1944; and Salmon and Nicoll, op. cit., pp. 17–20.

13. Some Members of the Resistance Groups in Europe, 'Draft Declaration II on European Federation', in W. Eichler, *Europe Speaks*, Militant Socialist International, 1944, and Salmon and Nicoll, op. cit., pp. 23–6.

14. Jean Monnet, *Memoirs* (translated by Richard Mayne), Collins, 1978, p. 65.

15. Ibid p. 83.

16. Idem.

17. The 'Algiers Memorandum' quoted in Pascal Fontiane (ed.), *Jean Monnet: A Grand Design for Europe*, OOP, 1988. For more on Monnet see François Duchêne, *Jean Monnet: the First Statesman of Interdependence*, W.W. Norton & Company, 1994.

18. See Salmon and Nicoll, op. cit., pp. 44–6.

19. For the text of these Resolutions see: A. and F. Boyd, *Western Union*, United Nations Association, 1948, and extracts in Salmon and Nicoll, op. cit., pp. 33–8.

20. Statute of the Council of Europe, May 1949, Command Paper 7778, HMSO.

21. Richard Mayne, *The Recovery of Europe*, Wiedenfeld & Nicolson, 1970, pp. 29–30.

22. United States Department of State Bulletin, 15 June 1947.

23. Convention for European Economic Co-operation, 16 April 1948, Command Paper 7388, HMSO.

24. Harry S. Truman, 'The Truman Doctrine: Special Message to the Congress on Greece and Turkey, March 12, 1947', *Public Papers of the Presidents of the United States*, pp. 177–9.

25. The Treaty of Economic, Social and Cultural Collaboration and Collective Self-Defence, March 1948. This was modified in 1954 by 'The Protocol Modifying and Completing the Brussels Treaty', October 1954, see Command Paper 7599, HMSO, 1949 and Command Paper 9304, HMSO 1954 for the texts. On 4 March 1947 the British and French governments had signed the Treaty of Dunkirk, a purely defensive treaty pledging each other military and other support in the event of hostilities with Germany. By 1948 this public concern had been replaced by the perceived Soviet threat.

26. See James A. Nathan and James K. Oliver, *United States Foreign Policy and World Order*, Little, Brown & Company, 1985, pp. 53–112; and Robert Osgood, *NATO: The Entangling Alliance*, University of Chicago Press, 1962.

27. The North Atlantic Treaty, Article V, *NATO Handbook*, October 1995, pp. 231–4.

28. See Salmon and Nicoll, op. cit., pp. 58–61.

29. J.-J. Servan-Schreiber, *Le Défi Américain*, published as *The American Challenge*, Penguin, 1969.

30. Jean Monnet, *Mémoires*, Vol. 2, Fayard Press, 1976, pp. 423–8, and note 17 above.

31. See Salmon and Nicoll, op. cit., pp. 44–6.

32. Compare Article 9 of the Treaty of Paris, 1951 with Article 157 Treaty of Rome establishing The European Economic Community, March 1957. Article 10 of the Treaty Establishing a Single Council and a Single Commission of the European Communities adopted the 1957 wording, and thus dropped even in the amended ECSC Treaty the word 'supranational'.

33. The European Defence Community Treaty, Article 1, Command Paper 9127, HMSO, 1954.

34. See Edward Fursdon, *The European Defence Community*, St Martin's Press, 1980, and R. Aron and D. Lerner, *France Defeats the EDC*, Praeger, 1957.

35. Draft Treaty embodying the Statute of the European Community adopted by the ad hoc Assembly 10 March 1953, Article 82, European Parliament Committee on Institutional Affairs, Selections of Texts concerning institutional matters of the Community from 1950 to 1982, pp. 57–77.

36. See 25 above.

37. For a discussion of 'high' and 'low' politics see: Roger Morgan, *High Politics, Low Politics: Towards a Foreign Policy for Western Europe*, Sage Publications, 1973.

38. Resolution adopted by the Ministers of Foreign Affairs of the Member States of the ECSC at their meeting at Messina on 1 and 2 June 1955; see European Parliament, Selections of Texts, op. cit., pp. 95–9.

39. The Treaty Establishing the European Coal and Steel Community, April 1951, Command Paper 4863, HMSO, 1972.

40. Treaty of Rome Establishing the European Economic Community March 1957, Command Paper 4864, HMSO, 1972.

41. Britain and the European Communities, Background to the Negotiations, H.M. Treasury, HMSO, 1961.

42. Cited in John Newhouse, *The Nuclear Age*, Michael Joseph, 1989, pp. 190–1.

43. See Salmon and Nicoll, op. cit., pp. 90–5.

44. *Bulletin of the European Communities*, 11–1970, OOP, 1970.

45. *Bulletin of the European Communities*, Supplement 11–1970, OOP, 1970.

46. Text of the Communiqué issued by the Heads of State or of Government at their meeting in The Hague, December 1969, *Bulletin of the European Communities*, 1–1970, OOP, 1970, emphasis added.

47. Text of the Communiqué issued by the Heads of State or of Government of the Countries of the Enlarged Community at their meeting in Paris, October 1972, *Bulletin of the European Communities*, 10–1972, OOP, 1972.

48. Final Communiqué issued by the Conference Chairman, Copenhagen, December 1973, *Bulletin of the European Communities*, 12–1973, OOP, 1973.

49. K. Kaiser, C. Kerlini, T. de Montbrial, E. Wellenstein, and W. Wallace, *The European Community: Progress or Decline?* Chatham House, 1983, p. 1.

50. European Parliament Committee on Insitutional Affairs Selections of Texts concerning institutional matters of the Community from 1950 to 1982, pp. 490–9.

51. *Bulletin of the European Communities,* 6–1983, OOP, 1983.

52. Commission Opinion on Greek Application for Membership, *Bulletin of the European Communities*, Supplement 2–1976, OOP, 1976.

53. See the Jean Monnet Lecture Delivered by the Right Hon. Roy Jenkins, President of the Commission of the European Communities, Florence, October 1977, in Salmon and Nicoll, op. cit., pp. 154–61.

54. Report on A People's Europe, *Bulletin of the European Communities* Supplement 7–1985, OOP, 1985.

55. Ad hoc Committee for Institutional Affairs: Report to the European Council, March 1985, Council of the European Communities 1985, OOP, 1985.

56. Draft Treaty Establishing the European Union, European Parliament Texts, 1984.

57. See EC Commission, *The Economics of 1992*, European Economy Series, 1988 no. 35 and P. Cecchini, 1992, *The Benefits of a Single Market*, Gower, 1988.

58. COM (85) 310 (Document Series), OOP, 1985.

59. The disagreement within the Cabinet over Europe was only one factor in her loss of support. The unpopularity of the government partly because of the introduction of the 'poll tax' was also important.

60. See *Agence Europe*, 20 April 1990, for the Kohl–Mitterrand letter and *Bulletin of the European Communities,* 4–1990, 6–1990 and 10–1990 for the Presidency Conclusions of the European Council.

61. Conclusions of the Presidency of the European Council, December 1992, Annex 1 to Part B: Decision of the Heads of State or Government, meeting within the European Council, concerning certain problems raised by Denmark on the Treaty on European Union, *Bulletin of the European Communities*, 12–1992, OOP, 1992.

62. Ibid, Annex 1 to Part A: Overall approach to the application by the Council of the subsidiarity principle and Article 3b of the Treaty on European Union.

63. Ibid, Conclusions of the Presidency of the European Council.

64. *Growth, Competitiveness, Employment: European Commission*, OOP, 1994.

65. See the new Title VII 'Provisions on closer co-operation' and Article 11 of the Treaty establishing the European Community.

66. New Article 7, para. 1 of the Treaty on European Union.

67. Treaty on European Union 1992, Article 6.2.

68. Treaty of Amsterdam amending the Treaty on European Union and the Treaty establishing the European Community, Article 1(1).

69. Rewording of Article 2 TEC.

70. New Article 6a of TEC.

71. See new Article 8 TEC, 1992.

72. Reformulated Article 8(1).
73. A new indent in Article 2 TEU whereby the Union asserts as an objective: 'to maintain and develop the Union as an area of freedom, security and justice, in which the free movement of persons is assured in conjunction with appropriate measures with respect to external border controls, immigration, asylum and the prevention and combating of crime.' and a new Title VI 'Provisions on Police and Judicial Co-operation in Criminal Matters'.
74. Revised Article 17, replacing old 1992 Article J.4.
75. For references to this decision and the associated decisions see *Bulletin of the European Union*, 5–1998, pp.11–17, OOP, 1998.
76. Conclusions of the Presidency of the European Council, Copenhagen, June 1993, *Bulletin of the European Communities*, 6–1993, OOP, 1993.
77. For all the *avis* published in 1997 on the applicant states *see Bulletin of the European Union*, Supplements 6/97–15/97, OOP, 1997.
78. Agenda 2000 for a stronger and wider Union, *Bulletin of the European Union*, Supplement 5/97, OOP, 1997.
79. Part of this process of preparation were the 'Europe Agreements' between the Communities, the Member States and individual Eastern and Central European states, the first of which were signed in December 1991. These were criticised as being too restrictive on the Community side and allowing insufficient trade opportunities to the prospective members. For a typical example see 'Europe Agreement establishing an Association between the European Communities and their Member States, of the One Part, and the Republic of Hungary, of the Other Part', December 1991, *Official Journal* L 347, 31.12.93.
80. See *European Union Financial Report 1997*, OOP, 1998.
81. Mrs Thatcher, Prime Minister, 'Speech at the Opening Ceremony of the 39th Academic Year of the College of Europe', Bruges, September 1988, in Salmon and Nicoll, op. cit., pp. 208–14.
82. Committee of Independent Experts 'First Report on Allegations Regarding Fraud, Mismanagement and Nepotism in the European Commission', 15 March 1999.
83. European Commission, *Growth, Competitiveness, Employment: The Challenges and Ways Forward into the 21st.Century*, White Paper, 1994, OOP, 1994.
84. The phrase used by Winston Churchill in his famous speech in Zurich in September 1946, extracts of which are reproduced in Salmon and Nicoll, op. cit., pp. 26–8.
85. An echo of Thomas Mann's famous call 'not for a German Europe, but for a European Germany'.
86. See note 81 above.
87. 'The Hague Congress Political Resolution', May 1948 in Salmon and Nicoll, op. cit., pp. 34–6.
88. Mr Malcolm Rifkind, Secretary of State for Foreign and Commonwealth Affairs, 'Principles of British Foreign Policy', September 1995, in Salmon and Nicoll, op. cit., pp. 227–81.
89. Wolfgang Schäuble and Karl Lammers, *CDU/CSU*, *'Reflections on European Policy'*, Bonn, September 1994, Fraktion des Deutschen Bundestages and Salmon and Nicoll, op. cit., pp. 255–61.

90. Prime Minister John Major's response was given at Leiden in September 1994, in Salmon and Nicoll, op. cit., pp. 261–3. In France, M. Balladur, a candidate in the 1995 Presidential elections in France in 1995 (he lost), had proposed a Europe of 'concentric circles' of states accepting obligations of different intensities.
91. See 31 above.
92. K.C. Wheare *Federal Government*, Oxford University Press, 1953 edn, p. 35.
93. Report of the Study Group on the role of Public Finances in European Integration, OOP, 1977, p. 20.
94. M. Jacques Delors, President of the European Commission, 'Speech at the Opening Ceremony of the 40th Academic Year of the College of Europe', Bruges, October 1989, *Bulletin of the European Communities*, 10–1989.
95. European Parliament, 'Draft Treaty establishing the European Union' February, 1984, EP Texts, 1984.
96. See the Treaty of Amsterdam 'Protocol on the application of the principle of subsidiarity and proportionality'.
97. Modified and re-named 'Provisions on Police and Judicial Cooperation in Criminal Matters' by Title VI of Amsterdam Treaty.
98. See Alexander C-G. Stubb, 'A Categorization of Differentiated Integration', *Journal of Common Market Studies*, Vol. 34, No. 2 (June 1996), pp. 283–95.
99. Emphasis added.

PART 2

THE INSTITUTIONS OF THE UNION

CHAPTER 4

THE EUROPEAN PARLIAMENT

INTRODUCTION

The theory of institutional structure

THE ARCHITECTS of the European Communities and of the European Union were not theoreticians but practical men and women of affairs well versed in administration and political purpose. The founding fathers had lived through weak government and oppressive dictatorship. They wanted to create a model of governance that would be effective, efficient and capable of taking decisions. It should also be one immune from legislative capture – that is, incapable of being taken over by a single uncheckable force, like the Nazi Party.

But in the beginning they faced a certain contradiction of aim. The first venture into European integration, the European Coal and Steel Community of 1951, had precisely as its purpose to remove the 'sinews of war' from the control of national governments, in this case primarily France, a democracy, and Germany, a demilitarised state still under occupation but being restored to democratic government.

Technocracy

The first Community sought to neutralise the excesses of nationalism by building a structure explicitly called 'supranational'. It did so by creating a powerful regulator and executive, in the High Authority. Its members did not depend on democratic legitimacy. They were appointed by common accord of the member states. But they were not representatives of the Member States. They were independent of them so far as the powers given to them by Treaty were concerned. They were the source of the implementing measures required to run the common market in coal and steel which the Treaty had created. For much of their work, they needed the assent of all the Member States, without abstention. This provided a form of democratic control, exercised by representatives who were democratically elected, each holding a veto that could thwart the hegemonic ambitions of any of its partners.

But the High Authority itself was consequently in the nature of a technocracy: its members were immune to the pressures inherent in a political system that depends upon the continuing support of an electorate. The High Authority was also shielded from the attentions of the Assembly that the Treaty had provided for. The Assembly could ask Questions, debated an annual Report, and, if it could find the required majority, fire the High Authority *en masse*. It had some budgetary power and could give Opinions when asked, except that the Treaty did not say that it had to be asked. It is given scant attention in the semi-official history of the ECSC.[1]

Technocrats rule

Technocracies have their place in the theory of political organisation. They belong to a utilitarian tradition that tends to underrate the importance of individual satisfaction in favour of pursuing the 'greatest good for the greatest number'. They can act and react quickly and with a singleness of purpose. They can escape from short-termism and behave consistently over the time needed to produce the benefits which, when realised, justify the absence of popular support for what they are doing.[2] The 'tiger' economies of Asia were once held up as examples of authoritarianism pursuing economic growth without political restraint. Whether the longer-term goals can be reached without some democratic expression is now a conundrum.

Separation of powers

Only a few years on from the ECSC Treaty, the direction and form of European integration changed. By 1957 the memory of totalitarianism had receded. Nationalism was no longer an unpleasant word. Supranationalism was on the wane because it was not perceived to be needed to neutralise war-making potential. The way was clear for a fresh approach to an organisation that in the preamble to its treaty gave itself more down to earth functions than the ringing eloquence of the ECSC Treaty, with its evocations of civilisation, world peace, an end to bloody divisions and a destiny henceforward shared.

The new underlying principle of structure and action was the *separation of powers*. This principle goes back to antiquity but reached its clearest expression in *The Spirit of the Laws* by Charles Louis Montesquieu in 1748, and especially in Book XI which purports to be an account of the English Constitution. Montesquieu's doctrine shines through the constitutions of Revolutionary France and of the United States of America. Put simply, it proposes that government should be based on the separation of the powers of the legislature (that cannot implement the laws it passes), the executive (that cannot make laws) and the judiciary (that is, independent of each and controls both).

The model for the new European Economic Community (EEC) and its contemporary, the European Atomic Energy Community (Euratom), is a best endeavour shot at the separation of powers. It consists of several institutions, endowed by Treaty with powers, or 'competencies'. The Commission is a kind of executive;[3] the Council and the European Parliament (EP) are types of legislature; and the European Court of Justice is the independent judiciary. It cannot be claimed that the separation of powers is water-tight. The members of the Commission are appointed by the Member States in conjunction with the EP. The judges are appointed by the Member States. The Commission has quasi-judicial functions, especially in the area of competition policy. Execution is in many cases decentralised to agencies that belong to the apparatus of the Member States (customs service, agricultural support, enforcement of regulations).

But the theoretical principle remains: the structure is designed to prevent any part of it from dominating the others. All are in the loop and if any one node declines the signal the process stops.

Incomplete separation

In the earlier time of the EEC, domination was not in fact avoided. The Council, the gathering of the Member States acting communally, was effectively the legislature. The constraint on it, apart from the obligation to remain within the powers conferred by the Treaty, was that it could not initiate legislation. With few exceptions, it could act only when it had a Commission proposal. At the other end, the decision on the proposal, it was unfettered. It was obliged to consult the EP on many of the measures proposed, but the opinion given (*avis*) was not binding. Progressively through Treaty amendment the Member States have diluted the Council's unilateralism. When the Treaty of Amsterdam came into force in 1999 significant legislation became a matter of co-decision between the Council and the EP. If they fail to agree, the measure under discussion is dead. There is no override.

The tripod

Action by the Community therefore depends upon the Commission proposing *and* the Council and the EP agreeing. The Court continues to ensure that all the institutions party to law-making observe the law. A fifth institution, also called a Court (of Auditors), checks for financial regularity. It is likewise independent of the other institutions. Its members are appointed by the Council, after consulting the European Parliament (see pp. 86–106).

The new technocracy

The technocracy of the European Coal and Steel Community retreated but was not completely effaced. It revived when the Community decided to create a sixth institution, without calling it one. The theoretical basis is again de-politicisation. The Commission is in theory apolitical – not that it has ever regarded itself as such – but since it is the 'motor of European integration' and the source of new integrative proposals, it is perceived to have a quasi-political agenda of its own. The Council is a confluence of politics, with a common stream of Europhilia, except when a Member State like Denmark or Britain takes the view that integration is going too far, to the detriment of national

Box 4.1   Institutions and bodies

The European Commission

The Council
   The Committee of Permanent Representatives   (Coreper)
The European Parliament
The European Court of Justice
   The Tribunal of First Instance
The Court of Auditors

The European System of Central Banks   (ECSB)
The European Investment Bank   (EIB)

The Economic and Social Committee
The Committee of the Regions   (CoR)

authority. When the fulfilment of a single market (on the theory of the welfare benefits of trade liberalisation) threw into relief the barrier of separate currencies the Member States found that they needed a new instrument for the management of common or single monetary policy. They could have set up a second Commission if they had reservations about the first. They could have directed it to work on the lines of the Commission, making proposals to the Finance Council on how to keep prices stable, with due EP involvement. They decided instead that political control was the last thing wanted to permit the taking of a long-term view and resistance to the urgings of pressure and single interest groups. Hence, the Executive Board of the European Central Bank, appointed by common accord of the highest political authority of the Member States, the Heads of State or Government, after *consulting* the EP (Article 112, ex-109a) and enjoying unprecedented independence from Community institutions or bodies, governments of the Member States or anybody else (Article 108). This is a classic example of Fukuyama's 'benevolent, market-orientated absolutism'.

Even before the ECB began its tasks, its independence, which can also be described as undemocratic, was under threat from, on the one hand, the European Parliament, which sought to extract assurances about the supervisory role it wishes to assert and, on the other, the governments of the Member States participating in the single currency, with their informal Euro-XI, that wants to conduct a dialogue with the ECB.

The creation of the European Union

The foregoing questions were made more complicated when the Treaty on European Union of 1992 created an entity styled 'European Union', which is only sketchily described in the treaty. It has no legal personality, no institutions of its own and no legal powers. With some word-play, Article 3 of the TEU provides that the Union 'shall be served by a single institutional framework' but the institutions of the Union are only optically single, since the Union is built on several pillars, usually counted as three, but the institutional peculiarity of the EMU makes the count more properly four (Box 4.2). The first is the classic Community, using what used to be described as the Community method – independent Commission with a monopoly of the initiative; Parliament with the right to be consulted (and now rather more power); Council, representative of the Member States, taking decisions; the Commission again monitoring Member States for compliance with the law; the Court of Justice applying the provisions of the treaties.

The second is the CFSP, inter-governmental, and reflecting the ambition to progress towards a common foreign and defence policy.

The third is the co-operation among ministers of justice and home affairs, likewise inter-governmental in the most sensitive areas, and now called 'police and judicial co-operation in criminal matters' (formerly Justice and Home Affairs), although in this pillar it is important to note that some competencies have been transferred to the Community pillar.

The 'fourth' is the monetary union, with its own institutions, independent of the Commission and of the other institutions and (ostensibly) of the governments of the Member States.

Box 4.2   The European Union: Four (or the three traditional) pillars

The European Union			
I	II	III	IV?
European Community ECSC Euratom	Common Foreign and Security Policy	Provisions on police and judicial co-operation (formerly Justice and Home Affairs)	EMU

The incomplete Union

Thus the Union of the end of the century shows itself as incomplete and multi-faceted. There is no catch-all word to illuminate what it is. Its newest creation, the ECB, is intended to be technocratic, but may have to yield to demands to be responsive and accountable. An earlier creation, the Co-operation on Justice and Home Affairs, also known as the Third Pillar, was inter-governmental and outside the checks and balances of inter-institutional balance. In the Treaty of Amsterdam it began to move towards both parliamentary and judicial scrutiny. The 'democratic deficit' of which the Council was accused was diminished by the proliferation of co-decision. The desire to lend the Community the legitimacy of parliamentary government in the Member States by including their parliaments in the decision-making process was cut across by the efficiency criterion that argued for majority voting in the Council.

The Community has always been in transition. Its journey was to 'an ever closer union'. It now is a Union, but not a perfect one – in fact just as incomplete as when the first President of the Commission described the Community as the 'uncompleted federal state',[4] a reflection returned to in the Conclusion.

THE INSTITUTIONS IN DETAIL

According to Article 7EC (ex-4), the tasks of the Community pillar are entrusted to five institutions.

According to Article 4 TEU (ex-E) the same five institutions exercise their powers as provided for in the Treaties establishing the European Communities, as amended, and by the 'other provisions of this [TEU] Treaty'. The confusion over whom the institutions belong to is dispelled (?) by Article 3 (ex-C) which says that the Union is served by a single institutional structure. Therefore the institutions which are proper to the Communities (Pillar I) also exercise their appointed powers in Pillars II and III of the Union, even if they are not the same powers. Two of the institutions lead a double life between the Community and the Union:

The five institutions are:

- the European Parliament
- the Council
- the Commission
- the Court of Justice
- the Court of Auditors

Missing from this list are:

- the European Central Bank, or the European System of Central Banks (which is not called an institution, although it is indistinguishable from one, indeed nowhere is there a definition of institutional status);
- the European Council, which, according to Article 4 TEU (ex-D), is inter-institutional;
- the Economic and Social Committee; and
- the Committee of the Regions, which are 'bodies'.

The institutions' involvement in the Community's decision-making process is pictured in Figure 4.1.

The European Parliament

The European Parliament (EP) began life as the Assembly. At this time, the members were 'representatives' and were also members of their national parliaments, which appointed them. On 30 March 1962 the Assembly decided to call itself the European Parliament. In 1986 the Single European Act made the change of name official. Members were the appointed representatives until 1979, when the first direct elections were held.

Fig. 4.1 The Union's decision-making process

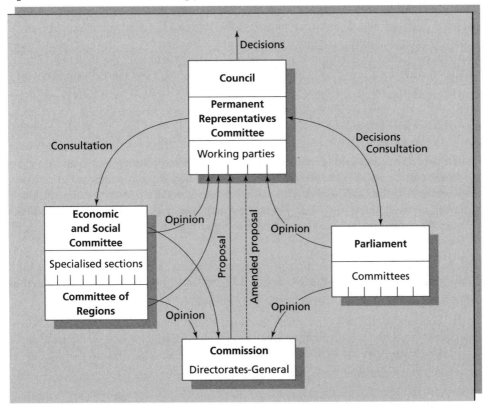

At their constituent meeting, in 1958, the representatives decided that they would not sit in national groups but in their political families.

EP–Council–Commission

Mr Ruud Lubbers, when Prime Minister of the Netherlands, once said[5] that in Western European parliaments there was government and opposition; in the Eastern bloc there was government in parliament; and in the European Parliament there was opposition. He might have added that this was inevitable, since there is nothing corresponding to the conventional forms of government in the European Community/Union. The consequence is that the relationship between the Council, which brings together democratically elected representatives of the Member States and the EP, of democratically elected members, is adversarial. In sum: in the beginning, the Council was the decision-maker. The history of the relationship is of a share of the decision-making power being transferred to the EP.

The contrast is the relationship between the EP and the Commission. The 1957 Treaty establishing the European Economic Community said that the Assembly would exercise 'advisory and supervisory powers' (old Article 137, later amended). 'Advisory' meant to other institutions, as provided for in Treaty articles. Supervisory could only mean of the Commission again as provided for in Treaty articles – there were no Treaty articles conferring a power of supervision of the Council. Thus the EP can dismiss the Commission *en bloc* by means of a motion of censure (Article 201, ex-144) and the Commission is bound to reply orally or in writing to questions put to it by the EP or by its members (Article 197, ex-140). The first Annual Report of the European Economic Community (prepared under Article 143, ex-120) described the Assembly's role as:

> The Assembly, composed of representatives of the various peoples, exercises democratic control over the activities of the Community. It has the right to pass a vote of censure on the Commission. This control, however, is not negative in character, but rather a spur, an inspiration and a help for the activities of the institutions and it brings the public opinion of the Community to the support of all steps or endeavours made in the service of Europe.

But the EP cannot affect the composition of the Council; and the latter decides for itself when it wants to be heard by the EP (Article 197, ex-140). From this an early British commentator, a former Clerk of the House of Commons, concluded:

> The control over the executive which the Parliament is given is considerable but not complete since there is no absolute sanction over the Ministers who form the Council; yet the Treaties give the Parliament enough power to render the work of the Commission very difficult without its co-operation.[6]

The 1998–99 crisis

The Parliament usually has ensured that co-operation is forthcoming,[7] but it was severed in 1998–99 in the furore over the conduct of the Santer Commission. That same furore unleashed a potential major constitutional crisis in the spring of 1999, and ultimately brought about the demise of the Santer Commission in March 1999. The crisis involved the European Parliament's powers:

- to 'discharge' the budget;
- to censure the Commission, although an issue also became its lack of power to censure individual Commissioners;
- its rights of appointment to the Commission.

Early in 1998 the European Parliament's Budget Committee expressed concern over the 1996 budget and postponed 'discharge'. The committee had problems with the execution of the budget, against a background of long-standing allegations of fraud, waste, cronyism and bungling. It gave the Commission until December to put its house in order. The Commission subsequently claimed to have met most of the concerns that had been raised, but the committee and MEPs remained unhappy. This unhappiness was increased when a 'whistle-blower', Paul van Buitenen, broke Commission staff rules (for which he was suspended) in a letter not only attacking specific abuses, but also the broader problem of Commission incompetence and unwillingness to deal with fraud and irregularities. Unhappiness further increased when the Commission, on the eve of the decisive Parliament vote on the discharge, said that if the Parliament refused to sign off on the 1996 accounts the next logical step would be for it to table a censure motion against the Commission. MEPs met the challenge and voted 270 : 225 against the discharge of the budget, and shortly afterwards picked up the censure gauntlet by tabling a motion of censure.

Under Article 201 (ex-144) the Parliament can censure (dismiss) the Commission as a body ('en bloc') by a two-thirds majority of votes cast and a majority of membership. No censure motion had ever previously been passed, although it used to be said that a Parliament vote refusing 'discharge' of the Commission's annual accounts – that is, its stewardship of the budget – would be a resigning matter.

However, prior to December 1998 such a refusal had come and gone twice without resignations. On this occasion the Santer challenge to the Parliament made what had previously been an obscure technical matter highly political and constitutional. Politics between the political groups in the Parliament also came into play as Pauline Green MEP, the leader of the Socialist group, made clear that part of the reason for her moving the censure vote was to embarrass some of the other groups who had voted against the budget discharge. In fact, in January 1999 Green and the Socialists voted against their own censure motion, arguing that they now wished to restore confidence in the embattled Commission. The censure motion was defeated 232 to 292 (i.e. no two-thirds or absolute majority). The motion was, of course, as it had to be under the Treaty, a censure of the whole Commission, although the real issue involved parliamentary hostility to individual Commissioners, especially Edith Cresson and Manuel Marín. The Socialists' opponents in the Parliament claimed that the change of tactic by the Socialists was an attempt to protect Socialist Commissioners. The concern regarding individual Commissioners led to a number of calls for the Parliament to be able to oust individuals.

Santer, the President of the Commission, and his colleagues, survived the censure, but his and their position was substantially weakened, and in order to survive Santer had had to make a number of compromises. Partly as a result of these and partly as a result of the mood of the Parliament – having rejected the censure motion – in January 1999 the Parliament adopted a resolution on improving the financial management of the Commission and calling for:

a committee of experts to be convened under the auspices of the Parliament and the Commission with a mandate to examine the way in which the Commission detects and deals with fraud, mismanagement and nepotism including a fundamental review of Commission practices in the awarding of financial contracts, to report by 15 March [1999] on their assessment in the first instance on the College of Commissioners.[8]

Subsequently, it was agreed that the first report would examine individual Commissioners, and the Commission's responsibility as a body in these areas. The Committee had no legal powers, but given the political circumstances Santer and the Commission agreed to facilitate its work and recognise its findings, although Santer had initially wanted a less specific and more long-ranging inquiry.

When the report was published on 15 March 1999, as noted above (p. 60), it was damning. Pressure was initially put on individual Commissioners to resign, especially Cresson, but when individuals refused to accept responsibility, Pauline Green and others made clear that a censure against the whole Commission would now be passed. Given this and the general reaction to the report, the Commission decided to resign *en bloc* – for some, not because of a sense of collective guilt or even of collective responsibility, but because individual Commissioners refused to accept individual responsibility. The Commission thus resigned but, in another twist to the story, remained in office in an 'acting' capacity for some months, until a new Commission was appointed.

The EP follows a two-stage procedure in the appointment of members of the Commission. First, it approves (or rejects) the person nominated by the Member States to be President of the Commission.[9] Second, it approves 'as a body' the President and the other members of the Commission whom the Member States have nominated (Article 214, ex-158). This caused some difficulties in the circumstances of the spring of 1999, especially since a new Parliament was to be elected in June and the new Commission was supposed to take over in January 2000.

The solution was for the outgoing Parliament to accept the Member States' nominee, Romano Prodi, as President-designate in the interim, but to make clear that they could not bind the new MEPs elected after June 1999. It was the new Parliament that decided, with the Member States and with President-designate, Prodi, who the new Commissioners were to be. There were calls for Parliament to be given power to censure (sack) individual Commissioners, but the treaties, even after Amsterdam, do not allow that. Prodi himself rejected this idea, although he sought to make clear that given his new role in choosing the Commissioners they would be bound, once in office, by a pledge to him to resign if he asked. He emphasised, however, that he would not call for such a resignation just because the European Parliament may have requested it.

THE UNIFORM PROCEDURE

In Article 190 (ex-138) the Treaty requires the European Parliament to

> draw up proposals for elections by direct universal suffrage in accordance with a uniform procedure in all Member States.

This is the only right of initiative, other than for its own housekeeping, which the Treaty vests in the EP. The proposals are to be examined by the Council, which will draw up the appropriate provisions and recommend them to the Member States. Forty years later, no uniform procedure exists. For twenty years, EP elections have been conducted using, with modifications, the procedures used nationally. This was the fall-back position written into Article 7 of the 1976 Act concerning the election of representatives of the European Parliament by direct universal suffrage. Before the decision was taken to hold direct elections, the EP made two attempts to propose a uniform electoral procedure. Both failed to be adopted by the appointed parliament – the Dehousse Report 1960 and Patijn Report 1975. There were two further attempts after the first election. The Seitlinger Report of 10 March 1982 was adopted, with amendments by the EP plenary, and sent to the Council. The scheme was proportional, allowing for national and regional lists (the latter preserve something of the constituency bond proper to the 'first past the post' system). Most Labour MEPs voted against, although the proposals were consistent with the regional list system which the Labour government had unsuccessfully proposed in a Westminster discussion of direct elections in 1977. Some Conservative MEPs voted for, despite the Conservative stance that had defeated the Labour government's proposal.

The Council wavered and gave up with the approach of the second direct elections in 1984. The focus of opposition was the British Conservative government, which remained implacably hostile to PR in any form and in any elected body (except for European elections in Northern Ireland, where PR was the only way of allowing the minority any voice). Immediately after the election, the EP tried again. The Bocklet Report, again proposing PR, was overshadowed by the intensive preparations of the Draft Treaty of European Union energised by the veteran Italian federalist Altiero Spinelli. The Bocklet proposals had a lukewarm reception in the Political Affairs Committee, where there was perhaps awareness of the previous sterility of debate and where members were perhaps chary of changing the procedure that had elected them. The third elections, 1989, were held under national procedure.

A new study was commissioned in 1989. The De Gucht Report, by a Belgian Liberal with extensive institutional experience, was unsurprisingly based on PR. His Committee took the view that all that was needed for uniformity was the acceptance of PR. The EP plenary did not endorse the proposals until 10 March 1993. The Council did not consider them in time for the June 1994 elections. If it had, the then British government would have continued to oppose any obligation to introduce PR generally. The third election used national procedures. The British government of the day was prepared to argue that the uniform use of national rules was enough uniformity to satisfy Treaty requirements.

When the Inter-governmental Conference got under way in 1996, the prospects for uniformity seemed no better. But the coming to power of a Labour government in May 1997 changed the outlook. Far from being officially hostile to PR, Labour in opposition had contemplated it domestically in its thinking about assemblies in Scotland and Wales (see Figure 4.2). The Treaty of Amsterdam took Article 190.4 (ex-138):

> The European Parliament shall draw up proposals for elections by direct universal suffrage in accordance with a uniform procedure in all Member States . . .

and added:

> . . . or in accordance with principles common to all Member States.

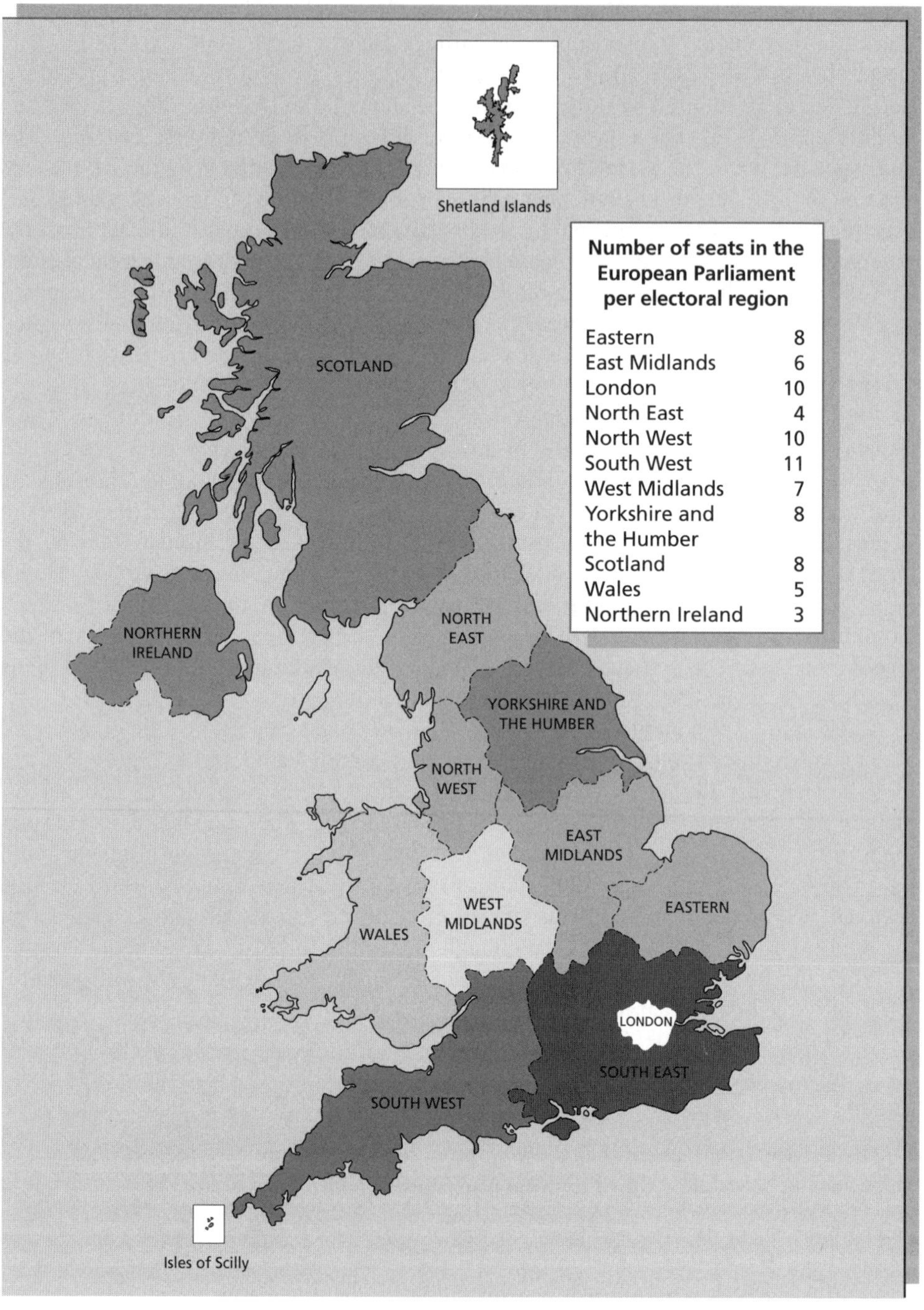

Fig. 4.2   Electoral regions in the United Kingdom of Great Britain and Northern Ireland, June 1999

Shetland Islands

Number of seats in the European Parliament per electoral region

Eastern	8
East Midlands	6
London	10
North East	4
North West	10
South West	11
West Midlands	7
Yorkshire and the Humber	8
Scotland	8
Wales	5
Northern Ireland	3

SCOTLAND

NORTHERN IRELAND

NORTH EAST

YORKSHIRE AND THE HUMBER

NORTH WEST

EAST MIDLANDS

WEST MIDLANDS

WALES

EASTERN

LONDON

SOUTH EAST

SOUTH WEST

Isles of Scilly

This, appears to have two effects. First, it gives encouragement to the De Gucht idea of limiting uniformity to an essential minimum. Second, the only principle common to all Member States, except Britain, on its mainland is PR. To square the circle, the British government, which took office on 1 May 1997, announced on 17 July 1997 that there would be a twelve-regional list form of PR for the elections held from 10 to 13 June 1999.[10]

The Institutional Affairs Committee of the EP, thus heartened, took up work again.[11] In July 1998 it presented a report and draft motion to the plenary session. The EP adopted the proposal that all elections to it should be by PR (see Table 4.1); that in Member States with population in excess of 20 million there should be regional lists[12]; and that there should be a threshold of 5% of the votes to secure a seat. A proposal that part of the membership should be reserved for cross-frontier candidates was not accepted.

Table 4.1   Electoral systems in the Member States for June 1999 elections

Member State	Electroral system	Constituency
Austria	PR with 4% threshold	Single national constituency
Belgium	PR	Four regional constituencies
Denmark	PR	Single national constituency
Greece	PR	Single national constituency
Finland	PR	Four regional constituencies
France	PR with 5% threshold	Single national constituency
Germany	PR with 5% threshold	Länder as constituencies
Ireland	PR/Single Transferable Vote	Four regional constituencies
Italy	PR	Five regional constituencies
Luxembourg	PR party mix	Single national constituency
Netherlands	PR	Single national constituency
Portugal	PR	Single national constituency
Spain	PR	Single national constituency
Sweden	PR with 4% threshold	Single national constituency
UK	PR	Eleven regional constituencies
+NI	PR/Single Transferable Vote	Single regional constituency

The number of seats per Member State in the 1999 election is given in Table 4.2.

Table 4.2   Number of seats in European Parliament per Member State, June 1999

Member State	Seats	Member State	Seats	Member State	Seats
Germany	99[13]	France	87	Italy	87
UK	87	Spain	64	Netherlands	31
Belgium	25	Greece	25	Portugal	25
Sweden	22	Austria	21	Denmark	16
Finland	16	Ireland	15	Luxembourg	6

Total 626

The number of seats is intentionally weighted in favour of the smaller states as a genuflection towards the sovereign status of all. With the accession of a large number of smaller states coming closer, this long-established principle is being reappraised, along with the other national coefficients, the weighting of votes in the Council and the number of Commissioners. As was proposed by the EP itself, the Treaty of Amsterdam fixes the maximum size of the EP after its enlargement at 700 (Article 189, ex-137). Unless there is another Treaty change, the accession of states with an aggregate population of 100 million would imply, in the European Parliaments of the next decade, some reduction in the present representation of the current fifteen Member States.

The most significant feature of the June 1999 elections was not the movement in the vote in a Centre-Right direction, so that the European People's Party replaced the Socialists as the largest political grouping, but the number of those who chose not to vote (see Table 4.3). Between June 1979 and June 1999 there has been a 15% drop in turnouts for elections to the European Parliament. In the June 1999 election the most spectacular decline (compared to 1994) was in Germany from 60% to 45%, while in the United Kingdom the turnout dropped from 36.5% to 23%.

Table 4.3 Turnouts in the Member States in June 1999 elections to the European Parliament compared to last election for the European Parliament (Austria, Finland and Sweden not voting in June 1994)

Member State	Year	Turnout	Year	Turnout
Austria	1996	68%	1999	49%
Belgium*	1994	90.7%	1999	90.5%
Denmark	1994	52.9%	1999	49.9%
Finland	1996	58%	1999	30.1%
France	1994	53.5%	1999	47%
Germany	1994	60%	1999	45.2%
Greece*	1994	71.9%	1999	70.1%
Ireland	1994	37%	1999	50.8%
Italy	1994	74.8%	1999	70.6%
Luxembourg*	1994	90%	1999	90%
Netherlands	1994	35.6%	1999	29.9%
Portugal	1994	40%	1999	40.4%
Spain	1994	59.6%	1999	64.3%
Sweden	1996	41.6%	1999	38.3%
UK	1994	36.5%	1999	23%
Eur 12	1994	56.4% EUR 15	1999	48%

* Compulsory voting

A number of reasons may be advanced for this decline:

- a lack of knowledge as to the powers and role of the Parliament;
- an awareness that the election was not about electing a government of the EU;
- a belief that the Parliament is tarred with the same corruption brush as the Commission – a view reinforced by problems about expenses;
- a belief that the Parliament is a toothless talking shop;
- the fact that there were really fifteen different national elections, rather than an election on European issues – a view reinforced by the feeling that the manifestos were general in nature; and
- a recognition that turnout in all elections – local, regional and national – has been falling across Europe.

While these arguments may carry some weight, the turnout hardly reflects the original federalist aspiration that if the people of Europe were given a voice they would demonstrate by acclaiming their support for the immediate transfer of authority from the nation-states to a united Europe. Indeed, the lesson of June 1999 seems to be the reverse; by non-voting the electorate were demonstrating their disenchantment with the integration project or their indifference or that they have taken umbrage at the single currency and its attack on identity and sovereignty. The electorate may be saying enough is enough. In any case, the turnout poses problems not just for the legitimacy and authority of the Parliament but of the European Union as a whole. In particular, it will be difficult for the 1999–2004 Parliament to challenge the right of Member States in the Council to take decisions or to appoint a Commission that reflects the Member States' wishes rather than that of MEPs. The Parliament may have the legal right to act in certain cases, but it now lacks the authority – power is about more than treaties and constitutions.

The vote in June 1999 also changed the political complexion of the European Parliament.

POLITICAL GROUPS

The European Parliament is composed of political groups and works through functional committees.

The *political groups* undergo changes after elections and during parliamentary terms. They are themselves composed of groups of national parties, some of them alliances of otherwise separate factions.[14] Among the 626 members of the EP that sat until the 1999 election, there were representatives of 99 national parties, along with a few independents (Table 4.4). The largest groups have always been the Christian Democrats, forming the European People's[15] Party (Centre Right) and the Party of European Socialists (Left). When these two work together, they form a commanding majority.

Table 4.4   Composition of the European Parliament by group after the June 1999 elections*

Group	MEPs	Group	MEPs	Group	MEPs
EPP/ED	233	Greens/EFA	48	EDD	16
PES	180	EUL/NGL	42	TGI	18
ELDR	50	UEN	21	Independent	18
TOTAL	626				

Provisional edition. Subject to change.

EPP/ED	The European People's Party and European Democrats, comprising Christian Democrat and Centre Right Parties from all member states including British Conservatives and Fine Gael members from Ireland. It is the largest group in the Parliament and also now includes an Ulster Unionist MEP.
PES	The Party of European Socialists, comprising members from all EU States including Britain and Ireland.
ELDR	European Liberal Democratic and Reformist Group, where the largest contingent is now from the UK. It includes one Irish independent who is Group Leader.
Greens/EFA	This comprises 38 MEPs from Green parties in eleven Member States who have formed a new alliance with ten MEPs from home-rule parties in Scotland, Wales, Flanders, the Basque country, Galicia and Andalusia. The UK Greens and Plaid Cymru are represented for the first time with two MEPs respectively.
EUL/NGL	The Confederal Group of the European United Left/Nordic Green Left NGL Group comprises of representatives of Left/Green parties from Denmark, Finland, Germany, Greece, Italy, the Netherlands, Spain and Sweden, as well as members of Communist parties from France, Greece and Portugal.
UEN	'The Union for a Europe of Nations' is pledged to defend the nation state and is led by twelve French national MEPs and is opposed to further integration. It includes six Fianna Fail members from Ireland, one Danish member from the People's Party and two Portuguese members from the 'Partido Popular'.
EDD	'The Europe of Democracies and Diversities Group' comprises six members from the French pro-hunting/defence of rural traditions group, the three new MEPs from the UK Independence Party, four anti-EU Danish members and three Dutch members.

TGI   This group brings together various parties of differing political com-
             plexions who have formed a Parliamentary alliance to register as a group
             and thus enjoy group privileges, i.e. the Bonino Radical Group from Italy,
             the 'Vlaams Blok' from Belgium, the 'Front National' from France and a
             Basque Separatist.

Ind   The rest of the Parliament is made up of independents, members of the
             'Allianza National' party in Italy, the Freedom Party in Austria and an
             Ulster Democratic Unionist.

The elections of June 1999 marked a profound change in the composition of the EP.
For the first time since direct election began in 1979, the European Socialist Party did
not win the largest number of seats. The European People's Party (predominantly
Christian Democrat, the descendants of the pre-war confessional parties) became
the largest bloc, with 233 members. The EPP is self-declared federalist and euro-
friendly, which are not hallmarks of British Conservatism, whose adherents were within
the EPP fold in the outgoing Parliament. There followed a negotiation in which the
British Conservative leader, William Hague, sought clarification from the leadership of
the EPP of what his supporters would be committed to if they maintained their relationship with the EP. Having apparently received sufficient assurance that they would not
be bound to a Europhile agenda, he was able to announce that the relationship would
continue.

The depleted Socialists opened their closed-door discussions with the EPP by sup-
posing that the 'Pact of Steel' still held. Under its terms, they should have the EP
Presidency for half the life of the new EP, in succession to the EPP incumbent. The EPP
dismissed this suggestion, as not in accord with the victory which the election had given
them. They courted instead the Liberal Group, and concluded a pact with it. It was
described as 'constitutive' and 'technical'. It provides that the EPP will hold the
Presidency for two-and-a-half years and the Liberals for the second half of the mandate. They will also work together on the reform of parliamentary administration. On
policy issues, they remain independent. At the first part-session, held in the new building in Strasbourg in July, the EPP candidate for President was elected on a single ballot.

The deeper significance was that the two centrist parties, EPP and Socialist, had split
so that for the first time there would be a Right–Left policy divide. The Right majority,
insufficient even with other right-wing parties, to command an overall majority, would
face in co-decision a Council with a majority of left-wing members.

An interesting feature of the 1999 result was that, in the UK, smaller parties, taking
advantage of the new electoral system, gained 23% of the national vote, with the
UK Independence Party gaining three seats with 8% of the vote. Elsewhere in Europe a
certain right-wing Euroscepticism appears to have crept into the European psyche.
In Denmark, for example, anti-EU parties won 5 out of 16 seats and in Italy
Silvo Berlusconi's right-wing Forza Italia Party won a majority of votes. Nonetheless, in
the EU as a whole the far-right failed to make any dramatic showing. For those who

97

did vote the election again seemed to be predominantly about national issues, serving in many cases as a sort of mini-opinion poll on the performances of incumbent governments.

FUNCTIONAL COMMITTEES

Once elected it can be argued that much of the real work of MEPs is performed in the functional specialist committees. In the 1994–99 Parliament there were twenty such Committees. The 1999–2004 Committees are shown in Box 4.3.

Committee chairmen are appointed by the political groups, employing the De Hondt system of proportionate share.[16] Each group has a stock of points that it uses up in acquiring chairmanships. Parliamentary committees are the mainstay of the conduct of business. Legislation on which the EP is consulted or co-decides is referred to the sectoral committee responsible, sometimes with turf disputes, and sometimes with other committees involved for their opinion. The committee appoints a *rapporteur* to draft a report and proceeds to discuss the proposed measure. Commission officials attend to explain and defend the proposal. The Council is rarely present, and virtually never at ministerial level. Within the committee there are co-ordinators acting as mild whips for groups which have several committee members. The committee votes by simple

Box 4.3   Committees of the European Parliament, 1999–2004

I	Foreign Affairs, Human Rights, Common Security and Defence Policy
II	Budgets
III	Budgetary Control
IV	Citizens' Liberties and Rights, Justice and Home Affairs
V	Economic and Monetary Affairs
VI	Legal Affairs and the Internal Market
VII	Industry, External Trade, Research and Energy
VIII	Employment and Social Affairs
IX	Environment, Public Health and Consumer Policy
X	Agriculture and Rural Development
XI	Fisheries
XII	Regional Policy, Transport and Tourism
XIII	Culture, Youth, Education and the Media
XIV	Development and Co-operation
XV	Constitutional Affairs
XVI	Women's Rights and Equal Opportunities
XVII	Petitions

majority on the report and the accompanying draft motion for a Resolution. If the motion, possibly as amended,[17] goes through, the outcome is submitted to a plenary, in accordance with the calendars worked out by the business bodies. In the debate, the committee chairperson and the *rapporteur* are the leading speakers. In all debates, political groups are given a time allowance that corresponds to their proportionate share of membership. Speakers are allowed a little latitude before being cut off.[18] Proceedings are simultaneously interpreted into all official languages and published in those languages.

The key actors in this whole process are accordingly the committee chairpersons, some of whom impose themselves, and the *rapporteurs*, who have acquired expertise in the subject. Committee meetings, like plenaries, are (usually) open to the public, although few attend. At least once[19] in a Council Presidency, Presidents of the different Councils appear before the committees that are shadowing their work to deliver a statement and answer questions from members. Properly used this could be a sharp tool in MEPs' hands, for example, in exploring in depth the proposals on which they are being consulted. They rarely attain the necessary degree of teamwork to make full use of the golden opportunity.

A committee with a particular external role is on Petitions (until 1987 within the purview of the Rules Committee). In its leaflet the Committee on Petitions assures Community citizens[20] that they 'may send a written request or complaint to the European Parliament, thus exercising their right of petition'. The matter has to fall within the scope of the EC's activities and may not concern a matter that is the subject of legal proceedings.

Committees of Inquiry

Of their own volition, the elected MEPs appointed temporary Committees of Inquiry to prepare reports on issues which members consider to be of importance. One example is the Committee of Inquiry into Racism and Xenophobia, 'one of the major social and political problems of our time'. The EP of 1984–89 was acutely aware of the problem since it had to contend with an increased presence of such extreme right-wing groups in its own chamber. The Treaty on European Union provides in Article 193 (ex-138c) for the EP to appoint Committees of Inquiry with a narrower remit relating to alleged contraventions or mal-adminstration in the implementation of Community law. The most notable use of this article was the Inquiry into BSE, 1996–97. Some members, detecting what they thought was a Commission cover-up, flirted with a draft motion of censure on the Commission, but were deterred by the majority.

Interparliamentary delegations

Another group of EP committees is the delegations to parliamentary bodies in non-member countries. Those with the CEECs and with Turkey, Cyprus and Malta are known as Joint Parliamentary Committees. Others are called 'Delegations for Relations with . . .' and collectively as Inter-parliamentary Delegations. Interestingly, these bodies give the EP a structured relationship with third countries that it does not have with parliaments in the Member States.

A much grander affair is the ACP–EU Joint Assembly, established under the Lomé Convention. The Assembly is composed of parliamentary representatives (or if there are none, appointed diplomats) from the ACP countries and an equal number of MEPs. It meets twice a year, once in a Member State and once in an ACP country. Its output is principally in the form of Resolutions proposed by members and worked over by the Bureau (of one co-president and ten vice-presidents from each side) before being placed before the Assembly for vote. Members on both sides would like to be able to question the joint ACP-EU Council of Ministers. The EU co-president of this body has been prepared to reply, solely on behalf of the EU, but the arrangements are minimal. Some of the Resolutions find their way into the work of the EP's Development and Co-operation Committee.

QUESTION TIME

It has been suggested above that the appearance of Council Presidents before EP Committees, although frequent, does little to enhance the democratic control which the EP would like to stand for in the institutional structure. When Britain became a member of the EEC, its representatives brought with them the institution of Question Time. The Commission is obliged by Article 197 (ex-140) to answer Parliamentary Questions. The Council does so voluntarily. The two take questions on different sessional days for an hour-and-a-half each. If it is not too much of a distortion to regard the EP as an approximation to the Opposition, Question Time might seem to be a first-class opportunity for MEPs to harry the Council. But the atmosphere is against the kind of heat that can be stoked up in the House of Commons. The hemicycle is not built for adversarial encounters. Members other than from Britain and Ireland are not versed in this kind of dialectic. Using the question as a device to make a mini-speech, they do not confront the Commissioner or Minister answering. Interpretation loses spontaneity. The Commission is criticised for giving answers that are excessively long – few Commission staff responsible for drafting have the sense of the occasion. The Council gives answers that are more cryptic because they have had to be cleared through all the Member States in its General Affairs Group (GAG). No useful purpose is served by asking the Council about something it has never discussed; and when it has discussed a subject, there is either a text that contains its conclusion, or a procedure that is still under way. Members sometimes make heavy weather by asking, for example, what the Council is going to do about 'dwarf-tossing'[21] in Australia, the employment of children as camel jockeys in Arab countries, or filling balloons with ozone and sending them aloft to fill the hole in the ozone layer. There is no Table Office to filter out unanswerable questions.

The Commission, and to a much lesser extent the Council, also answer written questions. It takes so long for a written question to receive its answer that little topicality survives.

LEGISLATIVE ROLES

Much play is made of the complexity of the inter-institutional legislative procedures.[22] There are six ways in which the European Parliament can be consulted over legislation or not:

- EP not consulted;
- EP consulted for its opinion, but its views are not binding on the Council;
- EP assent required but it cannot change the text;
- Co-operation (after the Amsterdam Treaty, this only applies in EMU);
- Co-decision (see Figure 4.3), although the word 'co-decision' does not appear in the treaties;
- The budgetary 'shuttle'.

After Amsterdam, however, only assent, co-decision and the budgetary shuttle (see pp. 313–16 below) are really significant. Which procedures apply to which articles are analysed in the Extended Glossary (pp. 531–58). The key co-decision procedure is shown diagramatically in Figure 4.3 and the areas it covers in Box 4.4. It remains true that much of the real impact of MEPs on legislation is through private influence and the committee system.

Box 4.4   The following issues are subject to co-decision

Pre-Amsterdam

Article	Subject
49	Free movement of workers
54(2)	Right of establishment
56(2)	Treatment of foreign nationals
57(1)	Mutual recognition of qualifications
57(2)	Co-ordination of provisions relating to self-employment
66	Freedom to provide services
100a	Internal market
100b	Internal market
126(4)	Education incentive measures
128	Culture
129(4)	Public health
129a(2)	Consumer protection
129d	Trans-European networks
130 I (1)	R&D: framework programmes
130s	Adoption of environmental action programmes

Box 4.3 (*cont.*)

and Amsterdam added:	
5	Employment incentive measures
119	Social policy – equal opportunities and treatment
129	Public health – quality and safety of organs and veterinary and phytosanitary measures
191a	General principles for transparency
209a	Countering fraud against financial interests of Community
New	Customs co-operation
213a	Statistics
213b	Establishment of independent advisory authority on data
6	Protection rules to prohibit discrimination on grounds of nationality
8a(2)	Provisions for facilitating the exercise of citizens' rights to move and reside freely within the territory of Member States
51	Internal market – rules on social security for Community immigrant workers
56(2)	Co-ordination of provisions for special treatment for foreign nationals (right of establishment)
57(2)	Co-ordination of provisions for taking up and pursuit of activities as self-employed persons
75 (1)	Transport policy – international to or from or passing across a Member State
84	Transport policy – sea and air
125	European Social Fund
127(4)	Vocational training
129d	Other measures (trans-European networks)
130e	ERDF implementation decisions
130o	Research measures
130s(1)	Environment – action to achieve objectives of 130r
130w	Development co-operation

THE PRESIDENT AND OTHER OFFICE-HOLDERS

The President of the EP is elected by a secret ballot of the members (see Box 4.5). The President serves for two-and-a-half-years, half a full session. Since a Liberal – the respected Madame Simone Veil – held the office in the first directly elected Parliament, there has been a Christian Democrat/Socialist succession, apart from one British Conservative, Lord Plumb (1987–89). This accommodation, known derogatively as the Pact of Steel,[23] has been criticised ineffectively by other groups. The result of the pact is that in 1989, 1992, 1994 and 1997 a victor emerged after only one round of balloting.

Figure 4.3   The co-decision procedure

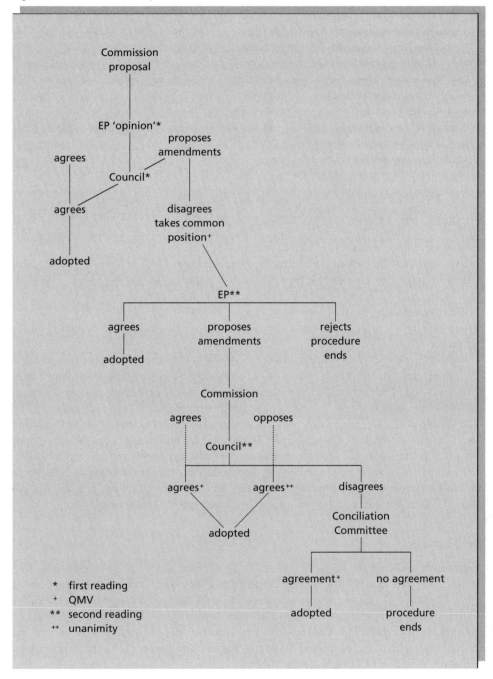

* first reading
+ QMV
** second reading
++ unanimity

Box 4.5 Presidents of the European Parliament since 1979

Simone Veil (France)	1979–82
Pieter Dankert (Netherlands)	1982–84
Pierre Pflimlin (France)	1984–87
Lord Plumb (UK)	1987–89
Enrique Barón Crespo (Spain)	1989–92
Egon Klepsch (Germany)	1992–94
Klaus Hänsch (Germany)	1994–97
José María Gil-Robles (Spain)	1997–99
Nicole Fontaine (France)	1999–

The President takes the chair at the bodies that arrange parliamentary business and run its workings, and at some of the part-sessions. (S)He has a representational function, *vis-à-vis* other institutions and in the world at large. (S)He attends and speaks at the opening session of meetings of the European Council.

Fourteen Vice-Presidents are elected by members. Some are old hands and some have built up reputations for the effective chairmanship during part-sessions, which is their principal activity. Three Vice-Presidents are standing members of the Conciliation Committee that acts in the co-decision procedure. Members also elect five Quaestors, responsible for overseeing parliamentary administration (including the perennial building projects).

Following a reform in 1993, ahead of the 1994 election, the EP reorganised its business structures. Its Bureau consists of the elected office-bearers: President, Vice-Presidents and Quaestors, the last-named having no vote. The Bureau manages forward part-sessions and disposes of internal administrative/inter-group problems. The Conference of Presidents, which previously had an informal existence, brings together the President of the Parliament and the leaders of the political groups. Before reform, the group leaders plus the Bureau composed the Enlarged Bureau, which was unwieldy. The other participant in the meetings of the Conference of Presidents is the Chairman of the Conference of Committee Chairmen, which meets to follow progress on the preparation of reports and the timing for their insertion into plenaries.

Ombudsman

A distinct remedy for the aggrieved citizen is the Parliamentary Ombudsman (*médiateur*), an office created in the TEU by Article 195 (ex-138e). The Ombudsman is appointed solely by the EP. On his or her own initiative, or on the basis of a complaint received, the Ombudsman investigates cases of possible maladministration on the part of Community institutions or bodies. The Ombudsman has access to the documents needed and the officials required to be examined. Matters that are the subject of legal proceedings, nationally or in the ECJ, are not admissible.[24]

Other appointments

Apart from its role in appointing the Commission, and its sole responsibility for the appointment of the Ombudsman (Article 195, ex-138e), the Parliament has other powers of appointment.

There were suggestions during the Inter-governmental Conference of 1996–97 that the EP should have a say in the appointment of the judges of the Court of Justice (as the US Senate decides on members of the Supreme Court nominated by the President), but such an aberration was not accepted.

The members of the Court of Auditors are appointed by the Council, after *consulting* the EP (Article 247, ex-188.b3). The EP, which is involved in budgetary control, prefers to regard this as a form of co-decision. Its negative opinion on individual candidates has in the past ruled them out of appointment.

The President, Vice-President and the four other members of the European Central Bank (ECB) are appointed by the Member States after consulting the EP (TEU: Protocol on the Statute of the European System of Central Banks and of the European Central Bank, Article 11). In the first appointments to the ECB, the designated President, Mr Duisenberg, said that if the EP did not approve, he would not accept appointment. The EP cannot censure the ECB; it is an independent body.

The EP plays no part in the appointment of members of the Economic and Social Committee, the Committee of the Regions or the Management Committee of the European Investment Bank.

THE PERIPATETIC PARLIAMENT

One of the EP's steady complaints about what the Member States have imposed on it is where it sits. There are three hemicycles to house plenaries: in Strasbourg, in Luxembourg and in Brussels. The Luxembourg building, carved out of rock-face, is out of use for parliamentary purposes. But the official headquarters of the Secretariat is on the Kirchberg Plateau in Luxembourg.

The original seat of the EP, decided by common accord of the Member States under Article 289 (ex-216), was Strasbourg. Although the city authorities provide generous facilities, most MEPs, other than French, resent the obligation to move to Strasbourg every month and would have preferred to be in Brussels, next to the Commission and the Council. When the EP started moving staff from Luxembourg to Brussels, and when the EP began to take steps to hold plenaries as well as committee meetings in Brussels, there were flurries of court cases crying foul.

The Treaty of Amsterdam incorporates a package settlement of a collection of location disputes agreed among the member states at the meeting of the European Council in Edinburgh in December 1992 (Protocol[25] on the location of seats of the institutions and certain bodies and departments of the European Communities and of Europol). It stipulates that the seat of the EP, where it will hold twelve-monthly sessions (two in one month for the Budget) is Strasbourg. It will hold additional plenaries in Brussels and its committees will meet there. Its General Secretariat remains in Luxembourg. Brussels plenaries, of two days at a frequency decided by the EP itself, are becoming common and a massive new building houses a hemicycle, committee rooms and MEPs' offices. (A new EP building in Strasbourg enabled the EP to quit the building that belongs to the Council of Europe.) Committees meet improperly in Strasbourg during part-sessions there. Most committee meetings are in Brussels, where some General Secretariat staff are based. The monthly move of MEPs, staff and their impedimenta from their home bases and from Brussels/Luxembourg to Strasbourg and back again adds greatly to administrative cost.

Perquisites

Another cost issue has been lax supervision of the generous allowances which MEPs can claim for attendance and travel. Control is said to have been tightened. As a more radical solution, a report in July 1998 suggested that salaries, which are equated to the salary of a member of the national parliament, should be levelled up. There has never been agreement among the Member States that an MEP's salary should be higher than an MP's.

The power of Parliament is growing

In the institutional power struggle, the EP has been on the winning side, notably in its 'supervision' of the Commission,[26] especially in the 1998–99 struggle, and in its co-decision with the Council. As the analysis in the Extended Glossary shows, there is still ground to conquer in the many Council decisions based on Articles where the EP has little if any input. There is also room for a better strategy of engaging the Council, at ministerial level, in the work of committees. But at least one veteran Committee Chairman has said that he prefers to deal with Deputy Permanent Representatives, who know their stuff, than with Ministers reading from their briefs.

NATIONAL PARLIAMENTS

One of the unsolved and possibly insoluble problems is the relationship between national parliaments and the European Parliament. Even before the first enlargement and long before direct EP elections, the late Andrew Shonfield[27] was warning of the danger inherent in organising competition between two separate democratic institutional structures. National parliaments are at the losing end. As the Community/Union extends its reach, subjects for which they were formerly part of the decision-making process recede from them. As the European Parliament gains power, national parliaments are further displaced.

The credentials of members of the Council rest on their accountability to their national parliaments. With the single exception of Denmark[28], this control is weak.

National parliamentary scrutiny is not seriously influential.[29] Ministers reporting back on EC/EU business are rarely harried on specifics. In the absence of a publicly available account of the meeting they attended, they can put 'spin' on their own performance and achievement.

The Treaty on European Union contains two pious Declarations (without binding effect). The first says that national parliaments should obtain Commission legislative proposals in good time in case they wish to examine them; and that contacts between national parliaments and the EP should be stepped up. The other invites the Conference of European Parliaments to meet 'as necessary' and promises that it will be consulted 'on the main features of the European Union'

The Conference of European Parliaments ('assises') can trace its origins back to a meeting in Rome in 1963 with the President of the European Parliament in the chair.[30] The principle, if not the format of such gatherings, which were not a success, was revived in 1989 in the body known as 'Cosac' from the French language acronym or 'CEAC' in English, standing for the Conference of European Affairs Committees (of national parliaments).

The Treaty of Amsterdam goes further. It contains a Protocol[31] (that is, legally binding) on the role of national parliaments in the EU. It notes that scrutiny of governments is a matter for domestic arrangement. It provides that all Commission consultation documents will be 'promptly' forwarded to national parliaments. It sets a minimum period of six weeks between legislative proposals being made available to the Council (whose Member States would pass them to the national parliament) and being placed on a Council agenda. It also provides that Cosac may make any contribution it deems appropriate for the attention of the Institutions of the European Union.[32] There are particular references to subsidiarity and human rights.

The Protocol is a pallid reflection of proposals that were current during the Intergovernmental Conference of 1996–97 envisaging the establishment of a Council/Committee of Parliaments charged with functions relating to Union activity[33] and especially upholding the rules of subsidiarity. The difficulty with all such proposals, as with Cosac itself, is that the EP is the only parliament in the Union which can describe itself as having a policy on anything (and even some of its members, of the extreme right or Eurosceptic ranks, would deny that the policies of the majority can be said to be those of the institution). All other parliaments, in differing degrees adversarial and necessarily so, cannot bring a single parliamentary position to an inter-parliamentary forum except on motherhood and apple pie issues. Although the Treaty of Amsterdam Protocol will afford those national parliaments that wish it a better opportunity to scrutinise legislative proposals, it is unlikely to give Cosac a higher profile or any effective role in Community/Union business.

LEGAL BASE

- Articles 137–144, 158 and 189b of the EC Treaty.

1. Discuss what is known as the 'democratic deficit'.
2. Should the Parliament elect the President of the Commission?
3. Are trans-national political parties, with a single European electorate using PR, possible or desirable?
4. Why did only 48% of the electorate vote in June 1999?
5. Can the Parliament control 'the executive'?
6. Is there any justification for limiting 'co-decision' to only some areas of policy?
7. Is it desirable or necessary to improve the relations between national parliaments and the European Parliament?

THE COUNCIL

THE POLITICAL theory behind the institution of the Council is straightforward. The architects of the Treaty were not building either the United States of Europe or the European Federation that was foreshadowed in the Schuman Declaration of 9 May 1950. All the members of the Community were equal – Monnet's dictum – and all maintained their identity as nation-states. There was to be none of the leader-principle from which Europe had suffered. Either all participated in a joint enterprise or it was abandoned. The Treaty had foreseen that at a later stage there would be majority voting, with weights assigned in a rough proportion to population size, skewed in favour of the less populous (see Box 5.1). For thirty years, however, the members of the Council preferred the politically more solid consensus, otherwise national veto power.

Any time and motion study would show that unanimity needs time to gather. A gambler could also have explained that in a Community of six there is one chance in five of reaching unanimity; with twelve, the odds against reaching it double and it becomes a bad bet. From

Box 5.1   The weighting of votes and qualified majority

France, Germany, Italy, United Kingdom	10 votes each
Spain	8 votes
Belgium, Greece, Netherlands, Portugal	5 votes each
Austria, Sweden	4 votes each
Denmark, Finland, Ireland	3 votes each
Luxembourg	2 votes

The total of votes is 87. The majority needed in the rare use of simple majority voting is now 44; for qualified majority it is 62, where the Council is voting on a proposal from the Commission; and in other cases, those 62 must include the votes of at least ten Member States.

this, qualified majority voting (QMV) has been described as 'upgrading the common interest'. When the Council decided in 1985 that it wanted to make a single market within seven years, it also decided that most of the 300 measures would be adopted by qualified majorities. The alternative was no single market. In presenting his proposal,[34] Lord Cockfield, the Commissioner responsible, mercilessly recalled all the undertakings which the Member States had entered into ... and disregarded.

COMPOSITION

In the current version of the Treaty establishing the European Community, the Council consists of a representative of each Member State at ministerial level (Article 203, ex-146). In the Treaty on European Union this replaced the earlier formula: 'The Council shall consist of representatives of the Member States. Each Government shall delegate to it one of its members.' The revision was required by constitutional change in Belgium. Regional governments assumed responsibilities previously discharged by the Central Government. Since the Central Government had lost competence to decide on the federalised subjects, it could no longer represent Belgium in discussions bearing on them. Regional ministers, who are not 'Ministers of the Government', took over in Community discussions.[35] The new Scottish Executive and the British government have still to settle upon a stable solution to how Scottish interests will be represented post-devolution.

The Single Council

The earlier formulation, at first sight, gives the impression that there is one delegate to the Council. This chimes with the fiction: 'there is only one Council'. In the early days, Ministers of Foreign Affairs composed *the* Council, accompanied on occasion by colleagues from line ministries. Even with only six governments represented, such meetings could become crowded. By 1960, Councils were beginning to meet without a Foreign Affairs presence. This was the beginning of the phenomenon of the Single Council meeting in multiple formations. Under the Austrian Presidency of the second half of 1998 there were meetings of Councils in twenty different formations. The appendix at the end of this book shows the history of Council meetings, prepared to mark the 2,000th.

No legal instrument is needed to inaugurate a new formation, just simple agreement among the Member States, usually to a Presidency suggestion. The spread of Councils of nominally equal status has required conscious co-ordination among them, bringing its own problems with it. Three Council formations are heavyweight and meet monthly or more often.

General Affairs Council

The General Affairs Council is manned by Foreign Ministers. Apart from external economic and political matters, ranging through Pillars I and II, it handles institutional questions. It also is a focus for inter-Council co-ordination, especially by virtue of its role as gate-keeper to the European Council[36] and of its members' right of attendance at European Council meetings (Article 4, ex-D). Finance Ministers have acquired the same right, without Treaty backing, when the European Council discusses their business. By their involvement in the preparations for European Council meetings, by their presence throughout the discussions, and from time to time by gathering in side-meetings to seek compromises, Foreign Ministers have a built-in oversight across the work of the Community/Union.

One small curiosity is that the Council has never developed a Council (External Trade), although the subject matter is one of the Community's heaviest charges and one for which it does not control the timetable. When required, Trade ministers attend the General Affairs Council. The British Trade Minister presided over one of its sessions in the first half of 1998.

All is not well with the General Affairs Council. There was a time when Departments of Foreign Affairs were the repositories of Community lore. Since they also owned the communications mechanisms and provided the Permanent Representative to the EC and members of his office, they provided leadership in the transaction of Community business. This pre-eminence is being eroded as specialist Councils and the national Ministries sitting on them consolidate their Community expertise. Departments of Foreign Affairs are accordingly in less demand as mentors, still less as leaders. The development of networks across parallel ministries has been elevated to what has been described as 'fusion theory'.[37]

In addition, meetings of the General Affairs Council are being hijacked by the endless round of encounters with third countries at Community headquarters in the framework of associations with third countries, partnerships, dialogues and all the other external relationships that the Community and the Common Foreign and Security Policy have been generating (see Chapter 9 on the Common Commercial Policy for some measure of the workload). There are numerous anecdotes about senior Ministers disappearing on the second day and agendas being abbreviated.

Reform is in the air, alongside the structural reforms that the Council is committed to addressing as a legacy from the 1996–97 Inter-governmental Conference. Some of the suggestions, which have not been systematised, envisage splitting the oversight function from the foreign affairs function. The latter would stay with Foreign Ministers. Since it would effectively devalue them it may not appeal to Ministries of Foreign Affairs.[38] The former – oversight, co-ordination, gate-keeping for the European Council, strategic thinking – would be the charge of a Council of Ministers for Europe. They would necessarily be a new breed – most of those who at present bear that designation are juniors in the Ministry of Foreign Affairs. Such a structure would semi-automatically imply reform at home. Ministries of Foreign Affairs would lose their centre-stage position; the Minister for Europe would need staff support; the central point would be in something like a Prime Minister's Department or a revamped Cabinet Office. The idea is not new (few reform proposals are) but in earlier forms it was usually suggested as a replacement for or upgrading of the (official) Committee of Permanent Representatives, as to which see below.

Agricultural Council

This Council, one of the longest-standing, has the onerous duty of managing the organised agricultural market. It grapples not only with great quantities of day-to-day legislation and the long-drawn-out negotiations on annual price-fixing and other benefits, but also the continuous effort to overhaul policy in response to financial pressures and the demands of external trade negotiation. According to one of the myths of Brussels, the Agriculture Ministers have formed an exclusive club. From its fastness they can collectively escape from the constraints which their Finance colleagues endeavour to impose upon them. It is probably closer to the truth to suppose that in domestic preparations for agricultural decisions, agricultural ministers correctly tell their ministerial colleagues what has a chance of getting through, which is close to the art of self-fulfilling prophecy.

The Agricultural Council gave the Community one of its distinguishing marks – the marathon meeting, going on all night and longer, and, if there is a deadline, 'stopping the clock' (*arrêter la pendule*) to ensure that it will be fictitiously respected.

The Economic and Finance Council (Ecofin)

The third of the big hitters brings together the power of Finance Ministers. Their Council was not traditionally one with a heavy legislative burden. They had much to do in the early 1990s in the financial services sector of the Single Market programme, but their crowning moments, from 1996 onwards, were in the successful preparation for and follow-up of Economic and Monetary Union established by the Treaty on European Union (that began its course as a treaty for EMU). This was an example of a block of work, central to the development of the Union, transacted entirely and competently by finance specialists, and endorsed by the European Council, with minimum involvement of the General Affairs Council.

Ecofin creates the frameworks for the Community budget, but the passage of the budget is the responsibility of the Budget Council, in which Member States are represented by junior ministers from Finance or other ministries.

With EMU, Ecofin assumes heavier responsibilities for economic policy co-ordination among the Member States. Neo-functional theory of integration suggests that just as the Single Market spilled over into the single currency, so other instruments of economic management such as fiscal policy come increasingly into Community purview for co-ordination if not for approximation or harmonisation. But the split between Member States which are founder members of the Monetary Union and the four others (Britain, Denmark, Greece and Sweden) has given birth to an inner circle. This is the French-inspired 'Euro-XI', an informal gathering of the eleven single currency countries, which wants to make itself at least the privileged interlocutor of the Executive Board of the European Central Bank. In politically incorrect language, commentators have called Euro-XI a 'counterweight' to the independent ECB. Sometimes called a 'Council', Euro-XI is not one in the Treaty sense, although it uses Community facilities. The four countries that are not participating in stage 3 of EMU were refused membership of Euro-XI on the understandings that they would be informed of its discussions and that only Ecofin had powers of decision. This does not diminish the potential significance of Euro-XI as a coalition within Ecofin and a possible agenda setter.

Specialist councils

Councils in other formations meet once or twice in a Presidency; or not unless there is business for them. They remain in being even if, like the Health Council, they go through a quiet period of some years. The agendas set by the Treaty of Amsterdam ensure that all known Councils will face substantial workloads.

'Jumbo' councils ('conjoint')

Some Councils overlap: Energy and Environment; Environment and Transport; Agriculture and Budget; Finance and Energy; Finance and Employment. One of several tools for keeping them in line[39] is joint-meetings. With double the number of participants 'jumbos' can become unwieldy. They serve the purpose of ensuring and displaying that two Ministers from the same government are on the same side. Whether they are better at problem-solving than a gathering half the size is debatable. The Austrian Presidency of the second half of 1998 held one. The preceding British Presidency held an *informal Jumbo*, combining two departures from orthodoxy (see below).

Informal councils

A Council meeting follows a set pattern. An agenda has been circulated and approved. Reports are presented and addressed at the meeting. If the subject is new-ish, discussion often begins with a *tour de table* in which, in rota, the ministerial representative sets out his or her position. There is not much spontaneity. The room is thickly populated with the ministerial entourages – the team led by the Commissioner (or more than one), the support staff from the Council Secretariat – all with much coming and going as discussion moves from item to item. There are not enough seats for all who believe that their presence is required. They are lodged in a *salle d'écoute* where they can watch the proceedings on CCT.

Council members have felt the need for a different kind of gathering in which they can engage in a more relaxed discussion without ground rules, without striving for specific decisions and with fewer witnesses. This is the genesis of the Informal Council meeting. There is a secondary reason. Informal meetings are held in the Presidency country, as a gesture of hospitality and as the occasion for Presidents to be seen by their own citizens, their media and perhaps even their own electors as Mr/Mrs Big in Europe.

The informal programme is usually a blend of outings, possibly relevant to the preoccupations of the particular Council; recreation, including repasts and folklore; and what some Presidents erroneously call the formal part, a meeting round the table, but with a reduced cast and an open agenda, introduced by the Chair. A standing rule, until late in 1999, was that translation was provided only for French, English and the language of the host Member State. The Finnish Presidency (July–December 1999) applied this language rule but in the face of a German boycott of informal meetings, which provoked others into demanding equal treatment, ended by providing translation into several languages while deploring the damage this did to informality.

It is not the purpose to take decisions, but perhaps to shed some new light on unsolved problems and to look forward to the issues to come. Events may dictate a drastic change of style and pace, as with the informal Ecofin in Bath in the British Presidency of August 1992. It developed into an angry dispute over backing for sterling in the ERM.[40] Informal meetings are in some danger of being institutionalised. The Austrian Presidency of the second half of 1998 listed eight of them (and in its five months, forty formal Council meetings), see Table 5.1.

Table 5.1   Austrian Presidency: July–December 1998 – calendar of meetings

	Date	Council
July	6	Ecofin
	8–10	*Informal* Employment and Social Affairs/Women (Innsbruck)
	13–14	General Affairs
	17	Budget
	18–19	*Informal* Environment (Graz)
	20–21	Agriculture
August		EU shut-down for holidays
September	5–6	*Informal* General Affairs (Salzburg)
	15–16	*Informal* Transport (Feldkirch)
	20–22	*Informal* Agriculture (St Wolfgang)
	24	Justice and Home Affairs
	24	Internal Market
	25–27	*Informal* Ecofin (Vienna)
	28–29	Agriculture
October*	1	Transport
	2–3	*Informal* Industry (Klagenfurt)
	5–6	General Affairs
	[5	European conference]
	5	Employment and Social Affairs
	6	Environment
	12	Ecofin
	13	Research
	19–20	Agriculture
	22	Fisheries
	24–25	*Informal* European Council (Pörtschach)
	26–27	General Affairs
	29–30	*Informal* Justice and Home Affairs

Table 5.1 (*cont.*)

	Date	Council
November	3	Consumers
	3–4	*Informal* Defence Ministers (Pörtschach)†
	9–10	General Affairs
	9	Internal Market
	12	Health
	16	Industry
	17	Culture
	23	Ecofin
	23–24	Agriculture
	24	Budget
	25	Telecommunications
	26	Youth
	30	Development
	30	Transport
December	1	Ecofin
	1–2	Employment and Social Affairs
	1(joint)	Ecofin/Employment and Social Affairs
	3–4	Justice and Home Affairs
	4	Education
	7–8	General Affairs
	7–8	Environment
	10	Research
	11–12	European Council (Vienna)
	14–16	Agriculture
	16	Energy
	17	Fisheries

* In Luxembourg.
† Although not officially recorded.

The Council lunch

In something of the same spirit as the informal Council meeting, the ministerial lunch on a meeting day has become an important event. Ministers and the Commissioner meet apart, with, in attendance only, the senior Council Secretariat official concerned (Secretary-General or Director-General) and the Chairman of the Committee of Permanent Representatives (Ambassador or Deputy). The room is organised for simultaneous translation. Under guidance from the President, table talk picks up what was being discussed before the break or looks forward to something new (see Box 5.2). Away from the eye-witness of their advisers and in the easier atmosphere of the lunch table –

encouraged by the Council's justly famous wine cellar – Council members may be able to discover hitherto undetected room for manoeuvre. There have been occasions when lunch has run on, with progress made. The Council has reconvened only for its President to record the agreement that has been reached.

Box 5.2   'Lunch items': General Affairs Council 21–22 February 1999

Relations with Russia
Ministers were informed by the Presidency and the Commission of the outcome of the EU–Russia summit in Moscow on 18 February 1999.

Situation in Angola
The Portuguese Minister briefed his colleagues on the situation in Angola following his recent visit to that country.

East Timor
The Portuguese Minister briefed his colleagues on his recent discussion in particular with Indonesian Foreign Minister Alatas and the UN Secretary General concerning the future of East Timor.

Source: Council 6110/99 (Presse 44-G)

Restricted meetings[41]

If discussion is sticky in the large company with which Council meetings open, the President may suggest a restricted, or super-restricted meeting. There is no arithmetical definition of restriction. One formula is 'inner table only', which leaves the Minister with two advisers. Tighter is 'Minister plus one' or, tighter still 'Ministers only'. The expectation is that in ever greater intimacy Council members will be able to do their deals, on their own political authority, without advice.[42]

THE SUPPORTING CAST

The Committee of Permanent Representatives (Coreper)

Article 207 (ex-151) says that a committee composed of Permanent Representatives prepares the work of the Council. Like much of the Treaty, it states a half-truth. There are two Corepers: 1 (Deputies) and 2 (Ambassadors).

The workload is too heavy for one. They serve different sets of Councils, with changing permutations. Coreper 2 works on foreign affairs, institutional matters, preparation for European Councils (and attendance at them, although not in the conference room) and for Councils with political charge – Energy, Research, Budget. Coreper 1 takes whatever Coreper 2 does not want. Its work was once described by an experienced Commission lawyer as 'well-paid penal servitude'.

Special Committee for Agriculture

Neither Coreper works for the Agriculture Council. It has its own faithfuls, the Special Committee for Agriculture (SCA), unknown to the Treaty. Unlike the Coreper, the SCA does not consist of Brussels residents, but of high-ranking officials visiting from capitals. If one of the tasks of the Coreper is co-ordination across Council meeting in different formations, agriculture escapes from its reach.

Other high-ranking committees

Some other Councils also have their own support troops, which in theory report through Coreper 2. For trade questions, the Article 113 Committee (full members) – post Amsterdam the Article 133 Committee – brings together directors – general from trade ministries in monthly meetings. Ecofin is served by the shadowy Monetary Committee of high officials from Finance Ministries. When monetary policy passed to the ECB in the third and final stage of EMU, the Monetary Committee tactfully changed its name to re-emerge as the Economic and Finance Committee, where the name shows its allegiance. It is unlike others of the kind insofar as its chairmanship does not go with the changing Presidency, but is arranged by the members. The Council for Justice and Home Affairs has as its support the K4 Committee (that, for consistency, should become the Article 36 TEU Committee but may hold on to its historical title). In a different category, but with the analogous task of 'contributing to the preparation of Council proceedings' relating to the fixing of the guidelines for national employment policy, the Treaty of Amsterdam, Article 130 (ex-109s) creates an Employment Committee. In these competing jurisdictions, Coreper 2 continues to reign supreme, showing its members' diplomatic skills as they integrate the specialist committees into the whole without ruffling them unduly.

Bureaucracy rules...?

The emerging transparency[43] of the Council does not hold for Coreper. Its methods expose it to the charge that the bureaucrats have taken over, practise their black arts, cook the reports and lead their ministerial masters to believe that there is no alternative to the decisions they have taken, and now need to have rubber-stamped. Thus Alan Clark described in his Diaries his attendance at a Council meeting:

> ... everything is decided, horse-traded off by officials at COREPER ...[44]

Clark's preferred alternative is that Ministers should instruct officials in Coreper on their 'line to take'. He apparently knew the word, but had not understood the context to which it belongs.

Creativity v control

There are at the extreme two ways of conducting the Brussels operation. One is proper to Member States in which there is weak policy co-ordination. This occurs typically in countries with a tradition of coalition governments, where it is often prudent to leave gaps; or where Ministers have constitutional independence. In such cases Permanent Representatives may be given only a broad mandate and trusted to use their professional skills to obtain a result which is both within it and the best available. The other extreme is that of Member States which put a premium on internal co-ordination. The co-ordination mechanism produces tight instructions, including the 'line to take'. Whether every Minister sees every paragraph is a matter of the organisation of ministerial time. The recipient of the instructions is subject to much greater exposure of his or her performance than would be the case at a desk in a ministry. Every meeting is reported back and the line taken can be compared textually with the instructions given.

Open instructions allow for local creativity and flexibility. Closed instructions ensure consistency and compel instructors in capitals to remain wholly up to date. In the real world, different delegations are closer to one of these models than to the other. In the first case, they need backing at intervals and a sense of trust. In the other, they must have some margin for negotiation. But to accuse them all of being out of control is a misreading of what they do, as well as a convenient washing of hands.

Coreper agendas and preparations

Like Council agendas, Coreper agendas contain items that are not scheduled for discussion because they are uncontentious. They are known as Part One points, equivalent to 'A' points (Box 5.3).

Box 5.3   Example of 'A' point

> Transport Council 30 November 1998
>
> **'Transportable pressure equipment**
> The Council adopted its common position with a view to adoption of the proposal for a Directive on transportable pressure equipment.'

Source: 13460/98 (Presse 420-G)

The working groups

When the Commission sends a proposal to the Council, it falls into the lap of a working group. This brings up the matter of committees.

Committee work is the essence of the Council. The word 'comitology' is sometimes wrongly used to describe how the Council works, that is, in committee after committee. Comitology in fact has a precise meaning, explained in the Extended Glossary (pp. 539–41).

The Council possesses an unlimited number of committees, around 300 at any one time. They serve Councils in different formations, to which they report through the filter of Coreper, or the SCA. They are composed of officials of national governments, or of para-state bodies. Their task is to carry out a first scrutiny of the Commission proposal and to establish how far the Member States can accept it, or what amendment would make it acceptable. Member States decide for themselves how they are to be represented on the working groups. Some delegates are Brussels residents; some come from capitals. They are not normally mandated by Coreper, which would in the usual course first address the Commission proposal when it received a report from the working group. Like Coreper, the working groups have no power of decision. They can record that (rarely) the entire proposal or (usually) parts of it give no difficulty to any delegation. In working group discussion, which is iterative, delegates establish that they understand what is proposed; debate with Commission representatives what the effects are; put forward amendments; discuss compromises; and isolate the key points which, if resolved at higher level, would ensure progress towards adoption. Some working groups, accustomed to working together, develop a club spirit that improves their interpersonal relationships. One of the most assiduous is the Budget Committee (whether a working group is called a committee is a matter of habit) which requires a special expertise, works to a fixed timetable and effectively passes through Coreper (currently Ambassadors, formerly Deputies) untouched.

Three committees deserve special mention

Les amis de la présidence are a shadowy group of shifting membership. They are Brussels residents, usually given a roaming commission in their Permanent Representations. They are summoned by the Presidency when it thinks that it needs some help to find a way through a problem. If they can, the Presidency presents the outcome, on its responsibility, in whatever is the appropriate forum at the appropriate level. There are suggestions that in an enlarged Union, there may be a stronger role for the *amis de la présidence*, bringing together at the behest of the Presidency the main players on a particular subject and asking them to find common ground which can then be offered to all delegations for consideration.

To ease the crowded agendas of their weekly meetings, each Coreper has a preparatory committee, each named after its first chairman. For Coreper 2 (Ambassadors) it is the *Antici* committee, for Coreper 1 (Deputies) the *Mertens* committee.

'Political agreement'

The Council track – Working Group, Coreper, Council is not synchronised with the EP track – Committee, plenary. The legislative procedure requires the Council to take account of the EP opinion. The Council could wait for the opinion before beginning its deliberations. This would mean time lost. The Council prefers to begin in the working groups before the EP opinion is given; and the working groups do not seek to keep themselves informed of what view the EP Committee is taking. In the reverse direction, the EP Committee simply does not know what the Council working group is doing.

One result can be that the Council can complete its stages and be ready to pronounce before the Opinion appears. But it cannot legally take a decision (in consultation of the EP) or reach a common position (in co-decision). Rather than interrupt its own flow, the

Council sometimes reaches what it calls 'political agreement' It knows what it wants, but awaits Parliament's Opinion. Political agreements are anathema to the EP because once reached they are hard to modify, even if the Opinion is a substantial contribution. One of the Commission's duties is to remind the Council that the EP Opinion (on which the Commission keeps itself fully informed) is outstanding.

('Political agreement' in a Council Press Release may not mean that it has outdistanced the EP. Rather, an agreement was reached but a new cleaned-up text was needed to formalise it. When the text appears, the item becomes an A point.)

THE COUNCIL PRESIDENCY

There is only a cursory and, by now, inoperative mention of the Council Presidency in the ECSC Treaty (Article 28). It does not rate a mention in the 1957 version of the EEC Treaty. In the 1965 Merger Treaty (making a single Commission for all the founding treaties) the Presidency is mentioned along with its six-month rota (see Table 5.2). By the time of the Single European Act, the word Presidency is used, in Part II, as if every reader would understand without further ado that the Council Presidency is being evoked. By 1994, beginning with the Greeks, the Presidency was calling itself, presumptuously, 'Presidency of the European Union' although the title *President of the Union* was studiously avoided. Holding the Presidency is an important political event for a Member State, emblazoned with various memorabilia – ties, umbrellas, pens. Few enter it with the modesty that the balance sheet of their achievement will justify.

The salience of the Presidency owes something to:

- the increasingly onerous representational function – someone is needed to personify the Council in its multitudinous encounters with third countries and in international fora;
- the dramatisation of European Council meetings as major political and media events, especially for the host;
- the need for choices to be made on priorities and for agendas to be announced well ahead of time;

Table 5.2   Order of the six-monthly Presidencies

Year	January–June	July–December
1997	Netherlands	Luxembourg
1998	United Kingdom	Austria
1999	Germany	Finland
2000	Portugal	France
2001	Sweden	Belgium
2002	Spain	Denmark
2003	Greece	

- the rebalancing of institutional weight in favour of the Member States rather than the Commission; and
- the need for a 'fount of compromise' when opinions are divided.

The Presidency fills the leadership gap in the Council structure. Member States accept leadership in the knowledge that it is restrained and that it will be theirs in due course.[45] Hegemony is avoided by the six-month cycle. The brief tenure ensures that egotistical initiatives are unlikely to yield material results before another short-lived leader takes the chair. But it is tacitly accepted that a Presidency will seek to push business in its inheritance that it particularly favours and likewise find technical reasons for underplaying proposals that it objects to.

The test of a Presidency is its ability to run the business of the Council efficiently, to stage a 'good' European Council meeting rich in conclusions and, most of all, to resolve differences of opinion. This last is the function of the 'Presidency compromise', which is often the beginning of a serious negotiation which has stalled.

In principle, the Commission, as both the source of the proposals before the Council and the 'motor of integration', might be a broker where there is divergence within the Council. Being intimately knowledgeable of the subject under discussion and concerned to move on, even if movement means weakening some part of what it believes right, it could be expected to find compromises that would unite opposing factions in the Council. It can and does, but is constrained by its alliances with the other half of co-decision, the European Parliament.[46] Delegations have turned to their Presidency to find the formulae that will enable the Council to reach agreements. The classical examples are the 'tour of the capitals' which the Presidency conducts to sound out prospects for big occasions, such as the annual agricultural price-fixing[47] and the detailed as well as overall compromises which the Presidency is expected to produce for the Budget Council as it works to the timetable it must observe.

Presidency in Parliament

Apart from representing the Council (and Union) vis-à-vis third countries, the Presidency also appears for it in the European Parliament. Council Presidents open a dialogue with the Committees that cover their subjects. In Pillar II, the CFSP, the Presidency consults and informs the EP (Article 21, TEU, ex-J.11); and similarly for Pillar III, Provisions on police and judicial co-operation in criminal matters (Article 39.2, ex-K11). The Presidency also represents the Council in the Trilogue (or Trialogue), that came into being under the Joint Declaration of 30 June 1980[48] as a means of reducing budgetary conflict. The participants were the Chairman of the Budget Council, the Commissioner for Budgets and the Chairman of the Committee for Budgets. The Trilogue has since spread to other fields (with appropriate membership) to the point of becoming a weekly fixture.

As the Council views its own enlargement in the next century, it faces hard decisions that it has hitherto ducked about its own structure. The Protocol on the institutions with the prospect of the enlargement of the European Union[49] makes *all* institutional reform contingent on the Council modifying the weighting of the votes of Member States, and in doing so compensating those Member States that give up their second Commissioner (Spain, Germany, France, Italy and the UK). It is difficult to see the less populous Member States giving them a stronger voice in the Council *and* accepting a further reduction in the size of the Commission.

The European Council meeting in Cardiff in June 1998 announced that it intended to proceed to hard thinking about institutional powers and performances under the Austrian Presidency. At a preparatory informal meeting in Salzburg on 5/6 September the General Affairs Council discussed the working methods of the Council, both in respect of foreign affairs and general policy matters.[50] It is reported that the Council Secretary-General, J. Trumpf, prepared a report containing radical proposals for the Council to mend its ways.

THE GENERAL SECRETARIAT OF THE COUNCIL

The General Secretariat of the Council was an act of spontaneous creation. A Luxembourg official, Christian Calmes, had been assigned to help the Coal and Steel Community to settle in. He used to recall that passing by the room in which the Special Council of Ministers was meeting, he was asked to make a note, in preference to leaving it to the High Authority. He became the first Secretary-General.[51] There was a change of style when Niels Ersboll was appointed in 1980. As a State Secretary[52] he had attended Council meetings as Danish representative. He rapidly became the grey eminence in the European Council, with a high reputation for his drafting and fixing skills and for commanding the trust of successive Presidencies, if not the affection of the President of the Commission.[53]

The first Treaty mention of the existence of a General Secretariat of the Council is in Article 207 (ex-151), an amendment introduced by the Treaty on European Union. Previously the General Secretariat owed its formal existence only to the Council's Rules of Procedure.[54] The Treaty of Amsterdam further amends the body by assimilating the Secretary-General to the new office of High Representative for the Common Foreign and Security Policy and creating the new post of Deputy Secretary-General (Article 207 in the new numbering). Their functions depend intimately on the profile of the High Representative whom the Council selected.

Composition and functions

The General Secretariat is over 2,000 strong, with 20% consisting of the language pools, in which English is displacing French as the first language. Committee secretaries make up some 200. There is a strong Legal Service, which gives the Council legal advice and acts for it in the Court. The bulk of the staff is concerned with the running of the world's most heavily stressed conference centre, typically housing two ministerial gatherings for three days each week and nine or ten committee meetings each day, with documents being presented in eleven languages.

The General Secretariat is organised functionally, with each of its Directorates shadowing several of the Commission's Directorates. Committee secretaries:

- see to the material administration of the meetings;
- produce reports after each session, recording delegations' positions and reasons given in support of them;
- act as the Council's memory;
- advise on the niceties of the Council's procedures;
- if asked, offer suggestions orally and in writing on how to unblock obstacles.

This last function, problem-solving, is available to the Presidency which asks for it. Some prefer to do their own. The distinguishing characteristic of the Council Secretariat is that it has no axe to grind, no agenda to achieve. It is there to serve the Presidency and through it the Council. With the entry into office of the High Representative, there will be a cultural change. That office will visibly, rather than in private, contribute 'to the formulation, preparation and implementation of policy decisions ...'[55] by producing 'argued policy option papers to be presented under the responsibility of the Presidency'.[56]

THE EUROPEAN COUNCIL

In the European Council – a periodic gathering of Heads of State or Government – the Member States have fashioned an instrument of admirable versatility. They have been helped to do so by building a constitutional screen between it and the institutions which have or claim the function of interacting with the Council, the near relative of the European Council. The European Council is above EP scrutiny or ECJ jurisdiction. It purports not to do any of the things that attract such control under the Treaties; instead it does them by proxy.

The European Council has also distinguished itself from the greyness of the Council by systematically playing to the media. Its meetings are staged events from the welcoming handshake of the host – happy to provide the photo-opportunity – to the 'family photo' on a convenient staircase, clustered round the host monarch, if there is one. Peripheral events, in the public eye, can be mildly competitive – bike rides for the fit and able, or collective attendance at cultural events. Souvenir ties, umbrellas, badges and medallions are freely dispensed. Hospitality is lavish. With 3,000 media people in attendance, a certain drama is almost *de rigueur* – meetings running over time amid rumours of deep divisions in the conference room, impending deadlock and the disgruntled departure of this or that participant. The final press conferences are Europhoric occasions (unless euphoria would be misplaced). The Conclusions have become fat documents varying from the rhetoric of intention to agonising detail of what are not supposed to be decisions.

The development of the European Council has introduced the idea that there is a hierarchy of institutions.[57] This is alien to the structure of the Economic Community,[58] in which the institutions represented a balance of forces within the separation of

123

powers. The European Council still has the aura of its precursor, European *summitry*. One visible sign is the solecism by virtue of which the Member State assuming the Presidency of the Council (and of the European Council) now styles itself 'Presidency of the European Union', of which there is no such thing. This slackness has further seen use of the term 'President of the Union', another non-office.

The European Council came into being in 1975. It succeeded meetings at the same level that began on the initiative of President de Gaulle in 1961. They were the Summits (see Box 5.4), which met at no fixed interval when one or other leader thought that it was time for a discussion with colleagues.

Box 5.4   Summit meetings

February 1961	Paris
May 1961	Bonn
May 1967	Rome (ceremony to mark 20th anniversary of signing of Rome Treaties)
December 1969	The Hague
October 1972	Paris
December 1973	Copenhagen
December 1974	Paris

The conversion of summits into the European Council was another French initiative, that of President Giscard d'Estaing. It occurred when the member states were discussing the Treaty task they had not set their hands to in twenty years – the transformation of a European Parliament composed of members appointed by national parliaments into one directly elected (in 1979, after several hitches). The European Council was an anticipatory response to the increased powers that an elected Parliament would predictably lay claim to and which could not be indefinitely resisted. These powers would be taken from the Council, which possessed them. The European Council, ostensibly having no Treaty powers, would not be affected.

The European Council began meeting in 1975. It first obtained Treaty recognition in the Single European Act 1986. In the latest formulation (Treaty of Amsterdam, consolidated version of the Treaty on European Union, Art. 4, ex-D) the European Council provides the Union 'with the impetus for its development and defines the general political guidelines thereof'. This is an important recognition of the role of the highest political authority of the Member States. It changes the defining concept of the Treaty establishing the European Community insofar as it makes the Member States proactive, rather than recipients of integrative proposals emanating from the custodian of the general interest of the Community, the Commission. It is not, however, completely new. The language is borrowed from section 2.1 of the Solemn Declaration on European Union adopted by the European Council in Stuttgart in June 1983.

The European Council consists of the Heads of State (France and Finland, accompanied by their Prime Ministers) and Government (Prime Ministers and Chancellors) and the President of the Commission, who are accompanied by the Foreign Ministers and a member of the Commission. It is practice for Finance Ministers and their Commission counterpart to sit in when economic and financial affairs are under discussion. Although retinues of some 1,500 accompany the great men and women, the only officials admitted are the Secretaries General of the Council and of the Commission and the serving chairman of Coreper (Ambassadors). A relay of Council officials listen in to the discussion and emerge to inform delegations stationed outside. Although called in *franglais* 'notetakers', they do not combine forces to prepare a record of the discussion. This exclusiveness, in sharp contrast to the dense attendance at Council meetings, goes back to the days when the European Council wanted the atmosphere of its meetings to be informal and even intimate, in the style of the 'fireside chat', without structured agenda and procedure. The European Council has not sought to model itself upon a Council meeting. It is, however, evolving. Its 'informal' meeting in October 1998 to consider institutional reform was restricted, with limited entourages and limited media targeting. This format is an innovation. The German Presidency of 1999 held two informal European Councils, describing them as 'coats off and no grand declarations'. Informality was a safeguard against failure to solve the problem of reform (Agenda 2000).

The proceedings open with a meeting with the President of the EP, who withdraws after making her statement. A proposed agenda has been circulated in the form of a letter from the President, setting out the themes that he proposes. Some impose themselves, some may be new openings. Members of the Council may respond with their own letters, suggesting what they think important. The Presidency letter explains how the proceedings are expected to run and receives suggestions. Ahead of the meeting the general shape of the meeting can be gauged. The meeting is prepared by the General Affairs Council and for it by Coreper Ambassadors. If the subject matter proves difficult, Foreign Ministers may meet close to the event in what they call a 'conclave', where attendance is highly restricted. The Chairman of Coreper Ambassadors and the Secretary-General of the Council begin drafting the conclusions. Late on the first of the two days for which the Council will sit, Coreper Ambassadors, briefed by their Ministers, begin drafting as much of the conclusions as can be tackled. By convention the conclusions[59] are issued in the name of the Presidency. In other contexts this can mean that they are not agreed but the conclusions of the European Council are worked over to be consensual, subject to occasional notes of dissent.

The proceedings of the European Council can be informal or otherwise.

(a) *Informal.* Over their first dinner, members may exchange views without too much focus, subject to the constraints of whispered translation. This may be a first, less intensive, round of what they are coming to later.

(b) *Overview.* The conclusions traditionally contain pieces in which the European Council reviews some of the bigger problems with which the Union is grappling. In commenting on unemployment, inflation, environmental protection, industrial competitiveness, the progress on the single market or on monetary union, the

European Council may commend the achievements of the Council/Commission or it may chide whichever institution is responsible for delay and, distancing themselves from the defences of national positions which are the cause (and which they endorse, nationally), the members of the European Council may order more speed. This is the mildly amusing spectacle of the members of the Council, who have suggested what their leaders should say, incriminating themselves for the sake of giving the latter a noble hue of resolution.

(c) *Dispute settlement.* This is what the European Council was NOT set up for – to take over when Ministers in sectoral council have been unable to reach agreement and show no sign of being able to do so. Officials, told to go away and agree, make fresh attempts in real time to overcome the problems and submit new texts, some of blinding technicality, which the European Council endorses. Although the Solemn Declaration on European Union of Stuttgart, 1983, wrongly says that the European Council can act as a Council (it means that the Heads of State and Government can do so), the European Council prefers to maintain its detachment and, having solved the problem, tells the Council to take the formal decisions.

(d) *Doubling as Council.* The Amsterdam Treaty says that the Heads of State and Government, being ministerial representatives, act as the Council of the Community on two occasions. Under Article 121 (ex-109j) they decide which countries are to join the monetary union; and under Article 122 (ex-109k) they do the same when other countries satisfy the convergence criteria. Under Article 7 TEU (ex-F1) the Council meeting at the level of Heads of State or Government acts where a Member State is suspended from the Union.

There is nothing to prevent ministerial (or presidential) representatives who are members of the European Council transforming themselves into a Council[60] on other occasions, while respecting the procedures proper to the Article under which they wish to act. They apparently did so in Milan in June 1985, when a majority of members decided to convene an inter-governmental conference under the old Article 236 (that became Article N of the TEU and 48 of the consolidated version of the TEU).

(e) *Doubling as the Inter-governmental Conference.* The final stages of the Inter-governmental Conferences which produced the Single European Act, the Treaty on European Union and the Treaty of Amsterdam were taken over by the Heads of State and Government, with contributions from the President of the Commission. The Inter-governmental Conference is of 'representatives of the governments of the Member States', without the addition 'of ministerial rank' (Article 49). The 'representatives' had been convened on the occasions cited as a European Council. They do not become signatories of the resulting Treaty.[61]

(f) *Acting as foreign policy spokesperson.* Meetings of the European Council have become the vehicle for declarations on foreign policy, not easily distinguishable in terms of importance from the series issued by the General Affairs Council (or its Presidency).

Anomalies in procedure

Different procedures for European Council/Heads of State or Government/Council at (HSG) Heads of State or Government level:

- Under Article 117 the President of the European Monetary Institute was appointed by common accord of the governments of the Member States, at the level of Head of State or Government (HSG). Before making the appointment the HSG *consulted* the Council, which is an institutional curiosity. Just as curiously, the appointments of the Executive Board of the European Central Bank differ (Article 112, ex-109a) since they are by common accord at the level of HSG but on a *recommendation* from the Council.
- In the procedure for establishing economic policy under Article 99 (ex-102a) the Council drafts the guidelines which the Member States are to follow. The European Council 'discusses a conclusion' and *ex hypothesi* reaches one. The Council then adopts a recommendation addressed to the Member States.
- In framing the Common Foreign and Security Policy under Article 13 of the consolidated version of the TEU (ex-J.3), the European Council defines the principles and general guidelines – autonomously. It also decides on common strategies, on a recommendation from the Council. The Council takes the necessary decisions.
- Under the new Employment Policy Article 128 EC (ex-109q) the European Council receives an annual joint report from the Commission and the Council. It adopts conclusions. The Council draws up guidelines which the Member States shall take into account. In fact, first time round and before the Treaty of Amsterdam entered into force, it did not work that way. The European Council meeting in Luxembourg in October 1997 drafted the first guidelines and asked the Commission to present draft guidelines 'in conformity with the present conclusions' for the Council to adopt before the year-end. It also looked forward to adopting the 1999 guidelines in Cardiff in December 1998.

To say the least, procedures in a Union that seeks simplification are becoming muddled.

Conclusions on the European Council

Some conclusions can be drawn about the existence of the European Council.

1. It has strengthened the standing of the Member States and their authority within the Union. This has not come about, as was feared and possibly even intended, at the expense of the powers of the European Parliament, which have been progressively extended.
2. In the hands of a skilled player like President Delors, the European Council can be recruited to back Commission initiatives, which, if launched lower down and where the Commission is not a paid-up member of the group, might have made heavier weather.

3. The European Council has not become, as was also feared, a final court of appeal from split Councils, which would thereby suffer a loss of credibility. Heads of State and Government do not want this chore and their ministerial colleagues do not want to admit failure.

4. The European Council is as transparent as an intense inter-governmental negotiation can reasonably be. However, it is not under institutional scrutiny. It purports not to take decisions, but it does so through its proxy, the Council. Non-decisions once taken are hard to modify even when the European Parliament has a part to play in them. The President of the European Council comes once in each Presidency to the European Parliament to give a decently confident speech about what his or her team achieved in its six months in office. MEPs may make noise, but there is no chance of a meaningful dialogue.

 ## LEGAL BASES

Council

- Treaty establishing the European Community (and parallel provisions in the other treaties).
- Article 7 (ex-4).
- Articles 202 to 210 (ex-145 to 154).
- Council Rules of Procedure, Council Decision 93/662/EC, OJ L 304/1, 10.12.97.

European Council

- Article 4 of the consolidated version of the Treaty on European Union (ex-D). OJ 340, 10.11.97.

 ## DISCUSSION QUESTIONS

1. National cabinets do not meet in different formations. Why should Councils of Ministers do so?
2. If a six-month Presidency is too short to carry through business, what are the alternatives?
3. Can transparency be combined with serious negotiation?
4. Why should some matters escape majority voting and co-decision?
5. Does it matter that the European Council is not an Institution?
6. Why not abolish the Council/European Council split and have the General Affairs Council meet at the level of Heads of State or Government, with Ministers of European Affairs replacing Coreper?
7. Does enlargement imply the end of 'fireside' chats and the introduction of rules of procedure for European Councils?

THE COMMISSION

THE EUROPEAN Commission is the largest Community institution. It employs two-thirds of all the established officials. Its total staff, including non-established, is of the order of 18,000. It is fashionable to suggest that this is small when compared with a typical big city administration. Such comparisons are odious because the functions of the two organisations are disparate.

The prescription for the tasks of the Commission, set forth in Article 211 (ex-155) does not contain the most important prerogative conferred on the Commission – the exclusive right of initiative. This is a jealously guarded privilege, proper only to Pillar I, the classic Community, where it is pivotal. It identifies the Commission as the custodian of the Community interest, independent of the national interests of the Member States, but not automatically in contradiction of them. The Commission's independence, which is twice referred to, is entrenched by Article 213.2 (ex-157). In a ceremony hinted at in Article 213, the incoming members of the Commission give a solemn undertaking (colloquially 'take an oath') before the Court of Justice that they will respect the obligations laid on them by the Article.

This makes clear that the Commission is not the Council's Civil Service acting under Council orders. It has its own duties and obligations. The status of its relationship to the European Parliament is less straightforward. The EP, with encouragement from members of the Council, including notably British governments (both Conservative and Labour), considers that the Commission is accountable to it. In an interview on German TV a former President of the Parliament, Klaus Hansch, contended that the Commission was dependent (*abhängig*) on his institution. Commission Presidents Delors and Santer sought to codify relations with the EP, giving just enough ground to persuade the Parliament that it has obtained the degree of accountability and influence which it sought.[62] But the events of 1998–99 (described above on pp. 88–90) transformed the situation, although it may be some time before the full implications of those events for Parliament–Commission relations are clear.

The European Parliament's 'supervision' of the Commission, to use the word which appeared in the original version of Article 137 (now amended in 189), rested on its 'club in the closet', the power of censure. Article 201 (ex-144) empowers the EP, if it can find the required majority, to dismiss the Commission *en masse*. No censure vote has ever been carried, although as seen above (pp. 88–90) some have been attempted by disgruntled MEPs, and the December 1998–January 1999 motion had major constitutional and political consequences.

To this power of censure others have been added in Treaty revision. The revision of Article 127 made in the Treaty on European Union provided for the governments of the Member States to consult the EP on their choice of Commission President. The German Presidency that conducted the first such consultation in 1994 gave an assurance that if the EP opinion was negative, the Member States would not override it. The logical progression, in the Treaty of Amsterdam, was to subject the Member States' choice to EP approval (Article 214.2). The resignation of Jacques Santer as Commission President in March 1999, on the eve of new elections to the European Parliament and before the process had begun to find a new Commission and President to take office in January 2000, caused major difficulties. By coincidence this occurred under another German Presidency (January–June 1999). It involved the European Parliament in the nomination procedure of Santer's successor by way of consulting Parliament's leaders and heads of political groups. Given the events of the recent months, it was particularly sensitive to the Parliament's view, although it refused to postpone the nomination of Romano Prodi until after the June elections.

The same article of the TEU (Article 214.2), unchanged, provides that the President and the other members of the Commission nominated by the governments of the Member States are subject 'as a body' to a vote of approval by the EP. It decided in October 1994 to hold hearings at which the individual nominees were examined. The Treaty reference to approval as a body did not deter MEPs from making clear their disfavour of certain individuals, but they accepted that any vote had to be about the nominees *en bloc* and accepted the entire Santer Commission despite reservations about individuals. The hearings were ill-judged, particularly since the examinees could not be expected to give an account of policies yet to be formulated by a future Commission acting collegially. The 1999 hearings were more productive.

The issue of the accountability of individual Commissioners came to the fore in the 1998–99 crisis, with the allegations against Commissioners Bonino, Cresson, Gradin, Liikanen, Marin, Miert, Papoutsis, Van Den Broek, Wulf-Mathies, and President Santer. While the Report on Allegations Regarding Fraud, Mismanagement and Nepotism in the European Commission generally absolved individual Commissioners of 'fraud and corruption' [para. 9.2.2.] and 'did not encounter cases where a Commissioner was directly and personally involved in fraudulent activities' [para. 9.2.3], it did find:

> instances where Commissioners or the Commission as a whole bear responsibility for in instances of fraud, irregularities or mismanagement in their services or areas of special responsibility. [para. 9.2.3]

The most severely criticised was Edith Cresson. As noted above (pp. 88–90), this whole saga and the Report raised the issue of individual votes on Commission appointments and individual censures, but so far these calls have been resisted.

Among the suggestions for further reform, the EP interest was at the heart of the idea that in the 1999 EP elections, the contesting parties should sponsor candidates for Commission President. How the candidates would pass to the next stage of nomination is unclear. It is, however, clear that the EP would expect its favoured son (or daughter) to be compliant and that the ability of the Commission neither to 'seek nor take instructions from any government or from any other body' (Article 213) would be yet further qualified.

INTERPRETING THE 'GENERAL INTEREST OF THE COMMUNITY'

With a few individual exceptions, Commissioners hitherto appointed have had their upbringing in the school of national politics. They therefore come to their posts with convictions that will help to shape the policies that they will advocate or agree to. The collegial deliberation should ensure that any idiosyncrasies are removed and that what emerges is free of personal or national bias. Whether it responds to a European interest is a matter for the other legislating institutions – the Council primarily concerned with national interests (that may include attachment to European ideals) and the EP with party ideologies and collections of single issues (environment, agriculture, human rights, overseas aid, etc.). Few Commission proposals emerge from the process unmodified.

Other sources of Commission initiatives are:

- The Council or one or more of its Member States, which may ask the Commission to make a proposal. The Council has the Treaty power to do so under Article 208.9 (ex-153). Calculations differ, but they agree that a high proportion of Commission proposals emanate from the Council or its Member States.
- The EP, which has a similar power under Article 192. 9 (ex-138b). This was a new power in the TEU (then Article 107a). It recognised the reality of demands that the EP was already making in Resolutions and other messages addressed to the Commission.
- Court judgements, which may point to loopholes and incompleteness.
- The staff of the Commission, at different levels in the hierarchy, who from their experience of the matters they deal with can show where legislation needs to be supplemented, improved or inaugurated.
- The world outside, especially from the ranks of consultants at large. There are said to be as many consultants, lobbyists, public affairs officers of major companies, trade association officials and regional representatives in Brussels as there are employees in the Commission. They have a sectional interest to cultivate but are also a source of expertise that the Commission is glad to have access to.

POWERS OF THE PRESIDENT

The person appointed as President of the Commission for a five-year term, renewable, puts his mark on the Commission that he leads. The ten years of President Delors were high-octane. The Presidency of his successor, Mr Santer, was (until the last few months) quieter and marked by the ironic motto: do less, do better. Until the Treaty of Amsterdam came into force, the President of the Commission was in principle one among equals, although in practice the incumbent could set himself above colleagues by strength of personality, with some help from the manipulation of procedure and power plays. The 1997 Treaty strengthens the President's hand:

- in the new Article 214 the Presidential nominee has the say over who else is nominated;
- in new Article 219 the members of the Commission are told that they work under the 'political guidance' of their President;
- under Declaration 32 the Inter-governmental Conference considered that the President must have discretion in the allocation and reshuffle of portfolios. The Conference clearly had in mind that the division of responsibility for external affairs between four Commissioners was a weakness in the Santer Commission.

The new Commission President, Romano Prodi, made clear in the aftermath of the Santer experience that he would use these new powers and would extract a commitment by individuals in his new team to resign if required to do so by him, although he was adamant that the Parliament did not have the right to sack individual Commissioners. The elevation of the President's status corresponds to the desire of Presidents and most Member States to see tighter co-ordination within the Commission and closer definition of responsibility.

MORE REFORM IN THE AIR

It was clear before the 1998–99 crisis that all was not well with the Commission any more than it is with the Council. At the meeting of the European Council in Cardiff in June 1998 there was strong criticism, notably from the German Chancellor, of the Commission's excessive activism and inept conduct of business. Mr Santer responded by correctly pointing out that Community legislation is not made by the Commission but by the co-deciding institutions. The focus was placed on the doctrine of subsidiarity and the ever-greater need to delimit the domain in which the Community acts, and correspondingly the domains in which the Member States retain their competencies.

Independently, the Commission had been examining itself closely. From 1995, the new Commission had been engaged in what it called 'a massive round of internal reforms'.[63] They included SEM 2000 (financial management) and MAP 2000 (management and administration policy). There was a hiccup in the summer of 1998, when an options document on the reform of conditions of service (the 'statut') came out prematurely and provoked militant staff protest. Reflection goes beyond matters of personnel management to consideration of 'fewer conventional portfolios and restructured departments' and of strengthening the Secretariat General 'to boost its capacity for co-ordination'. The consultation paper also grasps the nettle of 'the relationship between Members' offices and Commission Departments', otherwise known as the problem of the 'cabinets'. The new President, Prodi, has indicated sympathy for most of these proposals.

Mr Kinnock, one of the Vice-Presidents, has been given responsibility for masterminding the internal reform of the Commission. The other, Loyola de Palacio, has the equally demanding task of relations with the European Parliament.

The Commission President, as well as naming the new Commissioners, made it clear that (a) Commission reform was a core priority and (b) the Commission's departments would be adjusted to match the new portfolios (see Boxes 6.1 and 6.2).

Box 6.1   Prodi's reforms

- Commissioners will be housed alongside their departments rather than grouped together in a separate building.
- Commissioners' offices ('cabinets') will be smaller and more multi-national.
- The rules on senior appointments will be tightened and made more transparent.
- There will be greater internal mobility for senior Commission staff.
- The numbering of Commission departments will be abolished in favour of short, understandable names reflecting the department's main responsibility.

Box 6.2   Aims of Commission shake-up

- To reflect the new political priorities of the Commission.
- To make it more effective and less bureaucratic.
- To slim down the number of departments and group them more logically within single portfolios, thereby reducing overlap. Departments will be cut in number to 36, including the creation of several new ones.
- To focus staff resources where they are most needed: some 150–200 posts will be removed to other priority areas.

The main changes are:
- Dividing up external relations by subject (trade, development, enlargement and foreign security policy) rather than geographical region, giving one Commissioner an overall co-ordination role.
- Creating a new enterprise department, bringing together the current DGs for industry, small and medium enterprises and innovation policy.
- Creating a new department for justice and home affairs, in line with the Commission's new role under the Amsterdam Treaty.

Box 6.2 (*cont.*)

- Consolidating health and consumer protection into a single department.
- Creating a new department for education and culture, fusing the DG for education and training with part of the DG for information and culture.
- Creating a new media and communication service, bringing together the spokesman's service and part of the DG for information and culture.

THE CABINETS AND THE DIRECTORATES

Each of the twenty Commissioners – the number is fixed by Treaty, but may be altered by the Council under Article 213 (ex-157) – has two sets of staff.

The first is the personal office, or cabinet. The word shows its French origin. Cabinets are said to have been born in France when the monarchy was restored in 1815. Departments of State were manned by Bonapartists or their placemen. The new Ministers of the Crown needed help to control them.

The Commissioner selects his own personal staff. Some may come with the Commissioner from their previous activity. Some come from the staff of the Commission, knowing the ropes. Most are fellow nationals, but there is usually one of another nationality to improve the Commissioner's reach.[64] The members of the cabinet have two principal functions. The first is to act as the Commissioner's enforcer, ensuring that what he or she wants done is done and what is not wanted is squelched. In this sense the cabinet is a conduit, but with valves, between their Commissioner and the directorates which serve him or her.

The second function springs from the collegiate character of the Commission's work. Every Commission decision is taken in committee of all the Commissioners.[65] Decisions are by simple majority. To participate intelligently in the deliberations and to use the vote wisely, Commissioners must be up to date on the work and projects of their colleagues. On their personal staff they have people who shadow the other directorates general and are able to brief their Commissioner on agenda items, whether they bear on the Commissioner's portfolio or not.

The President, with the wider view, may need more staff. President Delors had a circle of members throughout the Directorates to help him and his cabinet to keep on top of the work of the entire Commission.

The Directorates

Each Commissioner has charge of a number of Directorates, which together make up his or her portfolio (see Box 6.3). Under the Directors-General the staff of the Directorates work on the proposals which the Commissioner is to present to the Commission meeting, or defend them in Council committee and EP debates. Some

Box 6.3   Directorates-General and services of the Commission (March 1999)

Secretariat-General of the Commission
Forward Studies Unit
Inspectorate-General
Legal Services
Spokesman's Service
Joint Interpreting and Conference Service
Statistical Office
Translation Service
Informatics Directorate

DG I	External Relations, Commercial Policy and Relations with North America, the Far East, Australia and New Zealand
DGIA	External Relations: Europe and the New Independent States, Common Foreign and Security Policy and External Missions
DGIB	External Relations: Southern Mediterranean, Middle East, Latin America, South and South-East Asia and North–South Co-operation
DGII	Economic and Financial Affairs
DGIII	Industry
DGIV	Competition
DGV	Employment, Industrial Relations and Social Affairs
DGVI	Agriculture
DGVII	Transport
DGVIII	Development
DGIX	Personnel and Administration
DGX	Information, Communication, Culture, Audio-visual
DGXI	Environment, Nuclear Safety and Civil Protection
DGXII	Science, Research and Development Joint Research Centre
DGXIII	Telecommunications, Information Market and Exploitation of Research
DGXIV	Fisheries
DGXV	Internal Market and Financial Services
DGXVI	Regional Policies and Cohesion
DGXVII	Energy
DGXIX	Budgets
DGXX	Financial Control
DGXXI	Customs and Indirect Taxation
DGXXII	Education, Training and Youth
DGXXIII	Enterprise Policy, Distributive Trades, Tourism and Co-operatives
DGXXIV	Consumer Policy and Consumer Health Protection
ECHO	European Community Humanitarian Office
TFAN	Task Force for the Accession Negotiations

Euratom Supply Agency

Office for the Official Publications of the European Communities tension, which may be of the creative variety, creeps into the relationship between the cabinet, as the voice of the Commissioner and the Directors-General, who by definition are likely to be experienced and strong-minded people. The consultation document delicately touches on the two-way problem: Member's offices interfere; departments do not always follow policy guidelines. Astonishingly enough, it finds it appropriate to suggest that 'meetings between the offices and the DGs could be held on a more systematic basis'.

Mr Romano Prodi announced the new members of the Committee and their responsibilities in early June 1999 (see Table 6.1).

Table 6.1   The new Commissioners and the organisation of the Commission, July 1999

Commissioner	Responsibilities	Departments
Romano Prodi (Italy) *President*	Secretariat-General Legal Service Media and Communication	Secretariat-General Legal Service Media and Communication Service
Neil Kinnock (UK) *Vice-President for Administrative Reform*	Overall co-ordination of administrative reform Personnel and Administration Linguistic Services Protocol and Security	Personnel and Administration Directorate-General (DG) Inspectorate-General Joint Interpreting and Conference Service Translation Service
Loyola de Palacio (Spain) *Vice-President for relations with the European Parliament and for Transport and Energy*	Relations with the European Parliament Relations with the Committee of Regions, the Economic and Social Committee and the Ombudsman Transport (including trans-European Networks) Energy	Transport DG Energy DG
Mario Monti (Italy) *Commissioner for Competition*	Competition	Competition DG
Franz Fischler (Austria) *Commissioner for Agriculture and Fisheries*	Agriculture and Rural Development Fisheries	Agriculture DG Fisheries DG

Table 6.1 (cont.)

Commissioner	Responsibilities	Departments
Erkki Liikanen (Finland) *Commissioner for* *Enterprise and Information* *Society*	Enterprise Competitiveness Innovation Information Society	Enterprise DG Information Society DG
Frits Bolkestein (Netherlands) *Commissioner for Internal* *Market*	Internal Market Financial Services Customs Taxation	Internal Market DG Customs and Taxation DG
Phillipe Busquin (Belgium) *Commissioner for Research*	Science, Research and Development Joint Research Centre	Research DG Joint Research Centre
Pedro Solbes Mira (Spain) *Commissioner for Economic* *and Monetary Affairs*	Economic and financial affairs Monetary matters Statistical Office	Economic and Financial Affairs DG Statistical Office
Poul Nielson (Denmark) *Commissioner for* *Development and* *Humanitarian Aid*	Development aid and co-operation Humanitarian aid	Development DG Humanitarian Aid Office
Günter Verheugen (Germany) *Commissioner for Enlargement*	Enlargement process including the pre-accession strategy	Enlargement Service
Chris Patten (UK) *Commissioner for External* *Relations*	External Relations Common Foreign and Security Policy Delegations in non-member countries Common Service for External Relations	External Relations DG Common Service for External Relations
Pascal Lamy (France) *Commissioner for Trade*	Trade policy and instruments of trade policy	Trade DG
David Byrne (Ireland) *Commissioner for Health and* *Consumer Protection*	Public Health Consumer Protection	Health and Consumer Protection DG

Table 6.1 (*cont.*)

Commissioner	Responsibilities	Departments
Michel Barnier (France) *Commissioner for Regional* *Policy*	Regional Policy Cohesion Fund Inter-governmental Conference	Regional Policy DG
Viviane Reding **(Luxembourg)** *Commissioner for Education* *and Culture*	Citizen's Europe Transparency Education and Culture Publications Office	Education and Culture DG Publications Office
Michaele Schreyer **(Germany)** *Commissioner for the Budget*	Budget Financial Control Fraud Prevention	Budget DG Financial Control DG Fraud Prevention Office
Margot Wallström **(Sweden)** *Commissioner for* *Environment*	Environment Nuclear Safety	Environment DG
António Vitorino **(Portugal)** *Commissioner for Justice* *and Home Affairs*	Freedom, Security and Justice	Justice and Home Affairs DG
Anna Diamantopoulou **(Greece)** *Commissioner for* *Employment and Social* *Affairs*	Employment Social Affairs Equal Opportunities	Employment and Social Affairs DG

Working methods[66]

The Directors-General and the cabinets, in harmony or otherwise, prepare the documents which the Commission is to consider at its weekly meeting. The meeting is preceded by the meeting of the '*chefs* (*de cabinet*)' under the chairmanship of the Secretary-General, top official and co-ordinator supreme. At the chefs' meeting, preliminary agreements can be registered, opposition can be motivated, ad hoc alliances can be sealed, points can be clarified. The key issues for discussion by the college are flagged.

The chefs' meeting itself is preceded by the 'special chefs', who are not chefs but cabinet members with responsibility for particular dossiers. The cabinet member who is nursing a proposal that a Commissioner is bringing forward has the opportunity to try it out on the other Commissioners' personal advisers. They have early warning.

Once a proposal is adopted and is in the hands of the Council and EP, the staff of the Departments at successive levels defend it, culminating in the Commissioner's appearance in the Council and in EP plenary. Officials from the Secretariat-General of the Commission sit throughout the discussion at both Corepers, virtually as supernumerary members, sometimes handling issues themselves, sometimes backing up their colleagues from the DGs.

THE COMMISSION'S OTHER RESPONSIBILITIES

The foregoing section concerns only one of the Commission's functions, the initiation of legislative and other proposals under the Treaty articles that authorise it to act. This function is not mentioned in the Treaty job description (Article 211, ex-155).

'Guardian of the Treaties'

The Commission is enjoined to ensure that the provisions of the Treaties and of the secondary legislation are observed. This is therefore evidence that the Community is not analogous to an international organisation. Respect for the obligations which the signatories have entered into is policed. The compliance force is the Commission, in conjunction with the Court of Justice. Member States do not re-enact regulations, which are directly applicable, but they are required to enforce them. They must enact directives. It is one of the Commission's duties to verify that they do. Mutual trust is not enough when detailed legislation is at issue.

It would clearly be beyond even a massively enlarged Commission to scrutinise the operation of every measure in every Member State. It tends to work reactively, often in response to complaints from another Member State, or from economic operators. If, after due notice, the erring Member State continues not to comply, the Commission can take it to the Court of Justice.

This function, imposed by the Treaty, can come close to busy-bodying, to what Douglas, later Lord, Hurd, then British Foreign Secretary, called invading the nooks and crannies of society. In 1998 the German government had its turn to be irritated by a series of Commission interventions and in some cases subsequent Court judgements: illegal aids to Volkswagen in former East Germany, business mergers blocked, German citizens allowed to shop abroad for medical treatment at cost to the German Health service.

Commission regulations and other acts

The Commission 'has its own powers of decision' (Article 211). Certain Treaty articles give it the power to make regulations or directives. It can impose anti-dumping duties subject to Council confirmation after six (in some cases nine) months.[67] It takes decisions to approve or ban mergers[68] and under the competition Articles 81 to 89 (ex-85 to 94) the Commission can take action to end distortions of competition, the abuse of a dominant position or unfair state aids within the Common Market. It also promulgates daily a host of regulations for the management of the organised agricultural markets, after non-binding consultation with the Member States in the management committees. But it is innocent of the headline reports of unpopular legislative measures. It may make the proposals (new Brussels ban on shrimp-flavoured crisps!) but the decision is not for the Commission.

The Executive Commission

Since the same word in French can mean Commission or Committee, MEPs for better clarity sometimes refer to the 'Executive Commission'. Article 211 stipulates that the Commission is to exercise powers conferred on it by the Council. In fact the characteristic of the Community is that much execution is decentralised in bodies in the governmental structures of the Member States: Customs service, VAT collection, Agricultural Produce Intervention Boards, Fisheries Inspectorate, Trading Standards Officers, Health and Safety Executive, Equal Pay Tribunals, etc. As an Executive, apart from managing the CAP, the Commission is principally involved in disbursement from the Budget in support of programmes and other actions which the Council or Council and Parliament have decided, including the supervision of development projects in countries which are beneficiaries of Community aid.

Commission representation abroad

The Commission represents itself, and to an extent the Community where there is exclusive Community competence, in third countries and (by virtue of Article 302, ex-229) in international organisations. There are also Commission representations in all the Member States acting as information and public relations outlets. In all there are 127 Commission offices outside the European Union, employing 700 officials and 1,600 locally engaged staff. This is a bigger external service than many of the Member States deploy. In some countries (USA, Japan, etc.) the Commission Representative is engaged in the diplomatic tasks of reporting, intelligence gathering, negotiating on Community responsibilities. In others the Commission-Office is running aid programmes and humanitarian assistance. There has been some reluctance among diplomats of the Member States to regard Commission Representatives as members of their club. Commission Representatives participate in local co-ordination, information pooling and joint reporting on economic developments in the host country. A single EU Foreign Service is a long way off.

RECRUITMENT

As in all the institutions, recruitment to the Commission is by open competition among nationals of the Member States. The response to notices of competitions for graduates is so overwhelming that there is a multiple-choice eliminator, run simultaneously at centres across the Union. This reduces the field to a manageable number for the written and oral tests (including a working knowledge of an official language other than the candidate's mother tongue). Success in the competition does not guarantee a job offer. That depends on the available budgetary means. Suggestions that the institutions should recruit jointly have been opposed, principally by the staff side in the Council's joint committees.

Staffing

There are no national quotas but there are shortage nationalities. In promotions to higher grades, care is taken to produce what is grandiloquently called a 'harmonious balance'. At the level of Director-General, Member States may successfully 'parachute' their choice of official into a post in which they think they have a special interest. Members of the cabinets of outgoing Commissioners are also on a fast track to senior posts. The Consultation document of the summer of 1998 is frank:

> A heavy managerial hierarchy, recruitment that sometimes depends too much on political considerations, a lack of internal communication and team spirit, less than perfect management of finances and staff – these are some of the most common complaints.

There are small hints at the possibilities of contracting out:

> We must consider delegating more of the straightforward administrative functions ... should the Commission shed some of the purely administrative tasks which it is not properly qualified to perform?

These are some of the early moves which will enable the Commission to respond to Declaration 32 of the Amsterdam Treaty in which it was noted that the Commission intends to:

> undertake ... a reorganisation of its departments ...

in which it must also take account of the more recent grumbles of some Member States. Not unnaturally, this dissatisfaction was multiplied by the revelations of the Committee of Independent Experts in March 1999. The British government in response produced a plan for reform:

- the next Commission President to be personally committed to reform;
- one of the Vice-Presidents to be 'personally responsible' for budgetary and personnel matters;
- promotion procedures to be changed;
- programme management to be improved;
- pay and personnel policy to be overhauled.

LEGAL BASES

- Articles 211–219 (ex-155–159) and powers dispersed throughout treaty.

DISCUSSION QUESTIONS

1. Since the Commission's right of initiative does not hold in Pillars II and III, why should it in Pillar I?
2. Has the Report of 15 March 1999 irreparably damaged the Commission as the motor of integration?
3. Can the Commission consist of less than one Commissioner per Member State?
4. Why not convert the Commission into the Council's civil service, producing proposals at the Council's request rather than on the Commissioners' orders?
5. Is a unified Union Foreign Service feasible?
6. Should the task of implementing and monitoring legislation be passed over entirely to the Member States, relying on their integrity and judicial review in the event of complaint?

EUROPEAN COURT OF JUSTICE AND COURT OF FIRST INSTANCE

THE EUROPEAN Court of Justice (ECJ) describes itself in the following terms:

> The Union . . . is governed by the rule of law. Its very existence is conditional on recognition by the Member States, by the institutions and by individuals of the binding nature of its rules. The Court of Justice, that is charged with ensuring that in the interpretation and application of the Treaties the law is observed, is responsible for monitoring the legality of acts and the uniform application of the common rules. The Treaties, the protocols annexed to certain conventions between Member States and certain agreements concluded by the Communities with non-Member States, confer various kinds of jurisdiction on the Court. It is called on to rule on direct actions brought by the Member States, by the institutions and by individuals; to maintain close co-operation with national courts and tribunals through the preliminary ruling procedure; and to give opinions on certain agreements envisaged by the Communities. The Court thus carries out tasks which, in the legal systems of the Member States, are those of the constitutional courts, the courts of general jurisdiction or the administrative courts and tribunals, as the case may be.[69]

Why does the European Community need its own Court? There are other international courts that rule on disputes among the parties or protect the rights of their citizens, and the Member States by definition possess courts which administer justice.

THE LEGAL ORDER

Although the European Community is established by a Treaty concluded by contracting parties, it has created its own legal order. The Treaty is more than an international agreement. It is the precursor of a constitution of the Community. In establishing the Community, the

Member States have limited their sovereignty, in a restricted but ever-widening area, in favour of the Community's legal order. The constitution that they have written in the Treaty concerns both the obligations and rights that the contracting parties have accepted and rights which their citizens can invoke. It cannot be left to the Member States' governments or judiciaries to interpret the terms of the treaty, free of other control. The central objective, the creation of a common market, presupposes that the Treaty will be interpreted and applied uniformly. It is to 'act as referee between Member States and the Community as well as between the Community institutions'.[70]

Supremacy of Community law

Another consequence follows, although it was not universally foreseen. The Community does not subsume the whole of the law-making powers of its Member States. There are many matters that it does not touch. There are others where national laws exist in the areas in which the Community also legislates. In the event of conflict, one or the other must be supreme. It is the law of the Community that takes precedence. This basic doctrine was inferred by the Court and expounded in a long line of cases. It has provoked controversy especially because it can assert that laws adopted by the due process of democratically elected and accountable parliaments can be declared incompatible with Community law. National Courts must then declare them invalid. At the extreme, this predominance of the ECJ has brought forth political demands that the law should be 'repatriated'; or that the Council should have the power to override an unwelcome Court judgement[71] or one having an effect not intended or desired by the Member States (see Box 7.1).

The governments of the Member States have never availed themselves of the opportunities they have had to downgrade Community law. Their supreme legal bodies have upheld the principle of its supremacy, sometimes with misgiving.

Box 7.1   Community legal instruments (Article 189 of the EC Treaty)

'the Council and the Commission shall make regulations and issue directives, take decisions, make recommendations or deliver opinions.

'A **regulation** shall have general application. It shall be binding in its entirety and directly applicable in all Member States.

'A **directive** shall be binding, as to the result to be achieved, upon each Member State to which it is addressed, but shall leave to the national authorities the choice of form and methods.

'A **decision** shall be binding in its entirety upon those to whom it is addressed. **Recommendations** and **opinions** shall have no binding force.'

JUDICIAL ACTIVISM

The ECJ's understanding of its own responsibilities gave rise in 1995 to a powerful attack on its methods of interpretation, the consistency of its judgements and the integrationist agenda which it was alleged to be following.[72] Eminent jurists[73] who defended the Court did not seek to justify all its judgements, but explained why it uses what is called the 'teleological' method of interpreting the Treaties and the legislation adopted under them.

The alternative is the 'blackletter' approach, which consists of trying to extract from the actual words of the statute the meaning that is to be given to them. The distinction is not categorical; international courts are accustomed to literal interpretation and to interpretation by reference to the general scheme of the act. Teleology is, however, more especially apposite in the ECJ's work because the texts which it is called upon to consider are not the handiwork of a single skilled legal draftsperson but the outcome of an international diplomatic negotiation, that has involved compromise with, at times, scant regard for the integrity of the text. In addition, the text exists in multiple language versions and no matter how expert the translator, there are inevitable discrepancies which obscure the meaning. (For example 'request' routinely corresponds to 'auffordern', but the German word is much stronger.) The controversy has not been stilled. As long as there is Euroscepticism, it will be encouraged by judgements of the European Court which appear to biased in favour of European integration and are attacked as 'judicial activism'. Cases in which the Court goes in the other direction will attract less notice.[74]

COMPOSITION

The composition of the Court is prescribed in Articles 220 to 245 (ex-164 to 168) EC (and corresponding articles in the other Treaties). The European Court of Justice (ECJ) consists of fifteen judges, enough for each Member State to provide one, which each does (see Box 7.2). The Treaty does not say that they should be of different nationality, or even that they should be European citizens, but all have been. They are appointed by common accord of the Member States, without any EP involvement, although it has been sought. There have been suggestions that the final choice should be in the hands of a Board of eminent national jurists,[75] but this is not generally thought to provide any better appreciation of candidates' qualities than the private consultations which governments conduct. One recurrent criticism is that too many of the appointees have had little courtroom experience in their native countries.

The appointed judges elect their own President by secret ballot. Appointments are for six years and are staggered so that there is partial replacement every three years. Appointments are renewable.

The Court is served by a corps unique to it, although having some French analogues. There are presently nine Advocates-General (AGs). Their task is to present to the judges

Box 7.2   The European Court of Justice

(a)	Governments of the Member States appoint the 15 judges and 9 Advocates-General by common accord for a term of six years
(b)	*Court of Justice*
	Full court of 15 judges
	Chambers: in groups of 3, 5 or 7

Types of Proceeding:

(i) actions for failure to fulfil obligations under the treaties (Commission or Member State v Member State)	(ii) actions for annulment (against the Council or Commission)	(iii) references from national courts for preliminary rulings to clarify the meaning and scope of Community law
	(iv) Actions of grounds of failure to act (against Council or Commission)	
		(vi) opinions
	(v) Claims for damages against the Community	

Court of First Instance
15 judges
(i) Direct actions by natural and legal persons, except anti-dumping cases
(ii) Staff cases
(iii) Actions under the ECSC Treaty
(iv) Ancillary actions for damages

an analysis of the case with an opinion, which is not binding, on the judgement which should be given. The Advocates-General are appointed for six years. There is a partial replacement every three years. Some AGs have later become judges.

The judges can meet as a full court, or in chambers, that is groups of three, five or seven. The number is odd because if there is division among them, the decision is that of the majority. This has been seen as a supranational quality.[76] There are no dissenting judgements. The main arguments in favour of apparent consensus are: dissenting judgements usually occur in appellate courts, which the ECJ is not; all judges take part in the formulation of the judgement, including those who inject doubts into the view of the majority; anonymity protects a judge against national political pressure; publicised dissent could solidify into a split based on different legal tradition and culture. The contrary argument is that the law will be enriched and citizens better served if dissenting opinions are publicised; and that the damaging effects have not been observed in courts in which opinion is divided. The AGs do not participate in the deliberations of the judges, which are led by the judge appointed as reporter and draftsman.

Court of First Instance

Attached to the ECJ is the Court of First Instance (CFI), which came into being by virtue of Article 235 (ex-168a), an amendment introduced by the Single European Act, and opened its doors on 24 October 1988. Such a new body had been proposed by the ECJ in 1978, as a means of reducing its excessive workload. The CFI is composed of fifteen members, who act exclusively in chambers (groups) and without the service of an AG. The CFI has jurisdiction for certain classes of action, which can be added to by Council decision, taken unanimously. There can be an appeal from its judgement to the ECJ but only on points of law. The CFI has relieved the burden on the ECJ and has built up expertise in its fields.[77] There are suggestions, so far considered premature, that it could be divided into specialised jurisdictions; and that there might be regional CFIs. See also below.

Despite disapproval expressed by the European Bar, the Council in April 1999 amended the legal basis of the CFI[78] by providing that it could give decisions when constituted by a single judge. To do so it approved amendments to the Court's Rules of Procedure, taking account of the increase in the workload of the CFI. The cases which may be heard by a single judge are restricted: disputes with officials of the institutions (Article 236, ex-179), legality of acts affecting natural or legal persons (Article 230, ex-173) and arbitration in contracts concluded by the Community (Article 238, ex-181).

PROPOSALS FOR RADICAL REFORM

In May 1999 the Court presented the Council with proposals for radical reform. One striking measure of its workload is the increases in cases coming before it, from 145 in 1990 to over 1,000 in 1998. A further upsurge is expected to flow from the judicial and law and order co-operation provisions of the Treaty of Amsterdam. The Court suggested that there should be branches in the Member States, closer to national judiciaries and conducting business in only one language. It also proposed procedures for filtering cases which come to it (i.e. filtering some out) and introducing 'fast-track' procedures for reducing delays. The Council shied away from anything so innovative as regional Courts. It cautiously asked for a report on what short-term expedients might be adopted.

A separate development in Community law comes not from the Court but from, notably, France in the person of its Justice Minister, Madame Elisabeth Guigou. This was a proposal that there should be a body of law, the *corpus juris*, dispensed by a single judiciary across the Community, which would act as Courts of First Instance in specified cases. Complicated arrangements for transferring judicial material from one national jurisdiction to another would be superseded. This proposal was among the matters discussed at a special European Council devoted to Justice and Home Affairs Co-operation under the Finnish Presidency in 2000. Alarm bells are ringing wherever traditional standards, such as *habeas corpus*, are thought to be under attack.

TYPES OF ACTION

The main classes of action which come before the ECJ (and in the specified matters, the CFI) are the *direct actions* and the *preliminary rulings*.

Direct actions are taken:

- by the Commission against a Member State which it considers to have failed to fulfil a Treaty obligation;
- by one Member State against another for the same reason;
- by a Member state, the Commission, or the Council against the legality of an act of the Council in co-decision with the European Parliament, of the Council, of the Commission, or of the European Central Bank and of an act of the EP intended to have legal effect *vis-à-vis* third parties, on grounds of lack of competence, infringement of an essential procedural requirement, infringement of the Treaty or of any rule of law relating to its application or misuse of powers. The EP, the Court of Auditors and the ECB can similarly bring actions to preserve their prerogatives.

Natural and legal persons may take proceedings against a decision addressed to them, or of direct and individual concern to them although it is in the form of a regulation or decision addressed to another person (Article 230, ex-173).

Requests for *preliminary rulings* reach the ECJ from courts and tribunals in the Member States. They concern the interpretation of the Treaty, the validity and interpretation of acts of the institutions and of the ECB and the interpretation of the statutes of bodies established by the Council, where the statutes so prescribe (Article 234, ex-177). National courts and tribunals *may* make such requests. Where there is no appeal from their judgement they *must* ask for a preliminary ruling. They must also ask for it if the validity of an act is being challenged before them. This last is not in the Treaty but in the jurisprudence of the ECJ.[79] Only the ECJ can give preliminary rulings. The requests cannot be heard by the CFI, and this is intended to ensure complete consistency. In giving preliminary rulings the ECJ does not try the case before the originating court. It tells the court what the relevant Community law is. It is for the court to incorporate such guidance into its consideration of the case. The ECJ is not therefore comparable to an appeal court, such as the Supreme Court of the USA.

The ECJ has other jurisdiction provided for in the Treaty, including the burdensome task of ruling on disputes between the Community and members of its staff, which is notoriously litigious and is exempt from the cost of actions, now a CFI responsibility.

Another important task of the ECJ relates to international agreements. Under Article 300.6 (ex-228) the Council, the Commission or a Member State (but not the EP) may obtain the opinion of the ECJ as to whether an agreement envisaged is compatible with the provision of the Treaty. The Court's opinion is decisive; to proceed against it the Member States would first have to amend the Treaty, if indeed an amendment would overcome the legal difficulty.

The foregoing depicts the ECJ as acting as a constitutional court, as an administrative tribunal and as an agent of judicial review. It also acts a civil court when it assesses damages for non-contractual liability. This occurs when a natural or legal person contends that it has suffered damage because a Member State has failed to transpose or has incorrectly transposed a directive and thereby deprived that person of a right which it could otherwise have exercised.[80]

Exclusions

The ECJ and the CFI are concerned with Community law, that is, legislation adopted in Pillar I of the Union. The ECJ has no standing in Pillar II, the Common Foreign and Security Policy. The common positions and the joint actions which the Council adopts in Pillar II are binding on the Member States (subject to the terms of the Articles on which they are based) under international law, and not under Community law. Some lawyers minimise the difference and regard Community law as a branch of international law.

Third pillar involvement

The Treaty of Amsterdam established a new basis for the standing of the ECJ in Pillar III. Article 35 (ex-K7) provides that the ECJ has jurisdiction to give preliminary rulings on the validity and interpretation of framework decisions,[81] to give decisions on the interpretation of Conventions established in Pillar III and on the validity and interpretation of measures implementing them. This provision is operative only as regards Member States that have made a declaration to the effect that they accept the Court's jurisdiction. Belgium, Germany, Greece, Luxembourg, Netherlands and Austria[82] made such a declaration at the signing of the Treaty. The jurisdiction of the Court does not extend to the operations of law and order authorities or to actions taken by the Member States to safeguard internal security. This restriction on the Court's jurisdiction in matters of civil liberties has come under heavy criticism.

Human rights

The 1957 Treaty said nothing about human rights, doubtless because the framers did not think the question relevant to the setting up of a common market. But as the Community extended its reach, questions began to be asked about human rights and whether the Community should accede to the Council of Europe's Convention for the Protection of Human Rights and Fundamental Freedoms. Asked in 1994 whether accession to the ECHR would be compatible with the EC Treaty, the Court gave the opinion[83] that the Community had no competence to accede. As explained above, in the face of such an opinion, accession would require a Treaty amendment (as well as an adjustment of the Convention which only *states* can accede to). The 1996–97 Inter-governmental Conference did not amend the Treaty in this sense. It preferred a new first paragraph of Article 6 (ex-F):

> The Union is founded on the principles of liberty, democracy, respect for human rights and fundamental freedoms, principles which are common to the Member States.

There follows, unamended from the TEU, which itself borrowed from a pronounce-ment of the Court:

> The Union shall respect fundamental rights, as guaranteed by the European Convention for the Protection of Human Rights and Fundamental Freedoms signed in Rome on 4 November 1950 and as they result from the constitutional traditions common to the Member States, as general principles of Community law.[84]

This in turn is linked with the new Article 7 (ex-F1) which contains a procedure for the suspension of a Member State in serious and persistent breach of Article 6.

Direct effect

Another major principle established by case law, to the surprise of at least some Member States, is that of *direct effect*, an expression which does not occur in the text of the Treaty.[85]

According to Article 189, regulations are directly effective without passing through a national law-making procedure but directives are not. The Court has ruled, however, that provisions in directives can be directly effective, that is, they create rights that can be invoked by the citizen in legal proceedings. Treaty articles can also have direct effect, the test being that the provision must be clear and unambiguous; it must be unconditional; and it must not depend for its operation on any further action by the Community or by the Member State.

By drawing together separate mentions in the EC Treaty, the Court inferred the exis-tence of a general principle of *equality* and non-discrimination. This was given Treaty status in the Treaty of Amsterdam, new Article 13 (ex-6a).

SOME BASIC LEGAL PRINCIPLES

The Court derived from German law a principle of *proportionality*: obligations should be the minimum necessary to secure the desired purpose. This principle became the com-panion of subsidiarity and appeared in the TEU in new Article 3b, third paragraph: 'Any action by the Community shall not go beyond what is necessary to achieve the objectives of this Treaty.' (Now Article 5.)

Legal certainty is a principle common to legal systems generally. The judgements of a court should put the law beyond doubt and provide predictability for the benefit of litigants and their legal advisers. The principle should therefore enable it to be said which persons in which transactions, not being part of the instant case, are affected by a judgement: in particular, whether a judgement is retroactive. One possible rule is that the interpretation of a statute is retroactive to the point where the statute took effect: this is the law and this always was the law. The Court has in some cases taken account of the profound effects that an apparent change in the law – or in what had been understood to be the law – could have, and it has limited retroactivity accordingly. This is tough on any persons who are unable to claim for themselves the benefit of the latest interpretation, and has given rise to charges of inconsistency.

A kindred principle is of *legitimate expectation*. This is a semi-subjective assessment of what a person can reasonably expect to be the law affecting a transaction when it is embarked upon. It does not, of course, mean that the law cannot be changed where there is good reason. Legitimate expectation has been the clarion call of Community staff associations whenever there have been Council moves to retrench on their benefits.

Subsidiarity was not a principle developed by the Court. It was of purely political inspiration (see the Extended Glossary).

L | LEGAL BASES

- Articles 220 to 245 (ex-164 to 188).
- Rules of Procedure of the Court of Justice (OJ L 176, 4.7.91), corrigendum OJ L 383, 25.12.92, p. 117, amendment OJ L 44, 28.2.95, p. 610.

D | DISCUSSION QUESTIONS

1. Many Community laws are made by representatives of governments or by the Commission they appointed. Many national laws are made by elected parliaments. Is it justified that Community law should take precedence in the event of a clash?
2. Does the ECJ interpret the law or make it?
3. Some appointments to the Court have been criticised for lack of courtroom experience. Are academic jurists appropriate judges?
4. Is the ECJ effective in upholding Community law and providing citizens and firms confidence that their rights will be protected?
5. Which is the most important judgement of the ECJ?

APPENDIX 7.1: FREQUENTLY CITED CASES

The appendix to this chapter contains a brief account of the cases that are most frequently quoted to illustrate the development of case law and the effect it has had on the Community.

The cases listed are those frequently cited in general literature, not law books. The original article references have been preserved for simplicity. There is a Table of Equivalencies in OJ C 340, 10.11.97, pages 85 to 91.

Case 29/62 Van Gend en Loon ECR 1

The landmark judgement that Article 12 EEC had direct effect. A customs charge imposed in the Netherlands was incompatible with the Treaty.

> The wording of Article 12 contains a clear and unconditional prohibition. This obligation is not qualified by any reservation on the part of states which would make its implementation conditional upon a positive legal measure enacted under national law. The very nature of this prohibition makes it ideally adapted to produce direct effects in the legal relationship between Member States and their subjects.

Case 6/64 Costa vs ENEL ECR 585

EC law is separate and supreme.

Sig Costa refused to pay a trifling electricity bill because the Italian government, in nationalising Edison Volta, had deprived him of his rights as a shareholder. The Italian government contended that the case was inadmissible since only national law was at issue. The ECJ demurred.

> By contrast with ordinary international treaties the EEC Treaty has created its own legal system, which on entry into force of the Treaty became an integral part of the legal systems of the Member States and which their courts are bound to apply.
>
> By creating a Community of indefinite duration, having its own institutions, its own legal capacity, the Member States have limited their sovereign rights, albeit within limited fields and have thus created a body of law which binds both their nationals and themselves.

Case 29/69 Stauder vs City of Ulm ECR 419

Herr Stauder, a pensioner, felt humiliated by the requirement that his name should appear on the voucher that enabled him to buy butter cheaply. He considered that his fundamental rights had been breached. The Court supported him, noting that in the versions of the Community measure in other languages the beneficiary's name did not require to be given. The most liberal interpretation must prevail.

Case 11/70 Internationale Handelsgesellschaft ECR 1125

It was a German rule that a sum must be deposited to obtain an export licence and was forfeit if the export did not take place within a certain time. The Court held that there had been no breach of fundamental rights but added:

> Respect for human rights forms an integral part of the principles of law protected by the Court of Justice. The protection of such rights, whilst inspired by the constitutional traditions common to Member States, must be ensured within the framework of the structures and objectives of the Community.

Case 22/70 Commission vs Council (ERTA) ECR 263

The first case to oppose the Commission to the Council as defendant. The Commission lost the case but won a major principle.

In 1969 the Council adopted a directive on road transport. Earlier, five of the Member States had participated in inconclusive negotiations for an international convention on road transport. When the negotiations were resumed, the Member States wanted to continue to participate in them in their own names, building on the earlier phase. The Commission objected. The Court did not uphold the complaint, telling the parties that they should have arranged co-operation among them. But the Court pronounced on the Community's capacity to conclude agreements:

> Each time the Community, with a view to implementing a common policy envisaged by the Treaty, adopts provisions laying down common rules, whatever form these rules may take, the Member States no longer have the right acting individually or even collectively to undertake obligations with third parties which affect these rules.
>
> As and when such common rules come into being the Community alone is in a position to assume and carry out the contractual obligations towards third countries affecting the whole sphere of application of the community legal system.

Case 4/73 Nold vs Commission ECR 491

Nold lost on a complaint that its right had been violated because it was unable to obtain Ruhr coal since it could not take the minimum amount provided for in a regulation. Giving judgement the Court said:

> In safeguarding these [fundamental] rights the Court is bound to draw inspiration from the constant tradition common to the member states and it cannot therefore uphold measures [Community measures] which are incompatible with the fundamental rights recognised and protected by the courts of these states. Similarly, international treaties for the protection of human rights on which the Member States have collaborated and of which they are signatories can supply guidance which should be followed within the framework of Community law.

Case 41/74 Van Duyn vs Home Office ECR 137

Ms Van Duyn, a Dutchwoman, wanted to take up a secretarial post with the Church of Scientology in England. The Home Office refused her permission to enter. Ms Van Duyn pleaded that Article 4(1) of directive 64/221 limited the discretion of a Member State to invoke a public policy proviso to refuse entry to a worker from another Member State; the refusal had to be based 'exclusively on the personal conduct of the individual concerned'. The British government argued that the Directive could not have direct effect. The ECJ ruled, inter alia, that the 'useful effect' of the Directive would be diminished if individuals could not invoke it in national courts. Ms Van Duyn lost the case because of the public policy proviso. This was hard in that British subjects were not prevented by law from doing the things that she would have done in the employment of the Church of Scientology.

Eight years later in the case of Adoui and Cornuaille vs Belgium the Court changed its stance by holding that the public policy proviso could not be invoked if the conduct of the individual concerned would not have given rise to a restriction if the individual had been a national of the state which wanted to keep the individual out.

Case 106/77 Simmenthal 2 ECR 629

Simmenthal objected to the compulsory payment of a fee for the health inspection of beef passing from France to Italy. The Italian government maintained that its regulations were posterior to Community regulations [and therefore under a recognised principle of law, overruled them] and that in any case only the Italian Constitutional Court could declare a national rule invalid. The Court, dismissing both arguments, reaffirmed the supremacy of Community law:

> ... any recognition that national legal measures which encroach upon the field within which the Community exercises its legislative power or which are otherwise incompatible with the provisions of Community law had any legal effect would amount to a corresponding denial of the effectiveness of obligations undertaken unconditionally and irrevocably by the Member States pursuant to the Treaty and would thus imperil the very foundations of the Community.

Case 120/78 REWE Zentrale vs Bundesmonopolverwaltung fur Branntwein ECR 649

This is the landmark judgement which, by establishing a principal of mutual recognition of regulatory action, paved the way for the completion of the Single Market through the 1992 programme.

A German public health law banned the marketing in Germany of Cassis de Dijon, a French liqueur drink (familiar as an ingredient of Kir). The Court said:

There is no valid reason why, provided that they have been lawfully produced and marketed in one of the Member States, alcoholic beverages should not be introduced into any other Member State.

[The Commission generalised this into the position that any product lawfully produced and marketed in a Member State must have free circulation in the others.

Mutual recognition became, with essential requirement, a keystone of the elimination of frontier barriers to the movement of goods. It extended the principle in 1993 to the free movement of services.[86]]

Case 108/81 Amylun vs Council (Isoglucose)

The Council had adopted a regulation within the sugar regime setting quotas and levies for isoglucose. It had consulted the EP as required, but when the latter dallied the Council adopted the regulation without having the opinion of the EP. The Court invalidated the regulation because the Council had not 'exhausted the possibilities of obtaining the opinion', e.g. by asking for a special session of the EP for the purpose or fixing an objectively justified deadline.

Having obtained the opinion the Council readopted the regulation and made it retroactive to the date on which the condemned regulation would have come into force. Simmenthal objected again but the Court ruled that retroactivity was justified because isoglucose needed to be put on the same basis as the sugar for which it is a substitute.

Case 294/83 Parti ecologiste Les Verts vs European Parliament

In 1983 the authorities of the European Parliament distributed, to the parties sitting in the EP, funds for their election campaign. The Greens thought the allocations were unfair to them and asked for the decision of the EP to be declared void. Article 173 of the treaty does not say that the Court shall review the legality of acts of the EP. The Court held that the 'general scheme of the treaty' enabled it to review all measures adopted by the institutions . . . that are intended to have legal effects. The Court drew the conclusion that an action for annulment may lie against measures adopted by the European Parliament intended to have legal effect *vis-à-vis* third parties.

[As has been seen above, the Treaty of Amsterdam duly amended Article 173 accordingly, that is to say, the Member States approved the Court's decision to extend its powers.]

Case 314/85 Foto-Frost

National courts may proclaim Community act valid but may not proclaim it invalid. They must ask for a preliminary ruling from the ECJ.

There is no provision to this effect in the EEC or Euratom Treaties. There was one in Article 41 of the ECSC.

Cases 6–9 /90 Francovich

Italy had failed to implement Directive 80/957 on the protection of employees in the event of their employers' insolvency. The Court held that a Member State is required to remedy harm caused to individuals by breaches of Community law for which it is responsible (non-contractual responsibility). Three conditions must be satisfied: the provision must confer rights on individuals; it must be possible to determine the content of these rights from the measure itself; there must be a causal connection between the breach of Community law and the harm suffered by the individual. It was news to some Member States that they had this liability.

Case 213/90 Factortame ECR 1–2466

In a part of the Merchant Shipping Act of 1988 the British Parliament had banned Spanish (and other) fisheries companies from acquiring British registration, and fishing in British waters, drawing on British fishing quotas.

The Court issued an interim injunction suspending that part of the Act that was on its face incompatible with Community law (because it involved discrimination). In the substantive case the incompatibility was confirmed. The British Court accordingly declared the offending part of the Act invalid in R vs Secretary of State for Transport *ex parte* Factortame. Parliament was in consequence obliged to repeal the relevant part of the Act.

[The case notoriously demonstrated that parliamentary sovereignty had been forfeited. This was startling but not new. Section 2(4) of the European Communities Act 1972 says as much, in complicated language.[87] Substantial claims by aggrieved Spanish fishermen against the British government are pending.]

Case T-194/94 Carvel vs Council

Mr Carvel, a *Guardian* journalist asked for a number of Council documents under the Council's Rules of Procedure (Decision 93/662/EC OJ 6.12.93,p1). He was refused some. The Court of First Instance held that the Council had failed to balance the interests involved and to exercise the discretion that the Rules of Procedure gave it.

Mr Carvel was supported by Denmark, the Netherlands and the EP.

Case C-106/96 UK vs Commission

The Commission had launched a programme to combat social exclusion, drawing on a budget line. The UK argued that there was no legal base for the execution of this line. The Court held that the expenditure, not being insignificant or for a pilot scheme, lacked a legal base.

This obliged the Commission to freeze a large number of programmes, including some in the CEECs while it urgently examined whether they were affected by the judgement.

THE LAST INSTITUTION, 'BODIES' AND CONFERENCES

THE COURT OF AUDITORS

THE EXPRESSION comes from the corresponding French Institution, *la cour des comptes*. The seat of the Court is Luxembourg.

The Treaty on European Union, Article 7 (ex-4), transformed the Court of Auditors from a 'body assimilated to an Institution' into an Institution of the Community. The change was intended to give the Court of Auditors higher status in recognition of its role in ensuring financial regularity in a Community accused of waste. It was accompanied by Declaration No. 21, TEU in which the Inter-governmental Conference emphasised the special importance which it attached to the tasks assigned to the Court of Auditors.

In the memorandum[88] which the Court of Auditors presented to the Reflection Group preparing the Inter-governmental Conference of 1996/97 it asked that it should be given the means to ensure that its rights and prerogatives should be upheld and interpreted by the Court of Justice – that is, it wanted the same power to take proceedings against Member States and institutions as is available to the other institutions and to the European Central Bank. This was granted in the Treaty of Amsterdam by an amendment to Article 230 (ex-173).

There is one auditor per Member State. They are appointed by unanimous decision of the Council. The EP is consulted and likes to say, not unreasonably, but not in accordance with the Treaty, that it co-appoints them. Not unreasonably, because of the budgetary and budget control powers of the EP. On occasion, the EP has opposed a nomination on the grounds that the candidate was not qualified. Although the Council is not bound by the EP opinion, it has preferred not to disregard it. The auditors appoint their own President and recruit their own staff.

The Court of Auditors draws up an annual report that is sent to the other institutions, along with the replies which the institutions have given to the Court's observations in the report. The report is debated by the Council, briefly, and more searchingly by the EP. On one famous occasion in 1988, the Court of Auditors reported that if the Community were a commercial enterprise, it would be insolvent.

Under Article 248 (ex-188c) the Court of Auditors is required to 'provide the EP and the Council with a statement of assurance as to the reliability of the accounts and the legality and regularity of the underlying transaction'. The Court's report is surprisingly confidential, but it is known that it has not always been able to furnish the certificate. In fact for consecutive years, to 1999, it was unable to do so. The Court of Auditors may also produce reports on the financial and budgetary aspects of specific subjects and forward them to the Council, the Commission and the EP.

Although the Court of Auditors is empowered to inspect records in the Member States, in conjunction with national audit bodies (Article 248.4), it has been known to have difficulty in obtaining from national agencies all the information it requires. This is despite the fact that its powers are more comprehensive than those of the National Audit Office in Britain. The latter, for example, is unable to audit transactions at the stage where they have passed to recipients from national paying agencies. The Court of Auditors can do so, with co-operation from the national audit.

The difference between irregularity in accounting for national expenditure and the same for Community expenditure is that the former deprives national authorities of revenue; the latter is in one sense an inward flow.

THE ECONOMIC AND SOCIAL COMMITTEE

The Economic and Social Committee (sometimes called Ecosoc, known among officials as Ces, pronounced à l'italienne: Ches) owes its existence to French and German counterparts. They formed part of the mechanisms of the near-corporate state, in which tripartite consensus of government, employers, workpeople, was sought (or lip service paid to it.)

The Economic and Social Committee is not an institution of the Community, much as some of its members would like it to be.[89] It sometimes calls itself the 'second Assembly'. Its function is to give advice to the Council and the Commission, and, from the Treaty of Amsterdam, to the EP, if asked. The Council and the Commission must consult the ESC where the Treaty says so and may consult it in other cases. The ESC may also give opinions on its own initiative. It was originally given this possibility informally. It was confirmed in the Treaty on European Union, Article 262 (ex-198).

Although consultation is in some cases obligatory, the Committee's opinions are not binding.

The constitution and functions of the ESC are set forth in Articles 257 to 262. The Committee consists of 222 members, appointed by the Council. The national breakdown is shown in Table 8.1.

The Member States submit lists of national candidates, two for each seat to allow choice. When composed, the Committee gives equal representation to three groups – employers, workpeople and, loosely, 'consumers', described as 'representatives of the

Table 8.1 Membership of the Economic and Social Committee

Seats	Member state
24	France, Italy, Germany, UK
21	Spain
12	Austria, Belgium, Greece, Netherlands, Portugal, Sweden
9	Denmark, Finland, Ireland
6	Luxembourg

general public' in Article 257, second para. The Council is supposed to obtain the views of representative European bodies on the list of candidates, but it never does. The Member States usually consult representative organisations and even invite their nominations. It was standard British practice, with which the Conservative government broke, to accept the nomination of trade union representatives from the TUC. Appointments are for four years, renewable. The committee changes *en masse* at that time.

Appointed members allocate themselves to nine special sections. The Treaty used to say that there must be sections for transport and agriculture, but this was deleted in the Treaty of Amsterdam. The sections are:

- Economic, Finance and Monetary
- External Relations, Trade and Development
- Social, Family Educational and Cultural
- Protection of the Environment
- Public Health and Consumers
- Agriculture and Fisheries
- Regional Development and Town and Country Planning
- Transport and Communications
- Energy, Nuclear questions and Research

The sections, under the guidance of their chairman and of the draftsman (rapporteur) appointed for each opinion, prepare a draft that is debated and voted on, with simple majorities, in a plenary session. The ESC produces between 150 and 200 opinions a year, including about 20 'own initiative'. Members of the groups generally vote together, but none can dominate.

The Committee appoints its chairman and officers ('Bureau') for a two-year term. The chair rotates among the interest groups. The Bureau organises the business of the ten plenary sessions that are held annually. The Committee appoints a Secretary-General; other staff are recruited by competition. The Council retains responsibility for appointments to the higher grades.

It is an open question whether members of the Council are aware of the opinions that they have received from the Committee. Committee members have access through their parent organisations to expertise on particular issues and can improve on the Commission's in-house technical capabilities. Their organisations can gain insight into the ongoing work of the Community when ESC members report back. Apart altogether from the formal business of the Committee, its existence is sometimes regarded as good in itself, since it provides a point at which influential people in their own spheres can meet and, in the American phrase, network each other. The Conservative government in Britain was unconvinced of its usefulness and made a mild attempt in the 1980s to have it wound up on economy grounds, but other Member States demurred.

THE COMMITTEE OF THE REGIONS

The Committee of the Regions (CoR) was created by Treaty on European Union Articles 263 to 265 (ex-198a to c).

The CoR was a political response to the demands of sub-national units to be involved in Community decision-making. Especially following the expansion of the structural funds, local bodies of different kinds had become the Commission's interlocutors. In the countries with a federal or proto-federal structure, autonomous sub-national bodies wanted to have direct opportunities to express their viewpoints (and protect their rights). A first step had been a Council decision to set up a Consultative Committee of Regional and Local Authorities.[90] In the Inter-governmental Conference which gave birth to the TEU, Germany took the lead in calling for a treaty-based body representing regions.[91]

Although the Treaty articles do not say so, members of the Committee, by use and wont, are elected representatives sitting in regional and local bodies. Their status is very different: the Minister-President of a German Land is a different political animal from a member of an English county council. Membership is divided roughly equally between local and regional bodies. Members are appointed by unanimous decision of the Council, with an equal number of alternates. The national breakdown of the 222 members is the same as shown above for the ESC. Appointments are for four years, renewable. The Committee elects its Chairman and officers for a two-year term. The Treaty of Amsterdam added a proviso that members of the committee may not be Members of the European Parliament (Article 263, para. 3).

Of their own volition, members of the CoR have begun to form loose political groups, with less fragmentation than there is in the EP – Christian Democrats, Socialists and 'Liberals', not in the traditional use of the word but as a grouping of the parties which advocate greater regional independence in their own political systems. Unlike the ESC, the Committee is not told to decompose itself into specialised sections, but it has done so. As in the ESC, the sections prepare draft opinions, which are voted in plenary by simple majorities. The CoR must be consulted by the Council or Commission where the Treaty says so and may be consulted in other cases. Whenever the Commission or Council consult the ESC, they tell the CoR that they have asked the ESC for an opinion. The CoR decides whether it wishes to give one on regional aspects of the subject. The CoR may also give opinions on its own initiative. It may also be consulted by the EP.

When the creation of the CoR was under discussion, the ESC served as a model; and at the suggestion of the ESC, the CoR originally shared staff with the ESC.[92] The CoR found this unsatisfactory and in its opinion on the Institutional Reform of the EU, pre-pared for the 1996–97 Inter-governmental Conference, it called for 'its own independent administration and its own budget'.[93] The Conference gave it satisfaction on this point but not on the demands that it should become an institution and have the right to pro-tect its prerogatives in the ECJ.

The CoR does not have the longevity of other bodies, and the Council is more preoccupied with its relations with the EP than with the non-institutions. The history of the ESC does not show it gaining in power or standing. But with decentralisation and subsidiarity in the ascendant, the CoR may have its day. It has in fact demanded that subsidiarity, which in present Treaty dispensations concerns only relationships between the Union and its Member-States, should be extended vertically to bring decisions 'as closely as possible to the citizen'.[94] A further sign of regional assertiveness was the demand by the government of the Flemish region that in the Council the five votes which Belgium casts should be split to enable the reality of the Belgian scission to be articulated.

THE EUROPEAN INVESTMENT BANK

The European Investment Bank is almost, but not quite, a Community institution. It was set up under Articles 266 and 267 (ex-198D and 198E), and a Protocol. It describes regional development within the Community as lying at the heart of its operations.[95] Two-thirds of its lending goes to Greece, Spain, Ireland, Portugal, Southern Italy and the Länder of Eastern Germany. The Treaty also stipulates that it will support develop-ment called for by the common market and projects of common interest to several Member States. The Treaty does not say that it will operate outside the Community, which it does.

The shareholders in the Bank are the governments of the Member States. A small part of the authorised capital is paid up. The EIB borrows on capital markets, where it has the highest rating (AAA), to lend on. The Bank can provide up to 50% of a capital project. On average the figure is a third.

The Board of Governors consists of the Finance Ministers of the Member States. The latter also appoint, from officialdom or from the banking profession, a Board of Directors, twenty-four in number, with twelve alternates. The Commission also appoints a Director, but is not represented on the Board of Governors. The Board of Governors, on a proposal from the Board of Directors, names the President and seven Vice-Presidents, who make up the Management Committee. They employ around 100 staff, at their HQ in Luxembourg, which is the financial (as well as juridical) centre of the Community. The EIB is not audited by the Court of Auditors but by external auditors chosen by an Audit Committee appointed by the Board of Governors and independent of the Management Committee.

Within the Community, the EIB lends for investment in communications, the envi-ronment, energy and industrial competitiveness.

Outside the Community, the EIB acts under mandates, with financial ceilings, issued by the Ecofin. It supports the Community's partnerships in the ACP countries and South Africa, in the Mediterranean, in the countries of Central and Eastern Europe and in Asian and Latin American countries. Lending in the CEECs has become the EIB's major operation outside the EU, accounting for 50% of the loans in 1996.[96]

CONFERENCES

The Member States of the Union/Community can hold a conference on anything they choose. For example, the first of the annual meetings of a *European Conference* was held in London on 12 March 1998. It brings together the fifteen Member States of the Union and the eleven applicants for membership. (Turkey was invited but declined to attend, considering itself humiliated by the decision not to open accession negotiations.) Such a conference, which is to be an annual event, and a component of the enlargement process, is outside the framework of the Treaties but that is immaterial.

The name *Inter-governmental Conference* (IGC) does not occur in the Treaties. Article 48 (ex-N) speaks of a 'conference of the representatives of the governments of the Member States' which is convened by the President of the Council to examine proposals made by a Member State or by the Commission for the amendment of Treaties. The article does not, unlike Article 203, specify that the government representative is to be at ministerial level.

The only purpose of an Inter-governmental Conference is to consider Treaty amendment. The end result, if any, is a new Treaty. The new Treaty is reached by common accord (of the representatives) and requires ratification in accordance with the constitutional procedures of each Member State. The amendments may be matters of procedure, of institutional changes or of policy development. The Commission participates in an IGC but is not party to the new Treaty. The European Parliament does not participate, is kept informed but less closely than it would wish and does not ratify. It makes its wishes known in a series of resolutions addressed to the Member States. If the IGC lasts longer than the term of a Presidency of the Council, the Conference Presidency likewise changes.

Although the Treaty is silent on the organisation of the Conference, it has settled down to comprise three stages. Foreign Ministers or their deputies take the brunt of the discussions. Finance Ministers may become involved within their sphere. Personal Representatives [of Foreign Ministers], often the Permanent Representatives in Brussels under another name, undertake some of the detailed negotiations. Heads of State and Government, meeting under the sign of the European Council, intervene at appropriate stages and conduct the final negotiations.

The Secretariat of the Conference is provided by the Secretary-General of the Council. The Council Legal Service drafts the resulting treaty articles. Draft articles are presented to the Conference under the responsibility of the Presidency.

An IGC lasts 'as long as it takes', usually through more than one Presidency. A new IGC began in 2000. The agenda is to be strictly limited to three interlinked issues:

- the size of the Commission;
- the weighting of Member States' votes in the Council and the question of what constitutes a majority; and
- a possible further extension of majority voting in the Council.

Another form of conference, *the enlargement conference*, meets when a European state applies to become a member of the Union under Article 49 (ex-O). If the application is entertained, accession negotiations open between the applicant and the Member States of the Union, for convenience meeting under the rotating Presidency of the Council, but not using any procedure prescribed by treaty. The Commission assists the Conference especially by proposing responses to the position papers which applicants are encouraged to send in. Position papers usually concern requests for transitional periods for the adoption of the *acquis*. The Council is not bound by the Commission's suggestions and has a free hand, acting unanimously (since the final decision on the admission of a new member needs unanimity).

The EP is not party to the negotiations although it would like to be. It is kept informed and contributes, usually through its President, views that have been expressed in its Resolutions. (The EP attended the European Conference in London on 12 March 1998.) It has the power of assent to the Accession Treaty (Article 49, para. 1, ex-O), by the absolute majority of its members, but without the possibility of amending the text placed before it. Like an amending treaty, an Accession Treaty (which also amends) is subject to ratification by the member States of the Union.

LEGAL BASES

- Court of Auditors, Articles 246 to 248.
- Economic and Social Committee, Articles 257–262 (ex-193–198).
- Committee of the Regions, Articles 263–265 (ex-198a–198c).

DISCUSSION QUESTIONS

1. Is the elevation of the Court of Auditors to institutional status significant?
2. Does the Union still need an Economic and Social Committee and a Committee of the Regions? What purpose do they fulfil?
3. The argument for the vertical extension of subsidiarity seems strong, what is against it?
4. Are 'conferences' simply a way of avoiding the Community 'method'?

B BIBLIOGRAPHY

The European Parliament

Blondel, J., Sinnott, R. and Svensson, P.: *People and Parliament in the European Union*, OUP, 1998.

Clark, G.: *Your Parliament in Europe*, UK Information Office of the EP, 1984.

Coombes, D.: *Seven Theorems in Search of the European Parliament*, Federal Trust, 1999.

Corbett, R., Jacobs, F. and Shackleton, M.: *The European Parliament*, 3rd edn, Cartermill, 1995.

Corbett, R.: *The European Parliament's Role in Closer European Integration*. Macmillan, 1998.

Duff, A.: *Electoral Reform of the European Parliament*. Federal Trust/European Movement, 1996.

European Parliament: Forging Ahead, OOP, 1989.

The Impact of the European Parliament through the Co-decision Procedure, OOP, 1997.

Hix, S. and Lord, C.: *Political Parties in the European Union*, Macmillan, 1997.

Katz, R. and Wessels, W.: *The European Parliament, the National Parliaments, and the European Integration*, Oxford University Press, 1999.

Nicoll, W. and Schoenberg, (eds): *Europe 2000*, Whurr Publishers, 1996.

Steed, M.: *Choice and Representation in the European Union*, Federal Trust, 1999.

Westlake, M.: *The Origin and Development of the Question Time Procedure in the European Parliament*, European University Institute, Florence, 1990.

Westlake, M.: *A Modern Guide to the European Parliament*, Pinter, 1994.

The Council

Bulmer, S. and Wessels, W.: *The European Council*, Macmillan, 1987.

Giscard d'Estaing, V.: *Le pouvoir et la vie*, compagnie 12, 1988 (pp. 120–3).

Hayes-Renshaw, F. and Wallace, H.: *the Council of Ministers*, Macmillan, 1997.

Johnston, M.T.: *The European Council*, Westview Press, 1994.

Morgan, A.: *From Summit to Council*, Chatham House, 1976.

Westlake, M.: *The Council of the European Union*, Cartermill Publishing, 1995.

see also references by insiders in:

Callaghan, J.: *Time and Chance*, Collins, 1987.

Carrington, P.: *Reflecting on Things Past*, Collins, 1988.

Howe, G.: *Conflict of Loyalty*, Macmillan, 1994.

Lawson, N.: *The View from No. 11*, Bantam, 1992.

Owen, D.: *Personally speaking* (to Kenneth Harris), Weidenfeld & Nicolson, 1987.

Piris, J.-C.: After Maastricht are the institutions more efficacious, more democratic and more transparent? *European Law Review*, Vol. 19, No. 5, October 1994.

Selsdon, A.: *Major, a Political Life*, Weidenfeld & Nicolson, 1997.

Thatcher, M.: *The Downing Street Years*, Harper Collins, 1993.

Tindemans, L. (Report): European Union, *Bulletin of the European Communities*, Supplement 1/76, OOP.
Tindemans, L.: *Europa zonder Kompas*, Standaard Uitgeverij, 1987.

The Commission

Cockfield, Lord: *The European Union – Creating the Single Market*, Wiley, 1994.
Edwards, G. and Spence, D.: *The European Commission* (2nd edn), Cartermill Publishing, 1997.
European Commission: *How does the European Union Work?* OOP, 1996.
Annual General Report on the Activities of the Community, OOP.
European Research Group: *A Europe of the Nations*, 1995.
Grant, C.: *Delors: Inside the House that Jacques built*, Brealey, 1994.
Jenkins, R.: *European Diary, 1977–81*, Collins, 1989.
Middlemas, K.: *Orchestrating Europe*, Fontana, 1995.
Noel, E.: *Working Together – the Institutions of the European Community*, OOP, 1991.
Nugent, N.: *The European Commission*, Macmillan, 1998.
Ross, G.: *Jacques Delors and European Integration*, Polity, 1995.
Tugendhat, C.: *Making Sense of Europe*, Viking, 1986.
Von der Groeben, H.: *The European Community – the Formative Years*, OOP, 1987.

European Court of Justice and European Union law

Borchardt, K.-D.: *The ABC of Community Law*, OOP, 1994.
European Commission: Community Law, OOP, 1974.
Hartley, T.C.: *The Foundations of European Community Law* (successive editions), Clarendon.
House of Lords: Select Committee on the European Communities, *Political Union: Law-making Powers and Procedures, Session 1990–91*, 17th Report, HL Paper 80.
House of Lords: Select Committee on the European Communities, *Europol, Session 1994–95*, 10th Report, HL Paper 51–1.
House of Lords: Select Committee on the European Communities, *The 1996 Inter-governmental Conference, Minutes of Evidence, Session 1994–95*, 18th Report, HL Paper 88.
Hunning, M.N.: *The European Courts*, Carterfield Publishing, 1996.
Mathijsen, P.S.R.F.: *A Guide to European Community Law*, Sweet & Maxwell, 1972.
Wall, E.: *Europe Unification and Law*, Pelican, 1969.
Weatherill, S. and Beaumont, P.: *EC Law*, Penguin, 1995.

Court of Auditors

Annual and Special Reports, Court of Auditors.
Carey, C.J. in Dinan, D. (ed.) *Encyclopedia of the European Union*, Lynne Rienner, 1998.
Laffan, B.: *The Finances of the European Union*, Macmillan, 1997.
Strasser, D.: *Les finances de l'Europe*, (5th edn; first edn 1995), Editions Labor.

European Investment Bank

EIB Annual Report (published by the Bank itself).
Albert, M. and others: *Investing in Europe's Future*, Blackwell, 1983.
Artus, P. and others: *Innovation, Technology and Finance*, Blackwell, 1988.

Economic and Social Committee and the Committee of the Regions

ESC: *The European Economic and Social Committee*, OOP, 1996–98.
CES Info, Monthly publication.
CoR: *Impact of the Opinions of the Committee of the Regions*, OOP, 1997.

Conferences

Corbett, R.: *The Treaty of Maastricht*, Longman, 1993.
Duff, A.: *The Treaty of Amsterdam: Text and Commentary*, Federal Trust, 1998.
Duff, A., Pinder, J. and Pryce, R.: *Maastricht and Beyond*, Routledge, 1994.
Laursen, F. and Vanhoonacker, S. eds: *The Intergovernmental Conference on Political Union*, European Institute of Public Administration, 1992.
Laursen, F. and Vanhoonacker, S. eds: *The Ratification of the Maastricht Treaty*, European Institute of Public Administration, 1999.

General

Archer, C.: *Organising Europe; the Institutions of Integration*, Edward Arnold, 1994.
Clark, A.: Behind closed doors in Brussels, *European Journal*, March 1994, p. 11.
Cram, L.: *Policy-making in the EU*, Routledge, 1997.
De la Serre, F. and Lequesne, C.: *Quelle union pour quelle Europe?* Editions complexe, 1998 (ch.6).
Duff, A.: *Reforming the European Union*, Sweet and Maxwell, 1997.
Edwards, G. and Wallace, H.: *The Council of Ministers of the European Community and the President-in-Office*, Federal Trust, 1977.
General Secretariat: (1) Presidency Handbook; (2) *Comments on the Council's Rules of Procedure*; (3) *Delegates' Handbook*, OOP, 1996.
Annual Review of the Council's Work, OOP.
Guide to Information about the Council of the European Union, OOP, 1998.
Hayes-Renshaw, F. and Wallace, H.: *The Council of Ministers*, Macmillan, 1997.
Hix, S.: *The Political System of the European Union*, Macmillan, 1999.
Ludlow, P. and Ersboll, N.: *Preparing for 1996 and a Larger European Union*, CEPS, Brussels, 1995.
Morgan, A.: *From Summit to Council*, Chatham House/PEP, 1976.
Nicoll, W. in Duff, A., Pinder, J. and Price, R. (eds) *Maastricht and Beyond*, Routledge, 1994.
Nugent, N.: *The Government and Politics of the European Union*, Macmillan, 1999.
Peterson, J. and Bomberg, E.: *Decision-making in the European Union*, Macmillan, 1999.
Richardson, J. (ed.): *European Union – Power and policy-making*, Routledge, 1996.

Vignes, D.: Le calcul de la majorité qualifiée – un casse-tête pour 1996, *Revue du Marche commun et de l'Union européenne*, No. 382, November 1994.

Wallace, H and Wallace, W.: *Policy-making in the European Union*, OUP, 1996.

Westlake, M.: *The Council of the European Union*, Cartermill Publishing, 1995.

NOTES

1. Spierenburg, D. and Poidevin, R., *History of the High Authority of the Coal and Steel Community*, Weidenfeld & Nicolson, 1994

2. See especially, Fukuyama, F., *The End of History and the Last Man*, Free Press (Macmillan), 1992, Ch. 10; and Sabine, G.H., *A History of Political Theory*, Harrap, 1960, under 'Hegel'.

3. In French, 'commission' is often what in English is a 'committee'. To avoid confusion, the European Parliament often calls the 'Commission' the 'Executive Commission'.

4. Hallstein, W., *Der unvollendete Staat*, Econ, 1969. Later editions were untendentiously entitled Die Europäische Gemeinschaft.

5. At the annual inaugural ceremony of the College of Europe in Bruges in 1986.

6. Sir Barnett Cocks, *The European Parliament*, HMSO, 1973, p. 7.

7. See W. Nicoll, 'The "Code of Conduct" of the Commission towards the European Parliament', *Journal of Common Market Studies*, Vol. 34, No. 2, June 1996, pp. 275ff.

8. Committee of Independent Experts, First Report on Allegations Regarding Fraud, Mismanagement and Nepotism in the European Commission, para. 1.1.1.

9. In 1994 Parliament was *consulted* on the appointment of M. Santer, but the German Presidency of the Council assured the EP that its opinion would be binding. The Treaty of Amsterdam catches up with practice.

10. National traditions dictate that elections are held on particular days of the week. The count does not begin until the polling stations have closed in the Member States where voting is on Sunday.

11. For discussion see A. Duff, *Federal Trust/European Movement, Electoral Reform of the European Parliament*, 1996; its sequel in A. Duff, (ed.), *The Treaty of Amsterdam*, Sweet & Maxwell, 1997, pp.150,151; *Forging Ahead*, OOP for the EP, 1989, p. 44; George Clark, *Your Parliament in Europe*, UK Information Office of the EP, 1984, p. 46.

12. The timing was unfortunate. The French government had just withdrawn a scheme for regional lists in the face of opposition in the Assemblée Nationale.

13. Until German unification, it had the same number of seats as the other big Member States.

14. For details of the kaleidoscope of Group composition see Richard Corbett, Francis Jacobs and Michael Shackleton, *The European Parliament*, Cartermill Publishing, 1995, Chapter 5.

15. In the singular.

16. The De Hondt system is one of the principal forms of proportional representation.

17. The Committee Report cannot be amended in plenary.

18. On at least one occasion a Member who wanted to be heard brought a loud hailer with him.

19. Details of Presidential attendance are given in the Annual Report of the Secretary-General of the Council.

20. A misnomer. Citizenship is of the Union (Article 8), although anomalously it is created in the Treaty establishing the Economic Community, as amended in the TEU.
21. Dwarf tossing was a 'sport' in which small people wrapped in protective gear were thrown competitively. Such spurious questions should be disallowed by the equivalent of a Table Office, but some get through.
22. The Principal Legal Adviser to the Council, J.-C. Piris, identified 22 of them in 'After Maastricht, are the Community Institutions more efficacious, more democratic and more transparent', *European Law Review*, Vol. 19, No. 5, 1994, pp. 469–70.
23. The original Pact of Steel was between Ribbentrop and Molotov in 1939 for the dismemberment of Poland.
24. All quotations are from the Committee's Report. The right wing group referred to is that led by M. Le Pen.
25. OJ C 340,10.11.97, p. 112.
26. See Nicoll, W., 'The Code of Conduct of the Commission towards the European Parliament', *Journal of Common Market Studies*, Vol. 34, No. 2, June 1996, pp. 276ff.
27. *Journey to an Unknown Destination*, Penguin Special, 1971.
28. The Market Committee of the Folketing debates upcoming Community business and mandates Ministers who will attend Council meetings. In principle if the Minister needs to shift position, he or she needs Market Committee assent. The fact that Danish governments are invariably coalitions, as is the Market Committee, helps to maintain coherence.
29. See Brian Cassidy MEP, 'The Devil is in the Detail', *European Business Journal*, Vol. 7, Issue 3, 1995, pp. 27–31: Lord Tordoff, 'A Watchful Eye', *European Business Journal*, Vol. 8, Issue 4, 1996, pp. 28–36.
30. Sir Barnett Cocks, *The European Parliament*, HMSO, 1973, p. 28.
31. OJ C 340, 10.11.97, pp. 113, 114.
32. In referring here to the Union, the Protocol implicitly accepts that national parliaments may involve themselves in second and third pillar affairs.
33. Andrew Duff, *Reforming the European Union*, Sweet & Maxwell, 1997, pp. 58–59; David Millar, *Crisis or Opportunity; Constitutional Issues: the European Parliament and National Parliaments*, Centre for European Union Studies, University of Hull, 1996.
34. COM (85) 310 of June 1985, *Completing the Internal Market*, White Paper.
35. See Cloos, Reinisch, Vigne and Weyland, *Le Traité de Maastricht*, Bruylant, Brussels, 1993, p. 413.
36. Not being an institution, the European Council is the subject of a separate section.
37. According to the writings of Wolfgang Wessels, a leading and respected German student of Community/Union matters: 'The major feature of this [integrative] process is a "fusion" of public instruments from several state levels linked with the respective Europeanisation of national actors and institutions', *Journal of Common Market Studies*, Vol. 35, No. 2, June 1997, p. 273.
38. Ministries of Foreign Affairs may also be apprehensive about (or receptive towards) ideas about a Union Diplomatic Service, applying the Common Foreign and Security Policy and absorbing the Commission's external representation. Consular services are already pooled on behalf of citizens of the Union (Article 20, ex-8c EC).

39. The other tools are: national policy co-ordination; the omnipresent Commission; the memory and longevity of the Council Secretariat; the Presidency (assuming that it is internally co-ordinated); the outside world calling attention to inconsistency.
40. For some reverberations, see Norman Lamont, *Sovereign Britain*, Duckworth, 1995. The fuller story was told in the BBC documentary 'The Money Changers', 1997.
41. 'The Council has not yet made use of the possibility given to it by Article 4(3) of the CRP to set a legal limit on the number of officials accompanying members of the Council.' Council guide: II, Comments on the Council's Rules of Procedure. There are limits on the numbers whose travel expenses will be reimbursed.
42. Restricted meeting, sometimes described as the same number of people in a smaller room, is only one of the mechanical devices which a President can muster to break blockages. For a light-hearted look at the others, see Nicoll, W., *The Great Game: the Council at Work and Play*, South Bank University Paper, 1996.
43. See the entry in the Extended Glossary.
44. Weidenfeld & Nicolson,1993, p. 139. The reader must be the judge of the objectivity of the account of the meeting described.
45. The extreme example of institutionalised leadership occurs in Article 24 TEU (ex-J.14). There the Presidency is given the power and duty to propose to the Council the conclusion of bilateral and multilateral agreements in the framework of the CSFP. In the first pillar, such a task belongs to the Commission, for example under Article 300 (ex-228).
46. See Nicoll, W., 'The "Code of Conduct" of the Commission towards the European Parliament', *Journal of Common Market Studies*, Vol. 43, No. 2, June 1996, p. 275.
47. With a combination of working breakfasts, lunches and dinners and morning and afternoon meetings, a President (and the President of the European Council) can jet round capitals in a matter of hours.
48. OJ C 194, 28.7.82, p. 2.
49. Annexed by the Treaty of Amsterdam to the Treaty on European Union and to the Treaties establishing the three Communities. OJ 340, 10.11.97, p. 111.
50. Council Press Release 10228/98, 13 July 1998.
51. On the troubled relations between Calmes and the High Authority, see Spierenburg, D. and Poidevin, R., *History of the High Authority of the European Coal and Steel Community*, Weidenfeld & Nicolson, 1994, pp. 59, 60.
52. Like Germany, Denmark gives its most senior officials Ministerial rank.
53. See Grant, C., *Delors, inside the House that Jacques Built*, Nicholas Brearley, 1994, pp. 190, 240.
54. OJ L 291, 15.10.87, Article 15, the revised version is in OJ L 304, 10.12.93.
55. Article 26, TEU, consolidated version, OJ C 340, p. 161, 10.11.97.
56. Declaration No. 6 adopted by the Inter-governmental Conference, 1997.
57. As will be shown below, the European Council is not an institution in the Treaty usage of the word, but it is often loosely called one.
58. But in the ECSC, the Commission had a leading status.
59. There may also be no conclusions if the meeting did not come to any.

60. The Stuttgart Declaration of 1985 gets its institutions wrong when it says (section 2.1.3) that the European Council can act as the Council. Not if the President of the Commission is a fully-fledged member (section 2.1.1).

61. Prime ministers of acceding countries often sign the Act of Accession.

62. See Nicoll, W., 'The Code of Conduct of the Commission towards the European Parliament', *Journal of Common Market Studies*, Vol. 34, No. 2, June 1996.

63. 'Tomorrow's Commission', Staff consultation document, 04/23/98, May 1998.

64. The circumstantial study of a cabinet is found in the works of George Ross, who spent months as a fly on the wall in the cabinet of President Delors in 1991. See 'Inside the Delors Cabinet', *Journal of Common Market Studies*, Vol. 32, No. 4, December 1994.

65. The Commission can decide to give one of its members a 'habilitation' to act in the name of the Commission.

66. In the history of the Commission there have only been three Secretaries-General, the late Emile Noel (in at the creation), David Williamson (imported) and currently Carlo Trojan (risen from the ranks).

67. Council Regulation (EC) No.384/96 OJ L 56, 6.3.96.

68. Council Regulation (EEC) No.4064/89, OJ L 395, 30, 12.89, as amended.

69. Report [to the Reflexion Group] of the Court of Justice on certain aspects of the application of the Treaty on European Union, May 1955, I.3.

70. T.C. Hartley, *The Foundations of European Community Law*, Clarendon Press, 2nd edn, 1988, p. 49.

71. This ludicrous proposition was reported to be held by the government of Mr John Major in the lead-up to the 1996–97 Inter-governmental Conference.

72. Sir Patrick Neill QC, *A Case Study in Judicial Activism*, reproduced in House of Lords, Select Committee on the European Communities, Session 1994–95, 18th Report, HL Paper 88, The 1996 Inter-governmental Conference, Minutes of Evidence, pp. 218ff.

73. Including Lord Howe of Aberavon QC, *Eurojustice Yes or No*, 1955 Bar Conference.

74. E.g. those quoted by Professor Alan Dashwood in his evidence to the House of Lords inquiry into the 1996 IGC., op. cit., p. 258.

75. House of Lords Report, HL Paper 105, p. 66, para. 260–261.

76. W. Weidenfeld and W. Wessels, *Europe from A to Z*, OOP, 1997, p. 121. This is strained given that most appeal courts decide by majority.

77. For example, on CAP regulations, on competition cases and in disputes between an institution and its staff. In 1993 it was made competent to hear actions brought by natural or legal persons. Its competence will no doubt continue to be extended.

78. Decision 88/591/ECSC,EEC,Euratom.

79. It may seem anomalous that a national court can rule on the validity of a Community act, but not on its invalidity. See Sir Patrick Neill, op. cit.

80. See the list of frequently cited cases in the annex to this chapter.

81. Framework decisions correspond roughly to directives in Pillar I. See Article K.6.2.b.

82. Declaration on Article K.7 as amended by the Treaty of Amsterdam.

83. ECR 1–1759 of 28 March 1996. *See The Human Rights Opinion of the ECJ and its Constitutional Implications*, University of Cambridge, Centre for European Legal Studies, paper No. 1, June 1996.

84. See the judgements given in cases concerning fundamental rights in the Annex.
85. 'Directly applicable' does occur. Direct effect and direct applicability can be taken to have the same meaning according to T.C. Hartley, *The Foundations of European Community Law*, Clarendon Press, 1990, Chapter 7. Other jurists can conceive of directly applicable measures, e.g. agricultural regulations, which do not have direct effect because they need Commission executive regulations as well. Still others define directly applicable as meaning taking full effect when passed and direct effect as meaning creating a right that can be invoked in a national court.
86. *Agence Europe*, 9 December 1993, p. 13.
87. For discussion see Eli Lauterpacht, 'Sovereignty – Myth or Reality?', *International Affairs*, RIIA, Vol. 73, No. 1, January 1997, pp. 137ff.
88. White Paper on the 1996 Inter-governmental Conference, Vol. 1, p. 388, European Parliament, 1996.
89. The Committee asked for institutional status in its Opinion on the 1996 Inter-governmental Conference. CES 1312/95, para. 12. It also asked, equally unsuccessfully, to attend the Conciliation Committee under the co-decision procedure.
90. Decision 88/487 EEC, OJ L 247/23, 6.9.88.
91. Cloos, Reinesch, Vigne and Weyland, *Le Traité de Maastricht*, Bruylant, Brussels, 1993, pp. 408–13.
92. TEU Protocol on the Economic and Social Committee and the Committee of the Regions. Deleted by the Treaty of Amsterdam.
93. CoR 136/95, p. 6.
94. Lemaire, J. and Miroir, M., *La Belgique et ses nations dans la nouvelle Europe*, Editions de l'université de Bruxelles, 1997, pp. 162–3.
95. EIB, *Annual Report*, 1996, p. 11. See also J.H.P. Paelinck, 'Investment and the development of Backward Regions in A. Heertje, (ed.), *Investing in Europe's Future*, Blackwell for the EIB, 1983, pp. 152ff.
96. The EIB in Central and Eastern Europe, Sir Brian Unwin, *European Business Journal*, Vol. 9, Issue 1, 1997, pp. 19ff.

PART 3

FIRST PILLAR POLICIES

COMMON POLICIES

THE COMMON AGRICULTURAL POLICY

THE COMMON Agricultural Policy (CAP) is the oldest of the integrative policies of the European Community. It is also the most bitterly criticised and the most stoutly defended. Its critics regard it as the acme of waste. Its supporters hail it as a resounding success. Towards the end of the century, it had become an expensive anachronism.

It is contended, on behalf of the CAP, that it has raised output to 120% of Community consumption. In a generation, output had risen twice over or more, while farming employment had fallen twice over. In real terms, prices have allegedly fallen by 2% p.a. It is counter-contended that by misallocating resources the CAP has reduced Community GDP by a steady 1% annually. It was pointed out in 1987 that it cost $410 to keep an EC cow going. This was more than the per capita income of half the world's population.

Famine

When European integration was debated in the late 1940s there were harsh memories of the famine which was widespread in Europe during and, even more, after the Second World War. The countries of Western Europe were heavily dependent on imports, which were a balance of payments cost and which left them insecure. It was a major policy objective to reach self-sufficiency in food. This was nothing new. Countries had traditionally safeguarded their farmers in the name of national security. Farm lobbies were powerful. They spoke for a large proportion of the electorate – around 25% of the working population across Western Europe – and they accounted for important shares of national product still around 5% in the early 1970s, and of export earnings. There were also romantic folk-memories among town dwellers who were only a generation or so away from the land. Henri IV of France had pronounced tillage and husbandry to be the two breasts from which France suckled and the 'true mines and treasures of Peru'. Thomas Jefferson, the American Founding Father, had written that those who work on the land are closer to God.

An economy can, within limits, decide what quantities of industrial goods it will produce. But even a command economy cannot decide how much food and other agricultural output there will be in any season. Khruschev tried and failed in the Virgin lands of Central Asia. Nature decides what grows. There may be surpluses or deficits. They can be evened out with buffer stocks, which may sell or may perish. Farmers and consumers alike look to governments to treat food supply as a public good and to stabilise markets and prices. Producers want to maximise outputs, using improved technology to maximise profit. Scientific progress – better crop varieties, improved machinery, agro-chemical inputs, biogenetics – automatically raises productive capacity by around 2% p.a. Consumer tastes shift. Beyond a certain level of consumption, they prefer food that is of better quality or more convenient to cook. Population growth settles down, with no increase in mouths to feed. Over a period in Western Europe, farm output rises by about 2% p.a. and food consumption by about 0.5% p.a. The share of food in family budgets falls. Health consciousness spreads, calorie and fat intakes are controlled, some foods – beef, cheese, eggs, GM tomatoes – become health scares. The secular trend is for farm income to decline relatively to other sectors where there is a better factor mix. Young people tend to leave the land for the perceived better employment prospects in the cities, and land fallen into disuse becomes a blot on the landscape. In the absence of any private responsibility, governments are expected to protect the national heritage of the countryside. Farm support policies have a mix of objectives to serve.

If any integration, then farming first

To 'grow more food', one of the British wartime slogans, some post-war governments protected national agriculture against imports by tariff and non-tariff barriers and by state subsidies. Their different systems were incompatible with each other and were explicitly designed to restrict cross-border trade. This had its costs, by depriving their citizens of access to cheaper food and by using a share of their tax money to sustain uncompetitive farming. As part of the impulse towards integration, attempts were made to free up agricultural trade, notably in discussions from 1949 onwards about a 'Green Pool' or 'Green Plan'. They failed, principally because they did not give the participants a plus-sum game.

When the Six decided to establish a Customs Union and to abolish trade barriers among themselves, there was no question of excluding agriculture from the free circulation of goods. It had to be part of the new structure. Since it would be only one of the parts, there would be opportunities for trade-offs with other sectors.

The Treaty

The first sectoral title of the Treaty establishing the European Economic Community, following the Title that secures free movement of goods, is devoted to agriculture. Annex II to the Treaty sets out the agricultural products to which the Title applies. Article 33 (ex-39)[1] establishes agricultural policy objectives: the development of agri-

Table 9.1   Employment in agriculture as a percentage of the working population

Member State	1970	1994	1996
Greece	41	21	–
Portugal	30	–	12
Ireland	27	12	–
Spain	27	–	9
Finland	23	–	7
Italy	20	–	7
Austria	15	–	7
France	14	–	5
Denmark	12	5	–
Netherlands	6	4	–
Sweden	14	–	3
Federal Republic of Germany	9	–	3
Luxembourg	9	3	–
Belgium	5	3	–
UK	3	–	2

Source: OECD.

cultural productivity and production, and the optimum employment of the workforce; an equitable standard of living for the farming population, including increase in individual income; stability of markets; security of supply; and reasonable consumer prices.

The Treaty sets forth how to dismantle internal agricultural protection, but not how to attain the objectives of Article 33. It instructs the Commission to make proposals. It did so by convening a conference at Stresa in Italy in July 1958 under the guiding hand of the first Commissioner for Agriculture, Sicco Mansholt, a former Dutch agricultural minister. Agricultural policy developments of the next decade bear his name. The conference established three fundamental principles for agriculture: a single market (implicit in the customs union); Community preference over imports; and financial solidarity – the Community would pay the cost of its agricultural policy. Only the last is genuinely innovative. It was also essential to replace national financial support for national agriculture by the Community, or, more accurately, partially replace it. The third principle also became the most difficult to implement and, because of its different budgetary effects among the Member States, the source of dissent and recurrent crises.

Foundation principles

It might have been possible to operate a single agricultural market free of price subsidy, allowing free play to competition. This did not, however, chime with the notion of sustaining agriculture at large or with the pre-history of farm policies The Commission toyed with the idea of a market built on quantitative import restrictions,[2] the antithesis of free circulation, but representing one possible interpretation of Article 34 (ex-40)

177

which allows for the 'stabilisation' of imports and exports. The Member States preferred the mention of price regulation in the same paragraph. Common prices became the sense of the principle of financial solidarity and the fundamental mechanism for the organisation of the European agricultural market. In the language used of the wider single market in later years, the agricultural playing field was levelled flat. The Community budget paid. This was a momentous decision, full of significance for Community policies and structures. Over time, nineteen market organisations (see Box 9.1) were brought into being (a market organisation can include several products).

Box 9.1   Market organisations

1962	Cereals, pig meat, eggs and poultry, fruit and vegetables, wine
1964	Rice, milk and dairy products
1968	Sugar, oilseeds
1970	Raw tobacco, flax, hemp
1971/72	Hops, seeds
1974	Dried fodder, Soya flour
1977/78	Silkworms, iso-glucose, peas, beans, pulses
1980	Sheep meat
1981	Cotton, cereal-based spirits, bee keeping, raisins and figs

Common prices

In general, European late 1950 agricultural price levels were higher than world prices. In addition, the policy was explicitly intended to increase agricultural production and reduce import dependency. This meant giving farmers a cash incentive to produce more, protection against cheaper imports and a guarantee of sales (see Table 9.2).

Table 9.2   Allocation of resources under the Guarantee section, 1997

Product	Allocation (ECU millions)
Beef	7,451
Dairy products	3,625
Olive oil	2,168
Accompanying measures	1,866
Sugar	1,834
Fruit and vegetables	1,679
Sheep and goats	1,447
Tobacco	1,043
Wine	0,805
Other products and measures	2,190
Arable crops	16,160

Source: Commission 1998.

The common prices were accordingly fixed at levels favourable to less efficient farming. Imports were restrained by putting a charge on them, known as a levy (now known as a duty). Disposal of unmarketed production was ensured by buying in at a guaranteed price, storing it for release if supply fell short, destroying it if it would not keep or selling it abroad with an export subsidy, known as a restitution, that is of the levy element in the domestic price, or giving it away as food aid to needy countries.[3] If it should happen that Community prices were below world levels, exports would symmetrically but only theoretically be subject to a charge.

The actual price mechanism varies from product to product and they are all endowed with fine-tuning devices. Cereals illustrate how the different fixed prices apply (Figure 9.1).

The *target price* is what the producer should receive in the market place. In the market organisation it is called the *guide price*. For tobacco it is the *norm price*. Target prices are set for cereals, sugar, milk, olive oil, rape and sunflower seed.

Figure 9.1   Levy and refund system for wheat

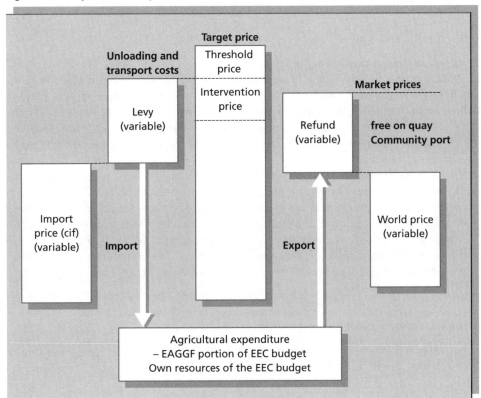

The *threshold price* is what imports should cost. When internal transport costs are added, it equals the *target* (etc.) *price.* To bring import prices up to the required level, a levy (duty) is imposed on the landed cost.

The *intervention price* is what the producers receive if they cannot get more on the market. Subject to limitations introduced later in the history of the CAP, they sell it to an agency, which may appear to be an entity separate from the national government or may be part of it. The agency stores supplies until a use is found for them.

The *sluice-gate price* is for pig meat, eggs and poultry meat. It is the cost price of the most efficient external producer; with the levy added it comes up to the Community price. If offered at less than the sluice-gate price, imports are hit with a supplementary levy.

A *basic price* is set for pig meat, triggering intervention.

Reference prices are the minima for imports of fruit and vegetables. If they are not respected, a levy is imposed.

All these support prices are on the way to becoming historical curiosities. The guarantee price system was a recipe for creating surpluses, especially of cereals, beef, dairy products, wine and tobacco (there was no external market for Community grown tobacco). Hence the notorious mountains and lakes.

Taking milk and sugar

Milk and sugar had their own problems.

Milk accounts for some 20% of agricultural output. About one-third of dairy farmers have fewer than five cows. Milk is not easily exportable. Consumption is static or falling because of cholesterol concerns. Production rises if unchecked by a steady 2% p.a. Milk was the first product to be subjected to a production limit, ultimately enforced by individual farm quotas (1984–88). Accounting was hideously complicated and easily falsified.

Sugar, made from beet especially in Germany, France and Italy, is in structural surplus. Price has not been the control mechanism. Production quotas are. The first slice of production, the A quotas, is price-guaranteed. The B quotas are subject to a heavily reduced intervention price. A and B sugar is subject to a levy to help to reduce the cost of marketing. C sugar is unsupported and must be exported. When quota size is calculated, account must be taken of the sugar, some 10% of the Community market, which the Community has undertaken to import from its Member States' former colonies (the ACP countries).

Green rates or funny money

The common prices so far mentioned are fixed in fictitious money, originally the Unit of account, later the ECU. Only agricultural produce was priced in what will not be a currency until there is a monetary union. So far as producers are concerned, prices are in their national currency. If exchange rates are stable, prices will remain common. Only one year after the CAP reached completion the French franc was devalued. This would have meant an increase of 11.5% in French franc prices. France did not want an inflationary surge and persuaded the Community to allow franc prices to remain unchanged. French farmers could, however, sell their produce in other Community markets at a price which, when translated into francs, gave them an 11.5% bonus. There was a first breach in the unity of the market. To correct the anomaly, French farm exports were hit by an 11.5% tax. The arrangement was shortly phased out, but the problem of fluctuating exchange rates remained. To cope with it and to preserve a semblance of common pricing, a system of representative or *green rates* and compensatory payments and charges was introduced. When a national currency was devalued the distorting effects were offset by Monetary Compensation Amounts (MCAs). Negative MCAs were levied on exports and granted on imports. Positive MCAs were paid when a currency was revalued; levied on imports and granted on exports. MCAs featured both in internal trade and in trade with third countries. Levies and subsidies were augmented or reduced by the MCAs. It applied logically enough to products subject to intervention (cereals, beef, milk products and wine) and perhaps with less justification to sugar, pork, eggs and poultry. It became fiendishly complex and came to be branded by the Commission as notorious.[4] It was partly alleviated by the relative price stability of the Exchange Rate Mechanism (ERM) in its original form of narrow fluctuation bands.

The system created different price zones in what was supposed to be a single market. Member States took advantage of it to award their farmers national price increases on home market sales on top of the agreed Community price fixing by devaluing their green rates, without much relation to the movement in their posted exchange rates, or to oppose Community price increases as wasteful while appropriating an increase in national currency terms. Green rates remained in vogue until they were abolished in Euroland (January 1999). MCAs were abandoned earlier and replaced by a Regulation which determined measures and compensation relating to appreciable revaluations (Regulation (EC) 724/97).[5]

Farm support begets crisis

The attempts to install the financial mechanisms to support the CAP led the Community into its first crisis of confidence, in the so-called 'empty chair' episode of 1965, when France accused its partners of foot-dragging.[6] This referred to the means to gather in Customs duties and levies on imports to pay the cost of intervention and export restitution. With this behind it, the Community completed the organisation of markets and the application of common prices by 1968. But by the same year the CAP was already in trouble. Commissioner Mansholt was the author of a rescue plan, which bears his name and is also known as 'Agriculture 1980'. This addressed the problem of farm size – making the point that three-quarters of the farms in the then Community provided work for only three-quarters of a worker's time. The Commission proposed, and the Member States accepted measures to help farmers who met the conditions to modernise and others between 55 and 65 to leave the land. This was the substantive start of structural measures for farming.

181

The Farm Fund, an integral part of the budget, consists of two parts. The Guarantee section, by far the larger, and despite all effort to the contrary, an encouragement to inefficient production; and the Guidance section, aimed in a modest enough way at improving efficiency. Later, the Guidance section was to be co-ordinated with other programmes into the Structural Funds, with their own collective mission and drive for expansion.

External effects

The CAP was never a comfortable policy in world trade circles. Although the Community remained the world's largest importer, and ran an import surplus and although its own economic growth improved market prospects for its suppliers, exporters elsewhere criticised the protection of the Community market by the levies. They also objected to its export subsidies (as well as its food aid, which was not always in the best interest of agricultural development in recipient countries). It was also troublesome at home. The annual price-fixing became a spectacle of 'marathon' meetings as farm ministers fought for national advantage and, enlisted by their lobbies, died in ditches to hold on at least to what they had. Apologists pointed to the undoubted achievements: by the 1970s the Community had moved from meeting only 80% of its food needs to providing 120%. Food shortage was a thing of the past. As to the cost, all depended upon what was put into the calculation. In the 1980s the Commission had a figure of 100 ECU (roughly £80) per head. This is a straight calculation of the cost in the budget. Critics in Britain had it as £250 per head including the cost of higher than world prices.

Budgetary discipline

By 1988 the Community budget, with farm-spending taking the lion's share, was out of balance. The Community decided to control spending, not by revising the mechanisms of the CAP but by means of financial disciplines. One control was to cap the total amount earmarked in the budget for guarantee spending. Its growth could not exceed 74% of the growth in Community GDP. This is known as the agricultural guideline. The other was the so-called 'stabiliser'. For every product in an organised market (except milk and sugar which had already been 'stabilised') a maximum guaranteed quantity was fixed. If production exceeded it, support payments were automatically reduced. With cereals again as an example: the maximum guaranteed quantity was 160 million tonnes a year. If production were higher, there would be an automatic reduction of 3% in the guaranteed price for the whole of the output of the next crop year and so on cumulatively. In view of the expected build up of arable crops and expected surpluses, set-aside was introduced. Farmers were paid for not planting land.

It was courageous but it did not work. Surpluses of beef and milk still accumulated. By 1991 only 2% of cereal acreage had been set-aside, much of it low yielding. Export markets in the former Soviet bloc weakened. A fall in the dollar debased world cereal prices and pushed up export subsidies. The maximum guaranteed quantity of 160 million tons of cereal held, but consumption fell because of competition from other ani-

Table 9.3   Some important dates in evolution of the CAP

Date	Event
1958	Conference at Stresa
1960	The Commission presents to the Council its 'Proposals on the working out and implementation of the Common Agricultural Policy'
1962	The first market regulations are adopted
1968	The CAP enters its final phase: common prices come into force
1972	The first socio-structural directives are adopted
1979	Ever-increasing milk surpluses lead to the introduction of a co-responsibility levy
1980	The Council of Ministers agrees in principle to the setting of production targets
1984	Milk quotas are introduced
1985	Publication of 'Perspectives for the Common Agricultural Policy: the Commission's Green Paper'
1988	Introduction of budgetary discipline and the 'stabiliser' system
1991	MacSharry publishes 'The development and future of the Common Agricultural Policy'
1992	MacSharry reforms adopted
1997	Agenda 2000 proposes further reforms

mal feeding stuffs, including imports. Cereal stocks rose in 1991 from 1.5 million tonnes to 18 million and were forecast to rise by another 10 million tonnes in the ensuing year.

Budgetary spending did not fall – it looked like increasing by 20% from 1991 to 1992. Something far more serious was required, and another name came to prominence: Ray MacSharry, the Agricultural Commissioner from Ireland, the country with a huge stake in traditional CAP.

Important dates in the evolution of the CAP are given in Table 9.3.

The MacSharry reforms of 1992

MacSharry sounded the alarm in 'The development and future of the Common Agricultural Policy', the published version of the papers COM (91) 100 and COM (91) 258. Although more radical than what had gone before, the reforms, which were adopted on 21 May 1992, upheld the fundamental principles – single prices, Community preference and financial solidarity. They therefore fell well short of what academic authorities and, especially in Britain, political groups were demanding, up to and including the repatriation of the CAP.[7]

The internal pressures for major reform coincided with the attack mounted on the CAP in the Uruguay Round of trade negotiations. Spokesmen for the Commission and some Member States maintained unconvincingly that the Community was acting autonomously and not caving in to pressure. The Community's position deserves to be stated in its own words:[8]

In deciding on the reform, the Council followed the three main guidelines laid down by the Commission:

- a substantial reduction in the prices of agricultural products to make them more competitive both within the Community and elsewhere;
- full and ongoing compensation for this reduction through compensatory amounts or premiums not related to the quantities produced;
- implementation of measures to limit the use of the factors of production (set-aside of arable land, number of animals per hectare of forage area, etc.) alongside the retention of more drastic rules, such as quotas.

At the same time, the Council decided to strengthen measures designed to protect the environment or improve links between agricultural activities and the protection of nature and the countryside, encourage certain categories of elderly farmers to cease farming and to transfer their land to other holdings and promote the use of agricultural land for other purposes such as forestry or leisure activities.

These decisions constitute major changes:

- First of all, support for the agricultural sector will no longer be provided solely or mainly through price support but also through assistance to producers in the form of compensatory payments or premiums.
- The Community, which is self-sufficient in the main agricultural foodstuff products, no longer needs to seek increased production except to the extent that an outlet can be found for surpluses.
- As the foremost world agricultural trader, the Community, by changing its rules, is stating its willingness to join the movement towards freer trade advocated at international level while preserving the basic principles and instruments of the CAP.

The generic word is 'decoupling'. Community support for its farmers would not be related to the quantity of their production. Correspondingly, units of output would not be directly subsidised. Domestic and international preoccupations would be answered at a stroke. The 1992 reforms, paralleling the 'Blair House' agreement on agriculture of November 1992, marked the way forward to the final act of the Uruguay Round, on which the Council pronounced itself as follows:[9]

> The European Union had two main objectives for agriculture: to achieve a better balance between supply and demand on world agricultural markets and to ensure that the results of the Uruguay Round were compatible with the machinery of the reformed common agricultural policy.[10]

The Blair House agreement subsequently underwent various clarifications. The [GATT/WTO] Agreement on Agriculture provides for the first time for the liberalisation of trade in agricultural products and the commitments cover market access, the gradual reduction of production support and also the observance of export disciplines. The lowering of customs duties will be spread over a period of six years for industrialised countries including the European Union (36% reduction) and ten years for developing countries (24% reduction). The industrialised countries also agreed to lower the level of their export subsidies to 36% in six years and to reduce the volume of subsidised exports by 21% over the same period. The 'peace clause' under which the participants must abstain from applying countervailing duties to their partners, will remain in force until 2003.

Enlargement

But there was not much peace for the CAP. In December 1995 the European Council meeting in Madrid confirmed that negotiations for the accession of new members would begin within six months of the conclusion of the 1996–97 Inter-governmental Conference. That conference carefully kept off CAP reform. Some Member States did not want it, considering that their farmers had 'suffered' enough. Others did not want to pursue reform in an IGC where unanimity is required and would not be available. In July 1997 the Commission produced 'Agenda 2000', its account of what the Union must do to put itself in shape for enlargement. The Commission expected (p. 15) that up to 2006 (see Tables 9.4 and 9.5) the strengthening and widening of the Union could occur without an increase in the available budgetary resources (1.27% of GNP). It proposed a further stage of price reduction for cereals, with some compensatory direct aids, a reduction in market support for beef, with some compensation in direct payments, and no major change for dairy products. 'However, dairy farmers should not be given the impression that the present system, with its intrinsic rigidities, can last for ever . . .' (pp. 29–31).

Table 9.4   Overview of the new financial framework 2000–2006 (1997 prices (ECU billions))

Appropriations for commitment	1999	2000	2001	2002	2003	2004	2005	2006
Agriculture (guideline)	43.3	44.1	45.0	46.1	47.0	48.0	49.0	50.0
Structural operations	36.1	35.2	36.0	38.8	39.8	40.7	41.7	42.8
of which: past adjustments	1.8							
Internal policies	6.1	6.1	6.4	7.3	7.5	7.7	7.9	8.1
External action	6.6	6.6	6.8	7.0	7.1	7.3	7.5	7.6
Administration	4.5	4.5	4.6	5.1	5.2	5.3	5.4	5.5
Reserves	1.2	1.0	1.0	0.8	0.5	0.5	0.5	0.5
Appropriations for commitments – Total	97.8	97.5	99.8	105.1	107.1	109.5	112.0	114.5
Appropriations for payments – Total	92.5	94.1	96.6	101.1	103.9	106.5	108.9	111.4
Appropriations for payments (as percentage of GNP)	1.25	1.24	1.24	1.22	1.22	1.22	1.22	1.22
Margin	0.02	0.03	0.03	0.05	0.05	0.05	0.05	0.05
Own resources ceiling	1.27	1.27	1.27	1.27	1.27	1.27	1.27	1.27

Table 9.5   Agricultural expenditure (current prices (ECU billions))

	1999	2000	2001	2002	2003	2004	2005	2006
Guideline (current prices)[1]	45.0	46.7	48.5	50.6	52.6	54.7	56.9	59.2
Agricultural expenditure (current prices)		44.0	45.9	49.7	52.1	53.2	53.9	54.5
Community of 15								
Reformed CAP	41.7	41.6	43.4	45.4	47.3	47.9	47.9	47.9
New rural development accompanying measures and horizontal fisheries measures		1.9	2.0	2.0	2.0	2.0	2.1	2.1
New Member States								
CAP (market measures)		0.0	0.0	1.1	1.2	1.2	1.3	1.4
Specific rural development accompanying measures		0.0	0.0	0.6	1.0	1.5	2.0	2.5
Pre-accession aid[2]		0.5	0.5	0.6	0.6	0.6	0.6	0.6
Margin		*2.7*	*2.6*	*0.9*	*0.5*	*1.5*	*3.0*	*4.7*

[1] Assumed 2% deflator per year from 1999 to 2006
[2] Equal to ECU 500 million at constant 1997 prices

The pre-Agenda 2000

Push became shove when the Commission set out its 1998 price proposals, envisaging reductions in support prices for beef of 30%, cereals 20% and milk 10%. The Agricultural Council was not amused, with opposition led by CDU-CSU Germany, the free social market with an unenviable reputation for agricultural illiberalism engendered by CSU strength in Bavaria. The 1998 agricultural price-fixing and associated measures, concluded at the end of the British Presidency, showed little progress towards Agenda 2000 objectives (see Tables 9.6 and 9.7). In May 1998, the Agricultural Council got as far as establishing the key issues it had to address:

> the necessity[11] and the appropriate time-scale for adjustment of support prices; the appropriate nature of compensation for price support cuts; the rules according to which Member States' discretion (for example, in modulating payments) should be exercised with regard to agricultural support; the role of production controls within the reformed CAP, for example, milk quotas; the promotion of the development of the rural economy and the rural environment including multifunctional agriculture, the degree of subsidiarity and simplification appropriate to these measures and the extent of the mechanisms and resources required; the appropriate balance of support between production sectors, producers and regions.[12]

All of which is a vast undertaking. Further steep price reductions for beef, cereals and milk proposed for the 1999 seasons became tied up with the hesitant negotiation of budgetary reform – including 'co-financing', a Commission suggestion (October 1998) that 25% of CAP cost should be transferred from the Community budget to national budgets. The 1999 proposals provoked militant demonstrations in Brussels in February, as ministers settled down to one of their marathons. When Agricultural ministers had concluded they had substantially reduced guaranteed prices for beef, cereals and milk products but at the uncovenanted cost of increasing the agricultural budget by approximately 5 billion euros. This could only further complicate the overall negotiations in the framework of 'Agenda 2000'.[13] The agreement reached encompassed the following elements:

- reform of the arable crops sector
- reform of the beef and veal sector
- reform of the milk sector
- reform of the wine sector
- reform of the rules applying to rural development support
- horizontal measures

although it was also admitted that these reforms were part of the 'Agenda 2000' package and that, therefore, agreement on the reforms depended on agreement on the 2000 package.

Table 9.6   EAGGF Guarantee Section expenditure as a percentage of Union expenditure 1988–1996 (% of actual expenditure)

Year	%	Year	%	Year	%
1988	64.2	1991	57.8	1994	55.0
1989	59.7	1992	53.2	1995	51.7
1990	58.0	1993	53.8	1996	50.5

Table 9.7   1998 Common Agricultural Budget

Item	ECU (millions)	Item	ECU (millions)
Arable farming	26,503	*Plant Products*	
Livestock	10,742	Cereals	17,255
Ancillary expenditure	909	Olive oil	2,256
Income aid	3	Fruit and vegetables	1,921
Accompanying measures	2,280	Sugar	1,674
		Tobacco	995
Animal Products		Wine	806
Beef	5,786	Others	1,596
Milk	2,976		
Sheep and goats	1,413		
Others	567		

World Trade Organisation

Aside from the accession of Eastern European countries with large agricultural sectors, the Community faced two other incursions into its agricultural support policies.[14]

The World Trade Organisation (WTO), set up at the conclusion of the Uruguay Round, had programmed a new cycle of negotiations on agricultural trade. After some hesitation the USA made this a fixture in the State of the Union address in February 1999. The CAP would once again be a target. Other exporting countries could take heart from statements by MacSharry's successor, the Austrian Franz Fischler. He had frequently said that it must be the Community's objective to raise competitiveness to the point where the Community could export without subsidy.

Renewed financial frameworks

The year 1999 was also the point at which the Council and the European Parliament needed to negotiate a new agreement on Community expenditure 2000–2006. With resources constrained and other desirable objectives of expenditure at home and abroad being canvassed, farm spending would again be targeted as part of a very large package, spreading across several Council formations.

Fraud

In an operation of the size and complexity of managing the Community agricultural market, it would be utopian to expect unqualified regularity and integrity. Some waste is politically driven, such as the encouragement given to the growing of tobacco. Some is intrinsic to the control mechanisms, such as subsidising olive-tree cultivation, whether each single tree produces olives or not. Some is forecasting error, such as overcompensating cereal growers for their 1986–87 crop when world prices unexpectedly held. Some is fraud. Fraud was usually estimated to cost some 6 billion ECUs annually. Recoveries are low. From 1994 agricultural expenditure, the Commission recovered from Member States 308 million ECUs improperly paid.[15] The Member States, as custodians of their citizens' payments, continually upbraid the Commission for inadequate control. It in turn contends that most of the fraud occurs in Member States' administration of the support schemes. It counter-demands that controls which Member States apply to the disbursement of Community funds should be at least as rigorous as the disciplines applied to their own public spending. The Audit Court, a Community institution, highlights fraud in its annual and special report and for the third consecutive year was unable to certify that, in the Commission's 1996 accounts, expenditure had been properly authorised. This was one of the factors which contributed to the Santer Commission's downfall in March 1999.

The bastion of Council authority

The decision-making process in Community agriculture differs from the model of other policy areas. The common feature is the Commission's sole right of initiative. Downstream from that, there is less parliamentary involvement than is becoming established elsewhere. As was the case with all legislation, the European Parliament is in the main only *consulted* on agricultural measures and its opinion is not binding. This is of a piece with the inter-institutional division of budgetary authority. The Council has steadily declined to allow the European Parliament to have the say on farm spending. The only ultimate weapon in the Parliament's hands is to reject the whole budget if it disapproves so strongly of the farm section that it will face up to the consequences.

The general textbook rule, now revised in the redistribution of powers, is that the Commission proposes and the Council decides. In the common organisation of markets, the Commission *decides*, after *consulting* the Member States in the Management Committees.[16] This dialogue produces a daily tide of Commission regulation, which in terms of pages of print is the bulk of Community legislation. The huge volume of individual decisions on running each of the markets has to be taken in real time and are market sensitive. The only scrutiny possible is by experts of the Member States. Disagreement between them and the Commission is extremely rare. The system gives rise to crude statistics of laws passed which are unfairly evoked by critics to show that 'Brussels' is a prolific bureaucratic law-maker beyond control.

THE COMMON FISHERIES POLICY

The Common Fisheries Policy (CFP) is a branch of the Common Agricultural Policy – by virtue of Article 3 of the Treaty establishing the European Community, as amended by the Treaty on Union and Article 32 (ex-38).[17]

'The Prisoner's Dilemma'

The control of fishing is a classic case of the Prisoner's Dilemma.[18] Since overall there are not enough fish to go round[19] the fishing countries must accept some restriction. Restriction will be effective only if each participant believes that all the others will play the game. If they do not, the restricting country is making a gift to the others. Similarly, the individual fisherman who sticks to the rules may be passing up an advantage if the others are not complying.

It is hardly surprising that the CFP has been widely pilloried within Britain, particularly in the last two or three years, and cited as another example of Brussels' ineptitude and its prejudice against British interests.[20]

Rationale

A Common Fisheries Policy was perceived to be necessary when (i) some stocks were threatened with exhaustion through over-fishing, and (ii) Member States extended their jurisdiction over the sea to 200 miles, as all those with coastlines had done in 1977.

The first meant that there was a common interest in restricting certain catches. The second meant that some traditional fisheries were placed in 'foreign' waters. Therefore within the overall restriction there had to be multiple bargaining involving fishing areas and fish species to uphold 'rights' quasi-sanctioned by history. Ministers responsible for agreeing on the catch limits and the share-out of catches had to reconcile the estimates of diminishing supply with the vociferous demands of their fishermen for a livelihood in the practice of their dangerous calling. Ministers usually did so at both ends. First, by disregarding the mathematically based forecasts of the size of future fish stocks; second by compromising on their opening bids for a share of what they now declared to be on offer.

There is no other product, industrial or agricultural, of which there can be said to be a shortage of supply on the Community Market.[21] All other pressures on employment opportunities in the Union arise from situations of internal or world surplus production, including substitutes.

Economic significance

The Community is a large importer of fish, some 8 billion ECUs annually. Exports are around 2 billion. The fleet comprises around 100,000 vessels, with a tonnage of around 2 million. Total catches are around 7 million metric tonnes, which is roughly 7% of world catches. There are about a quarter of a million fishermen with about four times as many employed on shore.

Britain has a longstanding grievance: the first CFP was hastily composed on the eve of British entry into the Community. After some years of piecemeal development, the CFP was recodified and strengthened in 1983. The reformed policy was given a period of stability, without further major change, up to 2002, when it was due to be reconsidered. It had to be adapted following the secession of Greenland from the Community in 1985. An agreement was reached with Greenland for continuing fishing opportunities in return for tariff-free access to the Community for Greenland fish and an annual payment of over 30 million ECUs from the Community budget. It was further adapted with the membership of Spain and Portugal in 1986, by virtue of which Community fishing capacity was increased by 75%, the tonnage of fishing vessels rose by 65% and fish consumption rose by 45%.

The Iberian Accession Treaties placed limitations on fishing in the sensitive zones up to 2002. When Sweden joined the Union in 1995, the end of the restriction was brought forward to 1995. There would otherwise have been flagrant discrimination (and Spain might have vetoed the enlargement).

Controls

The instruments of the controls are numerous. Every year the Commission proposes for most stocks and most areas (other than the Mediterranean) Total Allowable Catches (TACs). They are based on the outcomes of the deliberations of international bodies set up to regulate fishing (such as the North Atlantic Fisheries Organisation, otherwise NAFO) and the work of the number-crunching experts in the Member States whom the

Commission consults. Fisheries ministers habitually add a margin for political requirements. The TACs are published annually, usually in the December edition of the *Bulletin
of the European Union* (OOP). The TACs are divided up among the Member States with
traditional or legal rights according to a percentage agreed after much pain in 1983 (later
adjusted as above). A coastal band is reserved for fishermen from the coastal communities. This was a cherished British objective, argued for social reasons. It is regarded as a
derogation from the principle of common waters. In the 2002 revision of the Common
Fisheries Policy it has already been stipulated that there will be free access to all waters
unless the Council changes its mind. There is no requirement that catches should be
landed in the vessel's homeport or state of registration. When the Soviet Union had a
major fishing fleet, much Community-caught fish went 'Klondyking' to Soviet factories
moored near the fishing grounds.

The control difficulties are obvious. Who checks that the national share is not
exceeded? In principle, fisheries inspectors, but the Prisoner's Dilemma presents itself
again.[22] The Member States do not allow Community Inspectors, of whom there are
about twenty, to inspect landings, or indeed catchings. They inspect national inspectors
only. Some fish are caught accidentally in the course of fishing for other species. This is
the 'by-catch' which may be a substantial quantity of a species under TAC control but
eluding it.

Since 1983, fishing vessels require a licence. This is supposed to control the size of the
fleet, but the fleet has not significantly diminished.

Immature fish are protected from catches by regulations relating to the size of the
mesh in the nets. The regulations are enforced by inspectors at home-ports and aboard
fishery protection vessels. There is satellite surveillance of the whereabouts of fishing
vessels. Accosting vessels at sea in boisterous weather conditions for inspection of the
nets that captains are using is not a straightforward task if the captains do not want to be
inspected.

Some techniques of fishing are banned in particular areas. One of the more controversial is drift netting in which a large hanging circle of net is paid out and then closed,
pulling in everything swimming in the enclosed waters, including dolphins. It was
banned in the tuna fishing areas in 1998.

'Quota-hopping'

With the future of their business uncertain or worse, a number of British owners
decided in the late 1980s to get out, by selling their vessels and licences, especially to
Dutch and Spanish operators. As nominally British businesses, the new owners acquired
quota rights. 'Quota hopping' caused outrage among surviving British fishermen and
their political champions, as what were thought to be rightfully British fish, stoutly negotiated for, were lost. The British Conservative government sought to amend ownership
by requiring in the Merchant Shipping Act 1988, that there must be a connection
between the place of registration of the vessel and its ownership. This was struck down
by the European Court of Justice as discriminatory.[23] The then British government set

191

itself to obtain a change of Community Law in the Inter-governmental Conference of 1996–97 and put in a memorandum to this effect.[24] The firmness of its resolve was not tested. The Labour government that took office in May 1997 did not pursue a change in Community Law. Mr Blair, the Prime Minister, announced enigmatically after the first meeting of the European Council which he attended in Amsterdam in June 1997 that the Commission had said or done helpful things on the subject of quota-hopping. Whatever the helpful things were, they did not stop or limit the practice. A subsequent development was a ruling in the British courts that the government was liable for damages for the loss of earnings for the vessels which had been kept off the fishing grounds under the 1988 Act.

Organisation of the market

The market organisation in fish is modest compared with the rest of the CAP.[25] There are guide prices for certain species and compensation for withdrawal from auction if the price is not realised. Withdrawal is a rarity: in 1992, 50,000 tonnes in total landings of 7 million. There are also minimum prices for imports of certain species. The annual details are published in the December issue of the *Bulletin of the European Union* – if they are agreed to by then. There are regulations setting out the minimum quality standards for fish and fish products, governing size, weight, packaging and labelling. The Community encourages the formation of marketing co-operatives to micro-manage their own local market.

Community funds had been available under different schemes for the modernisation and preferably contraction of the fishing fleet. The Financial Instrument for Fisheries Guidance (FIFG) is covered by a budget entry of 36 million ECUs (1997). There is additional budgetary provision of around 750 million ECUs for fisheries measures.

Mediterranean

The Mediterranean fisheries are not subject to TACs and area controls for the simple reason that any attempt to define Community zones would have led headlong into conflict with non-member coastal states. According to rough estimates, the Mediterranean accounts for some 15% by weight of CFP catches. The real problem of the Mediterranean waters of the Community is not fishing but the preservation of tourist assets, coupled with the protection of the coastal environment.

Third country agreements

As home to one of the world's biggest fishing fleets, the Community has global fishing interests. It has concluded some thirty agreements with third countries to secure access to their fishing grounds. The most significant – and, in negotiation, troublesome – is with Morocco. The Community pays Morocco over 100 million Euros a year and gives preference to Moroccan tinned sardines. In return over 700 trawlers fish in Moroccan waters.

In its 'first-generation' agreements with other countries, the Community usually negotiated an annual fee along with other inducements. In 'second-generation' agreements, of which the first was with Argentina in 1992, the accent shifted to mutual development and co-operation in the conservation of stocks and in scientific research as well as in 'co-enterprise' between Community and Argentinean ship owners. The Community undertook to provide financing of 28 million Euros in return for fishing rights for 70 vessels and 250,000 tonnes of fish annually. New or renewed agreements are on the same lines.

Outlook

There is no way to reconcile the immediate interest of the Community fishing fleet and long-term sustainable stocks. This can only mean continuing political trouble domestically and between governments of Member States. This can produce the miserable spectacle of naval fishery protection vessels firing warning shots over the bows of trawlers from the other Member States that they believe to be poaching. As in the past, fishermen's patience will be periodically exhausted and they will carpet the street outside the Council building in Brussels with selections from their recent inadequate catches. The applicants from the coastal CEECs are signalling that they have fishing interests that will require to be accommodated in their accession negotiations. The communities enjoying the derogation of a reserved coastal band may face new competitors in what they have regarded as home waters. Many Community policies are unpopular, but few are so divisive. Insult is added to injury insofar as the rules are imposed by Regulations, which have direct effect and are not debated in national parliaments.

THE COMMON COMMERCIAL POLICY[26]

External economic relations, including aid to development.

The theoretical starting point

The economic theory that underlies the Commercial Policy of the European Community is that of free trade. It is the antithesis of trade protection and of mercantilism. Protection is the safeguarding of domestic enterprise by keeping out or cutting down imports of over-competitive goods and services; mercantilism is the exclusive exploitation of foreign markets by superior powers that own or otherwise dominate them. The theories of trade and comparative advantage are amply explained in the standard textbooks. Samuelson, more recently Piggott and Cook and from a different standpoint, Porter,[27] are as good guides as any. Although the Treaties do not say so, membership of the Community/Union presupposes: 'the existence of a functioning market economy as well as the capacity to cope with competitive pressure and market forces within the Union'.[28] There is some controversy whether the Community, by pursuing privileged trade relations with selected third countries, may be hindering the cause of global trade liberalisation. There is no dispute that the external impact of its Common Agricultural Policy flatly contradicts its trade policy.

The core Customs Union

The Common Commercial Policy (CCP) is the third and last of the policies labelled 'common' in the first version of the Treaty establishing the European Community.

Countries which have made a customs union among themselves, with a common tariff, own it collectively and are not individually free to vary customs duties.[29] They can only do so by agreement between them. It is also normal for the procedure for initiating their common action to begin with a Commission proposal, in the characteristic 'Community method', colloquially, and now inaccurately: Commission proposes, Council decides.

But it is less obvious that the Commission should also have the responsibility for acting on the Council's decision, and for representing the Member States in commercial policy negotiations with other countries, bilaterally or multilaterally. It would have been entirely possible for the Council to decide that it should be represented by itself – for convenience perhaps by a small executive panel of its members (e.g. the Troika which came along with Political Co-operation)), or, by analogy with later developments in working methods, by its Presidency.

In the context of 1955 and the building blocks of integration, the Commission was the logical and at that time formally designated 'supranational' body to act for the Council externally. There was also a precedent in the Treaty establishing the Coal and Steel Community. Although it does not establish a customs union but a Common Market,[30] the transitional provisions attached to the Treaty provided in Section 14 that in negotiations with third countries the High Authority would act for the Member States jointly, on their unanimously agreed instructions. On this basis the High Authority negotiated and was a party to *and* signatory of the Agreement concerning relations between the United Kingdom and the European Coal and Steel Community signed on 21 December 1954.

Negotiations

The division of functions is laid down in Article 133 (ex-113), EC. The Commission recommends to the Council the opening of negotiations with a third country. The Council adopts a 'directive',[31] by majority vote, which it addresses to the Commission. No involvement of the European Parliament is provided for in the Article. The Commission negotiates in accordance with the directive (seeking and obtaining its amendment if necessary) and initials the resulting treaty text, confirming its authenticity. The Council then concludes the agreement, authorises signature and brings the provisions into effect. Nowadays coal and steel products are *de facto* included in Article 133 negotiations, without separate procedure apart from the correct internal formalities. (Unless the Community wants to keep them out, as it did in the Europe agreement with Poland.)

EP involvement

By today's standards, the exclusion of the European Parliament from the process is striking. The historical explanation is that national parliaments were not customarily involved in trade negotiations. Under pressure, the Council agreed that it would informally and confidentially inform the Parliament of the negotiating directive; keep it informed of the negotiations and ask its non-binding opinion on 'significant' agreements, prior to signature (Luns/Westerterp procedure). This undertaking has given the EP moral rights, which have not been translated into Treaty terms in the two IGCs.[32] The EP strengthened its hand in its 'Code of Conduct' with the Commission. The Commission agreed to inform the EP of its recommendation for negotiations and to keep it informed of the course of negotiations.[33]

In the negotiations, the Commission is the sole representative and spokesman of the Council. Delegates of the Member States may participate as observers and usually do. This keeps the Council in touch with the negotiations and enables the Commission to concert itself with Member State representatives when it needs their advice.[34]

Euratom

The Treaty establishing the European Atomic Energy Community gives the Commission a bigger role. It therefore negotiates and *concludes* agreements with third countries and international organisations, subject to approval by the Council, acting by qualified majority. Again there is no role in the Treaty for the European Parliament. In their day there were important and still valid agreements on Euratom affairs. New additions are rare.

Pre-zero commitments

Prior to membership of the EC, Member States had trade agreements, otherwise known as Trade and Navigation agreements, or Treaties of Friendship, in their own names. Where the provisions were not superseded by the CCP or did not intrude upon its application, they have been tacitly extended if the parties so wish. Some third countries wanted to conclude early agreements with the Community, which made itself available. The first was with Iran in October 1963. It expired in 1974. This and some other agreements anticipated the full applicability of Article 113, which came at the end of the transitional period in 1970.[35] Even then, the CCP was not fully applied to the countries of the Soviet bloc, with which, at the latter's choice, the Community had officially no relations. It was extended to them, without material effect in 1974. Later developments are discussed below.

Bilateral non-preferential agreements

Bilateral trade agreements under Article 113 (now 133) were concluded with the Argentine Republic (1971), Uruguay (1972), Yugoslavia and Brazil (1973), Mexico (1975) and, with more political significance, China in 1978. Since the Community's trade relations with these countries, other than China, are governed by the GATT/WTO, the agreements serve limited purposes, whilst involving time-consuming work and travel. This limited kind of agreement, which was a symbol of a friendly relationship, has largely gone out of fashion. As the Community has extended its own activities, and as pressures have developed within the Member States, new non-preferential trade agreements have been expanded into Co-operation agreements, or Framework agreements. The purely trade provisions are largely formal, but the Community undertakes to co-operate with the other party in pursuing trade liberalisation, in upholding democracy and respect for human rights, in creating conditions for investment and in scientific research, education and culture and in conducting a political dialogue. The modern kind of agreement institutionalises discussion between the parties, which gives each side the opportunity to present its shopping lists. But such 'mixed' agreements also give rise to problems of leadership divide between the Commission, the actor under Art 133, and the member states, upholding their national competence, albeit collectively.

So far as trade relations are concerned, bilateral non-preferential agreements usually contain not much more than a most-favoured-nation (MFN) clause, declarations in favour of mutually advantageous trade and the arrangements for periodic discussion of developments. The MFN clause is a formality since the Common Tariff has only one column (unlike the US Tariff, which is split, giving political headaches).

Preferential agreements

Of far greater economic and political importance are the *preferential* agreements, which the Community concludes. They do not rest on Article 133 but on Article 300 (ex-228). Known as the Association article, although the word does not occur in the text, it has greatly evolved.

Agreements under Article 300 go beyond trade relations and into other forms of co-operation including development aid. They are concluded (following a negotiating procedure similar to those described for Article 133) only after the European Parliament has given its *assent*. The EP cannot amend the agreement, when laid before it, only approve or reject it. It can and does use the prospect of rejection to incite the Council to reopen the negotiation.

Lomé

The Preamble to the EEC Treaty states the founder members' intention to confirm the 'solidarity which binds Europe and the overseas countries'. This referred to members' African colonies or ex-colonies, which had had privileged trade relations with their metropoles. In 1963 the Community concluded an agreement, the *Yaounde* Convention, with eighteen African and Malagasay states. Mauritius joined in 1973. In 1971 the three British ex-colonies of Kenya, Uganda and Tanzania concluded the separate *Arusha* agreement with the Community. It never entered into force because ratification was not completed. It was overtaken by the effect given to Protocol 22 of the Treaty concerning the Accession of the UK to the Community in 1973, entitled: 'On relations between the EEC and the Associated African and Malagasay States and also the independent developing Commonwealth countries situated in Africa, the Indian Ocean, the Pacific Ocean and the Caribbean.' Yaounde was renegotiated with a wider membership of ex-British colonies, resulting in the first five-year *Lomé* Convention of 1975, with originally forty-four (now seventy-one) A(frican) C(aribbean) P(acific) members.

The Lomé Convention, renewed at five- and, later, ten-year intervals, provides for free trade between the ACP parties and the Community, but the former are authorised to maintain duties and import restrictions required for their budget and economic development. They do so. The text doubtfully satisfied the GATT requirement that free trade must be reciprocal. It had been a British objective in the internal Community preparations to ensure that reciprocity would be a dead-letter.[36] Ninety-nine per cent of ACP products enter the Community duty-free. The agreement also provides for aid, to be disbursed from the Community's European Development Fund, exclusive to Lomé and constituting by far the world's biggest single aid programme (see Table 9.8).

Lomé IV, running from 1990 to 2000, provides 12 billion ECU in grants, soft loans and interest-free subsidies. It has provision for Community funding to stabilise ACP countries' earnings from exports (Stabex) and mining (Sysmin) operations. Countries that violate human rights (e.g. Nigeria) are suspended from benefits. The convention sets up three institutions: a Council of Ministers (debates at large), a Committee of Ambassadors (a workshop) and a Joint Assembly of MEPs and ACP parliamentarians (or diplomats if a parliament is inoperative).

In April 1997 the Republic of South Africa nominally joined the Lomé Convention, but without access to the trade regime, aid, Stabex or Sysmin. Prior to the end of apartheid, South Africa had not been regarded as a developing country. Trade and development co-operation was under separate negotiation with a declared aim of (reciprocal) free trade by 2001. There were some hopes that the agreement could be reached before the end of term of President Mandela, but these were dashed at the Cardiff meeting of the European Council in June 1998. Cuba is to be admitted to the upcoming renegotiations of the Convention, strictly as an observer.

Table 9.8   European Development Fund Disbursements 1996

Country	$m	Country	$m
Ivory Coast	114.6	Mozambique	62.7
Mauritania	111.2	Mali	62.0
Angola	94.5	Uganda	59.7
Ghana	79.8	Jamaica	57.6
Zimbabwe	70.9	Ruanda	56.0
Haiti	67.4	Ethiopia	54.7
Guinea	63.9		

Source: European Commission.

Reappraisal of Lomé

In mid-1997 the Commission set in hand a fundamental reappraisal of the Lomé Convention, which was due to expire on 29 February 2000.[37]

For all the sweeping changes in world politics and economics since 1957, the Community's approach to relations with the ex-colonies of Member States had remained essentially unchanged. The results were described as 'patchy' and the account of them makes depressing reading. The statistical tables show a continuing deterioration in the economic situation of the Lomé group overall. The Commission's Green Paper is too sensitive to draw out that, with the collapse of expansionist Communism, EU Member States' view of the significance of their relations with Africa may have changed. It is also too polite to dwell on the political deterioration in Africa at large. It observes that with the tighter disciplines of the WTO, as compared with the GATT, non-reciprocal preferences and partial free trade areas may be in jeopardy. The annual waiver from WTO rules may not be secure: 'The principle of partnership has lost its substance.' The political dialogue with ACP countries about strengthening democratic institutions has not made much headway and the economic gap between the EU and the ACP group has widened. The ACP share of the EU market fell from 6.7% in 1976 to 2.8% in 1994 (see Tables 9.9 and 9.10). The ACP countries account for 2% of world trade and 1% of international investment flows. Even the notion of the existence of an 'ACP group' is something confined to the Lomé Convention. In Africa alone there are now a series of groups of countries joining together to pursue their common purposes.[38]

Table 9.9   EU imports from ACP–Africa as percentage of total imports

1965	1970	1975	1980	1985	1990	1995	1997
11	9	8.5	8.4	8.4	5.5	4	4

Source: Eurostat

Table 9.10   ACP: percentage share of EC trade

	EC imports	EC exports
1988	4.5	4.3
1989	3.9	4.1
1990	4.4	4.4
1991	3.6	3.8
1992	3.3	4.0
1993	2.7	3.0
1994	3.1	2.8
1995	3.3	3.1
1996	3.4	3.0
1997	3.0	2.8

Source: Based on Eurostat.

The Green Paper reaches no conclusions. It rehearses a number of options. Apart from a new political dialogue, encouraging respect for human rights and introducing conflict prevention measures and from improved targeting and management of aid, it envisages 'differentiation' among the group according to each member's needs and capabilities. On the trade side it looks at the pros and cons of reciprocity, and of reciprocity with differentiation. A more radical option is to take trade concessions out of Lome altogether and replace them by the extension of the Generalised System of Preferences (GSP) (see below).

The outcome of the debate which the Green Paper inspired was the decision to encourage the ACP countries to form regional free trade groupings (by 2005), to which the EU would accede (between 2005 and 2015). The least-developed ACP countries would in any case retain their preferences in the Community market up to 2004, when the Generalised System of Preferences is to be reviewed. Negotiations began early in 1999.

Generalised System of Preferences

The Generalised System of Preferences (GSP) is a departure from the basic rule of the GATT/WTO that signatories may not discriminate against other signatories. All must be treated as the most favoured nation. In Geneva jargon, trade measures are *erga omnes,* and despite sustained US opposition pre-existing preferences were 'grandfathered' and allowed to continue, although losing their relative value as tariffs were cut.

In the 1960s, alongside the growing concern for the plight of the Third World, there were discussions in the GATT about the possibility of the iron rule being modified to the extent of authorising trade preferences in favour of developing countries. A basis was provided by the negotiation of a new Part 4 of the GATT. The case for globalised preference was strengthened by the preferential agreements, which the EEC was negotiating or contemplating. They took liberties with the MFN rule and it needed to be adjusted.

In 1971, in the light of discussions in the United Nations Conference on Trade and Development (UNCTAD), in its heyday the great North–South arena, the Community began to establish generalised preference. Unlike the preferences in Agreements, GSP is non-contractual, for which the jargon word is autonomous. The Community gives and the Community can take away. In the first version, preference took the form of tariff quotas, allocated beneficiary by beneficiary. When the quota is filled, the full rate of duty is applicable. Each country awarding preference decides for itself the list of beneficiaries, the list of benefiting products and the scale of the quotas. In 1994 the system was changed. The emphasis was shifted from the country of origin of the goods to consideration of the effects on Community producers. Quotas were replaced by tariff reductions.

The industrial product par excellence – textiles

Initially, preferences were given for industrial goods, and their effects were limited accordingly. Over time, some agricultural produce was admitted. The industrial product for which several of the developing countries might have had a competitive advantage was textiles. Along with other importers, the Community had inherited from its Member States restrictions on textile imports to protect their once powerful home industries, now in decline. They did so at first bilaterally, later with GATT cover in the 'Long Term Agreement', which was succeeded by the MultiFibre Arrangement, due to terminate in 2005. Countries that signed up to the disciplines of the LTA/MFA were able to obtain Community tariff preferences on a proportion of their textile exports. The GSP was not intended to reduce consumer prices. The waived duty element was expected to accrue to exporters. At least part of it customarily found its way into importers' margins.

In the new GSP adopted on 19 December 1994, the Community made the enjoyment of the benefits contingent on respect for human rights. This was the first expression of policy[39] that it now adheres to in its external relations generally. It can be awkward. It proved impossible to negotiate an agreement with a human rights clause with Australia in 1997. It survived as a Joint Declaration, with references to a shared insistence on human rights.[40]

Although the USA had argued that the EEC's contractual preference under the Yaounde agreement should be cancelled when GSP came in, the Community maintained both and was undeterred from extending its contractual arrangements. GSP gave it a means of strengthening its commercial relations with the ex-colonies or imperial territories that did not join the Lomé Convention. How this was done is described below.

Mediterranean

Another area of contractual preferential agreements is with the Community's Mediterranean neighbours.

When the EEC Treaty came into force, Algeria was still a *département* of France although on the brink of civil war. It was recognised as an independent republic in 1962. France had special historical trade relations with Morocco and Tunisia. These were replaced in 1969 by Community Association agreements. In 1963 Turkey concluded an Association Agreement with the Community. At that time, association agreements under Article 228 were looked on as a prelude to full membership. (Greece had also concluded an Association Agreement in 1961. It was frozen during the dictatorship of the colonels in 1967–74. After the restoration of democracy the agreement was the starting point for the negotiations leading to Greek accession in 1981.)

In 1970 a preferential agreement was signed with Spain, which had asked for association in 1962. Simultaneously, at the insistence of the Netherlands, which was cool towards Falangist Spain, a preferential agreement was signed with Israel. In 1972 it was the turn of Egypt, Cyprus and Lebanon. The last named did not come into force.

With France and Italy vitally concerned about conditions on the Mediterranean littoral, the piecemeal arrangements that were emerging were found unsatisfactory. The Community accordingly adopted its 'Overall Mediterranean Policy'. It set out to conclude agreements with all Mediterranean countries, as associations, except in the case of Israel (1975) which was a trade agreement, developing later into an association and later still into a free trade area. The other agreements (Malta 1976, replacing the 1970 trade agreement; Algeria, Morocco, Tunisia otherwise 'Maghreb', 1976; Egypt, Jordan, Syria, otherwise 'Mashraq', 1977; Lebanon 1977) gave the Mediterranean countries tariff preferences, some of them seasonal, and established annual financial protocols as the vehicle for Community aid, in this case from the general budget not, as in Lomé, from the unbudgeted European Development Fund. The agreements gave the partner countries access to the European Investment Bank.

The accession of Spain and Portugal to the European Community in 1986 gave new impetus to the Mediterranean relationship. A highpoint came in 1995 with the convening of the Barcelona Conference in which the Community met Algeria, Cyprus, Egypt, Israel, Jordan, Lebanon, Malta, Morocco, the Palestinian Authority, Syria, Tunisia and Turkey. On the trade side, the conference adopted a target of a Free Trade Area by 2001. This launched a new round of bilateral negotiations and new agreements with Morocco and Tunisia (1995), Lebanon and the Palestinian Authority (although it is not a state, 1996). Descending from an old agreement with Yugoslavia there was also a new non-preferential agreement with FYROM (1996). The Mediterranean initiative faltered under the strains of the Middle East Peace Process, but recovered some ground at a conference in Palermo in June 1998.

Membership of the EC/EU

The Mediterranean houses countries that may become members of the Union. In 1987 Morocco applied to join the European Community. Since Morocco is not a European country its application could not be entertained under the relevant article, (then 237 EC, later Article O, TEU, now Article 49 of the Consolidated version of the Treaty on European Union). The Association Agreements with Cyprus and with Malta are preparatory to membership. Both applied in 1990. Malta withdrew in November 1996 following a change of government, but after another change revived its candidacy. Cyprus is among the countries with which enlargement negotiations opened in 1998. The shadow of division hangs over the slow-moving negotiations.

In 1996 Turkey entered the Community's customs union. Its application to join the European Union has been on the Council's table since 1987, making slow progress in the face of the several obstacles, including Turkey's role in divided Cyprus and other frictions with Greece. Even the progression to the customs union was delayed when Turkey arrested prominent political dissidents.

The EU's global network of agreements can be seen in Box 9.2.

Euro-Arab relations

When in the 1970s the Community was focusing on its relations with Mediterranean countries and consolidating trade preferences for them, the USA took some alarm. Its settled policy is to oppose preference, unless it complies squarely with GATT rules: the coverage must be comprehensive and the deal must be reciprocal. In the informal Casey/Soames understanding of the time, the Community said that its interest was in countries on the Mediterranean coastline, plus Jordan. For it to push further into the Middle East would have set it at odds with US interests in the oil-producing areas.

Box 9.2   The EU's global network of agreements

- Customs union agreements with Turkey, Malta and Cyprus.

- Free trade agreements with individual EFTA neighbours.

- 'Europe' agreements with Central and Eastern European states.

- Lome Convention and preferential agreements with Mediterranean States.

- A series of non-preferential commercial and economic co-operation agreements, for example, with states of Latin America and Asia.

- Special sectoral agreements like those with Third World exporters of textiles and clothing to give them assured access to the Community market.

Euro-Arab dialogue

After the oil shocks of 1973/74 the Community set in train the Euro-Arab dialogue with the objective of improving mutual understanding and providing a meeting place at which co-operation and emerging difficulties could be discussed. As a by-product, the dialogue could help to unify the policy approaches of the Member States of the Community, which had drifted apart in the aftermath of the increases in the price[41] of oil and the Arab oil embargo against the Netherlands and Denmark, suspected of being pro-Israel. The Euro-Arab dialogue suffered from a lack of cohesion and clear purpose – which it would have been difficult to specify – and faltered. The Community sought to make a new start in Luxembourg in 1980 but substance was still lacking. The Community's hostility towards Libya and Syria as supporters of terrorism was among the impediments. The advent of Spain as a Member State, and one with a special relationship with the Arab world, gave some new impetus, especially the holding of a Euro-Arab conference in Paris on 22–23 December 1989 and the project for a Euro-Arab University in Spain.

Already in 1987 the Community was looking for an alternative approach to a better relationship with Arab states. In parallel with the strategy that it adopted in Latin America, it eschewed bilateral arrangements in favour of creating links with regional groupings. It likewise wanted to open political dialogue on Middle East problems. In 1988 it concluded a Co-operation Agreement with the Gulf Co-operation Council (GCC), more formally, the countries party to the Co-operation Council Charter for Gulf Arab States. (Saudi Arabia, United Arab Emirates, Kuwait, Bahrein, Oman and Qatar). The Community proposed and the Gulf States accepted that the agreement should lead to a free trade area. Talks began, but stalled with no present prospect of movement. The Agreement is largely confined to an annual meeting of all the parties at foreign minister level and discussion remains abstract.

Central and Eastern Europe

A second collection of association agreements prefiguring membership has been concluded with the countries of Central and Eastern Europe and the Baltic states, the CEECs[42].

Until the Cold War ended Moscow treated the European Community as at one with the enemy. There were some contacts. It is known that the Vice-Minister of Foreign Trade of every Soviet bloc country except the USSR itself visited Commission HQ in Brussels clandestinely to negotiate technical easements of levies on their agricultural exports. In 1975, Fadeev, the Russian Secretary of the Council for Mutual Economic Assistance (CMEA or Comecon) made overtures to the Community. In response Edmund Wellenstein, the Commission's Dutch Director-General for External Relations, led a small delegation to Moscow for talks. He treated the CMEA warily, giving no impression that its competences were in any way comparable to those of the Commission, or that dialogue (described by an onlooker as dialectic) with Secretary General Fadeev was any substitute for direct relations with the CMEA member countries. The contacts fizzled out. Separately Romania, internally the ultra-Stalinist satellite, broke ranks to conclude a bilateral trade agreement with the Community in 1980. Community trade with the Soviet bloc remained at low levels.

The member states of the Community had pre-EEC treaty relations with the Soviet bloc countries. Since they could not discuss complaints about Community trade policy, their encounters were empty. There was one landmark meeting in the framework of the Franco-Soviet pact in which the French told the USSR that any commercial policy questions would have to be taken up with the Brussels Commission. Some Member States sought to give a semblance of substance to the relationship by negotiating bilateral 'co-operation agreements', which could address technology transfer, licensing, the encouragement of joint ventures, direct investment and other matters not falling within the exclusive competence of the Community (which the Member States did not formally recognise until 1974). There might also be talk of export credits, which came closer to the forbidden domain. The Commission gritted its teeth and tried to encourage the exchange of information among the Member States and with itself. In low-level encounters under Commission auspices spokesmen for the Member States gave little away.

The collapse of the Soviet bloc

With *perestroika* relations could become as normal as is possible between state trading countries and open economies. In 1986 President Gorbachev agreed that Soviet bloc countries could enter into contractual relations with the Community. The way was paved by a joint declaration of the Community and the CMEA. By 1988, a 'first generation' trade agreement (Article 113 at the time) had been concluded with Hungary, followed by Poland (1989), the USSR, Czechoslovakia and Bulgaria (1990), and afresh with Romania (1991). With German unification on 3 October 1990 the former German Democratic Republic became part of the European Community without an accession process.[43]

The Community agreed to liberalise its quantitative restrictions on industrial imports from the CEEC, whilst continuing to restrict agriculture and textiles. The agricultural quotas were tight – in 1997 the Community found itself in internal argument about such matters as an extra lorry load of jam a year from Romania. In 1993 the European Bank for Reconstruction and Development observed that 50% of the exports of the CEECs to the Community were subject to restriction. The turbulence on the European Union's Eastern frontier required something more than trade agreements with limited scope and small effect. In August 1990 the Commission proposed that the Community conclude 'second generation' agreements with some CEECs. They became known as 'Europe Agreements'.[44]

Europe Agreements go further than conventional association agreements. Since the countries concerned are European, association can be a step to membership and this is more or less recognised in the preambles.[45] Europe Agreements are summarised as follows:

> The agreements take as their basis respect for the principles of pluralist democracy, the rule of law and human rights. They provide for the gradual establishment of free trade between each of the countries concerned and the European Community (which dismantles duties faster than its partner) and closer relations in a number of areas of economic activity, stipulating adherence to the principles of the market economy. Special attention is devoted to political dialogue. Co-operation between the parties extends to economic matters, trade, culture and finance.[46]

With support from the Phare[47] programme, Europe Agreements form the core of a pre-accession strategy. Europe Agreements were concluded with the CEECs which stated that they aspired to join the Union, and all of them subsequently applied for membership alongside the bilateral treaties. With the early applicants, the 'Visegrad' countries, Poland, Hungary, the Czech Republic, Slovakia, followed by Estonia, Latvia, Lithuania (ex-USSR, but always treated by the West as occupied rather than belonging), Bulgaria, Romania and Slovenia, the part of the former Yugoslavia which had escaped most of the turmoil of the break-up, the Union established the 'structured dialogue' in which Councils concluded their meetings by meeting their counterparts from these countries to discuss Community business with them. This was the next best thing to admitting them to Council discussion. It was well-intentioned but became sterile, dismissed as the 'structured monologue'. The structured dialogue was wound up when accession negotiations loomed closer and were replaced by the 'European Conference', bringing the Union and the CEEC applicants together twice a year.

Phare

The aid vehicle for Europe Agreements is not annual financial protocols as it is with other associates but the Phare programme. Phare works through country programmes (including Bosnia–Hercegovina). So far as the applicant countries are concerned, Phare prepares them for membership of the Union. The priorities are institution building

(30%) and investment projects (70%). Aid for agriculture is due to be introduced in 2000. Phare funds, analogous to the Structural Funds available to Member States serving to familiarise the applicants with the latter have been available since 1998. By 2000, pre-accession aid is forecast to amount to 3 billion euros annually.[48] The European Investment Bank extended its operations to the CEEC. They have become its biggest external commitment.

The Phare programme has had its share of criticism. Zeal for good financial management can turn into red-tape. There have been stories of highly paid consultancies of questionable value and familiar complaints that the contracts have not been duly shared out among the Member States. Conversely, local management of programmes may be faulty. In the summer of 1998 the Union withdrew part of its assistance to Poland because of dissatisfaction with Polish use of the funds.

The Phare and TACIS programmes (see below) are overseen by the TAIEX (Technical Assistance and Information Exchange) unit of the Commission, which has input into the enlargement negotiations.

The former Soviet Union

The collapse of the Soviet bloc was followed by the break-up of the Soviet Union. It was destabilised by the abortive anti-Gorbachev *putsch of* 19 August 1991. The three Baltic States thereupon proclaimed their independence despite the presence and armed reaction of Soviet internal ministry troops on their territories. They were followed by the other republics. On 1 January 1992 the Soviet Union passed out of existence. The Commonwealth of Independent States (CIS, whose members other than Russia are also known as the New Independent States, or NIS) came into being. It began with the three Slav states: Russian Federation, Belarus and Ukraine, to be joined by Moldova, the Ukraine's and Poland's neighbour; two of the trans-Caucasian republics, Armenia and Azerbaijan; and the five Central Asian republics, Tajikistan, Turkmenistan, Uzbekistan, Kazakhstan and Kyrgyzstan. Georgia was at the time in the grip of civil war but joined later.

The Community's continuing commercial relations with the new independent states rested upon the trade agreement concluded with the USSR in 1980. Most of them wanted to establish their own presence. The Community proceeded to negotiate Partnership and Co-operation Agreements with most of them. In the conventional definition of Europe, Belarus and Ukraine might be considered to be European but none of the CIS is a candidate for membership of the Union.

The individual Partnership and Co-operation Agreements, which are non-preferential, are broadly similar. A political dialogue is established with the partner country, excluding questions of security. There are clauses concerning merchandise trade, movement of capital, establishment of companies and respect for intellectual property. The Union undertakes to assist its partner in its economic reform programme and in the fields of financial services, transport, energy (very important in oil-rich Kazakhstan and Azerbaijan), environmental protection, education and training and R&D. It also assists in the protection of human rights and the construction of democracy. There are provisions to suspend the agreement if the principles of democracy, human rights and the market economy are violated. Because of the width of the Agreements, they are subject to ratification by all the Member States of the Union and to the assent of the European Parliament. The trade provisions are brought into force in anticipation on the basis of a Council decision that does not require ratification.

Partnership and Co-operation Agreements have been negotiated with Armenia, Azerbaijan, Belarus, Georgia, Kazakhstan, Kyrgyzstan, Moldova, Russian Federation, Turkmenistan, Ukraine and Uzbekistan. Albania, not ex-USSR, also has one. Because of the unsettled conditions in Tajikistan, no agreement was contemplated. In September 1997, the Council decided that because of the failure of the Belarusian authorities to respect democratic principles, the European Communities and the Member States would not conclude the interim trade agreement or the Partnership and Co-operation Agreement.

TACIS

The aid element of the partnership is provided by the TACIS[49] programme. It delivers technical assistance within the framework of Indicative and Action programmes in the CIS[50] and in Mongolia. By far the greater part is taken by the Russian Federation, which dwarfs the others. The principal contribution by TACIS has been for restructuring state enterprises and for private sector development, for public administration reform, social services and education and for energy. In the six years 1991–96, it launched over 2,500 projects and committed some 2.8 billion ECUs. From 1996 to 1999, 2.224 billion euros was earmarked.

The European Union's approach to the CIS has been marked by its desire not to undermine Russian governments, which take a proprietorial view of their 'near abroad'. This inhibits Union involvement in CIS affairs. It might be more charitable to recognise that there is not a great deal it can do; and that it is frantically busy in other areas where its presence and resources count for more.

EFTA and EEA

Nearer home, the great politico-economic divisions in Western Europe and the acrimonious trade bloc to trade bloc negotiations of the 1960s were laid to rest. In the framework of the first enlargement of the Community, it concluded in 1972–73 bilateral industrial free trade agreements with the EFTA countries which had not become members – Austria, Finland,[51] Iceland, Norway, Portugal, Sweden, Switzerland. In a free trade area the participant abolishes restrictions on trade with the other party, but maintains its own tariff against imports from sources outside the area. Origin rules of some complexity determine whether goods qualify for area treatment. The FTAs were considered to work well, but their effectiveness was weakened when, from 1985, the Community forged ahead with its programme to create the Single Market by systematically eliminating non-tariff barriers. However inappropriate the label 'Fortress Europe' may have been, the

'1992' programme threatened to open up new divisions between the Community and its major trading partners in Western Europe.

The received version of events is that half way through the Single Market programme, the President of the Commission, M. Jacques Delors, became apprehensive that some of the free trade partners might be so attracted by the virtues of a single market that they might overcome their long-standing aversion to joining the Community. This could be dangerous. The Single Market programme, involving 300 or so pieces of legislation, was a heavy charge on resources. A further enlargement of the Community could be overload. Larger membership would bring with it the risk of diluting the Community, and there was at least one Member State that would welcome dilution. Already M. Delors had another move in mind – the economic and monetary union which he had reflected on in 1985 but had put aside as too difficult.

On 17 January 1989, when presenting the Commission's programme of work for the year, he

> launched the idea of a far-reaching discussion with the countries of the European Free Trade Association on the possibility of broader co-operation with us.[52]

It may have been a manoeuvre to discourage membership applications. The outcome was the creation of the European Economic Area – 'the world's largest and most important economic structure',[53] bringing together nineteen countries and their 380 million citizens.

(In contradiction of the received wisdom, in 1994, on the morrow of the Norwegian referendum which went against membership of the Union, M. Delors said that when he launched the EEA project it was not to delay accession but because it seemed a solution that would one day actually aid the accession of the EFTA countries.)[54]

The nub of the agreement was to admit the EFTA countries to the emerging Single Market. Its hallmark is the four freedoms of the circulation of goods, services, capital and (some) people – workers and self-employed. For the EFTA countries it meant adopting thirty years of Community *acquis*, the mountain of integrative legislation. There are chapters on agriculture (well short of free trade) and fisheries; on common rules and equal conditions of competition, on 'flanking policies' such as R&D, education, youth, the environment, social policy, consumer protection, SMEs, audio-visual sector and civil protection (emergency services). The EFTA countries also agreed to extend financial assistance to Portugal, Greece, Ireland and parts of Spain (over five years, soft loans totalling 1,500 million ECUs and grants of 500 million ECUs). The help would enable them to face up to increased competition in the Single Market.

Enlargement

Between 1989 and 1992 the world changed. The end of the Cold War deprived the different neutralist stances of Austria, Sweden and Finland of most of their meaning. The Single Market was well on the way and would be deepened but the EFTA countries in the EEA would have little say in the measures that the Community would continue to adopt. The Press release referred to above innocently but ominously applauds a continuous and permanent process of information and consultation during all the stages of the preparation of Community acts, the aim of which is to facilitate the adoption at EEA level of new Community legislation.

The EFTA countries could tell a hack from a handsaw. Austria applied to join the Union on 17 July 1989, Sweden on 1 July 1991, Finland on 18 March 1992, Norway on 25 November 1992 and Switzerland on 25 June 1992. Austria, Finland and Sweden joined in 1995. Norway negotiated membership but a referendum rejected it. In Switzerland the referendum on joining the EEA went against and, in consequence, Switzerland also froze its application to join the Union. The EEA has one fewer member than planned. On the rump-EFTA side it consists of Iceland, Liechtenstein[55] and Norway. Its other candidate members skipped over the EEA option and joined the European Union. Although there were mild suggestions that the EEA might serve as a way station for other countries with a vocation to join the Union, such as the CEECs, this path was not followed. The CEECs did not want to wait.

USA and JAPAN

The European Community's commercial relations with developed countries, notably the USA and Japan,[56] in conjunction with whom it is responsible for 50% of world trade, are conducted under the aegis of the World Trade Organisation (WTO), the successor to the General Agreement on Trade and Tariffs (GATT) – see Box 9.3. The WTO is the source of the rules on international trade in goods and progressively in services. The rules forbid discrimination and provide for sanctions against unfair practices. At intervals the parties agree to hold a 'Round' devoted to negotiating reciprocal reductions in barriers – tariffs, import restrictions, regulatory limitations. Another Round is expected early in the century. The results of tariff negotiations are 'bound'. Tariff reductions cannot be undone without equivalent compensation. The WTO also provides a dispute settlement mechanism, which, unlike its GATT analogue, is binding on the parties.

There is provision for self-defence by countries which consider that exports to their markets are unfair. Countervailing duties can be imposed on imports that have been state-subsidised. Anti-dumping duties are imposed on goods which, roughly speaking, are exported at a price below what is charged on the home market (after making allowance for the differences in cost structure between home market sales and exports)

Box 9.3   GATT and WTO

GATT founded in 1948 to govern international trade.

Multi-lateral trade negotiations took place within GATT in a succession of 'Rounds'.

The last – the Uruguay Round – was completed in December 1993 and it led to the World Trade Organisation in 1995.

and which damage home producers of the same goods. The European Community is strong on anti-dumping. Along with the USA, it was criticised in an OECD report in 1995 for acting in cases where there was no threat to domestic production. An alternative to anti-dumping duties is the acceptance of undertakings by dumpers that they will mend their ways. It was reported in 1994 that the EC had 151 anti-dumping measures in place, including twenty-three undertakings. They covered 0.71% of imports.

A protective device that is less prevalent than in the past is a Voluntary Restraint Arrangement (VRA) or Voluntary Export Restraint (VER). Since GATT rules made it difficult to impose new trade restrictions on fellow members, the latter might be persuaded to limit exports of sensitive products, perhaps in return for some concession in another field. Since such arrangements were nominally voluntary, they were GATT-proof. The Community still had in 1997 a few VERs on imports from CEECs

Regional or global trade liberalisation

The mosaic of EC trade relations which involve discrimination by treating imports from some places more favourably than others, and the emulation of Community trade policy elsewhere, gives rise to concern that the objectives of globalised trade liberalisation may be hindered. Classical theory teaches that a free trade area spreads its benefits. There is trade creation where the partner displaces home production, trade diversion where the partner displaces a third country supplier, and trade expansion where improved efficiency in the area enables it to import more from outside.[57] But the theory is not accepted by all researchers.[58] The alternative view is that regional trade blocs impede general trade liberalisation. What can be said is that world trade liberalisation has proceeded, including ultimately diminishing agricultural protectionism, at the same time as two unprecedently large blocs have emerged: the EC with its special relationships within itself and with many other countries and the North American Free Trade Area (NAFTA).

In 1996 France raised within the Community the question of whether the policy towards regional free trade might be going too far. The specific occasion was a Mexican suggestion for a bilateral FTA (which would have made a technically awkward link with the NAFTA). The French intervention was prompted less by concern about possible damage to the cause of world free trade than by concern about the loss of protection and of advantage for traditional partners. In its response to the European Council the Commission stated baldly that preferential agreements could help to strengthen the multilateral system and that it would be desirable that the WTO rules which might invalidate preferences should be 'clarified'.[59] There was no significant follow-up but the French intervention had a side-effect.

Non-commercial considerations

There are suggestions that the instruments of trade policy should be used in a supporting role to advance deserving causes: the conservation of the environment and the protection of exploited workpeople, including child labourers. The EC participated in international discussion of these problems, but is reserved about using trade policy to alleviate them. In preparing for the first WTO conference in Singapore in December 1996, the Community decided that it should not seek the harmonisation of social policies between countries of different levels of social development nor seek to prevent countries which possess an abundant labour supply from exploiting the comparative advantage of cheap labour. In the conclusions of the Singapore Conference there was the first ever expression of support for the efforts of the International Labour Office (ILO) to promote compliance with universally recognised labour standards. The Community also endorsed the twin objective of a high level of environmental protection and an open, equitable, non-discriminatory multilateral trading system. It was against the imposition of countervailing duties on imports from countries with low environmental standards. However, the Council asked the Commission in 1997 to ensure that rules governing the grant of GSP should require respect for the employment standards of the International Labour Organisation (of the UN) and for the International Tropical Timber Association.

Trade and politics

The Community used to be reserved about using trade instruments to buttress its own foreign policy objectives. It is still true that member countries show concern about the possible repercussions on their traders of the use of trade restriction against a country with which the European Union is having political difficulties in the framework of its Common Foreign and Security Policy (CFSP). There was previously disagreement among the Member States whether politically driven trade measures[60] were within the Community's competence. Uncertainty was dispelled by Article 228a (now 301) introduced by the Single European Act, which builds a bridge between trade and foreign policy.

Asia

Mention has been made of the role of GSP in the Community's relations with the Third World, along with its development aid programme, which makes it the biggest donor in the world. When Britain joined the Community in 1973, major Asian countries faced the loss of the Commonwealth preference that they had enjoyed in the British market. In a Declaration of Intent annexed to the Act of Accession, the Community said that it would take appropriate action. GSP was one part of the solution. Agreements under the old Article 113 were negotiated with India in 1973, Sri Lanka in 1975 and Bangladesh in 1976. Pakistan followed much later in 1985. From 1993 the Community set out to galvanise its relations with Asian countries by converting existing agreements into Co-operation Agreements, beginning with India and Sri Lanka, 1994. It pressed on with what has been called 'pactomania': Korea and Vietnam, 1996, and negotiations with Laos, Bangladesh and Pakistan.

Additionally the Community set out to strengthen its relations with the Asian regional grouping, the Association of South East Asian Nations, (ASEAN), comprising Malaysia, Singapore, Indonesia, Thailand, the Philippines and Brunei, with Burma (Miramar) a latecomer. It negotiated a Co-operation Agreement with ASEAN in June 1980 and has arranged for an annual post-ASEAN encounter. It also convened in Bangkok in March 1996 the Asia/Europe meeting, which was followed by another in London during the British Presidency of 1998. Participants were the EU, the ASEANS, Japan, Korea and China. Basing itself on its vast interests in the Pacific, the Union would like to attend the Asia Pacific Economic Council (APEC) in which the USA is a big player – and which may be moving towards free trade, the declared objective – but its requests have not been accepted.

Latin America

A focus on Asia is not to the liking of all Member States. Latin America, described in a Commission report of 1995 as the most dynamic of all markets for EU exporters (but later suffering a string of economic disasters), has also commanded attention. Rather than relying on bilateralism, the Community has been establishing relations with the Latin American economic groupings. In 1993 it concluded a Framework Agreement on Co-operation with the Andean Pact, instituted by the Treaty of Carthagena (Bolivia, Colombia, Ecuador, Peru, Venezuela, with Chile,[61] a possible future member). The agreement is summarised as follows:

> The agreement specifies three priority areas for co-operation among the partners:
> development of economic co-operation of the widest possible scope, promotion of
> trade expansion and diversification, in particular by granting most-favoured-nation
> treatment and development co-operation to increase efficiency in the agriculture,
> forestry and rural sectors. The agreement also provides for a wide range of programmes
> and measures intended to help consolidate, deepen and diversify the ties between the
> parties.[62]

In 1995, came an Inter-Regional Framework agreement with MERCOSUR, established by the Treaty of Asuncion of 1991 and aiming at a Customs Union (Argentina, Brazil, Uruguay and Paraguay). The agreement covers the fostering of democracy and respect for human rights, economic stability and growth, the expansion of trade and investment, scientific co-operation and political dialogue. In 1996 the Community reached an agreement with the parties to the General Treaty on Central American Economic Integration, Costa Rica, El Salvador, Guatemala, Honduras and Nicaragua.

Together these arrangements give the EU contractual links with all the Latin American states except Panama and Cuba (the latter now showing interest in Lomé). They give it basis for developing the relationship as and when the Latin American economic groupings move towards closer regional economic integration. They also establish an additional framework in which matters such as drug trafficking can be tackled.

EU/USA

Economic relations do not depend upon treaties. The Community's most serious trade issues are with countries with which it has no overarching trade or co-operation agreements: the USA and Japan. It treats with them bilaterally and multilaterally.

There is recurrent talk of an EC/USA Agreement in one form or another up to and including a Transatlantic Free Trade Area. Since the two sides have so many engagements with each other economically and politically, such an agreement would be vast in scope and would require the most sensitive negotiation. It would also offer countless hostages to fortune in the shape of the ratifying powers of the US Senate.

Alternatives have been sought in understandings that do not require ratification. The Transatlantic Declaration of 1990, also known as the Baker Declaration from its American author, was followed in 1995 by the Transatlantic Agenda and the joint *EU/US Action Plan* adopted during President Clinton's visit to Madrid. The European Council meeting in Madrid two weeks later described it as a 'quantitative leap forward in strengthening our relations'. These transactions gave new edge to the twice-yearly encounters between the Union, represented by the President of the European Council and the President of the Commission and the President of the USA. As Machiavelli said, it is not the business of sovereigns to resolve disputes that their subordinates have been unable to settle. The meetings are politically important but the real tasks are discharged in frequent meetings at working level.

Another of the products of the Agenda is the Transatlantic Business Dialogue (TABD) which brings together executives of American and European business. Their reports show that they are less concerned about tariffs and instruments of trade policy than about mutual recognition of standards and certification.

In March 1998 the Commission, on the initiative of Sir Leon Brittan, Vice-President, moved on. It proposed the *New Transatlantic Marketplace* (NTM).[63] This was for free trade in the industrial products that the EU and the USA exchange, to be secured in the multilateral WTO framework. It envisaged:

> the abolition by 2010 of all customs duties on industrial products provided that a critical mass of other trading partners do the same.

Negative French interventions in the spirit mentioned above killed the NTM. It was succeeded at the end of 1998 by the *Transatlantic Economic Partnership*.[64] This builds on the Joint Action Plan of 1995. It sets out the lines of co-operation between the EU and the USA both bilaterally and in multilateral trade and economic fora. Tariffs are not mentioned. Ironically the two sides were simultaneously locked in dispute over an EC ban on imports of beef from cattle dosed with growth hormones and the preference which the EC gives to ACP bananas over bananas grown in Latin America and marketed by the US food giants.

Canada and Japan

In 1990 the Community and Canada issued a joint declaration which inaugurated top-level meetings as well as others at lower level. This elaborated the arrangements flowing from the co-operation agreement between Canada and the EC signed in 1976 (Article 113). There is a similar joint declaration and top-level gatherings with Japan (1991).[65] The EC, USA, Canada and Japan meet at Ministerial level in the 'Quad' usually to seek to prepare themselves for the positions they will take in WTO discussions.

Trade in services

At the end of the Uruguay Round there was a constitutional question concerning Article 113. There was a view, championed especially by Spain, that the article could not be used as the legal base for agreements on services, a sector growing phenomenally. Under Article 228.6 EC (now 300) the Court can be asked to deliver an Opinion as to whether an agreement is compatible with the Treaty. The Commission, which had negotiated on all matters in the Round, but had no competence to conclude, argued that within the Final Act the General Agreement on Trade in Services (GATS) and the Trade Related Intellectual Property Rights (TRIPS) could properly be concluded. The Court gave a different Opinion.[66] Only services involving cross-border supplies were within Article 113. Consumption or supply of services abroad were not.

Regarding intellectual property rights, only the parts of the agreement concerning the control of counterfeit goods at the Community's customs frontier were within the ambit of Article 113. In the 1996–97 Inter-Governmental Conference the Commission urged that Article 113 should be amended to create Community competence for wider aspects of services. The Conference failed to agree and the anomaly remains.

As this extended section shows, the European Community (and thereby the European Union) has established contractual trade relationships with all but a tiny few of the countries of the world; and, with many of them, is in or is heading towards free trade. The question which keeps coming back is: What is to be the relationship between it and the trade blocs which the United States sponsors, presently the North American Free Trade Area, perhaps in future a Pacific basin entity and a Free Trade Area of the Americas? The connected question is whether trade liberalising agreements of defined geographical scope help or hinder global trade freedom under the WTO.

Trade

One of the central arguments on behalf of British withdrawal (or other retreat) from the EU is that Britain incurs a trade deficit with the rest of the EU and a surplus with the rest of the world.[67] This contention uses statistics of imports[68] and exports of goods and invisibles. Invisibles include services, transfers and investment income. To have intellectual validity, the Eurosceptic argument should exclude investment income and transfers, since they are not a measure of a country's trading performance.[69]

Table 9.11   Trade in goods (£ billion)

	EU	Non-EU	World
1997	– 4 038	–7 874	–11 912
1998	–5 300	–15 298	–20 598

Source: Office of National Statistics.

Table 9.12   Trade in services: balance (£ billion)

	EU	Non-EU	World
1997	–1 085	+12 996	+ 11 881
1998	–	–	+ 13 415

Source: Office of National Statistics.

In 1996, 55.8% of British exports of goods went to the rest of the EU. The 1998 figure was 58%. There was a deficit on trade in goods within an overall deficit (see Table 9.11).

The 1998 deficit with the non-EU (48% of visible trade) doubled because of an £8 billion fall in exports. The latest year for which full information is available on services in 1997 is shown in Table 9.12.

It is true to say, with the Eurosceptics, that in 1997 the UK was in surplus in trade and goods and services with the Non-EU but in deficit with the EU. The deficit with the EU is incurred on goods and services. Sunny Spain and the British contingent among its 50 million visitors account for the deficit in services with the EU. The deficit with the non-EU on goods rose sharply in 1998. For the European Union the pattern of trade is as shown in Table 9.13.

Table 9.13   Major partners by region in 1996

Major export partners	Trade in goods (%)	Major import partners	Trade in goods (%)
USA	18.3	USA	19.4
Switzerland	8.2	Switzerland	7.3
Japan	5.7	Japan	9.0
Poland	3.2	China	5.2
Norway	3.2	Norway	5.3

Source: Facts and Figures (CN-680 98–002–EN–C).

214

THE COMMON TRANSPORT POLICY

The Transport Policy is one of the three described as 'Common' in the 1957 version of the EC Treaty (in Title V, Articles 70 to 80, ex Title IV, 74 to 84). Transport is also the first of the subjects selected for study in the Messina Resolution[70] in the context of the setting up of a 'united Europe'.

> The expansion of trade and the movement of persons call for the common development of large-scale communication facilities.
>
> With this end in view, a joint study will be undertaken of a European network of canals, motor highways, electric railway-lines, and the standardisation of equipment, as well as on efforts to achieve a better co-ordination of air transport.

By its frontier-crossing nature, transport implies international co-operation. Before there was a Community there had been a European Conference of Transport Ministers,[71] which had the privilege of being represented on the Spaak Committee which planned the EEC Treaty.[72]

Limitations – not sea, not air

The original members of the Community, apart from the Netherlands, did not belong to the great maritime nations. They had about 15% of world merchant tonnage, roughly the same as Britain alone. In any case, the Messina document is clearly referring to movement between the Member States. It is not suggesting that national shipping should embrace a common policy. Although it refers to air transport, its context is again continental. The exponential rise in long- and short-haul air traffic lay ahead. The substantive article (71, ex- 75) shows that the policy concerns surface frontier crossing and the cross-frontier provision of transport services. Article 84 excludes air and sea transport from the original scheme.[73]

Caution on policy

Title V is unambitious. It highlights the 'distinctive features of transport', it worries over the 'effect on the standard of living and on employment in certain areas' of some of the things that might be done. It recognises that state aids may be given for transport operations, a reference to public service obligations, and it requires account to be taken of the economic circumstances of carriers.

This caution reflects the massive involvement of the state in national transport facilities. In the mid-1950s, 40% of public investment went into transport assets. Transport infrastructures were overwhelmingly public goods. In particular, the railways were, and much of the network still is, publicly owned. On mainland Europe, unlike Britain, the railways had been built by the State[74] and were operated as a public service, all at a loss. They were part of the cohesion of the nation, they alleviated the problems of the remoter areas and they had strategic value.[75] But the railways were coming under threat from road-borne traffic and from bulk-load oceanic carriage of coal and ores, which struck at some of their staple markets. Governments were deeply concerned to protect their investment and discourage the switch of freight to the roads, meaning underuse of the existing national asset. The context of the infant common transport policy was therefore that it was more or less confined to frontier crossing and that it would not be allowed to disadvantage rail further. It was still true in the 1980s that the sum of subsidies for rail in national budgets was approximately as much as the CAP in the Community budget.

Inland waterways

Another transport system that had its problems was the inland waterways. As the Messina text shows, there had been hopes of a post-war recovery, but they remained underused. Moreover, the biggest artery of them all, the Rhine and its spurs, was beyond the reach of the Community. It was in the hands of the Central Rhine Commission, composed of all interested states. Founded in 1815 at the Congress of Vienna, it survived the change and internecine conflict of a century and a half. The Community as such could not become involved in its management.

Small achievement

In the early years, and although air and road transport was undergoing massive structural change, the achievements of the CTP were small. In its first annual report, the Commission said:

> [transport's] peculiar characteristics – the special structure inherited from its historical past, its social and strategic role, the scale of existing and future investments, the advent and rapid expansion of new means of transport and the far-reaching intervention exercised by public authorities – all these explain why the negotiators of the Treaty of Rome were unable to lay down in detail the ways and means of integrating transport into the common market.

First Action Programme

In 1962 the Commission brought out an Action Programme for Transport. Attention was to be given to the standardisation of weights and dimensions of lorries (not much could be done about trains); to social rules for transport staff, to subsidies and to taxation. As a symptom of the 'distinctive feature', the early Regulations on competition policy were suspended in the case of transport for three years.[76] Such movement as there was was set back by the paralysis of EC business in the episode of the 'empty chair'.[77]

The Treaty articles concern essentially the avoidance of discrimination in the provision of service and in price structures. The path to the former in the late 1960s and early 1970s was the setting up of a 'Community quota', enabling road carriers in one Member State to pick up loads in another. The plan was for the Community quota to increase until the market had been opened up. It would be hard to see any element of liberalisation in the quota scheme. Road transport remained tightly regulated. To give effect to other treaty articles, rules were established on maximum prices (to protect users against collusion) and minimum prices (to discourage cut-throat competition and the debasement of safety standards). Under 'other appropriate provisions' weights and dimensions of freight vehicles, working conditions of drivers and the taxation of vehicles and diesel fuel were proposed and lengthily discussed.

Rail

On railways, the Council accepted in principle in 1965–68 the principle that there should be financial autonomy, that there should be commercial accounting and that there should be criteria for payments in respect of public service obligations. But this was small beer, especially as compared with the deepening of other common policies. The turning point did not come until the early 1980s and it was induced by two events.

Parliament, Court and Commission

The European Parliament, in 1983 officially the Assembly, was in the tail end of its first term as directly elected. It was looking for new dragons to vanquish. It and its predecessor, the appointed body, had frequently criticised the Council's lack of drive. It could not at that time itself initiate Court proceedings but it encouraged the Commission to do so. In the judgement which it delivered in 1985, in Case 13/83, the Court confirmed that the Council was in breach of its duty to create a Common Transport Policy but acknowledged that it possessed no power of enforcement against the Council. By then, however, there was other movement. The Commission that assumed office in 1985 took up with vigour the task of 'completion'. This was the 1992 programme for the Single Market, piloted by the British Commissioner, Lord Cockfield. The soundings that the Commission took in business circles showed that the regulation of transport jointly with different rates of VAT, were considered to be the most important barriers to intra-Community trade.[78] This referred particularly to road transport. By this time the roads were carrying around 70% of goods (t/km) and 80% of passengers (p/km).[79]

Single market in road haulage

The Single Market programme swept away national road transport protectionism. On 1 January 1993 all restrictions on the cross-frontier carriage of freight and passengers were removed along with cabotage[80] for freight. Cabotage for passenger traffic was more stubborn, not yielding until the Transport Council meeting of 10/11 December 1997.[81] Urban and suburban services remain excluded from the Regulation that the Council adopted at that meeting.

The removal of restriction based on nationality does not mean deregulation. Safety and other rules continue to apply across the board, a reminder of the 50,000 deaths that occur annually on the transport systems of the Community. Indeed the same meeting tightened up tachograph[82] requirements with, for example:

> Each driver will have to have his own microprocessor card on which all the driver's activities are recorded. [Brussels draftsmen lack a sense of humour.]

Sea transport

The Single Market programme had little effect on maritime transport, except that cabotage was freed up. Merchant tonnage on the registers of Member States had fallen by half in forty years. Continuing discussion concerned marine safety, working conditions and pollution prevention, often within the framework of international conventions.

Railway traffic

The railways were not greatly affected by the Single Market programme. National railway operators had other worries. Even as late as January 1998 the Commissioner responsible for transport was chiding them for their 'fragmentation' and 'national focus' and their 'negligible response to the removal of political and economic borders within the Single Market'.[83]

By then, however, there was a new dimension in transport policy. The Single Market programme was concerned with eliminating barriers. A new focus was on completing networks.

Trans-European Networks

This initiative can be traced back to attempts, beginning in the late 1960s, to resuscitate rail and strengthen its competition with road. Among the moves were the German Leber Plan of 1967 to restrict road haulage and inland waterway transport and, beginning in 1981 with the Paris-Lyon sector, the French programme for emulating Japan by bringing into service the TGV (equals High Speed Trains or HST). In early 1985 the Commission took up the notion of improved transport as the backbone of the Single Market and a contribution to regional development, including 'missing links' and HSTs.[84] This is part of the activity of 'positive integration', where removing regulatory barriers is the less glamorous 'negative integration'. More glamorous but also much more difficult: capital investment needs, environmental impact and other planning hurdles, national and subnational divergences over track alignment, technological differences in rolling stock and signalling systems, all have to be addressed. But the Commission clung to the plan and widened it out into the 'Trans-European Networks', otherwise TENs.

TENs were singled out for 'special priority' in the Conclusions of the European Council meeting in Strasbourg on 8/9 December 1989. They were elaborated in the Action Plan produced by the Commission in 1990. They related to transport, energy and communications (less understandably, training practices, which were soon dropped from the list). TENs acquired a title of their own, Title XII, Articles 129b to d in the Treaty on European Union (now Title XV, Articles 154 to 156). From the start, the realisation of TENs was seen to depend upon the injection of private capital in what came to be known as Public/Private Partnerships.[85]

TENs are a development theme of one of the legacies that Commission President Delors left to the Community in the 1993 White Paper on *Growth, Competitiveness and Employment*.[86] However the European Council meeting in Brussels in December pointedly disregarded the Commission's suggestion that the largest single share of financing should come from 'Union bonds', seemingly because it believed that this would give undue prominence to the Commission. It reverted to 'structures which can call on private capital'. The Commission's estimate of the cost of transport infrastructure improvement 1994–2000 was 250 billion ECUs. The selection of priority transport and energy projects was entrusted to Henig Christophersen, Denmark, a former member of the Commission. From his Group's report the Corfu meeting of the European Council (24/25 June 1994) endorsed a list of ten road and rail schemes and one airport. Three more schemes were added when the three new members joined; mention was made of interconnection with Eastern Europe; and a special window of the EIB was named as a major source of finance.[87] The question was whether enough private capital could be raised to pay for anything like the total cost of the TENs advocated by the Commission.

New moves on railways

In July 1998 the Commissioner, Neil Kinnock, reopened questions concerning the *existing* rail network. Noting that there were nine different charging systems and that access to track was in the hands of the Europe Train Forum bringing together existing rail operators, he proposed that (as had already been decided) rail track should be in the separate hands from rolling stock and that electronic devices should be installed to measure track usage and permit it to be charged for rationally and transparently.[88] In June 1998 the Transport Council had a first orientation debate on the Commission's proposals, summarised as follows:[89]

On 2 April 1998 the Commission submitted to the Council a communication that takes stock of the transposition of the obligations imposed by [Directive 91/440/EEC] in each Member State, such as management independence of railway undertakings, separation of infrastructure management and transport operations, reduction of debt and improvement of finances as well as establishment of access rights to railway infrastructure, limited to international groupings of railway undertakings and undertakings providing international combined transport services. In its conclusion the Commission suggests extending access rights partially (only for freight transport) and gradually (so that an increasing proportion of the infrastructure capacity would be available to undertakings other than each Member State's operator).

The Press Release records, with the mildness typical of the genre, a number of Member States were supportive on the whole while others expressed their doubts on extension of access rights and on competition within the rail market.

In June 1999 the German Presidency brought forward a bold proposal to liberalise state railways – that is, to allow for privatisation. This was a major initiative, emerging from a socialist government and a country where the railways have always been a publicly owned service – in Prussia, the rail system had been under direct army control. The presidency plan encountered immediate opposition, including the charge that there had not been the normal round of quiet consultation before such ventures are announced. With France and Belgium determinedly against privatisation and citing the alleged failure of private railway ownership in Britain, the plan made no headway.

Air transport, up and up

TENs had little bearing on the other great structural change in internal and external transport – the surge in air traffic. When flight became one of the favoured ways to travel between centres in the Community as well as to distant destinations, the fare structure came in for criticism. Many comparisons were made of the high cost of European air journeys as against internal flights in the USA. This had something to do with the duopolies that characterised international air travel.

As soon as flying began, countries declared that the airspace above them was national property. For national security as well as safety and commercial reasons they controlled overflying and landings on their soil by licensing. This became a matter of bilateral bargaining, in the form of Air Service Agreements (ASAs) concluded under the aegis of the Chicago Convention on Civil Aviation (1944). ASAs specified the flights allowed to carriers of the nationality of the two parties; and airline companies had to be 'substantially owned and effectively controlled' by nationals. This is the origin of the duopolies. Since supply of seats was limited and since in some of the ASAs there was price-fixing and revenue-sharing, the two national airlines concerned had little interest in competing on fares.

The movement towards a common market in airline services was in phases in which pricing freedom was introduced and traffic-sharing was eased from the strict 50/50 rule that had been common in the ASAs. The complete freeing up of the internal market took longer than the 1993 deadline for the Single Market. It became effective in April 1997.

> Any airline established within the Union will be able to offer services – scheduled or unscheduled – at the fares they choose between any number of airports in Member States, subject to a common set of rules on licensing, financial solvency and competition.[90]

For effects to show up in fares, standards of service, route coverage, airline structures and competition would take time.

In the forty years from the signature of the Treaty establishing the European Economic Community, air transport had moved from exclusion from integration to forming a single market in services.

The ASAs had disappeared in internal Community aviation. Externally, however, they remained the basis of the operations of airlines established in the Community, and the national ownership rule was the cornerstone of ASAs. This had two effects: airlines could not afford to lose or dilute their 'nationality' and service rights remained subject to negotiation by each Member State, acting on its own account. The first consideration inhibited merger and acquisition and encouraged *alliances* in which the national identity of each airline was preserved but co-operation was strengthened. The European Commission regarded the second as a weakness. The rules governing the nationality of airlines and the restriction on foreign acquisition are clean contrary to the anti-discrimination principles of the Union, and is clearly illustrated in the tussles over the ownership of trawlers in the context of the Common Fisheries Policy. The Commission has been careful not to attack them doctrinally.

Commission competence hunting

In 1996 the Commission became concerned at the spectacle of individual Member States negotiating new air service agreements bilaterally with the USA. The states concerned were unwilling to 'communitise' the negotiating process and entrust it to the Commission. Under pressure from Commissioner Kinnock, in July 1996 the Council authorised the Commission to open negotiations with the USA 'with the objective of establishing a 'Common Aviation Area'. In taking note of the progress of the discussions, the Council was careful, at its meeting on 9 October 1997, to recall that 'there was no change in the situation regarding bilateral agreements'.[91] When the Commission asked for its mandate for negotiations to be strengthened in the autumn of 1998, the Council remained cautious, but agreed that negotiations should be continued at an appropriate level in order for a conclusion to be reached.

The air traffic with the CEECs was a different matter. Since all were candidates for membership and assimilation to the Single Market, the Commission is the natural inter-locutor. In October 1996 the Council authorised the Commission to open negotiations regarding agreements on access to the air transport market. They are likely to merge into the enlargement negotiations.

Air safety

Concern over air safety has led the Commission and Council to consider the setting up of a European Aviation Safety Authority. On 17/18 June 1998 the Transport Council authorised the Commission to open negotiations with such an end in view. The purpose of the negotiations was stated to be[92]

> to conclude an agreement establishing an international organisation, to be known as the European Aviation Safety Authority (EASA) , with the objectives of primarily establishing a high uniform level of safety in Europe, by the formulation, approval, and uniform application of aviation safety regulations, and its promotion throughout the world.

The Council have sought Community membership of the European Organisation for the Safety of Air Navigation (Eurocontrol).[93]

L LEGAL BASES

Common Agricultural Policy

Treaty establishing the European Community
* Articles 32 to 38 revised numbering (ex 38 to 46, with 44, 45, 47 repealed).
* First financial regulation: 25/62, OJ 30, 204.62, p.991.
* Guarantee and Guidance: 17/64, OJ 34, 29.2.64, p.586.
* Mansholt Plan (consol): 797/85, OJ 93, 30.4.85, p.1.
* First anti-fraud: 283/72, OJ 36, 10.2.72, p.1.
* Price fixing: annual.
* Market management: daily, OJ L series.

Common Fisheries Policy

* Articles 3 and 31 (ex-38)
* Regulations:
    Framework:
* Council no. 3094/86, 7 October 1986, OJ L 288.
* Council no. 3760/92, 20 December 1992, OJ L 389.
* Council no. 3759/92 17 December 1992, OJ L 388.
* Council no. 2080/93, 20 July 1993, OJ L 193.
* Council no. 2081/93, 20 July 1993 OJ L 193.
* Council no. 2082/93, 20 July 1993 OJ L 193.
* Council no. 3690/93, 20 December 1993, OJ L 341.
* Council no. 3699/93, 21 December 1993, OJ L 346.
Annual
* Total allowable catches and quotas by area and species; see annual index, monthly *Bulletin of the European Union*, OOP.

Common Commerical Policy

* Articles 131 to 134 (ex-110 to 116).
* Article 300.
* Generalised System of Preferences: Council Regulation 3281/94 EC (valid to 2004).
* Phare: Council Regulation 3906/89 EEC.
* TACIS: Council Regulation 1279/96 EC.

Common Transport Policy

* Article 70 to 80 (ex-74 to 84).

DISCUSSION QUESTIONS

Common Agricultural Policy

1. In what way is the decision to finance an agricultural policy from Community-owned funds 'momentous'.
2. Discuss the possibility of 'returning responsibility for agricultural policy to the Member States' as recommended by the European Research Group.
3. 'The CAP is the cement of the Community – poor Community', Th. Hijzen, former DG, External Relations. Discuss.
4. Can a CAP involving price guarantees and production and income aids survive the enlargement of the EU to the East?
5. How is cohesion obtained between the CAP, the CCP and the budgetary framework?

Common Fisheries Policy

1. Despite Community controls, fishing stocks are regularly depleted. Are the controls at fault, or is it lax enforcement?
2. No 'Brussels policy' is more unpopular in Britain than the CFP. What could be done to obtain a better hearing for it?
3. Can 'quota hopping' be defended?
4. The Conservative Party has promised withdrawal from the CFP. Is this a feasible proposition?

Common Commercial Policy

1. The European Economic Area enables European countries effectively to participate in the Single Market without belonging to the Community. Why does it not serve to prepare the CEECs for membership?
2. What is the EU interest in the Mediterranean?
3. Can the ACP successfully be treated as a unit?
4. If the conservation of the environment is a supreme planetary concern, should trade weapons be used to promote action?
5. Does the formation of regional preferential trade groupings block globalised trade liberalisation?
6. 'Powerful in world trade, powerless politically.' Is this a valid view of the EU?

Common Transport Policy

1. Beflagged trains crossing frontiers are an icon on European Integration. Why did and does the integration of transport lag behind?
2. Can Public/Private Partnerships, in which Commissioner Kinnock invested hope, succeed?
3. When the TENs are built, should the Community, as inventor, obtain a rent?
4. Is the Commission justified in seeking to assume competence for negotiating Air Service Agreements on behalf of Member States; or should subsidiarity apply?

KEY ECONOMIC POLICIES

THE SINGLE MARKET

WITH THE blessing of the gift of hindsight, the 1957 Treaty establishing the European Economic Community is an anomaly.

Customs Union and freedom of circulation

The Treaty proclaims in Article 2 that there is to be a common market. It elaborates in Article 3: customs duties and quantitative restrictions on imports and exports of goods among the Member States and all other measures having equivalent effect are to be eliminated. Obstacles to the free movement between the Member States of persons, services and capital are to be abolished. Article 9 (now 23) is more specific: the Community will be based on a Customs Union. That means that it will have a single external tariff in place of the national tariffs of its Member States. Thirty-seven articles set out how and when the Customs Union is to be attained. Nine articles extend the common market to agriculture and to trade in agricultural products. Nothing is said here about restrictions on trade between the Member States that are not customs duties, charges having equivalent effect or quotas.

Free movement of persons is later reduced to free movement of workers (Article 48, now 39). Freedom to provide services is to be the subject of a 'general programme' (Article 63, repealed because spent). *To the extent necessary to ensure the proper functioning of the common market,* Member States are to abolish restrictions on capital movements between residents.

The anomaly is that a comprehensive programme for a common market is set out, with the exception of the elimination of the mass of regulations which the Member States individually and sovereignly imposed and enlarged on goods entering their territory on such grounds as safety, human, plant and animal health, consumer

225

protection, industrial standards, labelling, professional codes and even venerable manufacturing traditions. Generically, these are the non-tariff barriers (NTBs).

The non-tariff barriers

With no discernible order of priorities, the Commission produced over the years scores of proposals for the approximation under Article 100 (now 94) of provisions laid down by law, regulation or administrative action in the Member States directly affecting the establishment or functioning of the Common Market. Some were adopted, by unanimity, which was the rule. Some were not, in the absence of unanimity. Among them were some which involved protracted negotiation (including sustained resistance) on formidably technical matters.[94] A large arrears of unfinished business – 800 Commission proposals at one stage in the early 1980s – grew as Member States either found no agreement, or did not try for it.

The Single Market

Several forces converged to give impetus to the creation of a *single* market (see Table 10.1).

Table 10.1   The stages in the establishment of the single market

Date	Event
12.03.85	Delors, Commission President, presents the internal market programme to the European Parliament
14.06.85	The Commission publishes a White Paper on the internal market drawn up under Lord Cockfield
2/3.12.85	Luxembourg European Council endorses the Single Act; one of the changes introduces majority voting to facilitate the completion of the single market by the end of 1992
15.02.87	Commission adopts an action programme 'The Single Act: a new frontier for Europe' for the implementation of the Single Act
01.07.87	Single Act comes into force
18.11.87	European Parliament backs Commission programme
11/13.02.88	European Council in Brussels approves Commission's programme of 15 February 1987
31.12.88	Over 95% of the 1985 legislative programme is completed, but delays, especially in the area of free movement of persons
End of 1993	Commission presents its strategic programme for the operation and development of the Single Market

1. Jumping over barriers – the EP Kangaroo Group

In 1980, the late Basil de Ferranti, an MEP industrialist in the first directly elected Parliament, inspired by the troubles of a firm in his constituency which faced a non-tariff barrier in France, founded the cross-party Kangaroo Group and began lobbying in Brussels as well as in London.

2. K.-H. Narjes' plans and Council actions

In 1981 the British Presidency took up some of the stalled proposals – company law and inflation accounting, qualifications of architects, product liability – and made limited movement along the lines sketched out by the responsible Commissioner, Karl-Heinz Narjes. In December 1982 the Danish Presidency had some extravagant ideas which were cut down to size by the Danish Secretary-General of the Council, Niels Ersboll. The conclusions of the European Council meeting in Copenhagen of December 1982 instruct the Council to decide before the end of March 1983 on the priority measures proposed by the Commission to reinforce the internal market.

3. The Albert–Ball Report

Likewise, in December 1982 the European Parliament asked two economists, Professor (later Sir) James Ball of the London Business School and Michel Albert, formerly of the French Commissariat au Plan, to answer the question: *How can the European economy recover during the 80s?* Their report[95] contains a long list of proposals and recommendations, including one almost buried towards the end: the European Community needs: '*an internal market where goods and services circulate freely*'.

4. Internal Market Council

In January 1983 the Council responded to the trend by establishing the Internal Market Council, with membership of trade ministers. They would intentionally be bound to stray into areas that were the direct responsibility of ministerial colleagues. If a supply is created – internal market ministers, then a demand follows – a functioning internal market. The senior British trade minister at the time was Lord Cockfield.

5. European Round Table

In 1955–57, there had been limited business interest in the Economic Community and even some opposition to it as another layer of government, and a remote one. This cool-ness changed in the 1970s under the influence of the Belgian Commissioner Etienne Davignon and the business figures which he cultivated, including notably Pehr Gyllenhammer of Volvo (ironically from outside the Community although deeply involved in its business). From these contacts the European Round Table of Industrialists (ERT) emerged in 1983. It was not a lobbying organisation but a group of business lead-ers who were prepared to work themselves and use their resources to put forward plans for Europe's industrial future. The centrepiece was a unified home base.[96]

6. The Dekker programme

One of the participants was the CEO of Philips of Eindhoven, Wisse Dekker. His man in Brussels was a college friend and compatriot of the Director-General in the Council responsible for industrial affairs, Emile a Campo. A Campo had links out to the Kangaroo Group and to the Commission. With his guidance, Dekker produced in 1984 a blueprint for creating a united European Market. Presentation was deferred until the new Commission of President Jacques Delors was in place in January 1985.

The integrative urge revitalised

The thrust for integration that had weakened in the 1970s was revivified in different quarters. The German/Italian initiative of 1981 was for political union, without mention of the internal market.[97] The 1984 Draft Treaty of European Union,[98] the brainchild of Altiero Spinelli – sometime political prisoner of the Fascists, sometime industrial Commissioner, now an 'independent communist' in the European Parliament – was in the federal vein. The decisive moves now came from France.

President Mitterrand proposes

Late in 1983 President Mitterrand, looking to the coming French Presidency, sent to his European Council colleagues a memorandum entitled: 'A new Step for Europe: a common space for industry and research.' The response was muted. In 1984 M. Mitterrand went further. On 24 May he told an applauding European Parliament that France approved of the inspiration behind its draft Treaty on European Union. He drew further applause by stating that the time had come to return to voting on important questions.[99] At the meeting of the European Council in Fontainebleau in June 1984 (where he resolved the British budgetary problem), he obtained agreement to the appointment of a committee to suggest improvements in European co-operation.

The Dooge Committee

The Dooge Committee,[100] from the name of its Irish chairman, reported in March 1985, and deliberately did not seek consensus, which would not have been available. Among its fully agreed proposals was the completion of the internal market by the end of the decade in accordance with a precise timetable. It proposed to sweep aside differences in national standards by applying the simple rule of mutual recognition based on the principle (established in the Cassis de Dijon[101] case) that goods legally produced and marketed in one Member State should circulate freely in the entire Community. A majority of the Committee proposed that more decisions should be taken by simple, or qualified majority. A majority of the Committee also proposed the convening of an inter-governmental conference to draft a new treaty.

The first Delors Commission, 1985

For the new Commission that took office in January 1985 this was an attractive prospect:[102] government, business and EP support for a new drive to 'complete' the internal market. 'Complete' was a long delayed part of the triptych inherited from the Summit of 1969: complete, deepen, widen.

- A powerful recommendation for a new treaty with majority voting to speed work up.
- A suggestion that the classic and laborious method of harmonising might be replaced by mutual recognition pending the working out of new community-wide rules.
- A timetable approach set out by a leading industrialist.

These were a first list of outstanding proposals prepared by their predecessors. Jacques Delors considered other options, including monetary union, for the big story of his Presidency but selected the internal market. Lord Cockfield had been appointed Commissioner with the precise British aim of opening the European market up for goods and services. In the overused metaphor of the time, he was to build the 'level playing field'. These were the sentiments and personalities needed to advance the market.

- Lord Cockfield brought out a White Paper[103] on 14 June 1985. It contained 279 annotated and logically interconnected measures that should be adopted according to a defined timetable ending in 1992.
- The Single European Act was signed in February 1986 by twelve Member States (including the newly joined Spain and Portugal). It stipulates in Article 8a (now Article 3c):

  The internal market shall comprise an area without internal frontiers in which the free movement of goods, persons, services and capital is ensured in accordance with the provisions of this Treaty.

It also provides in Article 100a (now 95) that the Council shall adopt the measures for the approximation of the provisions laid down by law, regulation or administrative action in the Member States which have as their object the establishment and functioning of the internal market. With stated exceptions the Council is to decide by *qualified majority vote*.

All the pieces were on the board in a programme such as the Member States, accustomed to much wordage and operational vagueness, had never seen. The legal reform to underpin it existed. A Commissioner-President duo of immense determination and total commitment was thirsting to get to work. An enlarged Community was giving itself a fresh start.

The 1992 programme for the realisation of the single market became one of the most heavily publicised activities of the Community, both by the Commission and by authorities in the Member States. Implementation began slowly, provoking complaint from the Commission, but successive Presidencies and the EP buckled to the task of maintaining momentum. Downstream, Member States fell behind with the transposition of directives into national law and with enforcement. Constant encouragement was to be found in the

Figure 10.1   Additional growth to be generated through achievement of the 192 objectives

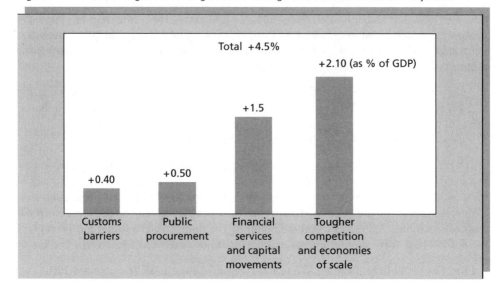

volume in which the Commission calculated the benefits to be obtained from *The Challenge*.[104] This book, written by a retiring Commission official, Paolo Cecchini, presented in accessible summary form the results of thirteen studies on the gains to be secured by the completion of the programme.

The medium-term consequences of market integration are presented in Table 10.2. This table shows the positive or negative effects on GDP, consumer prices, etc. of a number of measures connected with the single market: abolition of customs formalities, open public procurement, liberalisation of financial services and supply-side-effects.

Table 10.2   Macroeconomic consequences of EC market integration for the Community in the medium term

	Abolition of customs formalities	Open public procurement	Liberalisation of financial services	Supply-side* effects	Total
GDP (%)	0.4	0.5	1.5	2.1	4.5
Consumer prices (%)	−1.0	−1.4	−1.4	−2.3	−6.1
Employment (thousands)	200	350	400	850	1,800
Budgetary balance (% of GDP)	0.2	0.3	1.1	0.6	2.2
External balance (% of GDP)	0.2	0.1	0.3	0.4	1.0

*Economies of scale, increased competition, etc.
Source: 'The Economics of 1992', in *European Economy*, No. 35, March 1988 (Cecchini Report).

The new approach

Two basic principles of the programme, in what was called the 'new approach', were:

- the mutual recognition of national standards, as proposed by the Dooge Committee (and suggested by the Commission); and
- minimum requirement: previously, harmonisation directives had often become lengthy and complex as they covered all the aspects of the matter they were treating, but the new approach is to state essential requirements that are then amplified in European standards.

Standards established by CEN (mechanical), Cenelec (electrical) and ETSI (communications) are drawn up by representatives of the industries, replace national standards and are not mandatory. If not used, however, the goods may not be marketable. Minimum requirements are not enough where there are questions of inter-operability, and their closer specification is still needed. This is also true in pharmaceuticals, chemicals and vehicles.

Services

The Cassis de Dijon judgement related only to the free circulation of goods, but a parallel freedom for services was part of the 1992 programme. Financial services were of special importance. National legislation was highly protective of banks, stockbrokers, insurance companies, pension funds.

The driving principle in the approach to the liberalisation of services within the Single Market was the 'single passport' and 'home control'. Translated out of jargon this meant that any service provider could operate anywhere in the Community provided the operation (banking, insurance, dealing, etc.) had been licensed in the country of establishment, in conformity with Council regulations and Directives applicable to the sector.

The operation remained under the control of the 'home' authority and was independent of the regulatory authority in the receiving country. In practice this meant that the operation should be conducted through a branch. If a subsidiary were set up it would fall under the regulatory control of the country in which it was established. The measures adopted for services did not lead to an upsurge in branch operations. Most enterprises preferred to offer cross-border service from their home base, or to go into joint ventures with local established interests. It remains uncommonly difficult, for example, to insure a car outside the country of registration.

One of the more difficult problems to resolve, still awaiting an outcome, is the restrictions which some governments impose on the business decisions of pension fund managers. They are often required to invest in certain types of stocks and shares and to invest domestically. The Commission has argued,[105] to little avail, that returns could be improved and pensioners given a boost if these restrictions were relaxed. Meanwhile the treatment of pension funds remains a concealed restriction on capital movement.

Apart from material advantages which it brought and the mental satisfaction of achievement, the Single Market programme was on another agenda. President Delors' next stage was the single currency, which he had thought too fraught to embark on in 1985 – but a clear trace of it appears in the preamble and in the original version of Article 102a of the Single European Act (deleted because spent). It became the launch pad for the EMU programme set forth in the Treaty on European Union five years later, drawing on the work of the committee[106] over which M. Delors had presided:

> ... the single market was a means to an end as well as an end in itself; the credibility of the single market project finally paved the way for further integration and for the idea of creating an economic and monetary union.[107]

Judged strictly on itself, however, the 1992 programme appears to have been oversold. The assumptions about its benefits depended upon other assumptions about flanking conditions and policies, which were not fulfilled.

A survey of 7,000 manufacturing firms conducted by Eurostat in 1996 showed that there were only two sectors of the programme where 50% or more of the respondents were positive – the elimination of Customs documents and the crossing of frontiers. Improvement in road haulage scored high. There were low positive rates for patents, public procurement (very low) and company tax (that was not in the programme, but some work was done).

Savings on customs formalities were estimated at 5 billion ECUs per annum, about 0.5% of the value of intra-Community trade. 'Mutual recognition' was something of a disappointment; it was found to be beset by legal uncertainty and not helpful in opening up new markets.

The other major weakness has been in public procurement. The directives in the different sectors required transparency, publication in the Official Journal and, electronically, of calls for tender and respect for low bids. In 1996 cross-border procurement was 3%, which was virtually unchanged from 1987. The Commission has proposed more serious enforcement but there seems to be more to it than price. Long term trust between suppliers and purchasers is important, as well as proximity to head offices. It has been noted that in the USA only 6% of public civil engineering contracts go out of state.

Expansion of intra-trade

By 1995 the share of intra-Community trade in total manufacturing imports had increased by 6.7% from 1985. The most dramatic surge in the programme period was in cross-border investment, which rose seven-fold. The growth in merger and acquisition was largely domestic, suggesting that the first impacts of the programme were to promote restructuring at home, whether defensively or aggressively. There was some market concentration. The share of total sales by the four leading firms rose on average from 20.5% to 22.8% between 1987 and 1993 but there was also a reduction in domestic concentration in France and in Britain. In technology-intensive industries, concentration was more marked at 6% over the period.

The economic gains fall far short of what was foreseen in the Cecchini Report. With no supportive fiscal policy in the Member States, the GDP gains were forecast to be

4.5%. Ex-post study suggests 1.1% to 2.5%, which is worthwhile but is not what was held out. The recession that began in 1992 markets bears part of the responsibility. There may also be a long learning curve, in addition to business strategies which give more priority to defending existing markets than attacking new ones.

The programme was never scheduled to end in 1992. Additional market-opening measures remained and it became a priority of the British Presidency of 1998 to push on – both with new measures and with a drive for better national implementation all round. The monitoring tool is the Single Market Scoreboard, which analyses progress and results obtained. In particular it names and (politely) shames Member States which are behind with the transposition of Single Market directives into national law (regulations have direct effect). The October 1998 Scoreboard (Table 10.3) shows where the Member States stood.

Telecommunications and public procurement lag furthest behind

The exercise highlighted one almost philosophical problem. Community market-opening regulations, which often means national re-regulation, are decided by centralised institutions in Brussels and centrally by the Member States of the Community. Application is a task of central governments where the measures are not directly applicable. But monitoring, enforcement and compliance verification are often in the hands of local government agencies, or other agencies at one remove from the centre. They were not all new creations. Most of them already existed for other tasks from which they were

Table 10.3   Breakdown by area and Member State of non-transposed directives, 15.10.1998

	%	B	DK	D	EL	E	F	IRL	I	L	NL	A	P	FIN	S	UK
Telecommunications (15)*	66.7	4			10		2	1	2	6	4		4		3	
Public procurement (10)	60	1	1	1	5	4	1	1	2	1	1	1	4			1
Transport (48)	52.1	12	7	4	5	7	9	17	12	9	8	9	11	3	3	9
Intellectual and industrial property (7)	42.9				2			3	1	1	1		1			
Social policy (38)	26.3	2		3	5		3	1	8	9		2	4			2
Chemical products (74)	21.6	9	1	5	6	2	7	11	6	7	1	7	6	1		2
Veterinary checks (193)	18.1	10	2	8	13	7	23	14	19	14	4	17	17	2	6	13
Environment (92)	17.4	11	3	4	7	5	6	6	6	4	4	3	5	2	3	6
Cosmetic products (38)	15.8	1			2		3	4	1	3	1	3	2		1	
Food legislation (101)	14.8	3	1	4	4	3	4	10	7	3		6	11	1		2
Capital goods (99)	12.1	8	2	2	2	1	3	4	7	4		2	2	1	1	1
Motor vehicles (146)	8.2		1	1	1	1	3	1		7	1	1	1	1	1	11
Plant-health checks (172)	6.4	1	1	1	2	1	3	1	2	10	1	4	5	1		3
TOTAL		64	20	33	64	32	67	76	74	80	26	55	74	12	18	50

*number of Directives concerned in each sector.

converted. They have their own traditions and their own legal frameworks. This can mean that even after a measure has gone through its stages in the central institutions, and even after it has where necessary been transposed into national law, there can be gaping discrepancies in its application on the ground. This is an inevitable effect of the decentralisation that is built into Community administration. The shining example, in a different sphere, is that the Customs Union has no Customs Service and there is no proposal to create one.

The alternative is centralised administration, which would be politically unacceptable and would reinforce the notions about Brussels, the city of Towers – of ivory and of Babel.

External effects

Fortress Europe has been demolished. This unfortunate expression, coined by the Nazis to describe their readiness to repulse Allied invasion, came into use in the USA to foreshadow new barriers in more tightly protected European import markets. No such restrictive effects have been substantiated.[108]

THE SINGLE MARKET: ANNEX

The following are selected examples of Single Market legislation: showing its wide scope.

Decision 85/368/EEC (OJ L 199 31.7.85): Equivalence of professional qualifications
Directive 87/102/EEC (OJ L 42, 12/02/87): Consumer credit
Directive 88/295/EEC (OJ 127, 25.05.88): Public purchasing
Directive 88/378/EEC (OJ 187, 16.07.88): Toy safety
Directive 88/407/EEC (OJ L 194, 22.07.88): Trade in frozen bovine sperm
Directive 89/106/EEC (OJ L 40, 11.02.89): Building materials
Directive 89/440/EEC (OJ 120, 21.07.89): Public works contracts
Directive 89/552/EEC (OJ 298, 17.10.89): TV broadcasts
Directive 89/646/EEC (OJ L 386, 30.12.89): Credit establishments
Directive 4064/89/EEC (OJ L 395, 30.12.89): Mergers
Directive 90/336/EEC (OJ L 180, 13.07.90): Right of residence, students
Directive 90/387/EEC (OJ 192, 24.07.90): Telecoms open network
Directive 90/531/EEC (OJ L 297, 29.10.90): Public purchasing – water, energy, transport, telecoms
Directive 90/619/EEC (OJ L 330, 29.11.90): Second life insurance
Regulation EEC no. 3677/90 (OJ L 357, 20.12.90): Narcotics
Directive 91/263/EEC (OJ L 128, 23.05.91): Telecom terminals
Directive 91/477/EEC (OJ 13.09.91): Possession of firearms
Directive 92/32/EEC (OJ L 154, 05.06.92): Packaging and labelling of dangerous substances

Decision 92/421/EEC (OJ L 231, 13.08.92): Action plan for tourism
Regulation EEC no. 684/92 (OJ L 74, 20.03.92): International passenger coach travel
Regulation EEC no. 3911/92 (OJ L 395, 31.12.92): Exports of cultural articles
Directive 93/35/EEC (OJ L 151, 23.06.93): Cosmetics
Regulation EEC no. 259/93 (OJ L 30, 06.02.93): Shipment of waste
Regulation EEC no. 40/90 (OJ L11 14.01.94): Community trade mark

Possibly the Single Market development with the most conspicuous effects for the public at large was the judgement given by the Court of Justice on 15 December 1995 in Case 415/93, *Bosman*. The Court held that under Article 48 (now 39) no rules could require soccer clubs to field only a limited number players who were nationals of other Member States. This opened the way to multinational teams in national leagues. Hence the result in a France–England match played in 1999 was jocularly given as Arsenal 2: Arsenal 0.

COMPETITION POLICY

The paradoxes of policy

Competition policy – rules applying to undertakings and aids granted by states – is marked by three paradoxes.

In economic theory (and in some of the statutes by which regulators of privatised industry in Britain are governed, notably Oftel, for telecommunications) regulation will ultimately be replaced by conditions of full competition. But competition itself has to be regulated to keep it 'fair'.[109]

Second, competition is self-contradictory. There will be one surviving competitor serving the whole market without competition. Entry costs may make it impossible for there to be new competitors, unless there is technological change to reduce them. Before that stage is reached, public authorities would usually intervene to promote renewed competition, unless they positively favoured a monopoly.

Third, 'Europe both seeks and avoids competition'.[110] In attacking anti-competitive behaviour in the Single Market, the Union may also be damaging the international competitiveness of European undertakings *vis-à-vis* undertakings elsewhere which are not subject to the same disciplines. There is talk of international competition codes, but they remain talk. Meanwhile, the contradictions between internal and external competition and competitiveness create sustained tension within the Commission between the Commissioner responsible for competition and the colleague responsible for industry. There have been famous campaigns to try to stop the Competition Directorate-General – 'the ayatollahs of competition', according to one Industry Commissioner – from cramping firms' styles in the global economy.

Competition decisions proposed by DGIV are taken by the college of Commissioners, where there may also be solicitude for national industrial interests. A famous case was the state payment of FFr 20 billion to Air France, approved by the Commission but disapproved by the Court of First Instance in 1998 in a suit brought by British Airways and other airlines. In a widely criticised move, the Commission simply rewrote its letter of approval, changing the parts which the Court had ruled invalid.

A federal power

Competition policy in the European Union has another peculiarity. Violations of the rules are adjudicated by the Commission on its own authority, under the control of the Court of Justice. In this respect, the Commission is acting as a federal authority, possessing and exercising its own powers independently of the Member States. The Member States have in this rare case preferred a supranational control authority. Left entirely to themselves, they might not have striven officiously to curtail unfair practices that gave their enterprises an edge in the Common Market.

Nevertheless, some of the Member States are dissatisfied with the way in which their chosen instrument acts. They believe that they can detect the Commission in the act of using competition policy to serve other policy purposes, if not also disregarding the needs of national economies. Indeed, a former competition Commissioner, Mr Peter Sutherland, openly acknowledged that the powers that the Commission possessed could be used in versatile ways. The Commissioner responsible in the 1994–99 Commission, Mr Karl van Miert, said openly in his 1994 Report:[111]

> Indeed, the goals of growth, competitiveness and employment have led the Commission to take a positive approach to many agreements between companies in 1994.

(Conversely, 'There can be no getting away from the fact that measures to promote competitiveness are in some cases, at least in the short run, job-destroying'.[112])

The 'positive' approach to the regulation of competition has provoked suggestions that competition policy might be 'unbundled' and entrusted to a Community Cartel Office wholly independent of the Commission – and, perhaps or perhaps not, also independent of the Member States.[113] These suggestions, mostly of German origin,[114] have never been taken up in treaty revision.

A concentrated role

Another dissatisfaction in business circles is that the Commission acts as detective, prosecutor and judge in the examination of breaches of the rules. There is in fact another judge, in the ECJ in Luxembourg, which in this case acts like the federal appeals court, which it is not in its other modes. In fairness, it should be added that when the Commission summons suspected violators to a hearing, there is a Hearings Officer, formally independent of the Commission (although on its payroll) to advise parties of their rights and empowered to recommend to the Commission that the case should not proceed.

The powers

The purpose of competition is, in economic theory, the continuous improvement in efficiency in the use of the factors of production. It reduces costs, it improves quality, it innovates, it reduces waste. It is Adam Smith's invisible hand:

> By pursuing his own interest [every individual] frequently promotes that of society more effectually than when he really intends to promote it.[115]

In a similar vein, Mr van Miert, said:

> I shall not dwell here on the traditional objectives pursued by the Commission through its competition policy (improving the competitiveness of business both large and small, opening up markets, improving the allocation of resources, increasing consumer choice, etc.) . . .[116]

In terms of the Treaties, the purpose of competition rules is to forestall attempts to dissect by business behaviour a market made common or single by the abolition of state-imposed cross-frontier barriers. This is the thrust of Article 81 (ex-85) cartels, Article 82 (ex-86) monopolists or near it, and Article 87 (ex-92) state subsidies. These Treaty articles are complemented by Regulation 4064/89, merger control, OJ L series 395 of 30.12.89. It was amended by Council Regulation (EC) no. 1310/97 of 30 June 1997, OJ L 180, 9.7.97, as to which see below. The Treaty articles have not been changed in successive Treaty revision.

Article 81

Article 81, better known by its old style number 85, can be traced back to the anti-trust Article 62 of the ECSC Treaty. Article 60 was drafted under the influence of the team in the US Embassy in Paris that helped M. Monnet to give substance to his project.[117]

Article 81 imposes a flat prohibition, in paras 1 and 2, with an escape route in para. 3. Undertakings are forbidden to agree or concert with each other to divide up the market. They may, however, agree or concert if they thereby improve production or distribution or promote technical or economic progress. To obtain these reliefs, undertakings must notify their agreements or decisions to the Commission, which decides whether the prohibition is inapplicable. Sole distributorships, which benefit consumers, can qualify for exemption.[118]

When the Commission announced that it was ready to receive notifications, 35,000 were received. An unknown number of cartels remained, and are still unnotified.

Article 82 (ex-86)

This article prohibits abuse of the dominant position of one or more undertakings within the common market or a substantial part of it. It gives a non-exclusive list of types of abuse. Occupying a dominant position is not in itself an abuse, but, as will be seen later, it may attract unfavourable attention. Predatory pricing, discrimination and tying-in to one-sale sales of extra products (e.g. 'full line forcing') may be abusive.

Articles 83, 84 and 85 (ex-87, 88, 89)

These articles set up the arrangements for giving effect to the preceding articles. The most important measure is Regulation 17/62.[119] Unusually even for that integrationist period, the Regulation gives the Commission powers, uncontrolled by the Council, its Member States or the European Parliament, to investigate – the 'dawn raids' are stirring stuff – adjudicate and fine or absolve. In this it follows the precedent of the High Authority of the ECSC, which had penalty powers directly in Article 65 of the ECSC Treaty.

Article 86

Article 86 addresses the difficult matter of state or state-sponsored monopolies, which abounded when these articles were drafted. The article says piously that these bodies must not abuse their privileges. But it also recognises that some of them have *public service obligations* that can oblige them to behave in ways incompatible with the general rules. In practice, successive Commissions largely left Article 86 alone. The spread of privatisation which began in the 1980s places commercial enterprises on the market where there were previously state monopolies. The Commission's approach has been to secure the phased opening of 'services of general interest' or 'universal service' to free competition, but with regard for public service obligations. In the Commission's definition:

> Universal service reflects Europe's determination to complete the internal market while at the same time introducing greater competition in many sectors serving the general economic interest: balanced regional development, equal treatment for all citizens and high-quality service supplied to users round the clock.[120]

Article 86 unusually empowers the Commission to address *Directives* to the Member States. In the Commission's interpretation of this paragraph of the article (para. 3), these are not the *legislative directives* which occur in other treaty articles (and which generally speaking do not have direct effect – that is, they need to be legislated nationally), but statements of directly applicable law. Using these powers and that interpretation the Commission in 1988 issued a Directive to liberalise the market in telecommunications.[121]

Article 87

Article 87 bans state aids that distort[122] or threaten to distort competition and affect trade between Member States. State aid may be dispensed at several levels – central, regional or local – but all are caught. Some state aid is compatible with the common market (para. 2) and some may be (para. 3). Para. 3, for example, legalises regional aid schemes, of the kind that the Community itself operates. About 10% of the aid which states give or propose to give to enterprises is illegal.[123] After a period in which the Commission hesitated to lock horns with Member States, there have more recently been several famous battles between the Commission and state bodies, especially in the lineage of tough competition Commissioners – Peter Sutherland, Sir Leon Brittan and (in the 1995–2000 Commission) Karel van Miert.

The proposed grant of state aid must be notified to the Commission, which decides if it is justified. If not, it is banned and any aid already dispensed under the scheme must be repaid. Aid can include tax relief. A Member State that thinks that it has a good case can try to get a unanimous decision from the Council in its favour, even if the Commission is moving against it.

Authorised state aid

In some industries, continuing survival or necessary restructuring (the euphemism for closures) may depend on state aid. The conditions for granting it have been formalised in codes, which exist or have existed for textiles, shipbuilding and steel. Compliance with the rules of the code helps to secure approval.

In April 1997 the Commission published its fifth survey[124] of state aid in the Union. Although compared with previous surveys, the trend was downward,[125]

according to a widely held view this level is still too high and if Europe is to be competitive at world level it must be reduced.[126]

The sixth survey (published in June 1998) records a further fall. Member States provided 83 billion ECUs in state aid, 38.5 billion for manufacturing in the period 1994–96

In the context of the Single Market Action Plan, which is monitored in a Scoreboard, the Commission produces analyses of state aid to manufacturing (see Table 10.4).

Table 10.4   State aid to manufacturing industry: annual averages 1992–94 and 1994–96

Member State	In per cent of value added		In ECUs per person employed		In million ECUs	
	1992–94	**1994–96**	1992–94	**1994–96**	1992–94	**1994–96**
Austria	–	**1.3**	–	**626**	–	**448**
Belgium	2.5	**3.0**	1,310	**1,678**	920	**1,149**
Denmark	2.5	**2.9**	1,120	**1,383**	539	**671**
Germany	4.4	**3.7**	2,091	**1,888**	19,851	**16,639**
Old Länder	–	–	527	**455**	4,312	**3,192**
New Länder	–	–	10,816	**8,216**	15,539	**13,447**
Greece	6.5	**6.3**	987	**863**	722	**662**
Spain	1.8	**2.7**	512	**837**	1,311	**2,101**
Finland	–	**1.6**	–	**911**	–	**365**
France	2.4	**1.8**	1,174	**927**	4,931	**3,740**
Ireland	1.7	**1.5**	818	**838**	198	**215**
Italy	6.4	**5.8**	2,205	**2,151**	10,320	**9,760**
Luxembourg	2.6	**2.3**	1,555	**1,375**	55	**46**
Netherlands	1.5	**1.4**	760	**788**	694	**686**
Portugal	2.5	**1.9**	443	**371**	467	**382**
Sweden	–	**0.8**	–	**406**	–	**318**
United Kingdom	0.9	**0.9**	245	**263**	1,431	**1,513**
EUR 12	3.5		1,339		41,439	**37,563**
EUR 15		**3.0**		**1,238**		**38,318**

Source: The Single Market Scoreboard, October 1998.

239

Telecommunications

The so-called 'natural monopolies' of the telephone system and its outcrops were early candidates for pro-competition policies, in this case by deregulation. The eleven-year history is shown in Box 10.1.

Box 10.1   Deregulation in telecommunications

1988	Supply of terminal equipment
1990–93	Value-added services and data communication
1995	Satellite services and equipment
1996	Telecommunications using cable TV networks and alternative networks. Mobile phones
1998	All infrastructures and voice telephone services

Source: Commission.

Mergers

The Commission proposed in 1973 that there should be Community control of mergers in place of national controls. The Regulation was adopted sixteen years later – 4064/89, OJ, L 395, 30.12.89. Even by the standards of the Council's conduct of business before the reforms of the mid-1980s, this was an unconscionable gestation period. The Member States were wary. Because of the implications for employment, investment, production and exports, some preferred to keep the oversight (and perhaps even encouragement) of concentrations in their own hands. Others professed a free market philosophy – if undertakings want to merge, why obstruct their commercial judgement? They might have taken comfort from the lack of any consensual research conclusions regarding the effect of business concentration.

The Regulation requires the parties to a proposed merger to notify their plans to the Commission, which decides whether it would be compatible with the common or single market. Although Article 82 does not say that dominance is in itself abusive, in merger control it comes near to being so regarded. Compare Commissioner van Miert in his 1994 Report:

> The Commission's central objective in carrying out its responsibilities under the Merger Regulation is to prevent the creation or strengthening of dominant positions. The fact that companies enjoying dominance will charge higher prices and invest less in research and development than companies facing active competition is well documented.[127]

In the same vein, when in March 1998 a giant Anglo-Dutch publishing venture fell through, the Commission's parting comment was that the new business would have been

several times larger than any other publisher of professional information in the EU and

> could prevent a competitive situation in the supply of legal, fiscal and scientific
> information in the EU, with a significant impact on the terms and prices at which this
> information is made available to users and consumers.[128]

Although sometimes described as 'one stop shopping', Community merger control did not entirely replace national competition authorities even where cross-border mergers were concerned (see Table 10.5).

Small extension

In 1997 the Council agreed to an amendment of the 1989 Regulation by which it extended the Commission's reach, not by lowering the thresholds of the turnover of the enterprises concerned[129] as the Commission had proposed, but by reducing thresholds for certain cross-border transactions. Below the thresholds and subject to national law, national authorities may act.

Implementation

The Commission began quietly, not objecting to many mergers. In 1993 there were forty-eight notifications. By 1997 there were some 150 a year. By then the Commission was involved in some spectacular cases in which it found against the proposed mergers unless the parties accepted conditions which some of them found oppressive.[130]

Table 10.5 Number of final merger decisions taken by the European Commission each year and number of deals notified

	Final decisions	Notifications
1991	86	63
1992	70	60
1993	63	58
1994	102	95
1995	116	110
1996	132	131
1997	146	152
Breakdown by type of activity:		
Joint venture/control	49%	
Acquisition of majority stake	39%	
Take-over bid	7%	
Other	5%	

Source: Commission.

Extra-territoriality

In the span of competition policy, Community jurisdiction can look extra-territorial. This occurs when an undertaking with its seat outside the Community acts in ways that are incompatible with the Single Market. The principle was established in the Continental Can Co case before the Court.[131] Because of their shared interest, the Commission concluded an agreement with the US Justice Department to co-operate on appropriate investigations. The agreement was annulled as *ultra vires* but replaced by one which the Council had authorised.[132] It was in the terms of this co-operation that the two authorities accepted like undertakings from the Microsoft Corporation in 1996 regarding competitive practices.[133]

No 'dumping'

Within the Community there cannot be anti-dumping duties, because they are incompatible with the Single Market. 'Dumping' in the sense of selling at less than the price on the 'home' market is improbable, if only because purchasers in the home market have free access to goods selling elsewhere at the lower price. But selling in the rest of the Single Market at predatory prices might fall foul of Article 82. Community action against dumping by certain countries is shown in Box 10.2.

Box 10.2   Anti-dumping 1980–97

EC action against:			
China	69	Turkey	25
Japan	51	Eastern Europe	184
Former Yugoslavia	36	SE Asia	74
USA	35	Other	172
Total	656	Annual rate	36

Workload

In 1997 the Commission handled 1,338 new cases (1996: 1,246):

Articles 85, 86, 90	500
Mergers	162 (up 31%)
State aids	656 (new aid measures,516; unnotified aid,140)

One step under discussion to reduce the workload would be to exclude from control 'vertical agreements' between manufacturers and their distributors (which can already qualify for block exemptions). This is the only innovation in competition policy under review, in the form of responses to a Green Paper, in 1998. It would not be popular with consumer pressure groups.

TAXATION

Indirect taxes

Customs duties are a function of the Customs Union. They are fixed by the Council acting by qualified majority (Article 26), within the limits of GATT/WTO obligations.

Turnover taxes, excise duties and other forms of indirect taxation are required by Article 93 to be harmonised to the extent necessary to sustain the Single Market. The Council acts by unanimity, after *consulting* the EP (Article 93). In practice the original Community of Six decided that the turnover taxes in force in some of them should be replaced by a value added tax. Turnover taxes, which are cumulative, are difficult to neutralise accurately or consistently if they are remitted on export. There was a risk of excessive rebates, amounting to an export subsidy.

VAT also became a basis for part of the Community's 'own resources'.[134] A series of Directives was passed to establish it, culminating in the Sixth Directive adopted on 17 May 1977.[135] The unanimity rule enabled Member States to cling to features that they held dear. In particular, national VAT rates remained divergent. This was an obvious barrier dividing the common market. According to the Cecchini Report (the manifesto for the Single Market), every export/import transaction cost 153 ECUs, 1.5% of the average consignment value, because of frontier formalities, including charging VAT.[136]

The simple solution would be to charge VAT at the rate of the country of origin. This was the Commission's 1987 proposal, coupled with a clearing arrangement for reapportioning the yield among the Member States. The latter found the proposal tax-inefficient and costly to national exchequers. The Commission did not stand for a uniform rate. It advocated minimum rates, believing that small differences would be lost in other pricing factors and market pressure and would not be a barrier to cross-frontier trade. Taking account of the wide spread of national rates, it proposed a two-rate system to which all Member States could rally. They, however, preferred to keep closer to the status quo by operating three rates: a standard rate not lower than 15%, and two reduced rates not lower than 5%.[137]

As part of the package agreed in November–December 1989, the Member States accepted the 'Community principle' which the Commission had proposed – approximation of rates, no tax rebate on export and no tax imposition on import – but maintained that they could not bring it into effect by the end of 1992. For a transitional period, VAT would be charged in the country of destination (as hitherto). The transitional period would end on 1 January 1997. It did not. Work on a permanent system goes on more or less.

'Imports and exports'

One side-effect of the abolition of frontier checks is that the basis for statistics of intra-Community trade changed. The notion of 'imports and exports' disappeared.

Statistics are based on traders' returns to their tax authority. In Britain they run a month later than statistics of trade with the rest of the world. Intra-trade statistics are unreliable.

Excise duties are mentioned in the governing Article 93, but little progress has been made in approximating the rates. Member States prefer to maintain their freedom to vary them according to budgetary needs or health and environmental aims. The Commission proposed that rates should be brought more closely into line and that the principle of taxation in the country of destination should be maintained. The reason for the difference in the treatment of VAT is that excise duties are imposed at a single stage, when the product comes on the market. The only Council agreement was on the structure of tobacco tax, which is in two parts. There is a specific charge of x per 1,000 cigarettes plus an *ad valorem* charge, a percentage of the retail price (including VAT). No moves are pending to comply with Article 93.

Cross-Channel cigarettes and alcohol

The discrepancy between British and French excise on tobacco and alcohol has stimulated a substantial cross-Channel movement in individual small or not so small quantities of the goods.

So-called 'duty-free' sales at travel terminals and on board ships and aircraft are actually tax-free, that is, of VAT and excise. Tax-free shopping is anomalous in a Single Market. The Council decided in 1991 that it would end in June 1999. Agitation to retain it – because it is popular with travellers, is an earner for travel companies and provides jobs – mounted as the terminal date approached. With notably Britain and Germany converted to the virtues of duty-free shopping, the Commission in February 1999 stood firm and pooh-poohed estimates of the job losses that would go with abolition. With no new Commission proposal, the Member States were impotent, although they huffed and puffed.

Direct taxes

There are no plans to harmonise European Union rates of VAT, income tax or company tax. Yet inhabitants of Britain could be forgiven for thinking precisely the opposite. At the end of ... [1998] ... a large section of the British press claimed that Oskar Lafontaine, Germany's ebullient finance minister, was plotting to make the British pay more tax ... but there was little of substance to support the fantasies.[138]

There is no explicit Treaty requirement to harmonise or approximate *direct* taxation. It is argued that differences in national direct taxes and tax laws distort the Single Market because (a) they affect cross-border investment and (b) they can discriminate between enterprises which invest outside their own state and those remaining within a single tax jurisdiction.

The basis for action on direct taxation is weak. It relates to Articles 94 (better known as the old 100) and 95 which concern laws that directly affect the internal market. Article 95 stipulates that the Council qualified majority/co-decision procedure that applies generally is inapplicable to fiscal provisions: they require unanimity. (Tax, 'own resources' and treaty change are the hard core of unanimity.)

In broad terms, national direct taxation remains unaffected by Community provisions. The Member States have agreed on two packages that make some difference.

The first time the Community dipped a toe into direct taxation was in an agreement of 23 July 1990, falling within the period of the Single Market programme. There were three parts:

1. The 'Mergers directive'[139] established a common system for the taxation of mergers, divisions of assets and exchange of shares between companies of different Member States. Because of tax differences, assets accruing to merged companies had been liable to incur increased charges.
2. The 'Parent/subsidiary Directive'[140] is for a common system to prevent triple taxation – first on the subsidiary's profit in its country of establishment; second the withholding tax charged on profits distributed in the country of the subsidiary's establishment, and third on the subsidiary's distributed profits when incorporated in the parent company's profits. This is usually thought to be the most important of the three measures.
3. The 'Arbitration Convention'[141] to avoid double taxation on transfer pricing. This can occur when a tax authority increases the transfer price between a company and its associate in another Member State but the authority in the other Member State does not reduce the transfer price accordingly.[142] The Convention provides for the resolution of differences of opinion among tax authorities.

Soft law on taxes

The second step was unusual. There was no Commission proposal in the technical sense of the word. There was a Commission communication on harmful tax competition. It took account of a discussion opened among Finance Ministers at an informal meeting in Verona in April 1996. There is no Community law but a unique

> Resolution of the Council and the Representatives of the Governments of the Member States, meeting within the Council, of 1 December 1997 on a *Code of Conduct* for Business Taxation.[143]

The Resolution

The Resolution

> emphasises that a code of conduct is a political commitment and does not affect Member States' rights and obligations or the respective spheres of competence of the Member States and the Community in accordance with the Treaty.

In other words it is (a) a case of 'soft law', which gives strong guidance but falls short of creating an obligation and (b) a rare example of how subsidiarity replaces action by the Community.

The discussion from which the code of conduct emerged addressed distortions in the single market, preventing excessive losses of tax revenue or getting tax structures to develop in a more employment friendly way.

The code itself bears on only one aspect of the many problems. It states in its Article B that the favoured tax treatment of an enterprise, giving a

significantly lower effective level of taxation ... than that which applies generally in the Member State

is harmful and is covered by the code. Member States are not to introduce new anti-code measures ('standstill') and are to eliminate any they have ('rollback'). The code of conduct is qualified by half-a-dozen unilateral interpretations of some of its provisions.

Like its 1990 predecessor, the 1997 package is in three parts. The code is the first part. The second part is an Annex in which the *Council* asks the Commission to bring forward a draft *directive* on the taxation of savings. Luxembourg, sometimes known as 'downtown Frankfurt' because of the number of foreign banks it houses and the fiscal facilities it offers them, says that this should be part of a directive covering general arrangements for business taxation. The Commission has said that its proposal will be for a 'coexistence model' under which each Member State would either operate a withholding tax (on income earned by non-residents) or provide information on savings income to other Member States (to enable them to tax foreign income earned by their residents).[144]

Third, the Council asked the Commission to produce a draft directive on interest and royalty payments between associated companies. The Commission's proposal, dated 8 March 1998, is designed to eliminate taxes levied at source on payments of interest and royalties between associated companies in different Member States.

The proposed withholding tax

The absence of Community rules on direct taxation gave rise to repeated complaint about opportunities for tax evasion. The butt of most of the complaint was Luxembourg. Luxembourg does not levy tax on savings accounts of non-residents and has no obligation to tell non-residents' tax authorities what interest has been paid. Since fiscal decisions need unanimity, Luxembourg was consistently able to block proposals to establishing a withholding tax on non-resident accounts. Like Germany, Austria found such tax-evasion objectionable. At the launch of its Presidency it announced that it would push for the tax on external savings. As in similar episodes in the past, Luxembourg immediately stated its opposition, in which it was joined by the UK, concerned at some of its own fiscal devices. It is difficult to see a compromise between tax and don't tax, except as part of a bigger taxation package with something for everyone.

The German Presidency of the first half of 1999 took up the cause of distortion produced by different tax arrangements. There were several versions of its objectives ranging from an impossible corporate tax harmonisation to eliminating national practices which competed unfairly for investment. An artificial connection was made with the Single Currency. As Professor Otmar Issing of the European Central Bank pointed out,[145] fiscal policy should remain national because it is the instrument for local economic management when monetary policy has passed to the ECB. There were at no time proposals for Community involvement in national income tax.

MONETARY POLICY

The chicken-and-egg problem confronts the seeker after truth. Is a currency union established as a step towards a political union? Or must a political union follow ineluctably from the establishment of a currency union, which might be the corollary of a single market, itself the extension of a customs union? The answer is something of everything. Historical precedents are confusing. The stages leading to economic and monetary union are shown in Box 10.3.

Historical precedents

The Prussian-led Customs Union, *Zollverein*, which by 1833 had acquired 24 members, is usually regarded as one of the integrative forces that produced the German Empire of 1866. One of the imperial symbols was the mark, replacing a plethora of currencies with confusingly the same name for units of different value. The territorially contiguous Empire needed a currency, but did the currency need an Empire? The parallel Latin Monetary Union of 1865 to 1925, legalising the interchange of the currencies of Belgium, France, Greece, Italy and Switzerland, had no political union overtones, any more than the currency union of Belgium and Luxembourg has today.[146] The currency unions established in adjacent British ex-colonies did nothing to hold them together politically and were swept away with national independence.

Visionary undertakings

The first commitment to currency union and political union coincides with the first enlargement of the Community. Meeting in Paris in October 1972, the Heads of State and Government (now better known as the European Council), including those of the acceding countries, 'reaffirmed their determination irreversibly to achieve the economic and monetary union' . . . and 'affirmed their intention to transform before the end of the present decade the whole complex of their relations into a European Union'.[147]

They had in their hands the report the Six had commissioned in 1969 from M. Pierre Werner, Prime Minister of Luxembourg, containing a blueprint for a monetary union to be reached in three stages.[148] The principle of a single currency did not perhaps seem utopian at a time when exchange rates had been stable, and the cause might even have been advanced by the withdrawal in 1971 of the dollar link to gold, the key of the Bretton Woods system of fixed post-war exchange rates.[149] But the vision disappeared with the Yom Kippur War in October 1973, followed by the four-fold increase in oil prices decreed by the Organisation of Petroleum Exporting Countries (OPEC). The

Box 10.3   Stages on the way to economic and monetary union

1969	The Hague summit commissions report on possibilities of EMU.
1971	The Community agrees phased plan for the creation of EMU within ten years but the scheme fails because of world monetary instability and internal EC divisions.
1972	The 'currency snake' set up.
1979	European Monetary System (EMS) comes into force with eight initial members; creation of the ECU.
1987	Single European Act comes into force.
1988	Hanover European Council appoints a committee of experts (chaired by Jacques Delors) to examine ways and means of completing EMU.
1989	Madrid European Council approves Delors' Report and decides to begin first stage of EMU on 1 July 1990 and to prepare an IGC on EMU.
1990	First stage of EMU involving the removal of the remaining restrictions on capital movements, increased co-ordination of individual economic policies and more intensive co-operation between central banks.
1990	Sterling enters the ERM.
1992	September: Britain and Italy leave the ERM after Black Wednesday.
1993	Fluctuation bands of ERM widened to +/–15% except for Germany and the Netherlands.
1993	TEU comes into force.
1994	European Monetary Institute set up in Frankfurt.
1995	Commission 'White Paper' on single currency.
1995	Madrid European Council adopts the name 'euro'.
1996	Dublin European Council agrees basis of 'Stability and Growth Pact'.
1997	Amsterdam European Council agrees:
	• Stability and Growth Pact regulations
	• Legal framework for use of euro.
1998	Brussels European Council agrees:
	• Which States meet convergence criteria
	• Cross-rates of participating currencies
	• ECB office-bearers.
1998	Ecofin meeting determines value of euro in national currencies.
1999	EMU comes into being.

Member States of the enlarged Community, caught in the second[150] of its crises of confidence, abandoned Community solidarity in favour of unilateral salvation. Inflation rates diverged and exchange rates oscillated. Germany was the exception. It had already broken with the credit expansion trend of the early 1970s and stabilised itself.[151]

Any idea of creating monetary union by the end of the 1970s was dropped. Commission Vice-President Ortoli tried to keep a small flame burning by generously reinterpreting the phrase to mean 'in the 1980s'. The next move was not dictated by outside events but was another insider's initiative.

The revival

In the summer of 1977 the President of the Commission, Mr Roy, later Lord, Jenkins, was smarting under criticism in the *Economist* newspaper that his first six months in Brussels had been disappointingly inactive. He decided to revive the idea of monetary union[152] and delivered a seven-point speech at the European University Institute – the Commission's in-house study centre – in Florence in October 1977.[153] In less than a year the Community was on the move, driven by the combined forces of the German Chancellor, Helmut Schmidt, and the French President, Valéry Giscard d'Estaing. The two were old acquaintances from their days as finance ministers, but their motives were mixed. Schmidt may have been concerned by the revaluation of the Deutschmark against the dollar and looking for some cushioning effect from other European currencies by tying them more closely to the mark. Giscard believed, conversely, that France was at risk of spending its reserves to hold the franc up and that there should be better burden sharing between Germany and the others.[154] Britain was invited to participate in secret discussions with French and German finance officials, usually in airport buildings, and did so before withdrawing. The British Prime Minister, James Callaghan, told Schmidt and Giscard that a closer link with the mark would pull sterling up with deflationary consequences[155] (in the language of the period, this meant increased unemployment). The Community decided to go ahead without the British. It was an early example of what acquired a number of descriptions, including 'variable geometry', 'multi-speed', 'differentiation', 'graduated integration', 'enhanced co-operation' and more recently 'flexibility'.

The outcome of discussions in the European Council in Copenhagen in April 1978, Bremen in July and Brussels in December, was the European Monetary System (EMS) with at its core the Exchange Rate Mechanism (ERM).[156] It began on 13 March 1979, after a delay while France held out in the 1978 agricultural price-fixing.

The European Monetary System

The ERM is a hybrid – not entirely Community, not entirely outside it. The Commission proposed that it should be based on the default Article 235 EEC (now 308) but this was not accepted. Its bases are a Resolution of the European Council, which is not a legal instrument, a decision of the Council, which is, and an agreement between the participating central banks, which might be binding on the parties in international law. Member

States are not obliged to join. Sweden did not. Others have been in, out and in again. Third countries belonged to earlier exchange stabilisation arrangements for Member State currencies. Some of them have talked about joining the ERM but none has ever done so, possibly because of its link with monetary union.[157]

The ERM is in two parts. In the first part there is a parity grid for participating currencies. They may, without legal hindrance, fluctuate within a fixed band. If the fluctuation is wider, there is an obligation to intervene. The obligation is double-edged – to sell if a currency is rising, to buy if it is falling. The other more important part-mechanism is a divergence indicator. This measures changes in the value of a currency against the ECU. The ECU was a basket of the currencies of *all* Member States weighted for their economic importance. When a currency's relation to the ECU is no longer what its current economic weighting would make it and when the change is greater than 75% of the permissible fluctuation within the fixed band of the currency grid (as above), the country of the currency thus affected is required to act. The action can include fixing a new parity (by agreement with all the participants) and a new weighting within the ECU basket. To help countries to intervene on foreign exchange markets there is a very short-term credit facility, short-term support facility and medium-term financial assistance. This is illustrated in the following worked out example of a divergence threshold for a currency with a weighting in the ECU basket of 20% and a fluctuation band of 2.25%:

$$\frac{2.25 \times (100 - 20) \times 0.75}{100} = 1.35\%^{[158]}$$

After a settling-in and learning phase involving parity adjustments, the system stabilised and changes were infrequent. The original fluctuation bands were 2.25% except for Italy, 6%. For convenience, parities were usually expressed against the mark rather than the ECU.

> Between 1979 and 1985 exchange rate variability was half what it had been in 1975–1979; it halved again between 1986 and 1989.[159]

British aloofness

Despite such claims for the success of the system, Britain remained outside. This gave rise to tension within the Cabinet of Mrs Thatcher, whose Chancellor of the Exchequer, Mr Nigel, later Lord, Lawson, pursued an economic management policy of 'shadowing' the mark. Mrs Thatcher, whose personal economic adviser, Sir Alan Walters, was in open conflict with the Chancellor, yielded to the extent of putting down entry conditions at the meeting of the European Council in Madrid in June 1989. Although there are different versions of the 'Madrid conditions' for entry into the ERM, those announced to the meeting were: progress in reducing inflation in Britain and progress in the programme for the Single Market including in particular the abolition of exchange controls.[160] Fifteen months later the 'time was [deemed to be] right'.[161] At the Conservative Party Conference, under the Chancellorship of Mr John Major and alongside a 1%

reduction in interest rates, Britain announced that it was entering the ERM at a parity of DM 2.95 and within a 6% fluctuation band.

By that time there was a start along another monetary road that Britain did not want to take, from fixed but flexible exchange rates to fixed and irreversible rates and a single currency.

The Delors Committee

When the European Council met in Hanover in June 1988, it recalled that, in adopting the Single European Act in 1986, the Member States had confirmed the 1972 commitment to the progressive establishment of an economic and monetary union (Preamble, seventh paragraph). It appointed a Committee, chaired by the Commission President, M. Jacques Delors, an undisguised champion of monetary union, to study and propose concrete stages leading to EMU. Although the remit was 'how, if' it soon transformed itself into 'how'. The Committee[162] reported to the Madrid meeting. At the Strasbourg meeting in December 1989 President Mitterrand concluded that the necessary majority (of at least seven, which did not include Britain) existed for the convening of an Inter-governmental Conference under Article 236 of the Treaty (now 309) charged with working out amendment of the Treaty in order to bring in the final stages of EMU.

The Treaty on European Union, carrier of EMU

The outcome was the Treaty on European Union, signed on 7 February 1992, containing Title VI on Economic and Monetary Policy, with chapters 2, 3 and 4 devoted to the economic and monetary union, supplemented by Protocols on

- the European System of Central Banks and the European Central Bank
- the interim European Monetary Institute
- the excessive deficits procedure, and
- the convergence criteria.

Together they set forth how the Community proposed to move to locked exchange rates, a single currency, a single central bank and some of the monetary disciplines which member states would observe. The Treaty contains a conditional option for beginning the final stage of the process in 1996 (Article 109j3 – now 121). This date could not be kept. Automatically it began on 1 January 1999.

Britain out

Meanwhile, speculation in the foreign exchange market had driven Britain out of the ERM on 16 September 1992. The lira also left. The Spanish peseta was devalued. According to Dr Hans Tietmeyer of the Bundesbank a revaluation of the Deutschmark had been on offer[163] but was not accepted. There followed a year of turmoil with further devaluation of the peseta, the Portuguese escudo and the Irish punt. To relieve pressure, Germany cut its discount rate; and speculators attacked the French franc in July 1993. On 2 August, Community Finance Ministers sought to stave off heavy selling of the franc and other weakened currencies by widening the fluctuation band to 15%, except for Germany and the Netherlands. Alternatives discussed at the meeting were the winding up of the EMS, the devaluation of weaker currencies and (proposed by M. Delors) the exclusion of Germany from the system, which would allow others to reduce interest rates.[164] In essence:

> EMU means one monetary policy, interest rate and central bank. It also involves a fixed relationship between the currency units of participating member states and their replacement by a single common currency.[165]

Few observers would judge that the European Union is what economists call an 'optimum currency area'. They would consider that it lacks the essential attributes of labour mobility and a mechanism for fiscal redistribution. Each is usually considered desirable to cushion area shocks that are otherwise conventionally countered by exchange rate adjustments.

Entry criteria – convergence

To qualify for entry into the monetary union, a Member State must satisfy the following criteria:

- Government debt should not be more than the reference figure of 60% of GDP.
- The government deficit should not be more than the reference figure of 3% of GDP.
- Inflation should not be more than 1.5% higher than the performance of the three lowest inflation rate countries.
- Long-term interest rates should not be higher than the three lowest inflation rate countries.
- The currency should (belong to the ERM and) remain within the fluctuation band for two years.

Nothing is ever easy. The criteria gave rise to five years of debate. Those concerned with inflation and interest rates gave no trouble – all the conceivable candidates would pass. The reference figures were not absolutes but if they were not respected the common currency would be weakened from the outset. The annual deficit figure came to be regarded as adamantine (although Germany and France would have to struggle to get there), but the accumulated debt, 60% of GDP, was treated more leniently, such that Belgium, with a figure twice that size but falling, might be regarded as complying. The reference to ERM was troublesome. Some thought that it meant membership, one (Britain) thought that it meant respecting the rule against devaluation without actually belonging to the ERM.

British self-exclusion

The British Conservative government had negotiated an opt-out in the Treaty. It steadily grew more hostile[166] to the project and announced that Britain would not join in 1999. The incoming Labour government, favourably disposed to the project and to eventual British membership, announced in October 1997 that barring unforeseen developments, it would not join in the lifetime of the then parliament.

European System of Central Banks

The TEU creates a new institution, although not given that designation, to operate the monetary union. The European Central Bank is an amalgam of national central banks.[167] It is given as its primary objective price stability. It consists of a Governing Council, made up of its own Executive Board and the Governors of Central Banks. The Executive Board consists of a President, a Vice-President and four other members. They are appointed by a Council composed of the Heads of State and Government after consulting the European Parliament. They shall neither seek nor take instructions from Community institutions or bodies, from any government of a Member State or from any other body (Article 107, now 108). In other words, exchange rates among Member State currencies are no more and decisions about changes in interest rates are removed from governments. They are in the hands of the combination of liberal economics and technocracy labelled 'market-oriented authoritarianism'.[168]

The criteria

Between the entry into force of the TEU and the approach of January 1999 there was widespread controversy over the plan for monetary union. Its advantages were enumerated and dismissed. The loss of national control over national affairs was deplored or welcomed. The likely staying power of the currency, given the new name of *euro* in place of the ECU used in the TEU,[169] was upheld and discounted. The timing was criticised as premature, and insisted upon as necessary to maintain confidence. The candidature of countries like Italy, which wanted to be in but whose currency was not strong, was anxiously discussed. The dodges which governments got up to give eye appeal to their public finances – a one-off 'euro' tax in Italy, the state take-over of a pension fund in France, the revaluing of the gold stock in Germany – were attacked. Austere national budgetary measures which are a corollary of the convergence criteria and of the fight against inflation were politically unpopular and were blamed for exacerbating the desperate unemployment situation in most of mainland Europe.

The governments of the countries which are partisans of monetary union persevered to make the system as solid as they could. They did not include Britain, with its opt-out, and Denmark that had excluded itself altogether as part of the strategy for obtaining a favourable referendum result.[170] The unionist countries, supported by Germany, which had most to lose in a weakly euro, and with the 'outs' participating in the discussions, negotiated a Stability and Growth Pact to guarantee that public finances remain sound after monetary union has come in.

The Stability and Growth Pact has roots in Article 104 (ex-104) which established the 'excessive deficits procedure'. This created peer review of the budgetary situation in each Member State and in paragraph 11 sets up sanctions where annual deficits or public deficits exceed reference values. Curiously, in this instance, Community law in itself was not considered to be strong enough to command unqualified respect, or perhaps it was that sanctions were believed unlikely to be applied in practice. At the meeting of the European Council in Dublin on 13–14 December 1996, it was concluded that the Treaty should be reinforced by a European Council Resolution – itself without legal effect – which

> would invite all parties to implement the Treaty and the Stability and Growth Pact regulations strictly.

The Resolution was duly adopted at the European Council meeting in Amsterdam on 16–17 June 1997. For effect it depends on two Regulations:

- (EC) No. 1466/97 on the strengthening of the surveillance of budgetary positions and the surveillance and co-ordination of economic policies; and
- (EC) No. 1467/97 on the implementation of the excessive deficits procedure (OJ L 209, 2.8.1997).

Collectively the Treaty Article, the Resolution and the Regulations provide, subject to some easements, that if the deficit of a Euroland state (i.e. a state using the European Monetary Union) exceeds 3%, a fine will be imposed of 0.2% of GDP plus one-tenth of the percentage by which the deficit exceeds 3%, subject to a maximum in any year of 0.5% of GDP.[171]

Political interests

But there was also a cross-current. Although the primary aim of the ESCB is price stability, it is also enjoined to 'support the general economic policies in the Community with a view to contributing to the general achievement of the objectives of the Community as laid down in Article 2'.[172] Article 2 calls for a high degree of employment. The French Socialist government which came to power on the eve of the Amsterdam meeting had given the electors pledges on job creation. In the Inter-governmental Conference of 1996–97 there were demands for the employment responsibilities of the Community to be given more muscle. Alongside Treaty amendment, especially article 109n (now 125), which looks to labour markets responsive to economic change, the European Council balanced its Resolution on stability and growth by another on growth and employment, setting out measures '... to create more jobs and pave the way for a successful and sustainable third stage of economic and monetary union'.[173] Thus are circles squared.

There was another potentially more dangerous cross-current. As has been noted, the ESCB is independent of governments. It is not only federalist but is also bureaucratic.

This explicitly intended status proceeds from the conclusion that governments have been uniquely bad at managing exchange and interest rates – too much or too little and too late when it comes; never what American commentators call the 'Goldilocks scenario'. Bankers do not have to concern themselves with elections or party manoeuvres. But any government remains vitally concerned with what is happening to the voters because it will be taken out on it in the polling booths. Here again the new French government, uninhibited by pre-history, took a lead. It wanted some kind of counterweight to the ESCB. The C-word was never uttered. The euphemism was 'an economic pole' with the subliminal image of a bipolar system. This aroused strong German opposition and provoked a break for a spell of the Franco-German axis on which the Community turns. The ultimate compromise, which Germany embraced, preserved the special status and mission of the ECSB but created an 'informal Council' (sic) confined to the Member States participating in the monetary union. The word 'informal' was designed to relativise the body, but as the French Minister concerned, M. Dominique Strauss-Kahn observed that 'the G7 is informal'.[174] Germany gave the body another name 'E (or Euro) X' where X is the number of participants. It would discuss matters arising from the single currency and it would help to co-ordinate budgetary and even fiscal policy. It was not said that the body would have another function – it would be an inner closely-knit group within the Economic and Financial Council. At the ECOFIN meeting in November 1997, the British, Swedish and Danish ministers asked that they should belong but were refused.

ERM III

The complementary decision taken in Amsterdam was to rejig the ERM. The new version is to be a link between currencies outside the euro area and the euro. Central rate parities of such currencies are with the euro. The margin of fluctuation before intervention will be +/−15% or narrower at the request of the non-euro Member State involved (also known as the 'pre-in').[175] Membership remains voluntary and is not exclusive. One working innovation is that the ECSB can call for a change in parity. In ERM Marks I and II this was a matter for the Member State.

The Decision of May 1998

The British Presidency of the first half of 1998 had the unusual task of managing a meeting to take decisions that did not involve it. They were:

* Which Member States satisfied the convergence criteria?
* What are the cross-rates of participating currencies?
* Who are the office-bearers of the European Central Bank?

First question

According to a Report presented by the Commission[176] and leaving aside Britain and Denmark:

- All save Greece satisfied the inflation criterion.
- All save Greece were *not* the subject of a Council Decision on the existence of an excessive government deficit. But this was a euphemism. Few of the candidates met the criterion of 3% annual deficit, although all were near it. Two of them, Belgium and Italy, were years (on past trends, decades) away from meeting the criterion of 60% of GDP as public debt.
- All save Greece and Sweden were in the ERM, without severe tension.
- All save Greece met the long-term interest rate criterion.

In addition, eleven Member States had adopted or were adopting legislation to make the status of their central bank compatible with the independence of government of the European System of Central Banks.

Therefore Belgium, Germany, Spain, France, Ireland, Italy, Luxembourg, The Netherlands, Austria, Portugal and Finland participate in the third and final stage of Economic and Monetary Union.

Second question

Cross-rates were agreed without difficulty, ERM positions providing the guide. Euro rates were to come later: 'the irrevocable conversion rates for the euro have to be identical with the value of the official ECU expressed in units of the participating currencies on 31 December 1998'. The fixing of the value of the euro in national currencies was deferred to the eve of the Monetary Union.

Third question

The favoured candidate for President of the ECB was Wim Duisenberg of the Netherlands, serving President of the European Monetary Institute, precursor of the ECB. But for months the French President, M. Chirac, had been putting forward the Governor of the French Central Bank, M. J.-C. Trichet. This provoked what the British Prime Minister later acknowledged to be a 'mess'. The lunchtime conversation at which the appointment was to be settled dragged on for nine hours. Prime Ministers of eleven Member States twiddled their thumbs while the Prime Ministers of Britain and the Netherlands, the German Chancellor and the French President haggled inconclusively. The British Presidency was freely chastised for lack of preparation and poor management of the encounter. The inglorious outcome was that Mr Duisenberg was appointed for eight years but volunteered that in view of his age he would not serve a full term. His successor, for an eight-year term, would be French. M. Chirac said that the candidate would be M. Trichet. Mr Duisenberg had not actually said when he would go. Later he maintained that he would decide for himself, not, as French sources had stated, half-way through his term, which would coincide with the issue of euro notes and coins.

ECB opens its doors: Euro-XI meets

In short order, the ECB met early in June 1998 to arrange its portfolios. Euro-XI also met in June. The venue was Luxembourg, which is where the Council meets in June. But it was not in the Council building on the Kirchberg Plateau but in a castle which the Luxembourg government uses as a conference centre.[177] The British Chancellor of the Exchequer, Chairman of Ecofin, attended briefly but not being a member of Euro-XI left when it began to discuss business.

Euro-XI is not a Council in the Treaty sense, even of a gathering of Member States using the 'closer co-operation' facilities of Article 11 (new). Whether it is a political counterweight to the ECB awaits a verdict of history. It seems likely that it will discuss monetary matters and convey its conclusions to the ECB. It will also discuss associated matters, such as fiscal policy, on which occasions it will, so it has said, invite the non-euro countries to participate. Whatever else it does, it will become a more closely integrated group within Ecofin. This is a development which non-members may find unwelcome.

The economic part of EMU

The new Union is economic as well as monetary. In fact the economic union is wider. There are no opt-outs although there is differentiation. The core is the *excessive deficit procedure.*

Because of the complexity of the text and the instruments that it describes, it is easy to become lost between convergence, excessive deficit avoidance, stability and its sanctions and multilateral surveillance. The UK opt-outs are from compliance with convergence (and membership of the monetary union) and excessive deficit avoidance and the fine-tuning of the latter, as described above, into stability requirements. The UK is not exempted from multilateral surveillance.

In the second stage of monetary union, which lasted until 1 January 1999, Member States were enjoined to endeavour to avoid excessive deficits (Article 109e4, now 116). If they wanted to join the third stage they needed to do so. The existence of an excessive deficit is measured by the same convergence criteria (3% and 60%) in Protocol 11 as apply to eligibility to join the monetary union in stage three.

In the third stage, the Member States which have joined the monetary union *must* avoid excessive deficits (Article 104c1, now 104), as defined, under pain of the sanctions of the Stability Pact (above) which effectively replace those of Article 104c, especially paragraph 11. The Member States that have not joined the monetary union remain subject to the non-coercive provisions of Article 104c. They are examined by Commission and Council to determine whether they are incurring excessive deficits.

The results of this examination are routinely published, with no other penalty. Very soon after the launch of EMU, France and Germany came in for adverse comment on rising deficit.

Multilateral surveillance, a form of peer pressure, is instituted by Article 103 (now 99). It applies to *all* member states at *all* stages of monetary union and is wider in scope than the technical examination of deficits. In exercising multilateral surveillance, the Council studies the consistency of the economic policies of each Member State with the broad guidelines which have been previously adopted in a Council recommendation; and whether a Member State's policies might jeopardise the proper functioning of the economic and monetary union. In practice, in the second stage of monetary union, Council examination focused on Member States' convergence programmes and the many excessive deficits they had incurred, but which all, save Greece, succeeded in reducing. This form of peer pressure, without sanctions other than 'naming and shaming', was emulated when the Inter-governmental Conference wrote an Employment Title into the Treaty (VIII).

The monetary union is born

On 31 December 1998, Ecofin met to determine the value of the euro in national currencies. In effect they became transitional denominations of the euro, pending the circulation of euro notes and coins. It was noteworthy that the currency grid which Ecofin had decreed in May had held firm despite months of turmoil on foreign exchange markets provoked by the Asian economic collapse and the Russian repudiation of debt payments.[178] No British Minister attended a meeting of historic proportions. The irrevocable exchange rates for the former national currencies were fixed to several places of decimals, as shown in Box 10.4.

Box 10.4   National values against the 'euro'

Austrian schillings	13.7603	Italian lire	1936.27
Belgian francs	40.3399	Netherland guilders	2.20371
Finnish markkas	5.94573	Luxembourg francs	40.3399
French francs	6.55957	Portuguese escudos	200.482
German marks	1.95583	Spanish pesetas	166.386
Irish punt	0.787564		

The pound sterling was not so fixed. At 31 December market rates it stood at 1.41 euros. The dollar rate would be 1.16665.

Trading began when markets opened on 4 January 1999. The euro initially rose slightly against the pound. Anxiety that currency markets would not be able to cope with new pricing was dispelled. Within a few weeks the euro had weakened against the pound and the dollar.

From 1 January 1999 all non-cash transactions in Euroland have been expressed in euros. In cash transactions single or dual pricing may continue. New public debt will be issued in euros. Existing public debt will be progressively converted into euros. On 1 January 2002 euro notes and coins will come into circulation (an earlier date may be substituted). On 1 July 2002 (or earlier), national notes and coins will be withdrawn.

International Representation

Article 111.4 (ex-109) reserves to the Council decision on how the Community will be represented in international finance fora. Euro-XI decided in Vienna in November 1998 that the team for G7 meetings would be: President of Euro-XI (who might also be a national representative), President of ECB and Economics Commissioner. The inclusion of the last-named at G7 meetings was, however, opposed by the USA, which has in the past complained of European over-representation. After half a year of negotiation, an agreement on EU and Euroland was announced.

> When the G7 is considering, in Part 1 of its agendas, the state of the world economy and currency exchange rates, the President of the European Central Bank and the Finance Minister of the EU Presidency country will participate. The British, French, German and Italian Finance Ministers are there as of right. For Part 2, when the economic situation in particular countries is reviewed, the participants in Part 1 will be joined by the Governors of the Central Banks of France, Germany and Italy, and by the Commissioner for Economic Affairs. The Governor of the Bank of England will accompany the Chancellor of the Exchequer throughout and – unlike his French, German and Italian colleagues, will not be displaced by the President of the ECB.

The British position on membership of EMU

In October 1997 the new-ish Labour government set out its position. It could not over-enthuse about the euro because it had committed itself to a referendum. It discounted constitutional objections. It set out five tests to be satisfied before it could commend British membership of the monetary union to the electorate.

1. Sustainable convergence between the British economy and the economies of the members of the monetary union (in another formulation, this goes to the 'non-synch' in business cycles).
2. Sufficient flexibility [in Britain] to respond to economic change.
3. Effects on investment, including inward investment.
4. Effects of the British financial services industry ('the City').
5. Effects on employment.

The tests are loose and largely judgemental. The Chancellor of the Exchequer dismissed as inoperative the requirement[179] that an applicant must have belonged to the Exchange Rate Mechanism of the European Monetary System for two years. His view was not shared by other EU Finance Ministers. As to the Maastricht criteria, they were fulfilled.[180]

In 1998, for example, for the fourth consecutive year, Britain comfortably met the convergence criteria for government debt. The reference value in the Treaty on European Union – which some of the members of Euroland missed – is 60% of GDP. Also, for the second consecutive year, Britain easily met the criterion for the annual deficit, where the reference value is 3% of GDP. The numbers for Britain are shown in Table 10.6.

Table 10.6   The UK and the convergence criteria: government debt and annual deficit

	% GDP	
Date	Government debt	Annual deficit
1995	53.0	–
1996	53.6	–
1997	52.1	1.9
1998	49.4	–0.7 (net repayment)

Source: Office for National Statistics.

In February 1999 the British Prime Minister announced the National Changeover Plan. It set out the measures – some costing 'tens of millions' – to public funds needed to make the change if the referendum were to be in favour of it. The Prime Minister described the publication as a 'change of gear but not of policy'. Critics thought it was movement by stealth. In the June 1999 election campaign for the European Parliament, the Labour government campaigned on the position that it was not yet an issue of membership of the single currency, that the policy was still 'prepare and decide', that the Chancellor's tests were serious and that the referendum would be held. The Conservative opposition, which had a general policy of 'not in the next Parliament' – that is, not before 2006 or so – sharpened its attack on the single currency with, it appears, some success.

 LEGAL BASES

Single Market

- Article 3c in the consolidated version of the Treaty establishing the European Community (OJ 340/180, 10.11.97).
- Articles 28–31 (ex-30, 34, 36, 37).
- Articles 39–42 (ex-48–51).
- Articles 43–48 (ex-52, 54–5).
- Articles 49–55 (ex 59–66).
- Articles 56–60 (ex-73b–73g).
- Articles 94–97 (ex-100–102).
- Cassis de Dijon case, 120/78.

Competition Policy

- Articles 4–5 and 65–66 of ECSC Treaty.
- EC Treaty 3(g) and 58–94.

Taxation

- Indirect taxes: Article 93 (ex-99).
- Direct taxes: Article 94 (ex-100).

EMU

- EMS/ERM: See 'Texts concerning the European Monetary System', published by Committee of Governors of the Central Banks of the Member States of the European Community, 1979.
- Resolution of the European Council of 5 December 1978 (Brussels meeting).
- Agreement between the Central Banks of the European Community laying down the operating procedures for the European Monetary System, 13 March 1979. (This has no legal force.)
- Council Regulations (EEC) 3180/78 and 3181/78, 18 December 1978.
- Treaty on European Union; Title VI. Protocols 3, 4, 5, 6, 9, 10, 11.
- European Council Resolution on the Stability and Growth Pact, 16 June 1997 (no legal force).
- European Council Resolution on the establishment of an exchange rate mechanism in the third stage of economic and monetary union, 16 June 1997 (*Bulletin* 6/97, pp. 17ff.) (no legal force).
- Council Regulation (EC) no. 1103/97, OJ L162, 19.6.1997.
- Council Regulations (EC) no. 1466/97 and 1467/07, OJ L 209, 2.8.97.
- European Council conclusions, 12–13 December 1997 (*Bulletin* 12/97, pp. 12–13) (no legal force).

D DISCUSSION QUESTIONS

Single Market

1. Is there a necessary connection between the Single Market and the Single Currency?
2. Why did the British government of the day advocate QMV for most Single Market measures?
3. Compare the path to Single Market and the path to Single Currency.
4. What is the problem about free movement of people?
5. Why bother with a single market in insurance when policy-holders would prefer a local insurer?

Competition Policy

1. Is it appropriate for the Commission to exercise quasi-federal powers in competition policy?

2. Is there tension between an intra-Community competition policy and the Community desire to have strong companies that can compete in world markets?

3. Since the Commission pursues a wide-spectrum policy (and appears to temper it to, for example, employment considerations) is there a case for a separate Cartel Office which would not have these wider responsibilities and objectives? Similarly, an Anti-Dumping Office, separate from the Commission (just as the US International Trade Commission is independent of the commerce department)?

Taxation

1. Why are 'EU taxes' such a provocative prospect?
2. Should taxation at EU level come before or after a federal structure is in place?
3. Does EU taxation make sense with such economic divergence among the Member States?

EMU

1. What were the main arguments used by the British government against joining the ERM?
2. What are the main advantages and disadvantages of membership of economic and monetary union?
3. Does economic and monetary union imply subsequent political union?
4. Is a politically unaccountable European Central Bank compatible with representative democracy?
5. Is a referendum an appropriate way of securing support for a decision to join the EMU?

B BIBLIOGRAPHY ────────────────────────────────

Common Agricultural Policy

The Common Agricultural Policy of the European Community, Cmnd 3274, May 1967.
ADAS: *Reform of the Common Agricultural Policy*, 1995.
ADAS: *Agricultural strategy*, 1994.
Clerc, F.: *Le marché commun agricole*, Presses universitaires de France, 1970.
European Commission: *The Common Agricultural Policy*, OOP, July 1976.
European Commission: *Communication to the Council, Development and Future of the CAP*, COM (91) final, 1 February 1991.
European Commission: *The Development and Future of the Common Agriculture Policy*, OOP, Supplement 5/91 to the *Bulletin of the European Communities*.
European Commission: *Our Farming Future*, OOP, 1993.
European Commission: *The Common Agricultural Policy in Transition*, OOP, 1996.
European Commission: *Annual Report on the Agricultural Situation in the European Union*, OOP.

European Commission: *The New Regulation of the Agricultural Markets*, OOP, 1993.

Fennell, R.: *The Common Agricultural Policy, Continuity and Change*, Clarendon, 1997.

Grant, W.: *The Common Agricultural Policy*, Macmillan, 1997.

House of Lords: *CAP Reform in Agenda 2000*, March 1998, Stationery Office.

Kjeldahl, R. and Tracy, M. (eds): *Renationalisation of the Common Agricultural Policy?* Combined Book Services, Tonbridge, 1994.

Ockended, J. and Franklin, M.: *European Agriculture, Making the CAP Fit for the Future*, Pinter/RIIA, 1995.

Pinder, J.: *European Community, the Building of the Union*, OUP, 1991.

Salmon, T.C. and Nicoll, W., *Building European Union*, MUP, 1997.

Tracy, M.: *Government and Agriculture in Western Europe 1880–1998* (3rd edn), Simon and Schuster, 1989.

Von der Groeben, H.: *The European Community. The Formative Years*, OOP, 1985.

Common Fisheries Policy

Cann, C.: *Saving our fish*, CER Essays, 1997.

European Commission: *The New Common Fisheries Policy*, OOP, 1994.

European Parliament: *Manual of the CFP*, European Parliament, OOP, 1992.

Common Commercial Policy

Cable, V. and Henderson, D.: *Trade Blocs? The Future of Regional Integration*, Chatham House, 1994.

Church, C.H. and Hendriks, G.: *Continuity and Change in Contemporary Europe*, Edward Elgar, 1995.

European Commission: *Annotated Summary of Agreements linking the Communities with Non-Member Countries*, Update June 1996, DG1A European Union, World Trade, OOP, 1998.

Grille, E.R.: *The European Community and the Developing Countries*, OUP, 1993.

Hayes, J.P.: *Making Trade Policy in the European Community*, Macmillan, 1994.

Ludlow, P.: *Europe and the Mediterranean*, Brassey's, 1994.

Ludlow, P.: *Beyond 1992 – Europe and its Western Partners*, Centre for European Policy Studies, Brussels, 1989.

Nelson, M.: *Bridging the Atlantic*, Centre for European Reform, 1997.

Pedersen, T.: *The European Union and the European Free Trade Area*, Pinter, 1994.

Smith, M. and Woolcock, S.: *The United States and the European Community in a Transformed World*, Pinter, RIIA, 1993.

Tussie, D.: *The Less Developed Countries and the World Trading System*, Pinter, 1987.

Hoekman, B. and Sauve, R.: 'Regional and multilateral liberalisation of service markets: complements or substitutes?', *Journal of Common Market Studies*, Vol. 32, No. 3, September 1994.

Mayes, G.: 'The effect of economic integration on trade', *Journal of Common Market Studies*, Vol. XVII, No. 1, September 1978.

Woolcock, S.: 'The European acquis and multilateral trade rules: are they compatible?', *Journal of Common Market Studies*, Vol. 31, No. 4, December 1993.

Brack, D.: 'Balancing trade and the environment', *International Affairs* (RIIA), Vol. 71, No. 3, July 1995.

Common Transport Policy

Despicht, N.: *The Transport Policies of the European Communities*, Chatham House/PEP, 1969.

European Commission: *Growth, Competitiveness, Employment* (White Paper), 1994.

European Community Transport Policy, OOP, 1990.

Transport in the 1990s, OOP, 1993.

Trans-European Networks, OOP, 1994.

Transport in Europe, OOP, 1991.

Freeman, C., Sharp, M. and Walker, W. (eds): *Technology and the Future of Europe*, Pinter, 1991.

Britain in Europe, Stratagems Publishing, 1998, pp. 72–77.

Tyson, D'A.T.: *Who's bashing Whom? Trade Conflict in High-Technology Industries*, Institute for International Economics (Longman), 1992.

Single Market

Begg, I. (co-ordinator): *Economic and Social Research Council*, Single European Market, Reports, 1995–98.

Lord Cockfield: *The European Union – Creating the Single Market*, Wiley, 1994.

Cowles, M.G.: 'Setting the agenda for a new Europe', *Journal of Common Market Studies*, Vol. 33, No. 4, December 1995.

European Commission: *Action Plan for the Single Market* (CSE 97 final), OOP, June 1997.

Impact and Effectiveness of the Single Market, COM (96)520 final, OOP, October 1996.

Analysis of the Single Market, SEC (96) 2378, December 1996, OOP, 1996.

Hurwitz, L. and Lequesne, C.: *The State of the European Community*, Lynne Rienner (Longman), 1991.

Keohane, R.O. and Hoffmann, S. (eds): *The New European Community*, Westview, 1991.

Lord Simon: The Internal Market Council, *European Business Journal*, Vol. 10, issue 3, 1998.

Single Market Review (39 reports), Kogan Page, 1997.

Sbragia, A.M. (ed.): *Euro-politics*, Brookings, 1991.

Competition Policy

European Commission (DG IV): *European Community Competition Policy, Annual Report*, OOP.

House of Lords Select Committee on the European Communities: *Enforcement of Community Competition Rules*, Session 1993/94, HL paper 7, Stationery Office.

Nicoll, W. (ed.): *Lancaster House Competition Policy Inquiry*, ECERC, First Impression Graphics, 1987.

Wilks, W. and MacGowan, L.: 'Disarming the Commission, the debate over a European cartel office', *Journal of Common Market Studies*, Vol. 33, No. 2, June 1995, pp. 260–73.

Taxation

Department of Trade and Industry: (1) *The Single Market – the Facts*, 1992.

European Commission: *Approximation of taxes – why?* OOP, 1992.

European Commission: *Tax law and cross-border co-operation between companies*, OOP, 1991.

European Commission: *Taxation in the Single Market*, OOP, 1990.

Walsh, A.E. and Paxton, J.: *Into Europe*, Hutchinson, 1972 (Chapter 9 on VAT).

EMU

Andersen Consulting: *EMU, the Business View*, 1996.

Bank of England: *Financial Sector Preparations for the Year 2000*, periodical, by subscription.

Bank of England: *Practical Issues arising from the Introduction of the Euro*, monthly.

Barclays Bank: *European Monetary Union, a Guide for Business*, 1996.

Bergsten, C.F.: *Weak dollar, strong Euro?* CER, 1998.

Bishop, G. and others: *Britain and EMU, the Case for Joining*, CER, 1997.

Bishop, G. and others: *User Guide to the Euro*, Sweet & Maxwell, 1996.

Committee of Governors of Central Banks: *Texts concerning the European Monetary System*, 1979.

Currie, D.: *The Pros and Cons of EMU*, HM Treasury, July 1997.

Delors, J. (Chairman): *Report on Economic and Monetary Union in the European Community*, 1989.

Driffil, J. and Beber, M. (eds): *A Currency for Europe*, Lothian Foundation Press, 1991.

Duff, A. (ed.): *Understanding the Euro*, Federal Trust, 1998.

Emerson, M. and Huhne, C.: *The ECU Report*, Pan, 1991.

European Commission: numerous publications including: *One Market, One Money*, 1991; *Info-Euro*, periodical newsletter; *Euro 1999*, Part 1 Recommendation, Part 2 Report, 1998; *One Currency for Europe*, Green Paper, 1995; *Round Table on the Euro*, 22–24 January 1996; *EMU and the Euro*, 1997.

Federal Trust: *Towards the Single Currency*, 1996.

McCrone, G.: *Monetary Union and Economic Development*, Bank of Scotland, April 1996.

Nicoll, W., Norburn, D. and Schoenberg, R. (eds): *Perspectives on European Business*, Whurr Publishers, 1998.

Olszak, N.: *Histoire des unions monetaires*, Presses universitaires de France, 1996.

Sear, S.: *Managing the Impact of the Euro*, Gower Publishing, 1998.

Torres, F.S.: *Portugal, the EMS and 1992*, European University Institute, Florence, 1989.

Walters, A.: *Sterling in Danger*, Fontana, 1990.

OTHER POLICIES

SOCIAL AND EMPLOYMENT POLICY ────────

The theory of social policy

THE UNDERLYING political theory of social policy is that the state, as custodian of the public good, has a responsibility for ensuring that its citizens have the opportunity to pursue their happiness. The first advocate of social policy in the recent history of Europe was the German statesman more noted for his doctrines of 'blood and iron' and his unrelenting pursuit of the creation of the German Empire (Deutsches Reich), Prince Otto von Bismarck (1815–98).[181] Believing that the creation of the German State required a settled populace confident of its own future well-being, Bismarck introduced social insurance without precedent in Germany's neighbours. The tradition lives on in German social thinking. No small part of the German economic miracle of the 1960s and 1970s was attributed to the country's advanced social policies, both in welfare provision and in *Mitbestimmung*, worker participation in management of enterprises.

The first steps

In early discussion of economic integration among the Six, there was some concern that different levels of social security and of wages might give some countries a competitive edge over others. It was the situation much later described as 'social dumping'. The ECSC Treaty had faced the issue in its sphere. Article 68 provides autonomy in wage settlement for the Member States, except that if an undertaking paid wages which were abnormally low compared with wage levels *in the same area*, the High Authority could make recommendations, with binding force, to harmonise wage levels In addition, there were funds for retraining, job creation and new housing for resettled workers.[182] At Messina, the Six cautiously decided that it was 'imperative to study the progressive harmonisation of the regulations now in force in various countries, especially those relating to working hours, payment for overtime ... length of statutory holidays and holiday pay'.[183]

Continuing caution

By the time it came to the drafting and adoption of the EEC Treaty, caution was even more marked. The Preamble brackets together economic and social progress. It aims at the constant improvement of the living and working conditions of the people. The operative articles speak of the need to promote improved working conditions (Article 136, ex-117) 'so as to make possible their harmonisation while the improvement is being maintained'. To show that this was intended to mean that harmonisation would be quasi-automatic, the next paragraph envisages that it would ensue from the functioning of the common market, 'that will favour the harmonisation of social systems'. Otherwise the Treaty sets up 'close co-operation between Member States in the social field' (Article 137, ex-118), insists on equal pay for men and women for equal work (Article 139, ex-119) and in the wake of the ECSC creates a Social Fund to improve employment opportunities (Article 146 to 148, ex-123–125). Unemployment levels were not a prime concern. This was the era of full employment and of the recruitment of foreign labour, the *Gastarbeiter*. In its 1960 version, the Social Fund contributed 50% of the cost of national retraining schemes. In a reform of 1970 the Commission became more active in intervening when Community policy was affecting sectoral employment (see Box 11.1).

There was, however, no more explicit reference to harmonising wage and non-wage costs. Although a Member State like France might feel continuing concern that its social security arrangements and labour market regulation might weaken its competitivity, the

Box 11.1   Social policy: the early years

The question of how far social policy could or should be standardised across the EC was an important part of the negotiations on the Treaty of Rome. There were, and are, at least two opposing schools of thought:

- The 'neo-liberal' economists wanted to limit the social and other restraints on competition to a minimum in the belief that this would lead to maximum prosperity. They viewed social costs as just one of the many cost factors for firms which could be adapted as and when the economic situation required.
- The 'welfare-state' school favoured a welfare-state model for society and saw social exclusion expenditure as necessary in order to safeguard social standards and peace. They believed that identical social standards throughout Europe would prevent the kind of distortion of competition that arose when firms have different levels of cost to bear. States with high levels of social protection would otherwise lose jobs and capital because firms preferred to invest in states where labour cost less.

The Treaty of Rome represented a compromise.

Five generally preferred national independence to some model to be determined by the Community. The first President of the Commission, Walter Hallstein of Germany, might say in his first official speech that 'economic and social policy are inextricably woven together' but the Member States were content to leave it at that. Employer organisations and trade unions did not dissent.

Freedom of movement

The first actions were concerned with the free movement of workers, in partial fulfilment of Article 3c: 'the abolition ... of obstacles to freedom of movement of persons' and compliance with Article 39 (ex-48). This was achieved by the Second Council Regulation of 19 October 1968 (68/1612/EEC, OJ L 217) and was buttressed by a string of Court judgements between 1974 and 1985.[184]

Equal pay

The Court likewise reinforced the equal pay provisions of Article 141 (ex-119). In what some learned jurists have regarded as 'judicial activism' – that is, pushing a Treaty provision to its outer limits – the Court inferred that there is a general principle of non-discrimination in Community law and applied this principle zealously.[185]

German social policy as a model

The first major policy development came as a German initiative. In the spring of 1970 Chancellor Willi Brandt (SPD) announced that the Community should become the leading socially progressive area in the world and that it could not be done by the 'Europe of Businesses'. Germany fed its ideas into the Brussels complex where they converged with an initiative taken by Vice-President Mansholt (who later briefly became President). He called for a policy approach that laid less emphasis on the growth of production and more on the quality of life. Ideas of this kind were prominent in the 1960s before the world reeled under the shock of the surge in oil prices. The message reached the summit meeting in Paris of the Six plus the acceding states held in October 1972. The Heads of State and Government 'emphasised that they attached as much importance to vigorous action in the social field as to the achievement of the economic and monetary union' (which they had also agreed on). They asked for a programme of action providing for concrete measures.[186]

High employment

Unemployment was not at this time a burning issue. It was still under, or in Italy just over, 3%, except in Ireland. The programme had an employment motivation, for example, in the training schemes supported by the Social Fund, but the social policy measures which the Community proceeded to adopt were principally concerned with people *in* work. They included further improvement of free circulation of workers and in the social security service for migrants, closer definition of women's rights and a laborious programme for the mutual recognition of the diplomas prescribed in the national regulation of professions. As an example, the directive on the recognition of the qualification of architects took 17 years to pass, mainly because the other Member States were distrustful of the German *Hochschulen*, which they hesitated to equate to full tertiary education. It was this kind of frustrating experience that contributed to the faster tracks of the 1992 programme for the completion of the Single Market, although, as will be seen, there were no social measures in the programme.

Health and safety at work

The other area to which successive plans and programmes gave attention was health and safety at work. This was in the tradition of the awakening of the liberal philanthropic conscience of the nineteenth century, and the revelations of the appalling conditions of workers employed making matches, or sweeping chimneys or hauling tubs in mines. From 1974 onwards a steady steam of directives covered exposure to dangerous substances, the use of protective equipment, the posting of safety signs, the provision of safety information, etc.

Worker participation

Worker participation in the management of the enterprise was inspired by the then successful German model for co-operation between employers and workpeople. It was proposed in various Commission drafts. The most controversial was the so-called Vredeling Directive of 1980, named after the Dutch Commissioner who was its author. It proposed information and consultation in all enterprises above a certain size – originally 100 employees, later raised to 1,000. It made no more progress than similar proposals in the Fifth Company Law Directive, and in the proposed European Company Statute, first put forward in 1970. The Statute, which would create the European company, with one sole place of registration but with legal standing throughout the Union, still lies on the table.[187]

The Social Single Market

The 1992 programme, already referred to, held out the prospect of growth, more jobs, more prosperity but was about improved trading opportunities. In Brandt's phrase, it was for the businesses of Europe.[188] M. Jacques Delors, President of the Commission, ardent advocate of the Single Market and of monetary union, also had an acute social conscience. He said many times, in language which Hallstein could have used that 'there can be no social progress without economic progress and no economic progress without social cohesion'. More directly, he said in 1989, when the Single Market programme was well under way:

> Without some gesture at the European level in the direction of improved social provision there is a real danger that organised labour may react against the 1992 project, particularly when the economic and industrial casualties it will inevitably entail become obvious.

Casualties were all around whether from the 1992 project or not. Unemployment had become a scourge. But the Member States were not yet ready to regard unemployment as a matter for the Community. Nor were they talking the language of improved social security. At its meeting in Hanover in June 1988, the European Council considered 'that the internal market must be conceived in such a manner as to benefit all our people'. Its specifics were traditional: better working conditions, more health and safety measures, improved vocational training, mutual recognition of diplomas, dialogue with and between management and labour. The dialogue included the 'Val Duchesse' conferences which the Commission had initiated with representatives of employers and workpeople in 1985 and which began to give attention to a growth strategy for employment. Preoccupation with unemployment began to appear in the meetings of the European Council. The meeting in Madrid in June 1989 noted the traditional activities of social policy but added, in new language, '*job development and creation must be given top priority* in the achievement of the Internal Market' (emphasis added). In Strasbourg in December 1989, job creation had become not a target but an achievement (5 million new jobs, 1988–90). Unemployment in the Community then stood at 8.9%, and unemployment among the under-25s at 17.3%.

The Social Charter

At the Strasbourg meeting, eleven members of the European Council, Britain dissenting, adopted a social plan to match the 1992 programme: the Charter of the Fundamental Social Rights of Workers,[189] or Social Charter for short (Box 11.2). M. Delors had already unveiled the Social Charter at a meeting of the European Trade Union Confederation in Stockholm (not then Community territory) in May 1988.

Box 11.2   The Social Charter, December 1989

The Social Charter set out twelve basic principles on the fundamental social rights of workers:
1. The right to work in the EC country of one's choice.
2. The right to a fair wage.
3. The right to improved living and working conditions.
4. The right to social protection under prevailing national systems.
5. The right to freedom of association and collective bargaining.
6. The right to vocational training.
7. The right of men and women to equal treatment.
8. The right of workers to information, consultation and participation.
9. The right to health protection and safety at work.
10. The protection of children and adolescents.
11. The guarantee of minimum living standards for the elderly.
12. Improved social and professional integration for the disabled.

The following September, the Commissioner responsible for social affairs, Manuel Marin, published a discussion document on the Social Dimension of the Internal Market. The Charter was approved by the Economic and Social Committee and by the European Parliament. M. Delors had forecast to the latter in June of 1988 that by 1993 80% at least of economic, financial and *perhaps social* legislation would be flowing from the Community. It was among other threats of centralisation and federalism the spectre of corporatism that informed the memorable speech which the British Prime Minister, Mrs Margaret Thatcher, undauntingly delivered at the College of Europe in Bruges in September 1988 in which she stated what was to be an unshakeable principle of her European policy: '. . . and before I leave the subject of the Single Market may I say that we emphatically do not need new regulations which raise the cost of employment and make Europe's labour market less flexible and less competitive with overseas suppliers.' A year later, on the same platform, M. Delors defended the Social Charter, asserting, unconvincingly, that the different traditions of the Member States would be respected.

The 1990–91 IGC and the Social Protocol

The partial preservation of national competence for social affairs developed in a way which M. Delors could not have foreseen. In 1990 the Member States convened an Intergovernmental Conference for Treaty revision. It began as a basis for defining and programming economic and monetary union, but its coverage was greatly extended.[190] Eleven of the then Member States wanted to take up the substance of the Social Charter into the new Treaty. They also wanted to improve decision-making in this sector by enabling some of the ensuing directives (there are no regulations, because emphasis is placed on the responsibility of Member States: regulations are directly applicable, without the intermediacy of national legislation) to be adopted by qualified majority. The British Prime Minister, Mr John Major, upheld his predecessor's unwavering opposition. The outcome was what was called the opt-out. Behaving just as if they composed a Council, the Eleven (and later after enlargement the Fourteen) could adopt social measures. The United Kingdom was not bound by their decisions. It was not the first example of 'flexibility', as this kind of differentiation came to be known, but it was a historic one. The Social Protocol left intact the Community-wide social policy provisions already contained in the Treaty, which was to be a source of dispute.[191]

The effect of the Social Chapter of the Treaty on European Union was that, at the cost of dividing itself, the Community had made social policy central. The policy was focused on workers' rights. It did not seek to harmonise national policies, even in that narrow field. It provided for minimal prescriptions. It excluded pay, and the right to strike or to lock out. It had been said in earlier times that the reason for the meagre progress in the development of social policy was the unanimity requirement. This was not overpersuasive, since apart from the annual budget, all other Community decisions were taken consensually, even when majority voting could have been used. The Social Protocol applicable to 11/14 Member States produced little – a directive on setting up Works Councils in enterprises of a given size with establishments in more than one

Member State; and a directive on the minimal scales of parental leave. There was, however, a collision between the UK (of the Conservative government) and the others in connection with a directive passed under the 'old' social policy articles, applicable to all. It concerned maximum working time and it was presented as a health and safety measure. The British side negotiated on the original text and apparently succeeded in eliminating what it regarded as its worst features. On a vote, it abstained, which is usually regarded as a gesture rather than an attack. But it then took legal proceedings against the Council, contending that the measure could not be based on health and safety and implying that if the others wanted it they should use their Social Protocol. The Court found against the UK. For a while it looked as if there might be a constitutional crisis, in which the UK would refuse to implement the directive in defiance of the Court judgement.[192] The fuss died down when the Labour government came to power in Britain in May 1997 and agreed a month later in Amsterdam to abandon the opt-out.

By then the focus of social policy had moved on to the subject hitherto carefully avoided: what can the Community do about the citizen's greatest anxiety – unemployment and the insecurity of employment?

The scourge of unemployment

In fact, unemployment became a leading preoccupation, standing stubbornly at around 10% (not far short of 20 million Union citizens) half of it long term. It was usually described as primarily a matter for Member State action, with Community support. Care was taken to insulate national social security schemes from Community interference – thus the European Council at Luxembourg in June 1991 stipulated that the 'general approach must not in any way affect national social security and social protection schemes'. In Copenhagen in June 1993 the European Council broke with the banalities of its previous communiqués to proclaim:

> The European Council is deeply concerned about the present unemployment
> situation and the grave dangers inherent in a development where an increasing
> number of people in the Community are becoming permanently detached from the
> labour market.

This language was inspired by the statistical proof that, after cyclical recovery, the unemployment level is ratcheted higher than it was before its last rise. From then on, 'the fight against unemployment and equality of opportunity will continue in future to remain the paramount tasks of the European Union and its member states' (Conclusions of the European Council, Essen, December 1994).[193]

The 'fight for employment' drew on many policy sectors – the gains from the Single Market, education and training, the coming monetary union, trans-European networks, the investments provided by the Structural Funds, research and development, the information society, free movement of people, the 'double dividend' of protecting the environment – less pollution and more jobs in reducing it. It specifically addressed young people, the long-term unemployed and women. It offered as correctives:

- wage restraint, where wage increase agreements were to be below productivity gains;
- the reduction of taxes (including employers' social security payments) on the employment of labour, especially low-skilled, a euphemism for low-paid; and taxation on energy was a preferred alternative, but unless it was worldwide it would reduce EU competitiveness (worldwide meant especially, but improbably, in the USA);
- the reduction of regulatory rigidity, especially in labour markets, but without weakening social protection or weakening workers' rights;
- an attack on social exclusion, where sections of the population were not only dropping out of the economy but also of society.

Manifestos

Three documents articulate the objectives and programmes.

The White Paper on *Growth, Competitiveness, Employment,* which the Commission published in June 1993 after intensive consultation with the Member States, was one of M. Delors' final offerings to the Council and its Member States. It is a searching analysis of the weaknesses – low growth, rising unemployment, falling investment, falling competitiveness – against the USA and Japan. It rejects protectionism, creating a boom, reducing working hours and job-sharing and wage cuts. It identifies the well-known cyclical and structural varieties of unemployment and adds a third – technological unemployment. It enumerates the range of policies which the Community can marshal. On employment policy it highlights education and training ('the low level of training in the Community and especially the fact that too many young people leave school without essential basic training');[194] job-related growth ('Europe's employment rate is the lowest of any industrialised part of the world'); labour costs ('collective bargaining and related taxation and labour cost arrangements have the effect of causing gains from economic growth to be absorbed mainly by those already in employment'); the employment value of properly nurtured SMEs; statutory charges on labour – EU average, 1991, 49.6% of GDP, USA 29.8%, Japan 30.9%. It offers a new development model, increasing the use of labour resources and diminishing the use of environment resources.

The European Pact of Confidence for Employment bears the name of President Santer. It appeared in July 1996. It goes over familiar ground including the gains accruing from the Single Market and to be secured by monetary union; and the damage of fiscal imbalance, including the 'scissors effect' of taxation on employment ('between 1980 and 1993 taxation on labour rose by 20% whereas taxation on other factors of production fell by 10%'). With the Pact confirming sound macro-economic policy and measures for competitiveness, employers and workpeople would recover the confidence in the title which President Santer gave to his memorandum.

The Jobs Challenge is a declaration from the European Council meeting in Dublin on 13–14 December 1996. It reaffirms that employment continues to be the first priority. It reiterates that primary responsibility rests with the Member States. It calls for:

- labour market efficiency and investment in human resources to be enhanced;
- particular support for vulnerable groups;
- taxation and social protection schemes to be made employment friendly;
- markets for goods and services to be modernised;
- competitiveness to be advanced;
- local development to be promoted.

In sum:

> The European Council endorses the call [in the Confidence Pact] for a commitment by all the social and economic agents, including the national, regional and local authorities, the social partners and the Community institutions, fully to face their responsibilities in regard to employment within their respective spheres of responsibility.

The 'New Deal': the IGC of 1996–97

Meanwhile, the Member States were going some way beyond exhortation in the framework of the Inter-governmental Conference (IGC) on Treaty reform. When they began to face up to the commitment they had made in the Treaty on European Union[195] to convene another conference, they thought that they would escape the error of inadequate preparation by charging a study group with presenting a report. It worked in the second half of 1995. In its interim report it recorded that a majority of its members 'include unemployment, internal security and environmental degradation among the problems to be tackled as a matter of immediate urgency'.[196] In the final report this is sharpened up, although disputed:

> ... many of us want the Treaty to contain a clearer commitment to achieving greater economic and social integration and cohesion geared to promoting employment, as well as provisions enabling the Union to take coordinated action on job creation. Some of us advised against writing into the Treaty provisions which arouse expectations, but whose delivery depends primarily on decisions taken at business and state level.[197]

The advocates of an explicit free-standing employment policy duly proposed new treaty language.[198] The focus of opposition to non-market forces, the British Conservative government, left the scene in May 1997. Immediately prior to the final meeting in Amsterdam in June 1997, a Socialist government took power in France, elected on a platform of job creation.

The ensuing negotiations on a final text presupposed that there would be words about jobs. But the questions were:

- Should the Community declare that the objective is 'full employment', a concept with historical roots, or, as in the previous texts which it had borrowed from German law, 'a high level of employment'? The decision was to stick to the latter aim.
- How is responsibility shared between Member States and the Community?

275

- Were the regulation of labour markets, and the scope of state benefits for the unemployed, among the causes of rising unemployment? This was an offshoot of the wider debate about the 'Rhine Model' (in which state social welfare provision underpins favourable working conditions and productive employer/employee relations) and the Anglo-Saxon Model (in which the state has a reduced role and business is able to respond more smoothly to market forces – for example, by firing workers).[199]

Treaty status

The outcome was a new Title, 'Employment', VIa, in the Treaty establishing the European Community. It tasked the Community and the Member States with 'developing a co-ordinated strategy for employment and particularly for promoting a skilled, trained and adaptable workforce and labour markets responsive to economic change . . .' (Article, 125, ex-109n et seq.). The British Prime Minister had proposed 'flexible labour markets' but this was too tendencious for his French colleague. (The EU percentage unemployment rate for selected years is shown in Table 11.1.)

The highlight of the new Title (VIII in the new numbering) is a procedure for the examination of Member States' employment policies. This is modelled approximately on the multilateral surveillance of economic policy that the Treaty on European Union inserted into the preparations for monetary union. Employment policy is elevated to become a matter of common concern (Article 126, 2). The objective of a high level of employment pervades all other policies (Article 127). There will be incentive measures (cash, but not much and not new money) to encourage co-operation between Member States and support exchanges of information and best practices. There are otherwise no powers to legislate; and the incentive measures may not include harmonisation of the laws and regulations of the Member States (Article 129). An Employment Committee is set up, inspired by the Monetary Committee (which becomes the Economic and Finance Committee in stage 3 of monetary union).[200]

At the Amsterdam meeting, the French Socialist Prime Minister had additional objectives. Despite the budgetary rigour implied by the convergence criteria for monetary union, M. Jospin showed himself to be a stout proponent of monetary union and French membership in the first wave. However he and his Finance Minister colleague also presented themselves as advocates of 'Euro-X',[201] an informal gathering of the Finance Ministers of participating countries. Its function would be to discuss matters arising from the operation of the single currency and in particular the collateral competence of

Table 11.1   EU unemployment rate per cent (selected years)

1984	1991	1994	1996
10.4	8.0	11.3	10.3

Source: OECD.

the Member States in such fields as fiscal measures. It was officially denied that Euro-X would act as a counterweight to the statutory independence of the European Central Bank.[202] Such denials deserve to be treated with caution.

M. Jospin's other objective was to move employment higher up the Community agenda. The chosen instrument was a Special European Council, held in Luxembourg on 20/21 November 1997.

The Special European Council, November 1997

The Special European Council adopted a 'new approach' centred on the co-ordination of employment policies. The means were to be co-ordinated economic policy, ensuring sustainable growth and the harnessing of all Community policies to the task. For resources the European Investment Bank would put up 10 billion ECUs, which would call forth in partnerships another 20 billion. Additionally, the budget would be rearranged to yield 450 million ECUs for Small and Medium Enterprises (SMEs) (known as the 'European Employment Initiative'). In macro-economic policy, the Union would pursue stability, the strengthening of public finance (itself a requisite of admission to and continuing membership of the monetary union), wage restraint and structural reform. The Special European Council adopted the first guidelines for 1998, having four parts: professional insertion,[203] the spirit of enterprise, the adaptability of workpeople and of enterprises and equal opportunity.[204]

The Luxembourg Prime Minister, M. Jean-Claude Juncker, who presided[205] described the new basis for employment policy, along with the preparations for the enlargement of the Union, as the achievements of the Luxembourg Presidency of the second half of 1997.

Three points deserve to be singled out. First, Member State competence for employment policy is not transferred to Community institutions. They are a matter of *common* concern, not Community concern. Second, nothing is said about the cost to public funds of social security. Third, the guidelines call for the reversal of the tendency to increase taxes and other charges on work (that rose from 35% in 1980 to 42% in 1995).

The enigmatic 'Third Way'

The approach to a revitalised employment policy goes under the spin-doctoresque title: 'the Third Way'. According to Mr Blair, the British Prime Minister, the Third Way combines respect for traditional values with the dynamism of the market economy. Ideologues have some difficulty explaining what the Third Way is and are not helped by its free extension to other policies. The expression was in fact invented by President Chirac in the conclusions of a conference he called in Lille in 1996. In essence it is the search for, not the discovery of, a formula for securing the job-creating vigour of the USA without worsening income dispersion.[206] The taboo conclusion is that some economies are organised to protect the living standards of those with jobs rather than the lot of those without them.

STRUCTURAL FUNDS

Purpose

It is said in the section on the Community budget that Community expenditure lies where it falls. This is to overlook that part of budgetary expenditure that is directed in the shape of a resource flow for the benefit of the less-advanced Member States or regions within Member States. That said, the scale of budgetary expenditure makes it far below that of the intra-regional transfers within the public expenditure policies of the Member States. The Structural Fund (and the Cohesion Fund) represent an increment in the public expenditures of the Member States which benefit from them. Although small in the scheme of things, they can have great local significance and are accordingly lobbied for vigorously.[207] Although now commonly grouped together, the three structural funds had separate origins. The Cohesion Fund will be studied separately.

The European Social Fund

The European Social Fund (ESF) was established by the EEC Treaty of 1957 (Article 123, now 146). It was inspired by apprehensions among the Six, especially in France, that the functioning of the Common Market would affect employment negatively. There was no desire to entrust the new Community with a subject so politically sensitive as unemployment relief but a limited Community contribution to resettlement and retraining was judged to be an appropriate counterpart to the voluntary abandonment of national tariff policy.

The European Regional Development Fund

The ERDF was instituted[208] by virtue of an agreement reached with the United Kingdom in the course of the negotiations for its accession to the EEC in 1973. It was first endowed, with 150 million ECUs, in 1975 and placed in the charge of one of the first pair of British members of the Commission, George, later Lord, Thomson. It increased sharply in 1981 when it was used as a vehicle for the temporary relief of UK net budgetary payments. It increased further as policy developed and regional disparity remained sharp.

The EAGGF Guidance Section

The Agricultural Guidance Fund was set up under Article 40.3 (now 34) of the EEC Treaty. It was intended to contribute, alongside national actions, to the restructuring of the Community farm estate, in a modest enough way until the reforms of 1988.

Single European Act, 1986

The Single European Act (SEA) introduced to the Community lexicon the expression 'Economic and Social Cohesion', inscribed in a new Title V (now XVII). It reiterated that

Table 11.2   Structural Funds (ECU millions and per cent of budget)

	1975	%	1985	%	1988	%	1995	%	2000	%
EAGGF-G	76.7	1.3	685.5	2.4	1,140.9	2.7	2,530.6	3.7		
ERDF	150.0	2.5	1,610	5.6	2,978.8	7.9	8,373.6	12.2		
ESF	148.6	2.4	1,407.4	4.9	2,298.6	5.4	4,546.9	6.6		
Total	375.3	6.2	3,702.9	12.9	6,419.3	15.0	1,545.1	22.5	3,140	33.3

Source: European Commission.

one of the Community's objectives, enshrined in the Preamble to the EEC Treaty,[209] is to reduce the gap between the better-off and the less-favoured regions. The Community is to help by means of its Structural Funds (the three mentioned above) and the European Investment Bank. Cohesion was a euphemism for side-payments to the less-well-off Member States, including the new members, Spain and Portugal, who could not expect to do as well as the others from the opening-up of the big Single Market.[210]

As had already been strongly urged by the European Parliament, the Council agreed that the Structural Funds (see Table 11.2) should double between 1987 and 1993. The enlarged Structural Funds[211] were assigned five objectives:

1. Development and structural adjustment of regions whose development is lagging behind.
2. Conversion of regions affected by industrial decline.
3. Combating long-term unemployment.
4. Occupational integration of young people.
5. (a) and (b) Adjustment of agricultural structures and development of rural areas.

Objective 6 was added following the negotiations for the accession of Finland and Sweden in 1994:

6. Regions with sparse populations.

The map[212] shows the whole of Ireland, Greece and Portugal under Objective 1, along with most of Spain, Southern Italy, the Highlands and Islands of Scotland and the five Eastern Länder of Germany; Britain other than the South East, France other than the Paris and Lyons regions under Objectives 2 and 5, along with most of Austria and South East Germany and most of Sweden and Finland under Objectives 5b and 6.

Two-thirds of the expenditure is for Objective 1; Objectives 2, 3 and 4 obtain around 10% each; Objectives 5a and 5b around 5% each; Objective 6 obtains less than 1%.[213] Table 11.3 shows the distribution of Structural Fund assistance in the period 1994–99.

Reform in the air

Three considerations combine to force a rethink of structural policy.

Table 11.3   Structural Fund distribution 1994–99

Member State	ECU (million)
Spain	34,443
Germany	21,724
Italy	21,646
Greece	15,131
Portugal	15,038
France	14,938
UK	13,155
Ireland	6,103
Netherlands	2,615
Belgium	2,096
Finland	1,652
Austria	1,574
Sweden	1,377
Denmark	843
Luxembourg	104

Source: European Commission.

1. Does it work? The Commission answers: 'Member States and regions which lag behind and are eligible under Objective 1 have made progress towards real convergence.'[214]

   One measure is that GDP in Spain, Ireland, Greece and Portugal has risen from 66% of EU average to 74 % since 1988 (Ireland may even have reached the average). This is a measure of success (not wholly attributable to the Structural Funds) but would also suggest that funding needs to be looked at again.

   But equally, unemployment in the regions has not fallen; and the ten richest regions in the Community are still 4.5 times better off than the ten poorest. Regional disparity is not diminishing.

   Whether or not it works when it happens, Structural Fund administration is criticised as over-bureaucratic, to the point that possible beneficiaries are put off. The favourite anecdote is that the Hainault region of Belgium could use only 17% of what it had been allocated (Hainault doubtfully qualifies under the criteria).

2. Is it real? Structural Fund interventions are intended to promote schemes that would not have been undertaken without them. In other words, the schemes should be *additional* to what the responsible authorities would have funded from their own resources. Additionality is notoriously difficult to establish, since it means proving a negative. Co-financing, which is a condition of assistance, does not testify to additionality. It is therefore hard to say that structural fund expenditure has had in itself unique structural effects.

3. The impending accession to the Community of a group of countries with GDP well below the Community average opens up a new chapter of Member State and regional disparity, with the implication that the rules need revision in order to divert funds away from the present recipients and towards new Member States and regions with greater objective need. The alternative, which is close to unthinkable, is for the total size of the Community budget to be increased. Someone has to lose a share of the cake.

The complexity of objectives and the squeeze on funds underlie the Commission's proposals for reform. The proposals start from the contention that the time has come to reduce dependence on Community aid. The share of the working population living in areas at present eligible should be reduced from around 50% to less than 40%. The population covered by Objective 1 should come down from 29% to 26%. The objectives should be simplified to three:

• New Objective 1: Regions whose GDP is less than 75% of Community average.
• New Objective 2: Areas with high unemployment, facing industrial decline, rural areas suffering from depopulation, deprived urban zones, coastal areas dependent on declining fisheries.
• New Objective 3: Non-regional. ESF assistance to promote employment, combat social exclusion, provide training, and promote opportunities for women.

Funding would decline slowly from 32.1 billion ECUs in 2001 to 27.3 billion in 2006. The present Objective 1 would be phased out over six years,[215] Objective 2 over four.[216]

It is no surprise that the proposals have had a hostile reception from the Member States who calculate that they would lose. It is also no surprise that consideration of them moved with all deliberate speed pending the German federal elections of 1998. It became part of a wider review of budgetary finance and financing. The European Council Meeting in Berlin in March 1999 generally accepted the proposed changes, but changed the figure work. Funding would decline slowly from 31.4 billion euros in 2001 to 29.2 billion in 2006. There are to be a series of 'sweeteners' proposed by the Commission for the regions that are losing Structural Fund privileges (e.g. in Ireland and the Highland and Islands of Scotland).

In addition to the 'mainstream' objectives there were previously thirteen 'initiatives'. The Berlin European Council reduced them to three: INTERREG (cross-border development co-operation); EQUAL (transnational co-operation to 'combat all forms of discrimination and inequalities in the labour market'); and LEADER (rural development). Following discussions with the European Parliament, a fourth initiative was added: URBA (sustainable urban development in crisis areas).

COHESION FUND

If the doubling (or more) of the Structural Funds was a kind of side-payment to compensate for the differential economic outfall of the Single Market, the Cohesion Fund is an offset to the Single Currency.

Delors Report

The Delors Report[217] on EMU singles out common policies for structural adjustment and regional development among the four rules that are essential to the success of the monetary union. It suggests that experience shows that the effect on peripheral regions could be negative. While endorsing the enhanced role post-1988 of the Structural Funds, it argues that the object should not be a kind of pension for less-favoured areas, but should:

> aid the equalisation of the conditions of production through programmes of investment in fields such as the physical infrastructure, communications, transport and education, so that large scale displacement of the workforce does not become the main factor of adjustment.' (pp. 20–1).

The political response was Article 130d (now 161) of the TEU, calling for a further overhaul of the Structural Funds (see below) and for a *Cohesion Fund*.[218] The article neatly married the new fund to the trans-European networks, the subject of Title XV (ex-XII) so far as transport infrastructure is concerned and to projects in the field of the environment. In parallel Article 130s.5 (now 175) in the Environment Title XVI (now XIX) provides for financial support from the Cohesion Fund as an exception to the general rule that (a) the polluter pays and (b) Member States finance environment policy. The accompanying Protocol on Economic and Social Cohesion introduces two conditions of eligibility to benefits from the Cohesion Fund. The Member State hoping to qualify must have:

- less than 90% of average Community GDP; and
- a programme leading to compliance with the criteria for the avoidance of excessive deficits,[219] identical to the convergence criteria for eligibility to join the monetary union.

The Cohesion Fund was duly established on 25 May 1994.[220]

Distinct from Structural Funds

The differences between the Cohesion Fund and the Structural Funds are important. The Cohesion Fund does not have regional objectives. Its interventions could have regional effects. It is concerned with disparities between Member States, not between regions. Accordingly, the projects are agreed between Member States and the Commission, without the involvement of regional authorities. The Cohesion Fund is confined to Spain, Greece, Portugal and Ireland, and to environment and transport infrastructure projects. Disbursements from the Cohesion Fund are project-by-project. The Structural Funds proceed by programmes. The lower limit for a Cohesion Fund project is normally 10 million ECUs. At between 80 and 85% of cost, the Cohesion Fund takes a larger share than the Structural Funds. Cohesion Fund resources are much smaller (see Box 11.3).

Box 11.3   Cohesion and Structural Funds compared: 1993–99

Cohesion Fund	16,223 million ECUs
Structural Funds	172,506 million ECUs

Distribution

The Regulation lays down the country distribution (see Box 11.4). In 1993 the split was 38.7% for environment projects and 61.3% for transport. By 1996 it was roughly 50:50.

Box 11.4   Distribution of Cohesion Fund (%)

Spain	52–58	Portugal	16–20
Greece	16–20	Ireland	7–10

Facing enlargement

In the Commission's proposals for Agenda 2000, the Union facing its enlargement, the Cohesion Fund for EU15 remains flat at 2.9 billion euros to 2006. The condition that excessive deficit should be avoided is to be replaced by the requirement that beneficiaries (three of whom will be founder members of the monetary union) should comply with the Stability and Growth Pact. The criterion that beneficiaries should have less than 90% of average Community GDP should be reviewed half-way through the period.

All these proposals, and many more, were elements in the heavy negotiations between the Council, the EP and the Commission, with contributions from the ESC and the CoR, to establish the Financial Perspectives 2000–2006. They came to a head in the spring of 1999 and needed to be at least partly in place by the end of 1999. In the discussions, it has been argued that since three of the Cohesion Fund beneficiaries met the convergence criteria for EMU, they have no case for Cohesion Fund support. They strenuously uphold a different view.

INDUSTRY

The word 'industry' occurs in several articles of the 1957 version of the EEC Treaty, but there is no mention of an industry policy. The Euratom Treaty of the same vintage focuses on research but it has provisions that come close to a policy for the nuclear industry.

Euratom

Chapter VI vests in the Atomic Energy Community responsibility for the supply of nuclear materials, which could be a powerful weapon for the management of the industry using it (it is not so used). Article 40 requires those planning to invest in a scheduled list of activities in the nuclear field to inform the Commission, which will discuss forward plans with their promoters (Article 43), and with the consent of the Member States, persons and undertakings concerned, publish investment projects communicated to it. More generally the Commission is to 'facilitate co-ordinated development of [. . .] investment in the nuclear field'. If nuclear power had not lost its prominence and its promise, the provisions of the Euratom Treaty could have been used to establish arrangements for influential administrative guidance. As it is, Euratom is largely a dead letter, apart from the safeguards it established against the misuse of nuclear materials.

Coal and steel

The European Coal and Steel Community (ECSC) Treaty is more full-blooded. It uses the word 'intervention' in Article V, since that was what the High Authority was supposed to do. It can provide finance for investment and re-adaptation (Article 5) and exert direct influence on production. Under Article 54 it may require to be informed of new programmes and it may give reasoned opinions on them. A negative opinion, duly argued, would clearly affect the external financing of a new project.[221] Under Article 58 of the ECSC Treaty, in times of a 'manifest crisis' of oversupply, the High Authority may, with the assent of the Council, impose production quotas (as it did for steel production in the 1980s). Conversely, if ever there were serious shortages, the High Authority could propose to the Council the allocation of supplies. All the foregoing measures were consistent with the underlying objective of the Treaty, which was to remove the sinews of war from the control of European governments. They are not now in use.

Restructuring

The lack of an industry chapter did not inhibit the Community from involving itself directly in industrial affairs. Industrial restructuring – a euphemism for contracting – in steel under ECSC Treaty powers, in close consultation with Eurofer, the trade association, and in shipbuilding and textiles largely via permissible state aid was a major preoccupation. Interestingly, the Single Market programme did not include the type of adjustment assistance for enterprises negatively affected, which had been much discussed in tariff-cutting rounds in the 1960s and 1970s.

The Commission produced a string of communications on industrial organisation, in the car industry, on chemicals, on defence-related industry[222] and published an annual Panorama of European Industry. There are many plans and proposals for helping small and medium enterprises (SMEs) in all sectors. But it would have been difficult to discern the contours of an industrial policy. Industrial success was rather to be promoted by supply side improvement in R&D, in the rules of competition and, above all, in the enhanced business environment shaped by the Single Market. These are the subject of separate chapters. Vocational training[223] was another of the formulae for improvement.

When in 1990 the Member States addressed revision of the foundation Treaty, they began by not mentioning industry in the checklist prepared by the meeting of the European Council in Rome in December. When negotiation began, Belgium was the first to suggest a stronger base for an industrial policy. They proposed an Article reading:

> The Community has the objective of implementing a Community industrial policy aimed at orienting productive investments towards improved competitiveness in European companies and higher employment, taking advantage as much as possible of the benefits of scale of the Single Market.[224]

This *dirigisme* was opposed by the market-oriented countries, especially Germany, the Netherlands and the UK. They did not want there to be a *Community* industrial policy. The final text, in Title XIV in the new numbering and sole article 157, is an incomplete compromise with credit shared between Luxembourg, which provided most of the draft and the Netherlands which built in the saving for competition policy.[225]

There is no Community policy in the Article. The Community and the Member States are the actors. The Member States consult and co-ordinate with each other. The Community's contribution is to be found in what it does under other Treaty articles. Any specific measures aiming at industrial improvement require unanimity and involve simple non-binding consultation with the EP – the atavistic Community model. This Article remained unchanged in the Treaty of Amsterdam.

One industrial branch that has been given close Community attention is the development of the information society This was the expression preferred to the 'information highway' by the Committee which met under Commissioner Bangemann in 1993. It proposed ten initiatives, all of which could create industrial opportunities, as well as benefiting users:

> Tele-working (with job-creation), distance learning, networks for universities and research centres (i.e. principally the Internet), remote processing services for small business, road traffic management, air traffic control, health care networks, electronics tendering, a trans-European public administration network and city information highways (tele-shopping, home banking, educational courses, etc.).

Audio-visual policy, of support for producers (MEDIA and MEDIA II[226]), is designed to help an industry of economic and cultural importance to survive in a fiercely competitive market on the brink of explosion into the digital age.

A lesson learnt

The days of 'picking winners' have gone.[227] Governments (and Community institutions) regard it as their task to create favourable conditions for industry not to direct it, still less seek to manage enterprises. National champions are also no more. The massive restructuring of the European vehicle industry occurring at the turn of the century is independent of Community involvement, apart from the review of mergers under the competition policy.

RESEARCH AND DEVELOPMENT

The Treaty establishing the European Economic Community (1957) has nothing to say about industrial research and technological development. Its companion in time and place, the Treaty establishing the European Atomic Energy Community, deals extensively with nuclear research. It creates an in-house research laboratory (the Joint Research Centre (JRC), Ispra, in Italy, with branches elsewhere in the Community), provides for research programmes ('direct actions'), envisages research contracts which can be let out ('indirect actions'), calls for co-operation to avoid duplication and arranges for the dissemination of research results (see Box 11.5).

Box 11.5   The Joint Research Centre

The JRC has specialised institutes dealing with:

1. Central Bureau for Nuclear Measurements (Geel)
2. Institute for Transuranium Elements (Karlsruhe)
3. Institute for Advanced Materials (Patten-Ispra)
4. Institute for Systems Engineering (Ispra)
5. Institute for the Environment (Ispra)
6. Institute for Remote Sensing Applications (Ispra)
7. Institute for Safety Technology (Ispra)
8. Centre for Information Technologies and Electronics (Ispra)
9. Institute for Prospective Technological Studies

Euratom had only a brief operational period. Disenchantment grew when some of the Member States gained the impression that they were not getting their fair share of the contracts and became complete when nuclear power went out of favour in most Member States. Ispra was obliged to find a new role for its resources and staff. The nuclear fusion project, Torus at Culham in England, classified as an indirect action, also lost its appeal as a power source, if not as a new frontier in engineering, and is being run down.

Non-nuclear Research and Technological Development became the new chapter VI in the EEC Treaty by virtue of the Single European Act (1986) and was reinforced by the Treaty on European Union (1992) and the Treaty of Amsterdam (1997). In the consolidated version of the Treaty, it occupies Articles 163 to 173.

Losing out

By the mid-1970s the loss of European competitiveness compared with the USA and Japan was evident, especially in high-tech production. It had been charted and predicted in such works as Servan Schreiber's *The American Challenge*, Hedberg's *Japan's Revenge* and Efimov's *Il faut stopper less Japonais.*[228] At the time the industrial policy of the Community was focused on the 'sunset' industries, steel, shipbuilding, textiles, footwear, where the task was to manage decline.

The dynamic and visionary Commissioner Etienne Davignon, who took over the Industry DG in 1981, turned attention to the new science-based industries, especially electronic. In close consultation with industry leaders he inspired in May 1982 the Commission's proposal 'Towards a European Strategic Programme for Research and Development in Information Technology', better known as ESPRIT. Adopted by the Council (after British misgivings)[229] the programme offered part-funding for co-operation between enterprises and research bodies in 'pre-competitive' research. This could escape competition control by virtue of the let-outs in para. 3 of Article 81 (ex-85).

ESPRIT was popular and was followed by a string of catchy acronyms: RACE communication technology, Bridge, biotechnology, Brite/EURAM, technology and advanced materials, value, feasibility grants for small businesses, SPRINT, technology transfer, craft, cost-sharing among small firms.

The approach was systematised into the Framework Programmes, of which the 'Fourth' is shown in Table 11.4.

Framework programmes are proposed by the Commission and adopted under the *co-decision* procedure. At the insistence of the British Conservative government, the Council was unusually required to act unanimously. The new Labour government, which had announced that it was less allergic to majority voting, agreed to the change to voting the framework programme in the final stages of the negotiations of the Treaty of Amsterdam. Specific programmes are adopted by the Council using qualified majority voting (QMV) after *consulting* the EP.

The objectives of the programmes are set out in Article 164 (ex-130g): co-operation between undertakings and research bodies; international co-operation; dissemination of

Table 11.4   Fourth Framework Programme (1994–98)

Activity	ECU million
First Activity: Research, technological and demonstration programmes	10,045
Second Activity: Co-operation with third countries and international organisations	575
Third Activity: Dissemination and optimisation of results	352
Fourth Activity: Stimulation of the training and mobility of researchers	792
Total overall amount	11,764

Source: European Parliament Directorate-General for Research.

results; training and mobility of researchers. Financing is normally half Community and half participants in projects within a specific programme, but there can be 100% financing of the marginal costs incurred by non-profit-making bodies. Article 165 (ex-130h), echoing one of the provisions of Euratom, calls on the Community and the Member States to co-ordinate their programmes.

Does it work?

If it works, there seems to be a long way to go. In 1991, at the close of the Second Framework Programme, a Commission conclusion was: 'Europe invents, the USA invents and innovates and Japan innovates and sells.'[230] In 1993 the Commission published its powerful thinkpiece *Growth, Competitiveness and Employment*, M. Delors' swan song. Its first page contains the sobering finding:

Over the last 20 years:

- the European economy's potential rate of growth has shrunk (from around 4% to around 2.5% a year);
- unemployment has been steadily rising from cycle to cycle;
- the investment ratio has fallen by five percentage points;
- *our competitive position in relation to the USA and Japan has worsened as regards:*
  - employment,
  - our share of export markets,
  - *R&D and innovation and its incorporation into goods brought to the market,*
  - *the development of new products.* (Emphasis added.)

The Santer Commission's 1997 document. 'Agenda 2000' places the emphasis on *Knowledge Policies* (p. 12). It urges that the research and development effort 'must be given new impetus' and that Community R&D must 'provide real added value in relation to national programmes ... Europe should be able to transform scientific and technological breakthroughs into industrial and commercial successes'. In proposing the Fifth Framework Programme for 1998–2002, the Commission criticised the past:

> ... the Framework programme has been transformed over the years into a general framework for a series of activities which, while of undoubted quality, have been carried out on topics which are clearly too numerous and dispersed. As a result of the constraints weighing down on its decision-making and delivery mechanisms, it has become an unwieldy instrument at times incapable of reflecting the realities and keeping up with the speed of social, economic and scientific developments.[231]

The Commissioner responsible, Mme Cresson, therefore proposed 'a distinct break' with previous programmes. This translated as concentration on three 'thematic ' programmes under Article 164a; and three horizontal programmes under 164b, c and d. The thematic programmes were presented as:

1. Unlocking the resources of the living world and the ecosystem.
2. Creating a user-friendly Information Society.
3. Promoting competitive and sustainable growth.

The horizontal programmes are:

1. Confirming the international role of European research.
2. Innovation and participation of SMEs.
3. Improving human potential.

The programmes are to be implemented by means of 'shared-cost actions' and direct actions undertaken at the JRCs. The programmes include a Euratom section. There is also a role for COST and Eureka.

COST is the Commitee on Science and Technology, a vehicle for governments of the Member States to sign up to collaborative research projects, usually involving their national research facilities. Participation is optional. Eureka – which is not the property of the Community, and for which the Commission provides the secretariat but until 1988 no funds – is an agency for canvassing research projects and finding partners. It was devised by France in 1985 as a response to the US 'Strategic Defense Initiative' ('Star Wars' anti-missile programme), which was foreseen to yield civil spin-off likely to give US firms a gratuitous lead in the relevant technologies. Whereas Community R&D was described as 'top-down' in the sense that five-year programmes were written down and support invited, Eureka was 'bottom-up' in the sense that enterprises chose themselves the projects for which they wanted collaborators.

The programme headings in the Fifth Framework are broad enough to encompass research as wide-ranging as occurred under previous programmes. The greater concentration, which is the aim, will need to be ensured at the level of the specific programmes. The Commission described its new approach as 'research by objective'.

The Council, however, demurred at the proposals. More impressed by Madame Cresson's strictures on the past than by her proposals, it decided to reduce the Fifth Programme in real terms from the 16.3 billion euros proposed by the Commission and endorsed by the EP to 14 billion euros, of which 12.74 billion for the EC and 1.26 billion for Euratom. It added back a fourth thematic programme: improving the quality of life. The cutback in funding did not please the European Parliament, which found it at variance with the Council's strategies for improving competitiveness and creating employment opportunities. A compromise was painfully negotiated, with the British Presidency of the first half of 1998 playing a leading role, in contrast to its recalcitrance in earlier phases. It provides a total package of 14.9 billion ECUs[232]. The breakdown is shown in Table 11.5.

Table 11.5   Fifth Framework Programme (1998–2002): amounts (current prices) and breakdown

Activity	Actions	Issues	Million euros
First Activity	*Indirect actions (not Euratom)*	Theme 1 Quality of life and management of living resources	2,413
		Theme 2 User-friendly information society	3,600
		Theme 3 Competitive and sustainable growth	2,705
		Theme 4 Energy, environment and sustainable development	2,125
Second Activity		Confirming the international role of Community research	475
Third Activity		Promotion of innovation and encouragement of SME participation	363
Fourth Activity		Improving human resource potential and socio-economic knowledge base	1,280
	Direct actions (not Euratom)	Serving the citizen	739
		Enhancing sustainability	
		Underpinning European competitiveness	
	EURATOM		
	Direct actions	Nuclear fission	281
		Nuclear safeguards	
		Decommissioning and waste management	
	Indirect actions	Controlled thermonuclear fusion	
		Nuclear fission	
		Generic R&TD	
		Support for research infrastructures	979

EDUCATION AND TRAINING

> ... Determined to promote the development of the highest possible level of knowledge for their peoples through a wide access to education and its continuous updating ... [Preamble to the Consolidated Version of the Treaty establishing the European Community]

There are two strands in Union concern with education and training. The first is giving education a European dimension. The second is raising skill levels as part of the attack on unemployment.

The first exchanges

The first of these testifies to the ability of an individual to create a Community programme from scratch. In the early 1980s, a British official in the Commission, who had a background in higher education, Hywel Jones, conceived a plan for promoting educational exchanges with Community funding. It chimed with the interest there then was in finding or contriving actions that could be labelled as 'People's Europe'. The result, proposed by the Commission at Jones's urging, and accepted by the Council, was the *Erasmus* programme which enabled university students from Member States to pursue part of their studies in other Member States. *Comett* was a programme for facilitating the mobility of university teachers and for encouraging co-operation between academe and business. *Lingua* was for the teaching of Community languages in schools (with British resistance, since school education was held to be outside the purview of the Community). *Jean Monnet* funds set up teaching posts in university departments.

Treaty catching up

As often happens in the life of the Community, the text of the Treaty in due course caught up with ongoing practice. The Treaty on European Union introduced in Title III a new chapter, 'Education, Vocational Training and Youth', set out in new Articles 149 and 150 (ex-126 and 127). In drafting the education article, 126, the Member States were at pains not to use the allergenic word 'policy'. The Article calls for co-operation between the Community and the Member States in the development of quality education. Incentive measures are envisaged but they expressly exclude any harmonisation of laws and regulation in Member States. Unusually, but as if to point up what is in mind, the Article says that on a proposal from the Commission the Council may adopt recommendations. The Council would not usually need to start from a Commission proposal for a recommendation, which is without binding force.

In 1996 the original programmes, considered to be one of the success stories, were recast (Jones had meanwhile become the Director-General responsible). The *Socrates* programme is the instrument for student mobility. It also provides for support for courses with a 'European dimension' for students who do not move. There is support for school education in the *Comenius* subprogramme and for university studies in the *Erasmus* subprogramme. Other component parts are:

Grundtvig	Adult education
Lingua	Language training
Minerva	Open and distance learning.

The *Leonardo da Vinci* programme is concerned with vocational training including internships. It supports transnational pilot projects for vocational instruction. *'Youth for Europe'*, in its 1995 version, follows other programmes of the same name (see Table 11.6). It seeks to bring young Europeans together in common projects. Tempus II and Tempus III, awaiting renewal for 2000–2006, are part of Phare, the programme of assistance to CEECs which are applicants to join the EU.

All the foregoing programmes are open to the other members of the European Economic Area and are being extended to the CEECs which have applied for Union membership. There may be difficulties where part national funding is involved, as it is in student mobility.

Table 11.6   Budgetary endowments for the 'Educational Triptych' (million ECUs/euros)

	1995–99	2000–2006*
Socrates	850	1,550
Leonardo	620	1,150
Youth for Europe	126	–

*Proposed by Council.

The annual output is 127,000 mobile students and university level teachers; 40,000 young people in exchange schemes; 30,000 schoolchildren in language study visits; and 6,000 teachers in language training courses.

Sport

The European Union, a distant concept for most of its citizens, seeks to show a human face in its concern for sport. The Commission sponsors a tennis tournament. The ECJ judgement in the celebrated Bosman case in 1995 revolutionised cross-border transfers of professional soccer players. The European Council meeting in Vienna in December 1998 took some relief from its more abstruse matters by following up Declaration 29 annexed to the Treaty of Amsterdam, which

> emphasises the social significance of sport, in particular its role in forging identity and bringing people together . . .

It asked the Commission to study: competition rules and sport; sport and television; doping; sport in social policy and in employment.

Training

The drafting of Article 150 (new style), on training was less cautious. It says that the Community is to implement a vocational training *policy*. It inherited this language from the original Article 128 of the 1957 version of the Treaty. It enjoined the Council to lay down general principles for implementing a common vocational training policy. It is of no practical concern, but the drafting of the article would have permitted these principles to be adopted by *simple* majority, if that had then been practised in the working methods. The Council took the first steps in 1963.[233] It also set up the PETRA programme for helping to promote vocational training.

When they came to the Treaty on European Union, the Member States scrapped the old Article 128, hitherto the basis for the vocational training policy. But they made what was still described as a common policy respecting the responsibilities of Member States, which are undiminished. This is an interesting blend, or confusion, between Community policies and the rules of subsidiarity. Community measures may be taken but again they exclude harmonisation of national laws and regulations. There is no mention of recommendations.

New employment policies

Despite what appears to be a stronger legal base for action, Community intervention into the field is now part of Leonardo, or Youth for Europe. On the other hand, vocational training and improvement in general education have become a key component of the new employment policy set forth in the Treaty of Amsterdam.[234] In its White Paper on *Growth, Competitiveness and Employment*, the Commission preached the message of training as the 'catalyst of a changing society' (Chapter 7) and dwelt at length on the weaknesses of education and training systems in the Member States (especially school-leavers without any qualifications), in invidious comparison with the USA and Japan (p. 118). It put forward specific suggestions for action at Member State level, or by Member States in concert and at Community level. The Special Meeting of the European Council in Luxembourg in November 1997 took up the theme. Among the conclusions was agreement that every young person is to be offered a fresh start before the end of six months of unemployment in the form of training ('Youthstart'), retraining, work practice, a job or other employability measure.[235] School drop-out rate is to be reduced by improved education quality and young people are to be equipped with greater ability to adapt to change and with relevant skills. This part of the conclusions bears the fingerprints of 'new' Labour. The German input is shown by the absence of mention of any Community expenditure.

Without mention of education in any treaty texts, Ministers of Education in the Member States began meeting in 1980 'in the framework of the Council', the formulation which meant that they were using Community facilities, but had no Community powers.

CULTURE

Culture was formally imported into the Community by the new Article 128 of the Treaty on European Union (now 151). The decision to give the Community its cultural dimension had been taken at the meeting of the European Council in Rome in December 1990. Under the heading 'Extending and strengthening Community action' there appears:

> safeguarding the diversity of the European heritage and promoting cultural exchanges and education.

On hearing the word 'culture', the Member States reached for their scissors. The new Treaty article bristles with reminders that cultural diversity is precious. Even to adopt a recommendation (which is not binding on them), the Member States need a Commission proposal and they must be unanimous. Any legislative measures are to be adopted by co-decision, but throughout the procedure the Council must (exceptionally) act unanimously. Such inflexibility on one side of the Conciliation Committee, which is the heart of co-decision, puts a heavy strain on it. It is a sign of the domestic sensitivity of cultural policy that what can only be regarded as an anomaly survived in the Treaty of Amsterdam, when other unanimity requirements in co-decision were relaxed.

The Community's role is the modest one of *contributing* to the flowering of the cultures (in the plural) of the Member States.

In 1996 the Council and Parliament co-decided on the latest version of the programme for promoting co-operation in music, *Kaleidoscope 2000*.[236] In November 1997 the Council asked the Commission to prepare an action plan 'concentrating on teaching music from a very young age, on disseminating and composing music, including creating music using the new technologies, and on enhancing the skills of artists and other music professionals'.[237]

Another cultural programme is MEDIA, now II. One part of it[238] is for the encouragement of the development and distribution of European audio-visual works. The other part[239] is a training programme for professionals in the European audio-visual industry. (A less successful interlude, with cultural connotations but aims of commercial advancement, was the attempt to pioneer High Definition Television (HDTV), which was abandoned when industry chose the digital path to progress.)

In April 1998 – after the Oscars ceremony in Hollywood a few weeks before had been monopolised by the film 'Titanic', despite high hopes for British performers – the President of the Commission suggested that Europe should have its own Oscar system, paid for by the industry. The Council agreed. The sequel is awaited.

The protection of European culture was an aim of the 'Television without Frontiers' Directive of 1989.[240] It ruled that there was a single market in television broadcasting and that the only regulation was that of the originating state. It restricted the time available for advertising, set forth rules for the moral protection of minors (now a problem with the Internet, for which the Council has devised a code of conduct) and insisted on the right of reply. Its more controversial provision was to reserve the bulk of transmission time to European works. The quota system was applied loosely but continued to annoy the US film and TV production industry. In reviewing TV broadcasting in 1995 and 1996 the Commission reported that 'more than half of the television programmes broadcast by most television channels in the EU are of European origin'.[241] This may involve some juggling with the definition of European. A former Commissioner once maintained that non-European footage once transmitted on a European channel acquired European nationality.

One of the tasks of the Council (Culture), inaugurated by the actress Melina Mercouri when she was Greek Culture Minister in 1983, is the selection with Solomanic wisdom of the annual City of European Culture, or, when wisdom can no more, *Cities* (see Box 11.6). The accolade is keenly sought after as a major asset in tourist promotion and in stimulating the conservation of a city's architectural and artistic heritage. The Council invited St Petersburg to organise a cultural month in 2003. To avoid time-consuming haggle, from 2005 to 2019 there will be one city per Member State, beginning with Ireland and ending with Italy (new members to be accommodated when the time comes). In February 1999 the Council decided that instead of designating the European *Capital* of Culture by way of inter-governmental agreement, it should be brought into the Community framework based on the Article relating to culture in the Treaty on European Union.

Box 11.6   European Union Cities of Culture 2001–2004

2001	Rotterdam and Oporto
2002	Bruges and Salamanca
2003	Graz
2004	Genoa and Lille

A recent venture is the *Raphael* programme, agreed with some difficulty, unsurprising given the procedure, between the Parliament and the Council in September 1997. With total funding set at 30 million ECUs for 1997–2000, something less than half of the Commission's proposal, Raphael aims at the preservation and development of the European cultural heritage, arranging partnerships, improving public access and furthering co-operation with non-member countries and international organisations. The *Ariane* programme, agreed between the Council and the EP in July 1997, takes further an earlier scheme which was focused on literature written in the lesser known languages and therefore not easily accessible. Ariane offers financial assistance for the translation of books into other Community languages and establishes the Aristeion (Greek, 'best') prize for literature and translation. Funding for 1997–98 is set at 7 million ECUs. The programme then ends, unless renewed.

A jarring note is sometimes struck when the Commission refers to the 'culture industry'. The rest of the Union has not yet followed contemporary Britain into glorifying pop culture as a fountain of 'cool' creativity, and avant-garde or sociopathic performers as massive export earners.

A problem that is inconclusively looked at from time to time and again in 1997 is book pricing. Some Member States require forms of resale price maintenance (RPM) to protect writers and their outlets. Others do not allow producers' price-fixing. The two systems collide when books are imported from a free source to an RPM market.

PUBLIC HEALTH

Public health does not appear in the 1957 version of the Treaty establishing the European Economic Community. Nevertheless, Ministers of Health of the Member States began meeting 'in the framework of the Council' in 1977. They could dialogue and adopt plans under different names but had no powers, and between 1979 and 1985 meetings were irregular. Since 1989 the rhythm has been one meeting in each Presidency, almost as a moral obligation.

National regulation of health products and practices were divisive. When the stronger legislative basis for the Single Market was laid by the Single European Act in 1986 its new Article 100a (now 90) stipulated that in making proposals to unify the market concerning health, the Commission should take as a base a high level of protection. This requirement was further developed in the Treaty on European Union. At the suggestion of Germany, a new title, originally numbered X, was inserted, requiring the Community to *contribute* towards a high level of health protection; and a new objective was correspondingly added as Article 3.0.

The draft article included in the Luxembourg version of the draft Treaty on European Union proposal makes clear that the role of the Community is contributory and that the method is co-operation among the Member States. It singles out action on the major health scourges.[242] This was inspired by the programmes that the Health Council had already adopted over the years, especially for the prevention and treatment of cancer[243] and AIDS. Although stressing the health risks of smoking, the Health Council steers clear of the perils of alcohol (of which the Community produces excess for home consumption).

The Dutch draft of the Treaty on European Union specified in Article 129 (now 152) that drug dependency was among the major health scourges. In parallel with the other new titles under which the Community contributes to Member States' co-operation, it provided that any incentive measures adopted by the Community must exclude any harmonisation of the laws and regulations of the Member States.[244]

The Treaty of Amsterdam goes further. Article 152, now the sole article of Title XIII, replaces 'drug dependency' by 'drugs-related health damage' (Article 152, 1). It contains a reminder of the scandal in France when patients were infected with AIDS[245] by being given transfusions with infected blood. It has a two-fold reference to blood and blood products (Article 152, 4a and 5). It requires that Community action shall fully respect the responsibilities of the Member States for the organisation and delivery of health services and medical care (Article 152, 5). Health services are *par excellence* matters for subsidiarity (national precedence).

Despite the restrictions on Community action, the Commission continues to bring forward proposals to promote co-operation among Member States including particularly on blood supplies, which are a traded product (British supplies are imported to replace stocks possibly infected by the CJD agent).

The free circulation of medical personnel has been secured by directives some, e.g. on the recognition of the qualifications of doctors, long ahead anticipating the Single Market programme.

CONSUMER PROTECTION

The Community did not wait for a treaty base to begin to concern itself with the interests of consumers. The first mention of consumer protection is in the communiqué from the meeting in October 1972 of the Heads of State and Government of the Countries of the Enlarged Community[246] The first specific consumer protection legislation appeared in the late 1970s. In November 1989 the Council adopted a Resolution on consumer protection – making a link with the 1992 Single Market programme – and in 1990 the Commission produced its first action plan.

Treaty on European Union

When treaty reform was in the air in 1990, and when the Single Market programme needed a more human face, it was characteristically a Scandinavian Member State that highlighted consumer interests. The Danes circulated a memorandum in October 1990, in which they argued that consumer protection should be a priority objective of 'Community *co-operation*'.[247] Consumers are not mentioned in the conclusions of the European Council meeting in Rome in December 1990, which gives a list of subjects under the heading 'Extension and strengthening of Community action'. But a new 'consumers' title appeared in the Luxembourg draft of the Treaty on European Union dated 18 June 1991. It was preserved and completed in the revised Dutch draft that was adopted on 10 December 1991. With attention thus focused it was not surprising that, when former Commissioner Peter Sutherland and his High Level Group reported on the operation of the Single Market in 1992, they observed[248] that it had limited meaning for consumers. The nub of the problem is that while the frontier-free market *permits* consumers of goods and services to buy anywhere, they have less confidence in their *rights and their ability to enforce* them outside their home market. For example:

> ... despite the fact that the third life insurance directive removed all restrictions on advertising, consumers apparently are not so much making use of the possibility to purchase insurance services across frontiers.[249]

Few car-owners want to exercise their rights to insure outside the country of registration, and faced with a barrage of formalities fewer would try. These observations refer principally to direct cross-border transactions. They are not relevant to the sourcing of the goods which consumers buy on their home retail structures. But:

> In the end the only way to close the argument is to recognise that the single market is aimed at improving the lot of the consumer – not of the business person or worker – and that we're all consumers now.[250]

The new title, unaffected by the Treaty of Amsterdam, except for renumbering to become Title XIV, sole Article 153 (ex-129), falls into the group[251] which do not institute a Community policy but rather describe the Community as 'contributing', in this case to the 'health, safety and economic interests' of consumers. According to the Commission, the informal guideline is:

> As little regulation as is possible, but as much as necessary to protect consumers.[252]

The Article is unusual in citing (para. 3b), as a base for legislation, a different treaty article, 95, in the single market area of policy, which itself refers to consumer protection. Other measures which 'support, supplement or monitor the policy pursued by the Member States' can be taken by co-decision (para. 5).

Minimum harmonisation

In this field, there is 'minimum harmonisation'. Member States can maintain or introduce more stringent measures (para. 5) but they must be compatible with the Treaty. Whereas Article 95 (ex-100a) provides a saving for national measures to protect the environment or the working environment, it does not mention consumers. It might be possible to argue that a 'more stringent' national consumer protection measure was safeguarded by the let-outs in Article 30 (ex-36), but it would be wiser for any Member State which invoked Article 30 to point to human and animal health rather than consumer protection as such.[253]

Programme

Consumer protection will never end. There will always be new real or potential damage to consumer welfare or interests. In its 1996–98 'Priorities for Consumer Policy'[254] the Commission proposed the ten objectives[255] listed in Box 11.7. Correspondingly, the legislation ranges wide, as shown by the selection presented in Box 11.8.

Box 11.7   Consumer policy priorities

- Consumer education and information.
- Framework for consumer interests in single market.
- Access to financial services.
- Essential public utility services.
- Benefit of opportunities offered by the information society.
- Improve confidence in foodstuffs.[256]
- Sustainable, environmentally-friendly consumption.
- Enhanced consumer representatiom.
- Assistance to CEECs to develop consumer policies.
- Assistance to developing countries to promote consumer policy considerations.

The Commission's programme for 1998, under the motto 'do less, do better', contains only one new consumer protection measure, the distance selling of financial services. It is a second try.

BSE

The BSE crisis of the spring of 1996 seriously undermined the credibility of Community's consumer protection policies. An EP Committee of Enquiry lambasted the Commission for slackness, if not cover-up, and demanded reform under pain of a censure motion (which if passed dismisses the Commission collectively from office). In response, the Commission announced in February 1997 that, among other changes, it was

298

Box 11.8   Consumer protection legislation (examples)

76/768/EEC	OJ L 262, 27.9.1976	Products used in cosmetics
79/581/EEC	OJ L 158, 26.6.1979	Price marking foods
84/450/EEC	OJ L 250, 19.9.1984	Misleading advertising
85/374/EEC	OJ L 210, 7.8.1985	Liability for defective goods
88/314/EEC	OJ L 142, 9.6.1988	Price marking non-foods
93/580/EEC	OJ L 278, 11.11.1993	Potentially dangerous goods
94/3092/EC	OJ L 331, 21.12.94	EHLASS (domestic accidents)
95/629/EC	OJ L 162, 13.7.95	Reform of Consumer Committee
97/7/EC	OJ L 144, 4.6.1997	Distance selling
97/55/EC	OJ L 290, 23.10.1997	Comparative advertising

centralising responsibility for the seven scientific advisory committees (that had hitherto reported to different DGs) in the renamed DG for Consumer Policy and Consumer Health Protection, under Commissioner Bonino, a lady renowned for her activist campaigning for good causes. The Office for Veterinary and Plant Health Inspection and Control was removed from the Agriculture DG, where it had not distinguished itself, and placed in Madame Bonino's charge. The organisational changes were intended to mark a new departure, which was approved by the EP.

ENVIRONMENT POLICY

Symbolically, the period at which the EEC Treaty was being worked out was also the moment at which the first aerosols propelled by CFC gas came on the European market, as sun lotion, floor polish, car paint and so on. The Member States of the European Economic Community were to become the world's largest producers of the inert gases that make holes in the ozone layer and contribute to global warming.

The 1957 EEC Treaty does not mention the environment. Green politics did not begin until the 1960s.

The beginnings of policy

Within ten years concern for damage to the atmosphere, landscape, health, habitats, flora and fauna had become acute and a new political force in developed countries. The Club of Rome, an early Green movement, advocated a global policy of zero growth as the most effective means of arresting further damage. The Council of Europe declared 1970 to be European Conservation Year. The first landmark United Nations Conference on the Human Environment took place in Stockholm in June 1972. The European Summit (precursor of the European Council) which met in Paris on 19–20 October

1972, bringing together the Six and the countries which were on the eve of joining, declared that economic expansion was not an end in itself and that special attention would be given to the protection of the environment.[257] The Summit called upon the Commission to produce an action programme.

The original legal basis for action to protect the environment was the reference in the preamble to the Treaty and in Article 2 to the improvement in the standard of living and the default Article 308 (ex-235). It covers the situation in which the Treaty has not provided powers but action is necessary to attain one of the objectives of the Community. Article 94 (ex-100) provides for legislation to approximate national measures that affect the establishment or functioning of the Common Market. In its original form, this Article, like 308, required unanimity.

The new Title

As will be seen below, the Community proceeded to enact many conservation measures on this thin basis. When it came to the first major policy revisions, in the Single European Act of 1986, it created a new Title VII of three Articles devoted to the environment. It was not yet a matter of 'policy' but still of 'action', although the Title belongs to the Part called 'Policies of the Community'. Decisions were to be unanimous. The European Parliament was to be consulted, but the newly invented co-operation procedure was not applied. Member States were authorised to maintain *or introduce* more stringent protective measures than those adopted in common (minimum harmonisation). In the first Treaty evocation of the principle of *subsidiarity*, the new Title said that the Community was to act to the extent that the objective could be better obtained at Community level than at the level of the individual Member States (Article 130r, 4, which was deleted by the Treaty on European Union because a wider application of subsidiarity had been introduced).

The main environment policy Article from the SEA, 174 (ex-130r), set forth three principles: prevention, the rectification of damage at source and 'polluter pays'. It added that the protection of the environment should be a component of the Community's other policies.

In effect the new Title caught up with policy development. But confusion was sown by another Treaty amendment. Article 95 (ex-100a) is a key provision of the Single European Act, because it introduced qualified majority voting to the 'harmonisation' Article 100. In doing so, it mentioned environmental protection among the proposals that the Commission could bring forward with the object of the establishment or functioning of the internal market. There were therefore two possible bases, one still involving unanimity, the other using QMV. This discrepancy was to complicate the already difficult task of securing agreement on proposals.[258]

Further revision

By the time of the next Treaty revision in the Treaty on European Union, with the Green movements in Europe no less vociferous despite their eternal and internal wranglings, the Member States were ready to move on. In the Treaty on European Union of

1992 they added to Article 2, in the Part entitled 'Principles: sustainable and non-inflationary growth respecting the environment' that became the watchword of a new approach, designed to reconcile the economic progress which is a proclaimed objective of the Union and care for the environment. They amended old Article 130r by referring to '*policy* on the environment' and by subjoining a new 'precautionary' principle. Old Article 130s, on decision-taking, was amended by placing it under the co-operation procedure. This gave the European Parliament a greater involvement and the Council QMV, except for several categories where there would be simple consultation of the EP and unanimity in the Council: fiscal measures, town and county planning, land use and the management of water resources, and 'measures significantly affecting a Member State's choice between different energy sources and the general structure of its energy supply' (for example, the nuclear option). The Council could determine, unanimously, which of these matters it could decide by QMV, but still without the co-operation procedure, but it never did so. However, 'general action programmes, setting out priority objectives', otherwise known as 'environment action programmes', of which there had already been four, were to be adopted under the co-operation procedure. The Treaty also directed that 'environmental protection requirements must be integrated into the definition and implementation of other Community policies' (Article 130r, 2).[259] This requirement was deleted from the Article by the Treaty of Amsterdam (Article 174) to reappear as a free-standing Article 6.

Public views on the environment in 1995 are presented in Box 11.9.

Box 11.9   Public views on the environment (Spring 1995)

* 85% of Europeans believed that environmental protection was an immediate and urgent problem.
* 72% of Europeans considered that economic growth must be ensured but that the environment should also be protected.
* % of Europeans believed that damage to the environment was caused by:
  - factories releasing dangerous chemicals into the air or water   68%
  - global pollution   48%
  - oil pollution of the seas and coasts   40%
  - storage of nuclear waste   39%

In all, 69% of respondents believed that decisions with respect to the environment should be taken at the Community level rather than at national level.

Source: Eurobarometer (Spring 1995)

The Treaty of Amsterdam

The 1997 Treaty of Amsterdam lends further emphasis to environmental policy. All measures and programmes except those still protected by unanimity are subject to the simplified co-decision procedure. Given the credentials of the EP, this is the 'greening' of the Treaty, especially since environment protection pervades all other policies. In the recast Article 100a (now 95) it widens the possibilities for Member States to maintain *or introduce* national measures. This reflects the stronger Scandinavian membership of the Union – and perhaps the significance of the Danish referendum[260] for the new Treaty.

> This is the pertinent Article in what promises to be a long-running debate on genetically modified food. It says that even where there has already been harmonisation, Member States can introduce new measures to protect the environment. They must notify the Commission, which rules on whether the national measure is an (illegal) restriction on trade. The Commission acts autonomously, under the label 'Guardian of the Treaty'.

Like much else in the realm of the Community, the evolution of environmental policy can be tracked in the proceedings of the European Council.

Apart from desultory reference to marine pollution (the Amoco Cadiz disaster of 1978) and to acid rain attacking forests, it is not until the 31st meeting in Brussels on 29–30 March 1985 that there is a major statement about the environment and the announcement that 1987 will be the European Environment Year.[261] It is also here that, prefiguring the Single European Act, environment policy is described as the 'essential component of the economic, industrial, agricultural and social policies . . .'. The consequences of the explosion of the Chernobyl nuclear reactor are mentioned at the 34th meeting at the Hague on 26–27 June 1986. At its 39th meeting in Hanover on 27–28 June 1988, the European Council foreshadowed the language of the Treaty on European Union by declaring that environmental considerations must be *integrated* into all areas of economic policy-making. Thereafter the environment frequently features in European Council conclusions, often run together with the use of the Cohesion Fund to support environmental projects in the beneficiary states and with Trans-European Networks (TENs) serving environmental purposes.

There have been five Environmental Action Programmes – 1973–76, 1977–80, 1982–86, 1987–92 and 1993–2000. The last was entitled 'For Sustainable Development', in line with the new direction of the Treaty on European Union. Under the powers which have progressively been strengthened, over 200 legislative measures have been adopted. The protection of the environment was selected as one of the priorities of the United Kingdom Presidency in the first half of 1998.[262]

The measures in the programmes concern such areas as the quality of drinking and bathing water and water used in cultivating shell fish; acoustic pollution; air pollution, especially vehicle emissions; the protection of habitats; nuclear safety; eco-labelling; the LIFE fund for investment in ecological improvement; international agreements and conferences; waste disposal and waste management; chemical substances; safety standards in chemical plants; research into the environment under STEP and EPOCH; and public access to environmental information. Three deserve special attention: Environmental Impact Assessments, the European Environment Agency and exhaust emissions from small cars.

Environmental Impact Assessment (EIA) is an American innovation that some Member States had begun to copy. In November 1971 the Council decided that the effects of expansion projects on the environment should be taken into account at the earliest possible stage. This was the time of slow-acting consensuality as the decision-taking practice. The EIA directive appeared in 1988. It set up a standardised procedure for assessing the impact on the environment (humans, fauna, flora, landscapes, health, transport effects) of capital projects. The procedure provided for public participation in the inquiries. The assessments themselves were conducted by national authorities.

Although governments had willed EIAs into being to show their green credentials, they were troubled by the obligation to have recourse to them when the capital project was one which the government itself favoured or sponsored because of its economic or political advantages. Inquiries could take up time and protestors could both use the assessment process and appeal to the Commission to carry their point. In response to complaints the Commission began a series of proceedings against erring Member States (all twelve save Denmark) for incomplete assessments or avoidance of them. Nevertheless, the paradox of political gesture and administrative indifference remained. The 1985 version of the directive was further revised in 1996 under the co-operation procedure. It is clarified that the directive applies to such matters as the construction of long-distance railway lines, airports with a basic runway length of 2,100 m or more, motorways and waste disposal installations for the incineration, chemical treatment or landfill of hazardous wastes.

In 1990 the Council decided to establish a European Environment Agency.[263] The rationale behind the establishment of such agencies or observatories is none too clear: the job could be done by the Commission, as it does when, for example, it analyses the state of fish stocks. The Commission may be too closely identified with initiatives, agenda-setting and enforcement. The Member States wanted none of them. To them the Agency's mission is to provide hard objective information about the environment as a solid basis for policy decision, and to co-operate with the network of comparable national bodies. The European Parliament wanted a body with teeth for inspection and enforcement but the Member States resisted such an imposition. They then failed to agree on the seat of the Agency until the Belgian Prime Minister brokered a package deal at the European Council meeting on 29 October 1993. The Agency went to Copenhagen. In 1988 the Council looked at the Agency again and was 'in favour of strengthening the Agency's tasks rather than expanding its scope of action'.[264]

Vehicle emissions are notoriously pollutant. In February 1988 the Commission followed up a directive on emissions from medium-sized cars by suggesting the same CO, HC and N_{OX} emission limits for small cars (CO_2 cannot be controlled by the systems involved). The car-producing Member States other than Germany were opposed to the toughening of standards, even though the suggested limits did not imply the use of catalytic converters. The European Parliament wanted the more rigorous US standards. The softer Member States appreciated that they could not be overborne. However their position was undermined when the European Court of Justice decided in the landmark case of the Danish deposit-and-return rule for bottles that 'the protection of the environment was ... a mandatory requirement which would justify restrictions on the free movement of goods' (Case 302/86). This unexpected withdrawal from the holism of the Single Market and from the 'Cassis de Dijon' judgement (a product legally produced and marketed in one Member State must be accepted in another – Case 120/78) opened up the prospect of national standards becoming a bar to exports and the loss of economies of scale. The EP stood by the American standards. The Commission adopted them as an amendment to its original proposal. The Council could not change the amended proposal because this needed unanimity, which was not forthcoming. The car-producing countries had no option except to seek deferment of application. This case is often cited as a high point in the EP's use of its powers under the co-operation procedure.[265]

The achievements of Community environmental policy make mixed reading:

- In 1995 the Commission opened 265 infringement proceedings against Member States over environment law, something like one-fifth of the total number of proceedings.
- Every Member State was taken to the European Court of Justice for non-compliance with the 1979 directive on the protection of migratory birds.
- In 1991, of the 160 directives in force, not one had been fully implemented in every Member State.
- The Member States and the Commission arrived at the United Nations Conference on Development and Environment in Rio de Janeiro in June 1992 without a common position.
- In 1989 the Commission opened a debate on the cruelty to animals inherent in the use of leg hold traps, especially in North America (exporter of furs to Member States). Discussions were concluded in 1997 after negotiations with the third countries concerned.
- The directive on Environment Impact Assessments, which was adopted in July 1988, went through twenty-two drafts and had to be overhauled within five years.[266]
- A tax on the emission of carbon dioxide (CO_2) was suggested in 1990; after multiple discussions in different Councils (Energy, Environment, Ecofin) and the report of a High Level Group, it was still on the table in 1999.[267]
- A Commission Task Force examined the environmental implications of the increased economic growth forecast in 1985 to accrue from the Single Market programme. The Commission scrapped its ominous report.

Although all Member States proclaim the virtues of safeguarding the heritage of the natural environment and dwell on the dangers of climate change unless remedies are adopted, they are normally reluctant to incur present sacrifice for future advantage. They customarily affirm that environmental protection is not only compatible with industrial growth but is even a catalyst.[268] They are nevertheless apprehensive that the cost of protection may damage their competitiveness *vis-á-vis* the other Member States, or, if they act in concert, *vis-à-vis* other manufacturing countries. There are diverse perceptions of the pollution problem affecting each Member State. There are perhaps such mental reservation, such as, if Italy is the land of lemons because it has sunshine, Britain, with fast-flowing, non-international rivers, need not be too concerned about water-borne waste disposal. Authorities charged with purifying sewage discharge wryly observe that Brussels sewage is cheerfully discharged untreated into local rivers. There are also different starting points. Prevention at source is essentially a Teutonic approach, incorporated into Community philosophy in the first Action Programme of 1973 and anchored in the Treaty (Article 174.2, ex-130r). Britain traditionally backed the 'best environmentally practicable option' (BEPO), which would not invariably be total prevention.[269] Such differences are likely to remain, but to be overshadowed in coming years by the Herculean task of bringing environmental standards in the applicant CEECs towards established Community norms.

For the existing Community, the outlook is daunting:

- a 25% increase in hydrocarbon consumption by 2010
- a 25% increase in car ownership, 1990–2000
- a 63% increase in fertiliser use, 1970–88
- a 35% increase in solid urban waste, 1987–92
- a 35% increase in water use, 1970–85

Policy for the protection of the environment has been focused on the following issues, and the funding that was decided for primary environmental projects in 1990–95 can be seen in Table 11.7.

Air quality

According to the former Secretary of State for the Environment, Mr John Gummer, 50% of air pollution in Britain is blown in from mainland Europe (with reciprocal exports). Community action has been encompassed by wider international agreements and targets. The Community met the 1996 target of the UN Environment Programme for phasing out CFCs (the aerosol and refrigerator gas) and is on course for the required 35% reduction in HCFCs by 2004. It played the key role in the negotiation of the Kyoto Protocol under the UN 1992 Framework Convention on Climate Change for the reduction of emissions of greenhouse gases; and in June 1998 agreed on Member States' individual targets for the reduction of CO_2 emissions (a balance between some increases – Greece, Spain, Ireland, Portugal, Sweden[270] – and cuts in other Member States).

Water quality

As a start, and before there was a specific Title for environment policy, the Community concentrated on standards for water purity. Contemporary policy objectives are to integrate water quality protection with the management of freshwater resources. By 2010 all Member States are to ensure that water pricing reflects the full cost of supply. This collides with the alleged right of all to a clean water supply.

Biodiversity

The 1992 Convention on Biodiversity is the framework for the Community's programme to protect habitats and species. One of its first ventures outside the purely economic sphere proper to the then Community, was the populist 1979 Directive on the Protection of Migrant Birds.

Table 11.7   Funding for primary environmental projects, 1990–95

Project	Disbursements (million ECUs)
Land resources	143
Tropical forests	108
Biodiversity	47
Urban environment	40
Institutional strengthening	32
Climate change	31
Marine resources	19
Freshwater resources	13
Technology transfer	10
Pollution control	10
Total	452

Source: Commission

ENERGY

Energy is a Community Cinderella. Coal and nuclear power are the subject of separate treaties, but energy finds no place in the EC Treaty. The reason is the 'extreme politicisation' of the subject. This reached its finest hour in 1975 in the OECD Energy Conference in Washington when the Community participated as a bloc, but the Labour government in Britain insisted on having its own seat, behind its own nameplate. Oil is also often cited as the reason, along with fish, for the negative vote in the Norwegian referendum on Community membership in 1972.

The legacy of the oil price shocks

Member States' sensitivities are the legacy of the oil price shocks of the 1970s. In 1973 oil accounted for more than two-thirds of Community consumption of energy. Of the oil that the Community consumes, 80% is imported. Policies pursued in Member States to reduce their vulnerability have reduced the share of oil in energy consumption to less than 50%.

The Inter-governmental Conference of 1996–97 was due to consider the question of adding energy policy to the Community's activities. This was unfinished business from the negotiation of the Treaty on European Union of 1991 and it remained unfinished.

No energy chapter in the Treaty

In the IGC that resulted in the TEU, the Commission suggested a new chapter on energy, with the following substantive articles:

Article 1 The objectives of this Treaty shall, in matters governed by this Title, be pursued within the framework of a common energy policy.

   The common energy policy shall be closely co-ordinated with the policies pursued in the framework of the ECSC and EAEC Treaties.

Article 2 The common energy policy shall have the following objectives:
   (a) to guarantee security of supplies throughout the Union under satisfactory economic conditions;
   (b) to contribute to the stability of energy markets;
   (c) to complete the internal market in the energy field;
   (d) to define the measures to be taken in respect of each energy source in the event of a crisis;
   (e) to promote energy savings and renewable energy sources.

It shall ensure a high level of protection in relation both to the environment, and to health and safety.

Article 3 [Measures to be decided by co-decision]

Article 4 [Cartels and state aids permissible under certain circumstances][271]

The idea of a common energy policy was anathema to at least one Member State. The Luxembourg Presidency toned the Title down in its draft of the Treaty:

Article A Action by the Community in the sphere of energy, which shall support and complement that of the Member States, shall be aimed at the following objectives within the framework of a market economy.

Article B [Community *and* the Member States to co-operate internationally]

Article C [Measures to be adopted by the co-operation procedure][272]

Even this contributory role for the Community was too much for the Conference and all mention of energy was dropped from the final Dutch draft that was the basis for the TEU.

Measures adopted . . . and dismantled

In the wake of the 1973 crises, the Community adopted a large number of measures designed to reduce vulnerability. By 1995 much of the legislation was out of keeping with the abundance of energy on the market and with the doctrines of subsidiarity enunciated in the TEU and amplified in the Conclusions of the European Council meeting in Edinburgh in December 1992. Accordingly, and responding also to the call for simplification of Community law, the institutions made a bonfire of much of the regulation relating, for example, to the requirement to maintain stocks of coal at pitheads and to report requirements on energy firms.

307

The several programmes for improving energy use are being brought together in the 'Framework programme for measures in the energy sector' which the Commission produced at the end of 1997 in response to a Council invitation. The objectives are:

- security of supply;
- competitiveness;
- protection of the environment.

Among the programmes:

- SYNERGY is for international co-operation.
- SAVE (now II) concerns energy efficiency. One of its products is the CE marking of domestic refrigeration equipment that meets efficiency standards.
- ALTENER (now II) is for the promotion of renewable energy sources, including those which reduce CO_2 emissions. It has a budget of 22 million ECUs for the two years 1998–99.
- THERMIE was a research programme for energy technology. THERMIE II was opposed by Britain, France and Germany in 1994 and lapsed.
- CARNOT is for environmentally compatible technologies for the consumption of solid fuels.

Further, in TACIS (aid programme for the former USSR, excluding the Baltic States) there are measures for the safe transport of radioactive materials and for safety in nuclear facilities. KEDO (Korean Peninsula Energy Development Organisation) is a specific multinational programme to help North Korea to ensure nuclear safety in its Soviet-designed power stations (which have a positive heat gradient – the hotter they get the more they react).

One of the gaps in the Single Market programme when it completed its course at the end of 1992 was the supply of gas and electricity. Member State markets were traditionally supplied by state or para-statal monopolies, which were treated as essential public services. National enterprises and their counterparts in other Member States were excluded from production and delivery.

Electricity was tackled first. Beginning with a Commission proposal in 1992, the process ended with Parliament and Council Directive 96/92/EC concerning common rules for the internal market in electricity. The Directive opens up production to competition, and opens up the consumer market to the extent of 33%. It creates a right of access to the established network and allows Member States to impose public service obligations on suppliers.[273] The first stage of open markets began in February 1999.

Gas, on which the Commission had made a market-opening proposal in 1994, proved more difficult, especially as regards access to the established network. The Directive, agreed all round by April 1998, bans discrimination between undertakings and provides a choice of routes to access. The consumption market is opened up progressively, from 20% to 33% ten years from the entry into force of the Directive. Integrated storage, transmission, supply undertakings must unbundle their accounts to reveal whether there are abusive dominant positions or discriminatory practices. Public service obligations may be imposed on suppliers.

Three Councils – Ecofin, Environment and Energy – have repeatedly devoted much of a decade to the question of an energy tax, also called a CO_2 tax. In the beginning the tax was essentially an environmental proposal. Later, in the Commission's White Paper on *Growth, Competitiveness and Employment,* an energy tax was suggested as a replacement for statutory charges on labour.[274] An energy tax could be national, accruing to Exchequers and presumably harmonised, or it could be a Community impost – the first ever. Any tax proposal requires unanimity to pass it. Several delegations support it, including France and Germany; others are concerned at an extra burden on industry. In the absence of a multinational consensus on taxation measures to reduce energy consumption, unanimity has not been available within the Community.

After the collapse of the Soviet bloc and its trading patterns, it was clear that there was a complementarity between the energy needs of the Member States of the European Community and the vast and partly unexploited hydrocarbon resources of its Eastern neighbours (the Russian Federation is already a major supplier of natural gas through the pipeline which caused an EC/US rift in 1981[275]). In December 1991 fifty countries met in The Hague to discuss energy co-operation. They included all the countries of Western, Central and Eastern Europe, the New Independent States (including the Russian Federation),[276] the USA, Canada, Japan and Australia. The European Community was also represented.[277] The outcome was the European Energy Charter, concluded in 1994.

The first Article states:

> The parties are desirous of improving security of energy supply and of maximising the efficiency of production, conversion, transport, distribution and use of energy to enhance safety and to minimise environmental problems, on an acceptable economic basis.

The Community agreed to sign the Charter in mid-1997.[278] So far as it is concerned:

> ... the main aim is to meet the challenge of developing the energy potential of the independent states of the former Soviet Union and Eastern Europe while helping to improve security of supply for the European Community.[279]

The Treaty came into force in April 1998, having collected a sufficient number of ratifications, but not yet that of the Russian Federation.

Another Inter-governmental Conference for Treaty revision was scheduled for 2000, prior to the next enlargement. It may have to return to the question of whether there should be an explicit Community policy for energy[280] corresponding to the inclusion in Article 3u of the consolidated version of 'measures in the spheres of energy . . .'. It is almost certain that anything that comes out will not be a common policy creating Community competence but will be of the type in which the Community's role is to support what the Member States do.

THE COMMUNITY BUDGET

The Treaty rules governing the budget are set out in the title 'Financial Provisions'. Although the articles, which were extensively amended in the 1970s, have survived largely intact through three Inter-governmental Conferences for Treaty revision, in practice they are significantly replaced by working rules and inter-institutional agreements.[281]

The towering Eurocrat, the late Daniel Strasser, once said that 'An account of the tenure of budgetary power is . . . a kind of condensed history of European integration itself'.[282] As befits the man who invented 'La Saint Schuman',[283] his words were prophetic.

Coal and steel

In the first Community, the unelected High Authority for coal and steel possessed a taxing power (which the single Commission, its successor in the ECSC Treaty, still has). It imposed a levy on coal and steel production. Undertakings paid a price for the market conditions that the Treaty made for them. The supranational heyday was brief.[284]

EEC

The 1957 Treaty establishing the European Economic Community treated the new creation financially as if it were an international organisation like the others. It was funded by national contributions, with a GDP key, and a special key favouring Italy for national contributions to the Social Fund (ex-Article 200, repealed by the Treaty on European Union). Article 269 (ex-201) speaks of a future in which the Community would possess its 'own resources', especially from customs duties. Until then, the Member States were the paymasters. National contributions were carried in national budgets, voted through by national parliaments.

Own resources

The change to a Community endowed with its own resources as of right was slow to come. When it came it subjected the eight-year-old Community to its first test of strength. Own resources were needed to pay for guaranteed farm prices. The slow pace towards putting the necessary funds in place drove the France of President de Gaulle to boycott Community meetings in late 1965 in the episode of the empty chair.[285] It took three more years for the Member States to agree, at the Hague Summit in December 1969, to 'replace contributions from member countries by independent revenue'.[286] This was done by two instruments adopted in Luxembourg in April 1970: a Council Decision[287] to endow the Community with customs duties and a percentage of VAT; and the Treaty of Luxembourg of 22 April 1970.

Parliamentary control

The Treaty in particular partially corrected what would later have been known as a democratic deficit. Independent revenue meant independence from the national parliaments, which had previously, however cursorily, examined the national budget containing the Community contribution. The Assembly of the EEC, later the EP, was not given powers over revenue, but its say over expenditure was strengthened.[288] The Council remained the sole budgetary authority, responsible for declaring the budget adopted. This changed in the 1975 Treaty further amending certain financial provisions.[289] Under amended Article 272, 7 (ex-203), the President of the EP declares that the budget has been finally adopted. The EP had become a joint budgetary authority.

Revenue

Revenue remains the province of the Council and of the Member States. The Parliament, unlike others of the same name, does not vote supply. The source and composition of 'own resources' are decided by the Council (Economic and Finance, not in the Budget Council) after *consulting* the EP, subject to ratification by the Member States (Article 269, ex-201). This is one of the remaining bastions of Council unanimity. Privileges such as the UK rebate[290] cannot be repealed without the agreement of the privileged.

The Community's own resources (see Table 11.8) are:

1. Agricultural levies (on imports) and sugar and isoglucose levies (on production and storage).
2. Customs duties.
3. 1% of VAT (reduced from the 1988 level of 1.4%).
4. The fourth or additional resource, which is GDP based (as contributions were in the beginning) and is 'budget-balancing' (introduced in 1988).

Total revenue is capped up to 1999 (and, as was proposed in 'Agenda 2000: the Challenge of Enlargement', beyond) at 1.27% of Community GDP.

Table 11.8 Own resources 1997–99 budgets (million ECUs)

Resource	1997	(%)	1998	(%)	1999	(%)
Agricultural duties	2,015.5	(2.4%)	1,607.9	(1.95%)	1,921.1	(2.22%)
Customs duties	12,203.2	(14.8%)	11,144.3	(13%)	11,893.9	(13.77%)
VAT	34,587.7	(42.0%)	34,134.5	(39.9%)	30,374.2	(35.2%)
Fourth resource	32,947.2	(40.0%)	35,911.0	(41.98%)	41,530.0	(48.1%)
Miscellaneous	612.0	(0.7%)	688.0	(0.80%)	630.9	(0.73%)

Table 11.9   Expenditure in 1997 (outturn in payments)

Item	ECU (million)
EAGGF guarantee	41,350.0
Structural funds	28,598.7
Research	3,216.3
External action	4,866.3
Administration (all institutions)	4,331.4
Repayments and other	2,207.6
Total	84.727.5

Expenditure (see Table 11.9) is classified as Compulsory (CE) and Non-compulsory (NCE). Compulsory expenditure is defined as 'necessarily resulting from this Treaty or from acts adopted in accordance therewith' (Article 272, 4, ex-203). These terms of art have been the great battleground for the two branches of the budgetary authority. Since the EP has the last word on NCE, it strives to declassify CE. It has gained by attrition. The last block of CE remaining is the Guarantee Section of the European Agricultural Guarantee and Guidance Fund (EAGGF, or the pronounceable FEOGA, the French acronym). The 1996–97 Inter-governmental Conference was due to re-examine CE/NCE but for the nth time there was no result.

The reservation of decisions on CE appropriations to the Council, like the Member States' hold on own resource decisions, is among the constraints put on the Community budget. When it was faced with steeply rising expenditure in the 1980s, and especially when it proved impossible to balance the budget, the Council sought to impose tighter disciplines. It imposed on itself – and on the Commission – a guideline for the increase in EAGGF Guarantee spending (CE). It may not rise in any year by more than 74% of the annual growth in Community GDP. The budget itself had purported to restrain the rise in NCE by the application of the 'maximum rate of growth' (Article 272, 9, ex-203). The Council struggled to enforce this restriction in the face of parliamentary votes to overrun it, but its control was ineffective. Endless budgetary strife gave rise to the idea that there should be inter-institutional pre-agreement over the total size of the budget and its principal headings over a middle term, five or seven years. This could be accompanied by improved arrangements, without Treaty amendment, for negotiation between the two branches of the budgetary authority. This is the origin of the Financial Perspectives, which have become the instrument of expansion (for the expansive) or of control (for the restrictive).

The Financial Perspectives

The first Financial Perspectives, colloquially Delors Package 1, were negotiated for 1988–92. They followed the convention of dividing the appropriations between pay-

Table 11.10   First, second and third draft Financial Perspectives (commitments, including revisions) – ECU billions

	First draft		Second draft		Third draft	
	1988	**1992**	**1993**	**1999**	**2000**	**2006**
EAGGF Guarantee	27.5	35.0	36.7	43.3	44.1	50.0
Structural operations	7.8	18.1	22.2	36.1	35.2	42.8
Multi-annual policies	1.2	2.9 Int. pols	4.1	6.1	6.1	8.1
Other policies	2.1	5.9 Ext. actn	4.1	6.6	6.6	7.6
Repayments admin.	5.7	3.9 Admin.	3.4	4.5	4.5	5.5
Reserves	1.0	1.0	1.5	1.2	1.0	0.5
Total	45.3	66.9	72.0	97.8	97.5	114.5

ments (incurred in the financial year) and commitments, which involve subsequent payments and permit continuity of policy. The second Delors package, for 1993–99, was negotiated under the British Presidency of 1992, culminating in the memorable European Council meeting in Edinburgh in December 1992 (see Table 11.10).

With the Financial Perspectives go inter-instititional procedural agreements that are aimed at taking the sting out of the annual budgetary negotiations. The first principle, from 1982, requires that there can be no budgetary expenditure unless there is a legal base and that the institutions will co-operate to provide a legal base for budgetary entries. Some MEPs have romantically called this their right of legislative initiative.[291] If they put something in the budget, legislation will follow, or perhaps not if the Council does not like it.

It was also agreed that firm costings would not be cited in legislative texts. There had been problems when a legislative measure adopted by the Council with minimal EP involvement had cost the execution of the policy behind the measure. Such costings could not bind the EP in the discharge of its budgetary competences. As a half-way house in such cases, the Council at one stage used a formula devised by one of its English lawyers, 'the amounts deemed necessary', which preserved some trace of a financial framework for policy execution. It was later agreed explicitly that even this formula had no budgetary value.

The budgetary procedure

The 1992 deal introduced two new stages into the budgetary procedure.

According to Article 272, 3 (ex 203) the Commission is to produce a preliminary draft budget (PDB) not later than 1 September of the year preceding the budget year. This would not leave anything like enough time for a modern budget. There is a 'pragmatic calendar' agreed each year, in which the Commission produces its PDB in the early summer. The 1992 agreement inserted an earlier stage: *a discussion between the three institutions in the spring.*

This takes place in the 'tri(a)logue' (two forms of the word exist) which was created by the 1981 agreement between the Council and the EP. Strictly the trialogue consists of the Presidents of the three institutions. In practice the participants are the chairman of the EP Committee on Budgets, the Commissioner responsible for budgetary matters and the Chairman of the Budget Council, meeting with supporting officials. It was initially intended to meet as required to address problems that might arise as the budgetary procedure prescribed in the Treaty unfolded. Under the 1992 agreement it meets automatically in the spring to enable the three sides to expound their priorities; and it meets again in June, after the PDB has appeared, to discuss CE, that is the Agricultural Guarantee appropriations which the Commission has incorporated. These, in turn, are based on consultations between the Commission and the Member States in the framework of the FEOGA Committee. The resulting estimates are rarely discussed by the Budget Council or its supporting bodies.

In the legislative co-decision procedure the EP speaks first. In the budgetary procedure the Council, meeting shortly before the summer break, conducts the first examination of the PDB. It opens the proceedings by meeting a parliamentary delegation armed with a Resolution setting forth the EP's desiderata. MEPs call this a conciliation meeting. This is a misuse. Conciliation has a precise meaning, illustrated by the corresponding French word: *concertation.* The object of *concertation* is to reach agreement. The budgetary encounter at Council's first reading could not aspire to do so. In theory, the Council has not begun work. The Council adopts the draft budget (DB) at first reading. Since the PDB is not, in technical terms, a 'proposal' ('proposition') but a draft ('project'), the Council can amend it by qualified majority vote.[292] The Budget Council has always voted, long before the practice spread to Councils acting on the Single Market programme. Unlike other Councils, the Budget Council does not lavish effort on searching for consensus. Once a qualified majority has formed up, it is conclusive. This can create a problem. Voting line by line with shifting majorities, the Council can find that total expenditure exceeds revenue. In the late 1970s it adopted the simple rule, without debate, of reducing all appropriations except the smallest across the board proportionately to bring the total back within bounds. Called by courtesy the MacSharry rule after the Irish chairman (later a famed agricultural Commissioner) under whom it was first used, the rule was invented by a mid-ranking member of the British Permanent Representation and, like many good ideas, was initially greeted with derision.

The Council's first reading DB is debated by the EP at one of the two plenaries held in October. It returns to the Council, which considers the changes made by the EP in its first reading. The Council meeting is preceded by a second encounter with the parliamentary delegation. At this point the CE are unchangeable (unless the Commission were to amend its PDB) as are any budget lines which the EP did not touch. In November the Council carries out its second reading. By this time the outstanding issues, worked over by the Council's Budget Committee and by the Coreper, should have been reduced to a manageable number. The Council has before it a series of reports, prepared by the

Council Secretariat and presented by the Presidency, setting out what is agreed, what requires further ministerial debate and perhaps what the Presidency thinks might be the compromise to secure majority support round the table within the bounds of budgetary discipline and the Financial Perspectives.

The Council's second reading conclusions are transmitted to the EP for debate and vote in its December plenary in Strasbourg. The vote can be a rejection, by a majority of members (not of those present) and two-thirds of the votes cast (Article 227, 8, ex-203) or approval. The debate is in two parts: statements of what the EP wants, with the vote deferred to a later day in the session.

Peace may break out, as it did in 1998. In a resumed meeting, before the December plenary of the EP, its delegation met the Budget Council to resolve differences, principally over the insertion of reserves into the budget. With agreement reached, the December plenary could adopt the 1999 Budget. Warfare broke out in another theatre when the Parliament refused to discharge (approve) the Commission's accounts for an earlier year, contending that they gave evidence of fraud and mismanagement in the execution of the budget. Refusal of discharge is a sign of lack of confidence. It was followed in January by a threat to dismiss the Commission en bloc under Article 144 (201, consolidated version). Dismissal was averted by agreement between the Commission and the EP for improved controls and investigation into the allegations (and individual Commissioner's responsibility for irregularities).

The final stages

Commonly the Budget Council and the EP reach the final stages in disagreement. In the interval between the EP debate at the December plenary, which is based on a report from the Committee on Budgets and is the moment of prominence for the rapporteur(s) and the committee chairman, and the vote later in the week of the session, there are:

(a) a meeting of the Budget Council, whose members come to Strasbourg for a third reading unsanctioned by the Treaty; this has been superceded by
(b) possibly, a meeting of the trialogue, to explore possible ways forward if the EP debate shows it to be far from the Council's second reading DB;
(c) a one-on-one dialogue between the President of the Budget Council and the President of the EP Committee on Budgets for the deal to be done if there is one.

Council Presidents regularly go some way beyond the mandate their colleagues have given them in the 'third reading' to bring a conclusion back to a mollified Council.

If the two institutional representatives have come to terms, the EP plenary is invited to vote through the agreement reached. In a small ceremony the President of the EP exercises his Treaty duty of signing the budgetary document.

If, however, there is no agreement, the financial year that begins a few days later is marked by the dreaded 'one-twelfths'. Spending is limited to one-twelfth of the budget of the preceding year. This is not a soft option. Expenditure is not distributed evenly through the year and financial management becomes problem-ridden. The system is intentionally unwieldy to incite the Commission, Council and EP to set to afresh to adopt a proper budget.

Economy versus perceived need

It would not be a caricature to suggest that the heart of the conflicts which have produced round after round of inter-institutional litigation is the resolve of the Council majority to keep spending down and the aspiration of the EP to transfer spending from national budgets to the Community budget. The Council majority regularly intones – using the appropriate national references – that it cannot play Lady Bountiful in Brussels and Scrooge at home. As EMU approached, this plea was reinforced by the domestic budgetary rigour that the convergence and stability criteria imposed. The majority tends to gather strength, as an increasing number of Member States become net 'contributors'. The opposite view, articulated by MEPs although never ennobled as doctrine, is that increased Community spending is synonymous with continuing integration. This is exemplified, outside the budget areas, by the long-drawn-out struggle over the scale of the Fifth Framework Programme for Research and Development.

Net contributions

Alongside the inter-institutional squabbles, there is recurrent strife within the Council over the fallout of contributions to revenue (see Table 11.11).

Table 11.12 shows the members that continue to gain from the budget, with no relationship to national prosperity. The budget is redistributive, but not in accordance with an objective principle of need. Gross 'contributions' are not excessively discordant with GDP shares, but the net outturns, which are what hurt, are a source of political trouble.

Table 11.11 Net national contributions (gross payments minus receipts – ECU billion rounded) and as percentage of GNP

Member State	1996	%	1997	%
Belgium	1.4	0.68	1.0	0.50
Denmark	0.3	0.27	0.07	0.05
Germany	−10.5	−0.5	−10.9	−0.6
Greece	4.0	4.2	4.4	4.1
Spain	6.1	1.3	5.9	1.3
France	−0.1	0	−0.8	−0.06
Ireland	2.3	4.86	2.7	4.84
Italy	−1.2	−0.12	−0.06	−0.01
Luxembourg	0.8	5.49	0.7	4.89
Netherlands	−2.3	−0.75	−2.3	−0.71
Austria	−0.2	−0.12	−0.7	−0.4
Portugal	2.8	3.4	2.7	3.12
Finland	0.08	0.09	0.06	0.06
Sweden	−0.07	−0.35	−1.1	−0.59
UK	−2.1	−0.23	−1.8	−0.16

Source: Commission October 1998.

Table 11.12   Costs and benefits per head: average 1996–97 (euros)

Member State	Net benefits	Member State	Net costs
Luxembourg	1,769*	Italy	11
Ireland	635	France	14
Greece	382	UK	48†
Portugal	271	Austria	74
Spain	169	Sweden	101
Belgium	138*	Netherlands	140
Denmark	42	Germany	141
Finland	1		

*Includes administrative expenditure, not comparable to grants.
†After correction.
Source: European Commission.

Mrs Thatcher's government fought the battle of the handbag in the 1980s and emerged with the substantial rebate that took account of Britain's relatively low economic standing. Under Council Decision of 7 May 1985[293] the UK receives a 'correction' of 66% of the difference between what it would have been due to pay in VAT at a uniform rate for all Member States and its percentage share of total allocated expenditure (allocated expenditure excludes, for example, development aid for third countries). Germany also obtains a small rebate. As the Member States prepared themselves for new financing decisions post-1999, demands were made for revised burden-sharing, invoking the 'whereas' in the 1985 Decision which states: 'the European Council decided that any Member State bearing an excessive budgetary burden in relation to its relative prosperity may benefit at the appropriate time from a correction'.

At the meeting of the European Council in Cardiff in June 1998. The British Prime Minister stated from the chair that the British rebate was not negotiable. The German Chancellor, facing an election the following September, demanded fairer burden-sharing. It was agreed that the question would be on the agenda for a special meeting of the European Council to be held under German Presidency in the spring of 1999. Taking the initiative, Spain, a net beneficiary, proposed in July 1998 that gross payments into the Community budget should follow the GDP key. Portugal and Greece agreed. In October, comfortably after the German Federal election, the Commission published Table 11.11 (that it had hitherto traditionally declined to reveal). The Commission opposed any key based on relative prosperity as inconsistent with financial solidarity and with settled policy of helping less well-off members through spending. It suggested that a better balance could be secured by partially transferring the payment of income aids to farmers to national budgets. It noted that the 'budgetary imbalance of the UK is no longer unique'.

There was a good deal of ritualised breast beating in the spring of 1999 as the new German government in its first Council Presidency, girded itself up to address all the outstanding budgetary issues. It was undercut by the Agricultural ministers who, in their meetings of 22–26 February and 5–11 March 1999, limited themselves to a further round

Table 11.13 The Financial Perspective for EU-15 – commitment appropriations

	2000	2001	2002	2003	2004	2005	2006
1. Agriculture	40,920	42,800	43,900	43,770	42,760	41,930	41,660
CAP costs (excluding rural development)	36,620	38,480	39,570	39,430	38,410	37,570	37,290
Rural development and ancillary measures	4,300	4,320	4,330	4,340	4,350	4,360	4,370
2. Structural operations	32,045	31,455	30,865	30,285	29,595	29,595	29,170
Structural Funds	29,430	28,840	28,250	27,670	27,080	27,080	26,660
Cohesion Fund	2,615	2,615	2,615	2,615	2,515	2,515	2,510
3. Internal policies	5,900	5,950	6,000	6,050	6,100	6,150	6,200
4. External operations	4,550	4,560	4,570	4,580	4,590	4,600	4,610
5. Administration	4,560	4,600	4,700	4,800	4,900	5,000	5,100
6. Reserves	900	900	650	400	400	400	400
Monetary reserve	500	500	250	0	0	0	0
Reserve for emergency aid	200	200	200	200	200	200	200
Reserve for loan guarantees	200	200	200	200	200	200	200
7. Pre-accession aid	3,120	3,120	3,120	3,120	3,120	3,120	3,120
Agriculture	520	520	520	520	520	520	520
Pre-accession structural instruments	1,040	1,040	1,040	1,040	1,040	1,040	1,040
Phare (applicant countries)	1,560	1,560	1,560	1,560	1,560	1,560	1,560
Total commitment appropriations	91,995	93,385	93,805	93,005	91,465	90,795	90,260
Total payment appropriations	89,590	91,070	94,130	94,470	91,720	89,910	89,310
Payment appropriations in % of GNP	1.13	1.12	1.13	1.11	1.05	1.00	0.97
Available for accession (payment appropriations)			4,140	6,710	8,890	11,440	14,220
Agriculture			1,600	2,030	2,450	2,930	3,400
Other costs			2,540	4,680	6,640	8,510	10,820
Ceiling for payment appropriations	89,590	91,070	98,270	101,450	100,610	101,350	103,530
Ceiling for payment appropriations in % of GNP	1.13	1.12	1.18	1.19	1.15	1.13	1.13
Contingency margin in %	0.14	0.15	0.09	0.08	0.12	0.14	0.14
Ceiling for own resources in %	1.27	1.27	1.27	1.27	1.27	1.27	1.27

Table 11.14 Financial Framework for EU-21 – commitment appropriations

	2000	2001	2002	2003	2004	2005	2006
1. Agriculture	40,920	42,800	43,900	43,770	42,760	41,930	41,660
CAP costs (excluding rural development)	36,620	38,480	39,570	39,430	38,410	37,570	37,290
Rural development and ancillary measures	4,300	4,320	4,330	4,340	4,350	4,360	4,370
2. Structural operations	32,045	31,455	30,865	30,285	29,595	29,595	29,170
Structural Funds	29,430	28,840	28,250	27,670	27,080	27,080	26,660
Cohesion Fund	2,615	2,615	2,615	2,615	2,515	2,515	2,510
3. Internal policies	5,900	5,950	6,000	6,050	6,100	6,150	6,200
4. External operations	4,550	4,560	4,570	4,580	4,590	4,600	4,610
5. Administration	4,560	4,600	4,700	4,800	4,900	5,000	5,100
6. Reserves	900	900	650	400	400	400	400
Monetary reserve	500	500	250	0	0	0	0
Reserve for emergency aid	200	200	200	200	200	200	200
Reserve for loan guarantees	200	200	200	200	200	200	200
7. Pre-accession aid	3,120	3,120	3,120	3,120	3,120	3,120	3,120
Agriculture	520	520	520	520	520	520	520
Pre-accession structural instruments	1,040	1,040	1,040	1,040	1,040	1,040	1,040
Phare (applicant countries)	1,560	1,560	1,560	1,560	1,560	1,560	1,560
8. Enlargement			6,450	9,030	11,610	14,200	16,780
Agriculture			1,600	2,030	2,450	2,930	3,400
Structural operations			3,750	5,830	7,920	10,000	12,080
Internal policies			730	760	790	820	850
Administration			370	410	450	450	450
Total commitment appropriations	91,995	93,385	100,255	102,035	103,075	104,995	107,040
Total payment appropriations	89,590	91,070	98,270	101,450	100,610	101,350	103,530
of which enlargement			*4,140*	*6,710*	*8,890*	*11,440*	*14,210*
Payment appropriations in % of GNP	1.13	1.12	1.14	1.15	1.11	1.09	1.09
Contingency margin in %	0.14	0.15	0.13	0.12	0.16	0.18	0.18
Ceiling for own resources in %	1.27	1.27	1.27	1.27	1.27	1.27	1.27

of price cuts (as in 1998) within a *rising* agricultural budget. Ecofin, meeting on 15 March, resigned itself to the agricultural compromise. It recorded:

> As a matter to be solved in Berlin is the question of own resources, their providing and equality in burden-sharing within the EU ... the Presidency is convinced that within the framework of a global compromise all elements must be put on the table for discussion and that all Member States will have to make a substantial contribution to achieve a consensual solution.

Equipped with these pieties, the ensuing European Council meeting in Berlin on 23–24 March was overshadowed by the resignation of the Santer Commission the week before and by the NATO decision to launch air attacks on Serbia. Each placed a high premium on a display of solidarity. Heads of State and Government found no consensus for the radical financial reforms which had been in the air. They:

(a) trimmed the price cut affecting cereals;
(b) agreed of a recasting of the Structural Funds, largely in accordance with the Commission's proposals; and
(c) maintained the British abatement but excluded from the figure on which it is calculated the cost of the next enlargement.

The outcome would enable the Council to construct the table of the Financial Perspectives 2000–2006 and negotiate them with the European Parliament. Some Parliamentarians immediately announced that they disagreed with what they regarded as insufficient funding of 'internal policies' (see Tables 11.13 and 11.14).

The European Council's conclusions form one of the uncertainties surrounding the enlargement negotiations – they set up a financial framework, they maintained the working hypothesis that enlargement could be expected from 2002 and they earmarked pre- and post-accession budgetary allocations. But serious questions remained open:

- The agricultural decisions fell well short of the reforms that would enable the Union to play a leading part in the millennial round of world trade negotiations.
- 'Own resouces' remain subject to review, on which the Commission should report before 1 January 2006 (that is, in time for the next Financial Perspectives): and as part of that review, the question of creating new autonomous own resources is to be addressed.

Devices and desires

When budgets were materially out of balance, various devices were used to give them eye-appeal. A 'negative reserve' effectively reduced payment appropriations to the level which could be accommodated, while appearing to balance at a higher level. A few ECUs could be squeezed in by calculating the 'maximum rate of growth', when it was in vogue, to a second decimal place. Commitment appropriations were sometimes allowed to grow more liberally than payment appropriations, inflicting on later budgets a 'cost of the past'. When all else failed, the Member States had to agree to straight additional contributions, in 1984 and in 1985. Most of the bad habits have been reformed with the implementation of the Financial Perspectives. The Council no longer even bothers to record its agreement to an increase in the maximum rate of growth of NCE in the adopted budget (as is envisaged it should, for regularity, in Article 272, 9, fifth paragraph: ex-202)). Thanks mainly to reductions in world agricultural prices, budgets in the mid-1990s tended to be underspent, and amounts were transferred back to Member States.

But some dubious budgetary practices remain. In 'Agenda 2000: the Challenge of Enlargement' the Commission maintains that 'under certain conditions', the financing of enlargement to the East can be achieved 'within an unchanged ceiling of own resources'.[294] Few believe that it can happen, even with sacrifices from the existing Member States and with improved economic growth (which is now unreal) bringing in additional revenue.

The non-universal budget

Article 268 (ex-199) opens Title II with a categorical rule, known as the 'universality of the budget':

> All items of revenue and expenditure of the Community . . . shall be included in
> estimates to be drawn up for each financial year and shall be shown in the budget.

There were to be no hidden funds. In fact the Budget has never shown the European Development Fund. This is the financial instrument of the Lomé Convention. It is financed by Member States' contributions, has its own financial rules and is governed by a Steering Committee. There is no doubt that it is Community expenditure. But the Member States contend that development under Lomé is a mixed competence and are unwilling to give up their close control over the amounts made available for spending. The (European) Community budget does, however, cover Euratom, including its borrowing and lending operations, which were extended to the Economic Community in 1975, and the administrative costs of the European Coal and Steel Community. In an unusual further departure from universality, the European Police Unit (Europol) is funded by national contributions using a GDP key. This removes it from the scrutiny of the European Parliament.

Unfinished business included:

- Inter-institutional agreement on the next Financial Perspectives.
- Another look at the shaky distinction between CE and NCE; the EP wants more say over CAP spending.
- The future of the EDF in the new regime for aid to ACP countries.
- The demands for fairer burden sharing – see above.
- A continuing drive to curtail fraud, especially in payments under the CAP and especially within the decentralised responsibilities of the Member States. Fresh edge was given to fraud by the revelation in the autumn of 1998 that large sums of humanitarian aid could not be accounted for. Available data did not show where the money had gone or for what.

Summing up

Daniel Strasser's potted history shows the period of supranationality symbolised by the budgetary powers of the High Authority of the ECSC; the reassertion of Member State authority in the dawn of the EEC; the balancing of the role of the Member States by the cession of power to the European Parliament, even when unelected; the progressive strengthening of the EP, in the early form of co-decision represented by joint budgetary authority; the attempts by the Member States to recover ground by devising disciplines to be respected by all institutions.

Also, as a sad commentary, the Community, which likes to describe itself as one of law, has consumed resources which could have been put to better use by interminable legal battles over the handling of its budget. It also disregards the Treaty prescriptions of universality; it follows a timetable which is not what the Treaty says; it uses instruments which do not have a Treaty base; but it has renounced most of its more dubious practices. Above all, the continuing budgetary dominance of farm spending, even under the most far-reaching proposals yet (and those unlikely to be adopted) is a reminder of how far policy reform is behind.

FRAUD

One area in which the British governments have pushed for more power for the European Parliament and have pressed for more substantive Community powers, for example, in a powerful Court of Auditors) has been in the area of financial control and the identification and eradication of fraud. Given the endemic financial management problems of the Commission which culminated in the débâcle of the wrangling between the European Parliament and the Santer Commission in 1998 and early 1999, fraud has become even more of an issue. In an attempt to placate the EP, the Santer Commission did propose the setting up of an new anti-fraud unit within the Commission and appointed by it but independent of it, of other institutions and governments. Based on this Commission proposal, in March 1999 the Council pronounced its desire to see the setting up of a Fraud Prevention Office within the Commission, and to replace the existing Unit on Co-ordination of Fraud Prevention and to take over the duties concerning the protection of financial interests and the combating of fraud. There was to be a policy of 'zero tolerance'. The Council gave the new office quite sweeping powers of investigation.

 ## LEGAL BASES

Social and employment policy

Social policy:
• Article 136 to 145 (ex-117 to 122).
Social fund (one of the structural funds):
• Article 146 to 148 9 (ex-123 to 125).

Employment policy:
- Articles 125 to 130.

Structural funds

European Social Fund:
- Article 146 to 148 (ex-123 to 125).

European Regional Development Fund:
- Council Regulation 2083/93, amending Council Regulation 4254/88.

European Agricultural Guarantee and Guidance fund, Guidance section:
- Article 34.3 (ex-40).
- (Pre-legal) Presidency Conclusions of the Berlin European Council, 24–25 March 1999–08–31.

Cohesion fund

- Article 3k (ex-2).
- Article 161 (ex-130d).
- Protocol (TEU) on Economic and Social Cohesion.

Industry

- Article 157 (ex-130).

Research and development

- Title VIII EC.
- Articles 163 to 173 9 (ex-130f to 130p).

Education and training

- Articles 149 and 150 (ex-126 and 127).

Culture

- Article 151 (ex-128).

Public health

- Article 129.

Consumer protection

- Articles 95 (ex-100a) and 153 (ex-129a).

Environmental policy

- Articles 100r–100t.

The Community budget

- Title II, Financial Provisions, articles 268 to 280 (new numbering).
- Financial Regulation of 21 December 1977 , OJ L 356, 31.12.1977, p. 1, as amended by Council Regulation (Euratom, ECSC, EEC) no. 610/90 of 13 March 1990, OJ 1990 L 70, 16.3.90, p. 1.
- Joint Declaration of 30 June 1982 by the EP, Council and Commission, OJ 1982, C194, p. 1.
- Inter-institutional agreement of 29 October 1993 on budgetary discipline and improvement of the budgetary procedure OJ 1993, C 331, p. 1.

 DISCUSSION QUESTIONS

Social and employment policy

1. What is the Third Way?
2. In view of the diversity of social preference throughout the European Union (as witness the different national social security schemes) is it necessary for health and safety rules to be harmonised?
3. Is there a tension between social and employment policy?
4. In an economic and monetary union can the participants maintain indefinitely separate social security provision (given that Community-run social security could provide resource flows to needy areas)?

Structural funds

1. Have these funds achieved their purpose and can that purpose be achieved?
2. An alternative to the creaking machinery of the Funds would be a system of resource transfers such as exists in all Member States; with inter-regional transfers the responsibility of the Member State. Could this work in the EU?
3. Why should taxpayers in one part of the Union subsidise others in other parts of the Union?
4. The Committee of the Regions is only consulted on a regional policy. Since it consists of democratically elected representatives, should it not play a bigger role?

Cohesion fund

1. What is cohesion?
2. Can a Member State which has 'converged' claim that it should be at the receiving end of a resource flow? If it can, why are there no other resource flow provisions in the Economic and Monetary Union?
3. Is cohesion possible?

Industry

1. Is there a place for an active Community industrial policy?
2. Manufacturing industry throughout the Community (and elsewhere) is in decline. Is it inevitable?

Research and development

1. 'People of the same trade seldom meet together . . . but the conversation ends in a conspiracy against the public . . .' (Adam Smith: *Wealth of Nations*, Book 1, ch. 10, Pt 2). Can collaborative industrial research and the diffusion of its results be squared with the encouragement of competition?
2. Does contemporary Europe need a Joint Research Centre?

Education and training

1. Since education is intimately linked to national identity, is there any role at all for the Community?
2. If better training is a contribution to improved competitiveness, should it remain in national hands, in the 'open competitive economy' which the Community aspires to foster?
3. Does student mobility contribute to a more 'pro-European' outlook?

Culture

1. Having devised procedures which inhibit any decision-taking, would it not be more straightforward for the Council, if not the other institutions, to regard culture as entirely subject to the principle of subsidiarity?

Public health

1. The Community has banned tobacco advertising, effective from a future date. Germany is challenging the action. Is this a matter the Community should be involved in?
2. Is there a case for an arrangement similar to the new employment policy in which the Member States would treat health as a matter of common concern and examine each other's policies, with a view to picking out best practices?
3. Should there be a single market in health care?

Consumer protection

1. If decisions are taken as closely as possible to the citizen (subsidiarity), is a Community consumer protection policy appropriate or necessary?
2. Is the treaty-based category of 'contributory' support to national policies cosmetic only?
3. Can a CEEC joining the Union be expected to give priority to consumer protection legislation?

Environment policy

1. Is it anomalous that the first Treaty mention of subsidiarity occurs in the Articles concerning the protection of the environment?
2. What are the arguments for and against an 'energy tax', sometimes called a 'CO_2' tax?
3. 'There is no inevitable conflict between international trade and environmental protection' (European Commission). Is this the case?

Energy

1. Why is it apparently difficult for the Community to state that it has an energy policy?
2. What are public service obligations?
3. Write a report on the repeal of energy regulation in the Community.
4. What are the pros and cons of an energy tax accruing to the Community budget?

The Community budget

1. Why not national contributions, under national parliamentary control?
2. The first President of the elected EP said that real parliaments had revenue-raising power. Should this power be given to the EP as further evidence of its legitimacy?
3. How can a budget that redistributes resources without regard or need be justified?
4. In the interest of simplification, could the budgetary procedure be assimilated to the now widespread co-decision procedure for legislation?
5. Budgetary expenditure is decentralised and passes through agencies in the Member States on its way to beneficiaries. Would it be more efficient if the Commission acted directly *vis-à-vis* beneficiaries?

B BIBLIOGRAPHY ————————————————————————

European Commission: *How is the EU Protecting our Environment?* OOP, 1996.

European Commission: *Environmetal Protection: a Shared Responsibility*, OOP, 1996.

European Commission: *The EU and the Environment*, OOP, 1997.

European Round Table: *Climate Change*, Brussels, 1996.

European Round Table: *Greenhouse Gases*, Brussels, 1996.

Haigh, N.: *Manual of Environmental Policy: the EC and Britain*, Cartermill Publishing, 1992.

Johnson, S.P. and Courcelle, G.: *The Environmental Policy of the European Community*, Kluwer, 1995.

Skjaerseth, J.B.: 'The Climate policy of the EC: too hot to handle?', *Journal of Common Market Studies*, Vol. 32, No. 1, March 1994, Blackwell.

Weale, A.: 'European environmental regulation', *European Business Journal*, Vol. 7, issue 4, Whurr Publishers, 1995.

Social and employment policy

Hantrais, L.: *Social Policy in the European Union*, Macmillan, 1995.

Liebdried, S. and Pierson, P.: *European Social Policy between Fragmentation and Integration*, Brookings, Washington DC, 1995.

Maes, E.-M.: *Building a People's Europe*, Whurr Publishers, 1990.

Nicoll, W., Norburn, D. and Schoenberg, R. (eds): *Perspectives on European Business* (2nd edn), Whurr Publishers, 1998.

Structural funds

Ansell, C.K., Parsons, C.A. and Darden, K.A.: 'Dual Networks in European Regional Development Policy', *Journal of Common Market Studies*, Vol. 35, No. 3, September 1997.

Cafruny, A.W. and Rosenthal, G.G. (eds): *The State of the European Community*, Lynne Rienner, 1993.

European Commission: *How is the European Union meeting Social and Regional Needs?* OOP, 1996.

European Commission: *The Regions in the 1990s*, Periodic reports, OOP.

European Parliament: 'The Impact of 1992 and associated legislation on the less favoured regions of the Community', *Regional Policy and Transport*, Series 18, 1991.

Sbragia, A. (ed.): *Euro-politics*, Brookings, 1992.

Cohesion fund

European Commission: *Annual Report on the Cohesion Fund*, OOP.

European Commission: *The European Union's Cohesion Fund*, OOP, 1994.

Industry

Crouch, C. and Marquand, D.: *The Politics of 1992: Beyond the Single European Market*, Blackwell, 1990.

European Commission: *European Community Audiovisual Policy*, OOP, 1992.

European Commission: *Report of the Think Tank on the Audiovisual Policy in the European Union*, OOP, 1994.

European Commission: *The Information Society*, OOP, 1996.

European Commission: *Building the European Information Society for us All* (High-level expert group), OOP, 1997.

Federal Trust: *Network Europe and the Information Society*, 1995.

Federal Trust: *A Recovery Strategy for Europe*, 1993.

Middlemass, K.: *Orchestrating Europe*, Fontana, 1995.

Spierenburg, D. and Poidevin, R.: *History of the High Authority of the European Coal and Steel Community*, Weidenfeld & Nicolson, 1994.

Research and development

Dai, X., Cawson, A. and Holmes, P.: 'The rise and fall of high-definition television: the impact of European technology policy', *Journal of Common Market Studies*, Vol. 34, No. 2, June 1996.

European Commission: *Growth, Competitiveness, Employment*, OOP, 1994, ch. 4.
European Commission: *Padoa-Schioppa Report: Efficiency, Stability and Equity*, OOP, 1987.
McLoughlin, G.J.: In *Europe and the US, Competition and Cooperation in the 1990s*, Committee on
    Foreign Affairs, US House of Representatives, US Government Printing Office, 1992.

Education and training

European Commission: *Education and Training – Tackling Unemployment*, OOP, 1996.
European Commission: *Growth, Competitiveness, Employment*, White Paper, OOP, 1994.
European Commission: *Action for Employment in Europe: a Confidence Pact*, Bulletin
    Supplement 4/96, OOP, 1996.
European Commission: *Employment in Europe, Annual Report and Summary*, OOP.
House of Lords: *Student Mobility in the European Community*, HL Paper No 116–98.
Morrell, F.: *Continent Isolated*, Federal Trust Report, 1996.
Soper, T.: *Education without Frontiers: Mobility and the Single Market*, Overseas Students
    Trust, 1992.

Consumer protection

Booker, C. and North, R.: *The Castle of Lies – Why Britain must get out of Europe*,
    Duckworth, 1996.
Hildebrand, D.: 'Lawyers and marketeers, a European Partnership?', *European Business
    Journal*, Vol. 6, issue 2, 1994.
Wallace, H. and Young, A.R. (eds): *Participation and Policy-making in the European Union*,
    OUP, 1996.

The Community budget

Archer, C. and Butler, F.: *The European Community*, Pinter, 1992.
Franklin, M.: *The EC Budget: Realism, Redistribution and Radical Reform*, Chatham House
    Discussion Paper 42, 1992.
Hartley, T.C.: *The Foundations of European Community Law*, Clarendon, 1990.
Notenboom, H.: *Het Europees Parlement en de Financien*, SDU Uitgeverei, 1988.
Nugent, N.: *The Government and Politics of the European Community* (3rd edn), Macmillan,
    1996.
Ruimschotel, D.: *The EC Budget: Ten Percent Fraud?* European University Institute
    Florence, 1994.
Shackleton, M.: *Financing the European Community*, RIIA/Pinter, 1990.
Strasser, D.: *The Finances of Europe*, 5th edn (French), Editions Labor; 3rd edn (English),
    Praeger, 1984.
Weidenfeld, W. and Wessels, W.: *Europe from A to Z*, OOP, 1997 (also on CD ROM).
Westlake, M.: *The Council of the European Union* (includes extended bibliography),
    London, Cartermill, 1995.

NOTES

1. In the Treaty of Amsterdam, articles are renumbered as a contribution to simplification. Here the new numbers are used throughout, with the more familiar ex-numbers in brackets.
2. *The Agricultural Policy of the European Community*, 2/79, p. 12, OOP.
3. Surpluses could obviously not be released on to the home market. In some years there were gift supplies for charitable purposes.
4. *The Common Agricultural Policy in Transition*, OOP, 1996.
5. In principle, compensation was available from 1997 to 1999 to British farmers hit by the high pound. The British government did not apply for it, to the fury of the farming community. The reason was that the amount concerned would have been deducted from the British budgetary rebate described in the Budgetary chapter. The British government preferred to let the amount in question flow into its coffers than to reach the farmers directly.
6. See *Building European Union*, Salmon and Nicoll, Manchester University Press, 1997, pp. 90–5.
7. See as an extreme but not isolated example *A Europe of the Nations*, European Research Group, 1995, with its Foreword by Mr John Major.
8. Taken from *The Reform of the Common Agricultural Policy*, DG for Agriculture, 7 July 1992.
9. *Bulletin*, 4.94, pp. 74–5.
10. There are stories, not confirmed or denied, that, at a critical point in Blair House, the President of the Agricultural Council, then John Gummer, UK, was produced from a side-room to assure the doubting American negotiators that what the Community was ready to agree to was fully compatible with the CAP and would go through the Council. Since the Americans were enjoying 'fast track' they were in the unusual position of not having to defer to the Senate.
11. The word 'necessity' was added to the original Presidency draft by those Member States that were not convinced that price cuts were 'necessary'.
12. Press communiqué, 8683/98, 25/26, V, 98, p. 5.
13. The General Affairs Council was due to meet in Brussels in the same week but prudently displaced itself to Luxembourg.
14. It was later expected that the Millennial Round of Trade Negotiations would be far wider than agriculture.
15. *The Week in Europe* (newsletter of the Commission Representation in the UK, 7 May 1998, p. 2).
16. See 'comitology' in the Extended Glossary.
17. C. Booker and R. North argue in their *Castle of Lies* (Duckworth, 1996), p. 90, that the CFP is illegal; and the addition of the words 'and agriculture' to Article 3 of the Treaty is a retrospective attempt to legalise it. While this argument does not stand up, it is true that the first steps at a CFP were taken in some haste on the eve of the first enlargement of the Community in 1973. They became a belated part of the *acquis communautaire* which the new members were bound to accept under their accession treaties.
18. For an explanation of 'the Prisoner's Dilemma' see Matt Ridley, *The Origins of Virtue* (Viking, 1996, pp. 53–66).

19. The Community of Twelve had an annual deficit of 6 billion ECUs in its fish trade with the rest of the world.

20. Charles Cann, *Saving our Fish*, Centre for European Reform, p. 1, The extreme position of withdrawal is argued, for example, by M. Spicer in *A Treaty too Far* (Guardian Books, 1992), p. 80. It is amplified in *A Europe of Nations*, European Research Group, 1995, which recommends 'unbundling' the Community into mini-communities, including an Agriculture and Fisheries Community which Member States might join or not as they choose (pp. 19–20).

21. In the 1950s Nye Bevan, a former Labour Minister, once remarked that the British Isles were practically built on coal and surrounded by fish; and that it would take an organising genius to create a shortage of either.

22. One of us, some years ago, attended a fish auction in Skaagen in Northern Denmark. A uniformed fisheries Inspector was present. Asked what his duties were, he said that he supervised quality standards. What about tonnages? No, that was done in Copenhagen.

23. See Chapter 7.

24. *El Pais*, Madrid, 28 July 1996.

25. There are 10 million farmers against 300,000 fishermen. Farm support costs 30 billion ECUs. Fish prices are supported to the tune of 30 million.

26. In order, the first is the CAP in Article 38. The second is the Common Transport Policy in Article 74. The CCP is in Article 110.

27. Samuelson, P., *Economics*, McGraw-Hill, 1955; Piggott, J. and Cook, M., *International Business Economics: A European Perspective*, Longman, 1993; Porter, M.E., 'On Competition and Strategy', *Harvard Business Review*, 1991.

28. From the Copenhagen Conditions for accession to the European Union, European Council, Copenhagen, June 1993.

29. Members of a free trade area (FTA) abolish duties on imports from each other, but maintain national tariffs on imports from out of area.

30. Restrictions on trade within the Community were abolished. Member States retain national tariffs on imports. They were harmonised and could differ only by the cost of transport between Member States.

31. Not the same as a legislative directive. Commonly called a 'mandate'.

32. Article 300 (ex-228) requires the EP to be consulted and to give an opinion if any internal rules consequent upon an external agreement would be subject to co-decision.

33. W. Nicoll, *Journal of Common Market Studies*, June 1996, p. 280.

34. This makes the Community presence in the negotiating chamber cumbersome. But Member States are attached to the Article 113 committees. There may be a deep archetypal memory of the High Authority's negotiations with the UK. Although Member States were entitled to attend the sessions, they did not do so and there were accusations that the High Authority had not complied with instructions. See Spierenberg and Poidevin, *The History of the High Authority of the European Coal and Steel Community*, Weidenfeld & Nicolson, 1994, p. 216.

35. Under the Treaty, the transitional period went in three phases: up to 1962, 1963–66, 1967–70.

36. J. Hagestadt, *From Yaounde to Lomé*, 1975, monograph.

37. Green Paper on relations between the EU and the ACP countries on the eve of the twenty-first century.
38. For example, the UEMOA of Benin, Burkino, Faso, Ivory Coast, Mali, Niger, Senegal, Togo; the SADC of Angola, Swaziland, Tanzania, Zambia and Zimbabwe.
39. Europe Documents (Agence Europe, Brussels), No. 1928, 4 April 1995.
40. Council Press Release, 9305/97.
41. Report by the Commission on the behaviour of the oil companies in the Community during the period from October 1973 to March 1974. COM (75)675, 10 December 1975.
42. CEEC and CCEE are used indifferently. Some of them dislike being called 'Eastern', especially if their capital lies west of a Member State capital (e.g. Prague and Vienna).
43. Westlake, M., *The Passage to the Community's Legislative System of Emergency Measures related to German Unification*, European University Institute, Florence, 1992; also 'The Community express service: the rapid passage of emergency legislation on German unification', *Common Market Law Review*, 28, 1991.
44. Also as Europe (Association) Agreements, but the bracketed word was dropped.
45. For an example, see Salmon and Nicoll, *Building European Union*, MUP, 1997, pp. 250–3.
46. *Bulletin of the European Union*, 12/1994, p. 107.
47. So named in a French pun, from assistance for economic recovery in Poland and Hungary. Now extended to all CEECs.
48. European Commission, 'Agenda 2000', July 1997, Table 4, p. 89.
49. Tacis is now written in lower case because it is not confined to the CIS or to technical assistance.
50. Including Tajikistan, although there is no Partnership and Co-operation agreement.
51. In those days, Finland had to sound out Moscow for any objections. The Kremlin delayed replying which kept Finland away from the signing ceremony.
52. Jacques Delors, *Monthly Newsletter on the Single Market*, No. 10, November/December 1991, p. 1, OOP.
53. Council Press Release 5944/92,2, May 1992.
54. *Bulletin of the European Union*, 1/2 1997, p. 78.
55. Liechtenstein had to adjust its free trade area with Switzerland. This done, it held its referendum in April 1995.
56. A largely symbolic Co-operation Agreement with Canada was concluded in 1976.
57. For fuller discussion see *The European Union*, (eds) Brent F. Nelsen and Alexander C.-G. Stubb; *The Theory of Economic Integration*, Bela Balassa, Reinner, 1994, p. 125; *European Integration*, (ed.) Michael Hodge; *International Integration*, Ernst Haas, 1972, Penguin Books, p. 91.
58. See Vincent Cable and David Henderson (eds), *Trade Blocs?*, Royal Institute of International Affairs, 1994.
59. *Bulletin of the European Union*, 1/2 1997, p. 78.
60. Such as those taken in Spring 1982 at British urging during the Falklands War. See *The Falklands War*, Sunday Times Insight Team (André Deutsch), 1983, pp. 117–18.
61. There is a 1996 agreement with Chile.
62. *Bulletin of the European Union*, 1/1993, p. 65.

63. COM (1998), 125.
64. For text see *European Business Journal*, vol. 11, issue 2, spring 1999. For discussion see Brian Hindley, 'New institutions for transatlantic trade?', *International Affairs* (Chatham House), Vol. 75, No. 1, January 1999.
65. And with Russia from 1993.
66. *Journal of Common Market Studies, Annual Review 1994*, ed. N. Nugent, Blackwell Publishers, 1995, pp. 91–2.
67. See, for example, Burkitt, Bainbridge and Whyman: *There is an Alternative*, Campaign for Independent Britain, 1995; and Bill Jamieson, *Free to Choose*, Global Britain, 1998.
68. To the purist imports and exports within the Single Market are anomalous.
69. See *The Economist Guide to Economic Indicators*, (3rd edn), 1997, Chapter 10.
70. Quoted in Salmon and Nicoll, *Building European Union*, MUP, 1997, p. 59.
71. See the note by W. Nicoll in the *Revue du marche commun*, No. 311, November 1987, p. 625.
72. Ibid., p. 628.
73. In the Case 167/73 the ECJ said that the general rules of the Treaty apply to air and sea transport. The Council took a number of decisions under this Article by the required unanimity. One of the quirks was that it did not need a proposal from the Commission. This anomaly was rectified by Article 16(6) of the Single European Act.
74. In Prussia, the railways had been part of the Army; early engine drivers wore sabres.
75. The State Railway of Prussia came under the War Department and the engine drivers wore sabres. Until recent times, German rail employees were part of the civil service.
76. Council Regulation 124/62 suspended regulation 17/62.
77. Salmon and Nicoll, op. cit., pp. 90ff.
78. P. Cecchini, 1992, *Le Defi, Flammarion*, 1988, p. 49.
79. In its White Paper *Growth, Competitiveness and Employment*, 1994, the Commission estimated (p. 10), that the 1992 programme had secured a 3% saving on the costs of international transport.
80. The carriage of goods within a country by a non-resident carrier.
81. Council Press Release, 13140/97 Annex, p. iii.
82. The 'spy in the cab' installed by Regulation 543/69, of which Britain fell foul and lost a case in the Court.
83. *Evening Standard*, London, 16 January 1998.
84. See J.F.L. Ross, 'High-speed rail, catalyst for European integration?', *Journal of Common Market Studies*, Vol. 32, No. 2, June 1994, pp. 191ff.
85. H. Cowie, *Private Partnerships and Public Networks in Europe*, Sweet & Maxwell, 1996; C. Turner, 'The Financing of Trans-European Networks', *European Business Journal*, Vol. 7, Issue 2, pp. 37ff.
86. pp. 28–48.
87. Nicoll, W. and Schoenberg, R. (eds), *Europe beyond 2000*, Whurr Publishers, 1998, pp. 323ff.
88. *The European*, 27 July to 2 August 1998, pp. 12–13. See also Neil Kinnock, 'Transport in the 21st century', *European Business Journal*, Vol. 10, Issue 3, 1998.
89. Council Press Release 9551/98.

90. Neil Kinnock, 'The liberalisation of the European aviation industry', *European Business Journal*, Vol. 8, Issue 4, 1996, p. 8.
91. Council Press Release 11007/97.
92. Council Press Release 9551/98.
93. At one stage there was talk of incorporating Eurocontrol into the EC. See the note by W. Nicoll in the *Revue du marche commun*, No. 311, November 1987, p. 625.
94. One which has defied and continues to defy all effort is the approximation of the familiar electric plug. There is no interoperability. Or of telephone sockets.
95. *Towards European Recovery in the 1980s*, Touche Ross International, 1984.
96. Foundations for the future of European Industry (ERT), Amsterdam Conference, June 1983.
97. Solemn Declaration on European Union, European Council Conclusions, Stuttgart, 17–19 June 1983.
98. Salmon, T. C. and Nicoll, W., *Building European Union*, MUP, 1997, pp. 176ff.
99. 'The Luxemboug Compromise', Nicoll, W., *Journal of Common Market Studies*, Vol. XXIII, No. 1, September 1984, p. 41.
100. Ad hoc Committee for Institutional Affairs, Report to the European Council, March 1985. See Salmon and Nicoll, op. cit., pp. 190ff.
101. Case 120/78 Rewe-Zentral AG v Bundesmonopolverwaltung für Branntwein, OJ No. C 147, 22.6.78.
102. For conflicting theories of how it came about see the articles by Sandholtz and Zysman and by Moravcsic in *The European Union*, ed. B.F. Nelsen and A. G.-C. Stubb Rienner, 1994. For the business involvement see *Business means Europe – Who Built the Market?* Maria Green Cowles, in *Eminent Europeans*, ed. Bond, Smith, Wallace, Greycoat Press, 1996. For additional material see *Europower*, Nicholas Colchester and David Buchan, Economist Books, 1990.
103. COM (85) Final.
104. *Flammarion*, 1988, with preface by Jacques Delors.
105. *Bulletin of the European Union*, 6–97, p. 43.
106. Committee for the Study of Economic and Monetary Union: presented to the European Council meeting in Madrid in June 1989.
107. *Europe from A to Z*, ed. Werner Weidenfeld and Wolfgang Wessels, OOP, 1997, p. 202.
108. For two convergent views from opposite sides of the Atlantic, see Calingaert, M. in *European Business Journal*, Vol. 9, Issue 3, 1997; and Grimwade, M. in Volume 10, Issue 2, 1998.
109. For discussion see *Lancaster House Competition Policy Enquiry*, Paul Chapman Publishing for ECERC, 1988, p. 5 et seq.
110. *Europe from A to Z*, ed. Weidenfeld and Wessels, OOP, 1997, p. 49.
111. *European Community Competition Policy*, 1994, OOP, p. 3.
112. *European Community Competition Policy*, 1997, OOP, p. 5.
113. See F. Vibert, *Europe, A Constitution for the Millennium*, Dartmouth,1995, p. 187 and more widely for a radically different and logically cohesive distribution of powers.
114. See Disarming the Commission: the debate over a European Cartel Office, S. Wilks and L. McGowan, *Journal of Common Market Studies*, Vol. 33, No. 2, June 1995, from p. 259.

115. *Wealth of Nations*, 1776. Adam Smith famously warned against collusion among vendors and condemned monopolies unless they were temporary – new inventions and new books (Book V).
116. *European Community Competition Policy*, 1997 Report, p. 3, OOP.
117. *Eisenhower, Kennedy and the United States of Europe*, Pascaline, Winand, Macmillan, 1993, p. 23.
118. 'Community competition policy has always accepted that a vital part of many distribution or licensing systems is the allocation of exclusive territories to distributors or licensees and generally accepts not only exclusivity clauses in such agreements but also obligations on the distributor or licensee not to advertise or otherwise actively solicit customers outside its allotted territory.' 1994 Competition Report, p. 11. This exemption was said in 1999 to be the source of gross price disparity between cars sold in Britain and the same models sold elsewhere.
119. For the genesis of regulation 17 see *The European Community, The Formative Years*, Hans von der Groeben (first competition commissioner), OOP, 1987, p. 62.
120. *Competition in Telecommunications, Why and How?*, OOP, 1997, p. 13.
121. 88/301/EEC, OJ L 131, 27.5.88. France joined by Italy, Belgium, Germany, and Greece attacked the Commission's use of this article. The Court struck down three articles, not of the Commission's directive but of the principle behind it (case C-202/88). Thus encouraged, the Commission issued another relative directive in 1990 (90/388/EEC, OJ L 192, 24.7.90). Its announced intention to use the Article may have encouraged the Council to act on the liberalisation of 'value-added' telecommunication services.
122. Distortion is what a Member State does to the trade of another Member State. Discrimination is what it does to the trade of its own enterprises as well as to those in other Member States.
123. For an account of merger cases see *Orchestrating Europe*, Keith Middlemas, Fontana Press, 1995, pp. 514–19.
124. COM (97) 170 Final.
125. A natural monopoly is one which cannot be challenged because of the prohibitively high entry cost and the waste of resources inherent in building a parallel system. Thousands of miles of copper wire strung across the land to all but a few houses offers an example. Monopolies can be broken by allowing competitors access to the system; or by technology. For example, Mongolia had no telephone system, but is a heavy user of mobile phones.
126. 1997 Report, p. 61.
127. Op. cit., p. 4.
128. *Times*, 11 March 1998, p. 21.
129. 13/10/97 OJ L series 180, 0.07.97, coming into force on 1 March 1998. For details of the thresholds, see *Bulletin of the European Union*, OOP, 4.97, 1.3.53, pp. 22–3.
130. For an account of merger cases see *Orchestrating Europe*, Keith Middlemass, Fontana Press, 1995, pp. 514–10.
131. OJ L 7, 1972.
132. Agreement between the European Communities and the Government of the United States of America regarding the application of their competition laws OJ L 95, 27.4.95.

133. The US authorities considered that Microsoft had breached its undertakings. DGIV has been content to watch the US proceedings.
134. See below, pp. 311–12.
135. Council Directive 77/388/EEC, modified by Council Directive 92/77/EEC OJ L 315, 31.10.92 and Council Directive 92/111/EEC, OJ L 384, 30.12.92.
136. 1992 *Le Defi*, Flammarion, 1988, p. 55.
137. The 5% minimum prevented the incoming Labour government in Britain in 1997 from abolishing (if this is what they wanted) the tax on domestic consumption of energy which they, in opposition, had fought against their precedessors introducing. They reduced it by half.
138. Kitty Usher, 'The myth of tax harmonisation', Centre for European Reform, *Bulletin* (January 1999) p. 3.
139. 90/434/EEC OJ L 225, 20.8.1980.
140. 90/435/EEC OJ L 225, 20.8.1980.
141. 90/436/EEC OJ L 225, 20.8.1990.
142. For a full account of the effect of the three measures see *Tax Law and Cross-border Co-operation between Companies*, OOP, European Files series 1991.
143. *Bulletin of the European Union*, OOP, 12/97, pp. 168–71.
144. Council Secretariat Press Release, 66/19/98 Ecofin 9 March 1998, p. 13.
145. At a meeting in London of the Europe-Atlantic Group in January 1999.
146. N. Olszak, *Histoire des Union Monétaires*, Presses Universitaires de France, 1996. But the Latin Monetary Union collapsed when Italy overborrowed, using its sovereign power to do so.
147. For the text see Salmon, T.C. and Nicoll, W., *Building European Union*, MUP, 1997, p. 122.
148. Salmon and Nicoll, *Building European Union*, MUP, 1997, pp. 110–16.
149. Van Dormael, *Bretton Wood*, HM, New York, 1978.
150. The first time had been the empty chair of 1965–66.
151. Driffill and Beber (eds), *A Currency for Europe*, Lothian Foundation Press, 1991, p. 67.
152. Roy Jenkins, *A Life at the Centre*, Macmillan, 1991
153. Extracts in Salmon and Nicoll, op. cit., pp. 155–61.
154. Valéry Giscard d'Estaing, *Le Pouvoir et la Via Compagnie 12*, 1988, pp. 144–55.
155. James Callaghan, *Time and Change*, Collins, 1987.
156. Britain joined the EMS but not on the ERM, Giscard op. cit., says that he thought of the distinction. David Owens attributes it to Mr, later Sir, Michael Butler, his 'extremely bright' Foreign Office adviser (David Owen, *Personally Speaking*, Weidenfeld & Nicolson, 1987, p. 117).
157. On 1 January 1999 the ECU, which was not a currency but an expression of value, was replaced by the euro. The word ECU is preserved here for historical reasons.
158. European Commission, *The Economy of the European Community*, OOP, 1984, p. 50.
159. Commission Representation in London, Economic and Monetary Union, 1991, p. 1.
160. For differing versions of the story of Madrid, see Margaret Thatcher, *The Downing Street Years*, Harper Collins, 1993, pp. 710–13; Nigel Lawson, *The View from Number 10*, Bantam Press, 1992, pp. 932–6; Geoffrey Howe, *Conflict of Loyalty*, Macmillan, 1994, pp. 581–3.
161. Thus the correct expression 'Ripe' is apochryphal.

162. *Report on Economic and Monetary union in the European Community* (Delors Report) 1989.
163. *Irish Times*, 16 March 1996.
164. *Washington Post*, 23 August 1993; *European*, 31 July – 1 August 1993.
165. M. Levitt in *Perspectives on European Business 1998*, eds W. Nicoll, D. Norburn and R. Schoenberg, Whurr Publishers, p. 68.
166. The word used by Malcolm Rifkind, Foreign Secretary, early in 1997.
167. It is an additional requirement that central banks have to be independent of governments. The Labour government in Britain went most of the way shortly after it came to power.
168. F. Fukuyama, *The End of History and the Last Man*, Free Press (Macmillan), 1992, p. 123.
169. Germany thought that ECU sounded bovine and could be too easily satirised.
170. Conclusions of the European Council meeting in Edinburgh, December 1992, under Decision of the Heads of State and Government, meeting with the European Council, concerning certain problems raised by Denmark on the Treaty on European Union. Sweden also announced that it did not wish to be considered as a candidate. Soon after 1 January 1999, political factions in both countries were arguing for membership.
171. Europe documents no 2015/16, 18 December 1996, ratified by Resolution of the European Council meeting in Amsterdam on 16/17 June 1997, *Bulletin*, 6/97, pp. 17–18.
172. An example of the Community's predilection for wanting *x* while also wanting *y*.
173. *Bulletin*, 6/97, pp. 18–20.
174. *Le Figaro*, 7.11.97.
175. It is also made clear that the width of the band does not affect the convergence criterion which stipulates that a Member State must observe the 'normal' fluctuation margins. The Conservative government in Britain had sought to argue that the widening of the band made this criterion inapplicable.
176. Council Press Release, 8170/1/98, Rev. 1 2/3, V, 1998.
177. The July meeting of EuroXI was held in the Council building in Brussels, prior to the monthly meeting of Ecofin.
178. For background see D. Channon, 'Dragon devaluation plus dinosaur depression equals millennium global recession', *European Business Journal*, Vol. 10, Issue 4, p. 167.
179. Treaty on European Union, Protocol on the converence criteria referred to in Article 109j of the Treaty establishing the European Community, Article 3; also TEU Article 109j(1).
180. For the year 1998, British government net borrowing was 0.6% of GDP (Maastricht 3%). Gross debt was 49.4% (60%). Office of National Statistics, ONS (99) 75.
181. For such a towering figure there is a vast bibliography. An accessible source is Michael Balfour, *The Kaiser and his Times*, Cresset Press, 1964.
182. For some details, see Ulrich Weinstock in *Neun für Europa*, Diederichs Verlag, 1973, p. 166.
183. For the full text and context, see Salmon and Nicoll, *Building European Union*, MUP, 1997, p. 61.
184. See Marie-Elisabeth Maes, *Building a People's Europe*, Whurr Publishers, 1990, pp. 82–3.
185. For the line of cases see T.C. Hartley, *The Foundations of European Community Law*, Clarendon Law series, 1990, pp. 148, 150. The inferred principle is extended in Article 13 (consolidated numbering) of the Treaty of Amsterdam.
186. The communiqué says that the programme should aim, among other things, at 'closely involving workers in *the progress of firms*'. The original French text says 'la conduite de

l'entreprise'. Sir Roy Denman, who was present in the British Delegation, has described how this miracle of translation came about.

187. The Working Group on the European Company Statute is so venerable that its Presidency does not follow the rule of changing every six months. Delay is not entirely attributable to opposition to worker participation. There are also difficult fiscal issues.

188. In retrospect, in 1993 the Commission described the relationship between social and business development in the following terms: 'Initially, the Single Market did more for business than for the workforce. The time has come to develop its social dimension.' *Building the Social Dimension*, OOP, p. 8.

189. Extracts of the Social Charter are given in Box 11.2.

190. For background see Cloos, Reinesch, Vignes and Weyland: *Le Traité de Maastricht*, Bruylant, Brussels, 1993; also Laursen, F and Vanhoonacker, S: *The Intergovernmental Conference on Political Union*, EIPA, Maastricht, 1992.

191. The text of the Social Protocol is given in TEU Protocol. As will be seen, the two texts have little in common. Some of the objectives of the Social Charter are secured elsewhere in the Treaty. See Cloos, Reinesch, Vigne and Weyland, *Le Traité de Maastricht*, Bruylant, Brussels, 1993, pp. 302–315.

192. There were at the time extravagant British suggestions about subjecting Court judgements to political ratification.

193. This double dividend is dismissed in *Climate Change*, European Round Table of Industrialists, Brussels, 1997, pp. 7.

194. In 1997, half the Community unemployed had only basic school qualifications or less. One-third of the employed had basic schooling only.

195. Article N2 in the old numbering.

196. *Plus ça change*. These were also the priorities of the British Presidency of the first half of 1998.

197. All quotations are from the version included in *Europe 2000*, ed. W. Nicoll and R. Schoenberg, Whurr Publishers, 1996.

198. *The Treaty of Amsterdam, Text and Commentary*, ed. Andrew Duff, Federal Trust/Sweet & Maxwell, 1997, pp. 59–65. *Making Sense of the Amsterdam Treaty*, European Policy Centre, Brussels, 1997, pp. 50–2, 98–100.

199. See for discussion *Jobs and the Rhineland Model*, Ian Davidson, Federal Trust/Sweet & Maxwell, 1997. *Capitalism against Capitalism*, Michel Albert, Whurr Publishers, 1993. *Stop Go Crash Boom*, Chs 6 and 7, Michel Albert and Jean Boissonnat, Macdonald, 1989.

200. Alongside the new Employment Committee, composed of government employees, there are already the Economic and Social Committee, with treaty responsibilities, and the Standing Committee on Employment, in which the members of the Social Affairs Council meet employer organisations, trade unions and the body representing publicly owned industry. There was an Employment Committee before the Treaty of Amsterdam created it.

201. 'X' stands for the number of participant states, as in G7, which, as the French Finance Minister recalled, is also informal, but powerful.

202. The UK made a noisy attempt to join Euro-X without joining the monetary union. It was rebuffed but claimed success in the reaffirmation that only the Economic and Finance Council, with all Member States represented could take decisions. This reaffirmation was

superfluous. Readers may have been misled by the label *Euro-X Council*, which is not a Council in the Treaty sense.

203. Professional insertion is a notion close to 'employability', which the Commission had highlighted in its submission to the European Council. *Bulletin of the European Union*, OOP, October 1997, point 2.2.222.

204. The 1998 guidelines are given in full in ibid., 12. 1997, p. 92.

205. M. Juncker had other portfolios in the government and unusually for a Prime Minister, also presided at numerous Council meetings.

206. For a careful study of the dilemma, see Krugman, P., *Europe Jobless, America Penniless*, Foreign Policy, Washington DC, No. 95, Summer 1994, p. 19.

207. See McAleavy, P. and Mitchell, J., 'Industrial regions and lobbying in the Structural Funds reform process', *Journal of Common Market Studies*, Vol. 32, No. 2, June 1994, p. 238.

208. Regulation EEC No. 724/75, OJ L 73, 21.03.75, p. 1.

209. '... anxious [to reduce] the differences existing between the various regions and the backwardness of the less favoured regions ...'.

210. See De Ruyt, J., 'L'Acte Unique européen', *Etudes Européennes*, Brussels, 1987, p. 195.

211. The current regulations, including for EIB coordination, are:
     ERDF: 2083/93, OJ L 193, 31.07.93.
     ESF: 2084/93, OJ L 193, 31.07.93.
     EAGGF: 2085/93, OJ L 193, 31.07.93.
     EIB: 2081 and 1082/93, OJ L 193, 31.07.93.

212. Europe invests in its regions, DG XVI and DG X, 1997.

213. European Commission, *Frontier-free Europe newsletter*, Supplement No. 1, 1998.

214. Agenda 2000: For a stronger and wider Union, p. 15 COM(97) 2000, vol. 1, OOP.

215. Six years is the maximum length of a development programme.

216. Agenda 2000, p. 88.

217. Report of the Committee for the Study of EMU.

218. The Cohesion Fund, with its links to TENs and EMU, was a compromise solution to the alternatives demanded by certain Member States and rejected by others. See Cloos, Reinesch, Vignes and Weyland, *Le Traité de Maastricht*, Bruylant, Brussels, 1993, pp. 152–3.

219. In April and in December 1997, the Commission reported on conditionality. Although Greece, Spain and Portugal were in 'excessive deficit' by reference to the criteria, it concluded that assistance should continue. *Bulletin*, 4/97, p. 45 and 12/97, p. 57.

220. Council Regulation (EC) No. 1164/94, OJ L 130, 25.05.94.

221. Control over the steel industry featured in the 'renegotiation' of British terms of Community membership which the government of Mr Harold Wilson undertook in 1974–75. It was a negotiating objective to ensure 'the retention by Parliament of those powers over the British economy needed to pursue effective regional, industrial and fiscal policies'. The Report on the Renegotiations, Cmnd 6003, is low-key: 'In the particular case of steel, it has been established that neither the Commission nor the United Kingdom now has powers to control private sector investment.' Quoted in Salmon, T.C. and Nicoll, W., *Building European Union*, MUP, 1997, p. 132. The powers of the Commission, successor to the High Authority, were unchanged.

222. As recently as December 1997, in COM (97) 583.

223. See below, p. 292.

224. Quoted in *The Intergovernmental Conference on Political Union*, ed. F. Laursen and S. Vanhoonacker, European Institute of Public Administration, 1992, p. 43.

225. For an account of the negotiations in the IGC see Cloos, Reinesch, Vigne and Weyland; *Le Traité de Maastricht*, Bruylant, Bruxelles, 1993, pp. 288–92.

226. MEDIA II, Development and Distribution, Council Decision 95/563/EC, OJ L 321, 30.12.95. MEDIA II, Training Council decision 95/564/EC, OJ L 321, 30.12.95.

227. One of the biggest ventures, and failures, was the Commission/Community action to realise High Definition Television (HDTV), which was to lead the world. See *Journal of Common Market Studies*, Vol. 34, No. 2, June 1996 for an account of the 'Rise and Fall'.

228. Respectively Hamish Hamilton, 1968, Pitman, 1973, Hachette, 1974. For later analysis see the articles by Ball, Begg, Shepherd, Nicholson and Channon in *Perspectives on European Business*, 2nd edn, eds Nicoll, Norburn and Schoenberg, Whurr Publishers, 1998.

229. The Department of Trade hesitated. Any British financial cost from ESPRIT was scored against its budget, reducing availability for its own IT research programme, ALDIS.

230. M. Masioti, Chief Adviser, Commission, in Europe and Japan, 'Competition and Cooperation in Science and Technology', *European Business Journal*, Vol. 4, Issue 1, 1992, p. 50.

231. The Commission's Proposal for the *Fifth Framework Programme*, OOP, 1997, p. 2.

232. All amounts expressed in ECUs automatically became the same in euros on 1 January 1999. Amounts are 'indicative' and 'deemed necessary' and do not prejudice budgetary decisions. In practice the Fifth Framework Programme will be entered unchanged into the relevant years of the Financial Perspectives 2000–2007.

233. Decision 63/226 EEC of 2.4.1963.

234. See Chapter 11.

235. *Bulletin of the European Union*, OOP, November 1997, p. 12.

236. Decision no. 719/96/EC, OJ L 99, 20.4.1996.

237. *Bulletin of the European Union*, OOP, pp. 71–2.

238. Council Decision 95/563/EC, OJ L 321, 30.12.1995.

239. Council Decision 95/564/EC, OJ L 321, 30.12.1995.

240. 89/552/EEC, OJ L 298, 17.10 89; amended by Parliament and Council Directive 97/36/EC, OJ L 202, 30.7.1997.

241. Newsletter, *London Representation of the Commission*, 9 April 1998, p. 2. The definition of 'European' is elastic.

242. Quoted in *The Intergovernmental Conference on Political Union*, ed. F. Laursen and S. Vanhoonacker, European Institute of Public Administration, 1992, p. 383.

243. Consistent with the fight against cancer, the Health Council agreed to be non-smoking during some of its meetings, to the discomfort of Commissioner Vredeling, who noisily sucked his pipe, and to several of the assembled ministers.

244. Laursen and Vanhoonacker, op. cit., p. 451.

245. Including tragically the French delegate to CELAD, the pre-pillar 3 forum for planning the fight against drugs. Criminal charges were brought against the then Prime Minister,

Fabius, and Health Minister. For a historical reference see Lamnes, D., *The Wealth and Poverty of Nations*, Little, Brown, 1998, p. 184.

246. *Bulletin of the European Communities*, 10/1972.

247. Text in *The Intergovernmental Conference on Political Union*, ed. F. Laursen and S. Vanhoonacker, European Institute of Public Administration, 1992, p. 298.

248. *The Internal Market after 1992: Meeting the Challenge*, OOP, 1992.

249. Commission: *The 1996 Single Market Review*, SEC (96) 2378, 16.12.96, p. 106.

250. Colchester, N. and Buchan, D., *Europower*, Economist Books, 1990, p. 190.

251. Along with Education (Article 149), Culture (Article 151) and in a slightly different formulation Public Health (Article 152).

252. *Consumer Rights in the Single Market*, OOP, 1993, p. 5.

253. 'The S(ingle) M(arket) P(rogramme) put consumer safety before the free circulation of goods and services', Commission, *The Impact and Effectiveness of the Single Market*, COM (96) 520 final, 30.10.96.

254. COM (93) 378.

255. *Bulletin of the European Union*, OOP, 10/1995, p. 70.

256. Before BSE in beef, there had been salmonella in eggs and chickens, listeriosis in cheese, adulterated cooking oil, tampering with wine, etc.

257. Summit declaration preamble, para. 3.

258. J. De Ruyt, 'L' Acte Unique européen', *Etudes européennes*, Brussels, 1987, p. 218.

259. For the catalogue and sources of the TEU innovations, see Cloos, Reinesch, Vignes and Weyland, *Le Traité de Maastricht*, Bruylant, Bruxelles, 1993, pp. 319ff.

260. For further commentary see *Making Sense of the Amsterdam Treaty*, European Policy Centre, Brussels, 1997, pp. 102–3; Andrew Duff, *The Treaty of Amsterdam*, Sweet & Maxwell, 1997, pp. 75–7.

261. A small plot, with symbols and inscriptions, was created in the rue de la Loi in Brussels, outside the then Commission HQ, to commemorate the Year of the Environment. Ironically within a few years it had become an eyesore, until it was tidied up.

262. 'We will use the British Presidency to bring environmental considerations into the centre of the EU's decision making process', R. Cook, Institute of European Affairs, Dublin, 3 November 1997, quoted in *Britain's Agenda in Europe*, Federal Trust and Trans-European Policy Studies Association, December 1997.

263. Council Regulation EEC, No. 1210/90.

264. Council Press Release, 9402/98, 16/17, VI, 1998.

265. C. Hubschmidt and P. Moser, 'Why was the European Parliament influential in the Car Emission standards?', *Journal of Common Market Studies*, Vol. 35, No. 2, June 1997, pp. 225–42.

266. When the then Commissioner, Ripa de Meana, invoked EIA in connection with a road construction in the South of England, the then Foreign Secretary, Douglas, later Lord, Hurd famously remarked that the Commission was invading the 'nooks and crannies' of national life.

267. Meanwhile the eight 'northern' Member States had applied a national CO_2 tax. Energy taxes are stoutly opposed by captains of European industry in the European Round Table. See *Climate Change*, ERT Brussels, 1997, pp. 7–8.

268. Chris Patten, 'Industry and the environment', *European Business Journal*, Vol. 2, Issue 3, pp. 31–4. European Council, Copenhagen, 21–22 June 1993, conclusions, annex 1,7 'Taking into account the environment will create new jobs'. European Round Table, *Climate Change,*' The double dividend' (less pollution, more jobs) in an open market is yet to be proven', p. 8.

269. Albert Weale, 'The kaleidoscopic competition of European environmental regulation', *European Business Journal*, Vol. 7, Issue 4, 1995, pp. 19–25.

270. Sweden is deactivating its nuclear power stations.

271. Inter-governmental Conferences: contributions by the Commission. *Bulletin of the European Communities*, Supplement 2/91, OOP, p. 139.

272. Quoted in *The Intergovernmental Conference on Political Union*, ed. F. Laursen and S. Vanhoonacker, European Institute of Public Administration, 1992, pp. 380–1.

273. Public service obligations are a French preoccupation. They protect consumers against loss of supply and producers against competition in a liberalised market. See Commission, *Servicers of General Interest*, OOP, 1997.

274. White Paper, OOP, 1994, p. 153.

275. For an account of the sanctions which the USA impose on the Soviet Union in retaliation for the declaration of martial law in Poland, see *The Downing Street Years*, M. Thatcher, Harper Collins, 1993, pp. 253–6.

276. It was the first time the New Independent States of the former Soviet Union had participated in international negotiations.

277. Compare pp. 194–5 and 306 above.

278. The Commission signed under the ECSC Treaty and under Euratom.

279. *Bulletin of the European Union*, 5/97, p. 39.

280. The other outstanding subjects for which there is a question of a specific treaty base are tourism and civil protection, which is jargon for cross-border co-operation between emergency services.

281. Various radical proposals were made in the negotiation of the Treaty of European Union. None were adopted. See Cloos, Reinesch, Vigne and Weyland, *Le Traité de Maastricht*, Bruylant, Brussels, 1993, pp. 443–7.

282. *The Finances of Europe*, Praeger, 1977, p. 3.

283. Europe Day, 9 May, the anniversary of the Schuman Declaration. Otherwise, 7 May might have been divisively remembered as the day of German surrender in the Second World War.

284. The word 'supranational' is used in the original text of the ECSC Treaty to describe the status of the members of the High Authority. It was deleted in the 1967 Treaty revision. The subtitle of the virtually *Official History of the High Authority of the ECSC*, by D. Spierenburg and R. Poidevin is 'Supranationality in Operation' (Weidenfeld & Nicolson, 1994).

285. For texts see *Building European Union*, Salmon and Nicoll, Manchester University Press, 1997, pp. 90–4.

286. Communiqué, point 5.

287. OJ L 94, 19, 28.4.70.

288. The details are no longer important. As long as it did not increase expenditure, the EP could propose modifications. The Council needed a qualified majority to reject them. Otherwise put, a Council minority, in league with the EP, could protect them.

289. OJ L 359, 31.12.97.

290. Article 3.3 of the Council Decision of 7 May 1985, OJ L 128, 14.5.85.

291. An exception to this rule caused trouble in the past and still worries jurists. For some budget lines which concern pilot projects or which prefigure policies still to be articulated there cannot be a full-blown legal base. These are known in the jargon as 'actions ponctuelles', which has defied translation, except as the approximation 'one-off measures'. The Commission suffered a rude shock in the summer of 1998. In the case C-106/96 the ECJ ruled that it was illegal for it to execute various programmes which the EP had provided for in the budget, without a legal base.

292. Ordinarily, the Council needs unanimity to change a Commission proposal, even when the proposal can be adopted by QMV. This preserves the substance of the Commission's right of initiative, and is regarded as protection for states with low voting power against their larger partners.

293. OJ L 128, 14.5.85.

294. Page 55 and more fully in Part III of volume 1.

PART 4

SECOND AND THIRD PILLAR POLICIES

PILLAR II: THE COMMON FOREIGN AND SECURITY POLICY[1]

EARLIER CHAPTERS have traced the evolution and identified the tensions in the development of the European Community. There were contradictory features of this development. One was the clear understanding that the Community was never to be properly seen as confined to merely a formal application of the treaties, but rather belonged to a wider political environment, especially the aspiration to achieve political integration. Thus after the débâcle of the French-induced demise of the European Political Community, companion of the European Defence Community,[2] the Foreign Ministers of the six countries which switched to an exclusively Economic Community did not resile entirely from the objective of wider integration. Indeed they said at Messina in June 1955 that what they proposed in the economic field was only a first step '... towards the setting up of a united Europe ...', 'Such a policy appears ... to be indispensable if Europe's position in the world is to be maintained, her influence restored ...'.[3]

The contradiction lay in the fact that, despite such aspirations, the Member States have not been willing to go beyond an insistence on preserving national sovereignty in this area of policy and have been more hesitant about transferring power than in those other spheres of policy which have been the hallmark of half a century of European integration. In foreign policy caution has reigned. Member States have been mindful of the fact that 'foreign policy' touches directly on those factors which make a state a state; that is, the status of sovereignty. Given contract theory explanations of the origins and nature of the state – that it is to protect the lives and property of its citizens – and the role of external sovereignty in defining a state as a state, any encroachment upon foreign and defence policy by outside agencies threatens the very concept and existence of a state. The management of political relations between a state and other states is a criterion of statehood. The 'otherness' of other states forms a state's identity. Thus, the Member States of the European Union have always been extremely reluctant in practice to transfer any power of decision to another agency.

A further feature of developments in this area has been that because of this commitment to sovereignty, a separate policy and decision-making system has been adopted for questions relating to foreign policy, and this alternative system has at times been seen by some as a putative alternative to the Community method *per se*.[4] This alternative system first came into being in the form of European Political Co-operation (November 1970–November 1993) and is currently manifested in the Common Foreign and Security Policy (CFSP) provisions, although it has its roots much earlier.

FOREIGN POLICY CO-OPERATION, À LA FRANÇAISE

When General de Gaulle returned to power in France in 1958, he lost no time in proposing that the Six should engage in foreign policy co-operation. After some skirmishing, the Six agreed (on 23 November 1959) to meet quarterly, outside the framework of the Treaties and without the presence of the Commission:

> The consultations will concern both the political extension of the activities of the Communities and other international problems.[5]

Sadly for the Five, the proposal was a lure, the first move in a French reverse take-over bid to replace the economic communities by an inter-governmental organisation, a bid which unfolded in the Fouchet Plans, beginning in November 1961[6] and collapsing in May 1962. The EEC then became preoccupied with its own internal development, especially mixing the 'binding cement' of the CAP and the corollary of French-provoked first crisis of confidence in 1965–66.[7]

The Hague, December 1969: completing, widening and deepening

The end of the controversial de Gaulle era was marked by the summit meeting in The Hague in December 1969. It was heavy in symbolism. Within a month the Economic Community was due to complete its first, introductory phase and to move towards greater maturity (*completing*). The applications from other European countries, which France had squashed, were still on the table and were expected to be pressed. The prospect of enlargement (*widening*) suggested – since the depth of the British commitment to the construction of Europe could not be assessed – that it was time to turn to 'progress in the matter of political unification' (one component of *deepening*), on which Foreign Ministers were instructed to report.

The enigma of political unification or political union or united Europe or European Union or whatever

What is the 'political union' that falls so easily from the lips of politicians, agitators and commentators? The answer is that nobody knows for sure.[8] The only common strand in the scores of formulae and blueprints is that, apart from the forms of economic integration pursued and developed in successive Treaty revision from 1950 to 1997, there should be other functions erstwhile discharged by governments of Member States but transferred to institutions in which the Member States are collectivised and which are directly accountable to the citizens of the united/unified entity. Foreign policy suggests itself as a function of a state which could become a sphere of co-operation, or better, among states. In addition, co-operation in this area would:

(a) provide a complement to the external economic relations which are part of the activities and formal treaty remit of the Economic Community, and which it is bound to conduct in an economically interdependent world; and
(b) potentially allow the Member States to maximise their influence (colloquially, clout) in their international relations through the strength gained via their collective resources (if they were able to find a community of interest).

Davignon Report

Mandated by their political masters the Foreign Ministers commissioned a report from their advisers, who met under the chairmanship of the Belgian Political Director, Vicomte Etienne Davignon, later a successful Commissioner. Their Report, of October 1970, also known as the Luxembourg Report, proposed that the first stage in the desired but undefined political union should be devoted to foreign policy co-operation:

> The first fact is that, in line with the spirit of the Preambles to the Treaties of Paris and Rome, tangible form should be given to the will for a political union which has always been a force for the progress of the European Communities.[9]

In accordance with the doctrine of policy development by 'little steps', European Political Co-operation (EPC) was *not* to:

- be embedded in a Treaty,
- lie inside the framework of the Communities,
- require participating governments to enter into binding commitments,
- be subject to the procedures and constitutional balances proper to the Communities (Court and Parliament), and
- be served by a bureaucracy independent of the participants.

Governments committed themselves to no more than consultations with partners on foreign policy questions and to the adoption of common positions if they found that they shared them.

The Report was accepted. European Political Co-operation began in November 1970, and Ministers were to meet twice a year (once per Presidency). A Political Committee composed of their political directors would meet four times a year. The Commission was not a member but would be 'associated' when Community activities might be affected. There would be organised discussions with the European Parliament's Political Committee.

ENSUING DEVELOPMENT

European identity

At the first meeting of the Heads of State or of Government of the Enlarged Community in Paris in October 1972, it was resolved to transform before the end of the decade the whole complex of their relations into a European Union. In a report endorsed by the meeting in Copenhagen of the Heads of State and Government[10] (precursor of the European Council) in November 1973, ministerial meetings were stepped up to four a year (as already agreed in Paris); working groups could be set up, notably the 'European Correspondents' Group' (of foreign ministry officials); and the Coreu secure transmission link among foreign ministries was installed.[11]

The Copenhagen meeting devoted time to particularising the distinct 'European identity'. This was partly designed in some sense as a response to the American complaint (in the oft-quoted quip: 'we want to speak to them but they don't have a phone number'[12]) that Western Europe lacked policy coherence and, on important matters of international politics, was a political vacuum. It also reflected previous rhetoric about a European identity and European Union.

Despite this, there remained an absence of political will to move forward in a fundamental way. In addition to the reasons discussed above, that absence was caused by, and symptomatic of, the uncertain environment in international politics and economics generated by the Arab–Israeli conflict of October 1973 and the resultant energy crisis of the 1970s. Contrary to expectations that external crises might stimulate centripetal behaviour, it instead produced centrifugal pressures for each state to seek to arrange its own deal to its best advantage. The system at the time was also struggling to cope with the impact of the 1973 enlargement, which brought into discussions on these questions Britain and Denmark, who were and remain more hesitant about these matters. In this atmosphere, it is not surprising that the much vaunted European identity was a thin document; in essence a programme for the conduct of foreign affairs over a period ahead.

At the Paris Summit in December 1974 (the last before the inauguration of the European Council) it was agreed that the European Council would be dualist, treating both Community and European Political Co-operation (EPC), ending the practice of the Foreign Ministers meeting in different locations, even different cities on the same day to discuss EPC and Community business separately.[13] At Paris it was also agreed to ask the Belgian Prime Minister, Leo Tindemans, to write a report to clarify the notion of European Union.

Tindemans

The proposals of the Tindemans Report,[14] December 1975, were well ahead of their time. Little in it was implemented in the short term, but its influence was reflected in the developments of the next decade. The revolutionary proposals included:

* an end to the distinction between meetings within the Community structure and meetings on political co-operation;

- EPC should involve legal obligations;
- there should be a common foreign policy, for which the European Council should issue general guidelines; the Council would implement these guidelines, and it was proposed at this stage that 'the minority must rally to the views of the majority'.

In brief:

Our States will gradually wish to submit the greater part of their external relations problems to a common policy, and they will accept the constraints imposed in consequence. (p. 19)

Tindemans suggested that 'exchanges of views on our specific problems in defence matters' should be included. Tindemans made numerous other suggestions in a variety of areas, but most of these suggestions had to wait for the Treaty on European Union in 1992 for substantive progress.

London Report

In London on 13 October 1981, under British Presidency, Foreign Ministers adopted a further Report that:

(a) reiterated the commitment of states to consult each other before adopting foreign policy positions;
(b) brought the 'political aspects of security' into the ambit of EPC; this is the first ever mention of security in the EPC context; and
(c) envisaged going beyond consultations to taking 'joint actions'.

The London Report also formalised the idea of the Presidency being assisted by a small team of officials from the preceding and succeeding Presidencies, the 'troika', which was to operate at two levels: ministerial and a small official back-up provided by the three Foreign Ministries.[15]

Genscher–Colombo initiative

The Franco-German initiative of 1981 took its name from the Foreign Ministers of Germany and Italy. It gave rise to the 'Solemn Declaration on European Union' which was annexed to the Conclusions of the 26th European Council Meeting in Stuttgart on 17–19 June 1983, and sought to strengthen and increase the effectiveness of EPC by providing for the adoption of 'joint positions and joint actions', for intensified consultations and for 'the co-ordination of the positions of Member States on the political and economic aspects of security'. Common positions (same as joint positions[16]) would constitute a 'central point of reference for Member States' policies'. There was and is still no suggestion that Member State competence for foreign policy should yield to supranational authority.

Achievement

The system operated by consensus, but with no obligation to reach it. In the absence of consensus, the parties reverted to their freedom of action. So it was that the Conservative government in Britain, without any sense of oxymoron, could dwell on the synergy of political co-operation, without any actual sacrifice of independence, and the Irish Foreign Minister could say, in a pleasing Irishism, 'the obligation though binding in the sense that we have committed ourselves to co-ordinate our policies is not absolute since we are not obliged to reach agreement'.[17] Nonetheless, increasingly the Member States of the Community were viewed from the outside as a relatively coherent factor in international relations, and the gradual accumulation of collective actions began to give the appearance of constituting a policy line from which it appeared increasingly difficult for the Member States to depart and an embryonic *esprit de corps* between those most intimately involved developed.

The Middle East war of 1973 saw the EPC seeking to secure a cease-fire. At Venice in 1980, the EPC gravely upset the USA and Israel by a Declaration conspicuously supporting the self-determination of the Palestinian people and the inclusion of the PLO (at the time associated with terrorism) in the negotiations.[18] In the wake of the oil price shock of 1973 the Community combined with the EPC (as leader) to inaugurate the Euro-Arab dialogue, which was intended to lay the basis for a closer mutual understanding and partnership. When Argentina invaded the Falkland Islands in 1982 the Ten called for the withdrawal of Argentine forces. When the UK urged its Community partners to introduce trade sanctions, the Political Committee provided the essential political motivation for the use of a commercial policy instrument for the political purpose for which it was not devised.[19] In the course of its thirteen-year progression, EPC had been occupied also, unspectacularly but successfully, in aligning positions in the Conference on Security and Co-operation in Europe (1972–85) and on the detente policy which was the keynote of Member States' relations with the Soviet bloc. In meetings of the General Assembly of the UN the Member States sought to speak 'with one voice'.

However, against these centripetal trends, the record of UN votes did not show much European identity on major questions, and, for example, there was never any question of the two permanent members of the Security Council, France and Britain, putting themselves at the service of their partners in the Council. The record of EPC was mixed, since there was no common European foreign policy, and the pattern of apparent solidarity was by no means complete or wholly predictable, and was on occasion, such as the failure to agree to condemn the Soviet Union for shooting down a South Korean Boeing 747(KAL-007) in 1983, spectacularly breached.

Although not mentioned in any of the texts that were the foundation of EPC, Declarations became its stock in trade. They reflected implicit common positions. Joint actions were unknown. Given that EPC was deliberately not part of the European Community system, but separately run and organised by the Presidency of the Council, the Presidency assumed a higher profile than it had in the EEC, speaking for the participants and travelling to trouble spots as well as conference sites to convey EPC views and suggestions.

The Dooge Committee

As part of the mid-1980s perception that the Community needed new initiatives to break out of its malaise, it was agreed at the Fontainebleau European Council of 1984, under a French Presidency showing strong leadership, to appoint a Committee on Institutional Affairs. Chairmanship of the committee devolved on the succeeding Irish Presidency, in the person of Senator Jim Dooge, a former Irish Foreign Minister. He and his aides had a clear idea of what should happen next: Treaty revision and the completion of the Common Market.

As discussion of the Dooge Report gathered momentum, Britain, which had opposed much of it, came forward with a proposal for a new Treaty on political co-operation; and on the eve of the European Council meeting in Milan on 28 and 29 June 1985 France and Germany combined to circulate a draft 'Treaty on European Union', confined however to political co-operation. This was the genesis of Title III of the Single European Act – single because it concerns both the Community and the EPC. There is not much else that is common in its two parts.

The Single European Act, 1986, Title III

The Preamble states that the European Union comprises the Communities and EPC. The single article on EPC, article 30, codifies in twelve paragraphs the ongoing practices of EPC, most of which can be traced back to the reports and texts already examined. The only significant innovation – apart from the Treaty base itself – is the setting up of a Political Secretariat, distinct from the Secretariat General of the Council and manned by secondees from national diplomatic services – that is, the formalisation of the official level back-up of the existing troika.

The obligations contained in the Treaty are to consult, inform and take account of positions of other partners. In the Single European Act it was agreed that:

- due *consideration* would be given to the desirability of adopting and implementing common European positions (article 30.2b);
- these common positions were to be a *point of reference* (2c);
- the Member States would *endeavour* to avoid action which impairs cohesion (2d);
- they would refrain *as far as possible* from preventing consensus and joint action (3c);
- they would co-ordinate *more closely* positions on the political and economic aspects of security (6a);
- they would *endeavour* to adopt common positions in international gatherings (7a); and
- they would *take full account of* positions agreed in EPC (7b). (Emphasis added throughout.)

In other words, there were still no binding obligations to act in concert. The words 'common position' and 'joint action' are used in their ordinary dictionary sense, without a legal connotation. Articles 1 and 3 of the SEA maintained the rigid distinction between how the Community and EPC were to work and a distinctive legal base.

PRE-MAASTRICHT RECONSIDERATION LEADING TO PROGRESS? —

Two years after the Single European Act (SEA) came into operation in July 1987, the Europe to the east of the EC began its revolutionary changes and the axioms on which the infant European Union was based were falling away. The Soviet bloc and its military persona, the Warsaw Pact, collapsed. Germany was unified and the five Länder which had been the Democratic Republic became, as part of the Federal Republic, also part of the EU. As if this was not enough, some Member States were already coming to the view that the EPC system needed to be reconsidered as they wished to diminish the gap between intentions and outcomes that clearly still existed in terms of the endeavours of the Member States of the European Community to have a common, if not single, foreign and security policy. The blueprint for an Economic and Monetary Union had already pointed the way to a new Inter-governmental Conference (IGC) to devise the necessary Treaty amendments. Thus to the proposed IGC on monetary union was added another on political union. During the IGC (December 1990–December 1991) the crises in the Gulf and the fragmentation of Yugoslavia added to the perceived need for changes to the existing system of working. The outcome was the Treaty on European Union, February 1992.

Much of the argument in the IGC on political union was about whether the problems of agreeing and implementing a European Common Foreign and Security Policy reflected a lack of suitable institutional arrangements – that is, machinery – or whether they reflected a more profound issue of different analyses of the various issues at hand. The British, for example, argued vehemently that what was needed was a greater unity of analysis, not more or different machinery. They favoured a sector by sector approach, event by event gradually working towards a more effective common policy. A further part of the argument was the fundamental divergencies over not just the question of the vision of the future of the European enterprise – federal or inter-governmental, political or economic – but what role the future EU should play in European security and defence. At root this argument was about whether to encourage an embryonic European Security and Defence Identity (ESDI) through the Western European Union (WEU) with a strong emphasis upon the European dimension or whether to rely on NATO and the transatlantic link, keeping the USA involved. These basic differences made agreement difficult to achieve.

A solution?

The solution reached in Maastricht in December 1991 and embodied in the February 1992 Treaty was agreement around a form of words and arrangements that all could agree, but that nearly all could interpret differently. Most particularly, the French could argue that Maastricht recognised their argument for a greater role for the WEU and the potential for a more autonomous ESDI, somewhat detached from NATO, whereas the USA and the UK could argue that Maastricht accepted the primacy of NATO and the subordinate role of any ESDI within the NATO framework.

The Treaty on European Union (TEU) was deliberately ambiguous in this area, since this was the only way agreement could be reached. Given that the IGC involved Treaty amendment, unanimous agreement was, of course, necessary. This explains much about the Treaty on European Union and the ensuing difficulties in seeking to implement the Common Foreign and Security Policy (CFSP). In addition, ratification difficulties, which partly involved attempts to clarify what had so tenuously been agreed, delayed the coming into effect of the TEU until November 1993. By the time it came to be reviewed in 1995–96, it had been in operation less than three years.

Maastricht compromises

A major negotiating compromise was the 'pillar' construction of the European Union which created a barrier between the Common Commercial Policy (CCP), the external economic relations and trade relations of the European Community pillar and the CFSP, the foreign and security policy pillar. Although the TEU is replete with calls for consistency between the two, the divided responsibilities between the two systems and the separate, if parallel, decision-making systems do create a number of practical, legal and financial difficulties, making effective implementation of some policies difficult. This had already been apparent in the pre-CFSP system with near catastrophe in the Uruguay Round of the General Agreement of Tariffs and Trade in 1994. The 'pillar' solution, however, was a clear response to the view of several Member States that the 'tree' proposal,[20] was unacceptable precisely because it was perceived as creating too much central power and challenging state authority. So the EU remained divided at its heart when it came to seeking to be an international actor or having an international presence, or in making its weight felt across a range of policies. Each of the EU pillars had, and continues to have, its own rules and procedures.

Another compromise was in the general nature of the objectives of the CFSP. As specified in Article 11 (TEU), these are of the 'motherhood and apple-pie variety'. They are so general that there could be little objection, but they also provide little guidance for the implementation in specific cases. The objectives of the CFSP are couched in terms such as 'safeguarding common values, interests and the independence of the Union', 'strengthening the security of the Union and its member states', 'promoting international peace and co-operation' and 'enhancing democracy'.

A third compromise consisted of the fact that the mechanics of implementation left numerous escape routes for recalcitrant states, particularly given that it was made clear that the Council 'shall act unanimously' (old J.8.2 TEU), albeit that, where it unanimously agreed, it could adopt 'joint actions' by qualified majority vote. There was an attempt to tighten this up by an attached Declaration which saw the Member States agree to 'avoid preventing a unanimous decision where a qualified majority exists in favour of that decision', but again this was just words with no binding obligation. More representative was the reiteration in old Article J.2.1 (TEU) that the Member States 'shall inform and consult one another'. Thus the permanent members of the Security Council (Britain and France) now undertook to defend the positions and interests of the Union (old Article J.5.4) in the Security Council, but, as under EPC, were not obligated to toe a European Union line. These provisions reflect the real tenor of CFSP and raise the question of whether its introduction represented a significant advance on the SEA provisions on EPC.

The TEU formally introduced a distinction between a 'common position' and a 'joint action'. It can be argued that the key distinction is that the common positions are about intentions, objectives and priorities, while joint actions represent the rather more specific implementing part of the decision, relating to the use of EU and Member State resources directed towards achieving the concrete objectives adopted (including, for example, the deployment of manpower, expertise, finance, etc.). In practice, however, it can still be difficult to establish or discern the formal distinction between the two. The Council originally saw joint actions as the key instrument, backed up by common positions, but this distinction was not followed in practice. Common positions cover both fundamental orientations and concrete actions, and joint actions have on occasion been limited to ad hoc diplomatic or administrative measures. The similarity between the two, on occasion, is illustrated by a Common Position and Joint Action, which were both agreed on 8 June 1998 (see Boxes 12.1 and 12.2).

The TEU explicitly laid down that the objectives of the CFSP were to be achieved 'by gradually implementing . . . joint actions in the areas in which the Member States have important interests in common' (old J.3 TEU). Joint actions, when formally adopted, take the form of Council decisions .

They have been used, for example, with respect to the Former Yugoslavia – in the context of support for humanitarian aid in Bosnia-Herzégovina and the continuation of the administration in Mostar, the dispatch of observers to the Russian parliamentary elections, support for the South African transition towards democracy, support for the Middle East peace process, as well as support for the Stability Pact, the limitation of production and distribution of anti-personnel mines, and control of the export of dual-use goods .

A criticism of both joint actions and common positions has been that many of them 'merely transpose UN Security Council resolutions or extend the period of validity of earlier decisions'.[21] Thus in 1996, of the two common positions on the former Yugoslavia defined by the Council, the second simply removed a series restrictions on economic and financial relations laid down in accordance with numerous UN Security Council resolutions, although the first did call for the restrictions on arms exports to the states of the former Yugoslavia to remain in force, even after the UN arms embargo was lifted.

The CFSP however, has not just been about common positions and joint actions, since in addition there have been over 500 political statements and a huge number and variety of contacts and approaches – that is, the everyday activities which are an integral part of foreign policy, and which very much form the actual implemented outcome of policy decisions. Statements cover almost every topic of international relations, for example, declarations by the Presidency on 'the situation in the Palestinian Territories', 'concerning Chechnya', or on 'the occasion of the publication of the Anglo-Irish framework document on Northern Ireland'; and declarations by the European Union on the former Yugoslavia, Algeria or 'on the Frontier conflict between Ecuador and Peru'. However, many are of little real interest, since they merely express an opinion and their impact rarely extends beyond the sphere of rhetoric. For the numbers of Joint Actions, Common Positions and Declarations, issued between November 1993 and December 1998, see Table 12.1.

Box 12.1   Common Position of 8 June 1998

(Acts adopted pursuant to Title V of the Treaty on European Union)

COMMON POSITION
of 8 June 1998
defined by the Council on the basis of Article J.2 of the Treaty on European Union
concerning the prohibition of new investment in Serbia

(98/374/CFSP)

THE COUNCIL OF THE EUROPEAN UNION,

Having regard to the Treaty on European Union, and in particular Article J.2 thereof,

Whereas on 7 May 1998 the Council adopted Common Position 98/326/CFSP ([1])
concerning the freezing of funds held abroad by the Federal Republic of Yugoslavia (FRY)
and Serbia Governments; whereas a further reduction of economic and financial relations
with the FRY and Serbia was foreseen in case the conditions laid down in that common
position for the FRY and Serbian Government were not met;

Whereas, as such conditions have not been fulfilled so far, further action to reduce
economic and financial relations with Serbia should be taken;

Whereas, the restrictive measures set out in Article 1 will be reconsidered immediately if
the FRY and Serbian Governments move to adopt a framework for dialogue and a
stabilisation package,

HAS DEFINED THIS COMMON POSITION:

Article 1

New investments in Serbia are prohibited.

Article 2

This common position shall take effect from the date of its adoption.

Article 3

This common position shall be reviewed not later than six months after its adoption.

Article 4

This common position shall be published in the Official Journal.

Done at Luxembourg, 8 June 1998.

For the Council
The President
R. COOK

([1]) OJ L 143, 14.5.1998, p.1.

Box 12.2   Joint Action of 8 June 1998

JOINT ACTION
of 8 June 1998
adopted by the Council on the basis of Article J.3 of the Treaty on European Union
concerning the nomination of an EU Special Representative for the Federal Republic of
Yugoslavia (FRY)

(98/375/CFSP)

THE COUNCIL OF THE EUROPEAN UNION,

Having regard to the Treaty on European Union, and in particular Articles J.3 and J.11
thereof,

Having regard to the conclusions of the European Council, held in Amsterdam on 16 and
17 June 1997, concerning the Federal Republic of Yugoslavia (FRY),

Whereas on 29 April 1997 the Council adopted conclusions on the application of
conditionality with a view to developing a coherent EU strategy applicable to relations
with countries of south-east Europe which are not linked to the EU by an association
agreement;

Whereas on 19 March 1998 the Council adopted conclusions nominating Mr Felipe
González as EU Special Representative with a view to enhancing the effectiveness of the
EU's contribution to the resolution of problems in the FRY;

Whereas in its conclusions of 25 May 1998 the Council indicated that a Joint Action
should be adopted on the González mission:

Whereas the EU Special Representative will work in close consultation and concurrently
with the OSCE Chairman-in-Office to assist the FRY in promoting internal dialogue on
democratic reforms so as to contribute to the coherence of international efforts.

HAS ADOPTED THIS JOINT ACTION:

Article 1

Mr Felipe González shall be appointed EU Special Representative for the FRY for a period
ending on 31 December 1998.

The Council may review the content and duration of the mandate of the EU Special
Representative, including administrative and financial aspects, as appropriate before its
expiry.

Article 2

The mandate of the EU Special Representative will be to enhance the effectiveness of the
EU's contribution to the resolution of problems in the FRY and to pursue the subject of
FRY's future relations with the EU, its participation in OSCE and related matters.

Box 12.2 (*cont.*)

The EU Special Representative will carry out his mandate under the authority of the Presidency and as appropriate in co-operation with the Commission.

The EU Special Representative will be guided by, and report under the authority of the Presidency to, the Council on a regular basis and as the need arises.

Article 3

1. In order to cover the costs related to the mission of the EU Special Representative a sum of up to ECU 1 million shall be charged to the general budget of the European Communities from the date of adoption of this Joint Action.

2. The expenditure financed by the amount stipulated in paragraph 1 shall be managed in accordance with the European Community procedures and rules applicable to the general budget.

Article 4

1. The Member States and the Community may propose the secondment of staff to work with the EU Special Representative. The remuneration of personnel, detached by a Member State, the Commission or another Community institution to the EU Special Representative shall be covered respectively by the Member State concerned, the Commission or the other Community institutions.

2. The team of the Special Representative will be composed by the Special Representative on his own responsibility in consultation with the Presidency assisted by the Commission. The Council notes that the Presidency will keep it regularly informed of developments.

3. The Council notes that the Presidency, Commission and/or Member States, as appropriate, will provide logistical support in the region.

4. The privileges, immunities and further guarantees necessary for the completion and smooth functioning of the mission of the EU Special Representative and the members of his staff shall be defined with the parties. The Member States and the Commission shall grant all necessary support to such effect.

Article 5

This Joint Action shall enter into force on the date of its adoption. It shall apply until 31 December 1998.

Article 6

The Joint Action shall be published in the Official Journal.

Done at Luxembourg, 8 June 1998.

For the Council
The President
R. COOK

Table 12.1 Union and the world, 1993–98

	Joint actions					Common positions					Declarations				
	1994*	1995	1996	1997	1998	1994*	1995	1996	1997	1998	1994*	1995	1996	1997	1998
Central, Eastern, and South-Eastern Europe	*	5	6	4	10	*	6	2	3	8	*	12	17	26	37
Russia and CIS										1		13	15	13	13
Mediterranean countries												8	2	7	6
Middle East Gulf States		2		2	1		5	1	7	6		10	12	5	11
Africa			6	2	3			3	3	5		28	26	42	53
Asia												19	17	15	27
The Americas							1					12	16	13	6
Others		3	8	8	6		2	1		2		4	11	6	9
Total	14	10	21	16	20	8	13	10	13	22	110	106	116	124	163

*From November 1993 to December 1994
Source: European Parliament: Committee on Foreign Affairs, Security and Defence: Report on the role of the Union in the world: implementation of the common foreign and security policy for 1998 A4-0242/99.

Part of the political dialogue are the once-per-Presidency meetings between the Presidents of the European Council, the Commission and the US President; the once-per-Presidency troika and Commission meetings with the Japanese; and the annual meeting between the troika, Commission and representatives of the non-aligned movement. The Political Directors too meet both once or twice per Presidency or more regularly with, for example, their Canadian, Russian and Baltic counterparts. The embassy of the Member State holding the Presidency in third countries will also be the conduit for the passing of information, views and expressions of concern.

A real difficulty in achieving a positive policy outcome is that the Common Foreign and Security Policy is specifically excluded from the jurisdiction of the European Court of Justice (Article 46, TEU), although Title V of the Treaty on European Union substitutes for the options in Title III of the SEA, a series of legally binding obligations and states are bound by the general principle of *pacta sunt servanda*.[22] Common positions acquire a legal force – national policies must conform to them (old Article J.2.2) and joint actions commit the Member States (no longer the 'High Contracting Parties' of the SEA) (old Article J.3.4). In effect, however, the commitment is political and difficulties would need to be resolved politically. This might in some circumstances well involve turning a blind eye. Even if other Member States are unhappy, little apart from peer pressure can be exerted.

Defence

The contortions that the 1990–91 IGC involved regarding the CFSP and the fundamental compromises that were made are also clearly demonstrated in the security and defence fields. In the TEU the Member States agreed not only that a CFSP 'is hereby established', but that their discussions on such matter would for the first time 'include all questions related to the security of the Union, including the eventual framing of a common defence policy, which might in time lead to a common defence' (old J.4.1 TEU). However, the Member States in the very next paragraph distanced the European Union from direct involvement in the preparation and carrying out of defence related decisions by requesting the Western European Union 'to elaborate and implement decisions and actions of the Union which have defence implications'. The subcontracting of defence issues to the WEU is all the more extraordinary since, in 1991–92, of the twelve Member States of the EU only nine were in the WEU.

In a separate Declaration attached to the TEU, the WEU Member States agreed to perform this role, acknowledging that the WEU was to be built up in stages 'as the defence component of the European Union'. As a result of its new responsibilities the WEU agreed to:

- develop a closer working relationship with the EU;
- synchronise dates and venues of meetings and harmonise working methods;
- establish close co-operation between the respective Councils and secretariats of the EU and WEU;
- harmonise the presidencies of the EU and WEU; and

- develop a WEU planning cell, to enable closer military co-operation with NATO and military units answerable to the WEU.

There remained the strange omission in the Treaty and the declaration of any specific mention of what it was that came between 'to elaborate and implement'. It is simply implicit that it is the Council of the European Union that has the responsibility for taking such decisions. The use made of the WEU for joint actions has been rather limited, so far involving, for example, the provision of policing contingents for the administration of Mostar.

Further evidence of the sensitivies in the area of security and defence can be seen in the provisions (old J.4.3) that in this area the veto still applied and that Member States could pursue their own traditional policies of a 'specific character' or relating to NATO (old J.4.4), and indeed that groups of them could pursue their own co-operation arrangements. The bifurcation at the heart of decision making in such a sensitive area is especially important since, in the post-1995 enlargement, Austria, Denmark, Finland, Ireland and Sweden remained as non-members of the WEU, so that the fifteen theoretically could commit the ten (see Table 12.2). This became an issue in the 1996–97 IGC.

Other administrative adjustments

Since the new European Union enjoyed a single institutional structure, the Political Secretariat was amalgamated with the General Secretariat. The CFSP and external economic relations came together in a single Directorate-General of the Council. The

Table 12.2   EU Member States membership of security organisations in Europe, June 1999

Member State	NATO	PfP	WEU	OSCE
Austria	No	Yes	Observer	Yes
Belgium	Yes	n/a	Yes	Yes
Denmark	Yes*	n/a	Observer	Yes
Finland	No	Yes	Observer	Yes
France	Yes*	n/a	Yes	Yes
Germany	Yes	n/a	Yes	Yes
Greece	Yes	n/a	Yes	Yes
Ireland	No	?	Observer	Yes
Italy	Yes	n/a	Yes	Yes
Luxembourg	Yes	n/a	Yes	Yes
Netherlands	Yes	n/a	Yes	Yes
Portugal	Yes	n/a	Yes	Yes
Spain	Yes	n/a	Yes	Yes
Sweden	No	Yes	Observer	Yes
UK	Yes	n/a	Yes	Yes

n/a – NATO members are not 'Partners' since they are 'members'.
*These states have 'special' aspects to parts of their NATO membership.

Coreper (Part 2: the Ambassadors) retained and extended to the CFSP Council (that is, General Affairs Council) its responsibility for Council preparations. This meant some double-banking with the Political Committee which also served the CFSP Council. After some running-in problems, it was accepted that the Political Committee would continue as before although formally reporting through Coreper and that Coreper would send its work on, while itelf ensuring coherence with the external activities of the Community, and taking responsibility for the financial and institutional aspects of CFSP work. To enhance cohabitation between the Coreper and the Political Committee a group of CFSP counsellors, based in Permanent Representations in Brussels, was set up.[23]

The Commission, as well as Member States, may refer to the Council any question relating to the CFSP (Article 18), although it appears that this provision has been little used. Under the Maastricht provisions, CFSP administrative expenditure was a charge on the Budget, while operational expenditure may be charged to the Budget or to Member States (Article 28). This had a potentially important consequences, since the charging of expenditure to the Budget gave the European Parliament (as joint budgetary authority), which otherwise was simply informed of EPC activities, a *droit de regard* over CFSP actions.

The way ahead: to revise or to advance?

The timing of the advent of the CFSP could not have been less propitious. Although the Gulf War was over, the European Union had been conspicuously absent from it. The fighting in Yugoslavia inspired only futile EU efforts to promote cease-fires and negotiations.[24] In any case, long delays in the ratification of the TEU held the new powers of the CFSP in abeyance until November 1993.

The unsatisfactory and ambiguous nature of the Treaty on European Union arrangements for a CFSP were acknowledged by many of the participants, which is one reason why it was agreed that they should be reviewed, although it was not expected that there would be so little practical experience of CFSP before the review began. The Treaty on European Union made provision for the Treaty itself (Article N TEU) to be reviewed, and Articles J.4 (6) and J.10 envisaged revision of the CFSP, 'with a view to furthering the objective of the Treaty and having in view the 1998 deadline laid down in the modified Brussels Treaty of the WEU'.[25] The review of the TEU, although premature, was specified.

The questions that dogged the review process were in some respects the same as had arisen in 1990–91:

- The lack of shared visions as to the real objectives and nature of the CFSP.
- The divergences about the conceptions of the role of the EU in European security, perhaps indeed disagreement about the very nature of security in the late 1990s and the balance between arrangements primarily focused on the military and those primarily focused on the political and economic. If EPC had had problems in distinguishing the two spheres in the 1980s, in the 1990s the very nature of the

concept of and the basis of security itself was contested. The result was that the issue of what constituted the EC/EU's role in, and contribution to, European security became much more difficult.

- This related to such issues as whether NATO/WEU enlargement was a better route to European security in general and for Central and East European states, in particular, or whether the EU could fulfil that role.

The real issue, as in 1990–92, was that Member States were aware of the issues but were not yet able to resolve them.

Revision

One of the criticisms of the Treaty on European Union, seeking explanations for its unpopularity, was that the political union part had been unprepared. This time round, preparation of the revision of the Treaty was entrusted to a Reflexion (or Study) Group, composed of representatives of the Member States, a Commissioner and two MEPs. The Chairman was Spanish, Carlos Westendorp.[26] It was not expected or intended that the Group would find common ground. The Interim and Final Reports made no attempt to disguise the differences that existed on CFSP as on other issues, and, faithful to its terms of reference, the Group presented options rather than solutions or compromises. The Reflexion Group acknowledged that there had been a number of shortcomings in the operation of the CFSP, although it again had to acknowledge that there was no agreement as to the root causes of these shortcomings. The institutions were invited to prepare reports on policies and structures for the Reflexion Group to consider. There were reports from the Council, the EP and the Commission on CFSP.[27]

The Council submission was predictably anodyne. It suggested that both the expectations and the criticisms of the CFSP were exaggerated. Some Member States apparently found that the results achieved by the CFSP were 'not inconsiderable'; some saw them as 'falling far short of initial ambitions'. The report mildly observed that the functions of the different instruments – statement, common position and joint action – needed to be clarified; that the Coreu procedure should be further defined; that majority voting (Article J.3 (2)) had not been invoked; and the 'difficulties in implementing a joint action' (Article J.3 (7)) had not been fully appreciated. It noted that difficulties had also arisen over funding, over the aspirations of the European Parliament, the 'genuine merging' of Working Parties (EEC/old EPC) and the absence of a legal personality.

The European Parliament report was more full-blooded, noting 'a lack of and failure to implement cohesive and effective common foreign and security ... policies'. The solution it proposed, which went way beyond the Spinelli European Parliament 'Draft Treaty establishing the European Union' of 1984, was to integrate all external relations within the first (Community) pillar. Additionally, it argued a common defence policy should guarantee the borders of the Union.

The Commission was also blunt about the CFSP:

There was rarely the will to act together and maximise the Community's influence. It suffered, moreover, embarrassing failures to agree on important occasions.

The Commission was particularly concerned that the inter-governmentalism and consensual mode of the CFSP was infecting Community procedures for the conduct of external economic relations. It considered the rotating *troika* to be a weakness and called for better and earlier analysis of external conditions. The interconnection between the Union's CFSP and WEU did not, in its view, work satisfactorily.

These and other contributions to the debate were aware of the problems of lack of consistency in dealing with the challenges facing the Union. Reflecting the earlier divergences some saw the problems as merely those of 'running-in' the system; some attributed the difficulties to the level of high and unfulfillable expectations; and some to the lack of political will and inertia of attitudes. Many were disappointed by the result of the European Union's performance in the former Yugoslavia, which fell well short of the initial ambitions and expectations, and led to questions about the effectiveness of the instruments and means available. A majority saw a structural problem in what the Reflexion Group Report referred to as 'a mismatch between fairly ambitious, albeit somewhat vague, objectives and inadequate instruments for achieving them' (para. 148). Some blamed the institutionalisation of the pillar structure for this and other inadequacies. For many there was stark contrast between the operation of economic external relations under Pillar I, which allowed for qualified majority voting, and the operation of Pillar II, which basically did not. Moreover, the bifurcation between the pillars meant that there was a lack of synergy and co-ordination between the two pillars and areas of activity.

Reflexion Group critique

Specifically on the shortcomings of CFSP operation, the Reflexion Group itself identified the central issues as those of the formulation of policy, decision-making, and implementation, although it was noted that rigid divisions between these activities was inappropriate.

Formulation. The Group and a clear majority of states argued for an 'analysis, early warning system and planning unit' to be set up. The advantages of the proposal would be the outlining of options and possible responses, in other words the proper preparation of decisions. It was also hoped that such a unit would encourage the creation of common assessment of the issues, a common vision of what was to be done in order to guide the policy process, as well as expressing and arguing for the common interest, leading to more efficient policy outcomes.

Decisions. Here the debate centred on the possible use of qualified majority voting in one form or another as against the argument that the issues at the heart of the CFSP touched at the essence of national sovereignty and therefore required the continuation of the veto. Such was the deep-seated nature of this disagreement that it was recognised that it might be necessary to allow for the possibility of flexibility, by which those who feel it necessary for the Union to take a joint action would not be prevented from doing so. It is obvious here that this solution had some advantages in allowing some action to be taken, but the cost would be very high in terms of the perceptions of the Union as a serious, consistent, coherent actor in international affairs or on matters of European security.

Implementation. The Group identified three approaches to the question of implementation: the CFSP might be personified by appointing a 'Mr or Ms CFSP' to articulate the EU's position on foreign and security policy matters, to conduct personal meetings, and to act as a focus of contact for third parties; there could be a maintenance and strengthening of the central role of the Presidency; or the possible reinforcement of the Commission's role and responsibilities.

These divergences were not petty issues over structure, but rather represented fundamentally different views as to the nature and direction of the EU and its role in the new European security order. On the one hand, a maximalist position existed which, at least in the long term, wanted to drive for clearly defined policies with a real capability to carry them out in some form. This view was opposed by a minimalist vision of traditional alliance politics and inter-governmentalism, where all had the veto and nothing was agreed unless all agreed, yet another example of the tension between centripetal and centrifugal forces. In addition many of those holding this view wished to leave some central decisions to another organisation entirely, namely NATO. In the discussions it was clear that there was a strong feeling that the TEU's CFSP objectives were too general and that there needed to be a more specific statement of the Union's 'fundamental interests' either by geographical area, issues or priorities.

The European Union and the Western European Union

A further matter for consideration in the IGC was the vexed question of the EU's contribution to a more stable, secure and just European security order and the ways in which the European identity could be further developed, this more than twenty years after the infamous Copenhagen document.

The central issues in the 1990s remained those of:

- the relationship with NATO and the WEU;
- the respective roles of organisations in collective defence of territorial integrity;
- the managing of regional crises which stemmed from a variety of political, economic, ecological, social and humanitarian factors;
- the task of preventing conflicts and being active in the fields of crisis management and conflict resolution;
- how far the EU should go into the avowedly security field, particularly in such areas as those identified in the June 1992 Petersberg Declaration of the WEU.

In that Declaration in a section 'On strengthening WEU's operational role' the WEU members had indicated that in future:

Apart from contributing to the common defence in accordance with Article 5 of the Washington Treaty and Article V of the modified Brussels Treaty respectively, military units of WEU Member States, acting under the authority of WEU, could be employed for:

- humanitarian and rescue tasks;
- peacekeeping tasks;
- tasks of combat forces in crisis management, including peacemaking.[28]

The difficulty in 1996–97 remained the same as in 1990–91, namely the EU's reliance upon the WEU to do its 'dirty work' for it. In addition it was recognised by the WEU Member States themselves that many of the WEU's operational capabilities were still inadequate in many areas, despite the development of the Combined Joint Task Force (CJTF) concept between NATO and the WEU, whereby, for certain operations deemed only appropriate to the Europeans, the WEU could use NATO assets, including US military hardware and logistical capability. No agreement was possible on the precise nature of the relationship between the EU and WEU. Although most wanted the gradual integration of the WEU into the EU, there were differences over the pace of integration. Integration would have the advantage of helping in the development of the EU's operational capabilities, would help achieve coherence between the CFSP and defence as well as making a reality of the claims to solidarity because it would bring into play in the EU the guarantee of the Brussels Treaty.[29]

Other actors

A major difficulty for the EU states as they contemplated these questions was that the EU IGC was not the only forum in which such matters were being discussed or even acted upon. A major distinction between the 1996–97 and 1990–91 IGCs was the extent to which the arguments about the European security architecture and the position of NATO had already been resolved. By 1996 NATO had won the institutional argument and established its primacy. Even the French had abandoned their fierce support for an autonomous European Security and Defence Identity (ESDI), having learnt from the Gulf and Yugoslav experience just how important the Americans still were to European security and how inadequate in the mid-1990s the putative alternatives were. NATO, with the North Atlantic Co-operation Council (NACC) as the institutional basis for consultation and co-operation on political and security issues between NATO and the states of Eastern and Central Europe; Partnership for Peace (PfP) that endeavours to give practical effect to that co-operation; and forays into peacekeeping; had made its own adaptations to the changed environment before the EU 1996–97 IGC began, and perhaps rather like Rome in 1991 preceding Maastricht had, to some extent, foreclosed EC/EU options.

Similarly, the Western European Union had, through the Petersberg Declaration and the introduction of the Central and Eastern European states as 'Associate Partners', adjusted to the 1990s and had not just sat back waiting for the EU to decide its future.

There is a certain artificiality in this argument, however, since the ten WEU states were constituent elements of the fifteen EU states, and of the sixteen NATO states eleven were EU states, including the ten WEU states. Clearly these states were fully cognisant of what had happened in the other organisations, but the differences in response of these organisations is striking.

Divisions of opinion

Given the nature and extent of the divisions it is not surprising that the 1996 IGC staggered on until Amsterdam in June 1997, the delay in completion being symptomatic of the difficulties encountered in resolving the CFSP, as well as other issues. Towards the end of the negotiations informed sources suggested that the division of opinion on a number of CFSP matters was as follows, although the detailed positions were often more nuanced:

- *Increase majority voting in the CFSP*: Austria, Belgium, Finland, Germany, Ireland, Italy, Luxembourg, Netherlands, Portugal, Spain and Sweden were in favour; whereas Denmark, France, Greece, and UK were against.
- *Include defence in the EU*: Austria, Belgium, France, Germany, Greece, Italy, Luxembourg, Netherlands, Portugal, and Spain were in favour; whereas Denmark, Finland, Ireland, Sweden and UK were against.
- *Appoint Mr/Ms CFSP*: Austria, Denmark, France, Ireland, Italy, Portugal, Spain, Sweden, and UK were in favour; whereas Finland, Germany, Greece, Luxembourg, and Netherlands were against and Belgium was undecided.
- *Merge WEU/EU*: Belgium, France, Germany, Greece, Italy, Netherlands, and Spain were in favour; whereas Austria, Denmark, Finland, Ireland, Luxembourg, Portugal, Sweden and UK were against.
- No state opposed the setting up of an *analysis and early warning unit*, although Belgium, Denmark and Portugal were not as enthusiastic as the others.
- All bar Germany wished to retain the fundamentally *inter-governmental* character of CFSP and only three pushed for establishing common principles and objectives in the field of CFSP: Finland, Greece and Italy.
- No state formally pushed for the abandonment of *unanimity* on defence issues.

THE AMSTERDAM TREATY: A SECOND CHANCE TO GET IT RIGHT?

With the Amsterdam Treaty it could be argued that the Member States were given a much needed opportunity to provide clarification and to tidy up some of the inconsistencies contained in the Maastricht Treaty on matters relating to the CFSP and the EU/WEU/NATO relationship. Indeed, the section of the outcome agreed at the Amsterdam IGC dealing with the CFSP and External Economic Relations is headed 'An

Effective and Coherent External Policy'. Interestingly, perhaps as a sign of the difficulties experienced between 1993 and 1997 in determining and implementing the CFSP, the first item on the CFSP adds to Article **3*** (TEU) that the Council and Commission shall not only ensure consistency between external relations and the CFSP, but also in an added phrase 'shall co-operate to this end'. However, despite the changes and after twenty-five years of activity in the foreign policy area, the relationship between Council and Commission has still not been fully worked out, nor has a proper relationship between external economic relations and the CFSP been established.

The approach to defence was modified by the Amsterdam Treaty. The original J.4 (Article **17**) had referred to the 'eventual framing of a common defence policy'. In Amsterdam this became the 'progressive framing of a common defence policy'. The new paragraph 2 stated explicitly that the '[Q]uestions referred to in this Article shall include humanitarian and rescue tasks, peacekeeping tasks and tasks of combat forces in crisis management, including peacemaking', the Petersberg tasks. This form of words had been the subject of debate since – as the Irish draft treaty noted in December 1996 – the definition of peacemaking is not uniform in all relevant organisations, and there was a problem whether peacekeeping and peacemaking could involve the actual physical military enforcement of cease-fires or indeed military action against those who violated them. The restriction of the military security objectives of the CFSP in the short to medium term to the above three tasks leads to the question as to whether the Amsterdam Treaty brought the EU in reality any closer at all towards eventually framing a genuine common defence policy. The exquisitely balanced drafting of Article **17** shows the IGC delving deep into the deliberations of its predecessor.[30] English speakers are spared the arcane examination of the difference between a policy of common defence (which is the French reading) and a common policy of defence. British aversion to common defence (equals integrated command), which would undo the balance of the Atlantic Alliance, succeeds, but the genuflection to the Franco-German proposal for common defence remains live.[31] A common defence would presuppose agreement on what provokes defence of what. There is no security guarantee of the kind sought by the European Parliament, apart from a new shadowy reference in Article **11** to 'safeguarding . . . the integrity of the Union . . .'.[32]

It is the European Council that will decide on a common defence, although the Amsterdam Treaty makes clear that such a decision would need to meet the constitutional requirements of each Member State.

The WEU under Amsterdam

The instrument with operational capability is still the WEU, but it is no longer merely an integral part of the Union – it may be integrated into it, if the European Council unanamiously so decides. It is doubtful whether the Amsterdam Treaty provided any clear

---

*All references to Treaty Articles are to the Consolidated Version of the Treaty on European Union. They are shown in bold.

improvement with regard to the institutional obfuscation between the EU and the WEU. On the one hand, the WEU now has the responsibility for providing the Union with access to an operational capability notably in the context of the Petersberg tasks, but in a curious wording, while the European Council retains the competence to establish guidelines for the EU (Article 13 TEU) that competence now 'shall also obtain in respect of the WEU for those matters for which the Union avails itself of the WEU' (Article 13.3). When the EU avails itself of the WEU for the Petersberg tasks, it was agreed that

> all Member States of the Union (EU) shall be entitled to participate fully in the tasks in question. The Council, in agreement with the institutions of the WEU, shall adopt the necessary practical arrangements to allow all Member States contributing to the tasks in question to participate fully and on an equal footing in planning and decision-taking in the WEU'. (13.3)

That is, the neutrals and non-members of WEU will able to contribute to WEU operations in connection with the so-called Petersberg Tasks.

Despite all of this, the negotiators were unable to agree to anything more than the notion that the European Union 'shall accordingly foster closer institutional relations with the WEU with a view to the possibility of the integration of the WEU into the Union' (Article 17.1 TEU), although whether that would occur, and in what form, would ultimately be a matter for Member States to decide according to their own constitutional requirements. To complicate matters further, the new Treaty left substantially unchanged the other Maastricht provisions on the specific character of individual security policies and Member States' obligations to NATO, and the position of NATO and bilateral co-operation between two or more Member States. In other words, the new Treaty arrangement leaves unresolved the bifurcation at the heart of implementation in this area; the EU is still to avail itself of the 'WEU to elaborate and implement decisions and actions of the Union which have defence implications' (Article 17.3), which basically means that the fifteen still instruct the ten!

FORMULATION, DECISION AND IMPLEMENTATION

On the trinity of formulation, decision and implementation the new Treaty represents a rather mixed bag. While there is an attempt to move from purely inter-governmental decision-making to a system where the political stakes for being awkward are raised, and the onus is on Member States not to obstruct a policy unless they feel enormously strongly that 'important and stated reasons of national policy' are at stake (Article 23.2), it remains a question of political and moral obligation and no more.

Formulation

There is a 'Declaration on the establishment of a policy planning and early warning unit', which is to be established in the General Secretariat of the Council under the responsibility of its Secretary-General, now to be in addition the High Representative for the

Common Foreign and Security Policy. The High Representative heads up a policy planning and early warning unit, the subject of Declaration **6**. The unit is staffed by officials of Member States on secondment, members of the Secretariat-General, of the Commission and of the WEU. Under Article 26 the High Representative, thus assisted, contributes to the formulation, preparation and implementation of policy decisions. The High Representative can even, on his or her own initiative, produce argued policy option papers, which may contain recommendations and strategies for the CFSP (Declaration **6**). This raises awkward questions about the profile of the High Representative – is it to be an individual of ministerial timber, operating under Presidency orders but offering independent inputs, or simply a ranking diplomat, more visibly working under Presidential authority?

The tasks of the new unit are:

(a) monitoring and analysing developments in areas relevant to the CFSP;
(b) providing assessments of the Union's foreign and security policy interests and identifying areas where the CFSP could focus in future;
(c) providing timely assessments and early warning of events or situations which may have significant repercussions for the Union's foreign and security policy, including potential political crises;
(d) producing, at the request of either the Council or the Presidency or on its own initiative, argued policy option papers to be presented under the responsibility of the Presidency as a contribution to policy formulation in the Council, and which may contain analyses, recommendations and strategies for the CFSP.[33]

Member States and the Commission are to assist these processes by 'providing, to the fullest extent possible, relevant information, including confidential information'. This occasioned another Declaration noting the need for the General-Secretariat staff to have security clearance, although the staff involved had earlier attempted to thwart this proposal.

Also reflective of the problems of real solidarity, while the Treaty of Amsterdam equips the Council with a new information resource upon which policy advice will be built, the question arises of whether the Member States whose own services possess and process this information, including military intelligence as well, will share it with the new unit in accordance with para. 5 of Declaration **6**?

There are still affirmations of the need for appropriate measures to be taken to ensure coherence with the external economic and development policies of the Union as a whole by liaison with the Commission, but no detail on how this is to be accomplished, monitored or enforced. Indeed, the provisions on co-operating with the Commission remained as obscure and undefined as ever, although, as in Maastricht, there is a catch-all reference to the Council being responsible for 'the unity, consistency and effectiveness of action by the Union' (Article **13.3** TEU). This is an important issue since the different cultures of political and economic work has meant that the integration of the separate working groups has not been previously carried through to an acceptable or desirable extent. Little progress had been made before 1996–97 in reducing the overlap between various inter-governmental committees and ensuring practical co-operation between institutions.

Decision

There is a new category of decision – on common strategies (Articles **12** and **13** (**2**) TEU). The only characterisation of common strategies, which are decided by the European Council, on a recommendation from the Council (unlike the general guidelines which the European Council defines for itself) is that they are implemented in areas where the Member States have interests in common – which is a pleonasm – although they are to set out their objectives, duration and the means to be used. An early and notable common strategy is the 'Common Strategy of the European Union on Russia of 4 June 1999', of which extracts are reproduced in Box 12.3.

Box 12.3　Extracts from the 'Common Strategy of the European Union on Russia' of 4 June 1999 and European Council Declaration on the Common Strategy on Russia

The European Council
Having regard to the treaty on European Union, in particular Article 13 thereof;
Whereas the Agreement on Partnership and Co-operation (PCA) between the European Communities, their Member States and the Russian Federation entered into force on 1 December 1997, HAS ADOPTED THIS COMMON STRATEGY . . .

PART 1
VISION OF THE EU FOR ITS PARTNERSHIP WITH RUSSIA
A stable, democratic and prosperous Russia, firmly anchored in a united Europe free of dividing lines, is essential to lasting peace on the continent. The issues which the whole continent faces can be resolved only through ever closer co-operation between Russia and the European Union . . .

The European Union has clear strategic goals:

- a stable, open and pluralistic democracy in Russia, governed by the rule of law and underpinning a prosperous market economy benefiting alike all the people of Russia and of the European Union;
- maintaining European stability, promoting global security and responding to the common challenges of the continent through intensified co-operation with Russia.

The European Council therefore adopts this Common Strategy to stengthen the strategic partnership between the Union and Russia at the dawn of a new century.

This Common Strategy sets out the objectives as well as the means to be used by the Union in taking forward this partnership.

For their part, the European Union and its Member States will develop the co-ordination, coherence and complementarity of all aspects of their policy towards Russia.

Box 12.3 (*cont.*)

PRINCIPAL OBJECTIVES
The European Union has identified the following principal objectives:

1. Consolidation of democracy, the rule of law and public institutions in Russia.
2. Integration of Russia into a common European economic and social space.
3. Co-operation to stengthen stability and security in Europe and beyond.
4. Common challenges on the European continent.

Geographical proximity, as well as the deepening of relations and the development of exchanges between the Union and Russia, are leading to growing interdependence in a large number of areas. Only through common responses will it be possible to find solutions to challenges which are more and more often common to both parties.

The environment is the common property of the people of Russia and the European Union.

. . . a common interest in stepping up their co-operation in the fight against common scourges, such as organised crime, money-laundering, illegal trafficking in human beings and drug trafficking. The fight against illegal immigration is also a major preoccupation.

INSTRUMENTS AND MEANS
1. General Provisions
The European Council calls on the Council and the Commission in accordance with the responsibilities defined in Articles 3 and 13 of the Treaty on European Union to ensure the unity, consistency and effectiveness of the Union's actions in implementing this Common Strategy.

The European Union will work to achieve the objectives of this Common Strategy by making appropriate use of all relevant instruments and means available to the Union, the Community, and to the Member States.

4. Implementation and review
The European Council requests the Council:

* to ensure that each incoming Presidency presents to the Council, in the framework of its general programme, a work plan for implementation of this Common Strategy.

PART II
AREAS OF ACTION
The European Union shall focus on the folowing areas of action in implementing this Common Strategy:

Box 12.3 (*cont.*)

1. Consolidation of democracy, the rule of law and public institutions in Russia
   To enhance democracy, institution building and the rule of law in Russia, which is a prerequisite for the development of a market economy, the Union will undertake efforts to:
   (a) Strengthen the rule of law and public institutions
   - by providing support for, and by encouraging the necessary institutional reforms towards a modern and effective administration within Russia's Executive, Legislature and Judiciary at federal, regional and local levels; in particular, by developing the capacity of an independent judiciary, public administration and accountable law enforcement structures through the promotion of contacts between judicial authorities and law enforcement bodies of the EU Member States and Russia.
   (b) Strengthen Civic Society
   - by enhancing contacts between politicians of Russia and the EU, at federal, regional and local levels including with assemblies at all levels.

2. Integration of Russia into a common European economic and social space
   (a) Consolidate the process of economic reform in Russia.
   (b) Support the integration of Russia into a wider area of economic co-operation in Europe.
   (c) Lay the basis for a social market economy.

3. Co-operation to strengthen stability and security in Europe and beyond
   The EU wishes to deepen and widen co-operation with Russia and identify common responses to the security challenges in Europe and beyond through:
   (a) reinforcing political dialogue.
   (b) Russia's place in the European Security Architecture
   - by further developing co-operation with Russia in the new European Security Architecture.
   (c) Preventive diplomacy.

4. Common challenges on the European continent
   The European Union will, in particular, co-operate with Russia in:
   (a) energy and nuclear safety;
   (b) environment and health;
   (c) fight against organised crime, money laundering and illicit traffic in human beings and drugs; judicial co-operation;
   (d) regional and cross-border co-operation and infra-structure.

Box 12.3 (*cont.*)

PART III
SPECIFIC INITIATIVES

- The Council will examine the possibility of creating a permanent EU/Russia mechanism for political security dialogue.
- The Council will consider developing a consultation mechanism, in addition to existing troika expert level talks with Russia.

Dialogue on economic questions
The Union will consider the launching of a specific high-level EU/Russia dialogue to support the development by the Russian Government of measures to promote sustained economic recovery, based on a comprehensive economic programme, endorsed by the IMF, leading to a functioning market economy.

Trade and investment
Fight against organised crime.

- The European Union is proposing to set up a plan focused on common action with Russia to fight organised crime.

The Union proposes to cover, inter alia, the following areas:

- assistance in training for members of the judiciary and law enforcement authorities;
- the development of effective co-operation mechanisms to combat cross-border drugs crime.

The relevance of common strategies is revealed by Article **23**. Although the decision to adopt a common strategy requires unanimity, its implementation can be decided by a qualified majority.

The second case for qualified majority decision, if all agree, is for the implementation of a joint action or common position. However, the Member States remained caught in the tension between, on the one hand, wanting to both speed up the process of decision and enhance the prospect of decision, while wishing to safeguard their own capability to obstruct any proposed decision that they objected to. So the Amsterdam Treaty saw the introduction of a new Article **23** which, while designed to make it politically more difficult for Member States to obstruct the decision-making process, nonetheless offset this by providing them with the facility 'for important and stated reasons' to oppose a majority vote. It reads:

1. Decisions under this Title shall be taken by the Council acting unanimously. Abstentions by members present in person or represented shall not prevent the adoption of such decisions.

    When abstaining in a vote, any member of the Council may qualify its abstention by making a formal declaration under the present subparagraph. In that case, it shall not be obliged to apply the decision, but shall accept that the decision commits the Union. In a spirit of mutual solidarity, the Member State concerned shall refrain from any action likely to conflict with or impede Union action based on that decision and the other member states shall respect its position. If the members of the Council qualifying their abstention in this way represent more than one third of the votes weighted in accordance with Article 205(2) of the TEC, the decision shall not be adopted.

2. By derogation from the provisions of paragraph 1, the Council shall act by qualified majority when adopting joint actions, common positions or taking any other decision on the basis of a common strategy and when adopting any decision implementing a joint action or a common position. If a member of the Council declares that, for important and stated reasons of national policy, it intends to oppose the adoption of a decision to be taken by qualified majority, a vote shall not be taken. The Council may, acting by a qualified majority, request that the matter be referred to the European Council for decision by unanimity.

This paragraph shall not apply to decisions having military or defence implications . . .

This is an attempt to move decision-making some distance away from inter-governmentalism. This can be seen also in the introduction of the rule that where unanimity is required, abstentions do not ruin it (the normal Community rule), although the abstentionists can decide not to apply the decision (not the Community rule). This is the 'constructive abstention' discussed in the IGC, and it is clearly hoped that this solution might induce a Member State not to block the general wish. It is also a new way of attempting to dilute the national veto (although if non-appliers' voting weight exceeds one-third of the total, unanimity is lost). However, the older Brussels members might well recall the original wording of the Luxembourg compromise of 1966. There the key wording was the French delegation's insistence that 'where very important interests are at stake the discussion must be continued until unanimous agreement is reached'. As is well known the invocation of that phrase, or rather even the threat to invoke it, degenerated to being almost routine and helped to bring the Community to Euro-sclerosis between 1966 and 1985, despite numerous attempts to circumvent or limit its application and use. The wording of Article 23 may therefore not be enough to change the reality in day-to-day decision-making. Worse, this is the first of the recorded cases in which the European Council is textually turned into an appeal body from the Council.

Implementation

Again in terms of the coherence of implementation, the veto still looms large both with in the CFSP in general and in the defence and military area in particular. The Presidency retains a central responsibility for implementation, although oddly the phrase used here as in Maastricht is 'for the implementation of common measures' (Article **18**). In this task the Presidency is to be helped by its successor (not the old troika) and 'by the Secretary-General of the Council who shall exercise the function of High Representative for the common foreign and security policy' (Article **18.3**). This is the minimalist solution to the personification of CFSP in the form of a 'Mr and Ms CFSP' that was contemplated, and is indicative of fears that the appointment of an individual by the European Council and receiving instructions from it and the Council would be to raise the profile of this position so that 'Mr or Ms CFSP' might eventually establish a certain independence of view and even authority, as has indeed been the case with certain Presidents of the Commission in the past. The majority of the Member States found this unacceptable. The Secretary-General, High Representative, is to contribute to the 'formulation, preparation and implementation of policy decisions, and, when appropriate, acting on behalf of the Council at the request of the Presidency, through conducting political dialogue with third parties'. The High Representative is clearly to be kept on a short lead. The painfulness of reaching agreement is this area is revealed in the final paragraph of Article **18**. Having equipped itself with a High Representative, the Council can pile Ossian upon Pelion by also having recourse to the alternative – special envoys for special tasks. It might also be observed that the number of cooks responsible for implementing policy continues to grow, and the question arises as to whether this improves the dish or spoils the broth.

In response to the criticism referred to above about the difficulty of distinguishing between joint actions and common position, the Amsterdam Treaty attempted to define them more precisely:

- A joint action is said to 'address specific situations where operational action by the Union is deemed to be required' (Article 14).The Council adopts them.
- Common positions, on the other hand, 'define the approach of the Union to a particular matter of a geographical or thematic nature' (Article 15). The Council adopts them.

It would be comforting to trust that these precisions establish distinctions, just as it will be interesting to observe whether the Member States observe the new Treaty commitment that 'Joint actions shall commit the Member States in the positions they adopt and in the conduct of their activity' and that 'Member States shall ensure that their national policies conform to the common positions'.

Other features

The instability of the troika, on which the Commission commented, is addressed in Article **18**. On a French proposal, which others originally did not favour, the Presidency is assisted by the new office of 'High Representative' doubling as Secretary-General of the Council. The preceding Presidency is dropped from the CFSP troika and the Commissioner responsible for external affairs becomes a supernumerary member.

In the absence of an Executive within the CFSP, the Presidency opens negotiations for bilateral or multilateral agreements (Article **24**). The Presidency could commission the assistance of the High Representative under Article **26**. On the model of the Common Commercial Policy (CCP), the Council concludes them.

Going as far back as the Tindemans Report, and aware of the post-Cold War convulsions in defence industries in the Member States, they will, if they consider it appropriate, co-operate in the field of armaments (Article **17.1**, final subpara).

All non-military expenditure incurred in the application of the CFSP is a charge on the Budget. This entrenches Parliamentary control over the spending, although the EP has no say over the underlying operational decisions. Expenditure arising from operations having military or defence implications is charged to the Member States, other than those who have excluded themselves from the operation concerned (Article **28**).

ASSESSMENT OF THE AMSTERDAM MODIFICATIONS

The new CFSP responds partially to the critics who maintained that the trouble was weak mechanics. It opens up avenues by which the blockage of unanimity can be circumvented. It does not respond to the charge that the root fault is inter-governmentalism. One of the most important innovations for the future of the CFSP, and the EU itself, are the provisions on flexibility. If there is no agreement after due process, each Member State can pursue its own line of policy. Furthermore, there is also the differential memberships of the WEU and the EU with only ten of the latter being in the former, Austria, Denmark, Finland, Ireland and Sweden being 'Observers' in the WEU with no legal or other obligations to collective defence, although they can participate in WEU meetings.

In the summer and autumn of 1994, as noted in Chapter 1, the British, French and Germans all floated different ideas about how to cope with divergences which were apparent in the EU and which would be exacerbated by enlargement. The agreement reached at Amsterdam made provision for enhanced co-operation among Member States which wanted to move further and faster than some of their partners. Provided they satisfy the criteria of Article **11** TEC they may use Community instruments and institutions. But there is also a reserve veto power for any Member State if it has 'important and stated reasons'. The CFSP version of flexibility is in Articles **43** and **44** TEU. It incorporates the veto in subpara. **1h**. At the moment only speculation is possible as to the detailed implications of this innovation in the treaties, but it surely can be observed that it will not contribute to clear articulation of a Union position and it will add another wall between the EC, the EU, all Member States, and some Member States in areas covered currently by the CFSP. As continued evidence of the restrictive approach to these matters, little has been done to enhance the meagre role of the European Parliament and the Court of Justice remains excluded from the area.

The Amsterdam Treaty, in repairing perceived or alleged weaknesses, has dug another pit for the unwary. It was the essence of the Treaty on European Union that cohesion between the economic and the political would be improved by integrating them in the Council support service – the abolition of the separate Political Secretariat of the SEA and the merging of EEC and EPC Working Parties, which the Commission in its sub-mission described as incomplete. The Treaty of Amsterdam in effect musters a new Political Secretariat. Although the High Representative is an ex-officio Secretary General, the new post of Deputy Secretary-General must be more than a glorified Director of Administration, since he or she will head up the Directorates-General work-ing in Pillar I – except the DG for external economic relations, which logically must go with the CFSP. These fissures can be filled in, but at a cost in efficiency.

There is another hazard. The badge of the Secretariat-General, as at present consti-tuted, is that it is the only part of the institutional structures within the Union that does not have its own agenda. It does what it understands the Council wants done. Like the constitutional monarch, it asks only to be informed (in due time, of what is afoot), and to be able to advise and to warn. Can a High Representative display the same subordina-tion or impartiality – or is it in the nature of the office that he or she will negotiate with the Council or its Presidency towards some adopted aim?

The Treaty clarifies to some small extent the nature of the instruments of decision-making available to the CFSP, but the ingenuity shown in facilitating QMV carries the cost of a new and mysterious category: common strategies. Statements, which the CFSP issues at the rate of two a week, remain unmentioned in the Treaty base, including the recondite distinction between those made by the Union and those on behalf of the Union. As the European Parliament's Committee on Foreign Affairs, Security and Defence noted in May 1997 when reporting on the operation of the CFSP:

> the use of joint actions and common positions was confined to isolated matters and the Union did not venture to employ them to chart long-term comprehensive strategies in relations to key world issues.

This was regarded as all the more disappointing since:

> there are so few joint actions and common positions in comparison with the number of declarations, although the former are the real instruments of the CFSP.[34]

Another important aspect of Amsterdam, as demonstrated in the foregoing, is that it failed to resolve many of the key issues that had been identified both before and during the IGC regarding both the EU in general and the CFSP in particular. Just as in 1990–91 many issues were fudged or only tinkered with. This outcome does not bode well for a Union that was offering enlargement negotiations to the Czech Republic, Estonia, Hungary, Poland and Slovenia six months after the conclusion of the IGC in June 1997.

In 1996–97 the EU did not resolve the issues of formulation, decision and implemen-tation and it continued to find it difficult to define policy objectives and implement policy outcomes.

Similarly, the Amsterdam outcome for the functioning of the new European security order could only be regarded as a negative one. Security policy continues to cover all questions of defence, but the right time for common defence becomes the Greek calends, rather than *le moment venu*. WEU remains under Amsterdam the entity with operational capacity, except that it has none unless the Member States assign armed forces to it (and create untried command structures for them). The idea of the Franco-German Corps (to which others have meanwhile acceded) as the nucleus of a Union army has been devalued. The security guarantee is still not in the hands of the Union, but of the signatories of the Brussels and Washington Treaties.[35]

It would be difficult to argue that in the Amsterdam Treaty the Member States of the Union gave to the CFSP a key attribute of statehood – the autonomous ability to exercise the power of self-defence. Equally, it would be difficult to regard Amsterdam's progress in this area, thirty years later, as the 'first step' to political union in terms of the Davignon Report. But, just as had happened in the past in the development of the Community or Union, when it appeared that no substantive progress was being made or was even possible – yet within a short time there were leaps forward – somewhat ironically, before the Amsterdam Treaty was ratified or signed, the whole basis of debate and potential policy in the CFSP, especially in the defence area, changed.

POST-AMSTERDAM CHANGES IN MOMENTUM, PARADIGMS AND POLITICAL WILL

After the divisions and hesitancy in the two IGCs (1990–91 and 1996–97) on Pillar II questions, and before and just after the Amsterdam Treaty finally became operational on 1 May 1999, there were significant developments in the defence field which, by the summer of 1999, suggested that the prospects of providing the EU and the CFSP with an operational military capability had opened up. It was also in the summer of 1999, in June at the Cologne European Council that the Member States finally agreed the appointment of the CFSP 'High Representative'.[36] This was the 56-year-old Spaniard and NATO Secretary-General, Javier Solana Madariaga. Mr Solana had impressed the EU governments (and the USA) with his handling of the Kosovo crisis. The bombing campaign against Yugoslavia had enhanced his profile and reputation, especially in his contribution to maintaining the fragile NATO consensus. Unfortunately, it had taken two years, after the Amsterdam 1997 IGC conclusion, to agree on this nomination, and because of the NATO campaign against Yugoslavia Solana was not able to take up his new appointment for some months. Given the appointment of another senior politician, Chris Patten, as Commissioner for External Relations, including the CFSP, the relationship between the Commission and High Representative will be crucial and could lead to a turf war. The Cologne meeting also announced that Solana's Deputy was to be M. Pierre de Boissieu of France. While Solana's appointment suggests that the 'heavy-weight' school of thinking on the High Representative won the day, it should be noted that, as NATO Secretary-General, Solana was very much the servant of NATO governments, not their master.

The potential revolution in the CFSP post-Amsterdam came in the area of defence, especially in EU–WEU relations and in moves to provide the EU with an operational capability. From mid-1998 to the Cologne European Council in June 1999 significant shifts were underway after years of paralysis or, at best, slow progress. Decisions about ESDI (European Security and Defence Identity) suddenly took on a new dimension. In the spring of 1998, speaking to the French National Assembly, the British Prime Minister, Tony Blair, had called for Britain and France to 'do more together', and for their 'practical co-operation to advance much further and faster'.[37] Subsequently both British and French governments claimed to have ideas in the defence area. In public these ideas came to be aired in press reports that, given non-participation in EMU and Schengen, the British Labour government was looking for an area on which it could exhibit leadership in Europe. Certainly by October 1998 at the informal EU European Council in Pörtschach, Prime Minister Blair presented his colleagues with a paper calling for fresh thinking by Europeans on how to co-operate more closely and effectively on defence; although he explicitly ruled out a standing European armed force or abandoning NATO's primacy. He apparently told colleagues that the EU's foreign policy voice in the world was unacceptably muted and ineffective, especially given its economic weight and strategic interests. He referred explicitly to the Kosovo situation as an example of the need for action, and as an example of where the EU had shown itself hesitant and disunited. He does appear to have broached the possibility of a number of different institutional options, including the full merger of the WEU into the EU, a move that had hithertofore always been strenuously opposed by the British. Immediately after this informal European Council the Austrian Presidency convened the first ever meeting of EU Defence Ministers in Vienna (although it was so informal that neither the *Bulletin of the European Union* nor the *Austrian Foreign Policy Yearbook 1998* refer to it).[38] At that informal meeting the British widened the spectrum of institutional options by adding the strengthening of the WEU.[39] Meanwhile the French had already proposed transforming the WEU into an 'agence' at the disposal of the CFSP.

Speaking in November 1998, Blair called for the EU to be able to 'intervene where necessary'. He went on to repeat traditional elements of British policy:

> This does not mean duplicating NATO, creating a European standing army, or moving away from inter-governmental decision-making

but it did mean:

> First, rapid and comprehensive implementation of the European identity within NATO agreed at Berlin at the beginning of 1996. We need a European decision-making capacity and command structure which can operate rapidly and effectively if necessary. Second, proper decision-making structures in the EU, headed by European Council readiness to take strategic decisions on Europe-only operations. Europe needs genuine military operational capability – not least forces able to react quickly and work together effectively – and genuine political will.

He claimed to have 'no preconceptions' about institutions but that he did want a 'new debate'.[40]

Although the proposals remained somewhat vague, on 3–4 December 1998 the British and French governments agreed at St Malo a 'Joint Declaration on European Defence'.[41] This began by affirming that the EU 'needs to be in a position to play its full role on the international stage', making a reality of the Amsterdam Treaty. Crucially, it went on:

To this end, the Union must have the capacity for autonomous action, backed up by credible military forces, the means to decide to use them, and a readiness to do so, in order to respond to international crises.

Europeans would operate within the 'institutional framework of the European Union (European Council, General Affairs Council and meetings of Defence Ministers)', as well as respecting the NATO and Brussels Treaty and WEU obligations. Having said that, the Declaration identified the need: 'for the European Union to take decisions and approve military action where the Alliance as a whole is not engaged', and that to do so

the Union must be given appropriate structures and a capacity for analysis of situations, sources of intelligence, and a capability for relevant strategic planning, without unnecessary duplication . . . the European Union will also need to have recourse to suitable military means (European capabilities pre-designated within NATO's European pillar or national or multinational European means outside the NATO framework).

In sum,

Europe needs strengthened armed forces that can react rapidly to the new risks, and which are supported by a strong and competitive European defence industry and technology.

In December 1998 the Vienna European Council welcomed the St Malo Declaration and 'the new impetus given to the debate on a common European policy on security and defence'. It acknowledged that

for the European Union to be in a position to play its full role on the international stage, the CFSP must be backed by credible operational capabilities.

It appears that not only the British position was on the move, but so too was that of the 'neutrals', although the Vienna Conclusions included again the phrase that 'the reinforcement of European solidarity must take into account the various positions of European States . . .'. It made clear that these discussions were to be pursued further in the WEU and the EU, with the European Council returning to the matter in Cologne in June 1999, and the Council to bring forward, in agreement with the WEU, arrangements for enhancing co-operation.[42]

By March 1999, not least because of developments in Bosnia and Kosovo and the frustration of the apparent inability to back diplomatic persuasion with credible military threat, Tony Blair returned to the theme that:

Europe's military capabilities are too modest . . . we Europeans need to restructure our defence capabilities so that we can project force, can deploy our troops, ships and planes beyond their home bases and sustain them there, equipped to deal with whatever level of conflict they may face . . .

Be that as it may, he reiterated that

deployment of forces is a decision for Governments. I see no role for the European Parliament or the Court of Justice. Nor will the European Commission have a decision-making role on military matters.[43]

He also again reasserted that 'NATO . . . is an essential component to the Transatlantic Alliance' and that the proposals were not about 'weakening NATO'.

Given the removal of the British obstruction and developments in other fora, in the spring/early summer of 1999 three meetings and an interview opened up new possibilities in the defence–WEU/EU area.

On 23–24 April NATO leaders celebrated the 50th anniversary of the signing of the North Atlantic Treaty on 4 April 1949. Although overshadowed by the Kosovo crisis, NATO Member States paid considerable attention to the recent developments in the area of ESDI. The Washington communiqué welcomed those developments, and by its repeated references to the EU gave the green light to progress and even hinted that in time the EU would be the real US partner in European defence. The EU and NATO were to consult, and specifically the NATO meeting confirmed that the issues to be addressed included:

(a) Assured EU access to NATO planning capabilities able to contribute to military planning for EU-led operations.
(b) The presumption of availability to the EU of pre-identified NATO capabilities and common assets for use in EU-led operations.
(c) Identification of a range of European command options for EU-led operations.
(d) The further development of NATO's defence planning system to incorporate more comprehensively the availability of forces for EU-led operations.[44]

In similar vein, the Alliance's new Strategic Concept reaffirmed support for an ESDI within the Alliance, and noted that progress towards it would require 'close cooperation between NATO, the WEU and, if and when appropriate, the European Union'.[45]

Shortly afterwards a WEU meeting in early May set the ambitious target of the end of 2000 to create a common defence capability. At the same time the new President-designate of the Commission, Romano Prodi, speaking to the BBC,[46] claimed that a common European army was a 'logical next step' in creating a common defence policy, especially after the merging of a number of national defence industries, although he acknowledged that such a development would only come after 'years and years'. He acknowledged, citing neutrality, that some might opt not to join, but that if the EU went ahead with the idea, it would be inevitable that soldiers would be called to fight under a European flag and under a European commander. The alternative, he argued, was to be 'marginalised in the new world history'. Individual states would not be strong enough to prevent that happening to them however strong they currently appeared. Part of his argument was that while the European defence budget was two-thirds that of the USA, the EU's potential forces were only one-tenth of those of the USA.[47] The British, one of his main supporters as President, were embarrassed by these remarks and swiftly rejected these ideas.

All of this, however, paved the way for the Cologne European Council of 3–4 June 1999. The Cologne Council continued the re-thinking on CFSP. In Annex III to the Presidency Conclusions, the European Council re-affirmed its resolve that the 'European Union shall play its full role on the international stage' and determined that to that end, we intend to give the European Union the necessary means and capabilities to assume its responsibilities regarding a common European policy on security and defence.

It was seen as especially important that

the Council should have the ability to take decisions on the full range of conflict prevention and crisis management tasks ... the 'Petersberg tasks',

and to that end it concluded:

the Union must have the capacity for autonomous action, backed up by credible military forces, the means to decide to use them, and a readiness to do so, in order to respond to international crises without prejudice to actions by NATO ... to fully assume its tasks in the field of conflict prevention and crisis management the European Union must have at its disposal the appropriate capabilities and instruments ... We want to develop an effective EU-led crisis management in which NATO members, as well as neutral and non-allied members, of the EU can participate fully and on an equal footing in the EU operations.

Even more far-reaching was the decision to

task the General Affairs Council to prepare the conditions and the measures necessary to achieve these objectives, *including the modalities for the inclusion of those functions of the WEU which will be necessary for the EU to fulfil its new responsibilities in the area of the Petersberg tasks. In this regard, our aim is to take the necessary decisions by the end of the year 2000. In that event, the WEU as an organisation would have completed its purpose.* The different status of Member States with regard to collective defence guarantees will not be affected.[48] (Emphasis added.)

At the same time the European Council endorsed a report prepared by the German Presidency on the strengthening of the common European policy on security and defence, which *inter alia*, spoke of the ability of the European Council being able to 'take decisions on the whole range of political, economic and military instruments at its disposal when responding to crisis situations.'[49] The agreed Presidency document said that to do this might require:

* regular (ad hoc) meetings of the General Affairs Council, as appropriate including Defence Ministers;
* a permanent body in Brussels (Political and Security Committee) consisting of representatives with political/military expertise;
* an EU Military Committee consisting of Military Representatives making recommendations to the Political and Security Committee.

To achieve all this in the military field the Presidency document spoke of the need for forces with deployability, sustainability, interoperability, flexibility and mobility. It also noted that some operations might be EU-led using NATO assets, and others EU-led without recourse to NATO assets. In the former case, it was argued, it would be advantageous to pre-identify national or multinational European means.

Following this, the WEU and the EU agreed 'Arrangements for Enhanced Co-operation between the European Union and the Western European Union under the Protocol on Article 17 of the Treaty on European Union',[50] over twenty pages of detail on the modalities of co-operation. The headings included:

A. Improving the coordination of EU/WEU consultation and decision-making processes, in particular in crisis situations . . .
B. Holding of joint meetings of the relevant bodies of the two organisations . . .
C. Harmonisation, as much as possible, of the sequence of the Presidencies of WEU and the EU, as well as the administrative rules and practices of the two organisations . . .
D. Close co-ordination of the work of the staff of the Secretariat-General of the WEU and the General Secretariat of the Council of the EU . . .
E. Allowing the relevant bodies of the EU, including its Policy Planning and Early Warning Unit, to draw on the resources of the WEU's Military Staff, Satellite Centre and Institute of Security Studies . . .
F. Co-operation in the field of armaments, as appropriate . . .
G. Ensuring co-operation with the European Commission . . .
H. Security arrangements . . .

and there were six Annexes.

These developments perhaps do deserve the epitaph 'revolutionary', although as is often the case in EU policy developments, and as has been historically true in this area, caution needs to be exercised until the promised developments actually occur.

WHY THE CHANGE?

Nonetheless, it is striking that, after all of the procrastination, 1998–99 suddenly saw new momentum, a sea change in mindsets and new political will in this area. No single event or explanation can fully explain the reason for this, rather a number of factors seem to have come into play:

- There is little doubt that, since it came into office in 1993, the Clinton Administration in the USA had taken a more positive attitude to the principle of ESDI. It had already accepted that NATO assets *could* be made available to European members of NATO and the WEU.
- The change of government in the United Kingdom made it easier to reopen certain questions, and it was certainly keen to take a more proactive, even leadership, role in the EU. The self-imposed exclusion from the EMU and Schengen seem to have played a part in the government looking for an issue on which it could take a lead. Given British history, its major role in NATO, the size and capability of its forces, and the importance of the defence industry sector, defence was an appealing area.

- The French, too, had shifted position since 1990–91, as events in the Gulf war and subsequently in Yugoslavia, demonstrated to them that Europeans still needed NATO for some things.
- There were the continuing industrial and economic pressures on defence budgets, with consequent effects on projected force and equipment capabilities for individual states.
- The failure of Europeans to fulfil their self-identified destiny in the Balkans rankled, and the intransigence of Slobodan Milosevic, President of Yugoslavia and Serbia, over Kosovo, which culminated in the NATO military action of 1999. EU leaders seem to have concluded that diplomacy without a credible military threat or capability, in some situations, was fundamentally weakened.

Finally, for some there is little doubt that the EMU project seemed to have been successfully brought to fruition in January 1999, and the CFSP was perceived as the next big project. Like EMU, for some, its political overtones were as, if not more, important than the specifics proposed or discussed.

The year 2000 is nearly fifty years after the abortive European Defence Community was launched. In 1952 the EDC Treaty was signed but in 1954 not ratified. Clearly, after the Cologne decisions the landscape had changed, but there remained much to be done to transform the decisions in principle into reality.

CHAPTER 13

THE REFORMED VERSION OF CO-OPERATION IN JUSTICE AND HOME AFFAIRS

THE THREE PILLARS

IT WAS at one time customary to depict the Union in the metaphor of the three pillars. The first pillar was the European Community, which worked by using the 'Community Method'. The third pillar was Co-operation on Justice and Home Affairs, what Ministers of Justice and the Interior do, and was inter-governmental. Whereas the second pillar, the Common Foreign and Security Policy, was built up in public view, the foundations of the third pillar were obscured. The Amsterdam Treaty took up the criticism that third pillar inter-governmentalism was not working and built something like a lattice out of the first and third pillars. The new Treaty does not make a dusky area of the Union any easier to understand or perhaps to apply.

Amsterdam amendments

The embattled negotiators and their wordsmith draftsmen were faced with the combined sensitivity and seriousness of the issues: party political controversy at home, mounting crime, including drug traffic and abuse, the Treaty objective of free movement of people (a gift to the international criminal), public attitudes of xenophobia and racism, the deluge of applications for political asylum, long-held traditions governing the extradition of citizens, civil rights restrictions on the divulgence of police files, and Member States' unwillingness to abandon their veto rights or to submit to EP and ECJ control.

The unpublicised beginnings

Apart from free circulation of people as a Treaty objective since the beginning (Part One, Principles, Article 3c EC) the original Treaty was silent on justice and home affairs. But as problems magnified, the

Member States used their gatherings to set up informal co-operation. In 1975, acting on a British proposal, they created the TREVI group.[51] Its initial focus was to co-ordinate police action against terrorism. Its remit was extended to other forms of criminal activity, especially illegal drug trafficking and other organised crime. It concentrated on practical measures of police co-operation and worked in secret.

In 1986, again on a British suggestion, the Member States came together in the Working Group on Immigration (WGI). This was a response to an increase and projected further increase in the numbers of would-be immigrants. They included a rising number of applicants for political asylum, some of whom were not driven by a fear of persecution but by the search for a better economic future. The WGI was to address matters such as visa requirements, false documentation, 'refugees in orbit' – that is, presenting multiple applications – obligations of carriers not to bring in illegals and the question of the abolition or massive streamlining of immigration controls at the frontiers of Member States, including their airports. This bore on the parallel task of the Community's 1992 programme for a single market, in which all internal frontier controls would be abolished.

The British government seems to have envisaged that the WGI would be managed, on the TREVI model, by rotating presidencies. It was soon agreed, however, that the Council Secretariat would act. It had some experience on the Community side of the negotiations for a common format passport and of the blue 'Quintin'[52] roadside panels that the continental Member States began to erect as the only surviving sign of their frontiers. Unlike TREVI, the Commission participated in the WGI and in the meetings of Ministers of Justice and Home Affairs to whom it reported.

THE CO-ORDINATORS OF FREE MOVEMENT OF PEOPLE: THE PALMA DOCUMENT

By 1988 the gap between the lifting of frontier controls on goods and the continuing control of people was so stark that the Member States decided to create a new inter-governmental body: the co-ordinators of free movement of people. Like the WGI, it consisted of officials from Interior/Justice Ministries. There was some decent ambiguity about whether they were co-ordinating domestically or between the different parts of the Community/inter-governmental structures. The Commission – which was usually regarded, with the Council Presidency, as ensuring co-ordination – participated. Under the Spanish Presidency of 1989 the Co-ordinators adjourned for a weekend to Majorca and there produced an inventory of all the barriers to the free movement of people. This, in honour of the Mayor who addressed them, was called the 'Palma Document'. It became the basis of a programme for eliminating these obstacles. Whether the idea of doing for people what the 1992 programme was doing for goods and services is sound is at least debatable. The Palma Document tended to give undue prominence to trivial matters alongside the big issues. (What happens to legal alien residents of Member States? If there are no passports at frontiers, must there be identity cards and a police right to demand them of passers-by? Do airports have to be reconfigured to distinguish citizens of Community countries from others arriving on long-distance flights?) The Council Secretariat provided its committee services.

Customs co-operation

Customs authorities in the Member States had created their own liaison group to exchange information about contraband, drug trafficking and other criminal acts in the field of imports and exports. They met privately in the Mutual Assistance Group; Council staff were not involved.

The fight against drugs

In 1989, the French President, M. Mitterrand, launched CELAD, an action plan to fight against drug abuse. (One of his predecessors, M. Pompidou, had given his name to an anti-drug programme in the Council of Europe.) This brought another group into being, likewise serviced by the Council Secretariat. It interested itself among other things in diversion of 'precursors' used in the manufacture of narcotics and in the money-laundering of the profits of drug dealing. Action switched to the Community, which adopted legislation on both.[53]

Ministers of Justice meeting outside, but 'in the framework of' the Council

Ministers of Justice had begun meeting, in due course, annually to discuss judicial co-operation. They met under two different insignia. As Ministers of Justice they discussed matters which were deemed to have no direct connection with the Community. As 'Ministers of Justice meeting in the framework of the Council' they discussed and adopted Conventions under Article 293 (ex-220) which refers to 'the simplification of formalities governing the reciprocal recognition and enforcement of the judgements of courts or tribunals and of arbitration awards'. Not wanting to be seen as an organ of the Community, even when their starting point was a Treaty article, Justice Ministers entrusted their administrative support to the Political Secretariat which at the time worked for European Political Co-operation, the forerunner of the Common Foreign and Security Policy. It was not then part of the Council Secretariat.

Schengen

All the foregoing bodies were attended by representatives of all the Member States, some also by the Commission, and were more or less distantly connected with the Community. They remained aloof from the ECJ and the EP. But another closely related body decided to act completely outside the Community.

They had foreseen that the Community was a lost cause as far as their interests were concerned. In the negotiations leading to the Single European Act an orthodox new Article 14 (ex-7a) had been included. It was a legal basis for the Single Market programme, 'in which the free movement of goods, persons, services and capital is ensured in accordance with the provisions of this Treaty'. While the government of Mrs Thatcher was a strong proponent of the single market in goods, services and capital, it drew the line at the free movement of persons, despite the sense of Article 18 (ex-8a). In the speech that she delivered at the College of Europe in September 1988, Mrs Thatcher reiterated:

> Of course we must make it easier for our people to travel throughout the Community. But it is plain common sense that we cannot abolish our frontier controls if we are also to protect our citizens and stop the movement of drugs, of terrorists, of illegal immigrants.[54]

Under British pressure the single market articles of the SEA were qualified by a Declaration that they did not

> affect the right of Member States to take such measures as they consider necessary for the purposes of controlling immigration from third countries, and to combat terrorism, crime, the traffic in drugs and illegal trading in works of art and antiques.[55]

The Member States with common land frontiers could draw their own conclusion as regards future progress. The members of the Benelux Economic Union already had open frontiers towards each other. Germany and France decided to join with them by concluding in June 1985 the Schengen Agreement, to abolish 'gradually' the control of persons at their frontier crossings, consistently with, but independently of, the EC treaties, and to facilitate transport and the circulation of goods. They were subsequently joined at different dates by Denmark, Greece, Spain, Italy, Austria, Portugal, Finland and Sweden. Norway and Iceland, which belonged to the Nordic Passport Union with the Scandinavian members of the Community, became associates. Britain was not prepared to suppress its entry controls. Ireland is in a passport-free travel area with Britain, which it would have had to break to join Schengen, as it would have wished. The founding members of the Schengen Agreement described it as a 'laboratory' in which the problems of the free circulation of people would be addressed and resolved, becoming a model for the whole Community. The agreement covered such matters as the treatment of applications for asylum, a common visa, the free circulation of foreigners who had regularly crossed the external frontier, police co-operation, including 'hot pursuit' across frontiers, hotel fiches to be completed by foreigners, extradition, the carriage of arms and the smuggling of drugs, and the Schengen Information System (SIS) for the exchange of police information, with data protection rights.

The Secretariat was provided by the Benelux infrastructure.

THE TREATY ON EUROPEAN UNION

At the meeting of the European Council in Rome in December 1990, where scenarios for the forthcoming Inter-governmental Conference for Treaty revision were given their final touches, it was stated:

It should also be considered whether and how activities currently conducted in an inter-governmental framework could be brought into the ambit of the Union, such as certain key areas of home affairs and justice, namely immigration, visas, asylum and the fight against drugs and organised crime.

This was a German initiative. Germany was deeply concerned at the sharp increase in applications for asylum and other pressures of immigrant traffic. Eighty per cent of all applications for political asylum were addressed to France or Germany (see Box 13.1).

Box 13.1   Applications for political asylum: Community of 12, including double counting

1988	169,663
1989	208,136
1990	327,903

In 1991 there were estimated to be 900,000 claimants in Germany, at an annual cost to public funds of £2.5 billion.[56] In Britain in July 1998 there were said to be 50,000 cost-ing local authorities at least £500,000 p.a.

With the breakdown of political structures in the countries of the former Soviet bloc there came a sharp increase in gangland crime and apprehension that illicit trade in radioactive materials might be on the point of breaking out.

The Rome instruction was not for the replacement of informal inter-governmentalism by the extension of the reach of the Community. It was to consider how to bring Justice and Home affairs into the Union. The Treaty on European Union did so by building the third pillar.

Pillar III

It did this by gathering together the separate activities other than the Schengen Agreement and placing them in new Title VI, consisting of nine (now thirteen) articles prefixed by the letter **K**, now numbered **29** to **42** in the consolidated version of the Treaty on European Union.[57] It listed nine areas of common interest and authorised the Commission and the Member States to take initiatives for measures on six of them, with the initiative reserved to the Member States on three (Article **K**3: judicial co-operation on criminal matters, customs co-operation and

police co-operation for the purposes of preventing and combating terrorism, unlawful drug trafficking and other serious forms of international crime, including if necessary certain forms of customs co-operation, in connection with the organisation of a Union-wide system for exchanging information within a European Police Office (Europol).

There were to be common positions, joint actions and conventions (some of the latter would be inherited from the Co-ordinators). The Co-ordinators Group, authors of the

Palma Document, was converted into a Co-ordinating Committee under K4 (from which it took its colloquial name). The Commission was to be 'fully associated' with the work. The European Parliament was to be 'regularly informed', consulted by the Presidency on the principal aspects of Justice and Home activities and could ask Questions. Conventions established under this title may provide that the ECJ shall have jurisdiction to interpret them and to rule on any disputes regarding their application. The title was not to impede closer co-operation between two or more Member States (read Schengen).

The first sign of a possible future deviation from inter-governmentalism is Article **K8**, which provides that by unanimity the Council can decide to transfer the six activities in which the Member States share the right of initiative with the Commission to a reception article in Pillar I, the European Community. This was old Article 100c, concerning third countries whose nationals need a visa to cross the external borders of the Member States. (The Working Group on Immigration had toiled to produce common lists of countries whose nationals would need a visa, would not need a visa or could need a visa if the Member State to be visited so decided.)

Because of delay in the application of the TEU, the new Co-operation on Justice and Home Affairs (CJHA) got off to a poor start. Even so, its achievement was meagre by the time renewed treaty review came round. The Reflexion Group appointed to prepare the ground for the IGC reported:

> [the Group] has concluded unanimously that the magnitude of the challenges is not matched by the results achieved so far in response to them.[58]

But there was no agreement on the nature of reform. The CJHA had little to its credit. None of the Conventions it had discussed endlessly, going back to the days of informal inter-governmentalism, had come into force.[59] The only joint action was a modest enough German proposal to facilitate journeys by school parties.[60] There were numerous resolutions, a sure sign that agreement could not be reached on a stronger formulation.

The subordinate bodies and the Council had struggled with the Dublin Convention on responsibility for considering asylum applications. It had been negotiated and signed but did not come into effect until September 1997. Unfortunately it muddied the hitherto pure water of the doctrine that an application for asylum should be considered in the first safe Union Member State in which the applicant turns up. In conjunction with the Schengen relaxation of controls at internal frontiers, applicants could move on and even make their way to a non-Schengen country, in this case Britain. This began to cause mutual incriminations in the spring of 1998 when immigrants began to arrive in Britain with the alleged assistance of the Belgian immigration gendarmerie.

CONVENTIONS AND BLOCKAGES

The Convention on the Crossing of External Frontiers, put forward by the French Presidency in the autumn of 1989, cleared all its pre-ratification hurdles except the dispute between Spain and Britain over control at Gibraltar's frontier with Spain.

Europol

The Convention on the establishment of the European Police Office (Europol) is the 1991 version of an earlier German proposal that there should be a 'European FBI'. The choice of model was unfortunate if not inappropriate, since there is no federal jurisdiction in Europe and federal is a word best avoided in debate. It was also unlikely that the Member States would tolerate an independent police force operating on their territories. The shortened name, Europol, is also unfortunate insofar as it recalls Interpol, with HQ in Lyon, an organisation purely among police authorities, with no ostensible governmental involvement.

In the convention, which was finally ratified in June 1998, Europol has no operational responsibilities. By maintaining computerised records which can be consulted under tightly prescribed conditions, it is to facilitate exchanges of information and possibly to analyse intelligence. Serious problems arose over the maintenance of data and the protection of civil rights. There were also problems of judicial and parliamentary control.[61] In anticipation of the resolution of all the issues at stake and taking account of the specific mention of drug trafficking in Article K.1.9, TREVI ministers decided in September 1992 to make a start with a Europol Drugs Unit (EDU). The European Council meeting in Brussels in December 1993 decided, in the package deal for the apportionment of the seats of different Union bodies, that Europol should be based in The Hague, which is where the EDU opened its doors. It operated therefore without a charter and on the basis of an inter-governmental ministerial decision. The Member States seconded personnel.

The Decision states that :

'The Unit is to act as a non-operational team for the exchange and analysis of intelligence in relation to illicit drug trafficking, the criminal organisations involved and associated money laundering activities affecting two or more member states.'

In December 1994 the European Council added to the mandate: 'the fight against illegal trade in radioactive and nuclear materials, crimes involving illegal immigration networks, vehicle trafficking and associated money-laundering operations'. This effectively covered the whole of the terrain marked out for Europol proper.[62]

The final compromise which cleared the way to ratification of the Europol Convention gave Member States the option of permitting legal disputes on Europol operations to go to the European Court of Justice.

Drugs

Separately, in 1993, there was agreement to set up the European Monitoring Centre for Drugs and Drug Addiction, with its seat in Lisbon (EMCDDA). It was charged with the task of gathering information on, as a priority, the demand for drugs and the reduction of demand, as well as national and Community strategies, international co-operation on reducing supply, the controls over the drugs trade in Community acts and in international agreements, and the implications for producer, consumer and transit countries.[63]

DRASTIC REFORM AT AMSTERDAM

Starting from the rare show of unanimity in the Reflexion Group's Report to the effect that the CJHA was not meeting the challenge, the negotiators of the Treaty of Amsterdam drastically changed the balance of what had been the third pillar. For the first time in the history of the Community/Union,[64] they transferred what had been inter-governmental to the classical Community. In Title IV in the new numbering they placed Visas (already in old Article 100c), immigration and other policies related to the free movement of persons. New Article 62 installs the Commission-Council system for the crossing of external borders (ex-Convention material). Article 63 does the same for asylum, apparently aiming to replace the operative Dublin Convention. Article 65 covers measures in the field of judicial co-operation, previously raw material for convention treatment. For five years from the date of entry of the new Treaty into force there is an unconventional transitional regime in which the initiative is shared between the Member States and the Commission, decisions are unanimous and the EP is merely consulted. This was incorporated at the insistence of Germany, commonly regarded as one of the more federalist and EP-friendly of the Member States. It was the breathing space that the Chancellor thought he needed to carry the Länder, which have important law and order functions. After five years, the Council is to decide by unanimity for which parts of the Title the legislative procedure becomes in all respects co-decision.[65]

The Amsterdam Treaty goes much further and creates a tangled web of new *acquis* by the incorporation of all that is Schengen. It issues a blank cheque of Schengen *acquis* (said to cover 3,000 pages described in headline terms in a four-paragraph annex to a protocol). The Schengen Agreement thus becomes an example of the new *flexibility scheme* (Title VII) by virtue of which groups of Member States that want to enhance their co-operation can do so, and may use the Council's mechanisms and facilities for the purpose. In particular, the Council is charged with deciding which parts of the Schengen *acquis* find a legal basis in the Treaty establishing the European Community (as outlined above) and which have their basis in the Treaty on European Union, both as amended.

The odd men out

Denmark, although a signatory of the Schengen Agreement, declined to abandon the inter-governmental character of its provisions. It is free to enact Schengen provisions autonomously if it wishes to do so.

Britain and Ireland do not take part in the adoption of any of the measures of Title IV, Articles 61 to 68 (new numbering) and are not bound by such measures. But Britain and Ireland may, on request, take part in the adoption and application of a measure; or may adopt a measure after it has been adopted by the participating countries. The incoming Labour government hailed as a victory the part of the Protocol on Article 7a (see above for Mrs Thatcher's troubles in this area) which states that the UK can maintain its border controls. It was an easy enough victory. The present authors possess letters dated

11 March and 16 September 1996 from the Commissioner responsible for the internal market, Professor Monti, which affirm and reaffirm that 'such controls are not a violation of Community law in force'. If the matter had ever come before the ECJ, then that is the position which the Commission would have defended, however reluctantly.

It appears that there was a slip-up in the final flurried stages of the meeting of Heads of State and Government that approved the draft of the Treaty of Amsterdam. Britain and Ireland may at any time request to take part in some or all of the provisions of the Schengen *acquis* (Protocol integrating the Schengen *acquis* into the framework of the European Union, Article 4). To be accepted, the request needs the unanimous agreement of the Council. British ministers questioned whether this was what the meeting had agreed to, apparently proposed by Spain (Gibraltar again), but not to the point of reopening the text, which therefore stands. Early in 1999 the UK government announced that it wished to co-operate in selected parts of the Schengen provisions, namely those parts that did not impinge upon its right to maintain internal border controls.

The new and slimmer third pillar

The Consolidated Version of the Treaty on European Union contains a slimmed down third pillar, with the new designation *'Provisions on police and judicial co-operation in criminal matters'*. It concerns notably the work of Europol. It also sets forth inter-governmental procedures for the adoption of common positions; of framework decisions for the approximation of laws and regulations of Member States; of decisions which are binding but do not have direct effect; and of conventions (all in Article **34**). Article **35** admits the Court of Justice into the Title, where a Member State declares that it will accept the Court's jurisdiction. But the Court may not review the operations of the law and order authorities of the Member States (Article **35**).

The Treaty of Amsterdam changes the legal instruments, which give effect to third pillar policies (Article **34**). It renames joint positions 'common positions' and joint actions 'common actions'. It retains conventions, but innovates by introducing European Parliament consultation on them. It further innovates with:

(a) *Framework decisions* – 'For the purpose of approximation of the laws and regulations of the Member States; framework decisions shall be binding upon the Member States as to the result to be achieved but shall leave to the national authorities the choice of form and methods.' They are to decided upon unanimously by Council, may result from an initiative by either a Member State or the Commission, and involve consultation with the European Parliament.

(b) *Decisions for any other purpose* – These 'shall be binding' but 'shall not entail direct effect'. Again, the European Parliament is to be consulted. These decisions are to implemented by 'measures' decided by QMV (Qualified Majority Vote), although in this case the majority is to be '62 votes in favour, cast by at least 10 members'.

Organisation of work

Since November 1993, work on CJHA has been divided into three sections: asylum/migration, police/customs co-operation and judicial co-operation. In each section there are three or four working groups, meeting monthly. The Steering Committees, which were formerly interposed between the WGs and the K4 Committee, have been allowed to lapse (see Figure 13.1).

Asylum/migration

It took years to bring into force the Dublin Convention, which determines which Member State examines an asylum request when the same request has been presented in several. There is a blockage on the adoption of the July 1991 Convention on external borders control. It overlaps with the Schengen Agreement.

Police and customs co-operation

The big achievement is the final ratification of the Europol Convention in June 1998. The European Drugs Unit, belonging to Europol, has been active since 1994.

Figure 13.1   Organisation of Pillar III

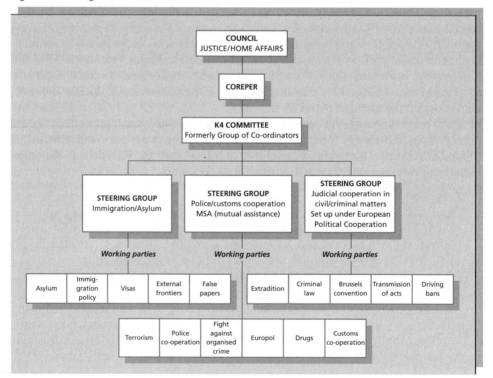

In 1996 a Joint Action was decided in regard to the approximation of anti-drug laws and practices in Member States, along with Resolutions on drug tourism, illicit cultivation and production of drugs and sentencing for serious drug trafficking.

In 1997 a Joint Action was decided concerning information exchange, risk assessment and the control of new synthetic drugs. Also in 1997 there were Joint Actions on the trafficking of human beings and the sexual exploitation of children, the lawful interception of telecommunications and hooliganism.

The fight against organised crime

The Action Plan on organised crime seeks to combat organised crime by stepped-up police co-operation controlled by judicial co-operation. It includes prevention measures, the improvement of legal instruments, the development of Europol capabilities and tightening money laundering. There is also a Joint Action on making it a criminal offence to participate in a criminal organisation in a Member State of the EU. Although symptomatic of hesitations in this area, this was only formally adopted after the Austrian Presidency reminded Member States of its importance.

Assessment

It defies belief that in a Union that has proclaimed the simplification of its procedures and its legislation, the Amsterdam mosaic of old inter-governmentalism, old Community and new 'flexible' Community can survive. But it was so hardly won that there will be reluctance to open it up again for a long time ahead unless there is no alternative. The Member States' hand might be forced by the predictable flow of litigation on the articles concerned, the measures taken under them and the effects on the citizens of the Union. When the time comes, and unless moods and minds have changed unrecognisably, the only possible direction of movement is towards further 'communitisation'.

Some Conventions adopted by the CJHA between 1990 and 1998 are listed in Box 13.2.

Rather like Pillar II, the CHJA is still evolving. It has changed since its inception and is a rare case of some areas of policy being moved from an inter-governmental pillar to the Community pillar. However, unlike the new momentum in regard to Pillar II, Pillar III continues to move at a slow pace. It also faces substantial hurdles in the context of enlargement, since there will be a continuing tension between the Single Market imperatives of free movement and the concerns about the porous nature of the Eastern borders of some of the applicant states. In addition, there is concern about their ability (even political willingness) to patrol their borders effectively. There has been some speculation that Pillar III may be an area where some new Member States do not immediately have to accept the whole *acquis* or that *flexibility* might be invoked or that the transition periods negotiated in the accession process will be very long.

Box 13.2   Conventions adopted by the CJHA and its forebears (excluding confidential conventions on police co-operation)

Convention signed on 15 June 1990, in Dublin, *concerning the determination of the State responsible for the examination of an asylum request in one of the Member States of the European Communities.* OJ No. C 254, 19.8.97.

Convention of 26 July 1995 *on the establishment of a European Police Office.* OJ C 316, 27.11.1995.

Convention *on the protection of the European Communities' financial interests.* OJ C 316, 27.11.95.

Convention of 26 May 1997 *on the fight against corruption involving officials of the European Communities or officials of Member States of the European Union.*

Convention of 26 July 1995 *on the use of information technology for Customs purposes*: OJ C 316 of 27.11.95.

Convention of 18 December 1997 on *mutual assistance and cooperation between customs adminstrations,* J C 24, 23.1.98 (colloquially 'Naples 2' replacing the 'Naples Convention' signed in Rome in 1967).

Convention of 26 May 1997 *on the service in the Member States of the European Union of judicial and extrajudicial documents in civil or commercial matters,* OJ C 261, 27.8.97.

Convention *on jurisdiction and enforcement of judgements in civil and commercial matters,* 16.9.1988 (the 'Lugano Convention' to which non-Member States can accede).

Convention of 10 March 1995 *on Simplified extradition procedures between the Member States of the European Union,* OJ No. 78, 30.3.95.

Convention of 27 September 1996 *relating to extradition between the Member States of the European Union,* OJ C 313, 23.10.96.

Convention between the Member States of the European Communities *on the transfer of proceedings in criminal matters,* 6 November 1990.

Convention beweeen the Member States of the European Communities *on the enforcement of foreign criminal sentences,* 13.11.91.

Convention on *Driving disqualification (withdrawal or suspension of licences): political agreement* May 1998.

Convention *on the mutual recognition of divorce: political agreement,* June 1998.

L LEGAL BASES

CFSP

- Consolidated version of the TEU, Title V, Articles 11 to 28 (ex-Articles J.1 to J.18). *NB*: This equivalence relates to the TEU as amended by the Treaty of Amsterdam, not to the Articles numbered J.1 to J.11 in the original TEU.
- Article 301 TEC (ex-228a) is a bridge between Pillars I and II.
- Protocol on Article 17 (ex-J.7 17). [This provides that the EU and WEU will draw up arrangements for enhanced co-operation within a year from the entry into force of the new Treaty.]
- OJ L 153/2, 19.6.1999 – Arrangements for Enhanced Co-operation between the European Union and the Western European Union under Protocol 17 of the Treaty on European Union.

CJHA

- Title VI, Articles 29 to 42.
- Title IV, Articles 61 to 69, incorporating: Schengen Agreement of 14 June 1985 concerning the gradual elimination of common frontier controls; and the Convention on the Application of the Schengen Agreement of 19 June 1990.

D DISCUSSION QUESTIONS

CFSP

1. 'This chapter of the Treaty marks a further step in the achievement of the ambition of the Brussels authorities to create out of the European Union a single European political entity, embracing among other things what are normally the attributes of a state – the conduct of relations with the rest of the world and provision for the defence of its territories and interests.' Lord Beloff in the *European Journal* (Sept./Oct. 1997). Discuss.
2. 'We do not believe that the formation of foreign or security policy would be improved by the use of majority voting.' House of Lords, Select Committee on the European Communities, the 1996 Inter-governmental Conference, para. 271. Discuss.
3. Define political union.
4. What are the arguments against the straightforward proposition to integrate all external relations in one Treaty Title?
5. In the light of Bosnia, Kosovo, French nuclear tests and Iraq after the Gulf War, can it be meaningfully said that the Member States are practising foreign policy co-operation or a common policy?
6. Why is movement towards a genuine common defence policy or common defence so difficult?

CJHA

1. Since Britain cannot be said to be an island so far as rail and air transport are concerned, what reasons does it have for remaining outside the Schengen Convention and its incorporation into the Treaty of Amsterdam?
2. Does the CJHA suggest that inter-governmentalism does not work?
3. Europol does not have an operational role. Is this a fatal weakness?
4. It has largely escaped notice that under Article 65 (new numbering) judicial co-operation in civil matters is transferred to Pillar I – although still provided for in Article 293 (ex-220). Has the significance of this move from inter-governmentalism been underestimated?
5. Can enlargement and free movement be reconciled?

 ## BIBLIOGRAPHY

CFSP

Cahen, A.: *The Western European Union and Nato*, Atlantic Council of the United States, 1990.

Monar, J.: 'The Finances of the Union's Intergovernmental Pillars', *Journal of Common Market Studies*, Vol. 35, No. 1, March 1997.

de la Serre, F. and Lequesne, C. (eds): *Quelle Union pour quelle Europe?* Editions Complexe, Paris, 1998.

De Ruy I.: *European Political Cooperation*, Atlantic Council of the United States, 1989.

Federal Trust Round Table: *Security of the Union*, 1995.

Fraser, M.: *Sink or Swim Together*, European Movement, 1996.

Gordon, P.: 'Europe's Uncommon Foreign Policy', *International Security*, Vol. 22, No. 3 (1997/9).

Hill, C. (ed.): *The Actors in Europe's Foreign Policy*, Routledge, 1996.

Holland, M. (ed.): *Common Foreign and Security Policy: The Record and Reform*, Pinter, 1997.

House of Lords: *Scrutiny of the Inter-governmental Pillars of the European Union*, HL Paper 124, Session 1992–93, 28th Report.

Nuttall, S.: *European Political Cooperation*, Clarendon Press, 1992.

Peterson, J. and Sjursen, H. (eds): *A Common Foreign Policy for Europe?* Routledge, 1998.

Salmon, T.C.: *Crisis or Opportunity?* Centre for European Studies, University of Hull, 1995.

Westlake, M.: *The European Union beyond Amsterdam*, Routledge, 1998.

WEU Secretariat General: *WEU Today*, Brussels, 1998.

Whitman, R.G.: *From Civilian Power to Superpower?* Macmillan, 1998.

CJHA

Anderson, M. and Den Boer, M. (eds): *Policing the European Union*, Clarendon Press, 1995.

Barrett, G.: *Justice Co-operation in the European Union*, Institute of European Affairs, Dublin, 1997.

Benyon J. *et al.: Police Co-operation in Europe: An Investigation,* Centre for the Study of Public Order, 1995.

Bieber, R. and Monar, J.: *Justice and Home Affairs in the European Community,* European University Press and College of Europe, 1995.

Delmas-Marty, M. (ed.): *What Kind of Criminal Policy for Europe?,* Kluwer Law International, 1996.

Duff, A.: *Reforming the European Union,* Sweet & Maxwell, 1997.

European Commission: *The European Union in Action against Drugs,* 1987.

European Commission: *The European Union and the Fight against Drugs,* 1997.

European Parliament: *Report on the Enquiry on Racism and Xenophobia,* 1991.

European Policy Centre: *Making Sense of the Amsterdam Treaty,* Brussels 1997.

Schermers, H. (ed.): *Free Movement of Persons in Europe,* Martinus Nijhoff, 1993.

Weidenfeld, W. and Wessels, W. (eds): *Europe from A to Z,* OOP, 1997, also on CD ROM.

 NOTES

1. The French acronym is PESC, in German GASP.
2. See Chapter 1.
3. Quoted in Salmon and Nicoll, *Building European Union,* MUP, 1997, p. 59.
4. Ralph Dahrendorf, 'A New Goal for Europe' in Michael Hodge's *European Integration,* Penguin, 1972, pp. 74–88.
5. Quoted in P. Gerbet, *La construction de L'Europe,* Imprimerie nationale, Paris, 1983, p. 275.
6. See Chapter 2 and relevant documents in Salmon and Nicoll, op. cit., pp. 80–4.
7. See Chapter 2.
8. 'It is not yet clear what this expression implies', Court of Justice Report on European Union, *Bulletin of the European Communities,* Supplement 9/75, OOP, p. 17.
9. Report by the Foreign Ministers of the Member States on the Problems of Political Unification, *Bulletin of the European Communities,* 11–1970, pp. 9–14.
10. The meeting has passed into history: the ministers of the Organisation of Petroleum Exporting Countries (OPEC) turned up uninvited, demanding dialogue; the French Foreign Minister, Jobert, refused to discuss Community affairs and EPC in the same place and the parallel Foreign Ministers' meeting had to repair to Brussels for the afternoon.
11. Now upgraded technically to CORTESY.
12. Henry Kissinger, *Years of Upheaval,* Little Brown, 1982, Chapter 5.
13. During the preceding Danish Presidency, French Foreign Minister Jobert had insisted on EPC being discussed in Copenhagen and Community work in Brussels on the same day.
14. European Union, a report by Mr Leo Tindemans, *Bulletin of the European Communities,* Supplement 1/76, OOP.
15. European Council, 21st meeting, London, 26–27 November 1981.
16. In French texts both 'joint' and 'common' are rendered as 'commune'.
17. Dail Debates 1978, Vol. 306, Cols 365–7.

18. Declaration on the Middle East issued by Venice meeting of the Heads of State or Government, 12–13 June 1980, *Bulletin of the European Communities*, 6–1980, pp. 10–11.
19. Sunday Times Insight Team, *The Falklands War*, Andre Deutsch, 1982, pp. 117–86.
20. The 'tree' proposal was that the basic institutional structure of the new Union should be based on the 'trunk' of the system with branches off for special areas like the CFSP.
21. Report on progress on implementing the common foreign and security policy (January to December 1997), European Parliament.
22. The obligations are binding in international law, but not Community law. The Member States are obligated by the principle: 'Every treaty in force is binding upon the parties to it and must be performed by them in good faith' (Vienna Convention on the Law of Treaties).
23. For a full account of the early mechanics of CFSP, see D. Galloway in M. Westlake (ed.), *The Council of the European Union*, Cartermill Publishing, 1995, Chapter IX.
24. See Trevor C. Salmon, 'Testing times for European Political Co-operation', *International Affairs*, Vol. 69, 1992, pp. 233–53.
25. Commentators used to say erroneously that the Brussels Treaty expired in 1998. The true position is that signatories can denounce the Treaty after 1998.
26. See W. Nicoll and R. Schoenberg (ed.) *Europe 2000*, Whurr Publishers, 1996, part 2, Introduction.
27. The institutional reports were published separately in various formats. They are conveniently brought together in the European Parliament's White Paper on the *1996 Inter-governmental Conference*, Vol. 1, Directorate-General for Research, Political Series W-18, 1996.
28. Western European Union Council of Ministers Bonn, 19 June 1992.
29. Article V of the 1954 amended Brussels Treaty of 1948, gives an automatic commitment to military help if one of the signatories is attacked.
30. Cloos, Reinsch, Vignes and Weyland, *Le Traité de Maastricht*, Bruyland, Brussels, 1993, p. 471.
31. F. Laursen and S. Vanhoonacker, *The Intergovernmental Conference on Political Union*, European Institute of Public Administration, Maastricht, 1992, p. 333.
32. The Irish Presidency's 'A General Outline for a Draft Revision of the Treaties' presented to the Dublin European Council in December 1996 carried the interesting 'comment': 'It has been proposed that Article J.1(2) be amended to include a reference to safeguarding the territorial integrity of the Union and the inviolability of its external borders. While this proposal remains under consideration, the Presidency suggests that the formulation . . . take account of the various concerns expressed.'
33. Declaration 11: Declaration on the Establishment of a Policy Planning and Early Warning Unit.
34. Report on progress in implementing the common foreign and security policy (January to December 1996), Committee on Foreign Affairs, Security and Defence Policy, Rapporteur: (Mr Tom Spencer, 28 May 1997, EP A4-0193/97. A report a year later suggested little had improved.
35. See note 26 above.
36. Cologne European Council, Presidency Conclusions, 3–4 June 1999, *Bulletin of the European Union*, 6–1999, pp. 7–37.
37. FCO Press release, 24 March 1998.

38. See *Austrian Foreign Policy Yearbook 1998*, Report of the Austrian Federal Ministry for Foreign Affairs, Federal Ministry for Foreign Affairs, Vienna, n/d, pp. 1–4 and 18–21.

39. See WEU: *Institute for Security Studies*, Newsletter 25 (February 1999) p. 1 for a brief overview of these developments.

40. FCO Press release. Speech by the Prime Minister, Mr Tony Blair, to the North Atlantic Assembly, Edinburgh, 13 November 1998.

41. FCO Press release, 4 December 1998.

42. *Bulletin of the European Union*, 12–1998, p. 16.

43. FCO Press release, 10 March 1999, Speech by the Prime Minister, Tony Blair, to NATO 50th Anniversary Conference, Royal United Services Institute, 8 March 1999.

44. NATO Press release, NAC-S(99)64, 24 March 1999.

45. NATO Press release, NAC-S(99)65, 24 March 1999.

46. Interview on the BBC's 'On the Record', 9 May 1999.

47. In 1998, defence expenditure in million euros for NATO Europe was 163,999 (2.2% of GDP); North America, 260,857 (3.2% of GDP); and the strengths of the armed forces were, respectively 2,858,000 and 1,579,000.

48. Cologne European Council Declaration on Strengthening the Common European Policy on Security and Defence, *Bulletin of the European Union*, 6–1999, pp. 7–37.

49. Presidency Report on Strengthening of the common European policy on security and defence, http://www/ue.eu.int/newsroom.

50. OJ L153/2, 19.6.1999.

51. The source of the title is the subject of different explanations. One is that they first met near the fountain in Rome. Another is that an early chairman was Dutch, called Fontane. A third is that it is an acronym for Terror, Revolution and Violence.

52. From the name of the Council official, deceased, who produced sucessive drafts of the Recommendation to this effect.

53. Precursors: Regulation EEC/3677/90 and Directive 92/109, EEC, Money-laundering: Directive 91/308/EEC.

54. Quoted in *Building European Union*, Salmon and Nicoll, MUP, 1997, p. 213. Mrs Thatcher drew on a recent incident in which a 'brave' Customs officer had intercepted a wanted terrorist at a frontier crossing between Germany and the Netherlands.

55. In her memoirs, Margaret Thatcher complains that she accepted this Declaration in good faith and felt betrayed when later it was argued against her that the Declaration had no legal value and could not be invoked to justify British border controls. In fact she knew from her experience of the Community and its legal system that a declaration cannot change the effect of a Treaty Article. See *The Downing Street Years*, Margaret Thatcher, Harper Collins, 1993, p. 556. For the discussion see 'Note the Hour and File the Minute', W. Nicoll, *Journal of Common Market Studies*, Vol. 31, No. 4, December, 1993, pp. 561ff.

56. Which Germany wanted to become a charge on the Community or shared with the other less solicited Member States. There is an indirect reference to this aim in Article 63,2h.

57. OJ C 340, 10.11.97, pp. 162–8.

58. Quoted in *Europe 2000*, W. Nicoll and R. Schoenberg, Whurr Publishers, 1996, p. 146.

59. For discussion see *The Treaty of Amsterdam*, Andrew Duff, Federal Trust, 1997, p. 19.

60. Decision 94/795/JHA OJ L327, 19.12.1994.

61. For an authoritative view, see Europol, House of Lords, Paper 51–1, Session 1994–95, 10th Report.

62. The European Council's dictum was made into a joint action by a Decision under Article K in December 1995. According to the British Home Secretary of the day, Rt Hon Michael Howard, neither the ministerial decision, nor the joint action are legally binding international instruments (House of Lords, op. cit., p. 12). Curiously, joint actions adopted in the CFSP, Pillar II, are binding in international law – although not readily enforceable.

63. For an account of the anti-drugs programmes, see *The European Union in Action Against Drugs*, OOP, 1997 (European Commission Secretariat General/DGX).

64. For an analysis of the organisational trends of Member State collaborative activities outside the framework of the Community, see 'La communauté en pénombre', W. Nicoll, *Revue du marche commun*, Paris, No. 311, November 1987, pp. 617ff.

65. Except for the list of states whose nationals need a visa, which from entry into force preserves the rule of old Article 100c, qualified majority vote and consultation of the EP. Similarly for the uniform format of the visa. Likewise, the Treaty already stipulates in Article 67.4 that the procedures for issuing visas and the rules on uniform visas pass to co-decision after the five-year period.

THE ATTITUDES OF THE MEMBER STATES AND APPLICANT STATES TO THE ISSUES OF EUROPEAN INTEGRATION, AND THE QUESTION OF ENLARGEMENT

THE ORIGINAL SIX

AS IS evident from other chapters, there have been and continue to be a number of important debates about the nature and shape of European integration, with some Member States wishing to proceed more quickly to deeper integration than others. In the 1990s these debates were sharpened and focused by the IGCs on Economic and Monetary Union and Political Union in 1990–91, which culminated in the Treaty on European Union, and the IGC of 1996–97 on the reform of the European Union, which culminated in the Treaty of Amsterdam of 1997.[1]

All fifteen Member States joined the Community or Union for their own reasons and in their own perceived interests. Some joined later than others: Denmark, Ireland and the UK in 1973, Greece in 1981, Portugal and Spain in 1986, and Austria, Finland and Sweden in 1995. Others are expected to follow early in the century. In many cases, but not all, the different interests, concerns and circumstances that affected the original decisions are still of some relevance today, and had some influence on policy positions in the Inter-governmental Conferences, as well as in the domestic debates about ratification of the Maastricht and Amsterdam Treaties.

While this chapter will examine the attitudes of Member States in order of their accession to the Community or Union, this is not to imply that those acceding at any one point shared an identity of interests. Among the original Six, for example, there have been and are significant divergences of outlook about the future shape of the Union, its domain and scope, and the destination of the enterprise. Of those joining in 1973, Ireland has been much more 'communautaire', largely it could be argued because it has been a clear net financial beneficiary, and has seen Community membership as a vehicle for escaping suffocating British influence. Both the Danes and the British have retained much of the original reserve, which characterised their attitudes as non-members, and remain more wedded to an inter-governmental approach. Greece provides an example of a state that joined 'late', and which with successive changes of government and transfers of resources via Community subsidies, has moved from agnosticism to selective belief.

Portugal and Spain, while generally having a similar outlook, have differed over whether there is a need to reduce the power of Brussels, which Portugal would like to see, and over a Community role in defence, which Portugal would prefer not to see. The different geo-political positions and histories of Finland and Sweden, as contrasted with Austria, have led to different approaches between them on issues such as the future of the CFSP, espe-cially defence, while Sweden has decided not to participate in the first wave of EMU.

Given such differences, any negotiation over the future of the Union was, and is bound to be, difficult. It is worth recalling that the original negotiations over the future were not trouble free: the EDC Treaty was de-railed by France in August 1954 and the negotiations before the Treaty of Rome founding the EEC nearly floundered. There was argument about the extent of centralised power in the context of how to reconcile French hesitations with the belief that it was necessary to go beyond the unanimity rule, which prevailed in other organisations. Differences over agriculture meant that the final text only states gen-eral objectives to be attained by the end of the transitional period, leaving the details to be worked out by the new Community itself. A difficult issue during the negotiations in 1956–57 was the relationship between the Six and their overseas territories, that is, former colonies. This was only resolved at the last minute by a Heads of State/Government meet-ing, and only then, because the French were able to argue that without a satisfactory arrangement there was little prospect of ratification. It is perhaps also worth recalling that Norway signed Treaties of Accession in January 1972 and June 1994, only to have to with-draw following referendums, in which the voters refused to endorse those acts.

The previous difficulties are especially relevant, perhaps given the traumas of the 1992 ratification process. In addition to the traditional attitudes and interests of the Member States, the 1990s debates took place against a background of recession and apparent public disaffection from the European Community and with national govern-ments apparently unable to turn the economic tide. In 1991–92 and then in 1996–98 the Community and Union appeared remote and irrelevant to many people, fearful of unemployment, and the debates about EMU did not seem timely to those current con-cerns. Given the civil war in Yugoslavia, the problems of inaction over Kosovo and the recognition of the potential for more troubles in Eastern Europe, many in Western Europe lacked confidence in the future and were fearful also of a wave of apparently uncontrolled immigration. Nationalism began to appear to be respectable.

One ought not, therefore, to fall into the trap of seeing an inexorable uniform pattern of progress towards some clearly defined predetermined goal. In fact, the record of both the Community and the Union might be better characterised as one of 'stop–go'. In the 1990s the question became rather whether it was to be 'two steps backward one step forward'.

THE BENELUX STATES

These three states had in some respects been the precursors of the EEC. Their govern-ments in exile in London agreed in 1944 to create a customs union after the war, elimi-nating all customs barriers between them and introducing a uniform tariff for imports.

This agreement came into effect in January 1948, and had the effect of demonstrating to those involved that they could profitably co-operate at the economic and political level. Nonetheless, this was not to be an end in itself, and the states concerned were interested in co-operation in a wider field, at least partly because they had direct experience of war on their territories. In keeping with these twin motivations of peace and trade, these states played a vital part in the *relance européenne* when on 20 May 1955 they jointly proposed to the other members of the ECSC the creation of a European atomic energy organisation and a customs union, with trade, agriculture, energy and transport under the guidance of a common authority. The Benelux memorandum played an important role at Messina and subsequent events, and the Belgian Foreign Minister, Paul Henri Spaak, chaired the committee, which drew up the draft treaties. It is noteworthy too that Belgium was the first Member State to make concrete proposals for an IGC on political union in 1990.

Belgium has had a generally uncritical view of integration for most of the post-war period. One observer has noted that: 'Being at the crossroads of Latin and German cultures, Belgium needs agreement and peace more than anyone else.' Europe provides a meeting point for most of the innumerable Belgian parties and for the two sides of the Flemish/Walloon divide. Moreover, as a free trade nation by tradition and by conviction, Belgium sees her relationship with Europe as a 'marriage of love and reason'.[2]

Much the same applies to the traditional position of Luxembourg. Geography, heavy dependence on external trade and small size all contributed to a positive attitude to integration. These factors held true for the Dutch too, but while supportive in general, they perhaps have not always been quite so enthusiastic, partly because there has been throughout the post-war period a rather stronger 'Atlanticist' element in their policy and a belief in the necessity for NATO and the American presence. They had, for example, reservations about the European Defence Community proposal.[3]

On most of the major issues in the 1990s the three states held broadly similar positions. They all favoured the movement to a single currency and were among the initial participants in economic and monetary union. Belgium had some difficulty in fully meeting the convergence criteria. Its problem related to the existence of an excessive debt burden, but the Belgian government was able to argue that the deficit was being reduced substantially and that the trend was in the right direction – this argument was accepted by the Commission and Belgium's partners. In the cases of both Luxembourg and the Netherlands there was a technical question about the conformity of national legislation with the requirements relating to the independence of their Central Banks, but this was regarded as being in hand and not an obstacle.

The three all favour the 'federal goal', which they regard as an essential element of European development. In a joint memorandum in March 1996[4] they emphasised their commitment to the irreversibility of integration, although they did acknowledge that in the new environment of the times they would accept differentiated integration, that is, that not all would proceed at the same speed to do everything. The Belgian government, in a memorandum to the Belgian parliament, openly stated that it saw flexibility as a way of avoiding future vetoes,[5] and while the Dutch government had reservations about it in principle, they argued that enlargement made some degree of differentiation inevitable, although they took the view that this related to a multi-speed approach to the same objectives.[6] All three were insistent that certain criteria would have to be fulfilled in order to maintain the integrity of the Union – the criteria they suggested were broadly reflected in the Amsterdam Treaty.[7] While all three supported subsidiarity, not surprisingly the Belgian government laid most stress upon it, noting that it considered subsidiarity 'to be an essential principle' for relations between 'the European Union, Belgium as a federal Member State and the Belgian Communities and Regions'.[8] However, it was nervous about what might be made of the principle, and argued that it was essentially about good administration, relating to efficiency, need and proximity; not a vehicle for the erosion of the Community *acquis*. It supported federal moves partly because of a lack of a strong national identity and its own internal 'Federalisation process'.[9] For Luxembourg, federalism was a mechanism for defence of its autonomy, reflecting the belief that the Union helped to protect the small against the powerful, a view shared by the Netherlands. At root, they all preferred an emphasis on and commitment to the 'Community method' over inter-governmentalism.

All three had supported the creation of a common foreign and security policy, although in 1990–91 the Netherlands was sensitive about the inclusion of defence as a Community competence stressing that any move should be compatible with NATO developments and role. The Dutch continued to emphasise NATO rather more than the other two. In the 1996–97 discussions they all supported the development of a Union defence policy, the integration of the WEU into the CFSP pillar and the incorporation of the Petersberg tasks into the CFSP. The three were originally and remained against the separation of the CFSP and the European Community's external economic role, and in 1996–97 again pushed for coherence and a single institutional framework. To this end they supported a greater role for the Commission in certain aspects of the CFSP, especially where joint actions needed to be implemented at ground level or where they were closely bound up with Pillar I, that is, European Community activities. They were all concerned with the need to improve CFSP decision mechanisms and capability, and offered a variety of proposals, with Luxembourg, for example, proposing the principle of 'unanimity minus one', which would allow a Member State to disassociate itself from a joint action without preventing it.[10] There was support too for an early warning and planning unit, which they wished to see building links between Member States, the Commission and the WEU.

Belgium and the Netherlands have been enthusiastic advocates of reducing the 'democratic deficit' and of greater powers for the European Parliament. Luxembourg has been more cautious, since it only has six MEPs out of the 626, but it too has accepted the arguments for the extension of co-decision. and the reduction of procedures in the European Parliament to: opinion, assent and co-decision. The three states have continued to be concerned at any possible erosion of the Commission's right of initiative, which they regarded as another defence for the small. They have placed great emphasis upon its role as the motor of integration, and wished its powers to be strengthened, especially with regard to the implementation of policies. They have supported moves towards one Commissioner from each Member State. There was strong support too for more Qualified Majority Voting (QMV), although their specific proposals varied in detail. The Dutch made clear that unanimity should continue for sensitive issues such as taxation, own resource issues (that is, budgetary contributions), and decisions of a constitutional nature. Luxembourg made a point of stressing its commitment to the existing system of rotating presidencies, making it clear that it would not accept any deviations from that principle. Given their concerns to protect both the interests of the small and the accumulated *acquis*, all three opposed any reduction in the powers of the European Court of Justice, favouring instead extending its role to the third pillar, Justice and Home Affairs.

Their support for integration and the 'Community method' over inter-governmentalism was further evidenced by their support for transferring aspects of Pillar III to the competence of the European Community. These aspects included all matters relating to freedom of movement and immigration, and envisaging the possibility of some voting. All were mindful of the problems in Pillar III, with the Dutch submitting a separate memorandum on the issues, containing a detailed critique of its operation and 'meagre results'. A particularly interesting joint proposal was that in the third pillar the Union should borrow from the first pillar the notion of Directives, which bind the Member States to the objective to be achieved but allow leeway on precisely how that objective is brought about.[11]

In 1990–91 all three had tended to favour the expansion of Community competencies into new policy areas. Belgium was most keen, especially on social policy, a real industrial policy and measures designed to show that the Community was more than a capitalist club. The Netherlands was wary of the potential costs. By 1996–97, rather than new areas of competence, the issue was regarded more as one of deepening and strengthening integration across the board, with the Belgians, for example, pushing for the creation of a common social core, and series of so-called flanking policies to strengthen the operation of the single market and the position of individuals within it.[12] Luxembourg argued that the 'social dimension' must be regarded as equally important as the Union's other major objectives. Most attention, however, centred on the issues of employment, economic revival and greater competitiveness. One area that was proposed for inclusion in the competence of the Union was that any new treaty should include specific reference to the protection of human rights, indeed they were among the states that argued for the incorporation of sanctions and even the suspension of certain membership rights if states breached these obligations – an argument that ultimately found expression in the Treaty of Amsterdam.

As can be seen, the basic position of these states was not very dissimilar on the major issues, although there were differences of emphasis and tactics. The evolution of public attitudes to European Union membership can be seen in Figure 14.1.

Figure 14.1   Belgian support for the European Union, 1981–98

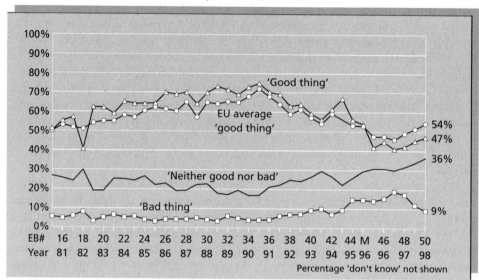

Source: European Commission, Eurobarometer, Public Opinion in the European Union, Report Number 50, 25th Anniversary: Eurobarometer Survey, Directorate-General for Information, Communication, Culture, Audiovisual, European Commission, March 1999, p. 22. [Hereafter Eurobarometer No. 50.]

Figure 14.2   Dutch support for the European Union, 1981–98

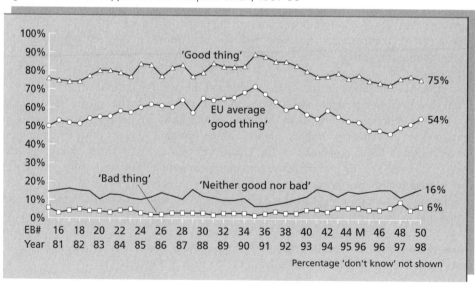

Source: Eurobarometer No. 50, p. 30.

410

Figure 14.3   Luxembourg support for the European Union, 1981–98

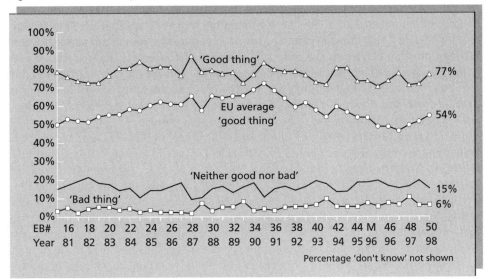

Source: Eurobarometer No. 50, p. 31.

FRANCE

If the Benelux states have some claim to be precursors of the European Community, France may rightly claim a large responsibility for its origin and original nature, particularly through the seminal initiative and endeavour of Jean Monnet and Robert Schuman. Like the Benelux states, France has a central geographical role in Europe having land borders with five other Union states and having been brought psychologically closer to the United Kingdom by the opening of the Channel Tunnel. It too has had first hand experience of war, especially of defeat and occupation, given the traumas of 1870, 1914–18 and 1939–45, especially 1940. Its geographical position and history have placed its relations with Germany, divided or united, at the centre of French concerns in the post-war period. This traditional concern was given a new dimension with the events of 1989 in Europe and the unification of Germany on 3 October 1990, one consequence of which was French support for EMU in the TEU negotiations and France's robust domestic economic policies in the period to 1998 to ensure the successful launch of EMU in 1999.

It was the concern with Germany that played a significant role in the impetus behind the ECSC, with fears of renascent German heavy industry. Four years later fears about rearming Germans played a key role in the French Assembly rejection of the EDC. But under the influence of Monnet and others, in the late 1940s and 1950s it was perceived that France needed to tie Germany into a political, security and economic relationship with France and other West European states, a perception reinforced by the looming Soviet threat.

411

Because of the EDC débâcle, France lost the lead on European matters to the Benelux states in the mid-1950s, but signed the Treaty of Rome in 1957. By this time a number of apprehensions about the Community were very apparent in France: fears over sovereignty and French national identity being lost to supranationalism; fears of German growing economic and industrial power; and concern at the underlying economic philosophy of the Treaty of Rome. Against these, however, were the memories of blood and war, and the high priority accorded to peace and stability, as well as the desire to see Europe as a distinctive entity. It might also be argued that the French have long felt that their true vocation was to be *a* or *the* European power.

Just a year after the signing of the treaties of Rome, de Gaulle came to power in France and dominated French policy for a decade. De Gaulle wanted France to be at the centre of Western Europe, but his vision was of a Europe that extended from the Atlantic to the Urals, a freer, less bipolar, wider and more genuine Europe. De Gaulle's Europe might be summarised as a Europe of independent states, independent of the United States, dominated in foreign policy by France, and open to Eastern Europe. His view of the future of the Community system was encapsulated in the Fouchet proposals for an inter-governmental political union, in which decisions would be made through a Council of Heads of State or Government on political, economic, cultural and security matters.

The key concern was that there be no surrender of national sovereignty. As de Gaulle put it in a press conference of 9 September 1965, 'nothing of any importance either in the initial planning or the later operation of the Common Market' should be decided except by the national governments. Otherwise the Member States would lose their national identities, and 'be ruled by some sort of technocratic body of elders, stateless and responsible to no one'.[13] These elements came together in the decision in 1966 to withdraw from NATO's integrated military structure, and the EEC French 'empty chair' crisis and boycott of July 1965 to January 1966 (see Chapter 2 above).

De Gaulle's immediate successors, Pompidou and Giscard d'Estaing, paid some lip service to Gaullist rhetoric, but followed very different policies in practice. One immediate difference under Pompidou, was the outcome of The Hague summit in December 1969 which opened the way for enlargement, paved the way for the development of common policies and reaffirmed the state's political commitment. Giscard d'Estaing also contributed positively to European integration in his role in the development of the European Monetary System with Helmut Schmidt of the Federal Republic and Roy Jenkins of the Commission.

Collaboration on EMS has not been the only example of Franco-German leadership in the Community. In 1981 French policy towards the Community entered a new phase with the election of François Mitterrand as President of France. This proved to be especially significant as Helmut Kohl became Chancellor of Germany in 1982, and for the next decade or so they enjoyed good personal and political relations, which led to a number of joint Franco-German proposals and memoranda to their partners in 1990–91 on the questions raised by the IGCs. In the mid-1990s, as Mitterrand's second seven-year mandate drew to a close, voter disillusion with his government grew and the European policies which the government upheld were not sufficiently explained. Furthermore, European integration seemed to some of the population, already worried by the perception of excessive immigration, to threaten to denature France. The idea that foreigners might vote in French municipal and European elections went hard in a country where, since 1789, sovereignty had belonged to the people. By the start of the substantive phases of the 1996–97 IGC, Mitterrand was dead, having been succeeded by Jacques Chirac, a Gaullist, in May 1995. Although there were more Franco-German joint memoranda,[14] these did not have the influence of those at the beginning of the decade, and on some key issues, such as whether the new European Central Bank was to be truly independent or not, the two states had sharply divergent views, a divergence which caused major difficulties in the summer of 1998. The French position was further complicated when in May–June 1997, on the eve of the Amsterdam meeting, Chirac's allies lost parliamentary elections in France, with the result that France re-entered a period of cohabitation, but on this occasion with a Gaullist President and a socialist government led by Lionel Jospin.

France has supported the movement to the single currency and economic and monetary union, and wished it to take place sooner rather than later. France's commitment in this area is evidenced by the economic policy it has followed since the early 1990s. Despite unemployment levels running consistently at 12% and growing public disaffection from both the government and European integration – factors that Chirac made much of in his election campaign – after a brief hesitation, he continued the policy of deflation. This was required in order to reduce the growing public deficit and to ensure that France met the Maastricht convergence criteria. The level of public debt continued to be a problem in the run up to the key decisions in the summer of 1998 on which states fulfilled the Maastricht criteria. France was able to persuade its partners that the trend was in the right direction, the deficit reducing from 5.8% of GDP in 1994 to 3% in 1997 with predictions of further reductions in 1998, although many inside and outside France were concerned that these figures were the result of some rather creative accounting and special one-off measures taken by the French government.[15] These difficulties were compounded by the French government's determination to push through structural reform of the French economy, partly for reasons associated with EMU, but partly because it believed they were long overdue. Fundamentally, French political leaders were determined to make EMU a success and to ensure that it came into operation on time. For France the political significance of EMU was probably more important than its economic implications. It was first and foremost a political endeavour and an instrument of political unity, and was, in essence, a revival of the Monnet 1950 strategy towards Germany, given the anxieties raised by German unification and potential in the 1990s and beyond. In addition, for France, a single currency had the added attraction of strengthening the Union *vis-à-vis* the USA and providing a counter-balance to the power of the USA and the US dollar.

Despite this strong commitment to EMU, France also believed that there should be political control of economic and financial policies. In 1990–91 it had opposed the idea of an independent European Central Bank (ECB) on the Bundesbank model. Fearful that the newly united Germany might as an economic giant dominate Europe and the proposed EMU, France argued that EMU had to be complemented by further political integration, and that the ECB must be under some political influence, if not control. They maintained this position after Maastricht despite the Treaty on European Union making the independence of the Bank clear and a matter of treaty, and it was a position shared by both Gaullists and socialists. In May 1998 there was a major crisis when the European Council came to consider the appointment of the first President of the ECB. President Chirac had for months pushed the claims of Jean-Claude Trichet, chairman of the Bank of France and architect of French monetary policy in the 1990s. President Chirac's purpose, however, was not one of personality or nationality, but rather a belief that such key economic decisions as the ECB would take needed to be responsive to political influence and judgement. The new Prime Minister, Jospin, argued strongly that there had to be a balance between a focus on monetary stability and concern for growth and employment. This became an issue in the decision on the appointment of the first ECB President. This became a fractious affair, with discussions dragging on and on, as the Germans and others continued to support the candidature of Wim Duisenberg of the Netherlands' central bank, a candidate whom it was believed would ensure the independence of the ECB. In a messy compromise, Duisenberg was appointed but stated his intention to step down before the end of his eight-year term. EU leaders came to an understanding that he would be succeeded, for an eight-year term, by a French nominee. The French made clear that this would be Trichet, clearly illustrating their continued belief that proper attention had to be paid to other factors beside price stability.

On the eve of the 1990–91 IGC, Mitterrand stressed to France's partners that the Union must have a 'federal finality',[16] but France did not mean quite the same thing as others in this phrase. Indeed, Mitterrand, at other times, was more inclined towards 'confederation'. It was the French who initially conceived of the idea of the pillar structure or temple approach to European Union, an approach reflected in the Treaty on European Union, but throughout the 1990s the perceived need to contain a unified Germany pushed the French to favouring deeper political integration. France remained committed to the original basic principles underlying integration, especially the notion that the enterprise had a political rationale and objective – the ending to war – and in the 1990s argued against any dilution towards an *à la carte* Europe, or movement towards a 'Single Market Plus' Europe, that is, a European Union which was almost exclusively concerned with economic issues. However, given the prospect of enlargement and the difficulties, even in a Union, of twelve, they came round to the view that some form of differentiated integration might be necessary or desirable. Although French ideas on what form this should take varied and the German and French views were not identical, by December 1995 President Chirac and Chancellor Kohl were able to write a joint letter to the President of the European Council, in which having stated their belief that all Member States should proceed together, they acknowledged that the reality had to be faced where one Member State might have temporary difficulties or reasons for not proceeding, and therefore the new treaty should contain a clause allowing the willing and able to develop closer co-operation.[17] Alain Jupé spoke to the French National Assembly in March 1996, of more restrictive, yet flexible circle of those nations, i.e. a small number of states, around France and Germany, which are ready and willing to go farther and quicker than others on matters such as currency and defence,[18] although such arrangements were not to undermine the overall unifying framework of the Union. The French envisaged potentially smaller numbers in some of the flexible circles than the Germans.

For a generation, France has not been keen on anything that presupposed its losing its leading role in Europe or its sovereignty. France was thus keen on inter-governmentalism. It had initially advocated the structures proposed for a CFSP and Justice and Home Affairs and in an internal document setting out its guidelines for the 1996–97 IGC emphasised the need to retain the distinctions between Pillars II and III, and the stress upon inter-govermentalism within them, although they seemed to accept that asylum and immigration would be brought into the Community sphere, as envisaged in the TEU.[19]

France had been strong advocates of a CFSP in 1990–91, especially in the context of a strong European security and defence identity firmly anchored within the new European Union, with the emphasis upon a 'European European' defence and an autonomous European security and defence identity (see Chapter 12). By 1996–97 the external environment had changed again, and in particular the French had observed that they had been rather marginalised in the Gulf because of their semi-detached relationship with NATO, that the European Community and European Union respectively had been ineffective in regard to the dissolution of Yugoslavia and the subsequent train of events, and that NATO and the Americans had largely won the arguments over the European security architecture. Therefore, this issue did not have the same salience for the French in the mid-1990s as it had earlier, indeed in December 1995 France announced it would rejoin parts of NATO's integrated military structure, and created an expectation that it might completely rejoin. In addition, they were pleased with the movement to the Combined Joint Task Force (CJTF), which would allow the WEU to use NATO, especially US, assets in operations that were deemed to be primarily of European interest. On defence, therefore, in the 1996–97 IGC France advocated developing the WEUs operational capabilities, in the context of a CJTF, the inclusion of the WEU Petersberg tasks into the remit of the CFSP, developing the WEU as an element in both the defence of the European Union and a means of strengthening the European pillar of NATO and reforming NATO from within, as well as the gradual integration of the WEU into the European Union. With the Germans, the French were willing to see some movement in the way decisions were made, especially by observing the distinction to the veto for matters of principle and qualified majority voting or constructive abstention in implementation, although it was to be clear that on defence questions no state could be made to act against its own wishes.[20]

France remained opposed to any increases in the power of the European Parliament or Commission; indeed, it would have preferred limiting the power of both. It was a strong advocate of the strengthening of both the Council and the European Council, itself a French creation. It argued that the Council should become more of a prime mover in making proposals and that the Presidency should last for a longer term to improve continuity. It argued both for more majority voting and the right of states to be able to invoke, where necessary, the existence of a national interest, which would justify postponing a vote and, in effect, allow the continuation of the Luxembourg compromise. More effort in any case should be made to take account of population size in votes. An interesting aspect of the French case in 1990–91 was the idea that the European Parliament should be matched by a Senate or Diet. The French idea involved the Diet, comprising MEPs and members of national parliaments having supremacy over the European Parliament and setting legislative guidelines for the Community. This had little support and was not pressed hard, but the idea did not go away. It was somewhat modified by 1996–97, adding to the idea of the creation of a second Chamber of National Parliaments the notion of 'High Parliamentary Council', to be consulted on all matters relating to subsidiarity, since by definition national parliaments were best able to judge such matters. This new body it was suggested could be created by institutionalising the existing Conference of European Affairs Committee (COSAC), which brings together six members from each of the national parliament's European Affairs committees and six MEPs. In general, France wished to maintain the prevailing institutional balance, or at least to prevent any significant shift to the centre.

On the other hand, France had been willing to see movement into new policy areas during the Maastricht negotiations. In an early joint letter in December 1990 Mitterrand and Chancellor Kohl proposed that the competencies of the Union be 'deepened and enlarged, particularly concerning the environment, health, social policy, energy, research and technology, consumer protection'.[21] As with other states, this was not such an issue in 1996–97, although the new Jospin government was concerned, as noted above, that there should be flanking policies to complement both the Single Market and EMU and to demonstrate greater awareness of the social dimension.

However, as France moved to being a net contributor to the Community budget, it also began to be cautious about some of the new policy proposals. For example, when early in 1992 the Commission produced the Delors II package on proposed future funding of the Union's activities for a five-year period, and which reflected a new emphasis upon distributive policies such as the Structural Funds and a new Cohesion Fund to help the poorest states, France argued that the plan should be scaled down.

A quixotic feature of the French debate in the 1990s was the referendum on 20 September 1991 on the question: 'Do you approve the law presented to the French people by the President of the Republic authorising ratification of the Treaty on European Union?' This was constitutionally unnecessary, since the necessary three-fifths majority of a 'congress' of the combined National Assembly and Senate had approved the treaty on 23 June 1991. But Mitterrand, largely for domestic political reasons – namely to boost his flagging popularity and to embarrass his divided opponents – decided to appeal to the people. He also hoped to demonstrate French commitment to the European ideal after the blow it had received from the Danes in June 1992. However, it very nearly ended the Maastricht process, given that the final outcome was 51.04% 'Yes' to 48.95% 'No' on a 69.7% turnout.

The main opposition was led by Philippe Séguin and Charles Pasqua of the Gaullist Rassemblement pour la République, although the party leadership supported a 'Yes' vote.

Arguments against related to the view that a 'No' vote did not mean the end of the Community; the franc would become simply part of the mark zone if EMU went ahead; the promised million jobs would not materialise; there would be a European tax; the 'democratic deficit' had not been addressed, and indeed it could only be addressed by reducing the power of the Commission and returning power to national parliaments, with the reminder that de Gaulle had claimed that 'democracy is inseparable from national sovereignty'; and the belief that events in the former Soviet Union and Yugoslavia showed that multinational federations were worthless. A more strident right wing view was espoused by Jean-Marie Le Pen of the Front National, who campaigned against the end of France, more immigrants, more taxes, more unemployment and more drugs. Also active were the farmers, who were complaining more about the reforms of CAP than Maastricht. A complicating feature of the campaign and voting was that the referendum was as much on Mitterrand himself as on the treaty.

The French did not repeat this experience with the Amsterdam Treaty, partly because of the change in domestic political circumstance and partly because the Amsterdam Treaty excited much less interest or debate, but the French were slow to ratify Amsterdam, perhaps partly because Amsterdam provided for new legislative powers for MEPs over the EU's structural aid funds, namely that MEPs will need to give formal approval to new regional and Social Fund rules before they become law. Pre-Amsterdam, MEPs were only consulted. As noted earlier, the French have never been keen on a greater role for the European Parliament.

Shifts in French attitudes to European Union can be seen in Figure 14.4.

Figure 14.4   French support for European Union membership, 1981–98

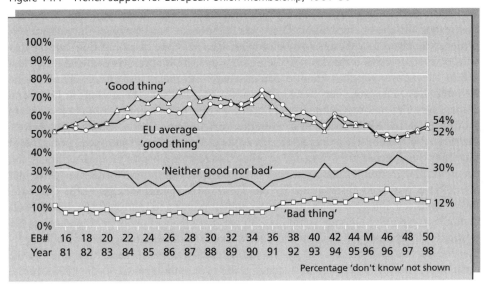

Source: Eurobarometer No. 50, p. 27.

THE FEDERAL REPUBLIC OF GERMANY

In 1949 the Federal Republic (West Germany) and the Democratic Republic (East Germany) were created, and the two Germanies existed until unification in October 1990, when the five Länder of the formerly communist German Democratic Republic acceded to the FRG.[22]

Throughout this period, and for some even since, the 'problem' of Germany has been at the heart of the European enterprise.[23] It was the problem that prompted Monnet to take his initiative in 1950, fearing that there was an 'increasing acceptance of a war that is thought to be inevitable' not because Germany might initiate something, but because other countries were treating her as the stake in their power games.[24]

Response in the Federal Republic was not unanimously favourable, some seeing the Schuman Plan as a method of stopping the revival of German industry, reflecting a French desire for cheap German coal from the Sarre and a brake on the recovery of steel-making in the Ruhr. For the SPD it was an attack on workers' rights and a real threat to the prospects for unification, which at that time was high on the German agenda. The decisive policy-maker, however, was Konrad Adenauer, elected Federal Chancellor on 17 September 1949, and the Chancellor for the next fifteen years. Adenauer placed a premium on Western values, had a profound distrust of the Soviets and their various unification offers, which invariably had conditions attached, such as neutralisation of a unified Germany, and also favoured the European ideal over the discredited nationalism that had besmirched Germany. There was also the belief that identification with Western European developments offered a path to moral, political, and economic rehabilitation, would strengthen the new democracy through interaction with other democracies, as well as strengthening national security, given the perceived threat from the communist East, especially the Soviet Union. There was real debate, however, over the relative priorities to be given to a Western orientation as against a hope of unification, but the distrust of the Soviets and the desire to be under a security umbrella provided by the West led to the opting for the Atlantic Alliance and European integration. The Federal Republic was thus a founder member of the ECSC, and once hesitations at home and abroad over German rearmament had been overcome, a member of NATO in 1955. In the late 1950s the SPD moved away from their original opposition, so that by, and from, the early 1960s there was a degree of consensus in West German European policy. West Germany, for a generation, was one of the strongest supporters of both political and economic integration, although at times this has taken different forms and particular issues have provoked reservation. In the 1970s an economically powerful Germany increasingly felt able to adopt a more independent policy and to provide European leadership. For example, Helmut Schmidt, who became Chancellor in 1974, was originally hostile to the Brussels bureaucracy and its works. Favouring inter-governmentalism, by the end of the decade, he was co-operating closely with Giscard d'Estaing on the creation of the EMS as a way of managing the economic turmoil of the 1970s. In the 1980s Foreign Minister Genscher was the principal author of the Genscher–Colombo initiative, designed to promote European Union, provide it with clear political objectives and a comprehensive political and legal framework capable of development, including the expansion of the definition of security to include defence. An accompanying statement, economic integration, called for a functional internal market and closer co-ordination of economic policy.

A positive attitude to European integration was aided by the fact that domestically the CAP was helpful in German politics. It had the effect of taking added value off the urban and industrialised parts of Germany and recycling it, via Brussels, to the agrarian parts, notably Bavaria. Since this did not involve budgetary processes in Germany, it was a money-laundering operation that might otherwise have provoked criticism. Moreover, as citizens of a federation – of Anglo-French creation – German leaders had no difficulty with a wider federation of Europe. In the German Basic Law, the competencies of government – *Kreis, Land* and *Bund* – are more or less clearly apportioned and the addition of a European layer is conceptually easy. But it is also a condition of the system that there should be democracy at every level. Accordingly, the European layer needs to be subject to a democratic control, represented in German eyes by the development of the European Parliament.

The velvet revolution in Eastern Europe in 1989 transformed the context of German policy, and for some of its neighbours raised the ghost of Germany's past. The response of Chancellor Kohl, who won round President Mitterrand, was to try to tie the new Germany firmly into a network of interdependent relationships and into deeper European integration. In April 1990 Mitterrand and Kohl sent a joint letter to the Irish Presidency arguing that the 'far-reaching changes in Europe', and the completion of the internal market, made it 'necessary to accelerate the political construction of the Europe of the Twelve' and to transform relations into a 'European Union' as envisaged by the Single European Act. They called, therefore, for intensified preparations for the IGC on EMU and for the Dublin European Council to 'initiate preparations for an inter-governmental conference on political union'.[25] This conference should have as its objectives: the strengthening of the democratic legitimation of the Union; increasing institutional efficiency; ensuring the coherence of the Union's economic, monetary and political action; and the creation of a Common Foreign and Security Policy. This IGC on political union was to be held in parallel to the conference on economic and monetary union.

Franco-German leadership was vital on a number of 1990–91 IGC issues, although they had also had several differences of view (even on the CFSP, on which they made several joint proposals, Germany being a little more cautious about a European defence identity than France), and Germany in particular was anxious not to marginalise the United Kingdom. As joint architects of the EMS and its ERM, France and Germany had a stake in sustaining it when it ran into trouble in 1992. In an indication of the strength of the Franco-German relationship, the German authorities were prepared to go to very considerable lengths to help the franc – lengths that were the envy of other weaker currency states.

By 1996 there had been significant changes in the environment within which German European policy was made, not least of which was the final hurdle that German ratification of the Treaty on European Union had to face from constitutional challenges before the German Federal Constitutional Court (FCC) in Karlsruhe. Although over twenty challenges were put before the Court, it proceeded with two: one from Manfred Brunner, former *chef de cabinet* of German EC Commissioner, Bangemann, and the other from four German Green MEPs. In essence the challenges were that the TEU violated the German Constitution, national sovereignty and democratic legitimacy. The FCC rejected the challenges on the grounds of inadmissibility or unsubstantiation, but in an 85-page judgement laid down a series of benchmarks as to what, in its view, were the limits to integration that were compatible with the German Basic Law, of which crucially it confirmed, the German FCC was the supreme arbiter. These benchmarks were:

- While the Federal Republic of Germany could join and belong to supranational international organisations, 'the condition for such membership is that legitimation and influence emanating from the people is also guaranteed within that community'.
- It must be remembered that 'democratic legitimation is achieved by referring the activities of European bodies to the parliaments of the Member States . . .' and that 'The pivotal factor is that the Union's democratic basis must be extended in line with the progress of integration and that living democracy is maintained in the Member States during that process'.
- Given the foregoing it took the view that 'the expansion of the responsibilities and authority of the European Communities is limited by virtue of the democratic principle'.
- In similar vein, it decreed that ratification of the TEU did not mean that the Federal Republic was 'subjecting itself to a nebulous "automatic" movement towards monetary union beyond its control'; rather each step might require 'subsequent approval' by the government, as influenced by the national Parliament, and strict adherence to the treaty convergence criteria.
- In a further comment on the TEU with potential implications for possible further judgements, it noted that the TEU 'establishes a union of countries in order to create an ever closer union among the peoples of Europe (organised as states) (Article A TEU), rather than a state based upon a European people'.
  It went on to apparently raise questions about the supremacy of the European Court of Justice: since it said it (the FCC) was 'examining whether legal instruments adopted by the European institutions and bodies remain within or overstep the boundaries of the sovereign rights granted to them'.
- While acknowledging that the FCC exercises jurisdiction over delegated EC legislation in Germany in a 'co-operative relationship' with the ECJ, it noted that it, the FCC, had responsibility for guaranteeing 'basic rights in Germany' and the 'guarantees contained in the Basic Law'.
- In a further cautionary comment, it observed that '. . . the result of an interpretation of the Treaty must not be tantamount to its extension; such an interpretation of powers would not be binding upon Germany'.[26]

As others have noted,[27] there is much here that is open to interpretation, but having half thrown down the gauntlet, in the subsequent period there has not been much legal activity. Nonetheless, this judgement left its mark on German policy-makers as they approached the 1996–97 IGC, as did, indeed, the other problems of ratification the TEU faced in Germany and elsewhere.

Neither the Bundesbank nor the public seemed to be as convinced of the benefits of the new arrangements as the government. In the ratification process the government was forced to bow to public pressure and agreed to make a German move to the third stage of EMU and the single currency subject to the approval of a two-thirds majority of both chambers of Parliament. Problems also arose when several Länder claimed that the Federal government had negotiated away some of their rights, and claimed that the government had no right to do so. In June 1992, fortified by the Danish 'No', they threatened to veto ratification in the Bundesrat. Eventually a compromise was reached which allowed the Länder to be directly represented in future Community negotiations on areas falling within their competence such as education, culture and the police. In the later IGC, negotiating positions had to be worked out by compromises between the Chancellor, the various ministries and the Länder. In 1995 representatives of the Länder submitted to EU Commissioner Oreja their thoughts which included:

- the need for a clear separation of powers between the EU and Member States;
- along similar lines, the compilation of a list of responsibilities per subject area for the EU, the broadly defined list of objectives of the EU should be replaced by a list of powers related to specific fields;
- a limited strengthening of the role of the Committee of the Regions.[28]

It was the Länder which were largely responsible for Chancellor Kohl's reluctance to extend majority voting in Pillars II and III in 1996–97, and among other things they secured a 'Declaration on Public Credit Institutions in Germany' attached to the Treaty of Amsterdam, which made clear that the Länder could continue to make available certain financial services, as long as there was no breach of competition policy.

The Länder have been a crucial factor in German support for subsidiarity. Indeed, the Bundesrat made subsidiarity a condition of support for Maastricht in November 1991. This was an example of the German determination that federalism should not be equated with centralism, but rather had to be seen as a decentralising concept both in Germany and in the Community. The Germans wanted subsidiarity to be one of the main issues in the 1996 IGC. In particular they looked for an extension to the 'subsidiarity list', whereby legal provisions of the EU are tested for their compatibility with Article 3b of the European Community Treaty. Interestingly, by seeking the deletion of the last clause of Article 3b – 'and can therefore, by reason of the scale or effects of the proposed action, be better achieved by the Community' – they attempted to reverse the burden of proof involved in the subsidiarity tests.

Chancellor Kohl was personally deeply committed to European integration, although he increasingly came up against the limits of internal support for certain aspects of the process, and some have wondered whether between 1992 and 1997 Germany 'turned from a champion of federalism into an advocate of inter-governmentalism'.[29] This may be over-stating the point, especially given the attitude of the Länder, but there is some truth in the view that there was a growing certain ambivalence in German attitudes to federalism. There appears to rather less inhibition as far as national interests are concerned. Germany's traditional 'culture of self-restraint' is less manifest, and whereas as recently as the 1994 CDU/CSU 'Reflections on European Policy' referred to 'fundamental' German interests, subsequently German politicians became less inhibited about referring to German 'national' interests.[30] Certainly not all of those involved in the German policy process shared Kohl's enthusiasm.

This could be seen especially in the increasing concern over the costs to Germany of a number of current and proposed policies and the perceived challenge posed to the mark by EMU and the single currency. Concern over costs and the German contribution is not new, but Germany's reduced disposition to continue in this vein reflected the experience of the higher than anticipated costs of unification, growing strains on the German budget because of unemployment, and the increasing sense that it was time that German national, or as it was often put, fundamental interests should receive more attention. From the German perspective what was needed was a general mechanism to limit inequitable net contributions, and they pointed to the fact that the 1984 Fontainebleau agreement which resolved the British problem, also contained a general clause which said that:

> it has been decided that any Member State sustaining a budgetary burden which is excessive in relation to its relative prosperity may benefit from a correction at the appropriate time.[31]

The Germans have been pointing to the fact that they are the largest net contributors, a fact confirmed by recent Commission figures (see pp. 316–17). Therefore, they have wanted the EU to stick to the budgetary ceilings agreed at Edinburgh, so that for the period 2000–2006 the ceiling of 0.46% of EU GDP should be maintained. Their own current contribution amounts to 0.6% of their GDP; they argue that this should be reduced to 0.4%. More precisely, Germany called for an assessment of gross contributions on the basis of the calculation of VAT and the gross domestic product of the Member States. In addition, it sought a greater flow of appropriations back to Germany and more efficient control of fraud and auditing. The Germans did not achieve this agreement in 1999.

EMU became a real problem for the Germans as the 1990s progressed once it became clear that the group of members would not be as narrow as Germany had anticipated. In addition, it was unpopular in Germany where for much of the period more than half of the population remained unconvinced of the argument for abandoning the Deutschmark and the independence of the fabled Bundesbank, a combination that was widely regarded as responsible for the German 'economic miracle' and stability, and a number of leading politicians of all parties expressed doubts and called for a delay in its introduction: Edmund Stoiber in Bavaria (CSU), Kurt Biedenkopf in Saxony (CDU) and most notably, given his subsequent position, Gerhard Schröder in Lower Saxony (SPD). Schröder had been particularly vigorous in his opposition, referring to the 'euro' in 1995 as 'monopoly money'[32] and even in 1998 referring to it as a sickly and prematurely born child.[33] By the time of the actual election campaign he had moderated his stance, and in any case the basic decisions had already been taken by Kohl and the European Council at Cardiff in May 1998.

The Germans had always insisted that those moving to the third stage of EMU would need to meet tough convergence criteria and agree on the independence of the proposed European Central Bank System from political control, on the Bundesbank model. Both of these prerequisites were brought into question as 1999 approached. Firstly, whatever doubts there were about whether others could meet a strict application of the convergence criteria, Germany itself had problems. These related specifically to the budgetary deficit position of the German government, as the deficit was proving difficult to reduce given high unemployment and internal political problems. Equally embarrassingly, while the Germans had always preached the need for strict rectitude in meeting the criteria, in May 1997 the German Finance Minister, Theo Waigel, attempted to force through a revaluation of the gold reserves held by the Bundesbank to change the percentage of deficit the Germans would report for 1997. He was forced to compromise but the episode damaged the German attempt to maintain the high ground, and their ability to enforce a narrow interpretation on others. The Commission 'Report on progress towards convergence . . .' noted the problem of Germany but chose to be optimistic that the trend was in the right direction, that Germany would be close to the reference point, and that there were in any case special factors relating to the costs of unification.[34] The question of the independence of the European Central Bank (ECB) proved equally difficult in 1998, but the Germans were forced to accept the compromise of their candidate, Wim Duisenberg of the Netherlands, agreeing not to serve the full eight-year term and being succeeded by the French nominee, Trichet, leaving somewhat open the question of how independent the ECB would prove to be. Germany had to accept the compromise to ensure that EMU would actually become a reality but their stance also confirmed that for Kohl, at least, EMU was more of a political priority than an economic question. It was part of his commitment to the call of Thomas Mann 'not for a German Europe, but for a European Germany'.

Attitudes regarding costs, and the need to meet or approach EMU convergence criteria, ran somewhat counter to the German enthusiasm for the Eastern enlargement of the European Union. At the beginning of the 1996 IGC process, although enlargement was not formally a matter for the IGC, the Germans made clear that the Copenhagen and Corfu decisions regarding enlargement should be implemented and that they placed a high premium on seeking to root stability in Eastern and Central Europe by bringing those states closer to the EU, with a view to accession. The idea of concurrent deepening and widening had gone largely unchallenged in Germany, but the SPD was the first major party to acknowledge the fears of some frontier regions in Germany about the consequences of enlargement for local labour markets and internal security, resulting from freedom of movement. The SPD made clear in the 1998 election that it would pay more attention to these fears and would seek to defer full freedom of movement. Mr Shröder himself spoke of the need for 'transition periods to avoid distortions in labour markets that can occur when high income disparities exist between new and old Member States'.[35]

This issue is likely to prove a real test of the relationship between the aspirational and operational aspects of the policies of Germany, since an operational policy is usually deemed to involve the disbursement of resources and, as noted above, the Germans are now less willing to disburse resources. Chancellor Kohl had accepted the idea behind 'Agenda 2000' as a basis for the future although he was opposed to the proposals on Structural Funds and in effect rejected the proposed reform of the Common Agricultural Policy. Although only 3% of Germans work in agriculture, the influence of the farm vote is not to be under-estimated. However, post the 1998 election and with the election of an SPD–Green coalition, Germany may prove to be more flexible, and it is possible that more will be heard of the idea of national co-financing of the CAP. Since Germany pays in around 30% of the CAP budget, while receiving only 15% back in agricultural payments, paying German farmers directly from Berlin would save around 50% of the total sum of around DM8bn annually (£3bn). Certainly Chancellor Schröder is anxious to push for 'developments that will result in a more equitable burden-sharing'.[36] The problem for the Germans is that budgetary and CAP reforms are inextricably linked to enlargement, and to the success of EMU, two prized German priorities.

A continuing feature of the German position has been the importance attached to strengthening the role of the European institutions and rectifying the 'democratic deficit'. Kohl sought to make movement on these matters a condition for approval of EMU, but eventually had to compromise. Germany has consistently pushed for the European Parliament to have co-decision with the Council on legislation, especially where the Council acts by QMV, for it to have a right of initiative, to be involved in the appointment of the Commission and its President, and to have a greater role in regard to the CFSP. It has opposed notions of a Second Chamber. It has also sought a new voting system in the Council, both with regard to a new weighting of votes and the introduction of a second majority requirement, relating to population. It was also anxious that the Commission's position should not be undermined and that, for example, it should retain the right of initiative.

More important than these specifics, perhaps, was the contribution made by the CDU/CSU, the two leading members of Kohl's coalition, in September 1994 on flexibility. While this was a party paper rather than official government policy, the paper by Wolfgang Schäuble (leader of the CDU after the 1998 election) and Karl Lammers, was one of the most interesting contributions to the debate about the future of Europe. Schäuble and Lammers feared that the EU 'contrary to the goal of ever closer union' was drifting towards becoming 'a loosely knit grouping of States restricted to certain economic aspects', little more 'than a "sophisticated" free trade area'. In addition to proposals about making the EU's decision-making more efficient and democratic, their principal proposal was for a hard core of states within the EU, comprising of five or six states (with some uncertainty about Italy), to become the new vanguard of integration. The core states would participate 'in all policy fields' and 'should also be recognisably more Community-spirited'.[37] The core would be 'open to every Member State willing and able to meet its requirements', but no state would be able to veto the will of the others to deepen integration. This contribution provoked a strong response from the British, and had to be amended in the IGC, but it clearly found expression in the Treaty of Amsterdam provisions on 'Closer co-operation' albeit that those proposals make closer co-operation by some contingent on the approval of all, if they wish to use the Union institutions. Part of the German desire was to prevent the emergence of an *à la carte* Europe, so the proposal was couched in a multi-speed perspective: all would arrive at the same objective in the end but at different times. Initially the SPD was concerned that the proposal might lead to the division of the EU into first- and second-class states, but Schröder took the position in 1998 that 'a Social Democrat government wants to strengthen the EU's capacity to act by allowing for more flexible combinations of Member States for certain policy projects than has been the case so far'.[38]

There was another area of concern to the Federal Republic and with regard to which it put forward a number of papers, namely the Justice and Home Affairs pillar. For the Federal Republic, preventing and combating organised international crime and drug trafficking was a priority, and it was anxious that Europol should be developed and that the Europol Convention should be ratified as soon as possible, that it should become a European police authority, which, in the long-term, would evolve into a European police office with operational powers. It also wanted the Schengen Agreement's provisions relating to external frontiers to be implemented, for Schengen to be integrated into the European Union and for much of Pillar III to be moved to the competence of the European Community, with all that implied about the role of Commission, Parliament, Court and decision-making procedures, since it believed that inter-governmental co-operation was inefficient and sluggish. Specifically, it wanted visa and asylum policy, customs co-operation and immigration under the Community pillar. It even proposed the attempt to harmonise definitions of offences and certain aspects of procedure.

On the CFSP, its general position again favoured strengthening the European Union's competence and capability. The Union should have more teeth and a greater capacity to take decisions. Thus the Federal Republic advocated more majority voting in areas with no military aspects, albeit that it was to be a double majority, that is, of Member States and population, and there was to be the possibility of 'positive abstention' whereby states in a minority would not block a decision. On this, however, the Germans argued that even those states that did not vote for the action should be required to provide logistical and financial support for decisions taken by the majority. The Germans on several occasions stressed the need for the CFSP to identify priorities, and named these in particular as: the establishment of a European peace order, the establishment of a genuine Euro-Mediterranean partnership, and the development of a broader transatlantic link. The first related directly to their view of the necessity of enlargement.

On defence, while reaffirming that NATO was the indispensable basis of European security, the Germans continued to advocate that Europeans should shoulder more responsibility. To this end, and to make the CFSP more effective, it supported proposals to increase the WEU's operational capability, greater inter-operability of armed forces and joint provision of equipment. Specifically on WEU capability it argued that the WEU should develop into a common defence structure capable of putting the actions under the Petersberg tasks into practice, and that the concept of combined joint forces enabling the WEU or coalitions of EU/WEU members to act should be developed. In the longer term it favoured the fusion of the WEU and the European Union. Pending that, the links between the WEU and the EU were to be strengthened. Together with the French, the Germans proposed the inclusion of a 'political solidarity clause' applying to all Member States, the incorporation of the Petersberg tasks into the CFSP competence and the establishment of an advanced research and analysis unit – that is, an early warning and planning unit.

Under Chancellor Kohl, the Germans laid a great deal of emphasis upon safeguarding Europe's industrial and economic power, especially by improving the environment for growth and employment. This had not only an economic dimension but fitted into his concern with making the European Union more relevant to its citizens. Partly because of this, he was also anxious to strengthen the social dimension of the EU. However, Kohl vetoed a number of social measures in the IGC on the grounds of cost, and while German negotiators accepted the new Employment title, they were among those responsible for limiting the authority of the European Community in the area, so that in the treaty outcome there is little more than exhortation. The SPD has laid rather more emphasis upon employment as part of its general attack on the record of Kohl. It also laid stress on social stability and the forming of a social union, and argued that the EU had a role in preserving the welfare state. In order to avoid 'social dumping', for example, the SPD wanted the EU to agree minimum standards of social protection and support for a European welfare model. Nonetheless, their main concern was to protect German standards.

Europe was not an issue in the German Federal election of 1998, although the CDU tried to emphasise Kohl's experience and weight in European affairs. The SPD did attack his attitude to the Employment title and his capacity to handle enlargement. They believed that employment should become the heart of European policy and they claimed there was a contradiction between Kohl's support for enlargement but refusal to address the reform of the CAP.

Perhaps reflecting the limitations of the Amsterdam Treaty and the prevailing German consensus on European questions, there was no real difficulty in ratifying the treaty. Its merits and shortcomings were debated but there were no doubts that the Treaty would be ratified. The only real controversy was that the Greens voted against because of the Treaty's lack of progress on democratic accountability. The new Chancellor, Gerhard Schröder just prior to the 1998 election, made it clear that he envisaged a Social Democrat European policy 'following a tradition of German European policy',[39] and the coalition agreement of October 1998 spoke of pledging the new government to 'drive the European integration process forward with new initiatives'.[40] Although many expect the post-1998 government to be less visionary and more pragmatic, and Schröder has indicated that 'a Germany standing up for its national interests will be just as natural as France or Britain standing up for theirs',[41] the new Green Foreign Minister, Joschka Fischer, is an enthusiastic pro-European.

The evolution of German attitudes to European Union can be seen in Figure 14.5.

Figure 14.5 German support for European Union membership, 1981–98*

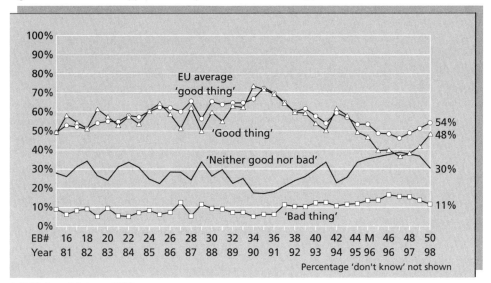

* Unified as of Autumn 1990.
Source: Eurobarometer No. 50, p. 24.

ITALY

Like Germany, Italy had a practical and psychological need to overcome the past, as well as to rehabilitate itself and re-establish its credibility. Like the Federal Republic, Italy, which for nearly thirty years was concerned at the power of the Communist Party of Italy (PCI) and a number of other destabilising tendencies, sought to protect itself by intimate involvement with the Community, NATO and the West in general, perceiving a linkage between such involvement and political stability at home. There was thus a pragmatic as well as an idealistic element in the original Italian choice to support integration.

There was a belief in some quarters in the European ideal, the past having discredited the nation state and sovereignty as a concept. These influences are reflected in the post-war Constitution which envisages agreeing 'on conditions of equality with other states, to such limitation of sovereignty as may be necessary for a system calculated to ensure peace and justice between nations',[42] in the early activities of Foreign Minister Sforza, who sought in 1947 a Franco-Italian customs union, and in the life and work of the federalist Altiero Spinelli. This mixture of pragmatism and idealism is one reason why it is not just in recent years that there has been a 'contradiction between the prevalence of pro-integrationist rhetoric in Italian political circles and their marked inability or unwillingness to translate this into policy action'.[43] This has been apparent on a number of occasions in the last forty-plus years, with, for example, the Commission reporting in 1990 that Italy had implemented fewer internal market directives than any other state, as well as paying least attention to judgements given against it in the European Court of Justice.[44]

Similarly apparent has been the lack of Italian political weight in the European Community or Union, for which a number of reasons can be adduced: internal political instability of governments has reduced the authority of Italian policy-makers in the higher circles of Community and Union policy-making; there have been problems in policy co-ordination within the governmental system and a lack of preparation; policy has often been reactive rather than proactive; and these difficulties have been compounded by recurring economic weakness. This latter has caused a number of difficulties for Italy, which were neatly summed up in the context of the EMS debate in 1978–79 by Guido Carli, President of Confindustria: 'Italy cannot afford to join this scheme, and she cannot allow herself to remain distant from it.'[45] Italy has not been able to influence many of the internal Community policies. For example, despite the importance of agriculture to the Italian economy over the last forty years, it has been others who have taken the lead on the issue and made it predominantly a policy for temperate agriculture. Italy has had some difficulty in matching France and Germany in terms of political weight and, indeed, has been concerned at the recurring prospect of a Franco-German hegemony. This concern was, for example, one factor in Italian support for British membership of the European Community.

It has, however, on a number of occasions taken initiatives and been diplomatically active. In the 1970s the Community gained greater priority in its own right in Italian policy, partly because the energy crisis and the enlargements to include Greece, Portugal and Spain focused more attention on the Mediterranean arena. Italy strongly supported these Community enlargements as shifting the centre of gravity in the Community more towards the south, and it promoted the idea of a Mediterranean Conference on Security and Co-operation in Europe. As in earlier periods individual Italians have made significant contributions, Colombo, for example, played a role in resolving the 1965–66 crisis as well as in the Genscher–Colombo proposals of the 1980s. Similarly, the Italian Presidency at the Milan European Council in June 1985 was crucial in bringing about the IGC that led to the Single European Act.

By a strange coincidence it was at the end of the Italian Presidency in 1990 that the two IGCs on EMU and Political Union were convened and in the middle of an Italian Presidency that the 1996 IGC was opened in Turin on 29 March 1996. In 1990–91 the Italian Foreign Minister, De Michelis, conformed to the pattern of ardent Italian rhetorical support for integration and federalism, and the Prime Minister, Andreotti, called for a 'federative union'.[46] Throughout the 1990s their rhetoric remained positive, reflecting Italy's strong pro-European commitment, and they continued to call for consolidation of the Union's federal dimension through greater internal solidarity and cohesion. They were keen to prevent any return to a Europe of nation-states since they believed that that would eventually lead to nation-states without Europe. Italy has wanted to retain the basic institutional balance and the notion of a single institutional framework for the Union. They have opposed 'opt-outs' and permanent exceptions and have warned against what they perceive as the tendency of certain states to want to create 'steering committees' of one sort or another. However, they reluctantly came to recognise that it might be difficult to avoid some degree of flexibility in new policy areas – the CFSP and Justice and Home Affairs – and perhaps others subsequently, not least because of enlargement. Flexibility came to be regarded as a way of resolving the deepening and widening dilemma, precisely by allowing a mixture of unity and flexibility. However, given their concerns the Italians argued that differentiated integration needed to be properly defined and it called for strict conditions to be met before such developments would be allowed:

- There must be adherence to the principle of institutional unity, especially there being a single Council, Parliament and Court.
- The *acquis* must be preserved.
- The arrangements should reflect the view that such developments were temporary, since they were arrangements to allow others to become gradually integrated in the policy areas.
- There must be predetermined conditions of entry and membership, with entry being open to all who were willing and able.
- The selection of areas was not to be arbitrary or discriminatory, the Italians fearing German plots against them, for example, following the wording of the Schäuble-Lammers proposals of 1994 (see pp. 424–5) and the German line on strict interpretation of the EMU criteria.

This approach was reflective of long-standing Italian concerns over notions of a two-tier or two-speed Europe, with the possibility that Italy would be excluded from the core of European developments, fears that were raised by the Tindemans' report of December 1975 and the movement to the European Monetary System in 1979. In general terms the Italians approached the review of the Treaty on European Union looking for solutions to its perceived deficiencies, preparations for enlargement, and making the European Union more democratic, efficient, simpler to understand and with more capacity and coherence in the subjects of Pillars II and III.

At the beginning of the decade, after the Iraqi invasion of Kuwait, Italy made the CFSP a priority, arguing, for example, in September 1990 that it ought to be the 'most visible objective to be realised'[47] in the IGC on Political Union. For them the Gulf showed that the competencies of the Union needed to be extended 'to all aspects of security without limitations' and they called for the 'transfer to the Union [of] the competencies presently being exercised by the WEU'. They argued this not least because it would imply a security guarantee among Member States, involve Defence Ministers in the work of the Union, and enable the Union to concert policy on crises outside Europe, although they did compromise on these questions and in 1991 sought to find common ground with the British. This involved a move in the direction of an 'Atlantic European defence'. By 1996 the Italians had moved a little in the direction of accepting that fundamental consensus on the principles and substance of foreign policy was a prerequisite for action. However, the Italians, contrary to the British view, believed this should allow simplified decision-making procedures and qualified majority voting on the implementation after general principles and guidelines had been laid down by the European Council. They were also keen that the CFSP should move beyond inter-governmentalism and that it should be established that a firm obligation to cohesion existed once decisions had been made.

In line with the view that the CFSP should be strengthened, Italy made quite detailed proposals with regard to a properly resourced secretariat with a capacity for analysis and forecasting in the CFSP area. It called for a new unit, which it saw operating under a Secretary-General for external policy, and which would take responsibility for the planning and implementing of decisions under the political guidance of the Council. It wanted a permanent body empowered to represent the Union in foreign policy and to ensure greater continuity, credibility and responsibility. In case this proved impossible, it made suggestions about having an elected Presidency for the CFSP, and for separating the CFSP role from the other functions of the Presidency.

On defence, Italy continued to argue that the WEU should be an instrument of the EU, and indeed absorbed into the EU. Not surprisingly, therefore, in the mid-1990s it was among those who supported the incorporation of the Petersberg tasks into the remit of the CFSP, and it argued that, pending absorption, the WEU structures should be brought under the aegis of the EU. In line with this approach, it suggested that WEU and EU membership should be harmonised and WEU operational capacity strengthened. However, rather like their final position in 1991, they were anxious that these developments should complement and not undermine NATO, which was to remain the basic pillar of collective defence and of ties between Europe and the USA. Finally, Italy was one the states to call for closer co-operation in the field of armaments.

On Justice and Home Affairs, the broad thrust of the Italians was the same as on the CFSP. They argued for increased use of Community procedures, particularly as regards asylum policy, the granting of visas and immigration; for simplification of the decision-making system; a review of the instruments in Pillar III, especially looking at whether they could be made more binding or even take on the more of the characteristics of Community directives; a role for the European Court of Justice and Parliament; a move to remove some of the constraints on the initiation of policy; and the incorporation of Schengen into the European Union in the context of differentiated integration.

A related area they saw as important was that of the need to spell out the basic constitutional principles of the European Union, especially with regard to the rights of EU citizens. They wanted a full list of civil and social rights to be enumerated, covering freedom of expression, association, and movement, etc., and action against racism and xenophobia. On rights, the Italians wanted them to be safeguarded by the European Court of Justice. As part of this overall approach, the Italians pushed as strongly in 1996–97 as they had in 1991 for a hierarchy of acts:

- Constitutional laws, requiring unanimity and national ratification.
- Legislative provisions, to establish the general framework for particular sectors or subjects, that would be determined by majority vote in the Council and co-decision with the Parliament.

- Regulatory and implementing decisions, which would be the responsibility of Council.

All of this was to be seen in the context of making the European Union more comprehensible to EU citizens, and more accessible and more responsive to the idea of a people's Europe.

On Community matters the Italians generally favoured strengthening the integrative aspects of the Community. They wanted majority voting to become the norm in the Council except for certain, 'constitutional' provisions, although they also favoured changing the weighting of the votes so that there would be a double majority of the states and population. They also supported the temporary use of constructive abstention in order to move things forward. Italy complained about the deterioration of the Council's working methods, and wished to see a revitalised secretariat and greater focus on co-ordination. They were keen to preserve the position of the Commission, emphasising that it should continue as guardian of the treaties while maintaining the right of initiative. Indeed, it was argued this should be extended to Pillar III. In similar vein, it argued that the Commission Presidency should have a stronger role, in order to increase both efficiency and external visibility. While it supported a reduction in the number of Commissioners, this was not to go beyond one per Member State, and there was a suggestion that the large states should be compensated by being able to nominate a 'Deputy' Commissioner.

The Italians had earlier taken a radical line in regard to the European Parliament, their own parliament having said it would not ratify the Treaty on European Union unless the European Parliament accepted it. They had earlier supported the European Parliament's 1984 Draft Treaty. In the 1990s they took the view that the European Parliament should have co-decision with the Council, a right of initiative, and the right to approve both the appointment of the Commission President and that of the Commission as a whole, and perhaps eventually the powers of a national parliament. On legislative role they linked their proposals to their views on a hierarchy of laws, which they saw as a way of aiding the movement towards just three legislative procedures: assent (to be extended at least to the revision of the treaties), consultation and co-decision, although this latter was to have a simplified procedure. The Italians wanted the European Parliament to have a greater role in Pillars II and III. They supported a ceiling of between 650–700 MEPs on the grounds of efficiency and also advocated the adoption of a single electoral system. Italy was a strong defender of the Court of Justice, wishing to see its current powers defended and indeed wishing to see a role for the Court in Pillar III and in protecting the rights of EU citizens. It endorsed the role of the Committee of the Regions, and supported strengthening the Court of Auditors' role, especially in anti-fraud cases. On many of these institutional issues Italy behaved almost as a small state, seeing integration as a protection for itself and as a way of enlarging its own scope of action.

Italy strongly supported the movement to EMU and the single currency, but opposed the German insistence on tough or mechanical convergence criteria, because of the difficulties Italy would have in meeting them, especially because of its public deficit, and the dangers of the transition to the third stage in fact leading to tiers among the members of the European Union and the two-speed Europe it had always opposed. Italy felt this especially after the Economic Affairs Commissioner warned the other eleven Member States in November 1991 that Italy's economy presented a considerable risk to EMU. But for an Italy which aspired to be a charter member of the EMU, and which increasingly was subject to internal problems of corruption and a sharpening of the North/South tension, a monetary authority, standing aloof from the political battle, looked like the most promising way of emerging from short-termism and political chicanery. The public deficit remained a contentious issue until 1998, with Italy being outside the TEU criteria from the first. The Commission, however, argued in March 1998 that 'there was a large and continuous reduction in the government deficit . . . from 9.5% of GDP in 1993 to 2.7% in 1997' with a further decline expected in 1998. The debt ratio was more of a problem but the Commission again argued that the trend was in the right direction.[48]

Italy has not been a strong advocate of enlargement either with respect to the fourth enlargement in 1995 or the next enlargement in 2003–2005. This is partly because it not only sees enlargement as a threat to deepening but also because enlargement poses some practical problems for the Italians. This was especially true in relation to Austria, but it is also the case that Italy fears that the Scandinavian members and the focus on the five Central and East European states will cause the Union to lose sight of its interests in the Mediterranean. In addition, Italy is now a net contributor to the Union budget and shares the anxieties of other net contributors. It can hardly oppose enlargement, however, and has thus emphasised the need for preparation, for institutional development, and the reform of policies, particularly the CAP.

Previously the Italians strongly favoured the wide extension of the competencies of the Union, but increasingly budgetary concerns have led to caution as they have become net contributors. Italy did support the inclusion of an Employment chapter in the Treaty of Amsterdam, but only on the basis of co-ordination. It argued for the strengthening of certain existing policies, especially those that might improve the public perception of the EU, such as consumer protection and social policy. It also argued for majority voting on environmental questions and the move to new policy areas in the fields of energy, tourism and civil protection. Given its overall position, Italy worries that over-emphasising subsidiarity could undermine the *acquis*, and Community action, but rather like flexibility has had to come to terms with it. It has sought, however, clearer definition of what it actually covers.

Italy has had to adjust its aspirational rhetorical position to the realities of developments in the 1990s, but it has managed to avoid the ignominy of being excluded from the first wave of EM participants. The changes in its public attitudes to European Union can be seen in Figure 14.6.

Figure 14.6 Italian support for European Union membership, 1981–98

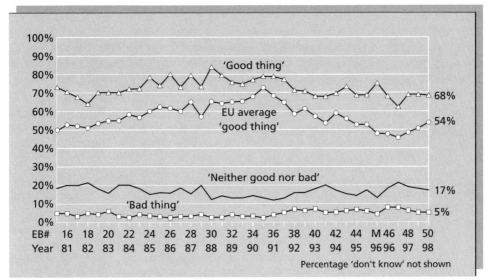

Source: Eurobarometer No. 50, p. 29.

THE FIRST ENLARGEMENT STATES

IRELAND

OF THE three states that joined in January 1973, Ireland has been by far the most *communautaire*. Yet until 1973 its history, its location, and its economic dependence upon the United Kingdom made it impossible for Ireland to join. Within Ireland the real watershed in attitudes was in the period 1958–61. Until then it had been outside the mainstream of European politics, having been non-belligerent in 'the Emergency' (that is, the Second World War), and so preoccupied with the Partition of the island of Ireland that it had both refused to join NATO in 1949 and pursued the so-called policy of the 'sore thumb' in European institutions it did belong to, especially the Council of Europe. 'Neutrality', Partition, irredentism, the claustrophobic relationship with Britain and protectionism were the key features of Irish policy.

In the late 1950s a sea change began in Irish politics. One factor was the growing perception that protectionism had not succeeded. Another, related, factor was the dramatic change in the external environment brought about first by the discussions of a free trade area in Western Europe, by the creation of the EEC and subsequently EFTA, by Ireland's exclusion from both (the latter largely at Britain's doing since Britain argued EFTA was for developed states only and should exclude agriculture), and most fundamentally, by Britain's decision to apply for EEC membership in the summer of 1961. Many felt that Ireland faced 'Hobson's choice' in 1961, it being clear that if Britain applied, 'we also will apply', since if Ireland's trading partners joined 'together in an economic union, we cannot be outside it'. It was not a choice of joining or leaving things as they were since the status quo was disappearing. If Britain did not join, neither would Ireland.[49] Ireland's bid was still-born because of de Gaulle's attitude to the United Kingdom.

When the climate for Britain changed, so too did the climate for Ireland, and by 1969 it had had a number of years to seek to adjust to the new requirements that it would face. On 10 May 1972 the Irish people voted 83% to 17% in favour of membership, with a turnout of 71%. In the debate the key arguments for were: the British decision; fear of jeopardising trade if they did not join; a belief that membership would free them from the suffocating relationship with Britain; the prospect of agricultural markets with guaranteed prices; the prospect of foreign investment; the alleged benefits of Protocol Number 30 in the Treaty of Accession (which, recognising the economic and social imbalances that existed in the Community between the regions, noted that they would need to be removed – a statement the Irish interpreted as a commitment to far-reaching regional policy); a vague hope that it might contribute to ameliorating 'the troubles' in Northern Ireland; and that there was no commitment to joining any alliance and, according to the proponents of membership, no threat to neutrality. The 'pro' campaign enjoyed the support of both major parties, Fianna Fail and Fine Gael.

The opposition was disparate and divided. The main opposition came from the Irish Labour Party, but also involved were Official and Provisional Sinn Fein. Labour attacked the terms, the capitalist orientation of the EEC, the problems posed to traditional Irish industries, as well as disputing the benefits to agriculture. They bitterly contrasted the Irish alleged pre-preparedness to enter military alliances and abandon neutrality with the principled stand of Austria, Sweden and Switzerland, who all said membership was incompatible with neutrality.

Since membership in January 1973 the Irish have benefited significantly from the CAP and other transfers. Garret FitzGerald, the Foreign Minister, summed up the Irish position in November 1975, noting that since Ireland was

> to a remarkable degree a net beneficiary of Community policies . . . Ireland must be careful not to appear too much in the role of constant 'demandeur' . . . Ireland must seek to compensate for this by playing a positive and constructive role in the present running and future development of the Community.[50]

In the period between membership in 1973 and the 1987 referendum Ireland received IR£5,745m (£6,030m) in net receipts from the Community and in 1986 the net budgetary transfers were equivalent to 13.5% of current government revenue. No wonder it was argued that to leave the Community would be 'economic suicide'.[51] In May 1998, on the eve of the referendum on the Amsterdam Treaty, the Irish Foreign Minister, David Andrews, suggested that that pattern of support was unaltered:

Table 15.1   Irish voting in referendums on EC membership, the SEA and the treaties of Maastricht and Amsterdam

	% Yes	% No	% Turnout
EEC entry 1972	83.1	16.9	71
SEA 1987	69.9	30.1	44
TEU 1992	68.7	31.3	57
Amsterdam 1998	60.4	39.6	56

Between 1973 and 1997, Ireland received total net funding from the EU to the tune of IR £21.5 billion.

The Structural and Cohesion Funds have been of exceptional importance . . . Between 1989 and 1999 these funds will account for an estimated 2.5% of our GDP each year.

The operation of the Common Agricultural Policy and Structural Funds have brought great advantage to agriculture and rural development. In 1996, for example, the combined impact of transfers and more favourable agricultural prices came to over IR£1.8 billion, equivalent to almost 4.5% of GDP.

Also:

- the EU Peace Programme 1995–99 aid to Northern Ireland and border areas of the Republic had contributed IR£400m;
- while the Single Market gave access to 360m people.

As a result, he claimed, Irish prosperity had climbed from 58% of the European average in 1973 to over 90% in 1998.[52] Whatever doubts individuals might have about aspects of Union membership, these figures were regarded by most as persuasive. Irish policy has been supportive, therefore, fairly consistently of a Community approach to issues and of a strong role for the central institutions. Ireland has been anxious about any inter-governmental tendencies, especially any that smacked of a 'directorate' or Franco-German hegemony, such as the EMS genesis, or of ideas related to two-tier developments. It therefore opposed the Tindemans' suggestion in 1975–76 of two tiers or two speeds, and as the 1996 IGC approached, again voiced opposition to 'the creation of an exclusive hard core of Member States which would result in the fragmentation of the Union and work to the detriment of its coherence'.[53] Ireland believed that provisions favouring certain Member States, by enabling them to pursue the same objectives at varying speeds, should be instituted only as a last resort and on a case by case basis. In a traditional reflection of Ireland's perspective as a small state, the government was clear that it would resist any suggestions that 'seek to make the decision-making process more inter-governmental, at the expense of Community mechanisms'.[54] Thus, its widely supported position on enlargement was that:

> The Government would not accept an enlargement process which altered the essential character of the Union to that of an expanded free trade area. The Union's unique supranational nature, characterised by the development of the common policies, must be maintained and strengthened as enlargement proceeds. Its achievements in areas of importance to the Union must not be put at risk, . . .[55]

not only in the institutional sphere, but also on CAP financing and cohesion.

Not surprisingly, the Irish were opposed to any attempt to use the IGC as an occasion to undermine the institution's 'basic functions under the Treaty' or to 'call into question the broad institutional framework which has served the Union well'.[56] Ireland would not therefore accept the loss of right to nominate a full member of the Commission nor any undermining of the Commission's role in initiating proposals, implementing and supervising Community laws, or acting as guardian of the treaties and the interests of all Member States. It was opposed to any weakening of the position of the Court of Justice. Similarly it was wary of changes to the weighting of votes and substantive change to the rotating Council Presidency. It would countenance more qualified majority voting, an extension of the co-decision procedure to strengthen the role of the European Parliament and a reduction in the number of legislative procedures. But while paying lip service to increasing the powers of the European Parliament, they were not as enthusiastic as some given fears over its possible urban composition and the small numbers of Irish MEPs. While also ready to countenance an enhanced profile for national parliaments, it was clear that this was not to be at the expense of the European Parliament, or lead to any further complicating of EU decision-making.

Partly because of its *communautaire* approach, its fear of a two-tier Europe and potential exclusion from key decisions, and its desire to lessen the suffocation caused by a large and powerful neighbour, and given substantial side payments, Ireland joined the EMS at its commencement. Of great symbolic importance was that on 30 March 1979 adherence to the EMS brought about the break with the link with sterling, for the first time in 150 years, and was the final demonstration to many of Irish independence from the UK. Ireland supported EMU and a single currency. As the 1996 White Paper put it:

> EMU is to the advantage of an open economy such as ours, which is heavily dependent on trade. Also, in EMU we would participate in the major monetary decisions affecting us instead of being in a situation where in practice we often must, as a small country, live with the consequences of decisions taken by others.[57]

The government and, more especially, some others were somewhat concerned about the prospect of Ireland joining and the UK remaining outside, admitting that 'it would clearly be preferable from Ireland's point of view if the United Kingdom were to enter EMU at the same time as Ireland',[58] but UK absence did not deter Irish participation in the first wave. The Commission Report of March 1998 was very positive about Ireland's performance relative to the convergence criteria, the only minor hiccup being the fluctuations in the value of the Irish pound against the other ERM currencies, but the Commission observed that the 'deviation of the Irish pound was mostly above its central rate and reflected the favourable conditions in the Irish economy'.[59]

Much more difficult for Ireland were matters relating to political co-operation, especially security. This had been an issue in the 1972 referendum and has remained a running sore through to the referendums on the TEU and Amsterdam Treaty where the alleged threats posed by the CFSP, and the 'eventual' or later 'progressive' forming of a common defence policy, were seen to bring into question significant aspects of Irish political culture and its traditional position on neutrality and its role in international affairs. This had also been an issue in 1986–87, the occasion being the ratification of the Single European Act. That referendum was necessary because the Irish Supreme Court took the view that Title III of the Act on EPC was contrary to the Irish Constitution's prescription that the government should be unfettered in its foreign policy. Given that EPC had occasioned the referendum, neutrality played a role in the debate.

Given this, Irish history and the identification in political culture of neutrality with independence from Britain, any proposals on a Common Foreign and Security Policy (CFSP) always formed a delicate question for Ireland. In 1990–91, however, it could afford to be somewhat relaxed on this issue because it did not believe that any major decisions were imminent, and the Treaty on European Union, echoing the London Report of 1981, did say (Article J.4.3) that the proposals 'shall not prejudice the specific character of the security and defence policy of certain Member States', a direct reference the Irish argued to their special position. Furthermore, real progress was to wait until another IGC in 1996, and any changes would require unanimity. Meantime the CFSP was purely inter-governmental. Ireland was still not committed to an alliance, or to a mutual defence agreement.

Ireland has always opposed membership in existing alliance systems, but in line with its long-standing policy it did accept that it would participate if the Community developed its own security system. The Minister of Defence in November 1991 acknowledged that Europe must have its own common defence system which would not be subservient to the USA and that Ireland would need to play a role in determining that system. Again it was fearful of being in a second tier of development, and so, although it opposed the Italian idea of a merger between the European Union and the WEU, it finally did accept the Franco-German idea of the European Council deciding on defence questions, with the WEU implementing those decisions. Ireland took the view that these matters had effectively been subcontracted to the WEU.

By the time of the next review, the Irish position had not moved far. The 1996 White Paper, *Challenges and Opportunities Abroad*, noted that the 'majority of the Irish people have always cherished Ireland's military neutrality, and recognise the positive values that inspire it . . .', and it assured the Irish people that 'that policy will not be changed unless the people of Ireland decide otherwise in a referendum'. But in further reassurance it went on to say that:

> The Government will not be proposing that Ireland should seek membership of NATO or the Western European Union, or the assumption of their mutual defence guarantees.[60]

Ireland had, however, taken up the 1992 WEU offer to EU Member States that were not members, to become 'Observers', which allows Ireland to attend and speak at WEU Ministerial Council meetings and participate in WEU working groups and committees, but does not involve any mutual defence commitment or military obligation. The question that has arisen, however, is whether Ireland should participate on a voluntary basis in operations of the Petersberg variety, especially given its long-standing tradition of contributing to United Nations peacekeeping forces. Ireland did contribute fifty personnel to IFOR/SFOR, who have acted in the role of military police, despite the fact that IFOR/SFOR, for example, is NATO-led under the political direction and control of the North Atlantic Council, and under the military control of SACEUR. A further complication is that Ireland has contributed military officers to OSCE missions to ease tension and help the settlement of the conflicts in, for example, Georgia and the former

Yugoslavia. In the 1996 White Paper, the Fine Gael/Labour coalition indicated that it was considering whether NATO's Partnership for Peace (PfP) was a 'co-operative security initiative . . . to which Ireland could contribute',[61] but it was assailed on all sides. The new Fianna Fail/Progressive government of May 1997 sought to avoid the issue but since the 1998 'Good Friday Agreement' on Northern Ireland, there have been signs that it is even beginning to look again at the issue, partly because of the difficulty in explaining why not.

In the context of the IGC the Fine Gael/Labour government identified three options for Ireland's relationship with the WEU:

- full membership;
- maintain Observer status;
- deeper EU co-operation on the Petersberg tasks but no defence commitment and maintaining the EU and the WEU as distinct identifies.

Basically the Irish argued their usual position, namely that movement towards a common defence policy must 'take account of the level of political and economic integration achieved by the European Union', be responsive to the broader developments in European security and reflect the different experiences and capacities of the Member States.[62] Despite these reservations on defence, Ireland was quite keen to see the European Union play a more active and coherent role in international politics. The Irish Minister of Defence did attend the 'informal' meeting of EU defence ministers held in November 1998 under the Austrian Presidency. While there was some criticism of this from the Green Party and other like-minded organisations, it attracted surprisingly little comment or controversy. Since then the Irish have gone along with the Cologne European Council Conclusions (see pp. 380–3).

The Irish have been adamant that decisions, especially on 'sensitive' matters, 'if they are to be sustainable and effective' must be 'underpinned by broad support'.[63] If this was present then the TEU provisions for QMV on decisions implementing foreign policy guidelines agreed on by the Council should be used more often, perhaps even allowing certain decisions to be taken by 'consensus minus one'. It supported the idea of a planning and analysis unit at the service of the Presidency and the Council, but within the Council Secretariat, and it argued for a higher profile for that Secretariat in order to help the Presidency in implementing the CFSP, and help enhance continuity.

It had appeared that Justice and Home Affairs would be less problematical. At the beginning of the IGC Ireland supported the transfer of immigration and asylum from Pillar III to Pillar I to facilitate more rapid and easier decision-making. It thought the Commission should have a right of initiative on all third pillar issues and that perhaps QMV could be introduced on some matters. Since Pillar III related directly to the citizen, Ireland argued for a greater role for the European Parliament or, failing that, for national parliaments in this area. Given the situation in the republic, efforts to combat drugs and drug trafficking were to receive high priority. By the end of the Amsterdam negotiations, a problem arose, namely the British attitude to freedom of movement of people and the incorporation of the Schengen *acquis* into the Treaty establishing the

European Union (Protocol Integrating the Schengen *acquis* into the Framework of the European Union). This occasioned separate Protocols on 'The application of certain aspects of Article 7a of the Treaty establishing the European Community to the United Kingdom and Ireland' and on the 'Position of the United Kingdom and Ireland'. These relate to exceptions from the freedom of movement, since the UK wished to be able to continue to check people at its borders to verify their credentials. The Irish did not advocate these exceptions, but felt forced into accepting them since they placed a higher premium on 'the Common Travel Area' between Ireland and the United Kingdom than on free movement between Ireland and the continent. If Britain opposed free movement on the pragmatic basis of the convenience of the maximising of freedom of movement in and out of Ireland, the Irish opted to opt out of EC and EU freedom of movement too. Thus, Ireland does not participate in the common policies for asylum, refugees and immigration, although in a Declaration of which the IGC 'took note', the Irish declared that they intended to participate on these matters 'to the maximum extent compatible with its maintenance of its Common Travel Area' with the UK, and as the UK began to shift position on this, Ireland has too.

Not surprisingly firm commitments to cohesion were a priority for Ireland in the negotiations of 1991. Ireland was the first state to make firm proposals in this area although it did not press its demands as stridently as Spain. Cohesion was important, given the economic realities of Ireland, their view of the original commitments, and since otherwise EMU was perceived as widening the regional disparities that already existed, especially in peripheral areas. The Irish insisted on inclusion of economic and social cohesion in the Treaty on European Union, and were rewarded with Title XIV on Economic and Social Cohesion as well as Protocol 15 on the same topic. As has been seen above, resource transfers have played an important part in Irish–EC/EU relations, and that continues to be the case.

Ireland also pushed for and gained another Protocol in the TEU. While Ireland favoured those aspects of social policy which touched on employment and worker rights, it was anxious lest there be any movement into areas touching upon issues of personal morality. Thus Protocol 17 attempted to make clear that nothing in the treaties affected the 'application in Ireland of Article 40.3.3 of the Constitution of Ireland', that is, the prohibition on abortion and the equal right to life of child and mother. There was later some confusion over what this meant, and whether it affected travel abroad for abortions or the right to information. Formal amendment initially was rejected by the other members, who did not wish to open up the prospect of renegotiation, but in May 1992 they approved a 'solemn declaration' to be attached to the Treaty saying that 'it was and is their intention that the Protocol shall not limit freedom either to travel between Member States or ... to obtain or make available in Ireland, information relating to services lawfully available in Member States'. Confusion, however, persisted.[64]

Like other Member States, as the 1990s progressed, so too did concern with unemployment and Ireland joined those in 1996–97 seeking Treaty amendment in this area, but it too joined the refrain that no measures on employment, or on strengthening social policy (which it supported), should jeopardise Member States' competitiveness.

Figure 15.1 Irish support for European Union membership, 1981–98

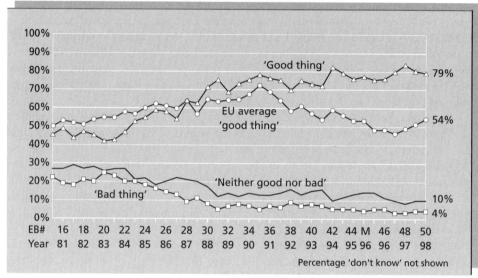

Source: Eurobarometer No. 50, p. 28.

Similarly, given the importance of inward investment to the Irish economy, they were anxious that what they regarded as disparities in the conditions of economic competition in the Member States should not be allowed to persist. Given local east coast concerns, they also looked for a strengthening of nuclear safety in the environment sector, because of problems with Britain over the nuclear waste allegedly being dumped in the Irish Sea.

Ireland has been strongly *communautaire* and has favoured political integration, especially as a protection for small states against larger neighbours. But given its relatively recent independence, it has also been sensitive to not going too far in the federalist direction, although it has argued that integration enhances Irish influence in Europe and the world. It has, therefore, strongly supported subsidiarity, especially in the social and environmental areas, although simultaneously it was worried that the principle could be abused and inhibits the development of policies in Irish interests. Irish attitudes to European Union are shown in Figure 15.1.

DENMARK ───────────────────────────────

The Danes have now had five referendums on European questions. Although these turnouts have been relatively high, particularly when European issues have been seen to touch on Danish independence, the lack of enthusiasm for Danish membership is

Table 15.2   Danish voting in referendums on EC membership, the
SEA, the Treaty on European Union and the Treaty of Amsterdam

	% Yes	% No	% Turnout
EEC entry 1972	63.3	36.7	90
SEA 1987	56.2	43.8	75
TEU 1992	49.3	50.7	82
TEU 1993	56.8	43.2	86
Amsterdam 1998	55.1	44.9	75

reflected in Danish turnouts for direct elections to the European Parliament. The average Danish turnout has been 49.5% compared to a European average of nearly 60%, and the Danish average is the second worst among the Member States. Indeed, Denmark, along with Britain, has been consistently the most sceptical of the Member States.

Part of the reason has been its geographic position between the Baltics, Scandinavia and Western Europe, and another has been its close ties with the UK market. Also it has been, and is, possible to characterise Danish policy as reflecting the tension between 'two opposing tendencies, towards involvement in and withdrawal from international politics', while historically there has always been a concern with its 'political relations with the great power neighbour'.[65]

It was a founder member of the OEEC and Council of Europe and was generally sympathetic to the British position. It was not involved in discussions on the ECSC, since coal and steel were of no relevance to Denmark. Of more relevance were Nordic efforts in 1947 and 1948–49, seeking to bring about a Nordic Customs Union and a Nordic Defence Union. These negotiations were unsuccessful but a passport union was agreed. At the time of the ECSC negotiations the Scandinavians were involved in discussions on a Nordic Council, which came into existence in 1952, but which because of the previous difficulties, avoided questions of high politics and was avowedly inter-governmental. Originally the Council had no statutes, permanent headquarters or secretariat, and it has no power to oblige governments to comply with recommendations. The Danes have often looked north as much as south, and this has been a continuing feature of their policy.

The Danes were one of those states that took the initiative in the OEEC to try to establish a free trade area that would include the Six, but to no avail. At other times too they sought to be a bridge between the Six and others, especially EFTA, but also to no avail. The Danes were founder members of EFTA in 1960, although they would have preferred a wider free trade area with agriculture included. They received a shock in 1958 when a Danish government commission questioned whether Denmark was ready for free trade or EEC membership without severe economic dislocation.[66]

In 1961 the Danes applied for EEC membership following the British application. Given the importance of the British (and German) market to them, the Danes wished to participate in the evolution of the CAP. Their application and negotiation were overshadowed by the British, but the applications of both countries foundered at about the same time. The year 1962 saw the codification of Nordic co-operation in the Nordic Council and some very limited institutional development. In the 1960s Denmark's EFTA membership benefited the Danish economy and the diversification of its markets. Again circumstances outside its control transformed the situation in 1969 with The Hague summit and subsequent British application. The Danish negotiations were not difficult, indeed the Danes proposed full membership without a transitional period; an offer rejected by the Six. Some difficulty was caused over the Faeroe Islands and Greenland[67] in relation to fisheries, and the Danes were also anxious about their former EFTA partners who were not applying for EEC membership.

The Danish constitution allows for the transfer of power to international organisation, if five-sixths of the Parliament (Folketing) agree, or failing that if a simple majority of the Folketing is supported in a referendum. To avoid making the question of membership an election issue in the winter of 1971–72, however, it was agreed that the issue be put to a referendum. In a vote in the Folketing in September 1972, a few weeks before the referendum, the opposition managed to muster more than one-sixth of the vote. In another twist, the Norwegian referendum took place a week before the Danish people voted, and produced a Norwegian 'No'. The real issue was summed up as 'Ever since the Six was formed, the Danes have faced the predicament of having a too significant economic interest in the Common Market to ignore it but too many restraining factors to join alone',[68] – hardly a ringing endorsement.

Denmark joined because it felt it could not afford to be outside and it was an economic decision to join a customs union, conditioned by the policies of others and external developments. It was not a vote for European political integration or federalism; and there has always been reservation about 'deepening'. Ironically there has been support for increasing the scope of integration to include social, environmental, industrial, regional and economic trade and monetary policy. The Danes have been positive about the CAP. They have also been against major reforms, against other protectionist tendencies in the EEC and barriers to trade, but for fixed currencies and the EMS. The oil, energy and economic crises of the 1970s combined to reinforce the lack of enthusiasm for membership, especially as it had been sold on economic grounds. They also had great difficulty with the common fisheries policy, being regarded as the least conservation minded.

In the 1980s the Danes continued to be comfortable with the economic dimension of integration, and supported moves to the internal market. They pushed hard on the environmental question, finally being satisfied that they could maintain their own high standards. Political integration continued to be a problem. The Danes voted against the calling of an Inter-governmental Conference at the Milan European Council in 1975. They had earlier resisted the Genscher–Colombo proposals, especially those seeking to integrate security, defence and foreign policy into the EC system, and were later against the linkage being made between the Single Market and institutional reform. They took the view that 'the difficulties facing the construction of Europe resulted from a failure to implement the existing treaties fully and could be remedied by the strict application of the Treaties'.[69]

444

Having been obliged to participate in a Treaty revision they did not want, the Danes made the best of a bad job by positively encouraging the IGC to strengthen Community competence in social affairs and in the protection of the environment. Their motives were mixed. They hoped and expected that the Community would be obliged to work for standards which were closer to those that Denmark had for long applied, thereby reducing any competitive disadvantage that Denmark might have inflicted on itself. But the government also wished to put some brakes on internal demands for further and costly improvements in the Danish welfare state, by deploying the argument that Denmark must not, in its own self-interest, get too far ahead of its partners. Denmark also secured, in a quiet way, the first of the opt-outs, which were later to become a feature of the Community's constitution. This was the so-called Danish clause of the Single Market article of the SEA. Article 100a, para. 4, enables a Member State to maintain higher standards than those accepted by the Community to protect the environment or the working environment, provided its higher standards do not restrict trade. In practice, the Danes never applied to the Commission to use this facility – nor did any other Member State.

The Folketing rejected the SEA in January 1986 by 80 to 75 votes on the grounds of the erosion of national sovereignty, and asked the government to seek to renegotiate. The other Member States refused, and the subsequent referendum endorsed the SEA, the government arguing that a 'No' would put Danish membership of the EC into question, and strongly playing the economic card, Denmark being a large beneficiary of the Community budget. Denmark, however, has consistently been one of the states to emphasise the upholding of national sovereignty.[70]

In the 1990s, like other states, Denmark had both the necessity and opportunity to consider its position *vis-à-vis* the future development of the European Union. In October 1990 Danish parties representing 75% of the Folketing agreed a memorandum setting out the basic Danish position on the IGCs. It was clear that 'the principle of subsidiarity should be stated as a basic principle in the preamble and should be applied in each specific area'.[71] Although not mentioned by name, there was clear antipathy to federalism in the document, with talk of 'gradual deepening' and 'gradual development' and several references to strengthening the existing Community.

Later in the context of the proposals of others, the Folketing demanded explicit references to a federal goal or vocation be dropped. On the other hand, after German unification many Danes were worried about the power of their neighbour, and some of them saw membership of the European Union as a way of containing Germany.

By 1995–97 these themes were still present in the Danish position, although given developments since 1991–93 they have been expressed in slightly different ways. At this later time, the debate concerned the nature and extent of differentiated integration. Originally a little ambivalent, since they realised that a multi-speed Europe was no panacea, and that issues in apparently discrete areas were often interrelated and could impact upon one another – in addition to the dangers inherent in notions of first-, second- and third-class member states – they came to accept it on the grounds of flexibility. It allowed those which wished to move faster to do so, and that, with enlargement, participation on different levels in different areas would make practical sense.

Continuing an earlier theme, the Danes still strongly supported subsidiarity, although they increasingly called for a greater delineation of what powers resided where. In the context of the 1996–97 IGC, the Danes identified three possible approaches to subsidiarity:

- the listing of an exhaustive 'catalogue of powers' for the Union and for member states;
- modifying the existing system; and
- specifying what was not within the Union's competence, simply defining more clearly and precisely where and when the Union should take action.

All of this was in the context of viewing the European Union as an inter-governmental organisation, where states should be able to determine for themselves those issues on which there should be common action. It is also to be seen in the context of a genuine concern to bring the Union closer to the citizen, to make it more transparent, and to simplify the treaties and the processes of EU governance.

In 1990 and subsequently, the Danes argued that the institutions had coped 'satisfactorily' in the past, there being, therefore, 'no need to consider any fundamental changes in the natural balance'[72] between the institutions and the institutions and the Member States. However, in both IGCs, along with supporting subsidiarity, the Danes argued for the strengthening of the role of national parliaments, and drew especial attention to the role of the Folketing Common Market Committee. In December 1995, this argument was put in the context of increasing the flow of information between the Union and national parliaments, giving the latter greater time and opportunity to adopt positions. In both IGCs, its proposals on strengthening the European Parliament were modest. In the first it was willing to allow greater scope for the co-operation procedure (but not co-decision), allow the European Parliament to require the Commission to put forward proposals called for by the Parliament, and allow it to hold hearings in Member States that had not complied with or implemented EC legislation. An ombudsman was to be responsible to the Parliament. In the second the proposals related to reducing the number of legislative procedures and to make the Parliament effective, placing a ceiling on its membership. In addition, it argued that the Parliament should have the right to reject the nomination of individual Commissioners. In essence, however, the Danish position was that real democratic control should rest with the national parliaments. Interestingly, the Danish Supreme Court in a judgement on a challenge to the validity of the Treaty on European Union made it clear that in their view it was the Danish courts that had the last word if there were a conflict between EU law and the Danish constitution.

In line with their view of democracy, accountability and Europe needing to be closer to the citizen, the Danes have consistently made the case for increased transparency in the institutions and decision-making, and of the possibility of some Council meetings being held in public. Perhaps somewhat tongue in cheek, it noted in one of its submissions to the 1996 IGC debate that while it might be difficult for some states to accept more openness in EU decision-making than existed at their national level, others found it increasingly difficult to accept less.

446

On the Council, the Danes, contrary to their generally cautious position about the transfer of power, have argued for more majority voting in some areas, particularly the environment, social policy and labour market matters, where they wanted progress. Indeed, as noted above, one reason for their sympathy towards flexibility was that they wished for stronger action in some areas, thus they argued that individual states should be in a stronger position to decide what was really important to them. The Danes, however, did not favour indiscriminate expansion of majority voting and were cautious about altering the qualified majority voting system. It feared that any change might alter the balance between large and small states to the disadvantage of the latter, although it did accept the idea that the system should ensure that the majority represented at least half of the Union's population – that is, a double majority. On the Presidency, the Danes presented some radical ideas, after accepting that there were problems with the current rotational system. They suggested that the duration of the Presidency might be extended and that there might be either an elected Presidency or a 'presidential group' whereby teams of four or five states (including a mix of large and small) would hold the Presidency for twelve to eighteen months. The Danes have always been cautious about foreign policy, security and defence co-operation. In October 1990 the memorandum agreed by most parties rejected 'the idea that European Political Co-operation should come to include co-operation in defence policies, inter alia the setting-up of common military forces'.[73] Denmark has still not joined the WEU and remains pro-NATO and Atlanticist, despite some reservations about NATO policy in the 1980s. It has wished to maintain the Edinburgh 'Decision' position and was clear that it was not up for negotiation in 1996–97:

> Nothing in the Treaty on European Union commits Denmark to become a member
> of the WEU. Accordingly, Denmark does not participate in the elaboration and the
> implementation of decisions and actions of the Union which have defence implications,
> but will not prevent the development of closer co-operation between Member States in
> this area.[74]

Nonetheless, Denmark has been aware that the security environment and debate have moved on since then. It has become an 'Observer' at the WEU, which allows it to be present and speak at WEU meetings but without a vote and having no legally binding obligation to come to the aid of WEU members. It remains opposed to an EU–WEU merger, although it has come to favour somewhat closer links between the two.

Denmark takes a broad view of security, believing that European Union co-operation on the economic and political aspects of security should be broadened to include the commercial, environmental and technological, so that minor problems could be prevented from escalating. In this vein it supported the emergence of an analysis and planning unit and the EU taking on board the Petersberg tasks on the basis that individual Member States could themselves decide to participate or not. Indicative of this approach was Danish involvement in some military aspects of crisis management, for example supplying UNPROFOR with 1,300 troops in 1993 and IFOR and SFOR with over 600 troops in the attempt to secure the implementation of the Dayton Agreement.

It favoured the continuation of consensus in the CFSP as a general principle, although the 1995 Foreign Ministry report made clear that Denmark was 'prepared to agree to joint actions being adopted even if one or two countries do not wish to participate' as long as there were suitable arrangements for 'those countries which do not participate in a joint action'.[75] It has pushed for greater co-ordination, unity and consistency between the CFSP and the EC both institutionally and practically, but believes in keeping the CFSP as a separate pillar. Inter-governmentalism was to prevail in this area with the Council as the decisive body.

The Danes have also been inter-governmentally minded on the third pillar, although they were rather more willing in Pillar III to conceive of certain areas being transferred to the Community pillar. However, their reservations in this sphere are exemplified by their sensitivity on the issue of citizenship. This was to form another part of the Edinburgh clarification or 'Decision'. This made it clear that the Treaty on European Union gave:

> nationals of the Member States additional rights and protection . . . They do not in any way take the place of national citizenships. The question of whether an individual possesses the nationality of a Member State will be settled solely by reference to the national law of the Member State concerned.[76]

Largely at Danish behest, this was reflected in the Amsterdam Treaty, which modified the TEU provisions on citizenship of the Union, crucially by adding: 'Citizenship of the Union shall complement and not replace national citizenship.' Fears about citizenship had been exploited in the 1992 referendum, and were fuelled by worries over immigration and a large, wealthy neighbour to the south.

If cautious on Pillars II and III, Danish governments have supported EMU, seeing it in 1990 as 'a natural extension of the creation of the internal market',[77] and believing that it should be based on tough criteria. The Danes hoped that EMU would help to keep inflation under control and that the ECSB would be an alternative to *de facto* domination by the Bundesbank. It accepted the case for an independent ECSB, but worried about democratic accountability, which should balance 'the necessary independence' of the ECSB. While accepting price stability as a supreme goal, the Danes wanted explicit references to the goals of full employment and environmentally sustainable development in the Treaty on European Union. They were also clear that in regard to 'fiscal and budgetary policy of the individual Member States the Treaty must reflect the principle of subsidiarity'.[78] Despite this official position, and apprehensive of Danish public opinion, Denmark negotiated a Protocol in the Treaty on European Union that made it clear that it might not participate in the third stage of EMU, and that if it notified the Council of its position it would have an exemption. After the June 1992 rejection of the Maastricht Treaty, at Edinburgh in December 1992 as another element of the 'Decision', Denmark declared that it would:

> not participate in the single currency, will not be bound by the rules concerning economic policy which apply only to the Member States participating in Stage III of

economic and monetary union and will retain its existing powers in the field of monetary policy according to its national laws . . .'[79]

Somewhat ironically, although the Commission Report of 25 March 1998 on progress towards convergence made no separate analysis of the Danish position given the Danes decision to opt out, Denmark, according to the general tables included, was in a better position to meet the criteria than most of those states which entered EMU on 1 January 1999.[80]

On new competencies in the 1990s the Danes made the enhancement of environmental policy a priority, increasingly focusing on the incorporation of 'sustainable development' as a treaty objective, on the need for a range of other policies to incorporate the environmental dimension, and even for the introduction of ecological taxes. The Danes have supported a Community social policy 'as a means of distributing the benefits deriving from the internal market. It is important that solidarity be shown'.[81] There were also Danish calls for a series of minimum standards to be laid down in this area and the avoidance of social dumping by multinational companies. By the mid-1990s there was concern that little had been achieved and the Danes pushed for the Social Chapter to be transferred fully to the Community pillar. In similar vein the Danes argued for unemployment targets to be set by the Union and the co-ordination of national policies to reduce unemployment – but this was to be co-ordination only. The 1990s also saw Danish calls for an examination of the introduction of minimum rates of income tax, VAT, and other taxes (Denmark is heavily taxed); consumer protection to be strengthened: stronger action on fraud and the non-implementation of Community legislation; a greater focus on human and democratic rights; and greater attention paid to health, education and cultural policies.

For the government, much of the approach to the 1996–97 IGC is encapsulated in the title of the 11 December 1995 memorandum: 'Bases for negotiations: an open Europe',[82] since the government felt that the IGC must have preparation for enlargement as a priority. Poland and the Baltic states, including Estonia, are of strategic and commercial importance to Denmark, while the Danes are not unaware that enlarging the Union will make it ever more difficult for it to become over-centralised and quasi-federal. The Danes accepted that while the IGC could prepare in some areas, it would have to be followed by reforms, especially in the areas of agriculture and the Structural Funds, although there were dangers here given that Denmark is still a marginal net beneficiary of Community funding.

During the 1990s the government was kept in constant check by the Folketing, which, for example, made the inclusion of a Protocol forbidding the sale of summer houses to foreigners a condition of support of the Maastricht Treaty (it was included in the Treaty as Protocol 1, and allowed the Danes to maintain the status quo), and by an awareness of the sensitive nature of public opinion on certain issues.

In 1992 only two small Danish parties opposed the deal agreed at Maastricht, and the Folketing on 12 May 1992 supported it by 130 to 25. Yet in the referendum on 2 June 1992 it was rejected by a margin of 46,269 votes (50.7% to 49.3%). The opposition was composed of a variety of disparate interests, but is perhaps best summed up in an old Danish saying: 'be prepared to sit next to someone but not on his lap' – a saying that has a particular salience, given Danish views of Germany.

The fears included:

- a loss of democracy, uncompensated for by a remote European Parliament;
- an acceptance of the internal market, but no belief in the need for political union – 'Ja til Europa, Nej til unionen', linked to traditional concerns about independence and sovereignty;
- concern that the Treaty did not go far enough on social and environmental matters, such that it would undermine the Danes' own higher standards,
- concern that the Treaty went too far on immigration and citizenships; and
- an exaggerated fear of young Danes being conscripted into a European army – even worse, an army dominated by Germany.

Against such fears the government and others tried to argue that there was a danger that the other eleven would go ahead with European Union leaving Denmark on its own, and that there was no possibility of renegotiations. In fact, after the 'No' it was made clear that the eleven would not proceed without the Danes, and in the second half of 1992 there was much discussion about the Treaty as the Danes sought clarification.

After a pause for reflection, and awaiting the vote in the French referendum, the government put together a package which seven of the eight parties in the Folketing accepted as a national compromise in October 1992 – the opposition Socialist People's Party accepting but the Progress Party still saying 'No'. The national compromise looked more radical on paper than in practice. It required a declaration making it clear that Denmark was not committed to the third stage of EMU, including a single currency (the Treaty already contained a provision for a Danish referendum). Denmark would not accept any obligation to join the WEU or a common defence of the European Union, again despite the fact that references to this in Maastricht implies no commitment to such defence. Other questions involved the Treaty's provisions on European citizenship, the closer co-operation on Home Affairs and Justice, assurances that nothing would be done to force Denmark to lower its existing national social and environmental protection standards, and a call for greater openness in EC decision-making, more explicit attention to subsidiarity and a strengthening of the role of both the national and the European Parliament. A further problem was the call that 'Danish agreement must be judicially binding for all Twelve Community Member States'. It was this that proved to be so difficult at the Edinburgh European Council in December, although the Danes and their Community partners, as seen above and in Chapter 3, believed that the 'Decision' at Edinburgh squared the circle.

In May 1998, 55.1% of Danes voted for the ratification of the Treaty of Amsterdam. Although emotions were very strong during the campaign, most of the controversial issues had been determined in the context of the 1992–93 campaigns and the Edinburgh 'Decision'. There was no issue specific to the Treaty of Amsterdam of the same controversial nature as a single currency or the CFSP. The Decision of December 1992 was not

Figure 15.2   Danish support for European Union membership, 1981–98

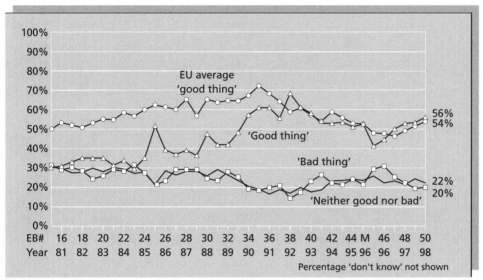

Source: Eurobarometer No. 50, p. 23.

challenged and the government could claim that it had achieved its objectives in the 1996–97 IGC. The negotiations with Central and Eastern Europe states would start on time, and specific Danish proposals on employment, environment, transparency, consumer protection, the fight against fraud, subsidiarity and the role of national parliaments were either completely or partially accepted. The 'No' campaign reiterated previous themes, argued that too much power had already drifted to Brussels and away from Danes, and sought to use the referendum as a plebiscite on Danish membership of the European Union. Their problem was, and remains, that while not European federalists, most Danes make a pragmatic judgement on whether particular proposals imply an unacceptable loss of national power as against the perceived economic benefits of membership. and most have been content to live with the compromises reached in the 1990s. The 1998 result was not followed by riots on the streets, as happened in May 1993 when Denmark saw its worst riots in five years. The evolution of Danish opinion can be seen in Figure 15.2.

UNITED KINGDOM

If the Danes have proved to be something of a thorn in the flesh of their partners, the United Kingdom has also been 'An Awkward Partner',[83] for the other Member States, and this awkwardness too has stemmed from deep-seated roots in British political culture.

One element of the problem has been the difficulty in adjusting to the secular loss of relative power and declining economic base since the mid-nineteenth century.[84] This trend accelerated as a result of both world wars, and with the loss of empire. The problem was exacerbated insofar as the trend was obscured by being on the winning side in both world wars, by the award of a permanent seat on the United Nations Security Council, with its accompanying veto, by the possession of the largest empire ever seen, and by the military power Britain still enjoyed in 1945, a power soon to be enhanced by the acquisition of the atomic bomb. Britain had also been the leading West European power on the allied side during the 1940–45 period. There was a widespread perception that Britain had 'won' the war and was a global power, and a pervasive belief in Britain's greatness. While there had been a 'Descent from Power',[85] that descent had been somewhat obscured and, given Britain's position in 1945, somewhat exaggerated.

The United Kingdom still had a global view of its position. Others might think almost exclusively in terms of European reconstruction and influence, but Britain believed that it was 'not solely a European power' and therefore had wider considerations on its mind.[86] But within this global context there were three spheres of influence that were regarded as particularly crucial to Britain: the 'special relationship' with the USA, its colonial heritage and inheritance, and the balance of power concern with developments in Europe. The problem for Britain was that the secular economic decline mean increasingly that it was unable or unwilling to provide the resources necessary to sustain these interests and roles, such that increasingly it began to focus upon the European dimension, while still occasionally hankering after a wider and larger role.

Britain played a leading role in some West European developments, being a founder member of the OEEC, the Council of Europe, the Brussels Treaty Organisation and NATO. Many in Europe had looked for British leadership on the question of European reorganisation, given Britain's wartime leadership and its role in the liberation of Europe. These hopes were reinforced by the famous speech Winston Churchill made in Zurich in September 1946, when leader of the opposition. Churchill called 'for a kind of United States of Europe', but, reflecting British concerns of the day and its paternalism, he went on to explain that Britain and its Commonwealth, the United States, and perhaps the Soviet Union, were to be 'the friends and sponsors of the new Europe', but not, although this point initially eluded many in Europe, an integral part of it.[87] In 1953 Churchill explained that Britain's relationship with Europe 'can be expressed by prepositions, but the preposition "with" but not "of" – we are with them but not of them'.[88]

Perhaps most importantly for Britain's attitude to European integration was its very different wartime experience from that of defeated and occupied nations. Far from believing that the war showed the need for a radical overhaul of the state and consequently of sovereignty, for Britain the British state had been vindicated by the years 1939–45. There was thus not the same perception of the need for radical readjustments such as federalism and the relinquishing of sovereignty. Therefore, British policymakers firmly opposed such developments, with no willingness to 'transfer control of the British economy, or other aspects of policy, from the British Government to a European body, either through the delegation of power or the acceptance of majority voting'.[89]

These reservations were shared by members of the first Labour majority government, and across the political spectrum. The preferred model was strictly inter-governmental co-operation in limited fields. It had already made that clear in the debate over the structure and powers of the Council of Europe, and the North Atlantic Treaty too relied upon consent, before any action could occur.

This attitude was deeply ingrained and the British never really appreciated the 'depth of drive towards real unity, as distinct from inter-governmental co-operation on the continent'.[90] This failure was profound and enduring, although to some extent the gradual realisation that the Europeans did care, did mean business, and were making progress towards their objective (see Chapters 2), was an important factor behind the gradual movement of British policy towards applying for EEC membership.

This realisation was abetted by the failure of the Maudling talks under the auspices of the OEEC in 1957–58. This British attempt to create a free trade area between the Six, who had just signed the Treaty of Rome, and the other members of the OEEC, floundered. The British government proceeded to negotiate with some of the other non-EEC OEEC states, and these negotiations led to the signing of the Stockholm Convention in January 1960, which founded the European Free Trade Association. EFTA was purely inter-governmental, involved only limited co-operation, excluded agriculture, and was limited to free trade, with no supranational bodies or powers. It was hoped that EFTA could still build some kind of bridge to the EC.

But just as EFTA was coming into being, questions began to be asked about the validity of that and other assumptions. It came to be appreciated that in any negotiations the Six were likely to insist upon a customs union. If so, the question became whether Britain would be better to join the EEC? Other factors working in the same direction were the recognition that the Six was not a flash in the pan, but was becoming a reality; that the British trading position faced real dangers since neither EFTA nor the Commonwealth was a viable alternative; that the British economy was not performing satisfactorily; and that the 'Descent from Power' was continuing. Fundamentally, it became a question of making the best of a bad job, as other avenues for progress, prosperity and influence were closed off or downgraded. It was not a radical shift of sentiment, but a pragmatic recognition of reality.[91]

After much internal debate and consultations with EFTA partners, the Commonwealth, the USA and the Six, Prime Minister Macmillan announced on 31 July 1961 that the government had 'come to the conclusion that it would be right for Britain to make a formal application for negotiations with a view to joining the Community if satisfactory arrangements can be made to meet the special needs of the United Kingdom, of the Commonwealth and of the European Free Trade Association', it being added that there was no guarantee of success, and there could be a situation where the cost outweighed the potential gains, especially if Commonwealth relations were disrupted. The Commonwealth was still at that time a potent force in British politics since the 'old' Commonwealth had helped Britain to defeat its enemies in two world wars. The House of Commons was told that Britain would have 'no influence' in Europe if it remained outside the Community, this being one reason why membership rather than association was being sought, and that there was 'a tendency towards larger groups of nations acting together in the common interest'. The application was lodged on 10 August 1961. Both Prime Minister Macmillan and Hugh Gaitskell, leader of the opposition, emphasised their antipathy towards federal developments. For Gaitskell there was 'no question whatever of Britain entering a federal Europe now'. Conservative anti-marketers agreed.[92]

The Conservative government appointed Edward Heath to negotiate to see what terms were on offer, and made it clear that it accepted the Treaty of Rome objectives. The major issues were the Commonwealth, agriculture and EFTA, as well as the length of the transitional period. The negotiations were, however, brought to an end by de Gaulle's unilateral 'non' in January 1963. De Gaulle's objections were not to the terms but to the prospect of French hegemony in the EEC being challenged.

In 1966 the Labour government that had come to power in 1964 announced that it would seek membership of the EEC again, 'provided the right conditions are established'.[93] All the previous factors came into play, plus the new recognition that technology demanded large markets. The formal application was made on 11 May 1967, although many in both the Cabinet and the Parliamentary Labour Party were unenthusiastic. It remained true that the economic arguments were finely balanced, while the political arguments were seen as compelling.

Negotiating issues were similar to those previously, but with a Labour government there was now also concern about the freedom of a Labour government to pursue industrial and social development in the less favoured UK regions. These concerns and the internal debate were again rendered superfluous by another de Gaulle objection in November 1967.

The situation changed with the change of government in both France and Germany. At The Hague summit in December 1969, the Six agreed to enlargement if the applicants accepted the treaties, their political finality, and the *acquis communautaire*. A British White Paper in February 1970 was cautious about the economic consequences of membership, but there was still seen to be no alternative. Wilson now argued that 'on fair terms we can stand and profit' by entry but he warned that 'should the negotiations not lead to acceptable terms for entry, Britain is and will be strong enough to stand on her own feet outside'.[94] Before real negotiations could start, the June 1970 general election intervened, and the Conservatives were returned to power. The new government was committed to negotiations and to seeking a fair settlement. The debate over the next few years revolved around whether the terms of entry were right. The government was headed by Edward Heath, who had made his maiden speech in 1950 welcoming the Schuman plan, and had led the 1961–63 negotiating team. Britain again made it clear that it accepted the treaties and the *acquis communautaire*. Labour would determine its position once the terms were known. The main phase of the negotiations was completed in June 1971 and a White Paper in July argued that the key question was whether British influence would be greater inside or outside the Community.[95]

In October 1971 the House of Commons debated entry and supported membership on the terms negotiated by 356 to 244. Despite a three-line whip to vote against, 69 Labour MPs voted in favour. The Conservatives had a 'free vote' and 39 of them voted against their own government. A new theme for Labour was the failure to consult the British people, as had happened in the other applicant states, and they also announced that a Labour government would seek to renegotiate the terms, especially the CAP burden, the blow to the Commonwealth, and the threat to regional policy.

The European Communities Bill, giving domestic effect to the Treaty of Accession, had a tortuous path through the Commons, but was finally passed by a majority of 17, and the United Kingdom became a member of the European Communities on 1 January 1973.

The decision was made, but significantly there was the lingering feeling that, Heath and a few others apart, there was no deep enthusiasm for the experiment of uniting Europe – a feeling reinforced by the party divisions on the European question. The British sojourn to Europe was motivated not by enthusiasm, but by the lack of visible alternatives:

> [T]he important thing about Britain's entry into Europe was that it had every appearance of being a policy of last resort, adopted, one might almost say, when all other expedients had failed. There was no suggestion of it being hailed as a brilliant success ... the impression remained that it was brought about in humiliating circumstances and when other options in foreign policy had lost their convincingness.[96]

This set the tone for British attitudes and policies towards the Community in the years that followed entry.

Entry did not resolve the debate about the nature of Britain's relationship with the Community. In February 1974 Labour fought the general election arguing that entry on the Heath terms was a mistake, and calling for renegotiations of those terms, particularly as regards the CAP, the financing of the Community, and retention of British control over regional, industrial and fiscal policies. Labour said they would give the British people an opportunity to express their view through either a general election or a consultative referendum. If the renegotiations were unsatisfactory Labour would not be bound by the terms of the treaty, but, if successful, Labour would play a full part in Europe. The election resulted in a minority Labour government, which immediately lodged the demand for renegotiations, citing problems with the goals of economic and monetary union and European Union, and with the CAP, trade with the Commonwealth and developing states, the budget, and certain regional and industrial policies. The other Member States demurred. Labour became a majority government in October 1974, with a majority of three, and the renegotiations took place between then and March 1975, when it culminated at the first European Council in Dublin. Wilson, the Labour Prime Minister, claimed that his government had been successful, arguing that changes to CAP would reduce prices; that there were guarantees for Commonwealth sugar producers and New Zealand; a corrective mechanism for British budgetary contributions was to be introduced (although it never operated and was soon forgotten); that there was progress on industrial and regional matters and that it was now clear that EMU had been tacitly abandoned.[97]

Seven Labour Cabinet members disagreed. They felt food was still too dear, the budget was unfair, and little had been done to ameliorate problems for Asian states or the balance of payments. More important still was the undiluted challenge to British democracy and sovereignty. In a key Commons debate in April 1975, while 396 to 170 MPs supported the recommendation that Britain should remain a member, a majority of Labour MPs on a free vote voted against the Motion, including seven Cabinet ministers and thirty junior ministers. The Conservatives, under their new leader, Mrs Thatcher, overwhelmingly supported continued membership, only seven MPs voting against. Mrs Thatcher argued that membership allowed the influence of being in a larger club, contributed to peace and security, and provided a secure source of food, whereas withdrawal would be a leap in the dark, and was not a genuine alternative.[98]

The referendum question on 5 June, in Britain's first ever national referendum, was 'Do you think that the UK should stay in the European Community (Common Market)?'

The government and the pressure group 'Britain in Europe' reiterated previous arguments stressing the availability of veto and that traditional sovereignty was a chimera. Membership provided a say in decisions. Parliament would still have the right to repeal membership at a later date. The 'No' campaign was headed by the National Referendum Campaign which claimed that pre-entry promises about jobs and prosperity had proved to be false and that the British were being asked to give up ruling themselves. They stressed that North Sea oil now allowed Britain to 'go it alone', and that there was an alternative to membership in a free trade area. The referendum result is shown in Table 15.3.

Of sixty-eight voting districts, only the Western Isles and the Shetlands voted 'No', with a general pattern of greater support in the south than in the north. Wilson claimed 'the debate is now over' and called for past divisions to be laid aside.[99] These hopes proved to be pious, particularly in his own party where many contended that the referendum had been an unfair contest, given the disparity of resources between the two sides. The Community also became an issue in the internal Labour Party divisions for the next ten years. The party executive secured control of the manifesto for the first direct elections in 1979 and called for fundamental reforms in the Community, and national parliamentary control over Community legislation, as well as raising the possibility of withdrawal again. The Conservatives in 1979 were much more positive about Europe, but in a harbinger of things to come, began to stress the need for a 'common sense Community which resists bureaucracy and unnecessary harmonisation proposals, holding to the principles of free enterprise which inspired its original founders'. The CAP should be reformed and 'National payments into the budget should be more closely related to ability to pay'. The power of the European Parliament was not to change.[100]

But after 1979 British policy towards the Community was made by Conservative governments, and has seen a continuation of the predominantly suspicious British attitude to European integration, although it was now accepted that the question of membership

Table 15.3 The British referendum 1975

Year	%Yes	%No	%Turnout
1975	67.2	32.8	64

was closed. The pervasive concern became, therefore, the attempt to remodel the Community in the British image, that image reflecting certain features common to both major parties and to traditional British post-war policy, although there were also distinctive Thatcherite elements.

This attempt to remodel the Community was originally hampered by the problem of the British budgetary contribution, which occupied the years 1979–84, (see pp. 29, 316–17), but it is important to note that many of Britain's partners saw it as a continuation of special British pleading. The environment did change as those partners began to realise that there were wider problems, and that the Community needed to raise more money to finance its objectives. Reform needed the support of all, and gradually linkage was established between an increase in resources, the reform of the CAP, budgetary discipline and a permanent formula for resolving the problems of budget imbalances. The real issue for Britain was the question of whether it was willing to become more *communautaire* in orientation and policy. Its partners pointed to its failure to join the Exchange Rate Mechanism (ERM), the continuing exchanges over the CAP, and the obvious lack of enthusiasm for the various proposals for institutional reform in the 1980s.

Britain clearly had a different vision of the future from the one held by many of its partners. While Britain favoured proposals relating to improving EPC, it opposed all reforms of the institutions that would strengthen the centre or radically alter the current institutional balance. Britain opposed the call for an IGC in 1985 at Milan, but participated in the IGC because it knew that any treaty change required unanimity. Any treaty amendments would have to be on a pragmatic and limited basis to have British support. Britain had made it clear earlier that it strongly supported the single market dimension of the discussions. It had called as early as 1984 for the creation of a 'genuine common market in goods and services', for the removal of the 'remaining obstacles to intra-Community trade' and the harmonising of standards, all of which could lead to the creation of 'what is potentially the largest single market in the industrialised world'. It also supported the 'development of a vigorous, efficient and cost effective industrial sector' able to compete with others.[101]

Parts of the SEA, therefore, fitted in very well with the Thatcher government emphasis upon deregulation and market forces, and reflected a British preference for measures of negative integration, that is, 'the removal of discrimination as between the economic agents of the member countries', as distinct from positive integration, namely 'the formation and application of co-ordinated and positive policies on a sufficient scale to ensure that major economic and welfare objectives are fulfilled'.[102]

Enthusiasm for the single market did not extend to all aspects of the SEA, not all of which seem to have been fully appreciated in 1986–87. Britain, for example, was not enthusiastic about the 'social dimension' which, as well as new measures to alleviate unemployment, also gave weight to workers' rights to consultation and to participation, and about the revived notion of monetary union going beyond the EMS.

In September 1988 Mrs Thatcher articulated her vision of the future in a famous speech at the College of Europe at Bruges. Some of this reflected the specifics of contemporary Conservative thinking on the free market, but some also reflected very traditional British policy, although expressed in Mrs Thatcher's own style. Britain had contributed to Europe for centuries, not least in bringing freedom in 1944–45. It sought no alternative to the Community, but did not want a European super state. Attention was to be given to specific tasks in hand, not 'arcane institutional debates' which were 'no substitute for effective action'. Mrs Thatcher went on to offer some 'guiding principles for the future' development of Europe:

- There must be 'willing and active co-operation between independent sovereign states'. It was not possible to 'suppress nationhood and concentrate power at the centre of a European conglomerate'. Europe should seek to speak with a single voice on more issues, but this did 'not require power to be centralised in Brussels or decisions to be taken by an appointed bureaucracy'. Success for Europe lay, as in Britain, in 'dispersing power and decisions away from the centre'.
- 'Community policies must tackle present problems in a practical way'; for example, although progress had been made in reforming the CAP it remained 'unwieldy, inefficient and grossly expensive'.
- Community policies must 'encourage enterprise' and there must be a greater awareness that the Treaty of Rome 'was intended as a Charter for Economic Liberty'. Its aim should be deregulation, free markets, wider choice and reduced government intervention. Rather than debating whether there should be a European Central Bank, there should be a focus upon immediate practical requirements, such as making easier the movement of goods and services. However, it was a 'matter of plain common-sense that we cannot totally abolish frontier controls', because of problems relating to drug traffic, terrorism and illegal immigrants.
- Europe should not be 'protectionist'.
- Europe 'must continue to maintain a sure defence through NATO'.

In concluding her speech, Mrs Thatcher reiterated that it was necessary to make decisions, rather than being 'distracted by Utopian goals'. In sum, the British wanted a 'family of nations, understanding each other better, appreciating each other more, doing more together but relishing our national identity no less than our common European endeavour'.[103]

The European issue continued to cause trouble for British political parties, especially now the Conservative Party. The Chancellor of the Exchequer, Nigel Lawson, resigned in 1989 over the conduct of government economic policy, especially as regards the exchange rate and disagreements with Mrs Thatcher over the ERM. The real crisis, however, was generated by the resignation of Sir Geoffrey Howe from the government in November 1990. He revealed that there were deep and continuing divisions over European policy, especially over monetary policy within the government, and that he and Lawson had only be able to persuade the Prime Minister to make a specific commitment to joining the ERM, albeit with conditions, at the Madrid European Council in June 1989 by threatening to resign. Britain joined the ERM on 8 October 1990 at DM2.95 (with a 6% plus or minus fluctuation band with a commitment to move to the narrower band when appropriate), three weeks before Howe's resignation, but he felt that the Prime

Minister was still not really committed to the idea. She clearly continued to have reservations, at least partly because of identifying the pound with sovereignty. At Rome in late October 1990, Mrs Thatcher had been isolated in her opposition to an early move towards the second stage of EMU and it was clear that she would resist the possible ultimate introduction of a single currency. There was a growing feeling that her trenchant negotiating style was now becoming counter-productive, both at home and abroad. Conservatives also had other concerns about the direction of the government and their position in opinion polls.

In the leadership elections, the new leader, John Major, defeated the pro-European Michael Heseltine, although Europe was not the decisive issue. Major shared some of Mrs Thatcher's views on Europe, and had made known as Chancellor his antipathy towards the Delors path to EMU, proposing instead a gradualist approach via the introduction of a parallel optional currency, the 'hard ecu'. He seemed, however, to believe that it was more productive to argue one's case positively and by seeking to be constructive than by continually adopting negative tactics and rhetoric. He had to be mindful that many in the party shared the Bruges' views of Mrs Thatcher, and, indeed, had formed a 'Bruges group'. The new Prime Minister, therefore, had to approach the IGCs in a rather cautious vein.

Not surprisingly, Britain was adamantly opposed to the federal vocation espoused by many. John Major told the House of Commons in November 1991 that 'We will not accept a Treaty which describes the Community as having a Federal vocation'.[104] The deletion of that phrase from the draft Maastricht text was seen as a British success. The British much preferred to stress the principle of subsidiarity. Britain regarded subsidiarity as 'bottom up', and therefore acceptable, and 'federalism' as centralisation, and therefore unacceptable. The government advocated the 'pillar' approach to the treaty and welcomed the fact that CFSP and home affairs and judicial co-operation would be on an inter-governmental basis. The government wanted unanimity to be retained for CFSP, and a right to take national decisions, if they were regarded as essential for the pursuit of British policy objectives. Britain would really have preferred to keep the current EPC system, albeit with slight modifications in its mechanisms. It did recognise that there were advantages in the Twelve speaking with one voice but, as noted in Chapter 12, felt joint analysis and objectives had to precede new institutional arrangements.

It was the same on defence. Britain continued to believe in the primacy of NATO, and that nothing must call into question the North American presence in and commitment to Europe. While Europe could do more for its own defence, the UK strongly opposed new structures as unnecessary and even worse as duplicating and undermining NATO. There could, however, be some WEU development, including the development of a planning cell and a European reaction force for operation outside the NATO area.

The British position on EMU was already clear by mid-1991. Britain believed in the necessity for strict convergence criteria before moving to the third stage, but would not accept a firm commitment on its part to a single currency. The decisions about joining and when to join were to remain matters for separate decision by the British Parliament. When pressed by opponents to EMU as to why the government did not block this part of the treaty, the government replied by showing nervousness that the other eleven might go ahead in this area on their own, leaving Britain aside.

The Treaty on European Union contained Protocol 11, which recognised:

> that the United Kingdom shall not be obliged or committed to move to the third stage of Economic and Monetary Union without a separate decision to do so by its government and Parliament.[105]

Britain also stood aside from the decision by the other eleven to proceed by agreement on social policy in order to implement the 1989 Social Charter, which it had not accepted. The Conservative government felt that these proposals would undo much of their labour and social policy of the 1980s, as well as costing jobs. The Conservative government was generally unenthusiastic about new policy areas for the Community, with John Major believing that 'We must constrain the extension of Community competencies to those areas where Community action makes more sense than national action or than action on a voluntary, inter-governmental basis'.[106] He did, however, support developments to make the single market effective, and accepted that pollution, for example, knew no frontiers. But all policies had to be judged in the light of the Conservative government's own political philosophy, and that meant a preference for the free market, and non-intervention in industrial practice, union relations, and wage bargaining. In line with traditional British thinking, the government's basic position on institutions was to support inter-governmentalism and no significant extension to the powers of the Community institutions.

Immediately after Maastricht, John Major's spokesman described the negotiations as 'game, set and match' for Britain, and on 19 December 1991 the House of Commons supported the negotiated outcome by 339 to 253. It repeated this verdict early in 1992 on the second reading of the European Communities (Amendment) Bill by a majority of 244. But this did not end the discord. On 5 November 1992 the government had a majority of only three on a motion inviting the House to proceed to further consideration of the Bill, a general election (won by the government), the Danish 'No' and the narrow French 'Yes', plus 'Black Wednesday' in September 1992 when the pound was forced out of the ERM by currency speculation and devalued, having radically changed the environment. This majority was only achieved with great difficulty, and the progress of ratification continued to prove difficult. Labour was ambivalent because of the Social Chapter 'opt out' but as part of its radical transformation in the 1990s did not wish to see the Treaty on European Union defeated.

The European Communities (Amendment) Bill had over 600 amendments tabled to it and its Committee stage took twenty-three days. The strongest challenges continued to be over the Social Chapter 'opt out' and the case for a referendum, while the government was defeated on an amendment that required that the persons elected to the Committee of the Regions must be elected local authority members. More significantly, Labour successfully moved an amendment which provided that the European Communities (Amendment) Bill, even when an Act, could only come into force (and thus the Treaty ratified) after both Houses had voted on the question of adopting the

Protocol on Social Policy. Following this, the Bill was passed by the Commons by a 180 majority in May 1993. The Lords approved it in July, having overwhelmingly rejected an amendment calling for a referendum on the Treaty. The final parliamentary stage concerned the separate vote on the Protocol on Social Policy. A Labour amendment making ratification dependent on adoption of the Social Chapter saw a tied vote in the Commons, and only failed because of the Speaker's casting vote. A government motion 'taking note' of the government's position was defeated and thus another vote was required if the Treaty was to be ratified. At this stage John Major decided to make support for the government's position on the Social Protocol a question of confidence in the government, in which case defeat would have led to a general election. His rebels backed down, the resolution was approved and the way cleared for ratification. This, however, was not quite the end of the problems since ratification then faced a legal challenge from Lord Rees-Mogg, who argued that:

- the UK Parliament had not specifically approved new powers for the European Parliament, as required by the Section 6 of the European Assembly Elections Act (May 1978);
- the government could not ratify the social protocol via Royal prerogative; and
- the Treaty involved the Crown transferring its foreign policy powers, which it was not entitled to do.

These arguments were rejected by the British courts and the UK ratified the Treaty.

The ratification of the Treaty on European Union in Britain and throughout Europe, far from ushering in a pause in the political debate, served only to open a new phase. The epicentre of the dispute in Britain was within the Conservative Party. The Labour Party had officially become Euro-friendly, although a minority in its ranks wanted Britain out, or at least no further in.

Opponents of further integration took heed from Britain's ignominious withdrawal from the ERM in September 1992 and the virtual collapse of the ERM in August 1993 when the French franc was devalued and fluctuation margins of 15% from the declared rates became the new norm. Euro-sceptics in Britain took all this as clinching evidence that monetary union, a prime objective of the Treaty on European Union, belonged to the realm of cloud-cuckoo land, as Lady Thatcher had once said. Seeing the European issue as a matter of constitutional principle, the Conservative rebels were not susceptible to the normal pull of calls for party unity. John Major's internal party critics maintained their opposition to further integration, or even the appearance or approach of further integration. In December 1994 this came to a crunch. Under the British Presidency of 1992 there been a new budgetary agreement to increase the Community's 'own resources' (see pp. 312–14). This required national ratification. Eight Conservative MPs defied the party 'whip' and voted against. In punishment, the party 'whip' was withdrawn from them and a ninth resigned from the party in protest. The Conservative government formally became a minority government, although it could expect to win any votes of confidence. Those who had lost the whip seized the issue of the admission of Spanish fishing vessels to waters off Britain, from which they had previously been excluded, to heighten the controversy, and announced proposals for British withdrawal from the Common Fisheries Policy and, among other things, to replace the European Parliament by an assembly of delegates from national parliaments.

This internal debate rumbled on in the Conservative Party and was the decisive consideration in the decision of John Redwood to challenge John Major for the leadership of the Conservative Party in the summer of 1995. Redwood, attempting to ride the tide of Euro-scepticism in the party, declared that a party led by him would never accept the end of the pound, nor any further transfers of power to the Commission or the European Parliament; the latter two of which Major concurred with. Although John Major won the leadership contest, his authority on European issues continued to be challenged and his government's approach to these issues had to reflect a sensitivity to the mood of the party and the government's precarious parliamentary position.

It is thus not surprising that post-Maastricht, John Major repeatedly emphasised British caution to a number of European proposals. In September 1993 he condemned the 'centralising vision' held by others, affirming that 'for us, the nation state is here to stay ... That is what [Europe's] people want: to take decisions through their Parliaments.' He hoped that his fellow leaders would no longer 'recite the mantra of full economic and monetary union as if nothing had changed'.[107] He sought to affirm the independence of the British view of the direction of integration in the spring of 1994 when he took the lead on seeking a reworking of the voting rules in the Council in the event of Union enlargement so that it would be easier to achieve a blocking minority, and some progress was made in this direction with the Ioannina compromise in March 1994. In the summer of 1994 he withheld his agreement to the appointment of the Belgian Prime Minister, M. Dehaene, as the new Commission President, on the grounds that Dehaene was an archpriest of the 'centralising vision' that he had condemned the previous September. In the autumn of 1994, in a speech in Leiden, he reacted to German ideas of a 'hard-core' of states pursuing further integration without those who did not feel able to join them, when he 'recoiled' from the idea that some Member States would be more equal than others.[108] The Conservative government's position was expressed more fully in September 1995 by the Foreign Secretary, Malcolm Rifkind, who began by asserting that the:

> best starting-point is Lord Palmerston's dictum 'the furtherance of British interests should be the only object of a British Foreign Secretary' ... the nation state remains the basic building block of the international system. It is nation states to which most people feel their first allegiance ... Variable geometry is already well established ... Sometimes one hears this described as a potential two-speed Europe. That is unwise. It implies a common destination arrived at in different time scales ... There may be some areas of integration that even in the long term will not be attractive or acceptable to a number of Member States ...
>
> If this reflects the reality of different interests, then the European Union will need to respond in a sensitive and flexible manner ...
>
> How then should Britain respond to proposals for further integration ... It should ... do so by a cool assessment of the British interest.[109]

It was from this perspective and against the background of intra-party hysteria that the Conservative government approached the 1996–97 IGC. However, matters were further complicated by the announcement on 20 March 1996 in the House of Commons – just nine days before the formalising of the IGC at a special Heads of Government meeting in Turin on 29 March to formally open the IGC – that a link between Bovine Spongiform Encephalopathy (BSE) and a new strain of Creutzfeldt–Jakob Disease (CJD) in human beings could not be ruled out. Despite the personal intervention of John Major in a telephone call to Jacques Santer and a brief delay, the Commission imposed an immediate ban on exports of British beef and beef by-products on 27 March. After much diplomatic effort the government hoped that the ban would quickly be partially lifted, but it failed to secure the necessary qualified majority (seven states with 39 votes voting against). In response on 21 May 1996 Prime Minister Major informed the House of Commons that his government would 'pursue a policy of non-co-operation' in European Union business:

we cannot be expected to co-operate normally on other Community business . . .
Progress will not be possible in the inter-governmental conference or elsewhere until we have agreement on lifting the ban on beef derivatives and a clear framework in place leading to lifting of the wider ban . . .[110]

The British government subsequently invoked blocking tactics in 117 cases before the Florence European Council in June 1996 came to the rescue by approving a Commission plan for a gradual lifting of the ban, but on condition of a wider than expected cull of British cattle and with no fixed dates. This, however, proved enough to allow the British government to claim victory and to allow a return to normality. The BSE problem was, however, to drag on beyond the life of the Major government. As if this was not enough, the Conservative Minister for Europe, David Davis, a key figure in representing the British government in the IGC, announced that the government would not allow the IGC to conclude without a satisfactory solution to the 'quota-hopping' issue.[111] This practice allowed EU, but particularly Spanish vessels, to buy up the licences of British owners leaving the fishing industry, and take up some of the British fishing quotas. As seen in Chapter 3, the incoming Labour government did not pursue this blockage on concluding the IGC in Amsterdam.

It is perhaps just as well that the Foreign Secretary, Malcolm Rifkind, initially stated that the IGC of 1996–97 would he 'little more than a 3,000 mile service of the Maastricht Treaty'.[112] The British wanted the IGC to be a practical examination of how the Treaty on European Union was working and the government made it clear that it would approach the IGC on the basis of

making the Union more relevant and acceptable to the people of Europe; improving practical European co-operation in areas where action at a European level is necessary; ensuring that the EU does not legislate where it is not needed.[113]

In addition, the government made it clear that it had no sympathy for 'more Europe', 'tighter political integration' or 'more centralisation; more uniformity'. It specifically noted that the Treaty references were to '"ever closer union among the peoples of Europe" (not, let it be noted, among the states of Europe, or among their Governments)'.[114] The government was clear that this phrase also did not mean an ever closer Political Union in the sense of an inexorable drift of power towards supranational institutions, the erosion of national parliaments, and the gradual development of a United States of Europe. Prime Minister John Major told David Frost in a television interview early in 1995 that he would not agree to any constitutional changes in the IGC.

Given the debates since 1994 about a potential 'hard core' and associated discussions, 'flexibility', or the issue of whether some states could proceed to deeper integration at a faster rate than others, was an important element of the IGC agenda throughout the 1996–97 IGC. The main thrust of the Conservative position was the requirement that any closer co-operation by some had to be 'agreed by all',[115] and indeed that it had to be open to all who were willing and able to participate. It also argued that there should be no presumption of convergence in the sense that it should not be assumed that initial non-participating states would eventually come on board – 'opt outs' could be permanent. The incoming Labour government of May 1997 was also cautious on flexibility, fearing a 'hard core' based on EMU, and also insisted that any flexible developments should be agreed by all, and should involve at least half of the Union's members.[116]

On most matters of substance, the position of the Labour government after May 1997 was not far removed from that of the Conservative predecessors. This can be seen in a major speech that Prime Minister Tony Blair gave to the French National Assembly in March 1998. Although he gained kudos by giving the speech in French, the essential themes relating to European integration were that while 'Britain's future lies in being full partners in Europe . . .', it needed to be appreciated, however, that there was 'deep concern amongst our peoples as to how they make sense and relate to the new Europe. They worry about their national identity . . . Brussels and the European institutions often [seem] remote and unsympathetic . . .', although the Prime Minister believed these' . . . these concerns can be answered . . .'.

He went on:

> . . . I believe in a Europe of enlightened self-interest . . . It is the nation-state's rational response to the modern world . . . the EU is a practical necessity. I happen to share the European idealism . . . but even if I weren't, I should be internationalist through realism . . . I have little doubt Europe will in time move closer still. But choosing where and how to move closer will determine whether our peoples accept these changes or rebel against them. There is a sense in which there is a third way in EU development also. We integrate where it makes sense to do so; if not, we celebrate the diversity which subsidiarity brings. In economic union, in trade and the single market, in the conditions of competition, it makes complete sense for us to co-operate ever more closely . . . In defence we can and should do more together . . . So in some areas, we integrate more closely. In others, how we run our education and health systems, welfare systems, personal taxes, matters affecting our culture and identity I say: be proud of our diversity

and let subsidiarity rule. We don't want a Europe of conformity, a United States of Europe run by bureaucrats ... For Europe to grow and prosper, Europe must be close to ordinary people's concerns. Europe must reflect the wider social and moral values we all share ...[117]

Both Conservative and Labour governments have emphasised subsidiarity, the former suggesting the inclusion in the new Treaty of elements of the subsidiarity guidelines that had been agreed at the Edinburgh European Council in December 1992. This led to the Amsterdam Treaty 'Protocol on the Application of the Principle of Subsidiarity and Proportionality', which made these provisions binding and gave them justiciable force (allowing them to be invoked before the European Court of Justice). Similarly, both have been adherents of the pillar structure of the Union.

The Conservative position on the third pillar, for example, was that while much could be done to improve efficiency and co-operation:

... change in the nature of the third pillar involving, for example, a much greater role for the Community institutions, would raise very real difficulties of principle. Nor would the government accept a transfer of subjects from the third pillar into the Community sphere, as some partners have suggested.[118]

While recognising that crime and terrorism accepted no national barriers, the government felt that third pillar matters touched on such sensitive issues of sovereignty, exacerbated in the British case by its island status, that there could be 'no question of supra-national' solutions and that unanimity had to prevail. Its proposals in this area, therefore, were limited to suggestions for improving the administrative machinery in the third pillar. In Opposition, the Labour Party committed itself to upholding the national veto over immigration and at the first meeting of its Minister for Europe, Doug Henderson, with the IGC Working Group of Personal Representatives on 5 May 1997, it was made clear that the new government would also insist on its right to maintain frontier controls.[119] Thus at Amsterdam, it too opted out of the incorporation of the Schengen *acquis* into the framework of the European Union. Early in 1999 the government indicated that it was willing to co-operate more closely on aspects of Schengen, but this co-operation was only to cover areas which did not impinge on the UK's right to maintain its own internal border controls.

Perhaps indicating the Conservative government's strength of feeling on the second pillar issues, the first substantive British document submitted in the context of the IGC was the 'Memorandum on the United Kingdom's approach to the treatment of European defence issues at the 1996 Inter-governmental Conference' of 2 March 1995. For the British, CFSP was to remain a separate inter-governmental pillar. Putting it bluntly, the Conservative government, in a view shared by their successors, told their partners that:

the nation state should be the basic building block in constructing the kind of international order we wish to see ... the nation state remains in particular the fundamental entity for co-operation in the field of defence ... defence of its citizens ... most fundamental duty of any Government ... it is a national Government's duty to

465

answer to national Parliaments when troops are sent into action . . . European action in the defence and security field should be inter-governmental, based on co-operation between nation states.[120]

Continuing traditional British policy, NATO's 'over-riding' continuing importance was stressed, especially the Article V commitment to mutual aid, as was the crucial commitment of the USA to European security. Given that US commitment, it was wrong to develop separate wholly European military structures, although the Europeans should shoulder more of the burden of European security. Thus there was support for the WEU remaining as both the European pillar of NATO and as the defence component of the EU. The WEU should leave collective defence to NATO, but should therefore develop its operational capabilities and Petersberg roles. This was all the more important since Europeans could no longer expect North Americans to participate in each and every aspect of European security. All these developments should be judged on a 'hard-headed assessment of what the European states can realistically expect to do together' and there should be a 'task-based approach' to defence. Thus 'future structures' should take account of 'the circumstances in which our armed forces are likely to be operating' and nations should be left to choose for themselves the operations in which they wished to participate; 'variable geometry' was the way forward.

As seen in Chapter 12, despite his sympathy with elements of this approach, Tony Blair, as Prime Minister, began to move British policy. Having raised defence with his European Council colleagues, in November 1998 he publicly cautioned against the 'renationalisation of defence'. It was in the same speech that he also argued that the unacceptably weak response to the Kosovo crisis had demonstrated that Europe needed a 'genuine military operational capability' and a 'European decision-making capacity and command structure' although none of this meant 'duplicating NATO'.[121] Britain became a major player in the evolution of thinking on a CFSP, the WEU and a European Security and Defence Identity.

More broadly on a CFSP, given its long-standing belief that common action could only properly flow from common policies derived from common analyses of issues, there was strong support for a planning and analysis unit, although also strong emphasis upon this being located firmly within the Council Secretariat. Similarly, while accepting the appointment of a single figure to represent the EU on the CFSP to the outside world, it was made clear that this person was to be responsible to the Member States, reflecting their collective view, not determining that view. The British wanted a person of Secretary-General rank within the Council Secretariat to fill the post. Not surprisingly, there was a commitment to retaining unanimity, although there was some recognition of the need to make real that commitment that a Member State should not stand in the way of a policy that had clear majority support. The Labour government faced the same paradox as their predecessors: on the one hand, they wanted unanimity and freedom for Britain to act as it wished, but, on the other, the Prime Minister believed that 'Europe's foreign policy voice in the world is unacceptably muted and ineffective'. Europe was 'hesitant and ineffective' and required a 'single, authoritative voice on the key international issues' and an ability to 'intervene effectively where necessary'.[122] Thus, they accepted the principle of 'constructive abstention'.

On institutional questions there were two issues in which the British played a leading role in forcing onto the agenda: fraud and financial mismanagement and the role of the European Court of Justice. While reluctant to allow the European Parliament more powers, the UK took the opportunity of the IGC to put pressure on the Parliament to exercise its existing powers in this area more fully and to paying greater attention to monitoring and restraining Community expenditure, and oversee more carefully the details of spending by the Commission. They also argued that the Council should have clearer powers to hold the Commission responsible in cases of fraud against the Community budget. On the ECJ, although the UK supported the role of the Court to ensure the even application of Community law and the prevention of *ultra vires* actions by the Union's institutions, it had become increasingly concerned over what it regarded as: judgements that imposed disproportionate costs on governments and business retrospectively, even when they had acted in good faith; and that the ECJ went beyond the letter of Community law and looked to its spirit. The British, therefore, suggested:

- limitations to the application of judgements with retrospective effects;
- that Member states should only be liable for damages where they had manifestly breached Community law;
- an internal appeals procedure;
- faster procedures for time-sensitive cases;
- a procedure to allow a Member State to test the legal base of Commission proposals; and
- a procedure for rapid amendment of Community law, which the ECJ had interpreted in ways not anticipated by the Council.[123]

The UK was unsuccessful in these areas.

As might be expected, the UK took a minimalist line on institutional change. Regarding the Commission, the main emphasis was upon improving efficiency and accountability, especially in the area of financial management and combating fraud. There were UK proposals for a so-called 'sunset clause' whereby Commission proposals would be automatically withdrawn if not adopted within a certain deadline; and for the greater use of fixed dates for the expiry of legislation or its review. It was also recognised that something needed to be done about the size of the Commission, but no strong line was taken on this.

The government had some sympathy for notions of 'team Presidencies' for the Council, perhaps comprising three or four Member States. It thought that this might be particularly useful in the CFSP pillar, where the team could always consist of a Member State with global interests to add credibility and weight to the EU's voice. More contentious was the issue of qualified majority voting. In evidence to the House of Commons Foreign Affairs Committee in February 1997, Foreign Secretary Malcolm

Rifkind said the government would oppose extending QMV in each of the eighteen cases listed as possible by the Irish draft treaty of December 1996.[124] Labour were rather more flexible, allowing for the possibility of more QMV on 'social and environmental policy, and industry and research, while insisting on the preservation of the veto on matters such as taxation, defence and security, immigration and decisions over the budget and treaty change'.[125] The British have, of course, pushed for a re-weighting of the votes in QMV.

The Conservatives were not enamoured by the European Parliament and did not support its having greater powers, particularly since they argued that the European Parliament had not properly exercised or exploited the powers it gained after Maastricht and should demonstrate that it could responsibly exercise the powers it already enjoyed. In particular, its role in restraining fraud and mismanagement was stressed. Labour was more willing to consider extending co-decision in those areas where majority voting applied in the Council. It was the British who invented and pushed for the 'Protocol on the Role of National Parliaments in the European Union'. Given that a Protocol is binding and justiciable before the European Court, its provisions have become important, especially the provision that requires:

A six-week period shall elapse between a legislative proposal or a proposal for a measure to be adopted under Title VI of the Treaty on European Union being made available . . . and the date when it is placed on the Council agenda for decision . . .

The UK has emphasised its view that:

National parliaments remain the primary focus of democratic legitimacy in the European Union, holding national Ministers in the Council to account.[126]

The Conservatives had opposed any new competencies for the EU, including those areas that the IGC was required to consider by the 1992 TEU: energy, civil protection, and tourism. Labour had made a manifesto commitment to signing up to the Social Chapter and to end that opt out. Although not formally part of the IGC, Labour's different position did lead to the Amsterdam Treaty incorporating the Social Chapter within the main body of the EC Treaty, although Labour refused to allow the extension of QMV in this area. Labour did support the inclusion of the new Employment Title in the Treaty but again in line with its underlying philosophy found the lack of legal obligation in that new Title coincided with its own preferences.

Many of the issues facing the post-May 1997 Labour government have transcended the IGC. Most notable have been:

- the British Presidency of January–June 1998;
- attitudes to enlargement and 'Agenda 2000'; and
- attitudes to EMU.

As discussed at length in Chapter 12, the Labour government has raised the issue of, and developed thinking on, defence.

The Presidency

When Tony Blair launched the 1998 (January–June) British Presidency at the Eurostar terminal at Waterloo station in early December 1997, he identified two general themes for that Presidency. One was to seek to 'demonstrate that Britain now has a strong voice in Europe'. The other was that it could play its 'part in building a Europe that works for the people and the people's priorities'. This meant that: 'We can only make Europe work for the people of Europe if, in turn, the people of Europe feel they have a stake in what Europe does.' Thus the mission was 'to make Europe work for the people: a Europe that is closer to the people's priorities: peace and prosperity, progress and partnership'. Key elements of that programme included:

- *Economic reform*: Building support for the 'Third Way in Europe. The focus for economic reform should be a social model based on improving the employability of the European workforce . . . This means education not regulation, skills and technology, not costs and burdens in business, and open competition and markets, not protectionism . . . The crucial tests will be completing the Single Market and in labour market reform.'
- *Crime*: A recognition that drug traffickers and money launderers do not respect national borders and therefore a push was necessary for a new European body for police co-operation, that is, Europol should be up and running.
- *Environment*: Particularly trying to bring about greater consistency between environmental concerns and other policy areas, like agriculture.

Some of its other priorities were inherited but Tony Blair was keen to:

- complete the move to EMU and establish the European Central Bank (see pp. 255–6 above);
- use British leadership to ensure that the enlargement negotiations made a 'flying start' [The negotiations were to start six months after the official signing of the Treaty of Amsterdam, which had taken place early in October 1997, that is, April 1998. These negotiations were opened under the British Presidency, along with the broader European Conference for all of the applicants (see pp. 511–12 above).];
- reform policy relating to Agenda 2000; and, in that context,
- press for 'the start of reform in the Common Agricultural Policy, Structural Funds and European institutions necessary to make enlargement a success'.[127]

In many of these areas the Presidency was limited by the political and economic environment, and the limitations of what could be achieved. On EMU issues there was some criticism that Blair had not properly paved the way for crucial European Council meetings. In particular, many regarded the May 1998 meeting, which was to appoint the new President of the ECB, as a sign of inexperience and bad handling. More successful was the launch of the enlargement negotiations at an appropriate pace; the workmanlike job on the Single Market by following up mechanisms for benchmarking and encouraging implementation; and administrative competence. On the CFSP, nothing happened, but Blair did take the initiative under the succeeding Austrian Presidency.

Attitudes to enlargement and 'Agenda 2000'

This issue continued well past the end of the British Presidency. The Labour government generally welcomed Agenda 2000, although it was careful to emphasise that it did not agree with all of its analyses and conclusions. A major worry was to ensure that EU policies would be funded sensibly and fairly in the years 2000–2006 and beyond. While accepting that existing members like Britain would receive proportionally reduced receipts, the government did not accept that the UK should contribute proportionally more or that the (in)famous Fountainebleau rebate system should be questioned. In 'Agenda 2000' the Commission had warned that it would be:

> necessary to adapt the definition of the expenditure on which the calculation of the rebate is based[128]

although it was put in the context of the rebate not being artificially increased given the change in the base of calculation brought about by enlargement. In fact, in Berlin 1999 the agreement accepted by the British reflected this Commission position. The British were relieved since, in the intervening period, the Germans and Dutch had tried to reopen the 1984 Agreement (see pp. 317–21 above).

The British accepted that reform was essential if enlargement was to be carried out successfully, and not surprisingly saw the CAP as a prime target of reform. In March 1998 Dr Jack Cunningham, the Minister for Agriculture, announced that the British broadly supported the Commission reform proposals. There were five key points for the UK in the negotiations: agriculture was to be sustainable and competitive; the environment was to be safeguarded; it needed to pave the way for enlargement and WTO negotiations; it needed to be affordable; and it needed to be fair, simpler and in conformity with subsidiarity.[129]

The British were also clear that reform of the Structural and Cohesion Funds could not be ducked, given that the new members were all much poorer. This, too, posed difficulties given that in any redefinitions and redistributions Britain would lose out, especially since in a key criteria – unemployment – the UK was now in a relatively better position; its levels being below the EU average. In fact, again at Berlin in March 1999 the solution was not as bad as expected. In particular, although the Highlands and Islands lost their lucrative Objective 1 status, a special transitional deal awarded them £199m until 2006 (see above, pp. 280–1).

More generally, the British have continued to look for institutional reform in the context of enlargement, especially in the Commission and on the question of qualified majorities and blocking minorities in the Council.

Economic and Monetary Union (EMU)

Part of the Presidency was made more difficult by the fact that Labour had made it clear that, like their Conservative predecessors, they would not be signing up to the first wave of EMU and the single currency. Labour had adopted their position in the run up to the

1997 general election and had also promised to hold a referendum before committing the UK to join. On 27 October 1997 the Chancellor, Gordon Brown, made a definitive speech about the Labour government's attitude to EMU. He began by identifying three principles of policy:

- 'In principle, a successful single currency within a single European market would be of benefit to Europe and Britain', but 'it must be soundly based. It must succeed.'
- Sharing 'a common monetary policy with other states represents a major pooling of economic sovereignty', but he regarded as 'wrong' the view that 'this should be a constitutional bar to British participation in a single currency, regardless of the economic benefits that it could bring.' He went on: 'I therefore conclude on the question of principle that if, in the end, the single currency is successful and the economic case is clear and unambiguous, the Government believe that Britain should be part of it.'
- The third principle was 'the consent of the British people. Because of the magnitude of the decision, we believe . . . it should be put to a referendum of the British people.'

To test whether joining would be in the national economic interest, he proposed five tests:

(i) 'whether there can be sustainable convergence between Britain and the economies of a single currency';
(ii) 'whether there is sufficient flexibility to cope with economic change';
(iii) 'the effect on investment';
(iv) 'the impact on our financial services generally'; and
(v) 'whether it is good for employment'.

He concluded on behalf of the government that, as of October 1997, Britain and the single currency did not meet those tests. Therefore, the UK would be 'notifying our European partners . . . that we will not seek membership of the single currency on 1 January 1999'. In addition, Gordon Brown went on to make clear that the current assessment was that there 'is no realistic prospect of our having demonstrated before the end of this Parliament that we have achieved convergence that is sustainable and settled . . .'. Therefore:

> barring some fundamental or unforeseen change in economic circumstances, making a decision to join during this Parliament is not realistic

but he was determined that preparations for joining should be made so that 'Britain can exercise genuine choice', a choice which would probably arise 'early in the next Parliament'. As far as the government was concerned, it was declaring 'for the principle of monetary union . . .'.[130]

The Conservative opposition under William Hague initially found it difficult to unite on its European policy, although Hague came out soon after the Brown speech to declare that the Conservatives believed it was a mistake to commit the UK in principle to joining a single currency. Rather he opposed 'Britain joining a single currency during the lifetime of this Parliament, and we intend to campaign against British membership of the single currency at the next general election'.[131] Because of continuing Conservative problems on the issue, Hague put his position to a referendum of his own party members in 1998. They endorsed the proposition that British membership should be ruled out for the life of this and the next parliament, that is possibly up to 2005–2007. There was some attempt to avoid answering the question: if the single currency was of proven advantage would the constitutional bar prevent membership? The Conservatives increasingly took the line that there needed to be evidence of how the Euro performed, etc., in good times and bad. There were also attacks on the lack of accountability of the European Central Banks.

The British general election in 1997 and the European Parliament elections demonstrated that public antipathy to Europe was rising. In 1997 opposition to the single currency was running at 2 : 1. Although not enough to save the Conservatives in 1997, since voters determined their electoral preferences on other issues, the emergence of the UK Independence Party in 1993 and the Referendum Party in 1995 seemed to indicate that some thought there was a mood of opinion on Europe that could be captured. The UK Independence Party stood for British withdrawal from the EU, and the well-funded Referendum Party stood on the single issue of seeking a referendum on the question:

Do you want Britain to be part of a Federal Europe? Or do you want the UK to return to an association of sovereign nations that are part of a common trading market?

The Referendum Party secured 3.1% of the vote on average and the UK Independence Party 1.2%, but this under-represents the importance of the issue and how people felt. Given the Conservative position on Europe many that were hostile to the EU voted for them, while the Labour Party sought during the campaign not to give too many hostages to fortune on the European issue.[132] While the Referendum Party faded away, in the June 1999 elections to the European Parliament the UK Independence Party won three seats (one each in the Eastern, South East and South West regions of England) with 8% of the vote, standing on a platform of taking Britain entirely out of the EU and returning it to its pre-'Common Market' state. On a very low turnout (see above, pp. 94–5) the Conservatives who ran their campaign with the message 'in Europe, but not run by Europe', secured 36% of the vote against Labour's 28%. Although a range of factors explain these results, attitudes to Europe were certainly a factor. Under the new electoral system, which did help the smaller parties, the Greens picked up two seats, the SNP two, Plaid Cymru two, the Liberal Democrats ten, and in Northern Ireland (using a different system – Single Transferable Vote) the Democratic Unionist Party, the Ulster Unionist Party and the Social and Democratic Party secured their usual one each.

The British have remained 'reluctant Europeans'. Coming as a late entrant, they have found it difficult to adjust politically and psychologically to a system they did not create. Ironically, with the emphasis on flexibility and subsidiarity and with the likely growing heterogeneity of the European Union after enlargement, the Union may be moving in a

Figure 15.3   British support for European Union membership, 1981–98

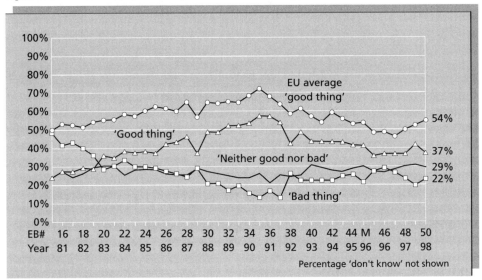

Source: Eurobarometer No. 50, p. 11.

direction favourable to long-standing British positions. However, before that can be asserted with confidence, the future of EMU will need to become clearer as will British participation or not in it. EMU will be the acid test of Britain's European policy and outlook. The trends in British attitudes to European Union can be seen in Figure 15.3.

THE SOUTHERN OR MEDITERRANEAN ENLARGEMENT

IN THE 1980s three more states joined the Community: Greece in 1981 and Portugal and Spain in 1986. The three had many experiences in common, especially recent experience of dictatorship, and levels of economic development that were well below the Community average.[133] Their accession also posed new issues for the Community, raised the importance of others and appeared as if it would shift the centre of gravity of the Community from the established democratic, industrialised northern states.

GREECE

The Greek accession in January 1981 marked the beginning of the 'Mediterranean' or southern enlargement. Given its geographic position, chequered political history, and relatively low levels of socio-economic development, Greece had not been involved in the mainstream of European integration, although it was a founder member of the OEEC, joined the Council of Europe in 1949 just after its foundation, and NATO in 1952. It lacked a common frontier with the Six.

In 1959 it requested an association agreement with the Six against a background of domestic economic crisis, and in 1961 the 'Athens Agreement' was signed. The Greeks favoured the EEC link over EFTA because they wished to strengthen their ties with the West and consolidate their internal political situation. There had been civil war in the 1940s and communist sympathisers received 25% of the vote in the 1958 election. Some, therefore, saw the EC as a contributor to stability. There were also hopes of the CAP, of some financing for economic development, and the attraction of foreign investment. Critics from the left saw the link as ending sovereignty, and involving imperialist links with capitalist powers. There were also more widespread fears that Greece would suffer in the competitive economic environment.

The 1961 Association Agreement was seen by both the Six and the Greeks as a first step towards membership, and not just as a trade arrangement. As a consequence it covered not just trade but a number of measures designed to bring the Greek economy closer to that of the Six. A major problem with the agreement was over agricultural harmonisation, and especially over the Greek aspiration to be directly involved in the making of CAP policy.

A hiatus in the development of relations occurred with the Colonels' coup of 21 April 1967, and in the following period the Community 'froze' the agreement. It was reactivated after the return to democracy in July 1974 when the Junta was replaced by a Greek Conservative government headed by Prime Minister Karamanlis, who remained in power until 1980.

As early as August 1974 the new government expressed its intention to apply for membership, and in June 1975 it applied. The political case was important to both sides: membership would mark a return to political respectability and the Community would buttress Greek democracy. The economic case was not undisputed, and indeed the Commission initially expressed a number of reservations on socio-economic grounds and because of the position regarding Greek–Turkish relations. Such reservations were brushed aside by the Council for political reasons, although there were some attempts to postpone the issue; threats which in turn led the Greek government to threaten to withdraw its application. Despite somewhat protracted negotiations the Treaty of Accession was signed in May 1979. The delay was largely for internal Community reasons, relating to its difficulty in adjusting quickly to the changed environment, the institutional implications of a broad enlargement (including Portugal and Spain) and a lack of Community political confidence and direction, as well as disputes over particular aspects of the negotiations, such as Greek–Turkish relations and agriculture. There was also some attempt to link the three applications in 'globalisation'. Once the political will to negotiate seriously was established the negotiations were not too difficult.

The situation again changed when ten months after accession there was a new government in Athens, formed by the PASOK party (Panhellenic Socialist Movement). PASOK had boycotted the accession vote because it did not wish to provide legitimacy for what it deemed to be an attack on Greek sovereignty, and in opposition in the 1970s had adopted a nationalistic radical position. It had pledged it would hold a referendum on the membership issue, although no such referendum took place. In practice in government PASOK's opposition to the Community was toned down.

The response over the next few years in terms of substantial funding and economic aid further lessened PASOK's hostility to the Community, although they never became fully converted to the concept of political union or EPC. They remained opposed to institutional development especially any enhanced role for the Commission or European Parliament. Nonetheless, while in 1983 they argued 'we cannot easily abandon traditional principles . . . [and] it would not be expedient for us to give the outside world the impression that we are obliged, since our accession to the Community, to adopt views diametrically opposed to those we have hitherto held' (this reaching its nadir at the Athens Council meeting in 1983, during the Greek Presidency, when the Greeks refused to allow the Community and its Member States to condemn the Soviet Union for shooting down the South Korean Boeing). By 1988 the Greeks were arguing that their Presidency would see 'every effort to ensure full application of the Single Act especially working out common positions, devising common measures and strengthening the principles of solidarity, mutual agreement and cohesion'.[134]

By the time of the airing of the possibility of the IGC on Political Union there was a new Greek government, the New Democracy Party, which had taken Greece into the Community returning to power. On 15 May 1990 it issued a 'Contribution to the Discussions on Progress Towards Political Union' which reflected the decisive shift that the new regime brought to these matters.[135] The memorandum made clear Greek support for further development of the Community, calling for rapid progress towards political union, which they linked to increased democracy within the Community, as well as playing a role in stabilising Eastern Europe. The memorandum also proposed European citizenship and the recognition of basic human rights by the Community. The Greeks wished to see an emphasis upon 'People's Europe'. Every effort was to be made to bring about what had already been agreed, especially 'cohesion' (the resource transfer). They favoured abandoning restrictions on types of security issues that could be discussed, and the inclusion of defence. At one point the Greeks seemed to threaten a veto of the whole exercise if they were not admitted to the WEU. This was important to them because of increasing Balkan instability, and their apprehensions regarding Turkey against whom they wanted a security guarantee. They, therefore, welcomed the Maastricht decision that 'States, which are members of the European Union are invited to accede to WEU ... or become observers if they so wish', whereas Turkey as a NATO but non-European Union member, was only offered 'associate' membership of the WEU.[136]

Greece at the time of the IGCs was an enthusiastic supporter of the federal goal, and the 'tree' approach. This reflects the view that unless Greece commits itself fully to political integration it could be left on the EC's economic and political periphery. Political union was to be based on subsidiarity and was to progress in parallel with EMU. They supported the movement to a single currency, despite knowing that they had little hope of joining this century. The Greeks were unhappy with what they regarded as prematurely strict convergence criteria, and know that fulfilling them is going to be a long hard haul. They staunchly reject the suggestion of a two-speed Europe and fear economic marginalisation. They pressed hard on the cohesion fund, believing that Maastricht had involved a commitment to a transfer of resources to the Structural Funds of the Community.

On fundamental issues there was a mixture of continuity and policy development in the 1996–97 Greek position compared to 1990–91. In the 1996–97 discussions for the Greeks, the major issues were: security, equality, cohesion, EMU and enlargement.

Various Greek memoranda to their EU partners in 1995–96 stressed the Greek view that strengthening the CFSP was a priority and that its objectives should be extended to 'include a clear guarantee concerning protection of the external frontiers of the Union and the Member States and a mutual assistance clause'.[137] This obviously reflected their preoccupations with the perceived security threat from Turkey, the disputes over Cyprus and the problems in the Balkans, with their continuing unhappiness over the newly independent former Yugoslav Republic of Macedonia. They felt somewhat let down by their partners, who, the Greeks felt, expected solidarity on matters affecting them but did not return the compliment on issues close to Greek hearts. Not surprisingly the Greeks favoured the evolution of a common defence policy and supported the 'phased absorption of the WEU into the EU', although in the meantime they accepted a division of labour between the WEU and NATO with NATO maintaining its primary defence position. In any event they supported the inclusion of the Petersberg tasks into the CFSP and the creation of an early warning and policy planning unit, but not a high-profile 'High Representative'.

Concerns regarding solidarity were also apparent in the Greek attitude to flexibility. On EMU, for example, the Greeks opposed some Member States proceeding before others to stage III, and more broadly they favoured 'institutional equality'. Thus they opposed notions of a 'multi-speed' Europe and stressed the importance of equal participation by all members. They rejected arguments for 'any form of differentiated integration which might destabilise the existing situation of unity and equality as between Member States'.[138]

The Greeks persisted in emphasising the need for transfers of funds to the less-developed areas of the Community, especially in their view once stage 3 of EMU had become a reality. They wanted a permanent commitment to the pursuit of economic and social cohesion and real convergence. An assessment by a Greek source suggests that although Greece has received massive financial support from Community funds, it has not closed the gap between it and the EC average.[139] This is partly because there has been difficulty in raising matching national finance. Nor have Greek industries gained greatly from the openings of the Single Market. Greece persists with the stabilisation programme, and in the peer review of its plans for 1998–2001, it gained approval, subject to further moderating wage increases and pursuing its structural reforms. In the EMU examination of March 1998, the reports were obliged to state that Greece did not meet the inflation, government deficit, ERM or interest-rate criteria – indeed, did not fulfil any of the convergence criteria – although the government had taken the appropriate steps regarding the position of the Greek Central Bank.[140] The Greeks continued to argue that the criteria should be relaxed so that no present EU member would be excluded, although it acknowledged that this might not be so for future members. In March 1998 Greece joined the ERM and in May 1998 the European Council noted the progress made by Greece. Greece intends to be qualified for EMU on 1 January 2001.

On enlargement, the Greek government was supportive as long as it did not become a 'pretext for the reversal of the economic and social conditions that support the present equilibrium within the European Union' and as long as any enlargement reflected the principle of 'sufficient resources' and was associated with appropriate budgetary changes.[141] The Greeks, of course, supported the accession of Cyprus and Malta as a priority concern. It was accepted that there would have to be reform of the CAP, etc. Although against differentiated integration, the Greeks accepted that some of the transition periods for new Member States might be quite long.

Figure 16.1   Greek support for European Union membership, 1981–98

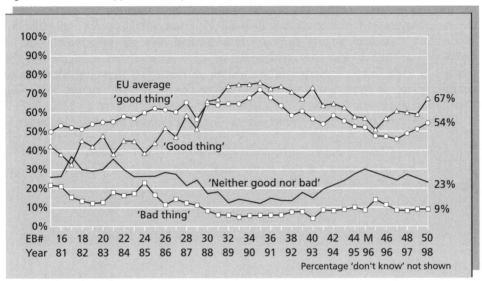

Source: Eurobarometer No. 50, p. 25.

On institutional questions, apart from the stress on equality, the Greeks opposed any move to question the Commission's existing role, 'powers, autonomy and exclusive right of initiative'.[142] They objected to any changes the composition of the Commission unless it was in the direction of one Commissioner per state. They fear any suggestion of a two-tier system. Similarly, they rejected changes to the weighting of votes in the Council, especially suggestions that there should be a relationship between population size and voting power. They argued that it was states that were represented in the Council, not people or populations. They were willing to see QMV extended on Pillar I questions *if* that were linked to the extension of co-decision in the European Parliament. They were content with the way the Presidency operated and did not envisage changes towards a 'team' Presidency. They continued to support unanimity for most issues of the CFSP, although a later memorandum did raise the possibility of communitarising at least elements of Pillar II and Pillar III. On Pillar III they wanted a Commission right of initiative, and a greater involvement of the EP and ECJ. On CHJA they were prepared to see more QMV, although it was clear that on issues that really touched on national sovereignty, the veto should remain. Greece wanted a general broadening of co-decision (with a few exceptions) for the European Parliament. Without being too specific, they supported a greater role of national parliaments and made some suggestions about some EP meetings involving national parliamentarians and increasing the role of 'assizes'.

The Greeks favoured the EC moving into new competencies or having enhanced powers on a number of matters, including: equality between individuals, consumer protection, and industrial policy. They advocated the institutionalisation of energy policy and the inclusion of tourism, and civil protection in Community competencies. Similarly, they supported the new Employment Title and saw it as part of the drive for cohesion. A particular concern of the Greeks related to a general strengthening of democracy in the EU and associated with this were proposals on strengthening the concept of citizenship. They specifically wanted greater stress on ending all forms of discrimination, on human rights and the accession of the EU to the European Convention on Human Rights.

Given their relatively late membership of the Community and their geographical position, the Greeks sometimes feel that they are not accorded enough respect or weight in the European Union, and a continuing theme of their policy is to try to assert their position as well as ensuring that they receive all the funding and other support they can. The evolution in Greek attitudes is shown in Figure 16.1.

PORTUGAL

Portugal experienced a dictatorship from 1932 to 1974. During this time the regime was profoundly nationalistic and was strongly committed to the Portuguese African empire. It was relatively isolated, but being reasonably benevolent, was tolerated by West European states, although excluded from the Council of Europe. It was a member of the OEEC, and because of its strategic position, and that of the Azores, was a founder member of NATO. Virulent anti-communism and attachment to colonies made Portugal very Atlanticist. It was a member of EFTA. There was a gradual change in policy outlook in the late 1950s and 1960s as the elite saw the external environment begin to change with integration in Western Europe, decolonisation pressures in Africa, and pressures for change at home. EFTA membership was no sign of commitment to the European idea, but rather reflected the importance of trade with Britain and not becoming isolated. Portugal, given its nationalistic outlook, favoured inter-governmental co-operation. EEC membership was at that time still ruled out by the nature of the regime, and by Portuguese fears of supranationalism, and of potential EEC exploitation of its colonies. The colonial aspect was a powerful factor in Portuguese policy considerations and hindered the development of policy in other areas, but gradually there came a growing awareness of problems in that relationship, of the increasing importance of imports from EFTA and of foreign investment, and that the old policies were not working. Trade dependence on the United Kingdom was crucial, and was such that until 1973 Portugal's position was determined by the UK's position.[143] With the British decision in 1961 Portugal had to ask for negotiations on trade links with the EEC, and in 1969–70 it again had to improve its relations with the Community. In July 1972, along with other EFTA members, it signed a vital free trade agreement with the Community. This encompassed the elimination of tariff barriers to exports from Portugal by July 1977 and some concessions on agricultural exports, although on the industrial side there were exceptions for about one-third of Portuguese exports, notably textiles, which were particularly sensitive. The agreement also contained an 'evolutionary clause', which provided for its revision and expansion.

The context of Portugal's policy and opportunities completely changed with the revolution of 25 April 1974, which ushered in the liberation of the colonies, and after a period of apparent anarchy, democracy. Portuguese policy-makers had to re-evaluate a range of external policies, while pursuing the revolution at home. Domestic convulsions caused a number of problems, but also caused Western Europe to rush in with emergency aid and concessions for Portuguese exports. These states took the political decision to seek to consolidate democracy in Portugal. Portugal applied for membership in March 1977 four months before Spain, with negotiations beginning simultaneously in 1978. The Treaty of Accession was signed in June 1985, Spain and Portugal becoming members of the Community on 1 January 1986. There was during this period little political debate, with the public mostly appearing indifferent. As can be seen, the negotiations were very protracted. Partly, as in the Greek case, this was because of internal Community difficulties on other matters, only some of which touched on enlargement. But there were also difficulties again on the whole question of agriculture and the perceived threat posed to French and Italian interests. More importantly, the Portuguese application became caught up in the greater difficulties of Spain, it being intended that the two should enter together. In the interim the Community provided Portugal with substantial pre-accession aid from 1980 onwards.

Membership is seen in Portugal as having been a success, contributing to rapid change, a transformation in the state's infrastructure, and an economic growth rate above the Community average. There is little opposition to membership, but much of the public remains indifferent. The Portuguese have been cautious about political union, the tone of their attitude being encapsulated in their memorandum of 30 November 1990 which started by saying that progress must 'be pursued gradually, be based on a pragmatic view of political, economic and social realities in Europe, respect national identities and diversity, preserve the existing institutional balance, ensure the correct application of the dual aspects of subsidiarity and solidarity'.[144]

The Portuguese approach in 1996–97 was very similar. In many ways its limited objectives seemed to revolve around limiting change, ensuring that there was no reduction in its own relative position and ensuring, like others, that its own particular interests were safeguarded. In keeping with this approach, a theme that was emphasised was the 'highest importance on preserving the basic institutional balance'. Portugal rejected 'any strategy or model which would permanently institutionalise a differentiation between groups of Member States ... since this would lead to the dissolution of the Union'.[145] It accepted that there could be different arrangements to deal with specific temporal and conditional circumstances, but these should not be allowed to turn into permanent rules for the future. It argued that the Union already possessed the mechanisms to deal with special cases. Portugal, like Greece, feared any movement away from the equality of Member States and the principle that all did and could participate in all Union activities.

Portugal advanced a number of other principles in its submissions to the IGC:

- respect for national identities;
- respect for human rights;
- support for political, economic and social solidarity;
- provision of 'sufficient means' to accomplish the objectives that had been defined.

Not surprisingly, Portugal was cautious on institutional change. With regard to the Council, it supported the existing weighting of votes although it acknowledged that with enlargements there would be a problem about maintaining an appropriate balance between the population of states and the ability to achieve majorities or blocking minorities, but it felt that the solution should be a matter of pragmatism rather than principle. It was prepared to accept some limited extension of majority voting, but argued both for recourse to a super-qualified majority in certain sensitive cases and the retention of unanimity on certain ultra-sensitive matters. It believed that the way the Presidency operated reflected the fundamental equality of Member States, and it therefore opposed any real changes to it, apart from some improvement in back-up support for it. It, for example, also opposed any ideas of a 'directorate' in the CFSP. It supported a significant role for the European Council in setting policy guidelines and wished it to retain this and its general political nature, rather than becoming institutionalised. On the European Parliament, the Portuguese felt, rather like the British, that it had not yet fully developed the additional powers given to it in the Treaty on European Union. However, given this, Portugal was ready to countenance some extension of co-decision, and some simplification of the co-decision procedure. It argued that consultation should be extended to Pillars II and III. Regarding the Commission, Portugal maintained that if there were to be changes it should be to one Commissioner per state. It objected to the European Parliament being able to censure individual Commissioners but said it would accept the European Council selecting the Commission President from a list of names supplied by the Parliament. It supported somewhat vaguely greater involvement of national parliaments in the work of the EU, but again reiterated that this must not alter the institutional balance. It was against any significant changes to the composition, nature and structure of the Commission and rather sanguinely suggested it remain as it was: 'collegiate, independent and dynamic ... [with] its exclusive right of initiative'.[146] It should, however, be more involved in issues concerning Pillars II and III. The Portuguese supported the Court of Justice's role and even advocated that it be given more responsibilities in the areas of individual rights, in Pillar III, in controlling the Community administration and in combating fraud.

On the CFSP, the Portuguese were adamant that they wanted it to remain intergovernmental and to retain the pillar structure. They did not support extending majority voting in this area but would permit 'constructive abstention' so that a majority could take action. While reluctant to move far on the CFSP there was a willingness to identify some areas or 'platforms' upon which, once agreement in principle had been reached, there could be majority voting. On the CFSP it argued that there should be one vote per state. Portugal could see a limited role for 'Mr or Mrs CFSP' but only if that figure was subject to close control by the Member States. It was rather more positive about a planning unit, but again saw it having a restricted role, supporting the Presidency and having no powers of initiative. As before, Portugal remained a firm supporter of NATO, its primacy and its fundamental responsibility for collective territorial defence of its Member States. It was also to have prime responsibility for major military action, although the WEU should be developed to allow it to deal with smaller-scale peace-keeping and crisis management missions and other Petersberg tasks. Any change to the WEU should respect NATO and although somewhat closer ties between the WEU and the EU should be developed there was to be no defence 'fourth pillar'.

On Pillar III matters, Portugal supported some issues being transferred to Community competence: asylum policy, and action against illegal immigration. It thought that possibly rules on crossing external frontiers, measures relating to free movement of third-country nationals and aspects of visa policy could be transferred. But again its general approach was one of caution, preferring to see in a number of other fields the reinforcement of inter-governmental co-operation, for example, in police co-operation and action against drug traffickers.

As in the earlier IGC, Portugal sought to ensure that a number of policies that complemented the major economic policies were developed. It felt strongly on cohesion, strengthening solidarity and job creation, and taking action to combat social exclusion. It supported a new Employment Title, and was an advocate of seeking to entrench the notion that employment concerns should be a key component of a number of policies. It felt that what it perceived as an imbalance between the focus on the Single Market and indeed EMU convergence criteria needed to be addressed by a series of flanking measures on employment, etc. In addition, in terms of new or enhanced competencies it supported Community activity in the areas of energy, tourism and civil protection, and enhanced action in the environmental field. It also supported the appropriate application of subsidiarity. Given its own position, it advocated special measures for outlying regions and islands. As in 1990–91 there was also an emphasis on Union citizenship, with Portugal favouring it being given a higher profile, more specific definition, and extension, as well as the EU acceding to the European Convention on Human Rights, and by the creation of a new Title: 'European Citizenship Charter'.

Portugal always fearing a two-speed Europe and it being placed at a perpetual relative disadvantage became a founder member of the single currency in January 1999. In the Commission Report of March 1998 Portugal received good marks for its legislation on the independence of its Central Bank, its inflation rate and price stability, its participation in the ERM and the exchange rate stability of the escudo and its average long-term interest rates. It did less well on the existence of excessive debt but was regarded as moving in the right direction, already having brought the government deficit to below the reference value, although the government debt ratio was only expected to meet the target.[147]

Portugal has rarely been in the vanguard of EU developments, tending to be rather cautious and tending to favour inter-governmental solutions, but its determination that it shall be treated equally with other Member States has on occasion seen it accept the advantages of Community or Union intervention, competence and action. In general, Portugal has been willing to accept some political developments as the price for

Figure 16.2   Portuguese support for European Union membership, 1981–98

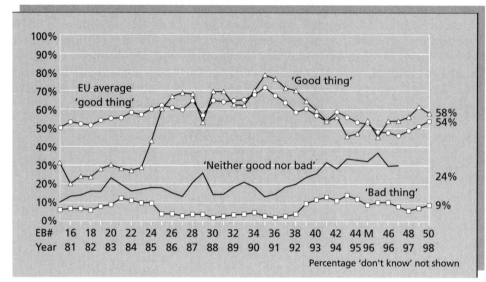

Source: Eurobarometer No. 50, p. 33.

maintaining that equality and for gaining economic and financial advantage. Portuguese attitudes to the European Union are shown in Figure 16.2.

SPAIN

Spain applied for EC membership on 28 July 1977. It had been excluded from consideration for many years because of the nature of its regime, and through having been too close to the Axis powers. It was also excluded from the UN, the Marshall Plan, the OEEC, the Council of Europe and NATO. Spain was not invited to take part in the movement towards closer European integration. Not surprisingly, its economic policy was self-sufficiency, and it looked to a vision of a community between it, Latin America and parts of North Africa rather than to Europe. In 1953 it made a bilateral defence deal with a United States consumed by fear of communism, and in 1955 as part of a package deal it joined the UN. By the mid-1950s it was acquiring some acceptability on the western side, but there remained many reservations on both sides. By the mid-1960s the question of Spain's relations with the rest of Western Europe needed to be addressed, as within Spain itself the policy of self-sufficiency and of resistance to change had been shown to be flawed. Modernisation became the key word, and it in turn became identified with Europeanisation. Europe was seen as offering access to wider markets, especially for agriculture and sources of investment capital. Britain's decision to apply was important too, given the size of the UK market for Spanish agriculture. In 1962 the

Spanish floated the idea of association with the aim of full integration into the Community, but this was still not acceptable to the Six. However, 1970 saw the signature of a preferential trade agreement, providing for free trade but not for Spanish eventual membership. The Spanish saw this as a major political development but for the Community it was a purely commercial arrangement. It was, however, part of the Community attempt to construct a global Mediterranean policy, a policy that could not exclude such a major trading partner as Spain. The 1970 agreement had a chequered career, with Spain being disappointed by the limited progress in its agricultural exports. The agreement formally lapsed when it was not adjusted to take into account the enlargement of 1973, but both parties continued to observe its major provisions.

The real turning point was the death of General Franco in November 1975 and in February 1976 the first post-Franco government announced that Spain wished to accede to the European Community. The initial reaction from the Community was favourable, and the formal application followed on 28 July 1977. While different groups in Spain had their own motivations for membership, an over-arching objective was to complete the process of emerging from the political shadows, and a necessary precondition was the return to pluralist, representative democracy. Spain saw the possibility of preference within the EC for Spanish agricultural produce, free access to the Community market, the possibility of attracting foreign investment, and both common cause with democracy and Christian Democracy. Given the return to democracy, it might have been thought that the negotiations would be quick, but in fact they were protracted. This was because the Community had its own internal problems, and because of disagreements in the negotiations over agriculture, fisheries and the reduction of tariff barriers for Spanish industrial goods. The Greeks at one point had also caused a hitch by linking progress on the application to their demands for aid to assist their own economic development, and what came to be known as the 'integrated Mediterranean programmes', a reservation only lifted in the spring of 1985. This allowed the Accession Treaty to be signed on 12 June 1985 and accession into the Community in January 1986. Within Spain there was general agreement with the decision. All parties emphasised the political dimension of the Community, and the opportunities for internal social and economic reforms.

In November 1988, along with Portugal, Spain joined the WEU. This was significant since the 1980 announcement by the centre-right government that it wished Spain to join NATO, which Spain did in 1982, had been bitterly contested by the socialist opposition. Spain also negotiated special arrangements subsequently which involved opting out of NATO's integrated military structure. The socialists promised a referendum on the issue and under Felipe Gonzalez Marquez came to power in October 1982. They modified their position on NATO and the subsequent referendum saw a 52.55% vote in favour of NATO membership, with 39.8% against (7.65% abstained). This vote, along with Community and WEU membership put Spain firmly in the West European camp, and in the initial year of membership, Spain signed the Single European Act in February 1986. In June 1989 Spain joined the Exchange Rate Mechanism, a decision which culminated in a successful Presidency in the first half of 1989, and in which Spain demonstrated its European commitment. During this time it had also played a positive role in EPC.

Accession to the Community, along with resource flows and heightened international respectability, hastened the transformation of Spain from the church-ridden, tightly controlled society of Franco's time. But it also brought problems. Nonetheless, Spain wanted to be a charter, or at least early member of a monetary union, and for this and other domestic reasons embarked in 1991 on a programme of austerity measures which ensured political unpopularity for the Socialist government. Although European policy took its share of the blame, there was no strong opposition to ratification of the Treaty on European Union.

Spain made an important contribution to the 1990–91 IGC in a number of areas, but especially by raising and focusing on European citizenship. It suggested that the Community had not unnaturally previously concentrated on economic questions, but that now it was appropriate to move to create a European citizenship that would provide 'special rights and duties that are specific to the nature of the Union'. Crucial were the 'freedom of movement, freedom to choose one's place of residence and the right of establishment'.[148] They also took the view that such rights would be created in parallel with the acquisition of new policies by the Community in the areas of social policy, health education, the environment and consumption. It was important, therefore, that the Community pay for these developments. These views came together in the emphatic Spanish insistence on economic and social cohesion. For them, 'If Europe is only a single market, Spain does not have an awful lot to gain in this operation.'[149]

Spain supported EMU and a single currency. It claimed not to see cohesion as compensation for involvement, but rather as a 'necessary political balance between efficiency, stability, and equity'.[150] It identified itself, Portugal, Greece and Ireland as having special problems of economic disparity, and called for a special fund to help implement cohesion, as well as a significant increase in structural funds within the budget. The matter of cohesion was regarded as crucial to Spain, and it argued in November 1991 that unless there was a satisfactory outcome on this issue it would block the negotiations on other matters. While disappointed by the money on offer, Spain was successful in establishing the Cohesion Fund. The arguments about money ran on, however, and Felipe Gonzales very nearly brought the Edinburgh European Council meeting to a collapse on this issue, making progress on all other issues conditional on obtaining satisfaction. Spain also emphasised the principle of sufficiency of resources for new policies.

The Spanish supported the federal goal, and were wary of subsidiarity as a potential mechanism for some members to pursue their own interests. They took the view that the enterprise was about sharing sovereignty rather than losing it. Spain largely preferred to maintain the existing institutional balance.

On the CFSP, Spain tended to support the inclusion of all aspects of security within it, including defence. It wished eventually to see a 'single' foreign and security policy but accepted that that might not be possible in the short or medium term. It did want EPC to be integrated into the Community framework, and the European Council to establish a list where 'common action' would take place among the Twelve. It was recognised that at the moment not all questions could be handled jointly. On defence Spain had few qualms about NATO but, recognising political reality, sought to straddle the argument between European defence (the WEU leading) and Atlantic European defence (NATO leading).

Many of these key themes of Spain re-emerged in the 1996–97 IGC and in the Spanish attitude towards the approach of EMU and enlargement. Just as Spaniards had been influential in key areas in 1990–91, in the 1996–97 IGC they played an even more important role, given that Carlos Westendorp (Spanish Secretary of State for European Affairs) was Chair of the Reflexion Group. Although there was a clear formal distinction between 'the Spanish position' and that of the Reflexion Group, Westendorp's nationality and position clearly informed the Reflexion Group's thinking.

As in 1990–91 the Spanish placed much emphasis on citizenship, on this occasion promoting the idea that where a Member State was seriously violating human rights or basic democratic principles then it should have its EU rights suspended.[151] In addition, it supported accession to the European Convention on Human Rights, the inclusion of provisions making it clear that socio-economic rights were as important as political rights, steps against discrimination, and movement to give fuller and more concrete expression to the citizens' rights already created in the Treaty on European Union.

In the mid- and late-1990s the Spanish continued to emphasise the importance of cohesion and, related to this, the principles of 'additionality of resources' and 'sufficient means'. In particular they argued:

(a) The costs of enlargement should be financed by additional resources being allocated to the new members, and significant increase in the Community budget. They also argued that the benefits of enlargement to the existing EU15 would more than compensate for the costs. They were particularly fearful of a new financial perspective that kept a lid on expenditure such that enlargement would be paid for by the current less-favoured states receiving less.

(b) There should be consistency between proposals and the resources available to pay, and especially that the means of funding policies should be properly identified so that the costs did not devolve to Member States.

The Spanish support an enlargement but have clear economic and financial concerns about it. They have opposed significant reform of the major policies, especially CAP, and has argued that rather than changing EU policies there should be transition periods for the new members, with hints that these periods might be quite long. They argued that the issue of funding should be addressed separately from the IGC, but as with other states it was never far from their minds. Other problems they identified on enlargement were:

- maintaining the power equilibrium institutionally, so that Mediterranean interests did not suffer;
- problems over potential migration; and
- the political and security problems associated with the applicant's borders and neighbours.

For the Spanish there was no doubt that a successful enlargement depended upon a simultaneous and genuine deepening of the Union.

Obviously closely associated with these economic and financial concerns has been the Spanish attitude to EMU. As noted above, Spain always wished to be in the first wave of EMU states. They were successful in this, although not without some pain. Spain was one of the states that pushed for the IGC to introduce proposals on employment, and that it should be agreed that job creation should be an objective of all EC policies. The tough decisions taken at the beginning of the 1990s meant that Spain was judged to have met the convergence criteria in the spring of 1998. Its inflation rate in the twelve months to January 1998 was below the reference value, the peseta had participated in the ERM for longer than two years and there had been exchange rate stability, and the long-term interest rates were below the reference value. The one area of difficulty, as with several other states, was in relation to the excessive deficit criteria, but it was argued the Spain had substantially reduced the government deficit with a further fall expected, and there was hope that the government debt ratio after rising in 1997 would decline in 1998 and subsequently.[152]

Spain has wished to be involved in all EU spheres of activity, and has thus been wary of proposals relating to differentiated or flexible integration. It firmly ruled out the idea of a Europe *à la carte*. As noted above, it was willing to envisage long transition periods for new members, but the *acquis* was to be preserved, even developed.

Similarly, it strongly favoured maintaining the current institutional balance, arguing for example that any reforms must respect both it and the character of the Union. Having said that, Spain did see that there could be advantages in abolishing the pillar structure; however, this was balanced by the view that the model would be similar to that of the EMU's relationship to Pillar I, so that in fact the essence of the pillars would remain, but not their formal existence. In general, there was continuity in the Spanish position in 1996–97 compared to 1990–91, although on specific details the arguments had clearly moved on. In 1996–97 it made a point of arguing for a genuine common electoral system for direct elections to the European Parliament. It accepted that the legislative procedures should be simplified but did not support granting the parliament the right of initiative. It did not see any need to change the Parliament's powers concerning the appointment of the Commission, nor increasing its role in the CFSP, making the point that national parliaments often had restricted roles in this area. It paid lip service to a greater say for national parliaments in general, but firmly opposed the creation of any new institution to represent them.

It was similarly cautious on changes to the Commission. It basically supported the Commission's existing functions and powers. It opposed proposals relating to the transfer of the Commission's executive powers to specialised agencies and the move to one Commissioner from each state. On this it argued that that would in effect nationalise the Commission. It said it was only prepared to accept it, if the Commission moved to weighting voting to reflect population size.

Similar caution was apparent regarding the Council. Thus, although Spain was willing to countenance a move to more majority voting, especially on matters related to the Single Market, it was clear that it regarded some issues as too important for this: primary law, own-resource issues, enlargement, areas of budgetary questions, environmental matters, and what it saw as quasi-constitutional issues. Where QMV was invoked, Spain argued that it was time that greater attention was paid to the population aspect, arguing for a double majority system taking into account not just votes but also population. Its other proposals on the Council system were largely merely modifying current arrangements: strengthening the co-ordinating role of the General Affairs Council and Coreper. Given its general approach, Spain defended the Court of Justice, wished to reinforce its position, and saw it having some role in Pillar III.

On Pillar III issues, Spain, after some initial hesitation, came to accept possible communitarisation in the areas of crossing of external borders, asylum policy, and joint rules for external frontier controls. It was willing to envisage the incorporation of Schengen into the Community pillar. Given domestic problems with terrorism, Spain thought that action against terrorism should be made a high priority. A specific proposal was that terrorists should not be able to claim that terrorist actions were political and thus escape extradition. Pillar III was one area where Spain saw a case for limited increased involvement for the Parliament, Court and Commission.

One reason for Spain arguing for the formal abandonment of the pillar structure was that it thought there continued to be problems of cohesion and consistency between the CFSP and the Community's external relations. It therefore opposed a single High Representative for the CFSP as not resolving the co-ordination issue and argued instead for greater co-ordination between the Commission, the Council Presidency and a 'political' Council Secretary-General, who would also be responsible for the proposed planning unit. This unit, however, was very much to be the servant of the Member States. Perhaps ironically, in June 1999 it was announced that a Spaniard, Javier Solana Madariaga, was to be the first High Representative, although acting in a rather different role than Spain had originally wished. Spain accepted the movement to some form of 'positive or constructive abstention' or on some issues a 'super-qualified majority'.

Spain was one of the states that believed that there should be some commitment to protecting the external frontiers of the Union. While willing to move a little on the CFSP and defence, Spain insisted that at the moment defence was so linked to national sovereignty that it had to remain an inter-governmental matter and a matter for consensus. However, it could see that this might change in the future. Again, while willing to see the WEU developed, especially in relation to the Petersberg tasks, it regarded NATO and the USA as still vital to European security. In the future, Spain could see merit in incorporating the Brussels Treaty Article V guarantee of collective defence and the WEU into the CFSP, although it acknowledged that this was some time off. It was in the Spanish proposals that specific reference was made to developing the EU's operational capacity.[153]

More generally, Spain had no radical suggestions for new competencies, and tended to the view that not much needed changing. It supported the new Employment Title, making employment a key feature of a range of other policies and more co-ordinated activity on job creation. On the environment it thought there was no need for any further strengthening competence, indeed specifically making the point that existing exemptions from QMV should continue to apply.

Figure 16.3   Spanish support for European Union membership, 1981–98

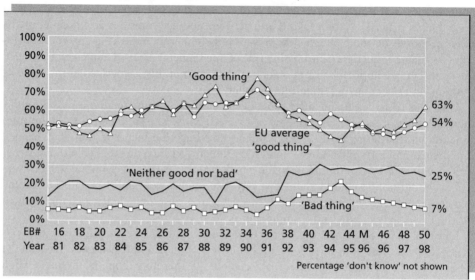

Source: Eurobarometer No. 50, p. 26.

Spain has gained in self-confidence and standing since it emerged as a democracy after the death of Franco in 1975. Its acceptance into the European Community and the part it has played in Europe since 1986 have been important factors in that change. Spain is broadly satisfied with its position, as long as its economic and financial rewards are not threatened. The attitude of its public can be seen in Figure 16.3

THE FOURTH ENLARGEMENT STATES

ON 1 JANUARY 1995 Austria, Finland and Sweden became members of what was now the European Union. In many ways this represented a reversal of policy for each of them since they had previously felt unable, or had been unwilling, to consider such membership. For the Austrians the perceived difficulty had lain in their relations with the Soviet Union. Austria had been occupied as a result of the war by the wartime allies, but in 1955 as part of a brief relaxation in international tension, the possibility of full Austrian independence emerged. However, there was a price to be paid. Although *not* a part of the Austrian State Treaty of 1955, in effect as a precondition of Soviet agreement, the Austrians expressed in the Moscow Memorandum of April 1955 their political will to practise a neutrality of the type maintained by Switzerland. Austrians have always insisted that this was a decision that they took of their own free will. After the withdrawal of foreign troops in October 1955, in the Federal Constitutional Law, the Austrian Parliament, in a law still extant, declared a policy of permanent neutrality. A second problem was that the Austrian State Treaty did prohibit 'all agreements having the effect, either directly or indirectly, of promoting political and economic union with Germany'.[154] The Soviets made it clear that they interpreted a relationship with the European Economic Community as a breach of that provision, a point made strongly by the Soviet leader Khruschev in 1962 and repeated, slightly less vehemently, by his successors in 1972. The Austrians never accepted this view, but at the very least it gave pause for thought and was an additional reason for maintaining their view that EEC membership was incompatible with neutrality.

The Finns were also constrained by the Soviets, reflecting the reality of their history, geo-strategic position and the nature of the Cold War international environment. Finland had lost in wars with the USSR twice in living memory: 1939–40 and 1941–44. They had lost territory – Karelia – but had not lost their independence or been occupied. Their position, however, was exposed, not least by the long border they shared with the USSR. Thus the Finns opted for a foreign and security policy predicated upon a good working relationship with the Soviet Union. This was most manifest in the 1948 Treaty of Friendship, Mutual Assistance and Co-operation. Although it contained no formal limitations on Finnish options, the treaty and the environment the Finns found themselves in meant that for forty years Finland, a small state, on occasions accommodated the views of its large neighbour – a policy which in the 1970s led to some (unfairly in Finnish eyes) coining and using the phrase 'Finlandisation'. Despite some alarms and occasional pressure, this policy worked. Finland occasionally tried to establish its own position via an emphasis upon its policy of neutrality, although it was many years before the Soviets accepted this.

Sweden was constrained neither by treaty nor constitutional law. Rather it had managed to keep European wars at arms length since the end of the Napoleonic wars and the Congress of Vienna in 1815. Subsequently it had evolved a tradition of non-involvement in European security. Perhaps because it was not based on either treaty or constitution, and partly because it was successful in helping Sweden avoid the ravages of war in 1914–18 and 1939–45, Swedes became almost inordinately attached to their neutral tradition. This attachment was further strengthened by the Cold War environment and especially by the Swedish view that its position played a key role in what was termed the 'Nordic balance'.[155] In essence, this meant that positioned as it was, Sweden's neutrality provided a buffer between NATO Norway and a 'Treaty of Friendship, Mutual Assistance and Co-operation' Finland, and perhaps reassured both NATO and the Warsaw Pact that it was not in the interests of either to disturb the balance. This was reinforced by Sweden engaging for a generation in, for its size of population, a very strenuous defence effort to make itself unattractive to attack. Until the late 1980s adherence to neutrality over-rode all other foreign policy goals. In 1971 the Swedish Foreign Minister said that: 'neutrality is determined by fundamental evaluations relating to security policy, not by economic interests'.[156] While not all permanently neutral, all three of these states empathised with the view expressed by an Austrian that:

> We have arrived at the point where the two spheres – neutrality and European integration – meet, or rather where they do not meet. *Integration in the real sense of the word and with its institutional requirements is not compatible with the status of permanent neutrality.* The neutral country is condemned to independence, condemned to staying alone. (Emphasis in original.)[157]

Despite this orientation, Austria and Sweden did not stand aloof from all European developments. Both were founder members of the OEEC (later OECD). Sweden joined the Council of Europe as a founder member in May 1949, with Austria joining in 1956 within months of the occupying forces leaving. Both Austria and Sweden were founder members of European Free Trade Association in 1960. Finland had to be rather more cautious, waiting until the Gorbachev revolution was underway in the Soviet Union before joining the Council of Europe in 1988. All three were signatories of the Helsinki Final Act of 1975 and played roles in the Conference on Security and Co-operation in Europe (later the OSCE). Indeed, Finland played a leading part in the calling for such a conference and much of the preparatory work took place in Finland. All three, of course, never applied to join NATO. Sweden was, however, a founder member of the Nordic Council in 1952 but Finland had to wait for a relaxation in Cold War tensions in the aftermath of the death of Stalin in 1953 before joining in 1955. Even then it had to accept, at the behest of the Soviet Union, that it would not take part in discussions on defence or security.

Austria, Finland and Sweden were not only involved in these ways. Despite having to be extremely careful not to subvert their neutral position and the perception of them as neutrals, all agreed with the Swedes that they were Western, given the 'many links deriving from a common civilisation and a common history'.[158] The Swedes and Austrians also had very strong trade links with the West. Between 1961 and 1981 about 80% of Swedish imports and exports were with OECD states and for Austria the figure was about 70%. Finland had a Western economy, but had a much closer trading relationship with the USSR and Comecon states, although in 1974 it agreed a free trade agreement with the European Community. Finnish trade with the USSR plummeted in the Gorbachev years (1985–91), given the upheaval in the Soviet economy, and this was one factor causing it to review its position at the end of the Gorbachev period. Despite the strict formal requirements of neutrality, none of the states was passive in international relations during the Cold War, seeking to contribute in a variety of ways to a relaxation of tensions.

Austria, Sweden and Finland participated in organisations that:

- did not involve any defence dimension;
- had no supranational decision-making institutions or capacity;
- had no overt political agendas concerning sovereignty and posed no significant constraints on their economies or their economic freedom.

Both Austria and Sweden were confirmed in their position by the apparent moves of the European Community after The Hague summit of 1969 towards political and monetary union.

All three, however, could not escape trade relations with the Community. Austria and Sweden in particular were somewhat left in the lurch when three EFTA partners activated their applications to join the European Community after The Hague summit – Denmark, Norway and the United Kingdom – and when Denmark and the UK joined in 1973. To remedy this, they accepted the proposal that bilateral free trade agreements should be negotiated with each of them, although not with EFTA as a bloc. These agreements were signed in July 1972 (along with similar agreements with other EFTA members individually). A similar agreement was signed with Finland, although its signing had to be postponed until October 1973 pending Finland discussing the issues with the Soviet Union. These agreements involved the abolition of customs duties on imports between the EC and the states concerned, but with each retaining its external customs tariffs on imports from third parties. The agreements largely settled, for more than a decade, the question of the relationship of these states with the EC.

What began to change the position of all three were the revolutions, beyond their control, in their economic, political and security environments at the end of the 1980s.

The first was the European Community's decision to seek to create a Single Internal Market by the end of 1992. The second was the convulsion in Eastern and Central Europe in and after 1989, which culminated in the demise of the Soviet Union itself at the end of 1991. The latter transformed the security environment, the basis of the three states' foreign and security policies of a generation, and raised the issue of what neutrality now meant, or indeed, if it had any meaning in the new order. The former rang alarm bells since the EFTA states feared that they might face new trade barriers at the Community's external borders, that they would not share in the benefits of the Single Market, and that equally importantly they would be excluded from key decisions which directly affected them.

Partly to forestall a rush of applications on the eve of the Single Market and when the Community was beginning to prepare for the EMU IGC, in January 1989 Jacques Delors, the Commission President, in presenting the Commission's programme for 1989 to the European Parliament, launched the idea of a far-reaching discussion with EFTA states on the possibility of broader co-operation. The underlying notion was to find a way in which these states might form part of the Single Market, with freedom of movement of goods (with agriculture excluded) and services. Many observers saw this as an attempt to head off membership applications, by offering an alternative that would be easier for the EFTA states, as well as the Community. This was the origin of the negotiations that led, on 21 October 1991, to political agreement on the European Economic Area (EEA). Formal agreement was reached on 2 May 1992 after the resolution of objections raised by the European Court of Justice, which considered certain aspects of the original agreement to be contrary to Community law. In the agreement the three states, and other signatories, undertook to organise themselves, in relation to the Single Market, in the same way as the Community, to ensure conditions of fair competition both ways. In the EEA the four freedoms of the Single Market – movement of goods, services, capital and people – were extended to the Area. The agreement was due to come into force on 1 January 1993, but this was delayed a year by the Swiss voters rejecting it in a referendum on 20 December 1992. Swiss voters were influenced by their rather more robust view of the requirements of neutrality along with other factors. (This rejection led to Switzerland withdrawing its interest in EC membership.)

If the EEA was intended as a brake on applications for membership it did not succeed. Even before serious negotiations had started, Austria applied for full EC membership on 17 July 1989. This was clearly motivated by the approach of the Single Market and was before the real unfolding of events in Eastern Europe. Sweden applied on 1 July 1991 and Finland on 18 March 1992. Before the EEA referendum result Switzerland applied on 26 May 1992 and the Norwegian parliament approved an application in November 1992.

The Commission's opinions on the applications from Austria, Finland and Sweden were positive, but started from the hypothesis that all the applicants accepted everything in the Treaty on European Union and all the legislation the Community/Union had already adopted – the *acquis* – although transition measures and periods were acceptable. The Commission did point out that account would have to taken of implications of neutrality, although it observed that 'This concept of neutrality is ... steadily evolving in the light of developments in Europe and worldwide.' It specifically noted in the Austrian case that 'Austria's permanent neutrality creates problems' but it went on to say that these 'should not however prove to be legally insurmountable in the context of the accession negotiations'. This issue was important not just because of the general context but because, Austria, in its letter of application for membership of 14 July 1989, had said in the second paragraph:

> Austria submits this application on the understanding that its internationally recognised status of permanent neutrality, based on the Federal and Constitutional Law of 26 October 1955, will be maintained and that, as a member of the European Communities by virtue of the Treaty of Accession, it will be able to fulfil its legal obligations arising out of its status as a permanently neutral State and to continue its policy of neutrality as a specific contribution towards the maintenance of peace and security in Europe.[159]

As had happened before, the Community had its own agenda, but it did agree at Maastricht in December 1991 that negotiations on accession to the Union could start as soon as the Community had terminated its negotiations on the future of own resources and related issues, it being taken as read that the Maastricht Treaty would be ratified by then. At the Lisbon European Council in June 1992, at British urging, it was agreed that the EEA agreement paved the way for the opening of negotiations with the EFTA applicants and that preparatory work could be speeded up. It was hoped to open negotiations immediately after the ratification of the TEU and agreement having been reached on future funding (colloquially the Delors II package). The Edinburgh European Council cleared the way on the latter and, in anticipation of TEU ratification, agreed to the opening of accession negotiations. These opened with Austria, Finland, Norway and Sweden on 1 February 1993.

The accession negotiations were notable for the problem that did not materialise as Austria, Finland and Sweden all accepted the Common Foreign and Security Policy without looking for any relief. In addition, given the EEA and that these states were relatively rich, the negotiations were not excessively difficult. Indeed, a distinction between the fourth and second and third enlargements was that this group of states were not expected to make demands on the Community budget. The Commission's original expectation was that the new members (including, as was expected at the time, Norway) would contribute about 6,000 million ECUs between them, but only receive 4,500 million ECUs in return, a favourable balance for the Union of 1,500 million ECUs. Only Finland would receive more than it gave. Issues that did cause problems included, for the Nordics, their tariff relationship with the Baltic states, and for all the applicants the fact that, by and large, their environmental, health and safety standards were higher than those of the EC, together with aspects of agricultural policy, certain specialised national state monopolies, and budgetary contributions. For Austria agriculture was a sensitive issue, but it was allowed a four-year transition. Also difficult was the issue of transit traffic through the Tyrol and Salzburg – an issue that had caused problems in the negotiation of the EEA – but which was again resolved by means of transition arrangements. A third problem was sensitivity over the sale of property in Alpine regions to foreigners. Again transition arrangements were agreed, but ultimately the Austrians had to accept non-discrimination.

For Finland the problems stemming from its short growing season and 'Arctic' farming were important, not least because they meant that production costs were relatively high in Finland compared to many of its future partners. Agriculture temporarily stalled the negotiations and Finland largely had to give way, not gaining the transition period it wanted and gaining only limited concessions on Arctic farming. There were other issues such as forests, aspects of sea transport, the nature of certain Finnish insurance provisions and really special cases like the position of the Åland Islands – the inhabitants of which approved the special arrangements finally agreed in a separate referendum.

For Sweden issues of concern were its budgetary contribution, the question of standards regarding food and the environment, issues relating to equality and unemployment, and peculiarly Swedish issues relating to the control of alcohol sales through the state-owned *Systembolaget* and the issue of a special form of snuff.

The negotiations proceeded briskly and were concluded by April 1994 – a record. The real issue was whether voters in the applicant states would vote for membership in the referendums each was committed to hold. The results of the referendums are shown in Table 17.1.[160]

Austria voted first on 12 June 1994, in a political situation where the ruling parties were losing ground, notably to the nationalists. Finland, fearful of instability in the Russian Federation, voted positively on 16 October 1994. Sweden voted more narrowly 'for' on 13 November 1994. It had been hoped that positive votes in Finland and Sweden (given that Denmark was already a member) might swing the vote in Norway, which had, of course, already voted 'No' in a referendum in 1972. But on 28 November 1994 the Norwegian electorate again voted 'No', in almost exactly the same proportion as in 1972.

In accordance with custom, representatives of the three acceding states began to attend Union meetings at official and ministerial levels in the autumn of 1994. On this occasion, given changes introduced in the TEU Article O, the European Parliament was required to give its consent to the accession of these states. It did this after the accession treaties had been signed but before the referendums. In May 1994 the Parliament voted

Table 17.1   Referendum results in Austria, Finland, Norway and Sweden 1994

State	% Yes	% No	% Turnout
Austria	66	34	81
Finland	57	43	74
Norway	48	52	89
Sweden	52	48	82

positively for Sweden (380), Finland (377), Austria (374) and Norway (374), with 518
MEPs eligible to vote and 259 positive votes being required. The votes were more contentious than expected because about 150 MEPs had supported an earlier motion to
postpone consideration of the applications to allow more time for negotiations with the
Council on Parliament's demands for more democracy and majority voting in decision-
making; but this was defeated with 305 MEPs voting against.

In the Member States of the Union, the ratification of the Treaties of Accession proceeded but there was a last minute hitch when Spain, in December 1994, said that it
would not ratify the three accession treaties if it did not receive access, six years earlier
than its accession treaty provided, to fishing waters off Britain and Ireland. This dispute
was resolved in a compromise covering area and the scale of fishing effort.

Austria, Finland and Sweden became members of the European Union on 1 January
1995. On 7 January Austria joined the European Monetary System. Sweden and Finland
decided to defer a decision on this until their economic situation had improved. Finland
joined in 1996 but for Sweden it became caught up in reservations about EMU. In any
case by the early summer of 1995 it already began to look as if the honeymoon was over
for Austrian and Swedish voters, as polls showed a sharp reduction in public support for
EU membership. The Austrian, Finnish and Swedish support for EU membership can be
seen, respectively, in Figures 17.1, 17.2 and 17.3.

Figure 17.1   Austrian support for European Union membership, 1995–98

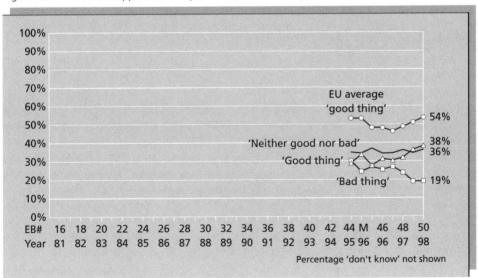

Source: Eurobarometer No. 50, p. 32.

Figure 17.2 Finnish support for European Union membership, 1995–98

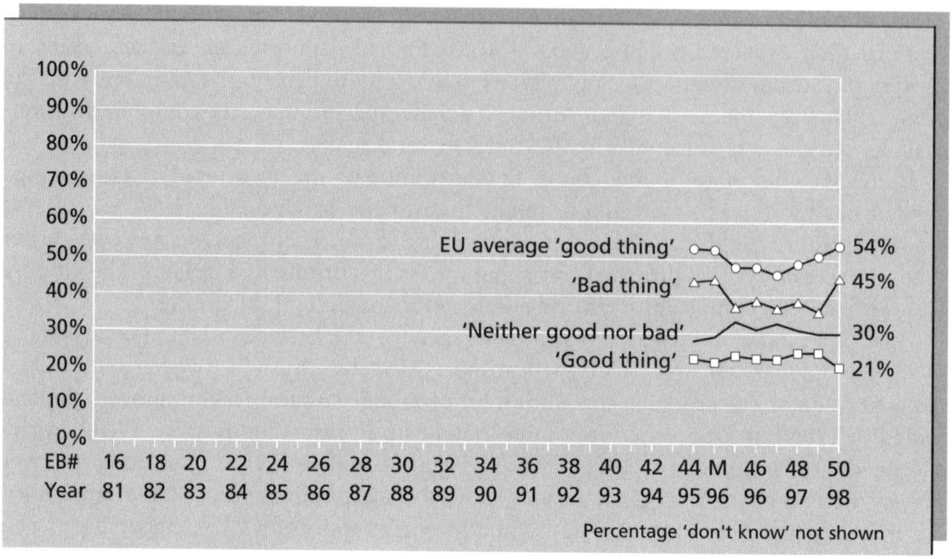

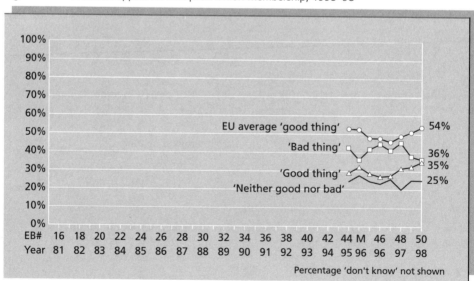

Source: Eurobarometer No. 50, p. 34.

Figure 17.3 Swedish support for European Union membership, 1995–98

Source: Eurobarometer No. 50, p. 35.

AUSTRIA

Although there has been some internal debate in Austria over the possibility of NATO membership in recent years (a debate that has rather waxed and waned), Austria has sought to maintain its neutral position. Its general orientation can be seen from the stress it has placed on the existing 1992 TEU objectives for the CFSP being appropriate and on the EU's contribution to European stability and conflict prevention. It did support the CFSP developing an operational capability in the sphere of the Petersberg tasks, although the Austrians added 'civil protection' to the new tasks to be included. Thus Austria has supported some strengthening of the ties between the EU and the WEU. Rather vaguely it supported the CFSP being gradually included in Pillar I. More specifically, it supported the planning unit idea but made it clear that it was to be adjunct to the Council Secretariat, should have no right of initiative and should not have a high profile. Except in cases of vital national interest, it was prepared to see a limited movement towards majority voting and some development in the notion of 'unanimously minus one' or 'positive abstention', but it rejected notions of some Member States being able to undertake action on behalf of the EU unless that action had been endorsed by the EU as a whole. It was adamant that any military-related decisions would require unanimity.

Austria was very wary of differentiated integration. In its IGC submissions it made clear that such flexibility should only occur in exceptional circumstances, should not allow any member or group a competitive advantage, and that all should have the opportunity to take part. If developments were to come in phases, the Austrians believed that all should agree the end objective. Austria was anxious that the current fundamental equality of Member States might be eroded. However, although it believed in the equality, it was also anxious to preserve the current institutional balance that gave them and other small states disproportionate representation in numbers of MEPs, in QMV voting, and in certain other institutions. It wanted the role of the smaller states to be preserved. It did recognise that there needed to be changes in the way the EU worked in the light of enlargement, which it supported, but the changes were to be marginal.

Austria was also cautious on institutional change. It accepted some increase in majority voting, on a case by case basis, but importantly including taxation, some areas of social policy and aspects of the internal market, but unanimity was to remain for other sensitive areas, especially own resources. Given its apprehension regarding losing equal status, it supported the existing rotating Presidency and reinforcing the Council Secretariat. Similarly, it accepted the move to one Commissioner per state. It was also prepared to see the Commission have a greater role in Pillar III. Otherwise it was one of those states that wished broadly to maintain the Commission's existing position. It believed that the European Parliament should play a greater role in selecting the Commission President, that the legislative procedures should be reduced to three and that co-decision could be extended. It did not accept giving the Parliament a right of initiative or other radical changes. On national parliaments, it echoed suggestions that material should be made available more timely, but did not push for greater involvement by national parliaments. Austria wished to defend the central role of the Court of Justice. As a federal state, Austria called for greater powers for the Committee of the Regions.

Although at an early stage the Austrians intriguingly raised the possibility of another parallel body to the Commission playing a greater role in Justice and Home Affairs, their later position was to support aspects of Pillar III being communitarised, in particular: visa and asylum policy, external frontier controls, immigration policy and aspects of actions against drugs and fraud. Criminal matters and internal security were to be left to Member States, but Austria did support the inclusion of Schengen into the treaty.

As in the accession negotiations, aspects of environmental policy particularly concerned the Austrians, and this area has remained one of priority for them. They have been keen that the principle of sustainable development should be in the treaty, and that it and other aspects of environmental policy should inform all aspects of Community policy. They also have pushed to be allowed to maintain higher national standards. In order to make environmental policy more meaningful, they advocated more QMV and co-decision on such matters, although for issues such as water and land usage they wanted unanimity to be maintained.

The desire for action on the unemployment front also ranked high on the Austrian agenda, but the specific proposals were modest, calling for 'high' levels of employment to be a Community objective and for the co-ordination of policy. They did link employment to social policy issues, being particularly annoyed at what they saw as the unfair advantage the UK had gained by opting out of the Social Chapter and seeking to have it incorporated fully into Pillar I. It favoured energy and civil protection becoming Community or Union policies as appropriate, but perhaps because of the size of its own industry rejected the idea that tourism become a Community policy.[161]

Austria became a founder member of stage 3 of EMU on 1 January 1999. It was one of the three best-performing economies as against the inflation target in 1997, the schilling had participated in ERM for more than two years and had proved to be relatively stable, and its interest rates at 5.6% average were well below the 7.8% reference value. On the excessive deficit criterion Austrian performed less well, being the object of a decision on the existence of an excessive deficit, but as in other cases it was argued that the trend was in the right direction, indeed in 1997 the government deficit was comfortably below the requirements.[162]

Austria has had some problems since January 1995, but the early years of membership have not been traumatic. It is interesting that it did feel able to accept the June 1999 Cologne European Council Conclusions on the future of the CFSP, the EU, the WEU and defence, although it still wishes to observe certain institutional formalities and distinctions in this area.

FINLAND

On 25 April 1996 the Finns and Swedes jointly submitted a memorandum to their partners on 'Towards an enhanced EU role in crisis management' which, like the Austrian position, was very reflective of their traditional position and orientation. This memorandum accepted the 'need for the European Union to enhance its role and capabilities in conflict management' and it went on to specifically refer to the Petersberg tasks and those aspects of 'conflict management where military organisations are used'. It argued for a reinforced linkage between the WEU and the EU, but was clear that 'at the same time, it is not necessary for the Union itself to perform military tasks'. It was, however, acutely aware of the need for the EU to be able to act, even 'in military crisis management', although it would be the WEU that actually acted – EU Member States would all have the option of being involved, even if not full WEU members. EU states to facilitate this were to provide the WEU with details of the forces they had available for such tasks. Typically they reiterated:

> an enhanced competence in the security and defence dimension of the Union will respect the specific character of the defence solutions of the members and will not affect their status as states pursuing independent or common defence. It is understood that co-operation in military crisis management is separable from collective defence.[163]

The Finns on their own behalf drew a distinction between political leadership being provided by the EU and implementation of crisis management being left to the WEU. They wanted to maintain the inter-governmental approach on all-important CFSP decisions. They did favour an analysis capacity, but stressed that it should be in the Council Secretariat. They did not support a high profile 'High Representative' as they did not see this resolving the consistency and cohesion issue between Pillars I and II. They wanted to broadly maintain the Presidency as it was. They were willing to see more co-operation on arms production.

Finland repeated several times that its vision of the EU was an 'association of independent states',[164] an association to which Member States had voluntarily transferred certain limited powers so that common agreed objectives could be fulfilled. Thus it emphasised the importance of equality in EU decision-making and made clear its objections to tiers of membership. Flexibility was only acceptable in exceptional circumstance, and was to be designed to bring about ultimately a common goal under agreed criteria. Finland has supported EU enlargement given that the above can be safeguarded. It has pushed particularly hard for the inclusion of the Baltic States, seeing this as making a strong contribution to Scandinavian security and the security of Europe in general.

The Finns, again with the Swedes, made increased transparency a major objective of the IGC and submitted a range of detailed suggestions as to how it could be improved. It pointed specifically to its own legislative provisions on access and transparency and pushed for some progress to be made in incorporating them into Community law. At a minimum it wished to see more Council legislative decisions taken in public and the inclusion of provisions in the treaty allowing for transparency to be broadened over the years. Similarly, the Finns wished their national concerns on environmental issues to be taken more seriously at Community level. They argued for the incorporation of the principle of sustainable into all sectoral policy areas, and for more QMV in the area so that higher standards could be achieved, but did not wish to open the door to their own standard being diluted.

Finland did not support radical changes in the powers of the European Parliament, specifically ruling out individual Commissioners' accountability with a view to dismissal or initial appointment. It did not support the Parliament gaining the right of initiative, nor greater rights over Pillar II, although willing to accept some movement on its role in Pillar III. Co-decision could be expanded. Like other small states it argued that it was necessary for small states to be somewhat over-represented as against a strict mathematical number directly related to population.

As regards the Council, as noted above, Finland strongly argued for the equal status of all Member States, and argued explicitly that population-based weighted voting would decrease its own influence. Similarly it felt comfortable with the existing arrangements for the Presidency since it enhanced the equality principle. It argued for more QMV on environmental issues, but also was clear that unanimity on some issues remained important.

Like other small states it saw no need for significant changes in the Commission's role, except that the Commission should have a strengthened position in Pillar III. Finns accepted the one Commissioner per state arguments, but were clear that the appointment of Commissioners must be left to each Member State. It did think that more implementation decisions could be transferred to the Commission, especially from the Council.

Finland defended the current position and role of the Court in relation to national legal systems and in ensuring that Community law was complied with. It looked for a moderate extension of the role of the European Court into Pillar III but not Pillar II. Perhaps given its geographical position, Finland explicitly drew a connection between freedom of movement and internal security, being anxious that the stress on the single market did not lead to dangers for the residents of the Member States. It rather hedged its bets on communitarisation of Pillar III – advocating more QMV, the transfer of some areas to Pillar I and a Commission right of initiative to remedy perceived weaknesses in its decision-making capacity but insisting that matters of real significance should not be placed under Community competence.

Finland believed, on employment, that the treaties should be amended to ensure that there was a proper relationship between employment and other aspects of economic policy. On employment it also said that it could see some advantages in a separate employment fund or administration at Community level. On energy and civil protection it was broadly for the status quo, while on tourism it spoke rather loosely about a Community framework. It wanted to enhance the awareness of the need to prevent social exclusion and favoured full incorporation of the Social Policy of the 1992 TEU to ensure that none had an unfair advantage, although states that preferred higher standards should be allowed to have them and basic social policy decisions should continue to be a national matter. It favoured moderate developments on health policy. Finland was also one of the states arguing for stronger provisions on sexual equality, non-discrimination and anti-racism and xenophobia. It also pushed for the development of European citizenship, but emphasised that citizenship of a Member State was a precondition of EU citizenship. Its submissions in this area concentrated on human rights, especially social rights. It wanted the EU to accede to the European Convention on Human Rights.

Finland joined in the move to the third stage of EMU on 1 January 1999. It met the inflation and long-term interest rate criteria easily. It had rather more trouble with the excessive deficit criteria, but by June 1997 had come under the reference value for government debt and the government debt ratio had more or less been continually under the target. The Finnish markka only joined the ERM in October 1996, less than the requisite two years at the time of assessment, but was deemed to have been stable in the relevant period and thus to have met the criteria.[165]

Finland has adjusted to EU membership since 1995. It has accepted the Cologne position on the CFSP, the WEU, the EU and an operational capability. In the summer of 1999 the Finnish President, Martti Ahtisaari, is judged to have played a helpful role in resolving the NATO–Yugoslav conflict, as an EU but not a NATO member. This just on the eve of Finland acceding to their first Presidency of the Union.

SWEDEN

As has been seen (pp. 500–1 above) Sweden submitted a joint memorandum with Finland on 'Towards an enhanced EU role in crisis management', a memorandum strongly reflecting Swedish traditions in UN peacekeeping and in seeking to contribute to international peace and security through offering mediation, etc. Sweden wanted to see the EU move into the Petersberg area of activity but not into collective defence. It emphasised to its partners that on security and defence it wished to be fully in control of its own decisions. It was going to maintain its neutrality and made it clear it had no intention of joining the WEU or any other 'alliance'. It drew a clear distinction between collective and territorial defence guarantees under the Brussels Treaty and working together on the Petersberg tasks. It could conceive too of some movement towards QMV on certain CFSP issues, but all major decisions needed to be inter-governmental and national. It could also see the benefit of reinforcing common preparation of decisions, if that was under the direction of the Council Secretariat, and of an individual representing the Union, if it was clear that the individual was under the control of the Council and acting under its mandate, especially that of the Presidency.

Sweden made no secret that it did not want the EU to develop in a federal direction. Rather it favoured co-operation. It was wary, however, of proposals for an *à la carte* Europe as it worried that these might undermine the Single Market. Nonetheless, proposals in this area should be examined on their merits, as long as they did not seek to undermine what had been achieved and the essential solidarity of the Union. One reason for its wariness was concern that changes might alter the basic equality of Member States and put the smaller states at a disadvantage. The Union had to be based on co-operation between independent, equal sovereign states, who had chosen to delegate limited powers in order to better achieve agreed objectives. That was to remain true in an enlarged Union as well. Sweden, like Finland, supported enlargement, especially the inclusion of the Baltic states, and accepted that there would need to be some changes to accommodate that, but those changes should not alter the existing principles on which the Union was based. Rather they should strengthen co-operation. Sweden made an additional point which was that all qualified applicants should be treated equally in terms of the conduct of negotiations.

Transparency was important to the Swedes and, like the Finns, they referred their partners to their national legislative provisions. Sweden did seek to gain acceptance that these same standards should apply at the European level. It wanted Council minutes to be made available, greater access to information, and by inserting principles on transparency into the treaties, wanted to ensure a culture of openness in the institutions, especially the Council.

On the Council Sweden favoured some increases in QMV but was anxious that the weighting of votes should not be changed in a manner that weakened the current position of smaller states – that is, in the direction of population weighting. Like several others it wished to maintain the institutional balance. It was clear that it would not support a reduction in its own influence. For reasons of equality of status and of influence it also objected to radical changes to the Presidency system although it did not oppose some tidying-up of that system. Given this orientation, the Swedes would accept no change to the composition of the Commission that led to less than one Commissioner per state. Otherwise it saw little need for change in the Commission, although it could have more influence in the third pillar, including the right of initiative in certain areas where it did not currently exist. It wanted the European Parliament's role to be strengthened but mostly in the areas of monitoring the administration and financial management. Extensions should be made to the Parliament's co-decision spheres and in a limited fashion to a right of initiative. Sweden was one of the states that advocated giving national parliaments more time to consider Commission proposals. In a continuing theme of improved efficiency, the Swedes called for the Court to be more expeditious in dealing with cases.

Sweden opposed communitarisation of Pillar III, except for a limited transfer on asylum and immigration. This pillar was to remain inter-governmental, although it also called for closer co-operation on police and judicial affairs. Sweden announced that it would join Schengen if there was stronger action on drugs. In fact, it accepted the incorporation of the Schengen *acquis* into the Community. Sweden coupled this with support for adherence to the European Convention on Human Rights and stronger provisions on equality between the sexes and non-discrimination. It also supported the full incorporation of the Social Chapter into the treaty, and including provisions for collective bargaining, like others being worried that there was currently an 'unlevel' playing field. Sweden advocated the incorporation of a title on employment with a commitment to a high level of employment, greater inter-state co-ordination of economic and employment policies and a special Employment Committee to review progress.

Again, like some others, Sweden wanted environmental concerns to be integrated into all other policies, and like other 1995 new members was keen to ensure that its own higher standards could be maintained rather than diluted. The principle of sustainable development was also important to them and they wished its status to be elevated in the treaties. They also advocated in the environment sphere the principle of substitution, greater QMV and improved access for citizens to information. Other areas of policy of interest were improvements in the field of competition, action against crime, and greater protection for consumers.[166]

As early as the 1970s Sweden had shadowed the attempts to stabilise exchange rate movements among EC members, and at the beginning of the 1990s it saw shadowing ERM as source of strength. However, it became caught up in the feverish speculation of 1992 and extreme exchange rate instability led to the cutting of ties between the krona and the ERM. It accepted EMU when it accepted the Treaty on European Union and the *acquis* on accession to the European Union, but there were problems relating to the convergence criteria. These problems were exacerbated when the Swedish economy ran into difficulties related to the European recession. In essence, the relatively high welfare payments in Sweden were predicated on low unemployment, and as unemployment increased this put strains on public finances. It also strained public support for the EU. Although the government submitted a draft convergence programme to the Riksdag in the summer of 1995, by the end of 1996 the Calmfors Commission of Inquiry, and then the Riksdag itself, determined that the price was too high and that Sweden would move to a 'wait and see' policy. Although Sweden has moved in the direction of meeting the convergence criteria – in the spring of 1998 it was judged to have met the inflation and interest rate targets – it had not been a member of the ERM, there had been exchange rate fluctuations (with official exchange rate target in Sweden), although public finances were improving there were still problems over the existence of excessive deficits, and there remained problems with its financial legislation not being compatible with the requirements relating to the European System of Central Banks. Little has happened since the Swedish shift in opinion in 1996–97 to suggest that Swedish participation in the third stage of EMU is imminent. It is now clear that such a decision would involve major political difficulties for leading Swedish parties, with the issue now being not just about the economic questions but also about sovereignty.[167]

The Swedes, having kept European integration at arm's length for a generation, have not suddenly converted to enthusiasm for the project. There has been and is a strong sense of a lack of viable alternatives.

THE NEXT ENLARGEMENTS OF THE EUROPEAN UNION

AS HAS been seen from the previous pages, enlargement is not a new phenomenon. The first enlargement of the European Community was in 1973 and saw the membership of Denmark, Ireland and the UK. The second saw the accession of Greece in 1981. The third saw Portugal and Spain joining in 1986. In January 1995 Austria, Finland and Sweden joined the European Union, which had come into being on 1 November 1993. These enlargements have not always been straightforward and on occasion there has been long delay between application and membership, for example, it was nearly nine years between the Portuguese and Spanish applications and their entry into the Community in 1986. The Norwegians have also shown that application and negotiation does not necessarily lead to membership, since twice – in 1972 and 1994 – the Norwegian people have rejected membership in a referendum. The past record of enlargement is mixed (see Table 18.1).

Some new members have proved to be very *communautaire*, others less, especially Denmark and the UK, and some attitudes to European integration have fluctuated over time, for example, in the Greek case.

In the case of the post-1993 enlargements the key Treaty Article is Article 43 (Consolidated text) (formerly Article O TEU) of the EC Treaty:

'Any European State may apply to become a member of the Union. It shall address its application to the Council, which shall act unanimously after consulting the Commission and after receiving the assent of the European Parliament, which shall act by an absolute majority of its component members. The conditions of admission and the adjustments to the Treaties on which the Union is founded which such admission entails shall be the subject of an agreement between the Member States and the applicant State. This agreement shall be submitted for ratification by all the contracting States in accordance with their respective constitutional requirements'.

In approaching the issue of enlargement, the basis was laid in The Hague communiqué of December 1969 which said that the original Six had agreed to enlargement:

Table 18.1   Applications and enlargement

State	Dates of application	Date of accession
Denmark	1961, 1967	1973
Ireland	1961, 1967	1973
UK	1961, 1967	1973
Norway	1961, 1967, 1992	
Greece	1975	1981
Portugal	1977	1986
Spain	1977	1986
[Greenland seceded in 1985]		
Turkey	1987	
Morocco	1987 (ineligible)	
[German Democratic Republic Länder acceded on German unification 1990]		
Austria	1989	1995
Sweden	1991	1995
Finland	1992	1995
Switzerland	1992 (but application frozen)	
Cyprus*	1990	
Malta	1990 (but withdrawn) 1998 (restored)	
Hungary*	1994	
Poland*	1994	
Slovakia	1995	
Romania	1995	
Bulgaria	1995	
Estonia*	1995	
Latvia	1995	
Lithuania	1995	
Czech Republic*	1996	
Slovenia*	1996	

*First wave of negotiations

'In so far as the applicant States accept the Treaties and their political aims, the decisions taken since entry into force of the Treaties and the options adopted in the sphere of development . . . .'[168]

These principles of accepting the Treaties, the *acquis*, and the political aspirations of the members have remained fundamental for thirty years and will remain fundamental for the next series of enlargements. In each previous case new members have had to accept the existing system – although it has been accepted that the periods of transition could be long, they have always been periods of transition and adjustment, not permanent opt-outs, which have been reserved for current members. In the past the prospect of enlargement has been linked to reforms in the institutions and movement to new policy areas – the Single European Act linked movement to the Single Market with movement to greater qualified majority voting, and even in 1973 there was an understanding that enlargement would lead to the introduction of a regional policy. In the 1990s there was much speculation on the possible relationship or lack of it between 'widening' (horizontal integration) and 'deepening' (vertical integration).

Enlargement has a number of implications for the European Union:

- There are a series of questions relating to the effectiveness of the EU, especially given the greater heterogeneity in experience, socio-economic and political systems and geo-political location on the wider map of Europe.
- These touch on issues such as the capacity of the EU to make decisions and to ensure that the decisions and the full *acquis* are implemented and respected.
- It raises the question of whether a Union of 20+ must by definition be different in character and nature from a Community of Six, and similarly whether a Union of 20+ covering three pillars, plus EMU, must be different from a Coal and Steel Community, or an EEC or Euratom.
- This in turn raises the question of whether there will be more opt-outs, variable geometry or use of flexibility.
- As can be seen from the attitude of many of the current members, especially the small, there are also large concerns over maintaining the institutional balance, and especially the rights of the smaller members to at least some form of equality of membership. This has arisen in the debate, for example, about the numbers of Commissioners and the nature and composition of the rotating Presidency. Larger states have become concerned that they might be outvoted by a weight of states that do not form a majority of the EU's population.
- There is also the question of finance, which was partly addressed by the European Council decisions in the spring/summer of 1999, but over which many doubts remain. Certainly few observers have been as sanguine as the Commission analysis published in 'Agenda 2000' in July 1997 when the Commission concluded that:

> There are various indications that it should be possible to cover the development of priority measures to be financed from the Community budget over the period 2000–2006 without raising the own resources ceiling from its level of 1.27% of GNP.

The 1999 budget should be adopted well below the 1.27% ceiling, saving a fairly substantial margin right from the beginning of the period.

With economic growth forecast to be running at 2.5% a year for the period 2000–2006 for the existing fifteen Member States and at 4% a year between now and

2006 for the applicant countries, then, if the own resources ceiling is maintained at its 1999 level in terms of GNP, by the end of the period there would be potential additional resources slightly in excess of ECU 20 billion (1997 prices)....[169]

Some of the potential implications of this and the progress on making the necessary financial decisions to bring this about are discussed on pp. 279-83. At the Berlin European Council in March 1999 some decisions were taken on 'Agenda 2000'.

• There are detailed operational issues, too, like the provision of translating and interpreting services from, for example, Estonian to Greek.
• There is also the issue of adjustments in Commission staffing, structure and culture.

There are, additionally, a number of questions that arise for the current applicant states:

• Can they accept the *acquis* and the full objectives and agenda of the EU?
• Will seeking to fulfil these requirements destabilise in some cases fragile economies, economies moreover that have already undergone the enormous post-1989 revolution? In other words, do they gain more stability by being in or out?
• How troublesome is the presumption of functioning marketing economies and the ability to compete in and face competition from the Single Market?
• Can they cope with and absorb all the changes – social, economic and political – that are required?
• What will happen if the enlargement is phased? Will some 'win' and others 'lose'? It was decided by the EU that the initial negotiations would be with Estonia, the Czech Republic, Cyprus, Hungary, Poland and Slovenia, but not with Bulgaria, Latvia, Lithuania, Romania and Slovakia. Will there be a continuous series of enlargements for the next decade?
• Is there any feasible alternative to membership?
• Will membership actually deliver on providing them with a sense of security? They all know that there is still no formal defence guarantee in the founding treaties of the European Union, but many of these states – rather like Finland in the 1990s – seem to take for granted that membership of the European Union will automatically increase their security, because they will be identified as members of the Union 'club'.

When it began to consider the post-EFTA states as candidates for membership and another enlargement, the European Community was clear that such enlargements could only occur on the basis of 'parallel progress ... as regards the internal development of the Union'.[170] By the Copenhagen European Council in June 1993, the Member States had agreed that:

> the associated countries in Central and Eastern Europe that so desire shall become members of the European Union. Accession will take place as soon as the associated country is able to assume the obligations of membership by satisfying the economic and political conditions required.

It spelt these out in the following way.

Membership requires that the candidate country has achieved:

- stability of institutions guaranteeing democracy, the rule of law, human rights and respect for and protection of minorities;
- the existence of a functioning market economy as well as the capacity to cope with competitive pressures and market forces within the Union.
- Membership presupposes the candidate's ability to take on the obligations of membership, including adherence to the aims of political, economic and monetary union.[171]

If strictly interpreted by the Union and the applicants, this is a daunting set of requirements, especially since the *acquis* includes not only the *acquis communautaire* (of the First Pillar) but also that of the Second and Third Pillars – CFSP and CJHA. In 1998 the British Presidency made the position clear (see Box 18.1).

Box 18.1 British Presidency résumé of principles for enlargement negotiations, European Conference, London, March 1998

'Accession implies full acceptance of the actual and potential rights and obligations attaching to the Union system and its institutional framework, known as the *'acquis'* of the Union. . . . The *'acquis'* has to be applied at the time of accession. Furthermore, accession requires effective implementation of the *'acquis'*, which implies in particular the establishment of an efficient, reliable public administration. The Union attaches a primordial importance to Justice and Home Affairs and the need for all applicant States to make rapid progress in this area even before accession. There is a need for a progressive alignment of the applicant States' policies and positions towards third countries. . . . The acceptance of the rights and obligations resulting from membership may give rise exceptionally to non-permanent transitional measures, to be defined during the accession negotiations. Transitional measures shall be limited in time and scope, and accompanied by a plan with clearly defined stages for application of the *'acquis'*.'[172]

These requirements are perhaps all the more daunting since one of the ironies of contemporary Europe is that countries which struggled to regain their sovereignty and resume control over their own destiny then rushed to share that destiny with their Western neighbours, ready, as the well known-phrase has it, to share their new sovereignty.

Subsequent European Council meetings after Copenhagen in June 1993 agreed to help prepare the applicants for accession by developing the 'Europe Agreements' that had already been signed with most of these states. These agreements were designed to provide a framework for political dialogue, to establish free trade between the states concerned and the EC/EU, to help the associate states progress towards the economic freedoms of the Community, and to help in the development of market economies. The EU, for example, in December 1994 at its Essen European Council meeting agreed to develop these arrangements into a comprehensive strategy for preparing the Central and East European states for membership. Partly, this was to be done by means of 'structured relations'.[173] Another year later, in Madrid, the EU states asked the Commission to prepare a composite paper on the issues arising out of enlargement, a request that led to the publication of 'Agenda 2000' in July 1997. At the same time the Commission also published its *avis* on each of the Eastern and Central European applicants. Of the twelve applicants,[174] six were adjudged, on the basis of those *avis*, at the meeting in Luxembourg in December 1997 of the European Council, to have satisfied the criteria that it laid down at its meeting in Copenhagen in June 1993. The Luxembourg European Council decided:

> to convene bilateral Inter-governmental Conferences in the spring of 1998, to begin negotiations with Cyprus, Hungary, Poland, Estonia, the Czech Republic and Slovenia on the conditions of their entry into the Union.

With regard to the others it declared that:

> at the same time the preparation of negotiations with Romania, Slovakia, Latvia, Lithuania and Bulgaria will be speeded up, in particular through an analytical examination of the *acquis*.[175]

To try to make these states feel less left behind the Luxembourg Council also agreed to the establishment of a 'European Conference' to bring together the EU states and all aspiring members of the EU, regardless of the stage of their application. The first convocation of this Conference was during the British Presidency (see pp. 469–70). As a sign of potential difficulties ahead, Turkey refused to attend, although the EU has maintained that the Commission should still seek to help Turkey to prepare for membership and that there would be regular reports on its progress towards meeting the Copenhagen criteria. Turkey had taken grave offence at the decision of December 1997 to exclude it from the first wave of negotiations, but one problem was that, for some, the Union could not have 'torturers and executioners' in its ranks. This was a more outspoken version of the Commission's conclusion in July 1997 that 'Turkey's record on upholding the rights of the individual and freedom of expression falls well short of standards in the EU'.[176]

It is perhaps indicative of certain qualms about future enlargements that the Amsterdam Treaty introduced for the first time the principle that the Council, meeting at Heads of State or Government level could:

> determine the existence of a serious and persistent breach by a Member State of the principles ... of liberty, democracy, respect for human rights and fundamental freedoms, and the rule of law ...

and

> decide to suspend certain of the rights deriving from the application of this Treaty to the State in question .... [177]

The other five

The five CEECs which did not receive a favourable opinion were brought within what was describe as an inclusive process by being invited to an annual 'European Conference' which held its first meeting in London under the British Presidency in 1998. They would remain under continuous review and it was not excluded that they might be reassessed and join the first group of five, belatedly.

Summary

The essence of the foregoing is:

1. Negotiations for membership opened in March 1998 with the Czech Republic, Estonia, Hungary, Poland, Slovenia and Cyprus.
2. There were initially no formal membership negotiations with Bulgaria, Latvia, Lithuania, Romania and Slovakia, but they might catch up, and various arrangements have been discussed to allow for that possibility.
3. Turkey is described as 'eligible' for membership, but the catch-up arrangements did not originally apply.
4. Negotiations concern the total adoption of the *acquis*. There may be transitional exceptions, purely temporary.[178]
5. Each negotiation is bilateral and is independent of the others; conclusion is also independent of progress elsewhere.
6. There is no end-date: 2002, sometimes evoked by the Commission, was simply a five-year horizon from the studies that produced the Opinions. A more realistic date is from the middle of the first decade of the century.

SLOW START

The Member States of the Union were collectively in no hurry to begin the serious stage of enlargement. They were also aware that when negotiations began to move, the applicants would require to be told several things which had not been decided – such as the next Financial Perspectives, the reform of the CAP, the size of the college of the Commission, the weighting of votes in the Council, the definition of a Qualified Majority, the distribution of seats in the EP, the language regime, and the transitional periods which the Union would want to enforce, quite apart from those the applicants would ask for.

Screening

The negotiations proper were preceded by a process known as 'screening'. It is conducted in meetings between the Commission's Accession task force and the six front-line applicants. The *acquis* is divided up into chapters. They are reviewed in bilateral meetings

Table 18.2   Summary of Commission opinions on the CEEC applications

Country	Democracy	Market economy	Competitive pressures
Romania	**Yes** but still needs to be consolidated by fuller respect in practice for the rule of law. Gaps remain in area of fundamental rights. Roma have to be integrated further.	**Considerable progress** but property rights are not yet fully assured for land. The legal system is still fragile. Complete restructuring of the financial sector in order to re-establish essential public and investor confidence.	**Serious difficulties** as much of its industry is obsolete and agriculture needs to modernise. Economy needs a number of years of sustained structural reform. Has not yet created the conditions which are conducive to a dynamic private sector.
Slovenia	**Yes** but some improvements are required in the operation of the judicial system and in restoring property to former owners. Corruption needs targeting.	**Yes** but the working of the market mechanism still needs some improvement.	**Able to cope** but there is a lack of competition in some sectors. Rigidities in the economy need to be reduced. Rapid wage growth combined with low productivity growth is a problem.
Slovakia	**No.** Instability of institutions, lack of rootedness in political life and shortcomings in functioning of democracy. Fight against corruption needs greater attention. Treatment of the Hungarian and Roma minorities needs improvement.	**Yes** but a restrictive price law was introduced in 1996 and the draft Enterprise Revitalisation Act would be a major step back from market mechanisms. The financial sector needs to be reinforced.	**Able to cope** (satisfactorily) but continued success requires more transparent and market based policies.
Bulgaria	**Yes** but needs to be reinforced by fuller respect in practice for the rule of law. Positive reforms announced in April 1997. Considerable efforts needed to pursue fight against corruption and to improve operation of judicial system.	**Limited progress** as price controls were not removed until this year. Recent renewed efforts towards economic reform. Complete restructuring of the financial sector is needed to re-establish public and investor confidence.	**Cannot yet cope.** Incomplete land reform prevents the emergence of a modern agricultural sector; slow privatisation and economic instability has weakened state enterprise and delayed development of dynamic private sector.
Estonia	**Yes** but need to address the naturalisation of Russian speaking non-citizens.	**Yes.** Progress has been good but land reform has been slow, and reform of the pensions system has yet to start.	**Able to cope** but needs to broaden its export base. The need to finance rising trade and current account deficits is a matter for concern. Substantial work needed in public procurement, intellectual property, financial services, taxation and competition.
Hungary	**Yes** but certain improvements are still needed in the operation of the judicial system.	**Yes** but reform of pensions and social security needs to advance rapidly.	**Able to cope** as the necessary reforms were implemented at an early stage.
Latvia	**Yes** but needs to accelerate rate of naturalisation of Russian speaking non-citizens.	**Considerable progress** made in stabilising the economy but effective implementation is lagging behind. Privatisation is not complete.	**Not able to cope.** Exports consist mainly of low value added goods. Industrial restructur as well as enterprise restructuring is still nee The banking sector is underdeveloped and weak in parts. Agriculture needs modernisir
Lithuania	**Yes.**	**Considerable progress** has been made, however, further progress is needed in the area of relative price adjustments, large scale privatisation and bankruptcy proceedings.	**Not able to cope.** Substantial enterprise restructuring is still required. Agriculture needs modernising and the banking sector remains weak.
Poland	**Yes.** Efforts to improve the operation of the judicial system and to intensify the fight against corruption will need to be sustained. There are certain limits to the freedom of the press.	**Excellent progress** but in order to guarantee longer-term stability, pension and social security systems need reform. Financial services are underdeveloped. A lot of trade related problems have arisen.	**Able to cope** provided it maintains the pace of restructuring and keeps the economy open.
Czech Republic	**Yes.** But there are some problems in laws governing freedom of the press. There is a problem of discrimination affecting the Roma, notably through operation of the citizenship law.	**Excellent progress** but in order to guarantee longer-term stability, corporate governance and the financial system will require stengthening.	**Able to cope** but import deposit scheme will need to be resolved in terms of Europe Agreement. Quality of exported goods is still low.

Country	Admin. capacity	*Acquis* problem areas
Romania	**Substantial reform needed** as it is currently vey weak. Does not have the capacity to apply community law.	**Has not yet implemented** key elements, especially environment, transport, employent, social affairs, justice and home affairs and agriculture.
Slovenia	**Substantial reform required.**	**No national programme** has been drawn up on the implementation of *acquis*. Progress needed in environment, employment, social affairs and energy.
Slovakia	**Substantial reform required.**	**If current efforts are significantly stepped up** the main part of the *acquis* could be adopted. Further work is required in the area of the environment.
Bulgaria	**Substantial reform needed.** Weakness of national co-ordination mechanism and overall public administration.	**Slow transportation of *acquis*** will not be in position in medium term. Needs special attention to the environment, transport, justice and home affairs, energy and agriculture. Will face difficulty in applying the Single Market *acquis*.
Estonia	**Reform needed.** Doubts about the capacity to implement the legal framework. Such a weakness will be temporary. Needs adequate structures of finance control at regional level.	**Substantial efforts needed** in the medium term to adopt main part of the *acquis*. Particular attention needed in environment, agriculture, fisheries, consumer protection and customs.
Hungary	**Good.** If current reforms continue, no difficulties will be expected.	**Should be in a position to adopt** main part of the *acquis* in medium term but progress needed in environment, customs control and energy. Despite efforts undertaken, concrete measures of implementation needed.
Latvia	**Reform needed** as it is very weak and this has had an impact upon the approximation and implementation of legislation.	**If current efforts are significantly** stepped up, the main part of this are *acquis* could be adopted. Further work is required in the area of the environment.
Lithuania	**Reform needed** as it is very weak and this has had an impact upon the approximation and implementation of legislation.	**Anticipated important obligations** of the Europe Agreement but substantial efforts remain especially in telecommunications, fisheries, customs, agriculture, energy and the environment.
Poland	**Good.** Overall the administrative infrastructure is either well established or recently set up and functioning normally, but the work of legislative adaptation is proceeding slowly in the field of technical rules and standards.	**Current efforts need to be stepped up** in areas where progress is lagging, especially agriculture, environment and transport. If this is done, Poland should be in a position to adopt the main part of the *acquis* in the medium term.
Czech Republic	**Good.** The administrative infrastructure is either well established or recently set up and functioning normally but substantial further efforts are needed.	**Current efforts need to be stepped up** in areas where progress is lagging, especially agriculture, environment and energy. If this is done, the Czech Republic should adopt the main part of the *acquis* in the medium term.

(preceded by a multilateral introduction). On the basis of the Commission's 'harmoni-grams', which record the stage each applicant has reached, the meetings consist of:

- an educational process in which the Commission explains the compass of the *acquis* in that section;
- the identification of matters for which there are no adoption problems, or purely technical adjustments to the Treaties and legislation adopted thereunder;
- the identification of substantive problems.

Substantive problems are to be reported to the Council as requiring attention in negoti-ation.

Loss of direction?

The first screening programme suggested that that part of the process would be over by the end of 1998. It was later revised to extend well into 1999. Meanwhile the Council had taken no decision to move to the substantive part, the contours of which would emerge from screening. The Commission sent it an interim Report in June but its first major con-tribution was to be a report at the end of 1998 – which, under the new screening sched-ule, would be only partial. When the Austrian Presidency took over in July 1998 there were signs of some gamesmanship. On its own authority it invited applicants to submit the 'position papers' containing their bids for transitions in the autumn, such that the real negotiations could be said to begin. This was not endorsed by the Council and appeared to be inconsistent with the function and purpose of screening. Why screen a chapter if position papers have already gone in? As a gesture, the Member States agreed to hold a negotiating session in late 1998, but it had little substance, and little progress was made in 1999.

OTHER STATES

Iceland has no interest in joining, since joining would deprive it of control of its fishing grounds.

Norway has twice negotiated accession and twice seen accession rejected in a refer-endum. Norwegian voters are said to value their independence, which is relatively recent in their history; and to want sovereign control over their oil resources and fish stocks. Switzerland applied for membership but froze the application when the referendum on participation in the European Economic Area failed to produce a positive result. With much difficulty, Switzerland negotiated a series of sectoral agreements with the EC. There are recurrent rumours that the Federal Council may wish to return to the ques-tion of membership. None of the ex-Yugoslav states, with the exception of Slovenia, are anywhere near a close relationship with the European Union, and the same is true of Albania. However, it may be that some states in the area will benefit from having supported NATO in its 1999 conflict with the Federal Republic of Yugoslavia and the ensuing sense that something should be done to show European gratitude to them. The Vatican, Monaco and Andorra have also not sought to join the EU, but rather have come to a series of pragmatic arrangements with it. Gibraltar is affected by EC legislation on free circulation of persons (but not of goods) and the provision of financial services. More importantly, the continuing Spanish claim to Gibraltar has shown the ability to throw a spanner in the works of what sometimes seem to be totally unconnected policies and developments.

LEGAL BASES

- Preamble to the EC Treaty
  Resolved by thus pooling their resources to preserve and strengthen peace and liberty and *calling upon the other peoples of Europe who share their ideals to join in their efforts.* (Emphasis added.)
- Article 49, consolidated version TEU (ex-O).

DISCUSSION QUESTIONS

1. Why has the Union agreed to its further enlargement?
2. Why do the CEEC applicants wish to join?
3. What can the Union do to maintain its cohesion with 20+ members?
4. Take any one applicant that was not in the 'first wave' and explain why it was excluded.

BIBLIOGRAPHY

Avery, G. and Cameron, F.: *The Enlargement of the European Union*, UACES, Sheffield Academic Press, 1998.

Crabbe, A. and Hughes, K.: *The Enlargement of the EU to the East*, Chatham House, 1998.

Henderson, K. (ed.): *Back to Europe: Central and Eastern Europe and the European Union*, London, UCL, 1999.

Nicoll, W. and Schoenberg, R. (eds): *Europe beyond 2000*, Whurr, 1998.

Preston, C.: *Enlargement and Integration in the European Union*, Routledge/UACES, 1997.

NOTES

1. See Finn Laursen and Sophie Vanhoonacker (eds), *The Inter-governmental Conference on Political Union: institutional reforms, new policies and international identity of the European Community* (Dordrecht, Martinus Nijhoff, 1992); and Andrew Duff (ed.), *The Treaty of Amsterdam: Text and Commentary* (London, Federal Trust, 1997).

517

2. See Adrian Poole (Belgium and Luxembourg) who cites *La Belgique et la Communauté Européenne, Textes et documents*, No. 317 (Brussels, Ministère des Affaires Etrangères du Commerce Extérieur et de la coopération au Dévelopment, 1979) p. 7, in Carol and Kenneth Twitchett (eds), *Building Europe* (London, Europe Publications, 1981), p. 145, and M.A.G. Van Meerhaeghe (ed.), *Belgium and EC Membership Evaluated* (London, Frances Pinter, 1992).

3. On the Netherlands see Philip Everts and Guido Walraven, *The Politics of Persuasion, Implementation of Foreign Policy by the Netherlands* (Aldershot, Averbury, 1989).

4. Memorandum on the IGC from the governments of Belgium, Luxembourg and the Netherlands, 7 March 1996. Many of the Member State submissions to the IGC are reproduced in: *European Parliament*, White Paper on the 1996 IGC, Vol. II, Summary of Positions of the Member States of the European Union with a view to the 1996 Inter-governmental Conference, European Parliament Inter-governmental Conference Task Force, January 1996.

5. Note on the IGC to Belgium Communities and Regions, Belgium Chamber and Senate, 28 July 1995.

6. Note of 14 November 1994 on the enlargement of the European Union: the opportunities and obstacles.

7. Luxembourg government Memorandum of 30 June 1995.

8. Note of 28 July 1995, op. cit.

9. Since 1991 Belgium has been converted into a federal state consisting of two self-governing regions – Dutch-speaking Flanders and French-speaking Wallonia – the Brussels region and the small German-speaking area.

10. 30 June Memorandum op. cit.

11. European Co-operation in the field of Justice and Home Affairs. Third Memorandum for the 1996 Inter-governmental Conference, 23 May 1995.

12. 30 June Memorandum, op. cit.

13. Aidan Cawley, *De Gaulle* (London, Collins, 1969), p. 443.

14. For example, 'Guidelines adopted at the Franco-German Seminar of Ministers of Foreign Affairs, Freiburg im Breisgau, 27 February 1996, reproduced in Patrick Keatinge, *European Security: Ireland's Choices* (Dublin, Institute of European Affairs, 1996), Appendix VIII, pp. 214–16.

15. EURO 1999, 25 March 1998, Report on progress towards convergence and the recommendation with a view to the transition to the third stage of economic and monetary union: Part 1: *Recommendation* (European Commission, Luxembourg, OOP, 1998), pp. 46–7. [Hereafter EURO 1999].

16. *Agence Europe*, 26 June 1990.

17. Letter of 6 December 1995 from the President of the French Republic, Jacques Chirac, and the Chancellor of the Federal Republic of Germany, Helmut Kohl.

18. *Le Monde*, 14 March 1996.

19. *Le Monde*, 20 February 1996.

20. See 'Guidelines' op. cit.

21. See *Agence Europe*, 10–11 December 1990.

22. Bonn had obtained a special Protocol in the Treaty of Rome by which trade between the two Germanies was regarded by the whole Community not as external trade but as intra-Community trade, not subject to the Common Customs Tariff.

23. See Simon Bulmer and William Paterson, *The Federal Government of Germany and the European Community* (London, Allen & Unwin, 1987) and C.C. Schweitzer and D. Karsten (eds), *Federal Republic of Germany and EC Membership Evaluated* (London, Pinter, 1990).

24. Jean Monnet, *Memoirs*, translated by Richard Mayne (London, Collins, 1978), pp. 288–92.

25. *Agence Europe*, 20 April 1990.

26. 'Germany: Headnotes to the Judgement of the Federal Constitutional Court, Second Division, dated 12 October 1993' [Official translation from the language service of the German Ministry of Foreign Affairs] reproduced in Finn Laursen and Sophie Vanhoonacker (eds), *The Ratification of the Maastricht Treaty: Issues, Debates and Future Implications* (Dordrecht, Martinus Nijhoff, 1994), Annex X, pp. 515–16.

27. Rita Beuter, 'Germany and the Ratification of the Maastricht Treaty' in Laursen and Vanhoonacker (eds), ibid., pp. 87–112.

28. Karl-Heinz Klär, Länder delegate to the Federal Government and for Europe, 3 March 1995, Memorandum to Commissioner Oreja.

29. Anne-Marie Le Gloannec, 'Germany and Europe's Foreign and Security Policy: embracing the British vision' in Carl Lankowski (ed.) *Break Out, Break Down or Break In? Germany and the European Union after Amsterdam* (Washington, DC, American Institute for Contemporary German Studies, 1998), pp. 21ff.

30. C.C. Clemens and W.E. Paterson, 'Special Issue on the Kohl Chancellorship' in *German Politics* Vol. 7, No.1 (1998).

31. *Bulletin of the European Communities*, 6–1994 and see pp. 316–17.

32. *Die Welt*, 22 November 1998.

33. *Bild*, 26 March 1998.

34. EURO 1999, op. cit., pp. 43–44.

35. Schröder, 'We want a strong Europe'. Speech to the Group of European Socialists, Strasbourg, 14 July 1998 mimeograph.

36. *Frankfurter Allgemeine Zeitung*, 14 September 1998.

37. CDU/CSU paper reproduced in Trevor C. Salmon and Sir William Nicoll (eds), *Building European Union: a documentary history and analysis* (Manchester, Manchester University Press, 1997), pp. 255–60.

38. Schröder, op. cit.

39. Ibid.

40. *Financial Times*, 10 November 1998.

41. Idem.

42. See Geoffrey Pridham, 'Italy' in Twitchett op. cit., p. 14 and 8–118 for an excellent short background on Italy's attitude to European integration. See also Fransesco Francioni (ed.), *Italy and EC Membership Evaluated* (London, Pinter, 1992).

43. Pridham, op. cit., p. 84.

44. Fifth Report on the Implementation of the White Paper (Brussels, Commission of the EC, 1990).

45. Guido Carli, President of the Confindustria, quoted in *Europaische Zeitung*, January 1979, cited in Pridham, op. cit., p. 103.
46. *Agence Europe*, 26 June 1990.
47. Italian proposals on CFSP, 18 September 1990, reproduced in Laursen and Vanhoonacker, op. cit., p. 292.
48. EURO 1999 op. cit., pp. 48–9.
49. Sean Lemass, Prime Minister, speaking to the *Dáil, Dáil Debates*, vol. 191, col. 205ff and 266, see Trevor C. Salmon, *Un-neutral Ireland: an ambivalent and unique security policy* (Oxford, Clarendon Press, 1989), p. 211 and passim; and Trevor C. Salmon, 'Ireland' in Twitchett, op. cit., pp. 191–216.
50. Speech to Royal Irish Academy, 10 November 1975, see Salmon, 'Ireland' op. cit., p. 203.
51. Calleary, Minister of State, Department of Foreign Affairs, Dáil Debates, Vol. 371, col. 2297 (1987). For a fuller discussion see Patrick Keatinge (ed.), *Ireland and EC Membership Evaluated* (London, Pinter, 1991).
52. Foreign Affairs Press release 7 May 1998.
53. *Challenges and Opportunities Abroad*, White Paper on Foreign Policy, Department of Foreign Affairs (Dublin, Stationery Office, 1996) p. 98, para. 3.154.
54. Ibid., p. 108 para. 3.187.
55. Ibid., p. 97 para. 3.150.
56. Ibid., p. 107 para. 3.183.
57. Ibid., p. 100 para. 3.163.
58. Ibid., p. 101 para. 3.168.
59. EURO 1999 op. cit., p. 48.
60. *Challenges and Opportunities*, op. cit., pp. 118–19, paras 4.4, 4.9–4.10.
61. Ibid., p. 130 para. 4.48.
62. Ibid., p. 146 para. 4.113.
63. Ibid., p. 111 para. 3.199.
64. The Protocol was designed to prevent legal abortion being introduced into Ireland under EC rules, but had the unintended effect of disallowing Irish women from travelling abroad.
65. Carsten Holbrad, *Danish Neutrality: a study in the foreign policy of a small state* (Oxford, Clarendon Press, 1991), pp. v and 57.
66. See Clive Archer, 'Denmark' in Twitchett, op. cit., pp. 168–90, especially p. 171.
67. Following home rule for Greenland and a referendum there, it withdrew from membership of the Communities in 1985.
68. G. Nielsson, *Denmark and European Integration* (PhD, University of California) quoted in Archer, op. cit., p. 179.
69. Mr Müller, footnote, in 'Report of the ad hoc Committee on Institutional Questions to the European Council', *Agence Europe Documents*, Nos 1349/1350, 21 March 1985, p. 2.
70. For the background on Denmark see Lise Lyck (ed.), *Denmark and EC Membership Evaluated* (London, Pinter, 1992).
71. Memorandum from the Danish government, 4 October 1990, reproduced in Laursen and Vanhoonacker (eds), op. cit., pp. 293–303.
72. Ibid.

73. Idem.
74. Annex 1 to Part B: Decision of the Heads of State or Government, meeting within the European Council, concerning certain problems raised by Denmark on the Treaty on European Union, *Bulletin of the European Communities* 12–1992, reproduced in Salmon and Nicoll, op. cit., pp. 240–1.
75. *Bases for Negotiations: Open Europe – The 1996 Inter-governmental Conference*, Danish government, 11 December 1995.
76. Annex 1, op. cit.
77. Memorandum from the Danish government, 4 October 1990, op. cit.
78. Ibid.
79. Annex 1, op. cit.
80. EURO 1999, op. cit., pp. 40–1.
81. Annex 1, op. cit.
82. *Bases for Negotiations*, op. cit.
83. See Stephen George, *An Awkward Partner: Britain in the European Community* (Oxford, Oxford University Press, 1990); and Simon Bulmer, Stephen George and Andrew Scott (eds), *The United Kingdom and EC Membership Evaluated* (London, Pinter, 1992).
84. Paul Kennedy, *The Realities Behind Diplomacy: Background Influences on British External Policy 1865–1980* (London, Fontana, 1981).
85. F.S. Northedge, *Descent from Power: British Foreign Policy 1945–1973* (London, Allen & Unwin, 1974).
86. Clement Attlee, Labour Prime Minister, *House of Commons Debates 5th Series*, Vol. 450, cols 1314–19, 5 May 1948.
87. Speech quoted in Randolph Churchill (ed.), *Sinews of Peace* (London, Cassell, 1948), p. 202.
88. Winston Churchill, as Prime Minister, *House of Commons Debates*, Vol. 515, cols 889ff, 11 May 1953.
89. Miriam Camps, *Britain and the European Community 1955–1963* (London, Oxford University Press), p. 4.
90. Ibid., p. 339.
91. Compare Camps, ibid., p. 274, who sees it as a 'radical change in British policy'.
92. Harold Macmillan (Prime Minister) and Hugh Gaitskell (Leader of the Opposition) in *House of Commons Debates*, Vol. 645, cols 928ff, 31 July 1961.
93. Harold Wilson, Prime Minister, *House of Commons Debates*, Vol. 735, col. 1540, 10 November 1966.
94. Harold Wilson, Prime Minister, *House of Commons Debates*, Vol. 795, cols 1080–97, 10 February 1970.
95. *The United Kingdom and the European Communities* (London, HMSO, Cmnd. 4715, 1971).
96. F.S. Northedge, 'Britain and the EEC: past and present', in Roy Jenkins (ed.), *Britain and the EEC* (London, Macmillan, 1983), p. 26.
97. Harold Wilson, Prime Minister, *House of Commons Debates*, Vol. 888, cols 1456ff, 18 March 1975.
98. For the major debate see ibid., Vol. 889, cols 821–1370, 7 April 1975.
99. Harold Wilson, Prime Minister, ibid., Vol. 893, cols 29–30, 9 June 1975.

100. Conservative and Unionist Party General Election Manifesto, May 1979.

101. Margaret Thatcher, Prime Minister, *Europe: the future*, paper produced for the Fontainebleau European Council, 25–26 June 1984, reproduced in *Journal of Common Market Studies*, Vol. 23, No. 1 (September 1984), pp. 73–81.

102. John Pinder, 'Positive integration and negative integration: some problems of economic union in the EEC', *World Today*, Vol. 24 (1968), pp. 88–110.

103. Speech by Mrs Thatcher, Prime Minister, to the Opening Ceremony of the College of Europe, Bruges, 20 September 1988, reproduced in Salmon and Nicoll, op. cit., pp. 208–14.

104. John Major, Prime Minister, House of Commons, 20 November 1991.

105. *Treaty on European Union*, pp. 191–3.

106. John Major, Prime Minister, House of Commons, 20 November 1991.

107. *Economist*, 25 September 1993.

108. See Salmon and Nicoll, op. cit., pp. 261–3.

109. Malcolm Rifkind, *Principles and Practice of British Foreign Policy September 1995*, reproduced in Salmon and Nicoll, op. cit., 277–82.

110. John Major, Prime Minister, House of Commons, 21 May 1996.

111. David Davis described it as a 'show-stopper', Foreign Affairs Committee, 4th Report, 'Developments at the Inter-governmental Conference' Session 1996–97 (HM), p. 22.

112. Malcolm Rifkind, House of Commons, 5 July 1995.

113. *A Partnership of Nations: the British approach to the European Union Inter-governmental Conference 1996* (London, HMSO, Cm. 3181, March 1996), p. 8.

114. Ibid., p. 4.

115. Ibid., p. 6.

116. *The Independent*, 9 May 1997.

117. Speech by Tony Blair, Prime Minister, to French National Assembly, 24 March 1998, FCO Press release.

118. *A Partnership of Nations*, op. cit., p. 23.

119. Opening statement by Doug Henderson, Minister for Europe, at the EU Inter-governmental Conference Working Group of Personal Representatives, Brussels, 5 May 1997, Britain and the EU: a fresh start. FCO Press release, 5 May 1997.

120. Reproduced in *A Partnership of Nations*, op. cit., Annex D, pp. 33–8.

121. Tony Blair, Prime Minister, to the North Atlantic Assembly, Edinburgh, 13 November 1998, FCO Press release, 16 November 1998.

122. Idem.

123. *A Partnership of Nations*, op. cit., p. 17.

124. Malcolm Rifkind, Minutes of Evidence to Foreign Affairs Committee 25 February 1997, p. 58.

125. 'New Labour: because Britain deserves better', Labour Party Manifesto, 1997, p. 37.

126. *A Partnership of Nations*, op. cit., p. 15.

127. Tony Blair, Prime Minister, 5 December 1997, FCO Press release, 8 December 1997.

128. 'Agenda 2000: For a stronger and wider Union', European Commission, *Bulletin of the European Union* Supplement 5/97 (Luxembourg, OOP, 1997), p. 68.

129. Jack Cunningham, Minister of Agriculture, Ministry of Agriculture and Fisheries Press release, 18 March 1998.

130. Gordon Brown, Chancellor of the Exchequer, House of Commons, 27 October 1997.

131. William Hague, Leader of the Opposition, Speech to the CBI Conference, 24 October 1997, Conservative Central Office press release.

132. David Butler and Dennis Kavanagh, *The British General Election of 1997* (London, Macmillan, 1997), pp. 7, 71–73, 103 and 305–6.

133. In 1977 Greece's GDP per capita was 46.6% of the Community average, Portugal's 27.4%, and Spain's 51.6%, see Loukas Tsoukalis, *The European Community and its Mediterranean Enlargement* (London, George Allen & Unwin, 1981), p. 9, and passim. for the background and membership debates.

134. See 'Statement on Greek Presidency of the Council' EC Bulletin, 7/8–1983, pp. 111–18; and 'Statement on the work programme of the Greek Presidency', *EC Bulletin*, 7/8–1988, p. 170.

135. See Greek Memorandum, 'Contribution to the Discussions on Progress Towards Political Union', 15 May 1990 in Laursen and Vanhoonacker, op. cit., pp. 277–81.

136. See WEU states declaration attached to the Treaty on European Union.

137. Memorandum of the Greek government of 24 January 1996 on the IGC: Greek positions and comments. This was submitted to Greece's partners by the new government of Costas Simitis.

138. Conclusions of Greek Inter-ministerial Committee, 7 June 1995.

139. Christos Bourouvalis, 'Greece' in Desmond Dinan (ed.), *Encyclopaedia of the European Union* (London, Lynne Rienner, 1998), pp. 256–7.

140. EURO 1999, op. cit., pp. 44–5.

141. See 138 above.

142. Memorandum of 24 January 1996 op. cit.

143. See Tsoukalis, op. cit., p. 53.

144. Ministry of Foreign Affairs: Memorandum of the Portuguese Delegation: Political Union with a view to the Inter-governmental Conference, Lisbon, 30 November 1991, in Laursen and Vanhoonacker (eds), op. cit., pp. 304 and 304–12.

145. Portuguese Foreign Ministry: 'Portugal and the IGC for revision of the Treaty on European Union', March 1996.

146. Idem.

147. EURO 1999, op. cit., pp. 53–4.

148. 'The Road to European Citizenship', 24 September 1990, reproduced in Laursen and Vanhoonacker (eds), op. cit., pp. 304 and 304–12.

149. Spanish Foreign Minister Ordonez, *Agence Europe*, 6 September 1991.

150. Idem.

151. Elements for a Spanish position at the 1996 Inter-governmental Conference 28 March 1996 – document sent by Spanish Foreign Ministry to Spanish parliamentary groups.

152. EURO 1999, op. cit., pp. 45–6.

153. Spain submitted a separate discussion paper on WEU on 6 July 1995.

154. Article 4 of the Austrian State Treaty. See Michael Cullis, 'The Austrian Treaty Settlement', *Review of International Studies*, Vol. 7, No. 3 (July) 1981, pp. 159–64 for background.

155. Nils Andren (ed.), *The Future of the Nordic Balance* (Stockholm, Ministry of Defence, 1977).

156. Swedish Foreign Minister, 1 November 1971, Documents on Swedish Foreign Policy 1971 (DSFP) Stockholm, Ministry for Foreign Affairs, 1971, p. 81.

157. Manfred Scheich, 'The European neutrals after enlargement of the Communities – the Austrian perspective', *Journal of Common Market Studies*, Vol. 12, No. 3 (1973–74), p. 237.

158. Swedish Minister of Commerce, 28 July 1962, DSFP 1962, op. cit., p. 146.

159. 'The Challenge of Enlargement: Commission Opinion on Austria's Application for Membership', *Bulletin of the European Communities* Supplement S4/1992, reproduced in Salmon and Nicoll, op. cit., pp. 246–9.

160. See Francisco Granell, 'The European Union's enlargement negotiations with Austria, Finland, Norway and Sweden' *in Journal of Common Market Studies*, Vol. 33, No. 1 (March 1995), pp. 117–41; Lee Miles (ed.), *The European Union and the Nordic Countries* (London, Routledge, 1996); David Arter, 'The EU referendum in Finland on 16 October 1994: a vote for the West, not for Maastricht', *Journal of Common Market Studies*, Vol. 33, No. 3 (September 1995), pp. 361–88; Wolfram Kaiser, 'Austria in the European Union', ibid., pp. 411–26; and on Norway, Ingrid Sogner and Clive Archer, 'Norway and Europe: 1972 and now', ibid., pp. 389–410.

161. For the Austrian positions in the IGC see: 'Guidelines of the Austrian government on the subjects likely to be dealt with at the 1996 IGC' submitted in June 1995 and 'Austria's positions of principle on the Inter-governmental Conference: Austrian government document of 26 March 1996.

162. EURO 1999, op. cit., pp. 51–2.

163. The IGC and the security and defence dimension – towards an enhanced EU role in crisis management, 'The Finnish–Swedish Proposal on Crisis Management', reproduced in Keatinge, op. cit., Appendix X, pp. 211–13.

164. 'Memorandum of the Foreign Ministry of 18 September 1995 on the views of the Finnish government concerning the 1996 Inter-governmental Conference' and 'Finland's starting-points and objectives for the 1996 Inter-governmental Conference report of the Finnish government', 27 February 1996.

165. EURO 1999, op. cit., pp. 54–5.

166. 'Note of July 1995 on the fundamental interests of Sweden with a view to the 1996 Inter-governmental Conference' and 'Communication of the Swedish government of 30 November 1995 on the 1996 Intergovernmental Conference'.

167. EURO 1999, op. cit., pp. 55–6, and information supplied by Dr Anders Widfeldt of the Department of Politics and International Relations, University of Aberdeen.

168. The European Communities: Text of the Communiqué issued by the Heads of State or Government at their meeting in The Hague, December 1969, *Bulletin of the European Communities* 1–1970.

169. 'Agenda 2000: For a stronger and wider Union', European Commission, *Bulletin of the European Union*, Supplement 5/97 (Luxembourg, OOP, 1997), p. 62.

170. Conclusions of the Presidency of the European Council, Lisbon, June 1992, *Bulletin of the European Communities* 6–1992.
171. Conclusions of the Presidency of the European Council, Copenhagen, June 1993, ibid., 6–1993.
172. 7095/98 (Presse 86-G).
173. Conclusions of the Presidency of the European Council, Essen, December 1994, ibid., 12–1994.
174. The Commission's Opinions on the CEEC applications are in Bulletin Supplements 6/97 to 15/97.
175. Conclusions of the Presidency of the European Council, Luxembourg, December 1997, *Bulletin*, op. cit., 12–1997.
176. Agenda 2000, op. cit., p. 56.
177. Articles 6 and 7 of the Treaty on European Union, Consolidated Version.
178. The only known permanent derogation in the fourth enlargement was for a type of chewing tobacco said to be part of the Swedish way of life and unknown (and unwanted) outside. Of course, temporary exemptions can be extended. . . .

CONCLUSIONS

It used to be modish to cite the 'bicycle theory of political kinetics'. It suggests that a political process cannot stand still but must always be in motion towards something other than the status quo. In this home-spun doctrine, when applied to European integration and regardless of the theoretical school or political persuasion invoked – federalism, functionalism, transactionalism, institutionalism, and their 'neo-' variants[1] – there is at least a provisional end-point in 'European Political Union'. In several models this is the *Federation* evoked in the Schuman Declaration, but the word has no precisely defined content and is used indiscriminately alongside *Confederation*, which, if it has a differentiated meaning, is a loose form of Federation.

THE COAT OF MANY COLOURS

An account closer to observed realities is that the body which calls itself the European Union to mark that it is more than the three economic communities is a little of everything. Its Central Bank is as much uniate as it is 'federal', which is what the Delors Report called it because it works through what were national banks.[2] Its Competition Authority, centred in the Commission's DG IV, is federal in the Wheare sense that it is not subordinate to other authorities. Its economic wing is nominally centralised, within stated powers, but since the Treaty on European Union came into force its highest political authority is inter-governmental and its working rule is 'Community action is the exception'. Its so-called Common Foreign Policy is simply an international pact. It does not have, and is not seeking to have, a Common Security Policy. The key economic and employment policies of its Member States are no more than *co-ordinated* under a principle of 'peer review'. Several of the policy areas dignified by a Title in the Economic Community are firmly national, with the possibility of a modest Community 'contribution'. Sensitive policy areas like

527

welfare state and national health provisions, income tax, wage policy (if any), education are virtually entirely outside Union purview.

There is no 'master plan'. There is no driving political ideology, apart from the contemporary attachment to the market economy and the concept of the rule of law. There is no 'next stage'. Just as nobody predicted German unification, so there is no predictability about what the Union will do next – is it fiscal harmonisation, or centralised social security, or regional courts as part of the European Court, or 'Ausgleich' – fiscal transfers among states, or the dismantlement of the managed agricultural market, or a European Defence Force under integrated command, or an independent competition authority, or a Second revising Chamber representing the states, or the official abandonment of joint research and development; or the formulation of a Common Energy Policy?

Whatever the developments or retrogressions are, they are the interplay between internal and external situations which the leaderships neither create nor control and the kaleidoscope of political power with the governance of the Member States.

At times, the flow is recognisably towards integration, as it was with the decisions to remove tariff and non-tariff measures affecting goods, regulation affecting services and control over major concentrations from national decision. At what may well be roughly the same times, it is towards national assertiveness, in the form of subsidiarity; the replacement of a Defence Policy 'in time' (that is mildly decisive) by a Defence Policy if the member states decide (which is a mere pleonasm); or by 'enhanced co-operation', which withdraws commonality from the Community.

So many men, as many opinions

The decision-makers, whose own exercise of power is ephemeral, have not subscribed to a common view. There was a generation that had shared a common experience of total war, dictatorship-cum-military occupation and a little later fear of Communist nuclear aggression. These mental wounds no longer burn. Although Lady Thatcher is no longer at the heart of Europe, her position remains unambivalent and unchanging:

> There is no European nation. There never will be. There is no European language, there never will be. We don't want to be dissolved into any amorphous group. We wish to keep our identity, our pride, our customs, and to co-operate with nations with their own pride, own monarchies, own customs.[3]

The counterpoint is the equally unchanging insistence of Chancellor Kohl, the spokesman for integrated Europe:

> Only the European Community can serve as the strong, dynamic nucleus and foundation of pan-European unification. It alone appears capable of giving Europe this quality, speaking with one voice in the world for the whole of Europe and adequately bringing this continent's weight to bear. To this end we must, however, endow it with the requisite structures and instruments.[4]

Completing, deepening, widening

To the pan-European completing-deepening (that are roughly the same process) and widening go together. The ever-closer union is not exclusive. To a closet sceptic, widening can only mean dilution – how can a much larger assemblage of countries at widely differing stages of economic development move as fast as a smaller group, which itself began with geographical neighbours and pre-existing high levels of mutual trade? The conflict within the triptych, which has been in the shadow, emerges unmistakably with the prospect of six new Union members within the first decade of the year 2000; and is testified to by the inability of the fifteen to lay the foundations of the adaptations which they have no alternative but to carry through. Power of decision and cash to spend have to be shared out – like St Augustine in his appeal for divine help to revert to chastity, the fifteen are taking their time to face up to the inexorable wrench. What vision do the new members have of the Union they want to belong to, but which they will help to shape? It can be confidently stated that they are just as uncertain, divided and self-contradictory as any of the fifteen have been, are, and will continue to be.

A contribution to a unified field theory

The only safe guide is that, using its own calculus, the government of each present and future Member State supports what the Union does as long it thinks it is in a plus-sum game. The added value does not have to accrue from every single act or in a set time frame; and it need not be tangible – integration itself may be a plus. The Union's anguish, shared with the political élites that drive it, is that the man and woman in the European streets see around them little sign of the proclaimed benefits. Moreover, it is inherent in any arrangement which harnesses together states and peoples with their own past and their own future expectations that it must be an unending series of compromises, cryptograms and ambiguities which contra-élites lovingly expose.

The task in hand is:

- to widen because the calculation is positive, part moral, part security-driven, part material;
- to complete, but without knowing or even needing to know what ultimate completion is;
- there is plenty to do in the coming decade;
- and to overcome the public morosity which confronts all forms of contemporary government by achieving results which can be felt, beginning with price stability without deflation, the sole task of the European System of Central Banks from the first day of the last year of the second millennium.

N NOTES

1. For discussion and bibliographies see: Clive H. Church, *European Integration Theory in the 1980s*, European Dossier Series, University of North London, 1996; Andrea Bosco, *What is Federalism*, South Bank (University) European Papers; Wolfgang Wessels, 'An ever closer fusion?', *Journal of Common Market Studies*, Vol. 35, No. 2, June 1997; Andrew Moravscic on 'Integration Theory' in Desmond Dinan (ed.), *Encyclopaedia of the European Union*, Lynne Rienner, Colorado, 1998.

2. A federal system has the choice of working through institutions which do not belong to it but act for it (as, in the EC case, customs services, intervention agencies) or which are its own (Inland Revenue, Social Security).

3. Press interview, September 1998 (fullest text in *Sage Magazine*).

4. Axel Krause, *Inside the New Europe*, Harper Collins, 1991, p. 308.

EXTENDED GLOSSARY

A points, B points, Part 1 points 'A' points on a Council agenda are not discussed but adopted *nem.con*. They are matters that have been agreed at working level. If a minister objects, which is exceptional, the point comes off the current agenda and appears as a 'B' point where it belongs. The Council adopting an 'A' point may not be the competent Council for that subject.

'B' points on a Council agenda are for substantive discussion.

False 'B' points are not for discussion, having been already agreed. But as a small courtesy to those affected by them, e.g. third countries, they are made to look as if the Council discussed them.

Part 1 points are the equivalent of 'A' points on a Coreper agenda.

Abatement, British 11–12 February 1988 the European Council meeting in Brussels agreed:

Correction of Budgetary Imbalances

The European Council conclusions of 25 and 26 June 1984 on the correction of budgetary imbalances remain applicable for as long as the new decision on Own Resources remains in force.

The mechanism decided at Fountainebleau was based on the difference between the United Kingdom's VAT share and its share of allocated expenditure, multiplied by allocated expenditure. The compensation represented 66%.

The following modifications are to be made:
(a) The VAT share shall be replaced by the United Kingdom's share of payments under the third and fourth resource.
[(b) transitional and spent]
(c) The compensation to the United Kingdom will be financed by the eleven other Member States on the basis of a GNP key. However, the contribution of Germany is reduced by a third and those of Spain and Portugal in accordance with the abatement provided for in articles 187 and 374 of the Treaty of Accession.

The review of the British compensation will be carried out in the framework of Commission report on the system of Own Resources.

Note. The formulation of the foregoing is

$$ \mathrm{uk_C} = \frac{\mathrm{uk}(r_3+r_4) \times 100}{r_3 + r_4} - \frac{\mathrm{uk_{REC}} \times 100}{B} \times \frac{66B}{100} $$

where $\mathrm{uk_C}$ is compensation, r_3 is the VAT resource, r_4 is the GDP resource, $\mathrm{uk_{REC}}$ is UK receipts and B is the amount of the allocated budget, excluding, for example, foreign aid on which there is no rebate.

Acquis Communautaire   This expression used to be translated as 'what the Community has achieved'. It is now not translated and means, approximately, everything that can be legally enforced against a Member State; otherwise put, all the obligations which membership brings with it. One of the principles of accession to the EU is acceptance of the *acquis communautaire* subject only to whatever temporary derogations have been negotiated.

When abbreviated to *acquis* the word may mean the same, or the user may intend it to be understood to include *acquis* that is not *communautaire* but comes from the third pillar.

Under the Treaty of Amsterdam the Schengen *acquis* become part of the *acquis communautaire.*

Agence Europe   Strictly, the title of this daily subscription newsletter is 'Europe'. It was founded and throughout his lifetime edited by Emanuele Gazzo. His incredibly close contacts with Ministers, Commissioners and officials enabled him (and the present staff) to report overnight on the whole span of the work of the Community/Union. His type-written daily, appearing in several languages, is obligatory reading for all concerned with European integration. Although Mr Gazzo himself never concealed his federalism, the policy of the newsletter is and was to remain strictly factual in its reporting, with the occasional editorial.

Agency   Agencies are bodies that belong to the Union structure, but not to its institutions. Some perform a service, for which they are accountable. Others observe and advise.

The advisory agencies prepare reports or undertake research independently of the European Commission. They are accordingly untainted by any integrationist agenda. Their reports or recommendations may inspire or influence Commission initiatives and Member State reactions. Some of the agencies in this category also run programmes and projects.

Quite apart from their intrinsic function, they play the politically useful role of being spread across the Member States, showing that it is not all focused on Brussels or mono-polised by the more populous Member States. Taking account of the European Parliament seat in Strasbourg[1] there is something for all the twelve states which were members of the Community when the last decisions under Article 216 (289 new style) were taken.

The service-providers are the EC Patent Office in Munich, the Translation Centre in Luxembourg (invented by the Belgian Presidency in October 1993[2] as part of the pack-age), the Office for Harmonisation in the Internal Market (trade marks, designs and models) in Alicante, and the Office for Official Publications of the European Communities (EUR-OP) in Luxembourg. The European Community Humanitarian Office (ECHO) has a different status, as part of the Commission. The European Police Office (Europol) in The Hague, is another service-provider, as is its Drugs Unit. An Office for Veterinary and Plant-Health Inspection and Control awaits establishment in Ireland.

The observing and advising agencies are the European Agency for Health and Safety at Work in Bilbao, the European Environment Agency in Copenhagen, the European Agency for the Evaluation of Medicinal Products (EMEA) in London, the European Centre for the Development of Vocational Training (CEDEFOP) in Thessalonika (shifted from Berlin), the European Training Foundation in Turin, the European Foundation for the Improvement of Living and Working Conditions in Dublin, The European Monitoring Centre for Drugs and Drug Addiction in Lisbon and the Community Office for Vegetable Varieties in Brussels.

Antici Group Named after the Italian official, who was its first Chairman, the Antici Group consists of middle-ranking officials of permanent representations who meet to prepare the agenda of the Committee of Permanent Representatives (Part 2, ambassadorial level). Their output is the draft agenda, circulated under the responsibility of the Presidency, and a shared understanding of the positions which delegations may take on agenda items.

The equivalent body for Coreper 1 (deputy permanent representatives) is the Merten Group.

Approval One treaty article stipulates that a particular decision taken by common accord of the Member States requires EP approval. It is 214, concerning the appointment of the Commission. The effect is similar to 'assent' (q.v.) except that in approval there is no starting Commission proposal. The appointment of members of the Board of the European Central Bank does not require EP approval, only consultation. But in the first appointments, in May 1998, the EP spontaneously held hearings at which the appointees appeared. The chairman-designate, Wim Duisenberg (The Netherlands) said that if the EP did not approve he would not take up the appointment.

Article 50 That is, of the Staff Regulations ('Statut'). Article 50 allows premature retirement with pension rights but without invalidity. It is an amicable, not to say generous, way of parting with officials of the grades A1 and A2 in the interests of the service. It used to be used to make vacancies for the appointment of staff of the nationalities of new Member States.

Article 235 Article 235, now 308 in the new numbering, is the default power. If something has to be done to fulfil an objective of the treaty and the treaty has not provided the necessary powers, Article 235 can be a legal base. Environment policy began with Article 235 before it acquired its own treaty chapter. The tests are rigorous – the action must be shown to be necessary. The Commission must propose the use of the article. The Council must be unanimous.

Assent Assent (in French: *avis conforme*) was introduced in the Single European Act. It was intended to give the Parliament some say without, however, giving it *co-decision* or even the degree of influence which it can exercise under the *co-operation* procedure (q.v.). In the *assent* procedure the Council, acting on a proposal from the Commission, comes to a decision, but the decision is inoperative until the European Parliament has given its assent. The EP assents by whatever is the majority required in the article under which the procedure is triggered. It cannot amend the Council position with which it is presented. By failing to find the sufficient majority, it can kill it. In doing so, it can explain what it found wrong with the proposed act. Assent was originally a way of acceding to the long-standing EP demand that it should approve international agreements. This power was in fact rare among the parliaments of Member States, where the Executives had treaty-making power, subject to parliamentary approval where the treaty required national law or budgetary provision. Assent was extended to a few other provisions in treaty revision. When the Treaty of Amsterdam came into force it applied in the following articles (in the new numbering):

7	suspension of a Member State
49	admission of a new Member State
105.6	prudential supervision of credit organisations
107	amendment of the ECSB Statute
161	objectives and organisation of Structural Funds (q.v.)
300.3 and 310	certain international agreements.

See also *Co-decision, Consultation, Co-operation* and *Non-consultation*.

Association Third states can become Associates of the Community by concluding agreements which go beyond trade facilitation measures and into, for example, investment protection, joint R&D, financial assistance. See also: *Enlargement.*

Ayatollahs The ayatollahs were the hard-working and hard-driving members of the cabinet of President Delors. They earned the title for their combination of zeal and intolerance of dissent. They have been finely described by George Ross, who spent six months watching them at work. See his article in *JCMS* 32.4, December 1994, pp. 500–23. See also Charles Grant, *Delors: Inside the House that Jacques Built*, Nicholas Brealey, 1994.

Bananas The EU gives a post-colonial preference to imports from the Caribbean. This disadvantages banana growers in Latin America. Production there is in the hands of US food giants. They egged the US government into a complaint to the World Trade Organisation. It repeatedly sustained the complaint, despite changes that the EU introduced. Early in 1999 the USA produced a 'hit-list' of $320 million worth of imports from the EU which would be subject to 100% increases in duties. Shortly after, in anticipation of its latest complaint being upheld, it required importers to deposit bonds to the value of the increased duties. The WTO dispute settlement system found in favour of the USA, but for a lower volume of trade, some $200 million. Since the duty increase had the WTO stamp of approval, there could be no question of EU retaliation. Some compromise had to be found to balance off the interests of the Caribbean producers and those of EU exporters.

BSE   Bovine Spongiform Encephalopathy, 'mad cow disease', infected the British cattle herd in the 1980s. For all the high-level assurances that British beef was 'safe' – a word which later underwent tortuous qualification – the British government announced in March 1996 that there could be a link between BSE and Creutzfeld–Jacob Disease (CJD), an incurable and fatal brain disease in humans. The European Commission, using its devolved powers, immediately imposed a worldwide ban on exports of British beef. Corrective measures failed to convince the Commission and the other Member States that the risk to human health had been eliminated. Thus spurned, the government of John Major decided on a policy of non-co-operation across the board. Although dramatic, this tactic was not seriously disruptive. It was abandoned after some weeks when a scheme was worked out providing for a massive slaughter of cattle exposed to the infection and a programme for the registration of the life history of all British cattle.

Bureau   The bureau, borrowed from French, is the Executive Committee of an organisation itself too large to be able to meet regularly and conduct business continuously. In the Union the EP, the Economic and Social Committee and the Committee of the Regions have set up bureaux that concern themselves with the organisation of work and with administration.

Cabinet   A ministerial cabinet, a handful of aides who serve the Minister outside the departmental structure, is a French practice, said to have been inaugurated at the restoration of the monarchy in 1815, when new ministers found themselves in charge of departments staffed by Bonaparte placemen or other loyalists. In the Union setting, the word generally refers to the offices of Commissioners.

Cabinet members are chosen by the Commissioner personally. Some may have come with the Commissioners in their former existences and may have political bonds. Others are selected from within the Commission's complement. The *chef de cabinet* is the Commissioner's grey eminence, with higher profile and responsibility than the typical ministerial Private Secretary provided by the British civil service. Unless there is evidence to the contrary, when the cabinet speaks, it is the voice of the Commissioner. The approximate number of cabinet members is fixed by the Commission, with an extra allowance for the President. It usually includes at least one who is not of the same nationality as the Commissioner.

The cabinet's responsibilities are the reflection of the collegiality of the Commission. Every Commissioner is involved in almost every decision. Whereas, in the British system, departmental ministers do not have in-house support for their participation in collective discussions outside their portfolio, Commissioners require explicit briefing on every agenda item. Cabinet members shadow the work of other Commissioners.

The weekly meeting of the Commission is prepared by:

1. The meeting of the inaccurately named 'special chefs'. They are the various cabinet members who specialise in subjects outside their boss's portfolios and seek to defend their boss's interests in upcoming proposals.
2. The weekly meeting of chefs (*de cabinet*) who prepare the Commission meeting. This involves powerfully advocating what master wants, knocking down opposition

(or noting what the contrary arguments are), making or floating compromises and bidding for priorities in time and resources.

The identification between the cabinet and the Commissioner can give rise to tensions between it and the directorates in the Commissioner's charge. Tension may be creative, when the (permanent) Director-General and the (ephemeral) *chef de cabinet* work well together or more often damaging when strong-minded people fall out. The cabinet system – which has embryonic analogues in the special advisers around British ministers – is criticised for wasting time and effort in internal frictions. Its strong point is the control which it gives Commissioners over their services and the capacity that it gives them for closely following and intervening in the work of their colleagues. This consequence of collective responsibility may have been of greater importance when the President of the Commission was officially one among equals, without formal authority to impose cohesion on them. This changes in the Treaty of Amsterdam. Under new Article 214, para. 2, the Presidential nominee must approve the nominations of his or her future colleagues; under Article 219 the Commission is to work under the political guidance of its President, giving him or her the last word on the distribution of responsibilities. The new Commission President, Prodi, has pledged to change the system of appointment to cabinets.

Censure Censure is the ultimate deterrent that the EP holds over the Commission. Under Article 201 (old article 144) the EP can dismiss the Commission *en masse* if it votes censure by a two-thirds majority of votes cast and a majority of EP members. Although censure votes have been tried or threatened – in 1997 over the Commission's conduct of the BSE crisis – none has ever carried. The power does not extend to the dismissal of an individual Commissioner and is therefore a blunt weapon. There is no such power of censure over the judges of the ECJ or the members of the Board of the ECB.

Mr/Ms CFSP Pillar II, the Common Foreign and Security Policy, has its distinctive organisation within the 'single institutional framework' which is evoked in Article 3 of the Treaty on European Union. Whereas in Pillar I the Commission represents the Community internationally in respect of matters falling within Community competence, Article 18 TEU provides that the Presidency [of the Council] shall represent the Union in matters coming within the CFSP. To provide some continuity, the Presidency was assisted by the troika of its immediate predecessor and successor. The changing cast meant, however, that the outside world had to get to know a new leader twice a year.

The Gulf War of 1991–92 and the Yugoslav crisis that began in 1990 found the Union unprepared to sustain a common foreign policy. This was entirely a matter of political will or unwillingness. But some Union personalities were unwilling to acknowledge that the weakness was in the sphere of policy. They blamed ineffective organisation. An originally French suggestion, supported by Germany, was that there should be what they called a new 'function'. In the Inter-governmental Conference of 1996–97, this crystallised into the creation of a post of High Representative.

According to the new Articles 18.3 and J.26, the High Representative for the CFSP is concurrently the Secretary-General of the Council. He is to assist the Council, 'in particular through contributing to the formulation, preparation and implementation of policy decisions' and at the request of the Presidency (which retains its representational responsibility) conducting political dialogue with third parties.

This makes the Secretary-General a different animal from the incumbents hitherto. They have been top-ranking officials from national administrations. It has never been their function to represent the Council or (officially) to formulate, prepare and implement policy decisions. Whatever they may have done behind the scenes, policy decisions have emanated from the Member States under Presidency leadership. One effect of the change made in the Treaty of Amsterdam is to divide the Council Secretariat in two, one half acting as a civil service for Pillars I and III, the other discharging different policy-making responsibilities.

The High Representative is to head up a policy planning and early warning unit staffed by personnel from the Council Secretariat and seconded from national services, the Commission and the WEU. This division within the Council Secretariat undoes the effort that was made in the aftermath of the TEU to integrate the former separate Political Secretariat into the Council Secretariat. The change in organisational structure is not self-evidently for the better. Additionally, the relationship between the existing unit serving the Political Committee and the General Affairs Council and the new policy planning and early warning unit remains to be decided.

Everything depends upon the profile of the first High Representative. The choice is between someone with an established political reputation, probably ex-ministerial, and high functionary from the world of diplomacy. The former, although under Presidency command, would manifest some independence of mind in CFSP debates. The latter would be more recognisably a subordinate to whom the Presidency or Council would delegate tasks. The Political Person would be unusual if he or she unerringly remembered that in Council discussions the High Representative has the right to speak on Pillar II matters but keeps his or her peace on others. In 1999 Member States chose the former.

Citizenship Citizenship of the European Union was a concept introduced into the Treaty on European Union by Spain. It was enlarged by the Treaty of Amsterdam and is now Part Two of the treaty establishing the European Community (consolidated version). Its location there is one of the reasons for dropping the word 'Economic' from the name of the treaty. It was placed in the first pillar so that Community measures could be adopted; the third pillar would not have allowed for them.

Union citizenship does not supplant national citizenship. Although it is said to impose duties on the Union citizen, there are none. The common European passport does not describe its bearer as a European citizen. The rights set forth in Articles 18 to 21 concern free movement and residence; voting and standing as a candidate in municipal and European elections – not national parliamentary elections – obtaining consular protection from the authorities of any Member State in a third country if the citizen's country is not represented there and petitioning the European Parliament or applying to the Ombudsman. Citizens may also use any official language (here including Irish) to write to any institution. The reply must be in that language.

Perhaps the practical value is that in official announcements and signposts Citizen of the European Union can replace 'National of a Member State of the European Economic Community'. Otherwise, European citizenship is purely symbolic.

Co-decision Co-decision (between the Council and the EP) was introduced in the Treaty on European Union as the outgrowth of the *co-operation* procedure. It proved cumbersome and was overhauled in the Treaty of Amsterdam by eliminating what had been called the 'third reading'. (This was a stage at which the Council could disregard a disagreement with the EP, but could be over-ridden by the latter.) In the same treaty co-decision largely replaced co-operation.

The articles to which co-decision applies after the entry into force of the Treaty of Amsterdam are:

12	discrimination on nationality
18.2	citizens' rights (Council unanimity)
40	freedom of workers' movement
42	migrant workers' social security
46	foreign nationals
47	mutual recognition of qualifications
67	immigration rules (immediately and after five years)
71	aspects of transport policy
95.2	Single Market (see *Consultation*)
129	employment incentive measures
137	social provision
141	equal pay
148	Social Fund
149–50	incentive measures: education and training
151	incentive measures: culture
152	public health measures
153.4	consumer protection
156	TENs
166.1	R&D framework programme
172.2	implementing R&D framework programme
175	environmental objectives (see also *Consultation*)
179	development co-operation objectives except ACP
280	anti-fraud
285	production of statistics
286	supervision of data protection

Cohesion Economic and social cohesion can trace its inspiration back to the preamble to the EEC treaty:

Anxious to strengthen the unity of their economies and to ensure their harmonious development by reducing the differences between the various regions and the backwardness of the less favoured regions.

538

Thirty years on, and with the actual or impending membership of states, rather than parts of states, which are 'less-favoured', the Single European Act introduced the new Title V, Economic and Social Cohesion, with Article 158 (ex-130a) picking up the language of the Preamble. The focus was still regional and the instrument was still the Structural Funds. In the negotiation of the Treaty on European Union, the Southern bloc, with Ireland, argued for enhanced resource flows in their direction, insisting that the Structural Funds were not enough (and neither was the sharp increase in private investment flows). The final compromises, of which the response to this demand was one element, included the establishment of a Cohesion Fund, which has no regional slant – although any local expenditure brings regional benefit. It confines the benefits to:

(a) the environment – it having been argued that compliance with environmental protection standards was imposing a disproportionate burden on the less favoured states;

(b) trans-European networks – from the point of view that improvement in transport infrastructures were a key to economic uplift.

A third condition was inserted in the Protocol on Economic and Social Cohesion, coming after the operative word 'AGREE':

(c) beneficiaries, having less than 90% of average GDP, must have a programme to fulfil the convergence criteria for EMU. This responds to the argument that budgetary measures necessary to comply with the criteria could handicap the efforts of the countries concerned to promote their own development.

The Cohesion Fund was duly established, with funding of 16.2 billion ECUs between 1993 and 1999 (Council Regulation (EC) 1164/94, OJ L 130, 25.5.1994). Funds are dispensed on a project-by-project basis, usually in conjunction with the European Investment Bank.

See: *Annual Report on Economic and Social Cohesion* (from 1996), OOP.

Comitology This *franglais* neologism is sometimes wrongly used. It does not refer to the vast structure of Committees which the Commission and the Council respectively use to carry their work forward,[3] but to three particular types of committee which concern the devolution of responsibilities to the Commission.

The Commission is sometimes called the 'Executive'. But Article 145 of the treaty (202 new style) makes it clear that in secondary legislation, decisions are taken on what powers to confer on the Commission for the implementation of the act.

In much secondary legislation powers are devolved to the Commission, subject to different degrees of collaboration with committees on which the Member States are represented. The respective power of the two sides, and of the EP, in relation to these committees is the stuff of *comitology*.

The Commission routinely objects that its power and therefore efficiency is prejudiced. The European Parliament complained that the committees escape its scrutiny and possible input. The Council was reluctant to curtail its control over matters which are conditionally delegated. Comitology was supposed to be overhauled in the Intergovernmental Conference of 1996–97 but was one of the many institutional matters

539

which did not make it to the Treaty of Amsterdam. On 20 December 1994 the three legislating institutions reached a 'modus vivendi'[4] in the terms of which the Commission informed the EP of its draft measures, took the utmost account of its observations (not 'opinion') and informed it of its intentions. If there was a subsequent reference to the Council in the circumstances described above, the EP was informed and conveyed its views to the Council. Matters that were urgent or secret were excluded.

The original and disputed text is the Council decision of 13 July 1987.[5] This sought to codify practices that had grown up organically and inconsistently. This version of comitology was modified[6] in June 1999, after much coming and going with the European Parliament. The changes give effect to the intentions of Declaration 31 attached to the Treaty of Amsterdam.

The Council's 1987 Decision and the 28 June 1999 changes distinguish three types of committee:

Type 1 is *advisory* (*consultatif*). The Commission presents its draft measure (which it proposes to adopt under its powers of implementation) to an advisory committee. The only obligation on the Commission is to take the utmost account of the Committee's opinion. A prudent Commission would think again if there were strong opposition. Advisory committees are not contentious, and are not affected by the June 1999 changes.

Type 2 is the *Management Committee* (*de gestion*). It is based on the Management Committees for organised agricultural markets, which have worked harmoniously and assiduously over the long years of the CAP. They are also used in the management of the Common Fisheries Policy.

The Commission presents its draft measure to the Committee. By qualified majority the Committee can issue a negative opinion. In the former *type 2a* the Commission could then defer the implementation of the measure for one month and the Council, to whom the file was sent, could meanwhile take a different decision. It can do so by qualified majority, since the measure is not a 'proposal' in the treaty sense. Changing a proposal needed unanimity. If the Council did not act, the Commission could proceed.

In former *type 2b*, the Commission had to defer implementation for three months and the Council could take a different decision. In default, the Commission could proceed.

Type 2 committees attracted EP criticism. Originally the EP was not informed and it objected to Council legislation of which it knew nothing. On the other hand, it would be impractical to involve the EP in the day-to-day management of agricultural markets.

In the 1999 reforms, there is only one type of Management Committee. The Commission submits a draft measure. If the Management Committee gives an adverse opinion, the measure is submitted to the Council. Meanwhile the Commission defers application for up to three months. The Council can take a different decision by qualified majority. In practice there is rarely a difference between Commission and Member States in the Management Committees.

Type 3 committees are regulatory (*de reglementation*). In the original scheme the Commission presented its draft measure to the Committee. If the Committee, by QM, gave a negative opinion, or failed to give any opinion since it had no majority in its ranks, the Commission had to defer implementation and send the file to the Council. In *type 3a* after three months of Council inaction the Commission could proceed with what it suggested. In *type 3b* the Council could, by *simple majority*, block the Commission's suggestion.

Under the June 1999 changes, the European Parliament is informed where the regulatory committee has not agreed with the Commission. The Council intervenes. It may adopt the proposal by QM. It may oppose by QM, which triggers a re-examination and the submission of what is now called an amended proposal (not a draft measure) or a new full-dress legislative proposal. If it does neither within three months, the Commission adopts the act.

The EP:

- is informed of all committee proceedings;
- may inform the Council if it considers that a regulatory measure would exceed the powers conferred by the legislation under which it is to be taken;
- may pass a resolution to the effect that a suggested implementing measure exceeds the powers given by the legislation concerned. The Commission can submit a new draft measure to the Committee; disregard the resolution; or submit a new legislative proposal to the Council and the EP. It must give the EP reasons for its action.

The June 1999 changes in comitology should take the sting out of long-standing disputes between the Council and the EP. Little local problems will probably recur. Almost simultaneously, in June 1999, there was a new twist in the draft. Council and EP directive on chocolate for human consumption (COM (95)722 final, OJ C 231/1 9.8.96). Its Article 6 involves a regulatory committee. The EP successfully objected to committee procedure for the possible modification of a sensitive rule governing vegetable fat content. This was taken out of classic comitology and made the subject of a specific conciliation procedure between the EP and the Council. If the precedent is followed, some new codification will be needed.

For analysis, see House of Lords Session 1998-99, Third Report, Paper No. 23, Delegation of Powers to the Commission: Reforming Comitology.

Compromise Commission proposals rarely go through the Council unscathed. It has been said that they are less like Bills, in the British parliamentary sense, than White Papers. The Member States, cultivating national interest, usually want changes and usually disagree both with the Commission and with each other. Having listened to discussion at several levels, the Commission may be ready to change its proposal, unless it disagrees with the trend of the discussion, or unless it has pledged itself to the EP to uphold some point on which the EP and the Commission have already agreed. If the Commission does not move, the Council has to find *unanimity* to change the proposal into something on which it can agree. This means a compromise between the usually conflicting demands of the Member States. Any delegation can propose a compromise – the Belgians and Italians are masters of the art – but they tend to look to the Presidency to bring one forward for further negotiation towards a consensual conclusion. Compromises have to contain something for everyone, but not too much for anyone. The working definition is that they please nobody.

541

Confessionals The confessional is one of the devices, which helps the Council to move towards agreement. Facing an impasse the President of the council calls an adjournment. The President invites named delegations or any who have something to say to him to meet with him or her privately. The President decides whether it would be helpful or not for the Commission to be present. The theory is that the awkward delegation can open up and perhaps even suggest the compromise it could just about accept. The President can also float trial balloons that it might be inconvenient to release in the session proper. After the confessionals, the President is expected to be able to put forward a compromise or a new agreement.

Consultation Consultation is the weakest of the interactions between the EP and the Council and in a purely quantitative measure it is still the commonest. Having obtained a proposal from the Commission, the Council asks the EP for its opinion (*avis*). Until the opinion is given, the Council cannot act. It sometimes proceeds to examine the proposal without waiting for the opinion (which is not binding on it) and may even reach what it then calls a 'political agreement'. This is resented by the EP. The Council can ask for urgency and can even suggest a time limit if there is an objective reason. The EP rarely accedes to an urgency request. It knows that in the terms of the isoglucose case, the Council must 'exhaust the possibilities of obtaining an opinion' before it can act without one. It is doubtful if it ever would. The articles that give rise to consultation are:

11.2	enhanced co-operation
13	discrimination other than nationality
19	candidacy in elections
22	rules of citizenship
37.2	CAP regulations
52	liberalisation of services
67	visa, etc., rules
71.2	transport policy
83.1	competition rules
89	state aids rules
93	indirect taxes except VAT
94	single market (old A100)
107.6	ESBC statute
111	exchange rate agreements
112.2b	appointments to ECB
121	members of MU
122	new members of MU
128.2	employment policy guidelines
130	appointments to Employment Committee
133	services under the CCP
159	specific cohesion actions
166.4	specific R&D programmes
172.1	R&D undertakings

175.2   aspects of environmental policy
202   delegation of Council powers
247.3   appointment of Auditors
269   own resources
279   financial regulations
283   staff regulations
308   default powers (old A235)

Protocol on the statute of the ESCB and the ECB (Treaty on European Union).

Art 11.2 appointment of the members of the Board of the ECB (consulted by the Council at the level of Heads of State and Government).

See also *Non-consultation.*

Co-operation   The co-operation procedure was introduced in the Single European Act in response to EP demands for additional powers. It reserved decision-taking to the Council but required it to pay more heed to the EP than it was obliged to do in consultation (see above). But the EP remained essentially advisory.

The Treaty on European Union went further towards Council–EP power sharing by introducing *co-decision* (q.v.). The Treaty of Amsterdam went further down the same road by replacing co-operation by co-decision except where co-operation existed in the area of the economic and monetary union. This preservation of co-operation in that sector owed nothing to regard for the procedure. It was simply that the Member States had decided that what the Treaty on European Union said about EMU was inviolable. There remain only a few articles that give rise to co-operation:

99.6   multilateral surveillance
102.2   financial institutions
103.2   no liability for Member State deficits
106   design of euro coins

Coreu   Coreu is the name of the fax link among the European correspondents (whence the name) in the foreign offices of the Member States.

Declaration   A declaration annexed to a treaty or entered in the minutes of the Council is not legally binding. It may be shared by all the treaty signatories and used to indicate what they intended. It may be made by an individual delegation or by a group of them in which case it usually indicates dissent, dissatisfaction or incompleteness which it/they wish to fill in.

Derogation   A derogation is permission not to comply with an obligation. The word has acquired a particular meaning in the expression 'Member State with derogation'. In the EMU this is a Member State which has not satisfied the convergence criteria or has put off the decision to join. In general usage derogations usually occur when a new policy is instituted and one or more Member States are given more time than the general run to implement it. Derogations must be temporary and objectively justified.

Transitional derogations feature in accession agreements. The joining country accepts the *acquis*, but is given time to assimilate some of it. A temporary derogation may also be imposed on a joining country to defer the enjoyment of some advantage, such as free movement of labour.

Permanent derogations are virtually unknown. Some appear as 'opt-outs'. One occurred in the accession of Sweden. It concerned a type of chewing tobacco that does not exist elsewhere, cannot be marketed in the rest of the Community, but is every true Swede's birthright.

ECU, Euro[7] The ECU was the currency unit used in Community accounting and in the Exchange Rate Mechanism. Its value was determined by the basket of the currencies of the Member States. There was mild controversy over whether it was ecu or ECU, with the implication that the ecu was a distinct currency. Because it sounds bovine in German, it was replaced by the Euro in the monetary union and for all Community accounting purposes. The Euro has a fixed value in relation to the national currencies that it progressively replaces by 2002.

Enlargement Some writers use enlargement to mean the 'widening' of the Union through the conclusion of contractual relations with a growing number of third countries. To avoid misunderstanding, it should be reserved to mean increased membership of the Union. 'Association' is sometimes described as a form of membership, which it is not.

Entry in the minutes Delegations at Council meetings may find it important to add a written commentary to a decision that the Council has taken. These are entered in the minutes. They may be on behalf of the whole Council, or of the Commission, or of the Council and the Commission together, or of one or more delegations.

The entries in the minutes may explain what the Council had in mind; or may contain undertakings as to future work; or may express disgruntlement with what the Council has decided.

They have no legal force, but they may help to understand what the Council thought it was doing. They cannot contradict the terms of the decision to which they refer, although they sometimes strain a possible interpretation. They may be politically important to a delegation that has to explain itself back home.

The coming of transparency brings the possibility of publicity for what were previously private messages. This may be welcome to a delegation that wants to mark its position. But there are other entries that those concerned would prefer to treat with discretion. One alternative is to enter them in the minutes of Coreper, which remain untransparent.

Euro-X Euro-X was the name originally given to the Council, which is not a Council, in which the Member States participating in the single currency would meet. When the number of participating Member States was known, the name became Euro-11.

Flexibility Flexibility, which goes under several other labels, means that not all the Member States incur an obligation.

Temporary derogations from the fulfilment of an obligation are familiar. They occur, for example, when a new member joins and, although accepting all the *acquis* is given extra time to apply parts of it. Similarly, a Member State may be given extra time to apply an act for which it is less well prepared than the others. The conditions are that the derogation is objectively justified and is temporary. In due course the obligation becomes universal.

Permanent derogations are not given to new members – although Sweden obtained one, and Finland and Austria are on the way to having made permanent a temporary derogation that prevents citizens in other Member States from acquiring holiday homes. The launch of new policies has seen permanent derogations for Member States that do not want to join in, but likewise do not want to stop the willing from proceeding. This was true of the British opt-out from the Social Protocol, the Danish self-exclusion from defence policy, the British, Danish and Swedish notifications that they do not wish to be considered for membership of the monetary union and the optional membership of the Exchange Rate Mechanism.

In the face of British isolationism in the Reflexion Group which prepared the 1996–97 IGC, France and German jointly proposed a departure to be known as enhanced or *closer co-operation*. Subject to appropriate conditions, a group of Member States would be able to agree to integrative measures while others stood aside. Although the incoming Labour government in Britain signalled that it would not cling to the national veto power as tenaciously as its predecessors had done, and agreed to the extension of majority voting, the idea of flexibility had by then taken hold and was incorporated into **Article 43** of the Treaty on European Union (consolidated version), which also applies to the Treaty establishing the European Community. This article stipulates the conditions that must be fulfilled if closer co-operation is to be practised. Those so practising it may use the institutions, procedures and mechanisms of the Union.

Article 11 of the Treaty establishing the European Community contains additional conditions and creates the right for a Member State which opposes a piece of closer co-operation to demand reference to a Council composed of Heads of State or Government, deciding by unanimity. The same right exists in relation to co-operation on Justice and Home Affairs in the Treaty on European Union, **Article 40**, except that the article erroneously evokes the European Council and not the Council composed of political supremos (the European Council cannot be a Council in the treaty sense).

In the CFSP Title of the TEU, a different form of flexibility is provided for. Under **Article 23**, up to one-third by weighted vote of the members of the Council may abstain and may make a declaration to the effect that the decision will not apply to them. In effect, this leaves the others to practise closer co-operation, but without all the qualifying conditions of Pillars I and III.

In the case of those CFSP decisions which, according to **Article 23**, can be taken by the dual form of QMV in **Article 205.2** of the Treaty establishing the European Community '*x*' votes cast by '*y*' Member States) an opposing Member State can demand reference to the 'European Council' (same error as above) for unanimous decision. No decisions having military or defence implications can be taken by QMV. It remains to be seen what use will be made of enhanced co-operation. One straw in the wind is that Euroland has not contemplated it for fiscal harmonisation.

See also *Unanimity* and *Derogation.*

Free Trade Area   The members of a Free Trade Area abolish customs duties on their imports from each other, but maintain these different national customs tariffs on imports from non-members. They must devise complex rules to define the taxable or non-taxable origin of imports.

Friends of the Presidency   A hopeful name given to ad hoc working groups, entirely staffed by Brussels residents, set up to tackle problems which are unlikely to be resolved in working groups with other obligations.

Guardian of the treaties   One of the sobriquets of the Commission, referring to its role under Article 211 of verifying that the Member States respect the obligations which they have entered into. Another traditional expression is Motor of European Integration, referring to the Commission's role as author of proposals.

Habilitation   The Commission decides collegially and by simple majority. For efficiency reasons it may authorise one of its members to act on its behalf, within a mandate it gives him or her. This is known in French as a *habilitation*, a word that is not translated.

Hierarchy of norms   During the negotiation of the Treaty on European Union, the Italian delegation suggested that there should be different decision-making procedures depending on the fundamentalism of the act ('norm') being discussed. Some acts should be subject to stricter rules for their adoption and amendment. At the other end some acts should have a simpler adoption procedure than any so far in existence. When the Commission took the idea up, it aroused opposition among most Member States because they inferred that the Commission was out to increase its powers. The TEU is silent on the subject. Prior to the Inter-governmental Conference that produced the Treaty of Amsterdam, it was agreed that the *hierarchy of norms* should be looked at again. The treaty is again silent on the subject.

Honorary titles   On retirement, officials of the Council, other than Directors-General, are given a nominal rank one step higher than they had reached, but without higher pension entitlement. Former Members of the European Parliament can call themselves Honorary MEP.

Human rights   Throughout the 1980s the European Parliament campaigned for fundamental human rights to be entrenched in the constitution of the Community. The Member States hesitated for different reasons. Some had already incorporated the European Convention for the Protection of Human Rights and Fundamental Freedoms (ECHR) into national law and were concerned at the possibility of overlapping jurisdiction. One (the UK) had not given, and at the time did not want to give, its citizens the possibility of obtaining protection in the national courts. The Council decided to test the question of incorporation by obtaining the opinion of the European Court of Justice. In its opinion of 28 March 1996 ([1996] ECR1-1759) the Court said that the Community had no competence to accede to the ECHR. Accession would require treaty amendment.

In the 1996–97 IGC the Member States decided against such treaty amendment. They confined themselves to amending ex-Article F (now 6), which already contained a reference to the ECHR, by declaring that the Union is founded on the principles of liberty, democracy, respect for human rights and fundamental freedoms.

Suspension for breach of human rights – a completely new Article 7 of the consolidated version of the TEU – sets up a procedure for suspending the rights of a Member State found to be in violation of the principles of Article 6. The procedure does not involve expulsion.

Human rights in agreements with third countries – the Community now incorporates into its international agreements a human rights clause. The two sides undertake to respect human rights and the Community reserves the right to itself to take sanctions against the other party if it should breach them. Sanctions were, for example, applied to the military regime in Nigeria.

Informal Council Informal meetings of the Council are held in the Presidency country, often in provincial centres. The rationale is that meeting together informally, with a light agenda and a programme of sightseeing or other entertainments, Council members will 'network' and in relaxed discussion, without conclusions, begin to see their way round problems. An alternative view is that the primary object is media attention for the President on his home ground and serves no serious purpose.

Under pressure of events, informal Councils may become very serious. An example was the informal meeting of ECOFIN in Bath in 1992 preceding the British exit from the Exchange Rate Mechanism. This became a tense and even bad-tempered negotiation in which the then Chancellor of the Exchequer, from the chair, insistently tried to extract from the President of the Bundesbank the promise of support for sterling, which was under attack on the foreign exchange markets.

A particular type of informal Council meeting is the Gymnich formula in which Foreign Ministers gather somewhere preferably secluded, with the minimum entourage and in the style of members of a club, to renew their acquaintanceships and pursue the exchanges for which they now have little time in their formal monthly meetings.

Jumbo A Jumbo Council is one bringing together two Councils of overlapping concerns but of different compositions. Examples are Environment and Transport, Finance and Environment (on taxation) and, briefly in the 1980s, Finance and Agriculture. The theory is that the two disciplines will find common ground on such matters as preventing pollution or containing expenditure. In practice, Jumbo Councils are unwieldy and inherently unlikely to move, although they may count as a media event. An even more time-wasting event is an *informal* Jumbo Council meeting. See *Informal Council.*

Jurists-Linguists The proper designation of this class of official is Legal Reviser. They are specialist members of the Legal Service of the Council. Trained in the law of their country of origin and well informed about other legal systems, they are also expert in legal terminology in languages other than their mother tongue. When the Council has adopted a measure the Legal Revisers examine the versions in the different languages to ensure that there is exact equivalence. It has to be said that national delegations, which are entitled to attend the meetings, sometimes regrettably seek to recover at the legal revision stage ground that they lost in the preceding debates.

Languages In the fifteen member Community there are eleven official languages for EC business:

547

English (UK and Ireland)
French (France, Belgium, and Luxembourg)
Dutch (Netherlands, Belgium)
German (Germany, Austria, Belgium)
Swedish (Sweden, Finland)
Italian
Spanish
Portuguese
Greek
Danish
Finnish

Although Irish is an official language in Ireland, the Irish government has not asked for it to be recognised as an official Community language. The treaties have been produced in Irish versions, having equal value with the others. Letzenburgsch became an official language in Luxembourg in 1984 but the Luxembourg government has not asked for it to be recognised. None of the several languages spoken in Spain is official in the Community.

The main working languages are English, French and German. English is displacing French as the original language for documents.

It is often said that eleven languages give an impossible number of language pairs. This is an arithmetical abstraction. Simultaneous translation into languages with fewer native speakers is by relay that is taken from the French or English stream, which can be twice removed from its original.

According to Declaration 29 annexed to the Treaty on European Union, the use of languages 'shall be in accordance with the rules of the European Communities'. In practice, English and French are used except for texts submitted to the European Council and to the Council and published texts, which appear in all the official languages.

Marathon The marathon is a meeting that continues non-stop day and night until it reaches what some call agreement by exhaustion. Farm ministers were famously marathon runners, emulated by the Budget Council before the budget was placed within financial perspectives. Some meetings of the European Council have become half-marathons. The one held in Brussels in May 1998 to launch the Monetary Union saw the working lunch continue until 11.30 p.m. More loosely 'marathons' describe any meeting which goes on for several days.

Non-consultation Despite the steady increase in the powers of the EP, it is still kept away from a significant number of treaty bases. The list is likely to diminish in further treaty revision or in inter-institutional agreements in which the Council undertakes to go beyond treaty requirements. The following are the articles that do *not* give rise to consultation of the EP.

Treaty on European Union
7.3   variation of the sanction imposed for breach of basic principles
13–28   the CFSP
29–41   excluding 34(2) (b), (c) and (d), police and judicial co-operation on criminal matters

Treaty establishing the European Community

14	Single Market guidelines (see also 128, employment policy guidelines, on which the EP is consulted; and 99 below)
44–45	freedom of specific establishment
49	extension of freedom to provide services to third country nationals
57	extension of freedom of capital movement to third countries
59–60	exceptional restrictions on capital movement (EP is informed of Article 60)
75.1	discrimination in conditions of carriage
80	extension of common Transport Policy to sea and air (but once extended, measures are co-decided)
88	Council approval of state aid
92	Council approval of exceptional charges on imports
99	economic policy guidelines (the EP is informed). See 14 above
100	exceptional financial assistance. The EP is informed
104	finding of excessive deficit. The EP is informed of any sanctions. Under
104.14	the EP is consulted on any amendment of the excessive deficit protocol
111	adjustment of ERM central rates. The EP is informed
119	mutual assistance to relieve payment imbalance
120	(valid until 1.1.99) exceptional protective measures
132	harmonisation of export credits
133	common commercial policy (for extension to services and intellectual property the EP is consulted)
139	Council endorsement of agreements between social partners
144	assignment of implementation of common social measures to Commission
151	recommendations on culture (Council unanimity)
152	recommendations on public health (Council QM)
187	provisions for association (Council acts *without* Commission proposal)
257	remuneration of members of ESC (there is no provision for remuneration of members of CoR)
289	seats of the institutions (including EP) – inter-governmental decision
290	designation of official languages
296	list of warlike stores excluded from the treaty.

Predictably, most of these will come under review in future IGCs.

Notenboom The Notenboom procedure in the EP was named for its author, a former Dutch MEP who was a leading light of the Committee on Budgets. When this item is taken on the EP plenary agenda, the Commissioner responsible for budgets gives an account of the current execution of the budget and MEPs can ask questions about expenditures of which they approve or not.

Own initiative The Treaty establishing the European Community lays down the cases in which the Council or Commission must consult the Economic and Social Committee. In addition the Committee obtained the facility of preparing reports 'on its own initiative' for transmission to the Council and Commission.

Political agreement   Press notices from Council meetings may say that the Council reached 'political agreement' on what it had been discussing. This expression has two meanings. The first is that the Council agreed but for one reason or another did not have a final text before it. The final version will later be adopted by the written procedure or as an A point on a Council agenda. The second meaning is that the Council was moving faster than the EP and had not received the latter's opinion. Without interrupting its own rhythm, the Council reached an agreed position. Without the opinion, it could not record a final agreement. The EP objects to the practice of political agreements, knowing that when the Council had completed its discussion, it will be reluctant to reopen it, even if the EP opinion seeks to do so.

Preamble   All treaties with the exception of the Treaty of Amsterdam open with a preamble. The Council's Rules of Procedure, Articles 11 and 14 state that regulations, directives and decisions must have a preamble. The preamble is an integral part of the measure, but is not itself a legal base. Its 'Whereas' (*considérant*) explain what the measure is for and are a basis for the operative articles.

Protocol   The protocols annexed to a treaty are an integral part of it and are just as legally binding as the articles. Protocols are frequently used to set out details that would be too bulky in the text of the treaty. Shorter protocols usually contain glosses on treaty articles, without contradicting them.

Réserve d'attente   The English equivalent is 'preliminary reservation'. It means that the delegation making it does not want to agree to what is on the table, needs time to consider, and may come back with agreement, suggested amendment or substantive disagreement (*réserve de fond*).

Screening   Screening, which was invented for the fourth enlargement, is the first phase of the negotiation of the accession of a new Member State. The Commission calls the applicant to a series of meetings at which it examines the stage reached in the adoption of the *acquis* and the likely ability of the Applicant State to implement it on accession. Screening does not involve the opening of negotiations on difficulties. It identifies possible difficulties on which the Commission then reports to the Council on the position that the Council should take in the negotiations. The screening of the five CEEC applicants and Cyprus began in March 1998.

Statut   The *statut* is the staff regulations, which are the conditions of employment of established officials (*titularisé*). Under the jurisprudence of the Court, officials also have 'acquired rights' to benefits and 'legitimate expectations' that their existing treatment will continue. The *statut* deals comprehensively with the rights and obligations of officials and their employers and is regarded as the charter for a service independent of the Member States. It includes the 'method' for pay determination. Annual adjustments are based on inflation and changes in the basket of the purchasing power of officials in public services in the Member States. There are no pay negotiations.

Stresa   Article 37 of the EC Treaty (now Article 43) required the Commission to convene a Conference of the Member States with a view to making a comparison of their agricultural policies. The conference opened at Stresa, in the north of Italy, on 3 July 1958, with the President of the Commission, Walter Hallstein, Germany, and a Vice-President, Sicco Mansholt, Netherlands, leading the discussion. The conference came to the view that, of the options offered by Article 40, the simple co-ordination of national markets would not work, rules on competition would not be sufficient and European market organisation would be required. This implied a common price policy, as foreseen in Article 40.2. From this there followed the need for a guidance and guarantee fund (Article 40.3). With the automatic addition of agricultural protectionism ('Community preference') the mechanisms of the CAP were brought into being and acceptance of them became a requirement of membership of the Community. Up to the 1970s it was politically correct to describe the CAP as the 'binding force of the Community'. It is now an anachronism.

Simplification Simplification of Community legal acts serves two objectives.[8] It may also improve public understanding, and therefore support of Community policies. The Irish Presidency of the second half of 1996 set out in their 'general outline for a draft revision of the treaties' a proposal that the treaties should be significantly simplified with a view to making them more readable.[9] Some overhaul of sections of the treaty, undertaken by the Council's legal service, showed that even the most fractured phraseology is not there by neglect, but by the wish of delegations to pack in considerations which they hold dear. So far as the treaties themselves are concerned, the IGC stopped at the final Irish proposal:

> A new Treaty in simplified and codified form could, if it were to be agreed, be presented at the end of the conference, separately from the substantive amendments (although it would also incorporate these amendments).

This is the codified version of the Treaty establishing the European Community that gives effect to Declaration 42 annexed to the Treaty of Amsterdam.[10] The consolidation of the EC Treaty (ECSC and Euratom have not had the treatment) is probably of less utility than a draft revision of the secondary legislation. According to the Commission's Report *Better Lawmaking 1996*[11] there are three procedures:

1. *Recasting* – An instrument is repealed. A new instrument, with amendments, is adopted. Normal decision-making procedures are used.
2. *Consolidation* – A new instrument is adopted replacing existing instruments without changing their substance. This is also called 'codification'. There is a fast track procedure[12] for adopting consolidated/codified acts without substantive amendment in the framework of consultative group for which the EP passes the new text via one committee and the Council via one working group, followed by Part 1 of the Coreper agenda, and an 'A' point on the Council agenda (without discussion).
3. *Informal consolidation* – The Commission publishes an information note without legal effect. It shows what an up-to-date regulation or directive would look like.

In addition, there is a special drive to simplify legislation on the internal market (SLIM). An example of unslimmed legislation is Directive 96/9/EC on the legal protection of[13] databases. The directive contains sixteen articles, covering five OJ pages. The preamble runs to 60 paragraphs, covering four and half OJ pages. Most of them were packed in by delegations seeking one way or another to qualify the effect of the directive, culminating in a generalised derogation approximately in favour of existing copyright.

The SLIM programme, launched in November 1996,[14] is working its way progressively through Single Market legislation to 'contribute to the better functioning of the Internal Market and hence to improve competitiveness and the creation of employment'.[15] A task far more important than any of the foregoing and one requiring sustained effort that is not forthcoming is the simplification and clarification of national legislation which transposes Community acts. It is what bites on enterprises and it is marred by tendencies to copper-plate the instrument concerned. Examples are lovingly chronicled by Christopher Booker.[16]

A third chapter devoted to simplification concerns *procedures*. There is a game of counting up how many decision-making procedures there are. Winners could score over 20. Despite this, Amsterdam did little to streamline procedures. It replaced co-operation by co-decision (except in EMU matters). It cut out the so-called third reading of the co-decision procedure under which the Council could over-ride the EP where conciliation had not been fruitful, subject to being over-ridden by the EP. The simplified rule is that if conciliation does not work, the proposal is dead.

Subsidiarity   Subsidiarity is variously 'national precedence' (John Major, former British Prime Minister) or 'gobbledegook' (Lord Mackenzie-Stewart, former President of the European Court of Justice).

The political basis of subsidiarity is that decisions should be taken at the level that is closest to the people affected by them. The difficulty is knowing where this level occurs. The word entered treaty language in the Treaty on European Union, which declares in its Preamble '. . . decisions are taken as closely as possible to the citizen in accordance with the principle of subsidiarity'. This is reiterated, without using the word, in the second paragraph of Article A. The wording of this paragraph was Prime Minister Major's amendment to the Luxembourg draft that read '. . . Union with a federal goal'.[17] He rejected any evocation of federalism (identified with centralisation). Its advocates would say that federalism incorporates subsidiarity (equals decentralisation).[18]

The TEU gave some precision to the notion in its Article 3b, second paragraph. This provides that except where the Community has exclusive competence (as over the Common Customs Tariff), it acts:

> . . . only if and in so far as the objectives of the proposed action cannot be sufficiently achieved by the Member States and can therefore by reason of the scale or effects of the proposed action, be better achieved by the Community.

The principle had been foreshadowed in the Single European Act Title on the environment. Article 130R4 stipulates that:

> The Community shall take action relating to the environment to the extent to which the objectives referred to in para. 1 can be attained better at Community level than at the level of the individual Member States.[19]

Theoretically, the principle of subsidiarity creates an alternative form of action common to some or all of the Member States. In practice, it has come to be described as meaning that 'action by the Member States is the rule; action by the Community is the exception'. In practice also, subsidiarity has become a respectable reason for inaction, *at any level*. Along with inter-governmentalism, it sets political and judgemental (but probably not legal) limits on the reach of the form of integration represented by the Community. It is sustained by the unwillingness of the Member States at large to confer new exclusive competencies on the Community or the Commission or European Parliament to propose them.

The British Presidency of the Community in the second half of 1992 gave the Conservative government[20] its opportunity to strengthen the nature and application of subsidiarity. It began the task in the meeting of the European Council in Birmingham in October 1992[21] and enlarged upon it in six pages[22] of the annex to the Conclusions of the meeting in Edinburgh in December 1992. This sought to establish guidelines and procedures for ensuring that the subsidiarity test is respected in new legislation and would be specifically applied to measures in the pipeline.

The legal status of the Conclusions of these meetings of the European Council is debatable. The British government of the day did not claim that they were part of Community law, but insisted that they were binding under international law. Any uncertainty on this point was dispelled in the Treaty of Amsterdam that contains a Protocol on the application of the principles of subsidiarity and proportionality. The Protocol, which is Community law, picks up, often word for word but also with omissions,[23] the language of the Edinburgh texts. So subsidiarity is legally entrenched. Whether it is justiciable or a political matter remains open.

Tour de Table   A device in the Council. To get a meeting off to a start the President asks members one by one to say what they think of an agenda item. Unless the subject is brand new, what delegations think of it is already known. *Tours de table* cannot survive an enlarged Union.

Transparency

> The business of government is difficult enough as it is, and no government could contemplate with equanimity the inner workings of the government machine being exposed to the gaze of those ready to criticise without adequate knowledge of the background, and perhaps with some axe to grind.
>
> Lord Reid in *Conway v Rimmer, 1968*

This mindset is out of step with Scandinavian concepts of government. It has also come to be regarded as one of the reasons for public distrust of Community institutions.

In a Declaration, non-binding, attached to the TEU,[24] the signatories broke with past practice with the statement: 'Transparency of the decision-making process strengthens the democratic nature of the institutions and the public's confidence in the administration.'

There are reasons other than sensitivity for official secrecy. In a negotiation, the actors cannot behave openly. They overbid (or bluff), they offer compromises (or sell-outs). The

Council decided that the risks to its negotiating styles were outweighed by the benefits of greater openness.

Common positions. In October 1992, the European Council[25] took the first step by deciding to publish Council common positions under the co-operation procedure, although publicity for these texts was not new – they had been available, at no cost to the applicant, from the Council library.

Open sessions of meetings. In December 1992 the European Council decided that there would be open sessions of the Council (not the European Council).[26] Open sessions are televised in real time to a room in the Council building and recorded for offer to television stations. These sessions are largely declaratory.

Votes in Council. In October 1993 the Council decided to publish the results of its votes on legislative measures.[27] Press communiqués issued after the Council meeting say who voted against a decision.

Code of Conduct. In December 1993 the Council and the Commission adopted a code of conduct on public access to documents.[28] The Council adopted a corollary decision on 20 December 1993.[29] Under this decision, access would be refused if disclosure could undermine:

> the protection of the public interest (public security, international relations, monetary stability, court proceedings, inspections and investigations; the protection of privacy; the protection of the Community's financial interests; the protection of confidentiality as requested by the natural or legal person who supplied any of the information contained in the document or as required by the legislation of the Member State which supplied the information.

There is also a blanket exclusion:

> access to a Council document may be refused to protect the confidentiality of the Council's proceedings.

The new rules did not work too well. The Council was taken to Court for refusing access and lost its case.[30] The Treaty of Amsterdam accordingly takes transparency further in its Article 207.3 (ex-151):

- Council votes on legislation, explanations of votes and any statements in the minutes to the public
- not new Article 255 (ex-191a)
- general right of access to EP, Council and Commission documents
- new Article 207 (ex-151)
- Council to define cases in which it is legislating
- interested parties will know which documents to ask for when the Council Secretariat, as is planned, lists them on the Council web site.

Access will still be a matter of case-by-case decision. Delegations can be expected to ensure that they take care not to be recorded saying things which they would not wish to have to defend in public and that documents that contain pointed references to national positions are edited before release.

Unanimity Depending upon the point of view, unanimity among the Member States is a solid foundation for action, or a blockage on progress. The negative attribute of unanimity is the national veto that it implies. The positive version is consensus, which nobody could criticise.

The ECSC Treaty recognises in its Article 28.3 that there are two degrees of unanimity. One is absolute – all Member States must agree. The other allows for abstentions, without a stated limit. In the TEU there is one case where excessive abstentionism defeats a proposal. In the EC Treaty, abstention does not invalidate unanimity, and the abstainer is bound by the agreement. There is no limit on the number of abstentions.

Abstention therefore has perverse effects depending on whether it features in QMV or in reaching unanimity. In the latter, abstention is harmless. In QMV an abstention counts as a vote against, because it does not contribute to the majority.

After three rounds of treaty revision, there are still a surprisingly large number of decisions for which the EC Treaty requires unanimity. There is also a general rule in Article 250 (ex-189a) to the effect that if the Council wants to change a Commission proposal, and the Commission does not obligingly make the desired change, the Council needs to be unanimous. The *exception* to this otherwise iron rule is found in the closing stage of the co-decision procedure (Article 251, ex-189b). When the EP and the Council have reached agreement on a joint text, it stands, whatever the Commission may think of it. The opposite is the case in the co-operation procedure (Article 252, ex-189c). There the Council needs unanimity if it is to amend the Commission proposal in its latest form.

Articles requiring unanimity (in the Council, in the European Council or in common accord of governments of Member States) – new article number [the old numbers can be traced in the Tables of Equivalence OJ C 340, 10.11.97, pp. 85–91].

Treaty on European Union (consolidated version)

7	finding that a Member State has breached fundamental principles
23.1	opting-out of a CFSP decision (but if more than a third of the votes are held by opters-out the proposal is lost)
23.2	objectors insist on reference to the European Council (see also Article 40 and EC 11)
24	conclusion of international agreements within the CFSP
28.3	ad hoc decisions on funding
34	adopting common positions and joint actions within CJHA
40	opposition to 'closer co-operation' forces reference to European Council (see also 23.2 and EC Article 11)
42	bridge to transfer powers to EC Treaty
49	consideration of applications for Union membership

EC Treaty (consolidated version)

11	opposition to 'closer co-operation' ('the Council, acting by qualified majority, may request that the matter be referred to the Council … sic' but the Council referred to is composed of Heads of State and Government and decides by unanimity)

13	action on non-discrimination
18	rights of citizens to reside and move. This and 151 are now the only two cases where in co-decision (Article 251) the Council acts by unanimity
19	rules on the right to vote and stand for election
60	political restrictions on capital movement are taken by QMV but the causative joint actions or common positions are taken by unanimity
62+67	for five years, unanimity for border control measures and visas, except QMV for the list of states whose nationals require visas and the procedure and conditions for using them
63+67	for five years, asylum and refugee policy, except QMV for burden-sharing, long-term visas and circulation of legal non-citizen residents
71.2	transport regulations having serious social consequences
72	exemption from otherwise obligatory national treatment for carriers
88	exemption from the ban on state aids
93	indirect taxes
95	fiscal measures, measures affecting free circulation, rights and interests of employed persons
100.2	exceptional cross-frontier financial assistance (for natural disasters, QMV)
104.14	amending the Protocol on excessive deficits
105.6	giving the ECB responsibility for prudential supervision
107	amending the statute of the ESCB, if proposed by the Commission (QMV if proposed by the ECB)
109	concluding agreements on exchange rates with external currencies
117	appointing the President of the European Monetary Institute; assigning it additional tasks (spent)
137+139	protecting workers' rights
144	social security for migrant workers
151	incentives to promote culture (co-decision with Council unanimity throughout – see also 18)
157.3	measures to promote industrial competitiveness
161	tasks, objectives and organisation of Structural and Cohesion Funds (EP assent)
175	environmental measures which are fiscal, concern town and country planning or concern energy choices and supply
187	association of dependent overseas territories
190.4	adoption of uniform electoral procedure for the EP
207	appointment of the Council Secretary-General (doubling as High Representative) and Deputy Secretary-General
214.2	common accord appointment of Commission President and Commissioners
215	deciding to leave a Commission vacancy unfilled
223	common accord appointment of Judges and Advocates-General
245	amending Statute of the ECJ; approving ECJ Rules of Procedure

247.3	appointing members of the Court of Auditors
257	appointing members of the Economic and Social Committee
263	appointing members of the Committee of the Regions
269	deciding 'own resources' (subject to national ratification)
290	rules on use of languages
296	list of warlike stores exempted from treaty rules
300.2	conclusion of international agreements involving internal rules which require unanimity
308	catch-all for powers needed but not expressly given

Schengen Protocol

2	implementing measures
4	agreeing UK/Ireland adopting parts of Schengen *acquis*. Protocol on the Statute of the European System of Central Banks and of the European Central Bank
11	appointment of the Executive Board of the ECB: common accord of Heads of State or Government

Written procedure   The Council usually takes its decisions or adopts its positions in the course of its meetings (see *'A' points*). The decisions or positions may be foreign to the Council taking them – the essence of the doctrine that the Council is one and indissoluble. There are situations, however, when an act has to come into force before there is a Council to adopt it. For such rarities, the Council uses a written procedure. In the working group or in Coreper, there is agreement that the written procedure should be used for speed. The Council Secretariat sends a message to Member State capitals. The message contains two questions, each to be answered by 'Yes' or 'No'. The first standard question is: Do you agree to the use of the written procedure? The second question is: Do you agree with the conclusion contained in document *xyz*? If a single Member State answers 'No' to the first question, the written procedure is abandoned and the matter is placed on the first available Council agenda (where it could, if QMV rules, be passed against the wishes of the Member State which objected to the written procedure). If no Member State objects to the use of the written procedure, the positive answers to the second question are counted if the matter is one where a QM decides, or one negative blocks the measure if unanimity is required. If a written procedure has been agreed to, the measure would be expected to pass.

NOTES

1. As well as the European Court of Justice, the Court of Auditors and the European Investment Bank in Luxembourg, the Jet Nuclear Fusion Project in Culham, UK, the Joint Research Centre in Ispra, Italy and the European Central Bank in Frankfurt.
2. European Council Meeting in Brussels, 29 October 1993. Annex II: 'Decision taken by Common Agreement between representatives of the Governments of the Member States on the location of the seats of certain bodies and departments of the European Communities'.

3. Some commentators see in the world of Commission and Council committees the real workplace of these institutions, where Commissioners and ministerial representatives of Member States cannot be more than secondary operators.
4. OJ C 293/2, 8.11.95.
5. OL J 197/33, 18.7.87, Council decision fixing the modalities for the exercise of competence conferred on the Commission for implementation. 87/313/EEC.
6. Council Press release 9008/99, 21–22 June 1999.
7. Euro is close to a designation suggested in 1974. Giovanni Magnifico used 'Europa' in an article in *New Europe* in spring 1974 in which he advocated a parallel currency as an interim measure. (Europe House Publishing Ltd.)
8. 'Whereas legislative and administrative simplification aimed at eliminating the excessive and unjustified costs which constitute a barrier to competitiveness . . .' Resolution adopted by the Council on 8 July 1996, Presse 2000-G.
9. Conclusion of the European Council, Dublin, 13–14 December 1996, IV, the IGC.
10. OL C 340/145 to 308, 10.11.97.
11. CSE 96 7 final of 27.11.96.
12. Inter-institutional agreement of 20 December 1994, OJ C 293/2, 8.11.95.
13. OJ L 77/20, 27.3.96.
14. Presse 326-G.
15. For example, Presse 356 G of 3.xii.96.
16. Regularly in the *Sunday Telegraph*, and see Booker, C. and North, *The Mad Officials*, Duckworth, 1994 and *Castle of Lies*, Duckworth, 1996, subtitled 'Why Britain must get out of Europe'.
17. Finn Laursen and Sophie Vanhoonacker, *The Intergovernmental Conference on Political Union*, European Institute of Public Administration, 1992, p. 358.
18. For a scholarly discussion see Cloos, Reinesch. Vigne and Weyland, *Le Traité de Maastricht*, Bruylant Bruxelles, 1993, p. 145. For an analysis of the organisational trends of Member State collaborative activities outside the framework of the Community, see 'La communaute en penombre', W. Nicoll, *Revue du marche commun*, Paris, No. 311, November 1987, pp. 617ff.
19. In L'Acte unique européen, *Etudes européennes*, 1987, De Ruyt notes (p. 215) that it is curious to invoke subsidiarity in relation to the protection of the environment, which crosses frontiers. The broad principle of what later came to be called subsidiarity, a borrowing from Roman Catholic doctrine, had been enunciated by Mr Roy (later Lord) Jenkins in his speech on monetary union in October 1997. See Salmon and Nicoll, *Building European Union*, MUP, 1997, p. 160. For more historical background, see Andrew Duff, *The Treaty of Amsterdam*, Sweet & Maxwell, 1997, pp. 96–106.
20. In the realm of subsidiarity, there is no significant difference between the British Conservative government and its Labour successor.
21. Birmingham Declaration – A Community close to its Citizens.
22. External relations also get six pages. Economic recovery gets two.
23. The Protocol does NOT say: that national powers are the rule and the Community is the exception; that subsidiarity cannot have direct effect; that the objective of presenting a single position of the Member States to third countries is not a justification for corresponding internal Community action.

24. Declaration on the right of access to information.
25. Presidency Conclusions, European Council, Birmingham, 16 October 1992 Annex 1, para. 3, *Bulletin of the European Communities*, 10–1992.
26. Presidency Conclusions, European Council, Edinburgh, 11–12 December 1992, ibid. 12–1992.
27. Ibid. 10–1993, p. 106 point 1.6.8.
28. Code of conduct concerning public access to Council and Commission documents 93/730/EC, OJ L 340/41, 31.12.93.
29. Council Decision of 20 December 1993 on public access to Council documents 93/731/EC, OJ L 340/43, 31.12.93.
30. Case 194/94 John Carvel and Guardian Newspapers v Council.

APPENDIX

BREAKDOWN OF THE 2,000 COUNCIL MEETINGS BY SUBJECT MATTER

This table includes special meetings – which are unnumbered – which explains why the number of meetings is slightly over 2,000.

Subject matter	1967	1968	1969	1970	1971	1972	1973	1974	1975	1976
Agriculture	8	18	15	15	12	12	15	16	15	14
Foreign Affairs	7	9	9	12	14	16	14	16	16	14
Financial Aff./Econ. and Fin. Aff.		4	2	1	7	4	9	7	8	7
Labour and Social Aff.	1	1	2	3	2	2	3	2	2	2
Transport	1	2	1	3	2	3	1	2	2	2
Technology/Industry	1		1	1						
Euratom	1	2	3	2	2	1	2			
ECSC		1								
Budget		1	1		1	2	2	2	3	2
Agriculture/Financial Affairs			2							
Agric./Financial/Foreign Aff.			4	1						
Foreign Affairs/Financial Aff.										
Energy			1				1	1	1	3
Public Works				2						
Justice					1			1		
Regional Policy					1					
Education					1			1	1	1
Environment							1	1	3	1
GATT							1			
Development Cooperation							1	5	2	2
Research									2	3
Patents									1	
Fiscal Matters/VAT									1	2
Fisheries										
Health										
Post and Telecommunications										
Steel										
Ecofin/Social Aff.										
ACP-EEC (preparation)										
Textiles										
Internal Market										
Consumer Protection										
Int. Market/Consumer Prot.										
Education/Labour and Social Aff.										
Industry/Steel										
Cultural Affairs										
	20	**38**	**40**	**40**	**44**	**40**	**50**	**54**	**57**	**53**

Subject matter	1977	1978	1979	1980	1981	1982	1983	1984	1985	1986
Agriculture	12	13	12	15	11	15	14	14	14	11
Foreign Affairs	12	15	13	13	12	12	12	17	14	11
Financial Aff./Econ. and Fin. Aff.	9	10	9	9	8	9	7	9	7	9
Labour and Social Aff.	2	2	2	2	2	3	2	2	2	2
Transport	3	2	2	2	2	2	4	4	3	4
Industry						2	1	1	1	6
Euratom										
ECSC										
Budget	3	4	4	5	3	4	4	3	5	5
Agriculture/Financial Affairs										
Agric./Financial/Foreign Aff.										
Foreign Affairs/Financial Aff.	3	1	1							
Energy	4	3	6	2	3	3	3	2	3	3
Public Works										
Justice		1			1		1			
Regional Policy										
Education					1	1	1	1	1	1	2
Environment	2	2	3	2	2	2	3	3	3	3
GATT						1				1
Development Cooperation	3	2	1	1	3	2	2	2	2	2
Research	2		2		1	3	5	4	2	4
Patents										
Fiscal Matters/VAT	1		1	1	2					
Fisheries	3	7	4	7	7	7	8	5	3	5
Health	1									1
Telecommunications	1								1	
Steel				2	4	1	5	1		
Ecofin/Social Aff.					1	1				
ACP-EEC (preparation)							1	3		
Textiles						1				
Internal Market							6	2	3	7
Consumer Protection							1	2	1	2
Int. Market/Consumer Prot.								1	2	
Education/Labour and Social Aff.							1			
Industry/Steel								2	4	
Cultural Affairs								2	2	1
	61	63	60	63	62	70	80	80	73	79

Subject matter	1987	1988	1989	1990	1991	1992	1993	1994	1995	1996
Agriculture	14	12	12	15	13	13	11	11	10	13
General Affairs	14	14	13	13	14	15	19	15	14	13
Ecofin	7	6	8	10	12	11	11	11	9	9
Labour and Social Aff.	2	2	5	3	3	3	4	4	4	4
Transport	4	4	4	4	6	4	4	4	4	4
Industry	5	2	4	4	2	2	5	4	3	4
Euratom										
ECSC										
Budget	6	4	2	2	2	2	2	2	2	2
Agriculture/Financial Affairs	1									
Agric./Foreign Trade				2						
Agric./Foreign Aff.							1			
Energy	3	2	2	2	2	2	2	2	2	3
Public Works										
Justice/Home Affairs	1		1		1	3	1	4	4	3
Regional Policy										
Education	1	2	3	2	1	2	2	2	2	2
Environment	4	3	4	4	4	4	5	4	4	4
Foreign Trade				1						
Development cooperation	2	2	2	3	2	2	2	2	2	3
Research	3	4	5	4	2	3	5	4	3	3
Patents										
Development/Environment										
Fisheries	3	5	4	3	4	5	5	5	4	5
Health	1	2	2	2	2	2	2	3	2	2
Telecommunications		1	3	2	3	3	3	2	2	5
Environment/Energy							1			
Environment/Transport							1	1		
ACP/General Affairs				1				1		
Internal Market	6	8	10	7	5	7	6	3	2	3
Consumer Protection	3		2	2	1	2	2	2	2	2
Int. Market/Consumer Prot.										
Education/Labour and Social Aff.										
Industry/Telecommunications								1		
Youth								2	1	
Cultural Affairs		1	1	2	2	2	2	2	3	2
Civil Protection	1	1		1				1		1
Tourism		1		1		1				1
Total	**81**	**76**	**87**	**91**	**82**	**89**	**96**	**92**	**79**	**88**

During the current year, 1997 (including the meeting on 21/22 April):

Agriculture:	4	Transport:	1
General Affairs:	5	Internal Market:	1
Ecofin:	3	Consumers:	1
Environment:	1	Fisheries:	1
Telecommunications:	1	Labour and Social Affairs:	1

Total: 19

INDEX